REFERENCE SOURCES
FOR SMALL AND MEDIUM-SIZED
LIBRARIES

SEVENTH EDITION

JACK O'GORMAN, EDITOR

AMERICAN LIBRARY ASSOCIATION

CHICAGO   2008

Jack O'Gorman is Coordinator of Reference at the University of Dayton's Roesch Library. With more than twenty-five years of experience in university, government, and business libraries, O'Gorman has an in-depth knowledge of reference sources. He has a bachelor's degree in mathematics from Walsh University and an MLS from St. John's University. He was the chair of the editorial board of *Reference Books Bulletin* from 2001 to 2004, and he continues as a member of that board. He has served on the RUSA Outstanding Reference Sources Committee and the Dartmouth Award Committee. He is the coeditor of *Recommended Reference Sources in Paperback* (Libraries Unlimited, 2000) and contributed to the fifth and sixth editions of *Reference Sources for Small and Medium-Sized Libraries.*

The paper used in this publication meets the minimum requirements of American National Standard for Information Sciences—Permanence of Paper for Printed Library Materials, ANSI Z39.48-1992. ♾

Library of Congress Cataloging-in-Publication Data

Reference sources for small and medium-sized libraries. — 7th ed. / Jack O'Gorman, editor.
    p.   cm.
    Includes bibliographical references and index.
    ISBN-13: 978-0-8389-0943-0 (alk. paper)
    ISBN-10: 0-8389-0943-4 (alk. paper)
    1. Reference books—Bibliography. 2. Small libraries—United States—Book lists. I. O'Gorman, Jack.

Z1035.1.A47 2008
011'.02—dc22   2007040026

ISBN-13: 978-0-8389-0943-0
ISBN-10: 0-8389-0943-4

Printed in the United States of America

12 11 10 09 08   5 4 3 2 1

CONTENTS

PREFACE   XV

1 *Reference Materials*   *1*

Bibliographies and Guides   1
  Books   1
  Periodicals   4
  Websites   5

Almanacs and Fact Books   6

Databases and Indexes   7

Dictionaries and Encyclopedias   8
  Print Encyclopedias   8
  Electronic Encyclopedias   8

Directories   9
  Postal Directories   11

Electronic Reference Resources   11

Internet Searching   13

Library Science   13

Search Aggregators   15

2 *Philosophy, Religion, and Ethics*   *16*

Philosophy   16
  Databases and Indexes   16
  Dictionaries and Encyclopedias   16
  Biographical Sources   17

Religion   17
  General Sources   17
    Bibliographies and Guides   17
    Databases and Indexes   18
    Dictionaries and Encyclopedias   18
  Bible   18
    Atlases   18
    Commentaries   18
    Concordances   19

Databases and Indexes   19
Dictionaries and Encyclopedias   19
Handbooks   20
Religion in the United States   20
Dictionaries and Encyclopedias   20
Directories   21
Biographical Sources   21
Religions   21
General Sources   21
Asian Religions   21
Christianity   22
Dictionaries and Encyclopedias   22
Directories, Yearbooks, and Almanacs   23
Biographical Sources   23
Islam   24
Judaism   24
Other Living Religions   26
Mythology   27

Ethics   28
Bibliographies and Guides   28
Dictionaries and Encyclopedias   28

3 *Psychology, Psychiatry, and the Occult   29*

Psychology and Psychiatry   29
Databases   29
Dictionaries and Encyclopedias   31
Directories   35
Handbooks and Manuals   35
Style Manuals   36
Tests, Measurements, and Questionnaires   37
Websites   38
Biographical Sources   39

The Occult   40

4 *Social Sciences, Sociology, and Anthropology   43*

Social Sciences (General Sources)   43
Databases and Indexes   43
Dictionaries and Encyclopedias   43
Bibliographies and Guides   45
Handbooks   45
Websites   46

Sociology   46
Bibliographies and Guides   46
Dictionaries and Encyclopedias   47
Handbooks   48

Abortion   48
Aging   48
Alcoholism and Drug Abuse   49
Criminology   50
Death and Dying   52
Ethnic Studies   53
   African Americans   55
   Asian Americans   56
   Hispanic Americans   57
   Native Peoples of North America   58
Family, Marriage, and Divorce   59
Gay and Lesbian Studies   60
Men's Studies   62
Sex Studies   63
Social Service and Philanthropy   63
Statistics and Demography   65
Urban Studies   66
Women's Studies   67
Youth and Child Development   68

Anthropology and Archaeology   69
Atlases   69
Dictionaries and Encyclopedias   70
Handbooks   71

5 *Business and Careers*   72
General Sources   72
   Bibliographies and Guides   72
   Biographical Sources   73
   Databases   74
   Dictionaries and Encyclopedias   75
   Directories   77
   Handbooks, Yearbooks, and Almanacs   78

Accounting   78

Advertising, Marketing, and Consumer Research   79

Banking, Finance, and Investment   81

Company and Industry   82

Economics   85

Entrepreneurship and Small Business   86

Insurance   87

Management   87

Real Estate   87

Careers and Vocational Guidance   88

CONTENTS

6 *Political Science and Law* **89**

Bibliographies and Guides 89

Dictionaries and Encyclopedias 90

Directories 92

Handbooks, Yearbooks, and Almanacs 93

Biographical Sources 95

7 *Education* **97**

Bibliographies and Guides 97
  General Sources 97
  Media and Curriculum Materials 97

Databases and Indexes 99

Dictionaries and Encyclopedias 100

Directories 101
  School and College Directories 102
  Scholarship and Financial Aid Directories 105

Handbooks, Yearbooks, and Almanacs 105

Statistical Sources 107

Biographical Sources 108

8 *Words and Language* **109**

General Sources 109
  Bibliographies and Guides 109
  Encyclopedias, Companions, and Atlases 109

English Language 110
  Bibliographies and Guides 110
  Encyclopedias and Companions 111
  Dictionaries 111
    Principal English-Language Dictionaries 111
    Desk Dictionaries 112
  Abbreviations and Acronyms 113
  Crossword Puzzle Dictionaries 113
  Etymology and Word and Phrase Origins 113
  Foreign Words and Phrases 114
  Handbooks 114
  Idioms and Usage Dictionaries 114
  Pronunciation Dictionaries 115
  Rhyming Dictionaries 116
  Sign Language Dictionaries 116
  Similes, Metaphors, and Clichés 117
  Slang and Euphemisms 117

Thesauri: Synonyms, Antonyms, and Homonyms   118
Style Manuals   119

Foreign-Language Dictionaries   121
Bibliographies and Guides   121
Arabic   121
Chinese   121
French   122
German   122
Greek   123
Hebrew   123
Italian   123
Japanese   124
Latin   124
Russian   124
Spanish   125

9 *Science and Technology*   *126*

Bibliographies and Guides   126

Databases and Indexes   126

Dictionaries and Encyclopedias   127

Handbooks, Yearbooks, and Almanacs   129

Biographical Sources   129

Astronomy   129
Dictionaries and Encyclopedias   129
Handbooks, Yearbooks, and Almanacs   130

Chemistry   130
Bibliographies and Guides   130
Dictionaries and Encyclopedias   130
Handbooks, Yearbooks, and Almanacs   131

Computer Science   132
Bibliographies and Guides   132
Dictionaries and Encyclopedias   132

History of Science   134
Bibliographies and Guides   134
Dictionaries and Encyclopedias   134
Handbooks, Yearbooks, and Almanacs   134

Internet   135

Earth Sciences   135
Bibliographies and Guides   135
Dictionaries and Encyclopedias   135
Databases and Indexes   135
Geology   135

Oceanography   136
Climatology   136

Engineering   136
Bibliographies and Guides   136
Dictionaries and Encyclopedias   136
Standards   137
Electronics and Electrical Engineering   137
Manufacturing Engineering   137
Vehicle Maintenance and Repair   137

Life Sciences   138
Biology   138
Bibliographies and Guides   138
Databases and Indexes   138
Dictionaries and Encyclopedias   138
Botany and Agriculture   140
Gardening   141
Paleontology   141
Zoology   142

Mathematics   143
Bibliographies and Guides   143
Databases and Indexes   143
Dictionaries and Encyclopedias   143
Websites   143
Biographical Sources   144

Physics   144
Dictionaries and Encyclopedias   144

Weapons and Warfare   144

10 *Health and Medicine*   *146*

General Sources   146
Databases and Indexes   146
Dictionaries and Encyclopedias   146
Directories   148
Handbooks, Statistics, and Diagnosis   149

AIDS and STDs   151

Anatomy and Physiology   151

Cancer   152

Children's Health   152

Complementary and Alternative Medicine   153

Drugs   153

Nutrition and Diet   154

Physical Impairments   155

Women's and Men's Health   155

11 *Households   157*

Beverages   157

Calendars   159

Consumer Affairs   160

Construction   161

Cooking   162

Etiquette   165

Festivals and Holidays   166

Foods   167

Home Improvement   169

Housekeeping   170

Interior Decoration   171

Maintenance and Repair   171

Parenting   172

Pets   173
Birds   174
Cats   174
Dogs   175
Fish   176
Horses   176
Unusual Pets   177

Tools   177

12 *Visual Arts   178*

Databases and Indexes   178

Websites   179

Architecture   180

Art   183
Dictionaries and Encyclopedias   183
Directories   185
Histories   185
Biographical Sources   186

Cartoons and Comics   188

Costume and Fashion   188

Decorative Arts and Antiques   190

Graphic Design and Illustration   191
Photography   192

13 *Performing Arts   194*

General Sources   194
  Bibliographies and Guides   194
  Databases and Indexes   194
  Directories   194
  Biographical Sources   195
  Awards   195

Dance   196
  Bibliographies and Guides   196
  Dictionaries and Encyclopedias   196
  Directories   196
  Handbooks   196

Film and Video   197
  Bibliographies and Guides   197
  Databases and Indexes   197
  Dictionaries and Encyclopedias   197
  Directories   198
  Handbooks   199
  Biographical Sources   200

Television, Radio, and Telecommunications   200
  Dictionaries and Encyclopedias   200
  Directories   201
  Handbooks   201

Theater   202
  Bibliographies and Guides   202
  Databases and Indexes   202
  Dictionaries and Encyclopedias   203
  Handbooks   204

14 *Music   205*

General Sources   205
  Bibliographies and Discographies   205
  Databases and Indexes   206
  Dictionaries and Encyclopedias   206
  Directories   208
  Handbooks   209
  Biographical Sources   209

Blues and Jazz   209
  Bibliographies and Discographies   209
  Dictionaries and Encyclopedias   209
  Biographical Sources   210

Classical Music   210
  Bibliographies and Discographies   210
  Databases and Indexes   211
  Dictionaries and Encyclopedias   211
  Biographical Sources   212

Country and Gospel Music   212
  Bibliographies and Discographies   212
  Dictionaries and Encyclopedias   212

Rock and Popular Music   213
  Bibliographies and Discographies   213
  Databases and Indexes   214
  Dictionaries and Encyclopedias   214
  Biographical Sources   215

World Music   216
  Bibliographies and Discographies   216
  Databases and Indexes   216

15 *Crafts and Hobbies*   217

Handbooks   217

Crafts   218
  Beading   218
  Knitting   218
  Needlework   219
  Quilting   220
  Scrapbooking   220
  Sewing   221
  Woodworking   222

Hobbies   223
  Antiques and Collectibles   223
  Coins and Paper Money   224
  Stamps   225

16 *Games and Sports*   227

Bibliographies and Guides   227

Almanacs   227

Chronologies   228

Dictionaries and Encyclopedias   228

Directories   229

Biographical Sources   229

Auto Racing   230

Backpacking   230

Baseball   230

Basketball   232

Bicycling   233

Billiards and Pool   233

Card Games   234

Chess   234

Exercise   234

Figure Skating   234

Fishing   234

Football   235

Gambling   235

Games   236

Golf   236

Hockey   236

Martial Arts   237

Olympics   237

Outdoors   237

Recreation   238

Running   238

Rules   238

Sailing   239

Soccer   239

Swimming   239

Tennis   239

17 *Literature   241*

General Sources   241
   Bibliographies and Guides   241
   Databases and Indexes   241
   Dictionaries and Encyclopedias   242
   Digests   242
   Handbooks   242
   Literary Characters   243
   Literary Prizes   243
   Multivolume Criticism   243
   Proverbs   244

Quotations   244
Biographical Sources   245

Special Interest   246
African American Literature   246
Asian American Literature   246
Gay and Lesbian Literature   247
Latino Literature   247
Native American Literature   248
Women's Literature   248

Specific Genres   249
Children's Literature   249
Prizes and Awards   252
Drama   253
Fantasy   253
Fiction   253
Gothic   254
Historical   254
Mystery   254
Novel   255
Poetry   255
Romance   257
Science Fiction   257
Short Story   257

Speech and Rhetoric   259

National and Regional Literatures   259
American   259
Arabic   261
British   261
Shakespeare   262
Classical   263
African   264
Australian   264
Canadian   265
Caribbean   265
Chinese   265
East Asian   265
Eastern European   266
French   266
German   266
Indian   266
Irish   266
Italian   267
Japanese   267
Latin American   267
Russian   268
South Asian   268

18 *History*   *269*

     Bibliographies and Guides   269

     Chronologies   270

     Databases and Indexes   270

     Dictionaries and Encyclopedias   271

     Handbooks, Yearbooks, and Almanacs   273

     Historical Atlases   274

     Primary Sources   275

19 *Geography, Area Studies, and Travel*   *276*

     Atlases   276

       World Atlases   276

       North American Atlases   277

     Dictionaries, Encyclopedias, and Gazetteers   278

     Handbooks, Yearbooks, and Almanacs   280

     Travel Guides   282

20 *Biography*   *284*

     Databases and Indexes   284

   INDEX   287

PREFACE

In 1969, Mary C. Barter, chair of the ALA Reference Sources Division, Basic Reference Books Committee, wrote in the preface of the first edition of *Reference Books for Small and Medium-Sized Libraries* that this title "has been prepared to meet a long-standing and widespread need. It is designed to serve as an authoritative buying guide for the purchase of reference collections for newly established libraries and for improving and expanding existing collections. . . . The list provides bibliographic information and evaluative annotations for the most convenient and productive reference sources in all broad fields on levels usually encountered in public libraries."

Over its thirty-nine-year editorial history, *Reference Sources for Small and Medium-Sized Libraries* has continued to serve this vital mission. Contributors with specialized knowledge in their subject areas drew upon their expertise in public, community college, and university libraries to recommend titles that you, the reader, will find useful for your library. Titles in this source are ones that reference collection development librarians should consider and will guide library science students in learning the art of reference services. With the changes happening in reference, this guide becomes even more important. Inclusion in this title is a valuable recommendation as to whether a title should be acquired, retained, or, by its absence, considered for weeding.

Size

The size of the library is an important criterion for inclusion. This guide is designed to be particularly relevant to smaller and medium-sized libraries. Using the following data from correspondence with staff of the ALA Library, the criteria for public libraries population served are

> Under 10,000 = very small
> 10,000 to 24,999 = small
> 25,000 to 99,999 = medium-sized
> 100,000 to 499,999 = large
> Over 500,000 = very large

Cost

Since the publication of the sixth edition, in 1999, many valuable free resources have become available via the Internet. *MedlinePlus* (www .medlineplus.gov) comes to mind right away. Where appropriate, these resources have been included. They are good candidates for links from within a library's website, or inclusion in the local catalog, so that it may act as a portal to the Internet at large. The cost of reference books was also a factor for inclusion in this title. For example, a print resource that was not included because of its price is the *International Encyclopedia of the Social and Behavioral Sciences.* Rather than specific pricing data, titles are given a price range as shown below:

Under $100 = $
$100–$500 = $$
$500–$1,000 = $$$
Over $1,000 = $$$$

Coverage

There are many changes from the sixth edition. Every title was reconsidered to determine whether it is still valuable in a reference collection. Every title was also examined by at least one of the contributors or the editor, and many of them also have been reviewed in *Reference Books Bulletin, Choice, Library Journal,* or other review literature. This critical and selective evaluation by the contributors caused the number of entries to go down 14 percent, to 1,695.

Important changes in society and technology are reflected in the reference sources recommended here. For instance, the broader attention to religions beyond Christianity and Judaism and a growing interest in international coverage and events are recognized in this edition. Another change is the role of the Internet and print literature. For instance, printed directory information is less important, but subject encyclopedias are increasingly important resources. Most of the titles listed are also available electronically. Librarians need to decide if their library should purchase an electronic or paper copy. One advantage of electronic reference books is the ease with which readers can use them remotely. Disadvantages are the multiple interfaces, difficulties readers face in getting to the source, and, of course, cost. In spite of these obstacles, librarians may need to migrate their collections toward electronic resources.

Reference publishing is at a crossroads. With so many good titles being published, reflecting quality scholarship and improved indexing, this might be considered a golden age of reference publishing. At the same time, reference works face competition that did not exist in 1999, when the last edition of this book was published. Public library patrons, undergraduates, and even graduate students will turn to the Internet and quickly and easily find information, but it is not necessarily scholarly or accurate.

Reference itself is changing. Renovations, more public seating, and group study spaces have meant that reference collections have shrunk. It is important to keep certain classic titles in reference, and this source includes some older titles that should be retained. Some of the titles are also suitable for circulating collections, for example, items from the crafts or household chapters. If the library can afford it, purchasing two copies of some titles might be appropriate. Taken together, all of these changes mean that *Reference Sources for Small and Medium-Sized Libraries* remains a valuable guide for reference librarians, collection development librarians, and library science students.

Approaching This Guide

In addition to an author-title index, this title can also be approached systematically. The table of contents and chapter arrangement identify areas of interest that selectors can review by subject. Contributors highlight not only the best sources on a subject but a range of sources within that subject. This will aid subject selectors in developing their reference collections. In keeping with editorial tradition, the twenty chapters have been arranged to reflect the major divisions of the Dewey Decimal Classification, although not in strict Dewey order.

Acknowledgments

Thanks to Patrick Hogan and Steven Hofmann of ALA Editions. Thanks to the RUSA Advisory Board, Charlette Dugan, Betty Gard, Corinne Hill, Charlene Rue, Alec Sonsteby, and Julienne Wood. Thanks also to Robin Chung, Amy Guy, and Whitney Winn, from UCLA, for their help in checking the bibliographic records. I would also like to thank the chapter contributors. We are a close-knit group, and we had a lot of fun with this project. A very special thanks to my wife, Kathy, for all of her love and support throughout this process. I am very proud to see it all come together, and I hope that you enjoy the book.

1 Reference Materials

JACK O'GORMAN, SUE POLANKA, AND BARBARA M. BIBEL

This chapter is different from the other chapters in this book because of its content. The others are arranged by subject, while this one is a general bibliography and resource listing. It combines the first three chapters from the previous edition and includes bibliographies and guides, almanacs, general-purpose databases, and Internet search sites. It also lists both print and electronic encyclopedias, electronic reference resources, and library science materials. Many of the other titles in the book are listed or included in sources here. For example, they may be available via Gale Virtual Reference Library, Oxford Reference Online, or Credo Reference, or they may be listed in *Books in print* or *Ulrich's periodicals directory*.

Entries in this category are at the cusp of changes in reference services yet also include reliable and well-known sources. Examples include the Librarians' Internet Index and the *Guide to reference*. Librarian and patron usage patterns have changed, and the largest challenge facing both is accessing accurate information. Using the sources recommended here will help with that challenge. Some formats, such as almanacs and printed encyclopedias, resist these changes, and libraries will want to retain them in print. What might the future hold for bibliographies and ready-reference materials? Obviously, there will be more electronic publishing. We can envision an electronic-reference-book center, where publishers sell the content at an affordable price, and users search via a single search interface chosen by the libraries.

Bibliographies and Guides

Books

1   **The American Library Association guide to information access: A complete handbook and directory.** Sandra Whiteley and American Library Association. 533p. Random House, 1994. ISBN 0679430601; 0679750754 (pbk.). $
025.5   Z711

This guide to the research process gives advice to high school, undergraduate, and independent researchers. It discusses the five treasures of information: libraries, archives, newspapers, government publications, and government agencies. Resources are also presented by topic. Its age may make the electronic products out of date, but the sources covered are classics and continue to be used in either print or electronic format. The subject chapters include bibliographies of general sources, periodicals, government agencies, associations, specialized libraries, LC Subject Headings, and other sources of information. Index included.

2   Book lust: Recommended reading for every mood, moment, and reason. Nancy Pearl. 287p. Sasquatch Books, 2003. ISBN 1570613818. $

011   Z1035

More book lust: Recommended reading for every mood, moment, and reason. Nancy Pearl. 286p. Sasquatch Books, 2005. ISBN 1570614350. $

011   Z1035

You should have three copies of these books. One in reference, one in circulation, and personal copies for when you're jonesing for something to read. Chapters are by categories, which can be whimsical. There is a title index for serious folk, but everybody else can enjoy browsing through "Chick Lit," "Dreaming of Africa," "Here Be Dragons," or "Zero: This Will Mean Nothing to You." Recommendations come in the text or in lists. The second title, *More book lust,* is, according to the author, more of a companion than a sequel. This book comes from titles that the author had to leave out of the first volume along with suggestions from librarians, readers, and friends. Some categories include "Other People's Shoes," "Gone Fishin'," and "Fractured Fairy Tales." Author Pearl is famous as the librarian action figure. The well-thought-out recommendations will delight both patrons and librarians.

3   Fundamental reference sources. 3rd ed. James H. Sweetland and Frances Neel Cheney. 612p. American Library Association, 2001. ISBN 0838907806. $

011   Z1035

What makes a fundamental reference source? Although there is no universal list, sources used to teach reference or frequently used by working reference librarians provide guidance to bibliographers. This title discusses the nature of reference services, sources of bibliographic information, indexing and abstracting services, directories, biographical information, dictionaries, encyclopedias, statistics, and geographic information. It does not suggest that every title must be held by every library but rather provides suggestions of titles most likely to be useful. Entries include short annotations and bibliographic information. Appendixes include an acronym list, guidelines for particular types of reference works, and a subject index.

4   Great books for boys: More than 600 books for boys 2 to 14. Kathleen Odean. 384p. Ballantine, 1998. ISBN 0345420837. $

028.1   Z1037

Raising boys presents its own challenges. Encouraging them to read can help them grow into emotionally healthy men. This title recommends more than 600 books that "appeal to boys and satisfy their needs and interests." Adventure, sports, humorous stories, and folktale parodies are included. The five main categories are picture books and storybooks, folktales, books for beginning readers, books for middle readers, and books for older readers. Entries contain author, title, illustrator, publishing information, age range, and annotation. If titles were Newbery or Caldecott winners, this is mentioned in the annotation. A chapter on resources for parents is included.

5   Great books for girls: More than 600 books to inspire today's girls and tomorrow's women. Rev. ed. Kathleen Odean. 420p. Ballantine, 2002. ISBN 0345450213. $

028.1   Z1037

Mary Pipher, author of *Reviving Ophelia,* states about this title: "I recommend it for all those who want girls to grow up strong, free, bold, and kind." The revised edition includes 294 new books and more than 600 total books portraying girls in a positive light. The author draws upon her experience as a children's librarian to find stories of girls and women "who face the world with courage, either from the first or after overcoming their fears." The chapters include picture books and storybooks, folktales, books for beginning readers, books for middle readers, books for older readers, and poetry. Entries contain author, title, illustrator, publishing information, age range, and annotation. If titles were Newbery or Caldecott winners, this is mentioned in the annotation. Magazines and websites for girls are included along with author and title indexes.

6   Guide to reference. Robert Kieft, ed. American Library Association, forthcoming 2008. $$–$$$$ www.guidetoreference.com.

Since its publication in 1902, *Guide to reference books* has become the standard reference for reference sources and is used to answer users' questions, train staff, educate LIS students, create local bibliographic materials, and develop collections. *Guide to reference* will be the first online edition and the first to incorporate sources on the Web, thus emphasizing the guide's traditional role as a portal to the reference literature. Organized by academic disciplines with new categories such as "Interdisciplinary Fields," "The Web as Reference Tool," and "Online General Reference Libraries." Content and internal category organization significantly revised to reflect new sources and changes in publishing and information-seeking behavior. There are plans to add content for teaching reference work and updating staff knowledge. User interface affords multiple browse and search functions as well as interactive features.

7 How to use the library: A reference and assignment guide for students.
Frank Ferro and Nolan Lushington. 324p. Greenwood, 1998. ISBN 0313301077. $
011   Z1035

Written at a high school level, this guide will help beginning researchers with their homework assignments and term papers. The book's three parts include an explanation of the research process, an annotated list of core resources by subject, and indexing. Part 3 includes subject and title indexes as well as a guide to homework questions, a glossary and bibliography, and a listing of the Dewey Decimal and Library of Congress classification schemes. Although this title is a little older, the reading level and content make it useful for school library research.

8 Introduction to reference work. 8th ed.
William A. Katz. 2v. McGraw-Hill, 2002. ISBN 0072441070 (v. 1); 0072441437 (v. 2). $
025.5   Z711

Frequently used as a text, this title has the beginning or inexperienced reference librarian as its audience. Volume 1 deals with basic information sources and is arranged by form of materials. Volume 2 covers reference sources, processes, evaluation, and techniques, including online reference. The updated edition addresses not only printed sources but electronic ones, where the reference librarian acts as a "key professional information expert."

9 Madame Audrey's guide to mostly cheap but good reference books for small and rural libraries. Audrey Lewis. 206p. American Library Association, 1998. ISBN

0838907334. $
011   Z1035

"Well . . . what are you waiting for? Go and spend a little money on books!" is how Lewis concludes the introduction of this source. Designed for small and rural libraries to help with their reference collection development, this title lists, in rough Dewey order, recommended reference books costing less than $200. Entries include bibliographic information and short annotations. Titles with very good coverage are indicated with stars. Useful for smaller libraries and for medium-sized and larger libraries to check their reference collections.

10 Magazines for libraries: For the general reader and school, junior college, college, university, and public libraries.
14th ed. Cheryl LaGuardia and William A. Katz. 1132p. R. R. Bowker, 2005. ISBN 0835247767. $$
016.05   Z6941

This title is an important selection tool with an annotated listing of journals recommended by subject specialists. Useful for libraries to determine which periodicals or databases they should subscribe to. Entries are listed alphabetically by title within subject categories and include publication details, for instance, where the journal is indexed and whether it is peer reviewed, and abbreviations indicating the audience. Some 6,850 annotations of recommended journals for public and academic libraries are listed. The introduction includes a discussion of such trends as direct linking to full text, metasearching, and open-access journals. Includes an excellent discussion of issues around search aggregators.

11 The Oxford guide to library research.
3rd ed. Thomas Mann. 293p. Oxford Univ. Pr., 2005. ISBN 0195189973; 0195189981 (pbk.). $
025.5   Z710

The third edition of this title presents what research libraries can offer that the Internet cannot. The author has a PhD and is a former private investigator. Currently, he is a reference librarian at the Library of Congress Reading Room. The audience is readers who need to know about modern research methods. It could be an excellent text for library science students or for university research-methodology classes. It focuses on books and other resources available to large research libraries and has a structure around nine methods of subject searching: controlled-vocabulary searching, subject classified book stacks, keyword searching, citation searching, related record searching, subject bibliographies, Boolean searching, using the subject expertise of people, and type of literature searching. It also covers encyclopedias, indexes to journal articles, review articles, published bibliographies, search limiters, finding materials in other libraries, reference sources, and special subjects and formats. Interestingly, there is an appendix on wisdom.

12   Recommended reference books in paperback. 3rd ed. Jovian P. Lang and Jack O'Gorman, eds. 315p. Libraries Unlimited, 2000. ISBN 1563085836. $
011   Z1035.1

A selection of 1,006 notable reference books chosen for their quality, economy, and price. Entries are arranged in broad subject categories and include bibliographic information and evaluative annotations. Paperbacks can be a viable, low-cost alternative for reference books. Organization is loosely based upon the *American reference books annual* (*ARBA*). Includes author, title, and subject index.

13   Reference and information services: An introduction. 3rd ed. Richard E. Bopp and Linda C. Smith. 617p. Libraries Unlimited, 2001. ISBN 1563086212; 1563086247 (pbk.). $
025.5   Z711

The third edition updates library science students on modern reference practices. Part 1 covers concepts and processes, including ethics, library instruction, the reference interview, bibliographic control, and the evaluation and management of reference services. Part 2 offers general principles for the selection and evaluation of reference sources. It includes bibliographies of basic reference sources by types. Sample search strategies are included.

14   Resources for college libraries. American Library Association and R. R. Bowker. www.RCLweb.net.

Presents a core collection for undergraduate libraries. The resources include recommended reference titles and web resources. Organized into broadly defined subject areas such as humanities, languages and literature, history, social sciences and professional studies, science and technology, and interdisciplinary and area studies. Entries indicate if they have previously appeared in *Books for college*

libraries or *Choice*. The print version of the 2007 edition is also available. For the electronic edition, pricing is based upon FTE enrollment. E-mail RCLweb@bowker.com for more information.

15   60 years of notable children's books. Sally Anne Thompson and Association for Library Service to Children. 227p. Booklist Publications, American Library Association, 2003. ISBN 0838982654. $
011.62   Z1037

A bibliography of selected notable children's literature from 1940 through 1999. Selection criteria include titles that are still relevant to young readers and youth services librarians. Chapters are by decade, and entries are listed alphabetically by author. Bibliographic citations include title, author, editor, illustrator, original publication date, and print availability. Titles from the 1970s through the 1990s have designated letters *Y, M, O,* and *A* for the age range for readers. Annotations are short, usually one or two sentences. Includes theme-list appendix and author-illustrator and title index.

Periodicals

16   Booklist online. American Library Association, 2006–. www.booklistonline .com.

The online version enhances the printed *Booklist. Booklist online* has both free and subscription-based components. It "contains over 100,000 reviews and thousands of features dating back to 1992." *Booklist* is essential for any public library and very helpful to many academic libraries. Reference librarians will be most interested in the Reference Books Bulletin (RBB) section. The signed reviews are detailed, comparative, and conclude with a clear recommendation. If one is not sure about purchasing an expensive source, one should wait for the RBB review. An annual cumulation of RBB reviews is also published. *Book links* is a related publication. As a journal for school librarians and teachers, it publishes advice for "using books in the classroom," including theme-based bibliographies, discussions, and articles about reading.

17   Choice: Publication of the Association of College and Research Libraries, a division of the American Library Association. Association of College and Research Libraries, American Library

Association, 1964–. ISSN 0009-4978. $$
028   Z1035

Choice reviews online. American Library Association. www.cro2.org.

Required for all academic libraries and valuable to medium-sized and larger public libraries. Each issue includes reviews of a sizable number of reference sources appropriate for the undergraduate library. The reviews are brief, critical, comparative, and signed. An annual list in May points out the "Outstanding Academic Books and Nonbook Materials." In spite of all the automation, three-by-five-inch cards are still a popular way to distribute reviews to subject selectors. In 2006 *Choice reviews online* was redesigned to allow advanced searching, listing outstanding academic titles, and My Monthly Reviews and My Lists features. Users can browse, e-mail, print, and download any reviews, bibliographic essays, forthcoming title lists, and outstanding title lists.

18   **Library journal.** Library Journal, 1976–. ISSN 0363-0277. $$
020   Z671

A must for even the smallest library. A good part of each issue is devoted to book reviews, including reference books. The reviews are brief, signed, timely, and critical. There is also an annual list of outstanding reference sources (April 15) and of notable government documents (May 15). Online databases are frequently discussed in articles and columns. The book reviews are also available on three-by-five-inch cards.

19   **Reference and user services quarterly.** Reference and User Services Association, 1997–. ISSN 1094-9054. $
025.5   Z671

The "Sources" section of *Reference and user services quarterly* (formerly *RQ*) contains reviews of databases, reference books, and professional reading. The reviews are critical, comparative, and written by practicing librarians or educators. The "Reference Books" and the "Professional Materials" sections also list books received but not reviewed. Useful for the evaluation and selection of reference sources.

20   **Reference services review: RSR.** Pierian Press, 1973–. ISSN 0090-7324. $$
011   Z1035

A timely acquisition for medium-sized to larger reference departments. Rather than isolated reviews of just-published books, *RSR* provides a generous number of review essays, most focusing on a particular subject or type of reference source. Whether the articles are literature surveys, comparative reviews, core collections, or examination of databases, they are highly informative and cover the broad range of issues and sources important to reference service.

21   **School library journal.** Reed Business Information, 1961–. ISSN 0362-8930. $$
027.8   Z675

One of the standard selection tools for libraries serving children and young adults. Approximately half of each issue is devoted to reviews, including audiovisual materials, computer software, and more than 2,800 books each year. Because so few reference sources are published for young people, however, most of these reviews are for circulating books. Of particular interest to reference librarians is the annual "Reference Books Roundup" in the May issue. The reviews are also available on three-by-five-inch cards.

22   **Voice of youth advocates.** Scarecrow, 1978–. ISSN 0160-4201. $
027.62   Z718

An essential purchase for libraries serving young adults. Although *VOYA,* as it is commonly called, contains news notes, comments, and features, it is most useful for its reviews and collection development articles. The journal examines a variety of materials, including reference sources. The reviews are usually two to three paragraphs long and evaluate the sources in light of their value and appeal to young adults.

Websites

23   **Alibris.** Alibris. www.alibris.com.

Alibris is a website dedicated to the sale of books, movies, and music. It acts as a middleman for out-of-print and older in-print titles and titles unavailable via other channels. The site offers consolidated shipping, collection development support, and other features, such as wish lists and book fetch. When librarians search for a book, they see the available copies, their prices, and a ranking of the reliability of the booksellers. According to the website, the inventory has millions of books. Items ship from the sellers or directly from Alibris, but Alibris guarantees the shipping. Shipping discounts are applied when you order more than one item from the same seller. Other book sites include AddALL and Abebooks.

24 Amazon.com. Amazon.com.
www.amazon.com.

Amazon.com began as an Internet-based bookstore but has expanded into other retail services. It is an innovative leader in the sales of books, for example, offering a feature called "Surprise me! See a random page in this book." Includes readers' reviews as well as the more useful editorial reviews from *School library journal* and *Booklist*. The busy pages can sometimes make it hard to use as a reference source; thus, librarians may want to use the advanced search features to find specific titles. Amazon.com also acts like a middleman for the sale of used books from third-party vendors. An excellent source of information about the identity and availability of books.

25 Books in print. R. R. Bowker, 1948–.
www.booksinprint.com/bip/.

This resource is a large web-based bibliographic database. Forthcoming, in-print, and out-of-print books, audiobooks, and videos can be searched by keyword, author, title, exact title, and ISBN. Browsable by subject categories and by author, title, and subject index. Contains 5.6 million records, with a preview feature from Ebrary with 12,500 titles in mid-2006. Includes full-text reviews from *Booklist, Publisher's weekly, Library journal,* and *Choice*. Also contains contact information on more than 200,000 publishers, distributors, and wholesalers. In spite of some concerns about consistency with the data, this source is useful for collection development and acquisitions. Smaller libraries may be able to get by with other Internet-based book resources without subscribing to Books in Print.

26 WorldCat. OCLC (Online Computer Library Center). www.worldcat.org.

OCLC's WorldCat is "the world's largest network of library content and services," offering access to more than one billion items in 10,000 libraries worldwide. Users may search for books, music, videos, and digital items; find a nearby library that owns them; and borrow the items if they have a card at a participating library. They may also search for similar items. Basic and advanced searching is available. Users may access the database directly or via Google, Yahoo! or a local participating library's website.

Almanacs and Fact Books

27 Canadian almanac and directory. Copp Clark, 1948–. ISSN 0068-8193. $$
971   AY414

Standard source for all things Canadian. Includes customs information for Canadians returning from abroad, table of precedence for Canada, and words to the national anthem, provincial flags, arms, and emblems in a color section. The table of contents is in English and French. Some parts are in French, such as forms of address for heads of state. In addition to traditional almanac information, it contains directory information, such as addresses and officers of associations, institutions, professional and trade organizations, and government departments. New with this edition are AM and FM stations and Internet Service Providers. Detailed subject index.

Consumer Reports buying guide, see **905**.

Chase's calendar of events, see **901**.

28 CQ researcher online. Congressional Quarterly and EBSCO, 1991–. http://library.cqpress.com/cqresearcher/.

CQ researcher online is a great place for high school and lower-level undergraduates to begin their research. Detailed information on current hot topics is presented, including charts, pro and con discussions, and bibliographies for further reading. Includes "in-depth, unbiased coverage of health, social trends, criminal justice, international affairs, education, the environment, technology, and the economy." Each issue is on a single theme and offers about 12,000 words on that topic. The online version has coverage back to 1991.

29 Facts on File: Weekly world news digest with cumulative index. Facts on File News Services, 1940–. ISSN 0014-6641.
016.9   D410

Facts.com is the online version of *Facts on file*. It presents a digest of world and national affairs arranged under broad headings. Yearbook cumulations begin in 1940, making this a great place to check for older information. Five-year indexes are also available.

Famous first facts, see **1623**.

30 Guinness world records. Guinness Media, 1955–. ISSN 1475-7419. $
032   AG243

The guide to the superlatives of the natural and human worlds: the first, the last, the tallest, the shortest, the most, the least, and so forth. Arranged by broad topics into ten sections. Colorful photos, including some "actual size," make for visual excitement. New categories are identified with a red star, and updated records are identified with a yellow star. Includes a discussion on how to be a record breaker. Detailed subject index.

Holidays and anniversaries of the world, see **947.**

31 Issues and controversies on file. Facts on File, 1995–. ISSN 1081-941X. $$
973   JK1

Published by Facts on File, this loose-leaf service contains articles of current interest. For example, the April 28, 2006, issue has articles on gentrification, the U.S. role in the world, and religion and the Bush presidency. Charts, graphs, photos, and sidebars make this readable source appropriate for high school and first- and second-year undergraduates. Bibliographies and recommended additional sources are found at the end of each section.

32 Statistical abstract of the United States. U.S. Census Bureau. U.S. Govt. Print. Off., 1878–. Annual. ISSN 0081-4741. $ http://purl.access.gpo.gov/GPO/LPS2878.
317.3   HA202

An indispensable collection of social, political, and economic data selected from many statistical publications, both governmental and private. A section of international statistics is included for comparative purposes. Each table cites it source and thus also serves as a guide to other statistical publications and sources. Classified arrangement and detailed index. The single most important statistics fact book on American life.

33 The time almanac. Information Please, 1998–. ISSN 1529-1154. $
031   AY64

This source presents current events; U.S. government and history; U.S. states, cites, and stats; disasters; awards; people; calendars and holidays; space and aviation geography; and an extensive subject index. Includes a special section on happiness and color photos of events of the previous year. Published in conjunction with Information Please and available electronically from www.infoplease.com.

34 The world almanac and book of facts. Newspaper Enterprise Association, 1923–.

ISSN 0084-1382. $
317   AY67.N5

An essential ready-reference tool containing a plethora of information. Includes statistical material for the current and preceding years, important events of the year, associations and societies and their addresses, and many other items. Also contains solid subject indexing for easy access. Some color photos highlight the previous year. Also available as a database on FirstSearch. Belongs in libraries of all size.

Databases and Indexes

35 EBSCO academic search premier. EBSCO. www.ebsco.com.

Every library needs a general purpose database. The ones that come to mind are EBSCO Academic Search Premier, Gale's InfoTrac, ProQuest's Periodical Abstracts, and OCLC's ArticleFirst. Because of its coverage, indexing, interface, ease of use, and limiters, EBSCO Academic Search Premier is recommended. Includes PDF and HTML full-text links, ability to limit to scholarly peer-reviewed journals, and is OpenURL link enabled. Indexes 8,000 publications and has "full text for more than 4,450 of those publications." Some back files available to 1975, and cited reference searching for more than 1,000 journals.

36 LexisNexis academic. LexisNexis. www.lexisnexis.com.

Academic institutions should consider subscribing to LexisNexis Academic. Includes more than 5,000 full-text sources, including national and international news, magazines, wire services, and university newspapers. Good business coverage along with Securities and Exchange Commission reports such as 10-Ks and 10-Qs. Interface has some difficulties; for example, previous six months is the default, but the power of the content more than makes up for any design flaws.

37 Readers' guide to periodical literature. H. W. Wilson, 1904–. ISSN 0034-0464. $$
016.05   AI3

If your library keeps one printed index for when the network goes down on a Saturday afternoon, this is it. The standard author-subject index to about 260 of the most popular general and nontechnical magazines. Book reviews indexed by author in a separate section. Also available is *Readers' guide retrospective, 1890–1982,* which provides good coverage between the *19th century masterfile* (formerly *Poole's*) and databases with more modern coverage such as *Academic search premier.* Available on WilsonWeb as *Readers' guide full text, mega edition.* Indexing of periodicals back to 1983, and thirty new journals were added in 2005.

Dictionaries and Encyclopedias

Print Encyclopedias

38   Compton's. Encyclopaedia Britannica.
26v. Encyclopaedia Britannica, 2005. ISBN
1593392370. $$$
031   AG5

Geared toward students ages ten to seventeen, this encyclopedia has 37,000 entries and a *Fact-index* volume. Although 430 articles were rewritten for the 2005 edition, many are not current. The *Fact-index* volume contains brief articles and tables that are more current than material in the main body of the work. This is an adequate encyclopedia but not a preferred choice. Available online as part of the *Encyclopaedia Britannica online school edition.*

39   Encyclopedia Americana. 30v.
Scholastic Library Publishing, 2005. ISBN
0717201384. $$$
031   AE5

An encyclopedia suitable for junior and senior high school students as well as adults and college-level students. Cross-references are plentiful throughout the 45,000 articles. The index is comprehensive and analytical. Americana contains an exceptionally large number of U.S. place-names and biographies. The sciences, mathematics, American history, and the social sciences are particularly well developed. There are bibliographies at the end of major articles, nearly 400 of which have been updated for this edition. Ninety-seven articles are new or replacements, and there are more than 600 minor revisions and 186 major ones. Although a continuous revision policy is in place, updating is sometimes not as thorough as one would like.

40   The new Encyclopaedia Britannica. 32v.
Encyclopaedia Britannica, 2005. ISBN
1593392362. $$$$
031   AE5

This most famous, scholarly, and venerable of English-language encyclopedias is suitable for an adult audience and competent high school and college students. The unique three-part structure is by now familiar: the *Propaedia,* a one-volume outline of recorded knowledge and contents guide to the *Macropaedia*'s articles; the *Micropaedia,* a twelve-volume ready-reference set; and the *Macropaedia,* a seventeen-volume compilation of longer, scholarly, signed articles with bibliographies. The *Micropaedia* provides cross-references from articles to more extended treatment in the *Macropaedia* or to other related *Micropaedia* coverage. The other two parts of the set also give adequate assistance to the seeker of information in broad topical areas of philosophy, law, history, and religion, with access to specific subjects aided by the two-volume comprehensive analytical index. There are 81,000 articles in this edition. Eighty-four are new, and 3,900 are rewritten or revised. This encyclopedia is available online.

41   The World Book encyclopedia. 22v.
World Book, 2005. ISBN 0716601052.
$$$
031   AE5

Appropriate for elementary grades through high school and for general use in the home, *World Book* is also a favorite with reference librarians. The 17,300 signed articles are arranged alphabetically, word by word. Numerous cross-references and an exhaustive (more than 150,000 entries) analytical index ensure easy access to the contents of the set. The social sciences, arts and humanities, life and physical sciences, literature, and biography are covered in a clear, lively style. Technical terms are explained as they are introduced, and maps are placed near related text. Illustrations account for about one-third of the layout, and some 80 percent are in color. This edition has 77 new articles; 230 articles and 300 bibliographies are extensively revised. The index volume, titled *Research guide and index,* provides basic information on preparing written and oral reports. This encyclopedia is available online.

Electronic Encyclopedias

42   Encyclopaedia Britannica. Encyclopaedia
Britannica. www.eb.com.

Britannica offers two online versions: *Encyclopaedia Britannica online* and *Encyclopaedia Britannica online school edition.* Both include *Encyclopaedia Britannica* and *Britannica student encyclopedia* (*Compton's*), but the school edition offers a more child-friendly interface for the *Britannica elementary encyclopedia* and *Compton's* by Britannica. In addition to 120,000 encyclopedia articles, the online version includes articles from more than 450 periodicals from EBSCO and more than 300 professional and academic journals from ProQuest. There are more than 170,000 Internet links as well as 3,000 video clips, 158 sounds, and 334 animations. Other resources available include *Britannica's original sources, Webster's third new international dictionary, unabridged,* an atlas, and *Enciclopedia universal en español.* Updated every two weeks, with selected content updated daily. A thirty-day preview is available.

43   Grolier online. Scholastic.
http://go.grolier.com.

The Grolier Online suite offers online access to *Encyclopedia Americana online, Grolier multimedia encyclopedia* (grades 5 and up), and *New book of knowledge online* (elementary grades). In addition to the encyclopedias, users may access American Heritage dictionaries, an atlas, and 1,100 age-appropriate periodical articles from EBSCO Content Solutions. Other databases available from Grolier Online include *America the beautiful, Lands and peoples, The new book of popular science,* and *La nueva enciclopedia cumbre.* Update schedule varies. A thirty-day preview available.

44   Wikipedia. Wikimedia Foundation.
www.wikipedia.org.

This free encyclopedia is available on the Web in several languages. Anyone may contribute an article or edit an existing entry. There is no editorial oversight or authority control. This makes for an eclectic mix. Some entries on arcane subjects are written by experts and cover material that is hard to find. Others may be problematic. Congressional aides have been known to clean up their bosses' entries, and someone unjustly accused a journalist of assassinating both Kennedy brothers in one article. Use with caution, and verify information in another source.

45   World Book online reference center.
World Book. www.worldbook.com.

The World Book Online Reference Center offers all of the content of the print set plus more than 8,500 articles specially created for the online version. It has more than 100 videos, 10,000 sounds, 100 360-degree photographs, and 7,000 Internet links. It also has a dictionary, an atlas, parent and teacher resources, and a selection of periodical articles from

EBSCO Content Solutions. *Surf the ages* (imaginary websites from the past), *World Book research libraries* (primary source documents), and *Enciclopedia estudiantil hallazgos* (a Spanish-language encyclopedia for elementary school students) are unique resources on this site. Updated monthly; some features updated daily. No free trials offered.

Directories

46   American library directory: a classified list of libraries in the United States and Canada, with personnel and statistical data. Information Today, 1923–. ISSN 0065-910X. $$
021   Z731

Includes U.S. and Canadian public, academic, and special libraries arranged by state or province, city, and institution. Entries include name and address of school, key personnel, and library holdings. Income expenditures, e-mail addresses, subject specialties, automation and publications, and a code for type of library are also included. Additional sections include listings of networks and consortia; library schools; library systems; libraries for the blind, deaf, and disabled; state and provincial public library agencies; the interlibrary loan code; and armed forces libraries overseas. Includes an organizational and personnel index and an editorial revision form to send changes to Information Today.

47   Directories in print. 2v. Gale, 1989–.
ISSN 0899-353X. $$$
300   Z5771; AY2001

Describes and indexes 16,000 directories of all kinds, arranged in twenty-six broad subject categories. A detailed subject index and thesaurus has more than 4,700 terms and cross-references. Entries give title, subtitle, publisher's address, telephone number, description of contents, arrangement, coverage, frequency, usual month of publication, pages, indexes, price, editor's name, ISBN, GPO, or other pertinent number. Volume 1 covers descriptive listings; volume 2 contains the subject and title and keyword indexes. Includes supplements as they appear. Available in electronic format as part of Gale's Ready Reference Shelf.

48   Encyclopedia of associations. Frederick G. Ruffner, Margaret Fisk, and Gale Research Company. 5v. Gale, 1961–. ISSN

0071-0202. $$$
060   AS22

Essential information on more than 22,000 national membership organizations representing numerous business, social, educational, religious, fraternal, ethnic, and avocational interests. Convention and meeting dates and locations and titles of organizations' directories and publications are included in the entries. There are also the *Encyclopedia of associations: International organizations* and *Encyclopedia of associations: Regional, state and local organizations.* Volume 1 includes the Great Lakes states, volume 2 includes northeastern states, volume 3 covers southern and middle Atlantic states, volume 4 includes south central and Great Plains states, and volume 5 covers the western states. Libraries should subscribe to the national and at least their regional directory. Available online as part of the Gale Digital Archives.

49   The foundation directory. Foundation Center, Foundation Library Center, and Russell Sage Foundation. Foundation Center, 1960–. ISSN 0071-8092. $$
061; 060   AS911

Lists the 10,000 largest nongovernmental, nonprofit organizations that provide grants in the United States. Part 2 lists the next 10,000 foundations. Data elements covered for each include donor, purpose, assets, expenditures, officers, and grant application information. Arranged by state, with four indexes: by state and city; donors, trustees, and administrators; foundation name; and fields of interest. Foundation giving patterns are shown, with up to 10 selected grants provided where possible. Average grant award is noted to give a typical range of grant awarded. The 1,277 new entries are indicated by a star and listed in the index of new foundations. Does not include organizations whose giving is restricted by charter to one or more specified organizations.

50   Gale directory of publications and broadcast media. 5v. Gale, 1990–. ISSN 1048-7972. $$$
302.23   Z6951; PN4867

Some reference sources keep their old names for a long time. As the cover says, this title was formerly known as the *Ayer directory of publications.* It is a geographical listing of newspapers, magazines, radio stations, and other publications in the United States and abroad. The first two volumes include the United States and Canada. Volume 3 contains

the indexes, while volume 4 has regional market indexes. Volume 5 includes international coverage. Indexes include a subject index, agricultural publications, foreign-language publications, fraternal publications, magazines, newspapers, trade and professional publications, and a master index. Newsletters and directories are excluded. Defunct organizations are removed from entries and listed in the index as ceased or unable to locate. Entries include title, publisher contact information, e-mail address, description, subtitle, date founded, frequency, circulation, online availability, ad rates, and editors. Great for finding local newspapers and radio stations. Part of Gale's Ready Reference Shelf.

51   International directory of little magazines and small presses. Dustbooks, 1974–. Annual. ISSN 0092-3974. $
070.5   Z6944

Aspiring authors will appreciate the in-depth coverage of small-press publishing opportunities. Magazines and book publishers or presses are included. Entries include contact information and type of materials published, with information supplied by the publisher. For example, "We produce fiction and nonfiction series for young adults. No picture books." Includes subject indexing in area publishers have printed materials.

52   Organizing black America: An encyclopedia of African American associations. Nina Mjagkij. 768p. Garland, 2001. ISBN 0815323093. $$
369   E185.5

In the nineteenth and twentieth centuries, many African Americans joined together to establish organizations that served their communities. This guide lists 567 associations established by African Americans, interracial organizations that served black constituencies, and organizations that worked in the interest of African Americans. For example, the National Negro Business League is listed along with the National Medical Association, which was founded when the American Medical Association excluded blacks. These organizations worked to end slavery, segregation, and racism. With desegregation, many of these associations ceased to exist. The signed entries from 184 contributors include bibliographies. The entries describe the "origins, goals, founders, membership, achievements, and failures, and the ways in which the organizations influenced blacks in America."

53 Toll-free phone book USA: A directory
of toll-free telephone numbers for
business and organizations nationwide.
Omnigraphics, 1997–. ISSN 1092-0285. $$
384.6   HE8811

Lists toll-free numbers for more than 46,200
U.S. companies, associations, educational institutions, travel providers, and government agencies.
Listings include mailing address. Alphabetical and
classified arrangement. Convenient for toll-free
calling. Librarians and users can also call 800-555-1212 for 800 and 866, 877, and 888 directory information.

54 Ulrich's periodicals directory. R. R.
Bowker, 1932–. ISSN 0000-2100. $$$
011   Z6941

A classified list of current domestic and foreign
periodicals, including irregular serials and annuals. Provides complete publishing and subscription
information and indications of where each title is
indexed or abstracted. Entries include title, frequency, publisher contact information, and indication if a journal is refereed. Also includes a list of
serials that have ceased or suspended publication
since last edition. Indexing includes ISSN, title,
subject, cessations, and availability on CD-ROM or
online. Also available in electronic format.

Postal Directories

55 **Canada Post.** Canada Post Corporation.
www.canadapost.ca.

The official website for Canada Post offers postal
information in either English or French. Users can
use the site to get a postal code, calculate a rate,
find a post office, change an address, and other
services. The search interface for the six-character
alpha and numeric postal codes is well designed.

56 **United States Postal Service.** USPS.
www.usps.gov.

This site is the U.S. Postal Service's location for
Internet-based services. Use it to find a zip code,
calculate postage, print a shipping label, schedule
a pickup, find a post office, track packages, buy
stamps, and so forth. Also available free to depository libraries is the *National five digit ZIP code and
post office directory,* which performs a similar function in print.

Electronic Reference Resources

57 ABC-CLIO's history reference online.
ABC-CLIO. www.abc-clio.com.

More than 340 encyclopedias, handbooks, dictionaries, and guides focusing on U.S. and world
history, current issues, politics, and geography are
included. Some 85 percent of the titles were published between 2000 and the present, with many
multivolume encyclopedias included. One search
box, with options to search the full text, author, or
title fields, is available. Users may also browse the
collection by general subject, then title. Results,
uniquely grouped by book title, are sorted within
the title according to relevancy. Once a title is
selected, users can view full text and have easy
navigation through the rest of the book via the
table of contents and forward/back page options.
Citations, at the entry level, are available in APA,
MLA, Chicago, and Harvard styles. A new window is opened for each book title that one uses.
Does not offer options for library customization,
nor are there store, mark, and export or e-mail
options.

58 **Credo reference.** Credo Reference. http://
corp.credoreference.com.

Credo Reference, formerly Xreferplus, is an online
reference service with more than two-million
entries from 207 reference titles. With a focus on
ready-reference content, it includes subject dictionaries, biographical data, statistics, quotations,
and audio and image files from more than fifty
publishers. Two subscription options are offered,
Credo 100 and Credo Unlimited. Unlimited is the
entire collection of more than 200 titles, which
in 2007 grew by 300 titles. This service can also
be accessed through the Gale Virtual Reference
Library. What makes it unique is the cross-referencing across titles, publishers, and disciplines.
Also available are the visualization search capabilities, pronunciation files, images, dynamic table
functionality, chronology builder, and an interactive world atlas. The library administration system
allows customization with library logos and links,
provides usage statistics, and offers promotional
and educational materials. Credo Reference is
available as a subscription database. Specialized
reference titles are priced separately and may be
added to either package.

59 **Gale virtual reference library.** Gale.
www.gale.com/gvrl/.

11

The Gale Virtual Reference Library (GVRL) contains 700 reference titles from more than twenty-five publishers, including Gale, Wiley, Sage, and Cambridge, with a focus on multivolume encyclopedias from a variety of fields. Purchased title by title, the GVRL can be as large or small as needed. Using the PowerSearch interface, which is clean and well structured, the content is easy to navigate via keyword searching or browse options. Results are ranked by relevance and may be sorted by document or publication title. Articles are delivered in HTML (showing actual page breaks) with links to PDF versions. Unique features include search history access and marking, storing, and exporting items for print, e-mail, or download to bibliographic software. Articles can be approximately translated into eight languages. E-books include all front and back matter with hyperlinked table of content and indexes. Those who also subscribe to Credo Reference may access this content via this product. The cost of individual titles is 10 percent above print, plus an annual hosting fee.

60 Greenwood digital collection.
Greenwood. www.greenwood.com.

This collection includes 3,600 titles from Greenwood, Praeger, and Libraries Unlimited, including encyclopedias, dictionaries, and primary documents. About a quarter of the titles are reference and cover more than twenty-four subject areas. Browse the collection by title, subject, or author, or perform a quick or advanced search of the entire collection. Results, ranked by the number of hits, include highlighted search terms within the text and may be sorted by date, author, or title. Individual full-text entries, including tables and charts, are in HTML format as they would appear on a page in the printed book. Up to twenty pages may be printed at one time. Greenwood offers two unique features, My Bookshelf and My Bookmark and Notes, accessed via a user-initiated log-in. Libraries who wish to own the content may purchase titles individually or as packages. Prices are generally 10 percent above the print list price no matter the size of the institution. There is also an annual access fee per institution.

61 Oxford reference online. Oxford Univ. Pr.
www.oxfordreference.com.

This database contains more than 100 quick-reference titles in nearly every field. Also available is the premium collection, adding the Oxford Companion series, the *Oxford dictionary of quotations,* and other

information. Search this product on three levels; globally, subject area, or as a single reference title. An intelligent search feature, activated after an unsuccessful search, widens the search to full text and then to pattern and stem searching. Individual entries include full text and illustrations (if available), links to *see also* references within the title, browse next and previous entries, an e-mail option, and the entry citation in modified MLA format. Once users begin to navigate away from the results page, it is difficult to get back. Options for printing, exporting, or selecting the style format are not yet available. A cross-referencing tool allows users to highlight a word in the full text and locate this word in other Oxford titles. The premium collection offers additional special features. Oxford Reference Online is a subscription collection and titles are not owned by the library. Those interested in ownership should investigate Oxford's Digital Reference Shelf product.

62 Reference universe. Paratext.
www.paratext.com/ru_intro.htm.

Reference Universe searches the article titles and indexes of more than 28,000 subject encyclopedias and reference books, both print and electronic. This gives librarians and researchers the ability to search the content of reference books, content that is not available in the catalog. Keyword and browse search options are available with several options to limit results, including a limit to titles owned by one's library. Search results are listed first when search terms are found in the book title and second when terms are in the article title or index. Reference Universe also provides a means to search across electronic-reference-book platforms, including ABC-CLIO's, Credo Reference, Oxford's, Greenwood's, and Gale Virtual Reference Library. A search on "right to life" retrieves encyclopedias and articles in law, science, religion, ethics, and medicine; the first twenty titles are from more than ten different publishers. This variety by topic and publisher opens up opportunities for researchers to explore their topics from multiple perspectives. All titles are linked to the library catalog for quick access to call numbers for print and links for e-books. If libraries own the electronic book, links are provided at the title and article level. Searchable Table of Contents and indexes and links to book reviews from *ARBA, Choice,* and *Book news* make Reference Universe an effective collection development tool as well. Contact the publisher for pricing information.

Internet Searching

63 Google. Google. www.google.com.

When Vannevar Bush wrote about the Memex in "As We May Think" (*Atlantic* 176 [July 1945]: 101–108), it seems as if he had Google in mind. Google's story is beyond the scope of this book. *The Google story,* by David Siegfied (Delacorte Press, 2005), or *The search: How Google and its rivals rewrote the rules of business and transformed our culture,* by Mary Whaley (Portfolio, 2005), gives good descriptions of the search engine. In short, Google combines a very simple interface with powerful indexing to create the Web's most popular search engine. Much to many librarians' concern, information found via Google is considered reliable by many users. Information should always be verified for authority, source, content, and lack of bias. According to *Hoover's,* in 2006 Google indexed 8 billion web pages. Google Scholar is OpenURL link enabled and thus allows users to see if their libraries subscribe to materials found in a search. Additional features include translation, Google Maps, Google Earth, Google Books, and Froogle, for shopping. Google is not the Web's only search engine, and librarians and users may want to look at Search Engine Watch (www.searchenginewatch.com) for information about additional search engines.

64 Librarians' Internet index. Librarian's Internet Index. http://lii.org.

Librarians critically evaluate websites for the Librarians' Internet Index (LII), formerly the Librarians' Index to the Internet. Founded in the early 1990s as a Gopher bookmark file, the LII has gained recognition as an authoritative Internet search site. Websites come to the LII via the newsletter *New This Week,* which features "dozens of high-quality websites carefully selected, described, and organized by our team of librarians." The newsletter is also available via an RSS feed. Contains 20,000 entries organized into 14 main topics and about 300 related topics. Librarians also check and remove dead links. Funded by the states of California and Washington.

65 Yahoo! Yahoo! www.yahoo.com.

Begun by two graduate students at Stanford University, Yahoo! was originally based upon the Gopher at the University of Michigan Library. Yahoo! is a popular e-mail, chat, game, news, and entertainment site on the Internet. Includes search capability for video, audio, news, directory, shopping, and more. Although smaller than Google, Yahoo! search is a very popular feature. Entertainment, news, and directory information are strengths of Yahoo! For more information about Yahoo! Randolph Hock's *Yahoo! to the max* (CyberAge Books/Information Today, 2005) is recommended. The Internet portal also offers Yahoo! Search Subscriptions (www.search.Yahoo.com/subscriptions/).

Library Science

66 Administration of the small public library. 4th ed. Darlene E. Weingand. 256p. American Library Association, 2001. ISBN 0838907946. $
025.1   Z678.6

In the fourth edition of this title, the author continues her focus on change in libraries, marketing, and perception of the library as a business. Also included are vision, service, managing multiple objectives, cost, demands, grants, program budgeting, and nonmonetary compensation. The book addresses small communities such as suburbs, college towns, company towns, and market towns. Planning, governance, personnel, finance, and policies are all discussed. Appendixes include the "Library Bill of Rights." Will help a library manager continue to demonstrate the crucial role of libraries in the life of a small community.

67 The Bowker annual of library and book trade information. R. R. Bowker Company, Council of National Library Associations, and Council of National Library and Information Associations (U.S.). R. R. Bowker, 1962–. Annual. ISSN 0068-0540. $
020   Z731

A compendium of statistical and directory information relating to most aspects of librarianship and the book trade. Contains professional reports from the field, international library news, library legislation, grants, and survey articles of developments during the preceding year. Also contains a useful entry on how to obtain an ISBN. Index included.

68 The branch librarians' handbook. Vickie Rivers. 203p. McFarland, 2004. ISBN 0786418214. $
025.1   Z685

In the introduction, the author states: "Managing a branch library will be one of the most exciting challenges of your professional career." This guide is intended to offer encouragement and answer questions about running a branch library. The audience of this practical guide is the library branch manager. It covers such topics as working with your boss and your staff and managing yourself professionally and as a worker. Supervision, getting to know your staff, day-to-day operations, procedures, disaster planning, service desks, and special-needs patrons are also discussed. This useful guide will help make branches better neighborhood libraries.

69 **Encyclopedia of library and information science.** 2nd ed. Miriam A. Drake. 4v. Marcel Dekker, 2003. ISBN 0824720776 (v. 1); 0824720784 (v. 2); 0824720792 (v. 3); 0824720806 (v. 4). $$
020   Z1006

With more than 3,000 pages, and more than 450 professional contributors, this work presents modern issues in library science. This second edition also has a 2005 supplement and has been published electronically by Dekker.com, part of Taylor and Francis Books. End pages include brief table of contents. A selection of entries include academic branch libraries, a history of cataloging, pertinence and relevance of search results, and presidential libraries. Each signed article has references and suggested further readings. Includes subject index. Optional for smaller libraries.

70 **The librarian's copyright companion.** James S. Heller. 257p. W. S. Hein, 2004. ISBN 0837733006. $
356.7305   KF2995

This title is designed to help librarians with copyright issues. Copyright principles, owners' rights, infringement, fair use, and the library exception are all discussed. Digital licensing issues and audiovisual works are also included. The extensive appendixes include copyright websites; a bibliography; class copying guidelines; a model policy for university photocopying, including library reserves; interlibrary loan; fair use for electronic reserves; educational uses of music; a sample copyright permission letter; AALL fair-use guidelines; a sample law-firm copyright policy; image guidelines; and selected provisions of the copyright act.

71 **Managing for results: Effective resource allocation for public libraries.** Sandra S. Nelson, Ellen Altman, Diane Mayo, and Public Library Association. 362p. American Library Association, 2000. ISBN 0838934986. $
025.1   Z678

Third in a Public Library Association series, this source aims to help public librarians map out their futures. The other two titles are *Planning for results: A public library transformation process* (1998) and *Wired for the future: Developing your library technology plan* (1999). This book deals with issues around resource and staff allocation and managing facilities, technology, and collections. It will help library managers develop budgets, justify grants applications, review internal data collection, organize data, and determine the effectiveness of services. Appendixes include activities for the planning cycle, gap analysis, analyzing numeric data, library scanning, and current resource-allocation charts.

72 **The practical library manager.** Bruce E. Massis. 149p. Haworth Information Press, 2003. ISBN 0789017652; 0789017660 (pbk.). $
025.1   Z678

A short guide to running a library. Topics include managing staffing challenges, assessing the impact of technology, building staff competencies, and implementing training programs. It also discusses "clicks and bricks," challenges presented by virtual libraries, library consortia, and a bibliography of classics for the library manager. Appendixes list American Library Association–accredited library schools and sample surveys.

73 **The public library start-up guide.** Christine Lind Hage. 166p. American Library Association, 2004. ISBN 0838908667. $
025.1   Z678

The factors that relate to beginning a library include community support and public relations as well as construction and collection development issues. This title is intended as a step-by-step guide through the process of establishing a library. The author has extensive public library experience, including a start-up, and advises librarians who are facing these challenges.

Search Aggregators

74 **Library of Congress portal application issues group.** Library of Congress. www.loc.gov/catdir/lcpaig/portalproducts.html.

Search aggregators are software programs that combine results from a variety of databases and interfaces into a single search result. Public and academic libraries should have a search aggregator; however, it is not possible to recommend which one because a library's choice is dependent upon its ILS vendor, consortial situation, and other variables. The Library of Congress portal application issues group provides a good discussion and comparison of the different products. Also, the section on search aggregators in *Magazines for libraries* is very good.

2

Philosophy, Religion, and Ethics

BARBARA M. BIBEL

There are few general reference sources in philosophy, so librarians will welcome the appearance of new editions of classics in this field, like the *Encyclopedia of philosophy*. Sources in religion, however, are abundant. New ones appear daily. As our population becomes more diverse, our collections should reflect changing interests. Sources on Asian religions, Islam, and nontraditional religions and movements should join the Judeo-Christian materials that are on the shelves. Some sources on mythology, superstition, and folklore are included in this chapter because they reflect the ancient social traditions that are the basis of Western culture.

Philosophy

Databases and Indexes

75   **Philosopher's index.** Philosopher's Information Center, 1967–. ISSN 0031-7993; ISBN 9780974982502. $$
     105   B1

This is the principal index in the field, covering philosophy and the philosophy of other academic disciplines. It has an author index with abstracts as well as subject and book-review indexes.

Also available online and on CD-ROM via CSA, OCLC, and Ovid. Contact providers for pricing information.

Dictionaries and Encyclopedias

76   **Cambridge dictionary of philosophy.** 2nd ed. Robert Audi, ed. 1039p. Cambridge Univ. Pr., 1999. ISBN 0521637228 (pbk.). $
     103   B41

Compiled by an international team of 436 scholars, this edition has 400 new entries with 50 covering contemporary philosophers. The definitions are clear and thorough and cover non-Western philosophy, applied ethics, and the philosophy of the mind as well as traditional philosophical subjects.

77   **Encyclopedia of classical philosophy.** Donald J. Zeyl, ed. 630p. Greenwood, 1997. ISBN 0313287759. $$
     180.3   B163

The only current encyclopedia devoted to classical philosophy, this covers the teachings, schools, and philosophers of ancient Greece and Rome.

78   **Encyclopedia of philosophy.** 2nd ed. Donald Borchert, ed. 10v. Gale, 2005. ISBN 0028657802. $$$$
     103   B51

First published in 1967, this classic is the first stop for research in philosophy. The new edition contains material from an international group of scholars. It has over 2,100 articles, including more than 450 that are new, and 1,000 biographies of major philosophers. It covers both Western and non-Western thought.

79   Masterpieces of world philosophy. Frank N. Magill, ed. 704p. HarperCollins, 1991. ISBN 0062700510. $
100   B75

Magill has written critical essays on 100 influential philosophical works. He summarizes the major ideas in the text and provides historical background and an overview of the relevant literature on the topic.

80   New dictionary of the history of ideas. Maryanne Cline, ed. 6v. Gale, 2005. ISBN 9780684313788 $$$
903   CB9

The first *Dictionary of the history of ideas* was published in 1973–1974 and "became a landmark of scholarship on European thought." This older work is available online at www.historyofideas.org. The *New dictionary of the history of ideas* is a new work of scholarship that expands coverage into North America, Africa, Asia, Latin America, and the Middle East. This source is "designed to introduce a general audience to the main ideas and movements of global cultural history from antiquity to the twenty-first century."

81   The new encyclopedia of unbelief. Tom Flynn, ed. 800p. Prometheus Books, 2006. ISBN 1591023912. $$
211   BL2705

This is a comprehensive reference work covering the history, beliefs, and thought of those who choose to live without religion: atheists, agnostics, secular humanists, and skeptics. An international group of over 200 scholars wrote more than 500 entries covering topics such as sexuality, intelligent design, and morality.

82   Routledge encyclopedia of philosophy. Edward Craig, ed. 10v. Routledge, 1998. ISBN 0415073103. $$$$
103   B51

The shorter Routledge encyclopedia of philosophy. Edward Craig, ed. 1077p. Routledge, 2005. ISBN 0415324955. $
103   B51

This is one of the standard reference sources in philosophy. More than 2,000 entries cover the philosophy of the mind, philosophy of science, applied ethics, non-Western philosophies, and contemporary thought. The shorter version is a single volume containing the full text of the most important articles and condensed versions of the others in a single volume. The online version (www.rep.routledge.com) is a new edition with more than 100 new articles, revisions and updates of others, and web links to philosophy sites. For pricing of the online edition, contact the publisher.

83   World philosophers and their works. John K. Roth, ed. 3v. Salem Press, 2000. ISBN 0893568783. $$
109   B104

Here, 285 alphabetical entries cover 226 of the world's greatest philosophers and five significant ancient works of undetermined authorship. Articles contain a biography of the author or a discussion of the context and possible authorship, an overview of the work, and a bibliography. Subject and title indexes and a chronological list of philosophers and works will help students find what they need.

Biographical Sources

84   Biographical dictionary of twentieth-century philosophers. Diane Collinson et al., eds. 968p. Routledge, 1995. ISBN 0415060435. $$
109   B104

With more than 1,000 entries, this dictionary provides essential, difficult-to-obtain information on twentieth-century philosophers from all over the world. Entries include biographical highlights, major publications, secondary literature, and key concepts.

Religion

General Sources

BIBLIOGRAPHIES AND GUIDES

85   Recent reference books in religion: A guide for students, scholars, researchers, buyers, and readers. 2nd ed. William M. Johnston. 330p. Fitzroy Dearborn, 1998. ISBN 1579580351. $
016.2; 200.16   Z7751

A superb guide to the field of religion. Lengthy annotations describe scope, strengths, weaknesses, and competitors of works. Covers the major world religions as well as works on mythology, folklore, and ethics.

DATABASES AND INDEXES

86 ATLA religion database. American Theological Library Association. www.atla .com/atlahome.html.

This database indexes journal articles, essays, and book reviews from more than 1,500 journals covering all aspects of religion. It is available online and as a CD-ROM, updated twice a year. The journals represent all major religions and denominations, and the scope is international. Contact publisher for pricing information.

DICTIONARIES AND ENCYCLOPEDIAS

87 Encyclopedia of angels. 2nd ed. Rosemary Ellen Guiley. 416p. Facts on File, 2004. ISBN 0816050236. $

202   BL477

An overview of angels that includes their origins, natures, functions, and manifestations. The second edition includes 600 new entries, many revisions, and new images. Entries include Abraham, dreams and visions, Joan of Arc, and Gnosticism. This is a definitive source on the subject.

88 Encyclopedia of religion. 2nd ed. Lindsay Jones, ed. 15v. Macmillan Reference USA, 2004. ISBN 0028657330. $$$$

200.3   BL31

Mircea Eliade's classic work was published in 1987. The second edition includes almost all of the 2,750 entries from the original, updated, as well as approximately 600 new ones. An international team of scholars collaborated to preserve Eliade's cross-cultural approach while emphasizing religion's unique role in individual cultures. Also available as an e-book.

89 Oxford dictionary of world religions. John Bowker, ed. 1136p. Oxford Univ. Pr., 1997. ISBN 0198662424. $

200.3   BL31

The concise Oxford dictionary of world religions. John Bowker, ed. 736p. Oxford

Univ. Pr., 2005. ISBN 019861053X. $

200.3   BL31

Offers clear information in brief definitions of terms from all of the world's religions. An introductory essay on religion and 8,200 alphabetical entries provide a great deal of information. The concise dictionary is an abridged version.

Bible

ATLASES

90 Bible atlas. 3rd ed. Yohanan Aharoni et al. 224p. Wiley, 1993. ISBN 9780025006058. $

220.9   G2230

First published in 1968, this atlas covers religious, political, military, and economic events associated with the Bible from 3000 BCE to 200 CE. It has monochrome maps and substantial text commentary.

91 Oxford Bible atlas. 4th ed. Herbert G. May; ed. by Adrian Curtis. 240p. Oxford Univ. Pr., 2007. ISBN 9780191001581 $

220.9   BS630

This atlas has information from the most recent advances in biblical, archaeological, and topographical research.

COMMENTARIES

92 International Bible commentary. William R. Farmer et al., eds. 1986p. Liturgical Press, 2005. ISBN 9780814624548. $

220.7   BS511.2

A new Catholic Bible commentary with bibliographical references and an index. Scholars from all over the world have contributed to this multicultural interpretation of scripture.

93 New interpreter's Bible. Leander E. Keck et al. 12v. plus index Abingdon, 1994–2004. ISBN 0687063477; 0687039169 (index vol.); 0687019990 (CD-ROM). $$$; $ (index vol.); $$$ (CD-ROM)

220.7   BS491.2

The *New interpreter's Bible* provides authoritative exposition and exegesis of the Bible using both the New Revised Standard Version and the New International Version as base texts.

94 The new Jerome biblical commentary.
3rd ed. Raymond E. Brown et al., eds.
1475p. Prentice-Hall, 1999. ISBN
9780138598365. $
220.7   BS491.2

A single-volume Catholic commentary that offers line-by-line explanation as well as thorough topical articles on hermeneutics, canonicity, Old Testament themes, and biblical theology. There are also articles on Gnosticism, Jesus, and the early church.

CONCORDANCES

95 New Strong's exhaustive concordance of the Bible. Rev. ed. James Strong.
1968p. Thomas Nelson, 2001. ISBN
0785245405. $
220.5   BS425

A classic source since 1894, the latest edition of Strong's concordance features expanded word studies so that readers can gain better understanding of the Hebrew, Greek, and Chaldee words used in the Bible. This concordance is based on the King James Version. There is also a 2005 publication, *New Strong's concise concordance of the Bible.*

DATABASES AND INDEXES

96 New Testament abstracts. Weston Jesuit School of Theology, 1956–. ISSN 0028-6877. $
220.05   BS410

Provides abstracts of books and articles from 350 Jewish, Catholic, and Protestant periodicals.

97 Old Testament abstracts. Catholic Bible Association of America, 1978–. ISSN 0364-8591. $
220   BS410

Provides abstracts of books and articles from 350 Jewish, Catholic, and Protestant periodicals.

DICTIONARIES AND ENCYCLOPEDIAS

98 Anchor Bible dictionary. David Noel Freedman. 6v. Doubleday, 1992. ISBN 038542583X. $$
220.3   BS440

Nearly 1,000 scholars with various religious affiliations participated in creating this comprehensive six-volume set. It contains 6,200 entries with bibliographies and serves as a companion to the Anchor Bible Commentaries series. This scholarly, well-written source is an important text in Biblical scholarship.

99 HarperCollins Bible dictionary. Rev. ed. Paul J. Achtemeier, ed. 1280p. HarperOne, 1996. ISBN 0060600373. $
220.3   BS440

This revision of a favorite source is a nonsectarian scholarly work based on the Revised Standard Version. It includes an outline of each book of the Bible and all the important names, places, and topics. Major articles cover recent archaeological findings and explain the variety and significance of the many versions of the Bible. It has a color map section and many black-and-white photographs as well as an index and cross-references.

100 The international standard Bible encyclopedia. Rev. ed. Geoffrey W. Bromley, ed. 4v. Eerdmans, 1979–1995. ISBN 0802837859. $$
220.3   BS440

This revision of a standard Bible encyclopedia is more scholarly and more conservative than the first edition. It defines, explains, and identifies terms and topics that interest students and clergy.

101 Mercer dictionary of the Bible. Watson E. Mills et al., eds. 993p. Mercer Univ. Pr., 1998. ISBN 0865543739. $
220.3   BS440

A balanced dictionary of current biblical scholarship containing 1,450 signed articles. Feminist thought is included where appropriate.

102 The new interpreter's dictionary of the Bible. Katharine Doob Sakenfeld. 5v. Abingdon, 2006–2008 (in progress). ISBN 0687333466. $$
220.3   BS440

This new dictionary will have articles on 7,100 topics, including persons, places, things, and theological concepts. It is based on the New Revised Standard Version and written by more than 800 scholars from forty countries and a variety of perspectives.

103 Zondervan pictorial encyclopedia of the Bible. Merrill Chapin Tenney, ed. 5v.

Zondervan, 1975. ISBN 0310331889. $$
220.3   BS440

This encyclopedia has a conservative critical and theological approach to the persons, places, objects, customs, historical events, key themes, and doctrines of the Bible. The color illustrations are a valuable feature. Articles are signed, and the longer ones have bibliographies.

HANDBOOKS

104   Oxford companion to the Bible. Bruce M. Metzger and Michael D. Coogan, eds. 874p. Oxford Univ. Pr., 1993. ISBN 0195046455. $
220.3   BS440

The *Oxford companion to the Bible* offers criticism and historical background on the full range of questions surrounding the Bible and its content. It has maps, a bibliography, and an index.

105   Roget's thesaurus of the Bible. A. Colin Day. 900p. Book Sales, 2004. ISBN 9780785817086. $
220.3   BS432

This book uses Roget's category concept to group together similar subjects and opposite subjects, making it easy for users to locate Bible verses and passages.

106   Who's who in the Bible. Reader's Digest editors. 480p. Reader's Digest, 1994. ISBN 0895776189. $
220.9   BS570

Biographical information on 500 figures from the Hebrew and Christian scripture and the Apocrypha of the Revised Standard Version. Color illustrations, maps, sidebars with interesting facts, and a list of biblical names make this a very useful source.

Religion in the United States

DICTIONARIES AND ENCYCLOPEDIAS

107   Dictionary of Christianity in America: A comprehensive resource on the religious impulse that shaped a continent. Daniel G. Reid et al. 1306p. InterVarsity, 1990. ISBN 083081776X. $
277.3   BR515

This source offers authoritative information and historical perspective on the development of Christianity in English-speaking North America. The 4,000 signed entries cover denominations, movements, and individuals. Many entries have bibliographies.

108   Encyclopedia of African-American religions. Larry G. Murphy, J. Gordon Melton, and Gary L. Ward, eds. 962p. Garland, 1993. ISBN 0815305001. $$
200.89   BR563

This encyclopedia provides cultural background on current practices in African American religion but does not trace them back to their African origins. The alphabetical entries include 777 biographies.

109   The encyclopedia of American religions. 6th ed. J. Gordon Melton, ed. 1243p. Gale, 1998. ISBN 9780810381470. $$
291.097   BL2525

A comprehensive guide covering more than 2,100 North American religious groups. It includes information about their historical development, theologies, and lifestyles. Information about small, obscure religious groups is especially valuable. Several indexes and an extensive bibliography make this work very useful.

110   Encyclopedia of American religious history. Rev. ed. Edward L. Queen et al. 2v. Facts on File, 2001. ISBN 0816043353. $$
200.973   BL2525

This encyclopedia examines the people, religions, and social movements that played important roles in American history. The articles are signed and have brief bibliographies.

111   The encyclopedia of Native American religions. Rev. ed. Arlene B. Hirschfelder and Paulette Fairbanks Molin. 390p. Facts on File, 2000. ISBN 9780816039494. $
299.7   E98R3

The 1,200 alphabetical entries in this work describe the practices, ceremonies, sacred places, myths, and principal figures associated with Native American religions. The work also examines the impact of missionaries and contact with Europeans and other Americans and their effects on these traditions.

DIRECTORIES

112   Handbook of denominations in the United States. 12th ed. Frank Spencer Mead et al. 430p. Abingdon, 2005. ISBN 9780687057849. $
200.973   BL2525

This source describes the Christian, Islamic, and Jewish denominations in the United States and offers statistics, principal doctrines, and history. The first edition of this source was published in 1951. Entries include name, date founded, membership, number of churches, description of beliefs, and contact information. Includes 235 religious denominations in the United States, from Shia Islam to Roman Catholic Church to Primitive Baptists.

BIOGRAPHICAL SOURCES

113   American religious leaders. Timothy L. Hall. 430p. Facts on File, 2003. ISBN 0816045348. $
200.92   BL72

This source offers brief profiles of more than 270 American religious leaders. They represent all faiths, including Native American religions. The biographies are brief. The book has a bibliography, a glossary, and alphabetical, religious affiliation, and chronological indexes.

Religions

GENERAL SOURCES

114   The encyclopedia of world religions. Rev. ed. Robert S. Ellwood and Gregory D. Alles. 528p. Facts on File, 2006. ISBN 0816061416. $
200.3   BL80.3

This encyclopedia provides reliable, unbiased information on the world's religions, both ancient and modern. More than 600 alphabetical entries cover both specific religions and concepts, such as fundamentalism. A good resource for public and school libraries.

115   How to be a perfect stranger: The essential religious etiquette handbook. 4th ed. Stuart M. Matlins and Arthur J. Magida, eds. 432p. Skylight Paths, 2006. ISBN 1594731403. $
291.38   BJ2010

This fascinating and useful manual will help users understand religious rituals and feel comfortable when attending a service or ceremony at an institution of a faith different from their own. A religious glossary, calendar of holidays and festivals, and a summary of proper forms of address for religious leaders are included. Unfortunately, there is no index.

116   Introduction to the world's major religions. Emily Taitz et al. 6v. Greenwood, 2005. ISBN 0313336342. $$
200   BL80.3

Each of these six volumes covers one of the world's major religions: Judaism, Confucianism and Taoism, Buddhism, Christianity, Islam, and Hinduism. They offer good overviews of the history, texts and major tenets, branches, practice worldwide, rituals and holidays, and major figures and have glossaries, bibliographies, and indexes.

ASIAN RELIGIONS

117   Buddhism. Rev. ed. Madhu Bazaz Wangu. 128p. Facts on File, 2002. ISBN 0816047286. $
294.3   BQ4032; BQ277

This concise encyclopedia gives users the history and development of Buddhism and information on its three major schools of thought, its philosophy, and its precepts.

118   Confucianism. Rev. ed. Thomas Hoobler and Dorothy Hoobler. 128p. Facts on File, 2004. ISBN 0816057281. $
299.5   BL1852

Confucianism is a system of ethical behavior and social responsibility that evolved into one of the world's great spiritual traditions. This encyclopedia presents the basic tenets of Confucian thought, its evolution in response to Chinese history, and its relevance in the modern world.

119   Encyclopedia of Hinduism. Constance Jones and James D. Ryan. 512p. Facts on File, 2007. ISBN 9780816054589. $
294.503   BL1105

This new encyclopedia provides a good overview of the Hindu religion: history, scriptures, practices, gods and goddesses, and culture.

120   **Shinto.** Rev. ed. Paula R. Hartz. 128p.
      Facts on File, 2004. ISBN 0816057257. $
      299.5   BL2220

Shinto is an ancient Japanese tradition. It is deeply
ingrained in Japanese culture. This book explains
the rituals, traditions, and values and their role in
contemporary society.

121   **Sikhism.** Rev. ed. Nikky-Guninder Kaur
      Singh. 128p. Facts on File, 2004. ISBN
      0816057265. $
      294.6   BL2018

Sikhism is one of the world's youngest religions,
founded in India only 500 years ago. Sikhs believe
in the Ultimate Reality, a formless force that is above
all things and yet present in them. They reject distinctions based on social class and race. This concise volume explains the beliefs and practices as
well as the political problems facing Sikhs in India
and the struggles of Sikhs living in the West.

122   **Taoism.** Rev. ed. Paula R. Hartz. 128p.
      Facts on File, 2004. ISBN 0816057249. $
      299.5   BL1920

Taoism is a philosophical and religious tradition
that developed in China. It has no one god or
founding prophet and states that each person must
follow his or her own path to the Tao (way of life).
This book examines the tradition and its influence
on the world's cultures.

CHRISTIANITY

Dictionaries and Encyclopedias

123   **Blackwell encyclopedia of modern
      Christian thought.** Alister E. McGrath,
      ed. 720p. Blackwell, 1995. ISBN
      0631198962. $
      230.0903   BR95

This source presents the views of the most eminent
theologians of the eighteenth through the twentieth
centuries on the key issues of the times.

124   **Encyclopedia of early Christianity.**
      2nd ed. Everett Ferguson, Frederick
      W. Norris, and Michael P. McHugh,
      eds. 2v., 1213p. Garland, 1997. ISBN
      0815316631. $$
      270.1   BR162.2

More than 150 scholars collaborated to create
1,200 entries covering the early church from the

life of Jesus to the seventh century. The scholarly
but accessible presentation makes this an important part of the reference collection.

125   **Encyclopedia of Protestantism.**
      J. Gordon Melton. 628p. Facts on File,
      2005. ISBN 0816054568. $$
      280   BX4811.3

More than 800 alphabetical entries cover people,
places, theological issues, and historical and modern views of Protestant movements. The introduction provides a definition of Protestantism and a
historical outline of the Reformation.

126   **Mormonism for dummies.** Jana Riess
      and Christopher Kimball Bigelow. 384p.
      Wiley, 2005. ISBN 0764571958. $
      289.3   BX8635.3

Two Mormons explain how the Church of Jesus
Christ of Latter-day Saints differs from other
Christian churches. They cover the history, beliefs,
and rituals as well as the debates over race, polyg-
amy, and the status of women.

127   **New Catholic encyclopedia.** Rev.
      Berard Marthaler, OFM Conv., ed. 15v.
      Gale, 2002. ISBN 0787640042. $$$$
      282   BX841

The first new edition of this monumental work
in more than thirty years is the work of more
than 200 contributors under the auspices of the
Catholic University of America. A total of 12,000
entries are completely revised and updated to
reflect the new (1983) Code of Canon Law. There
are hundreds of new articles, including biographies of contemporary religious figures and coverage of controversial issues such as gender and
reproduction.

128   **New international dictionary
      of Pentecostal and charismatic
      movements.** Stanley M. Burgess and
      Eduard M. van der Maas, eds. 1328p.
      Zondervan, 2002. ISBN 0310224810. $
      270.8   BR1644

This dictionary has 1,000 entries and 500 photographs that provide information on Pentecostal
and charismatic movements in sixty countries and
regions of the world. Bibliographies and indexes to
people, places, and subjects provide easy access to
the content.

129 New Westminster dictionary of liturgy and worship. 1st American ed. Paul F. Bradshaw. 493p. Westminster John Knox Press, 2003. ISBN 0664226558. $
264 BV173

This work presents an ecumenical approach to the liturgies of the various Christian sects. It covers revisions made by the Catholic and Protestant churches as well as historical background.

130 Oxford dictionary of the Christian Church. 3rd ed. F. L. Crosby and E. A. Livingstone, eds. 1840p. Oxford Univ. Pr., 2005. ISBN 9780192802903. $$
270.03; 260.3 BR95

More than 6,000 alphabetical entries cover Christian history, beliefs, practices, traditions, and people. An authoritative one-volume work. This edition is not a major revision: some changes were made to accommodate an electronic version, some new articles were added, and bibliographies were updated.

131 Oxford history of Christian worship. Geoffrey Wainwright and Karen B. Westerfield Tucker, eds. 960p. Oxford Univ. Pr., 2005. ISBN 9780195138863. $
264 BV15

This is a comprehensive and authoritative treatment of the history of the origins and development of Christian worship. It looks at Catholic, Orthodox, Protestant, and Pentecostal practices in all parts of the world.

Directories, Yearbooks, and Almanacs

132 Catholic almanac. Matthew Bunson. Our Sunday Visitor, 1904–. Annual. ISBN 1592762301. $
282 BX845

This annual compendium of facts about the Catholic Church includes a chronological summary of the year's events from the Vatican, the United States, and the world as well as handbook information on Catholic topics. It is well edited and indexed.

133 Official Catholic directory. National Register staff. P. J. Kenedy and Sons, 1817–. Annual. ISSN 0078-3854. $$
282 BX845

This directory provides current information about churches, clergy, schools, hospitals and other institutions in each diocese of the United States. It also contains statistics, a pilgrimage guide, and information about the Catholic church worldwide.

134 A place for God: A guide to spiritual retreats and retreat centers. Timothy K. Jones. 480p. Doubleday, 2000. ISBN 0385491581. $
647.94 BV5068

This is a guide to 250 retreat centers, mostly Catholic, in the United States. It is organized by state and includes information on the type of accommodations and nearby sites of interest.

135 Yearbook of American and Canadian churches. Eileen W. Lindner. National Council of Churches, 1973–. Annual. ISSN 0195-9403. $
277 BR513

This source includes directory, statistical, and historical information about religious and ecumenical organizations, service agencies, churches, educational institutions, and depositories of religious materials. It also has lists of religious periodicals. Print subscription includes a one-year subscription to the online version.

Biographical Sources

136 Butler's lives of the saints. Alban Butler; Paul Burns, ed. 640p. Liturgical Press, 2005. ISBN 9780814629031. $
282.092 BX4654.3

This concise and updated version of Butler's work offers one saint per day per month through the calendar year. They are selected from the new full edition, published 1995–2000, in twelve volumes.

137 Dictionary of saints. Rev. ed. John J. Delaney. 720p. Doubleday, 2005. ISBN 0385515200. $
282.092 BX4655.8

This compendium of 5,000 saints has been revised to include those newly canonized and beatified. It includes listings of feast days, patron saints, and saints' symbols.

138 Encyclopedia of saints. Rosemary Ellen Guiley. 432p. Facts on File, 2001. ISBN 0816041334. $
282.092 BX4655.8

The 400 entries in this encyclopedia describe the lives of saints within a social and historical context. Detailed appendixes provide information on patron saints by topic, a calendar of feast days, beatified and canonized popes, and an explanation of the canonization process and glossaries of heresies and terms.

139   Oxford dictionary of popes. Rev. ed. J. N. D. Kelley and Michael Walsh. 368p. Oxford Univ. Pr., 2006. ISBN 9780198614333. $
282.092   BX955.25

The new edition of this work is current with expanded coverage of John Paul II's life and an entry for Benedict XVI. It is arranged chronologically with an alphabetical index.

140   Oxford dictionary of saints. Rev. ed. David Hugh Farmer. 607p. Oxford Univ. Pr., 2004. ISBN 9780198609490. $
270.092   BR1710

This book offers concise accounts of the lives of more than 1,400 saints, including martyrs from Korea, Vietnam, and the Spanish civil war. It also has maps of pilgrimage sites in Europe and brief bibliographies.

ISLAM

141   The American Muslim. The American Muslim. www.theamericanmuslim.org.

According to their website, the American Muslim strives to "provide an open forum for the discussion of ideas and issues of concern to Muslims in America" and to "provide a forum for and encourage intercommunity dialogue particularly on divisive issues, and to encourage interfaith dialogue to find common ground for cooperation on issues of mutual concern." It also seeks to "help people of faith (Muslims, Christians and Jews) who share our concern for dialogue, peaceful resolution of problems to find each other so they can work together" and "provide a balanced, moderate, alternative voice focusing on the spiritual, dimension of Islam rather than the more often heard voice of extreme political Islamism."

142   A concise encyclopedia of Islam. Gordon Newby. 256p. Oneworld, 2002. ISBN 9781851682959. $
297.03   BP40

This illustrated reference guide to Islamic tradition contains more than 1,000 entries covering

people, places, events, beliefs, and rituals. It includes the different branches and movements within Islam: Sunni, Shia, and Sufi. A chronology, a bibliography, and a list of the ninety-nine divine names complete the work. *Encyclopedia of Islam* (2008), edited by Juan Campo, is available from Facts on File.

143   Encyclopedia of Islam and the Muslim world. Richard C. Martin, ed. 2v., 823p. Gale, 2004. ISBN 9780028656038. $$
909   BP40

This two-volume set with about 500 articles presents the work of 500 international scholars. The audience is high school through university readers. Contains 170 photographs, drawings, and charts and a glossary of commonly used Arabic and Islamic terms. This set will be useful for libraries of all sizes because of the interest in learning about Islam.

144   The holy Qur'an. Alawi D. Kayal; M. H. Shakar, trans. 10v., 640p. Kegan Paul International, 2002. ISBN 9780710307668. $
297   BP109

With the high interest in Islam, libraries of all sizes should have a Qur'an. This edition is a good choice. The bilingual text in English and Arabic is the accepted way to publish the Qur'an. Multivolume format will come in handy for patrons.

JUDAISM

145   American Jewish yearbook. American Jewish Committee, 1899–. Annual. ISSN 0065-8987. $
296   E184

This almanac has information about Jewish life and culture, including population statistics, directories of Jewish organizations and periodicals, a religious calendar, necrology, and coverage of international Jewish politics, communities, and periodicals.

146   Biblical literacy: The most important people, events, and ideas of the Hebrew Bible. Joseph Telushkin. 656p. Morrow, 1997. ISBN 9780688142971. $
221.6   BS1140.2

Rabbi Telushkin acts as a guide for a tour of the Hebrew Bible, pointing out the important people, places, and ideas within the text.

147 **The book of Jewish values: A day-by-day guide to ethical living.** Joseph Telushkin. 544p. Crown/Harmony/Bell Tower, 2000. ISBN 9780609603307. $
296.3   BJ1285

This book offers advice based on Jewish sacred texts for living an ethical life in a morally complex world.

148 **A code of Jewish ethics.** Joseph Telushkin. 576p. Crown/Harmony/Bell Tower, 2006. ISBN 9781400048359. $
296.3   BJ1285.2

This is the first of three volumes of Rabbi Telushkin's major treatise on Jewish ethics. Using scripture, Talmud, and rabbinic commentary, he discusses ethics in personal life. The next two volumes will focus on interpersonal issues and family, friends, and community.

149 **Dictionary of Jewish lore and legend.** Alan Unterman. 261p. Thames and Hudson, 1997. ISBN 0500279845. $
296   BM50

This illustrated volume explains the colorful characters and legends in Jewish folklore and the traditions upon which they are based. Both Ashkenazic and Sephardic lore are included. Information on mystical movements, customs, festivals, and home life is given.

150 **Encyclopedia Judaica.** Fred Skolnik and Michael Berenbaum. 22v. Thomson Gale, 2006. ISBN 0028659287. $$$$
909   DS102.8

This classic resource has been thoroughly revised and updated. The new edition has 22,000 signed articles by American, Israeli, and European scholars, including more than 2,500 new entries dealing with gender issues and Jewish life in New World geographic areas. It also has more than 600 maps, charts, and other illustrations.

151 **The essential Kabbalah: The heart of Jewish mysticism.** Daniel C. Matt. 240p. HarperCollins, 1996. ISBN 0062511637 (pbk.). $
296.1   BM525

An eminent Kabbalah scholar has created an anthology in translation of the principal Jewish mystical texts.

152 **The essential Talmud.** Adin Steinsaltz. 304p. Jason Aronson, 1992. ISBN 9780876681602. $
296.1   BM503.5

One of the greatest living teachers of Talmud offers an introduction to this Jewish text, describing its structure and the methods used to study it.

153 **Etz Hayim: Torah and commentary.** David L. Lieber, ed. 1560p. Jewish Publication Society, 2001. ISBN 0827607121. $
222   BS1223

The Torah: A modern commentary. Rev. ed. W. Gunther Plaut and David E. Stein. 1604p. Union for Reform Judaism, 2004. ISBN 0807408832. $
222   BS1225.53

These two Torahs with commentary present the first five books of the Hebrew Bible divided into weekly readings along with commentary from scholars. *Etz Hayim* is from the Conservative movement, and *The Torah: A modern commentary* is from the Reform movement.

154 **A guide to Jewish prayer.** Adin Steinsaltz. 464p. Schocken Books, 2002. ISBN 9780805211474. $
296.45   BM660

Rabbi Steinsaltz explains the origins and meaning of prayer, the structure of Sabbath and festival services, the history of the synagogue, and the different rites of Ashkenazic, Sephardic, Yemenite, and other cultural groups.

155 **How to run a traditional Jewish household.** Blu Greenberg. 520p. Simon and Schuster, 1985. ISBN 0671602705. $
296.74   BM700

This concise guide to Jewish living provides clear explanations of dietary laws, family purity laws, traditions, and holidays and how they are integrated into home life.

156 **The Jewish holidays: A guide and commentary.** Michael Strassfeld. 256p. HarperCollins, 1993. ISBN 0062720082. $
296.43   BM690

Seasons of our joy: A modern guide to the Jewish holidays. Arthur J. Waskow.

272p. Beacon Press, 1991. ISBN
9780807036112. $
296.43   BM690

These two guides explain the Jewish festivals and
the traditions associated with them. They discuss
the theological basis of the holidays and offer
appropriate readings. Waskow's book includes
recipes for special holiday foods.

157   **Jewish women in America: An
historical encyclopedia.** Paula E.
Hyman and Deborah Dash Moore.
2v., 1800p. Routledge, 1997. ISBN
0415919363. $$
920.72   DS115.2

Sponsored by the American Jewish Historical Society,
this award-winning work contains authoritative bio-
graphical entries on more than 800 women as well
as 110 topical entries on organizations, movements,
vocations, culture, and so forth. Spanning the years
1654 to the present, these volumes include more
than 500 photographs and an extensive bibliogra-
phy. A masterful reference source.

158   **The JPS guide to Jewish traditions.**
Ronald L. Eisenberg. 806p. Jewish
Publication Society, 2004. ISBN
0827607601. $
296.4   BM50

This is a comprehensive guide to Jewish life and
culture. It explains life-cycle events, the Sabbath
and festivals, the synagogue and prayers, and such
miscellaneous topics as food, animals, plants, and
magic and superstition.

159   **JPS Hebrew-English Tanakh: Standard
edition.** 2040p. Jewish Publication
Society, 1999. ISBN 0827606567. $
221.44   BS895

**The Jewish study Bible: Jewish
Publication Society Tanakh
translation.** Adele Berlin, Michael
Fishbane, and Marci Zvi Brettler.
2818p. Oxford Univ. Pr., 2003. ISBN
0195297512. $
220.447   BS895

The *JPS Hebrew-English Tanakh* contains the com-
plete Hebrew text based on the Leningrad Codex
side-by-side with an English translation based on
modern biblical scholarship. *The Jewish study Bible*
uses that translation along with introductions and

extensive commentary by eminent scholars to help
readers fully understand the text.

160   **Judaica reference sources: A selective
annotated bibliographic guide.** 3rd
ed. Charles Cutter. 392p. Libraries
Unlimited, 2004. ISBN 1591581338. $
016.909   Z6366

An annotated guide to resources dealing with all
aspects of Judaica. It has author and title indexes
and extensive cross-references. Also available as an
e-book.

161   **Oxford dictionary of the Jewish
religion.** R. J. Zwi Werblowsky and
Geoffrey Wigoder. 792p. Oxford Univ.
Pr., 1997. ISBN 9780195086058. $$
296.03   M50

This one-volume work serves as a reference to the
various facets of Jewish religion and its teachings.
With its focus on religion rather than culture, it
provides an excellent scholarly reference work for
the library and home. It includes significant bibliographic citations for each entry.

OTHER LIVING RELIGIONS

162   **Baha'i faith.** Paula R. Hartz. 128p. Facts
on File, 2002. ISBN 0816047294. $
297.93   BP365

Although this is among the youngest religions,
it now has six million members worldwide. This
book explores the history, beliefs, and practices of
the Baha'i faith.

163   **Encyclopedia of cults, sects, and new
religions.** 2nd ed. James R. Lewis, ed.
775p. Prometheus Books, 2001. ISBN
9781573928885. $$
200.3   BL2525

This book has 1,000 entries covering a wide range
of historically significant and obscure religious
groups. The entries are brief and objective.

164   **Encyclopedia of new religious
movements.** Peter Clarke, ed.
800p. Routledge, 2005. ISBN
9780415267076. $$
200.9034   BL31; BL98

This new encyclopedia covers new religious movements all over the world. Entries cover people,

movements, concepts, and ideologies as well as topics such as exit counseling.

165 **Essential Wicca.** Estelle Daniels and Paul Tuitean. 350p. Crossing Press, 2004. ISBN 9781589010996. $
299   BF1566

This book clarifies the principles, underlying beliefs, and practices of Wicca. It includes 100 illustrations and a glossary as well as information about group rituals and festivals.

166 **New Age encyclopedia: A mind-body-spirit reference guide.** Rev. ed. Belinda Whitworth. 288p. Career Press, 2003. ISBN 9781564146403. $
299   BP605

This source provides an overview of new age beliefs and practices, including various bodywork techniques, numerology, and spirit guides. It also has a directory of addresses for organizations and websites.

167 **New religions: A guide; New religious movements, sects, and alternative spiritualities.** Christopher Partridge, ed. 448p. Oxford Univ. Pr., 2004. ISBN 9780195220421. $
200.9034   BP603

This book is organized according to a new classification that associates movements, sects, and spiritualities with the religious traditions from which they arose; for example, Baha'i is an offshoot of Islam. It covers movements inspired by indigenous and Pagan traditions as well as more mainstream groups.

168 **The Rastafarians.** 20th ed. Leonard E. Barret Sr. 328p. Beacon Press, 1997. ISBN 9780807010396. $
299   BL2532

This is a classic study of the culture, religion, history, ideology, and influence of the Rastafarians.

169 **Santería: The religion; Faith, rites, magic.** Migene González-Wippler. 384p. Llewellyn, 2002. ISBN 9781567183290. $
299.67   BL2532

The author presents the gods, beliefs, practices, herbs, and sacrifices that are part of the Santería religion. The book includes photographs and interviews with Santería leaders.

170 **Voodoo in Haiti.** Reprint. Alfred Metraux. Schocken Books, 1972. OP.
133.4   BL2490

This older title is a classic study that explains the origins of Voodoo and its rites and traditions. The most widely held edition is the one from 1972 published by Schocken Books. This is a reprint of Metraux's classic work, which Oxford University Press published in 1959. If libraries own an older edition, it may be sufficient for their collection. It is also available from Textbook Publishers (www.textbookpublishers.net) as an on-demand title.

171 **Zoroastrianism.** Rev. ed. Paula R. Hartz. 128p. Facts on File, 2004. ISBN 0816057230. $
295   BL1572

Zoroastrianism is one of the world's oldest monotheistic religions. This book traces its history and explains its beliefs. It also looks at Zoroastrian communities in Iran and India.

Mythology

172 **Dictionary of gods and goddesses.** Michael Jordan. 416p. Facts on File, 2004. ISBN 0816059233. $
202   BL473

This dictionary has entries covering more than 2,500 gods and goddesses from ancient and modern religions in all parts of the world.

173 **Facts on File encyclopedia of world mythology and legend.** 2nd ed. Anthony S. Mercatante; rev. by James R. Dow. 2v., 1120p. Facts on File, 2004. ISBN 9780816047086 $$
291.1   BL303

This thoroughly revised and updated edition covers more than 3,000 myths and legends from around the world, both ancient and modern. It has 400 illustrations, a bibliography, and extensive cross-referencing.

174 **Oxford companion to world mythology.** David Leeming. 516p. Oxford Univ. Pr., 2005. ISBN 9780195156690. $$
201.3   BL312

The author explores the role of mythology in history and examines all aspects of the world's major mythological traditions. The work is illustrated and has appendixes with family trees of the major pantheons; equivalency charts for the major gods of Greece, Rome, Babylon, and Sumer; an extensive bibliography; and an index.

175   **Penguin dictionary of classical mythology.** Pierre Grimal and Cecil Parrott; Stephen Kershaw, ed.; A. R. Maxwell-Hyslop, trans. 480p. Penguin, 1992. ISBN 0140512357. $

292.1   BL715

The first English translation of a French classic, this is a superb guide, with thirty-four pages of genealogical tables to clarify relationships.

176   **Tree of souls: The mythology of Judaism.** Howard Schwartz. 704p. Oxford Univ. Pr., 2007. ISBN 9780195327137. $

296.1   BM530

The first anthology of Jewish mythology has nearly 700 Jewish myths gathered from the Bible, the Talmud, Midrash, kabbalistic literature, and pseudographia as well as medieval and Hasidic lore.

Ethics

Bibliographies and Guides

177   **Bibliography of bioethics.** National Reference Center for Bioethics Literature. Kennedy Institute of Ethics, Georgetown Univ., 1975–. Annual. ISSN 0363-0161 $

016.174   Z6675; R724

This bibliography is derived from bioethics citations in the databases of the National Library of Medicine. Users may search the database at www.georgetown.edu/research/nrcbl/nrc/index.htm.

Dictionaries and Encyclopedias

178   **Encyclopedia of applied ethics.** Ruth Chadwick et al., eds. 4v. Academic Press, 1997. ISBN 0122270657. $$$$

170.3   BJ63

This award-winning work divides the realm of ethics into twelve major subject areas, including medical, scientific, legal, business, and media

ethics. It has 281 signed articles on specific topics within these areas such as abortion, advertising, animal research, and auditing practices. Each entry includes a contents outline, a glossary, a defining statement, and a bibliography.

179   **Encyclopedia of ethics.** 2nd ed. Lawrence C. Becker and Charlotte B. Becker, eds. 5v., 2032p. Routledge, 2001. ISBN 0415936721. $$$

170.3   BJ63

The editors of this edition worked with 325 scholars to update all of the articles and add 150 new ones. New entries include fiduciary relationships, the Holocaust, gay ethics, bad faith, and political correctness.

180   **Ethics.** Rev. ed. John K. Roth, ed. 3v. Salem Press, 2004. ISBN 158765170X. $$

170.3   BJ63

This new edition has 1,007 essays, 200 of which are new. The main emphasis is applied ethics, and it is a student rather than a scholarly work. It covers people, concepts, cultures, and works. It has an annotated list of organizations with web addresses, a biographical directory of people mentioned, and a timeline of primary works of moral and ethical philosophy.

181   **Medicine, health, and bioethics: Essential primary sources.** K. Lee Lerner and Brenda Wilmoth Lerner, eds. 513p. Thomson Gale, 2006. ISBN 1414406231. $$

174.2   R724

This book contains 175 primary documents dealing with health, medicine, and bioethics. An introduction to each document provides historical context and information about its significance. Information about the author and resources for further information are included. Also available as an e-book.

182   **Westminster dictionary of Christian ethics.** Rev. ed. James E. Childress and John Macquarrie, eds. 700p. Westminster John Knox Press, 1986. ISBN 0664209408. $

241   BJ1199

Scholars from many backgrounds contributed to this ecumenical work addressing ethical questions relevant to philosophy and theology.

3 *Psychology, Psychiatry, and the Occult*

SARAH BARBARA WATSTEIN

It is safe to say that the fields of psychiatry, psychology, psychoanalysis, and neurology have all, in their own ways, transcended traditional boundaries. Today, contemporary psychology is part and parcel of our daily lives, and lay and professional readers alike share an increasing interest in psychology. Terms, theories, and concepts fascinate all levels of library users, from high school students to practicing psychologists, both academic and clinical. Busy practitioners, researchers, and students seek quick access to all important psychological terms, concepts, theories, and practices. Their interests span every major branch of psychology, including applied, clinical, cognitive, developmental, educational, forensic, industrial, physiological, social, and theoretical. Adolescent sex offenders are the focus of our users' information, reference, and research questions as much as other topics—Z-score, conduct disorders, and shamanism. Information about important figures in the history of psychology is also important. The well-tempered small and medium-sized library will have a solid core collection of easy-to-use, very informative, and authoritative psychology reference sources.

Psychology and Psychiatry

Databases

183   EBSCO psychology databases. EBSCO. www.ebsco.com.

EBSCO provides access to the *Mental measurements yearbook* and the *PEP archive,* the definitive source of peer-reviewed scholarly and scientific articles from the field of psychoanalysis, produced by Psychoanalytic Electronic Publishing. EBSCO also offers access to all online databases produced by the American Psychological Association, including PsycARTICLES, PsycBOOKS, PsycEXTRA, and PsycINFO. Descriptions follow in alphabetical order.

184   Mental measurements yearbook. Buros Institute. www.unl.edu/buros/.

Produced by the Buros Institute at the University of Nebraska, the *Mental measurements yearbook* (*MMY*) provides users with a comprehensive guide to more than 2,000 contemporary testing instruments. Designed for an audience ranging from novice test consumers to experienced professionals, the *MMY* series contains information essential for a complete evaluation of test products within such diverse areas as psychology, education, business, and leadership. All *MMY* entries contain descriptive information (e.g., test purpose, publisher, pricing) and edited review(s) written by leading content-area experts. To be included in the *MMY*, a test must be commercially available, be published in the English language, and be new or revised since it last appeared in the series. First published by Oscar K. Buros, the *MMY* series allows users to make knowledgeable judgments and informed selection decisions about the increasingly complex world of testing. *MMY* online provides coverage from volume 9 to the present. Also useful for browsing is the printed *Mental Measurement Yearbook.*

185   PEP archive. Psychoanalytic Electronic Publishing. www.p-e-p.org.

The *PEP archive* is the definitive source of peer-reviewed scholarly and scientific articles from the field of psychoanalysis. Produced by Psychoanalytic Electronic Publishing, the database offers the full text of 20 principal psychoanalytic journals and more than 40 classic psychoanalytic books dating as far back as 1920. The materials in *PEP archive* originally encompassed more than 400 volumes and a total of 250,000 printed pages. Points of interest include the full text of Freud's correspondence with his chief collaborators (such as Abraham, Fleiss, Jones, and Jung) and all major works by Bion, Klein, and Winnicot. Contributions by Anzieu, Fairbairn, Laplanche and Pontalis, Rosenfeld, Spence, and Stern are also represented. In all, the database includes more than 50,000 articles, book chapters, book reviews, letters, and commentaries and 4,000 figures and illustrations. Besides psychology and psychiatry, students and professionals researching anthropology, linguistics, nursing, physiology, neurosciences, and women's studies will find the *PEP archive* indispensable. *PEP archive* is co-owned by the American Psychoanalytic Association and the British Institute of Psychoanalysis.

186   PsycARTICLES. American Psychological Association. www.apa.org/psycarticles/.

PsycARTICLES, from the American Psychological Association (APA), is a definitive source of full-text, peer-reviewed scholarly and scientific articles in psychology. The PsycARTICLES database covers general psychology as well as specialized, applied, clinical, and theoretical research. The database contains more than 45,000 articles from fifty-nine journals—forty-eight published by the APA and eleven from allied organizations. It includes all journal articles, letters to the editor, and errata from each journal. Coverage spans 1985 to the present. PsycARTICLES is indexed with controlled vocabulary from APA's *Thesaurus of psychological index terms.* The coverage from 1894 to 1984 in PsycARTICLES historical col-

lection doubles the size of the database to more than 100,000 articles, covering most APA journals to volume 1, issue 1.

187   PsycBOOKS. American Psychological Association. www.apa.org/psycbooks/.

PsycBOOKS, from the American Psychological Association (APA), is a database of more than 16,000 chapters in PDF from more than 1,000 books published by APA and other distinguished publishers. The database includes most scholarly titles published by APA from copyright years 1953–2005. It also includes 100 out-of-print books, more than 400 classic books of landmark historical impact in psychology, and the exclusive electronic release of more than 1,500 authored entries from the APA and Oxford University Press *Encyclopedia of psychology.* PsycBOOKS is indexed with controlled vocabulary from APA's *Thesaurus of psychological index terms.*

188   PsycEXTRA. American Psychological Association. www.apa.org/psycextra/.

PsycEXTRA, produced by the American Psychological Association (APA), is a bibliographic and full-text companion to the scholarly PsycINFO database. The document types included in PsycEXTRA consist of technical, annual, and government reports; conference papers; newsletters; magazines; newspapers; consumer brochures; and more. This database complements PsycINFO and the other APA databases with extensive coverage of gray literature relating to psychology and the behavioral sciences; it contains more than 85,000 records with nearly a quarter million full-text pages. PsycEXTRA is indexed with controlled vocabulary from APA's *Thesaurus of psychological index terms.*

189   PsycINFO. American Psychological Association. www.apa.org/psycinfo/.

PsycINFO, from the American Psychological Association (APA), contains nearly 2.3 million citations and summaries of scholarly journal articles, book chapters, books, and dissertations, all in psychology and related disciplines, dating as far back as the 1800s. Some 97 percent of the covered material is peer-reviewed. The database also includes information about the psychological aspects of related fields such as medicine, psychiatry, nursing, sociology, education, pharmacology, physiology, linguistics, anthropology, business, law, and others. Journal coverage, which spans 1887 to present, includes international material selected from more than 2,100 periodicals in more than twenty-five languages.

PsycINFO is indexed with controlled vocabulary from APA's *Thesaurus of psychological index terms.*

Dictionaries and Encyclopedias

190 AA to Z: Addictionary to the 12-step culture. Christopher Cavanaugh. 196p. Doubleday, 1998. ISBN 9780385483407. $

616.86 HV5804

Records the language, history, and set of customs unique to the twelve-step-program culture. *Addictionary* is hardly a traditional dictionary. The alphabetic dictionary of Alcoholics Anonymous (AA) jargon is supplemented by a "Sponsorship Guide," suggested reading list, and step work sheets. AA began in 1935; today, it has an estimated two million members worldwide with a presence in 180 countries (www.aa.org). Additionally, its program of recovery serves as a model for many other twelve-step fellowships. Today, the recovery subculture is both established and entrenched in our own. Here is a book that helps twelve-step participants, students of twelve-step programs, and the general reader get a closer look at this.

191 Ariadne's book of dreams: A dictionary of ancient and contemporary symbols. Ariadne Green. 292p. Warner Books, 2001. ISBN 0446677523. $

154.6 BF1091

Dream educator, researcher, and urban shaman Ariadne Green is the creator of DreamThread, a multimedia company whose mission is to illuminate the value of dreams through the Internet. The company hosts a highly popular website that analyzes dreams and provides opportunities for discussion. *Ariadne's book of dreams* is a compendium of symbols ranging from ancient times to today. Complete with an alphabetical listing of symbols and their possible meanings, as well as techniques for dream recall and evaluation, this book is a comprehensive resource for dream interpretation in the new millennium. Dream-interpretation books are increasingly popular; most supermarket checkout lines feature them on their magazine and book stands. *Ariadne's book of dreams* stands out for its interpretation of contemporary symbols.

192 The Blackwell encyclopedia of social psychology. Miles Hewstone, ed. 694p. Blackwell, 1996. ISBN 9780631202899. $

302.03 HM251

Social psychology, the branch of psychology that studies persons and their relationships with others and with groups and with society as a whole, is no longer a field that lacks a standard reference work. *The Blackwell encyclopedia* certainly qualifies as the definitive resource for all students, teachers, and researchers of social psychology eager to know more about a particular phenomenon, concept, or theory. Each key topic is addressed by internationally recognized authorities, making the encyclopedia both comprehensive and authoritative. Four types of entry comprise the work: feature items providing extended treatments of centrally significant topics, shorter essays giving detailed yet compact analyses of important areas, extended glossary items, and straightforward glossary items.

193 The concise Corsini encyclopedia of psychology and behavioral science. W. Edward Craighead and Charles B. Nemeroff, eds. 1112p. Wiley, 2004. ISBN 9780471220367. $$

150 BF31

Edited by high-caliber experts, and contributed to by quality researchers and practitioners in psychology and related fields, *The concise Corsini* includes more than 500 topical entries. Each entry features suggested readings and extensive cross-referencing accessible to students and general readers.

194 The Corsini encyclopedia of psychology and behavioral science. W. Edward Craighead and Charles B. Nemeroff, eds. 4v. Wiley, 2002. ISBN 9780471244004. $$

150 BF31

The history of this classic reference is worth noting—previous editions of this reference for "the community at large" appeared in 1984 and 1994, followed by a one-volume condensation. Editors Craighead and Nemeroff indicate that two-thirds of the prior edition has been updated and one-third replaced; several reviewers have challenged this claim and have documented other editorial problems. Others continue to champion this work and its execution. Some 1,000 contributors have produced 1,200 articles, and an international flavor continues to characterize the work. Despite its mixed reception, this remains an essential, solid, and important reference work in psychology and behavioral science.

195   **A dictionary of psychology.** Andrew M.
      Colman. 861p. Oxford Univ. Pr., 2006.
      ISBN 9780192806321. $
      150   BF31

With 10,500 entries ranging from neuroanatomy
and psychoanalysis to statistics and pharmacology,
this work might very well be the best single-volume
dictionary of its kind. Entries are extensively cross-
referenced for ease of use and cover word origins
and derivations as well as definitions. Readers will
also find more than eighty illustrations complementing the text, appendixes covering more than 800
commonly used abbreviations and symbols, and a
list of phobias and phobic stimuli, with definitions.
Thumbs-up to Coleman for coming close to exhaustive coverage of topics in the field of psychology.

196   **The dream encyclopedia.** James
      R. Lewis. 416p. Gale, 1995. ISBN
      9780787601560. $
      154.6   BF1091

Interest in understanding the unconscious mind
continues unabated. Dreams remain a popular
subject with reference works and with mass-
market paperbacks. Although the jury is still out
insofar as the classic dream reference is concerned,
Lewis's work remains a serious contender. With
250 entries, *The dream encyclopedia* covers the role
of dreams from the Gilgamesh epic to the theories
of Sigmund Freud. Added value is provided by a
separate section with definitions of more than 700
dream symbols and a list of sleep-research centers
and dream organizations around the country.

197   **The encyclopedia of addictions and
      addictive behaviors.** Esther Gwinnell
      and Christine Adamec. 344p. Facts on
      File, 2005. ISBN 9780816057078. $
      362.29   RC564

The diverse area of drug use and addiction remains
of high interest (slight pun intended) to lay readers, students, and professionals alike. More than
300 entries comprise this volume. Readers interested in the symptoms, possible causes, treatment,
rate of occurrence, social and ethnic influences,
and emergency treatment of addictions, among
other topics, will not be disappointed. Eighteen
helpful appendixes provide information on state
mental health agencies, rates of substance abuse
by high-schoolers, demographics of people who
have received treatment for substance abuse, and
more. Numerous tables and graphs help communicate complex statistical data. Whatever your

interest—drinking, drug addiction, or addictive
behaviors not associated with substance abuse, such
as gambling, eating disorders, or shopping, this
work serves to further our knowledge and understanding of addictions and addictive behavior.

198   **Encyclopedia of applied psychology.**
      Charles Donald Spielberger. 3v. Elsevier
      Science and Technology Books, 2004.
      ISBN 9780126574104. $$$
      158   BF636

Applied psychology, any of several branches of
psychology that seek to apply psychological principles to practical problems of education or industry or marketing and so forth, is ably covered in
the *Encyclopedia of applied psychology*. The work
encompasses applications of psychological knowledge and procedures in all areas of psychology. The
topics include, among others, aging (geropsychol-
ogy), assessment, clinical, cognitive, community,
counseling, educational, environmental, family,
industrial/organizational, health, school, sports,
and transportation psychology. Entries, drawn
from the above-referenced areas, provide a clear
definition of topic, a brief review of theoretical basis
relevant to the topic, and emphasize major areas of
application. Professional practitioners, researchers
in psychology, and anyone interested in applied
psychology will find this work to be of value.

199   **Encyclopedia of evaluation.** Sandra
      Mathison. 481p. Sage, 2004. ISBN
      9780761926092. $$
      001.4   H62

The field of evaluation has certainly come into its
own, as a practice, as a profession, and as a discipline. This volume documents the development
of the field—its history, key figures, theories,
approaches, and goals—and defines its fundamental concepts and methods.

200   **Encyclopedia of human development.**
      Neil J. Salkind. 3v. Sage, 2005. ISBN
      9781412904759. $$
      155   HM626

The scientific study of progressive psychological
changes that occur in human beings as they age,
developmental psychology was originally concerned with infants and children and later other
periods of great change such as adolescence and
aging. It now encompasses the entire life span.
This cross-disciplinary field examines change
across a broad range of topics, including motor

skills and other psychophysiological processes, problem-solving abilities, conceptual understanding, acquisition of language, moral understanding, and identity formation. Here are state-of-the-art research and ready-to-use facts from the fields of psychology, individual and family studies, and education. With more than 600 entries organized from A–Z, this three-volume work features cross-disciplinary coverage, a readers' guide (organizing entries around themes or specific topic areas), several "anchor" essays, and a general bibliography.

201   Encyclopedia of human emotions.
David Levinson. 2v. Simon and Schuster, 1999. ISBN 9780028647678 (v. 1); 9780028647685 (v. 2). $$

152.4   BF531

What is it about our internal state of being, particularly our feelings—our strong feelings, such as joy or anger—that continues to intrigue? One thing is clear: emotion is complex. Indeed, the term *emotion* has no single universally accepted definition. The study of emotions has traditionally been part of psychology, neuroscience, and, more recently, artificial intelligence, and what was known about the nature, causes, expressions, and societal role of emotions was scattered and difficult to pull together. Billed as the first reference source devoted to human emotions, this work contains 146 entries covering not only specific emotions and their behavioral expressions but also theoretical issues that cut across emotions and biographies of individuals who have made significant contributions to the study of emotions. Photographs, drawings, and literary references complement many entries.

202   The encyclopedia of memory and memory disorders. Carol Turkington and Joseph Harris. 296p. Facts on File, 2001. ISBN 9780816041411. $

153.1   BF371

Memory is the ability of an organism to store, retain, and subsequently recall information. Although traditional studies of memory began in the realms of philosophy, the late nineteenth and early twentieth century put memory within the paradigms of cognitive psychology. In the recent decades, memory has become one of the principal pillars of a new branch of science that represents a marriage between cognitive psychology and neuroscience: cognitive neuroscience. Turkington and Harris here provide an updated survey of information on the neurobiology of memory, memory-loss prevention, and how

to differentiate normal memory decline with aging from the severe cognitive impairment of advanced Alzheimer's disease. Resources, suggested reading, a glossary of terms, and an extensive index are included. Readers interested in major concepts, disorders, and diseases will find many of their questions answered by this work. The first edition of this work, edited by Richard Noll and Turkington, was published in 1994.

203   The encyclopedia of mental health. Ada P. Kahn and Jan Fawcett. 468p. Facts on File, 2001. ISBN 9780816040629. $

616.89   RC437

Mental health is a concept that refers to a human individual's emotional and psychological well-being. According to the World Health Organization, there is no one "official" definition of mental health. Given the landscape, this desktop reference is a most welcome addition to the psychology reference corps. Here are definitions of theories, syndromes, symptoms, treatments, and contemporary issues in mental health. More than 1,000 entries are included; extensive cross-referencing facilitates access. A brief directory lists organization contacts on mental health and general health topics. A bibliography is also a useful addition.

204   The encyclopedia of psychiatry, psychology and psychoanalysis. Benjamin B. Wolman. 649p. Holt, 1996. ISBN 9780805022346.

616.89   RC437

Carefully culled from the twelve-volume *International encyclopedia of psychiatry, psychology, psychoanalysis, and neurology,* this abridged volume succeeds as a concise, current reference to psychology and related fields. More than 2,500 entries provided by experts in the field are included. Arranged alphabetically, the entries range from brief descriptions to multipage articles. The format and layout of this volume make it an easy-to-use reference tool. Topical headings in bold type, provision of subheadings in the lengthier articles, a comprehensive index that includes cross-references to all of the subheadings, brief biographical descriptions of major figures in the fields, and an extensive eighteen-page bibliography are examples of several features that distinguish this work.

205   Encyclopedia of psychology. 2nd ed. Raymond J. Corsini. 4v. Wiley, 1994.

ISBN 0471558192. $$$$
150   BF31

A comprehensive scholarly encyclopedia covering all aspects of psychology. Articles are on subject areas as well as on important contributors to the field. Volume 4 contains an extensive bibliography, biographies, and name and subject indexes. There is also an appendix: the psychologist's code of conduct and ethics and sample contracts.

206   **Encyclopedia of psychology.** Alan E.
       Kazdin. 8v. American Psychological
       Association and Oxford Univ. Pr., 2000.
       ISBN 9781557981875. $$$
       150   BF31

The *Encyclopedia of psychology* is widely recognized as the first place to turn to for authoritative information on this increasingly multidisciplinary and multicultural field. All areas of psychology are covered, as are related fields of sociology, social work, nursing, and allied health. Signed, alphabetically arranged entries range from 500 to 700 words in length—1,500 entries and nearly 400 biographies in all. Access is facilitated by an extensive system of cross-references and a comprehensive index. The efforts of some 1,400 contributors are highly commended. This is the dominant source for classic and contemporary knowledge in psychology.

207   **Encyclopedia of school psychology.**
       Steven W. Lee. 656p. Sage, 2005. ISBN
       9780761930808. $$
       370.15   LB1027.55

Nonspecialists, practitioners, and vocational counselors will appreciate this timely introduction to the scope of psychology applied to education. School learning, motivation, and educational assessment are the focus of this comprehensive guide. Arranged in alphabetical order, the work contains more than 250 articles by 175 of the more influential school psychology scholars at all levels. Layout, added features, and indexing add to the value of this source.

208   **The Gale encyclopedia of mental
       disorders.** Ellen Thackery, ed. 2v. Gale,
       2002. ISBN 9780787657680. $$
       616.89   RC437

Mental disorders and conditions are the focus of this two-volume set. Included are entries for all 150 disorders classified in the *Diagnostic and statistical manual of mental disorders, text revision.* Also featured are entries for prescription, alternative, and over-the-counter drugs as well as the various

therapies used to treat mental disorders. Readers interested in definition, description, causes and symptoms, demographics, diagnosis, treatments, prognosis, and prevention will not be disappointed. All entries have a resource list of print and electronic sources and organizations to contact. Black-and-white photographs and charts illustrate the text. Other features include ample cross-references and boxes with definitions of key terms; a full glossary and thorough index conclude the set. Carefully focused scope and structural consistency are two of the hallmarks of this work.

209   **The Gale encyclopedia of psychology.**
       Susan B. Gall. 435p. Gale, 1996. ISBN
       9780787603724. $$
       150   BF31

Covering the entire spectrum of psychological terms, theories, personalities, and experiments, this comprehensive reference work features entries ranging from 25 to 1,000 words. More than 400 articles are arr anged alphabetically. *See* references and bibliographies of sources for further reading complement many entries. A subject index and list of articles by subfield conclude the volume. A glossary, general bibliography, and list of organizations provide added value. Readers interested in pursuing topics covered in high schools and introductory college courses will not be disappointed.

210   **The Penguin dictionary of psychology.**
       3rd ed. Arthur S. Reber and Emily S.
       Reber. 831p. Penguin, 2001. ISBN
       9780140514513. $
       150   BF31

The third edition of an appealing work features clear, concise definitions; helpful appendixes; and jargon-free language. New to this edition are social psychology and neuroscience terms, British spellings, and a new co-compiler. Approximately 17,000 definitions are included. All areas of psychology and psychiatry are covered in this wide-ranging work.

211   **Popular psychology: An encyclopedia.**
       Luis A. Cordón. 274p. Greenwood,
       2005. ISBN 9780313324574. $
       150   BF31

The gap between contemporary popular psychology and the discipline practiced by professional psychologists continues to grow, fueled in part by the frequency and quality of coverage of the field in the media. Cordón is to be credited for taking on the misinformation about the field of psychology in a concise and useful guide. Psychological theories and ideas, disorders, and treatments, as well as pop psychologists, are covered in some 120 or so entries; almost all include a limited "Further Reading" list. An annotated bibliography that includes websites completes the work.

212   Wiley's English-Spanish, Spanish-English dictionary of psychology and psychiatry. Steven M. Kaplan. 593p. Wiley, 1997. ISBN 9780471192848. $ 150   BF31

This unique and useful resource provides concise, comprehensive, and current coverage of virtually every word or phrase used in the study and practice of psychiatry and psychology. More than 62,000 entries are included—more than 30,000 in each language—covering all disciplines and subdisciplines, both research and clinical. The equivalents provided are designed to be understood by a majority of fluent speakers, especially those trained in these fields. Psychiatrists, psychologists, students, translators, and interpreters will appreciate the quick, easy access to equivalent terms in Spanish and English. Readers looking for definitions need to look elsewhere—this is a bilingual dictionary giving the Spanish equivalents of English words and the English equivalents of Spanish words.

Directories

213   American Psychological Association 2004 membership directory on CD-ROM. Joe Simpich, April Arrington, and Bruce Roth, eds. American Psychological Association, 2003. ISBN 1591471389. $$
150.60   BF11

This volume lists members and affiliates of the American Psychological Association (APA). The directory includes the "Ethical Principles of Psychologists and Code of Conduct and Psychology Laws in the United States and Canada." The directory also contains the APA bylaws, present and past officers, past locations of the annual convention, membership statistics, and a list of psychological specialties and major fields. Readers can search for addresses, fax numbers and e-mail addresses, highest academic degree, home and office phone numbers, licensure or certification, major field, names, principal present employment, private practice listings,

psychology specialty area, state psychological association membership, and university affiliation.

Handbooks and Manuals

214   Diagnostic and statistical manual of mental disorders: DSM-IV-TR, text revision. American Psychiatric Association Staff. 943p. American Psychiatric Publishing, 2000. ISBN 9780890420249. $
616.89   RC455.2.C4

A revised edition of the ultimate mental health reference, the *Diagnostic and statistical manual of mental disorders, text revision (DSM)* is used worldwide by all practitioners requiring diagnostic criteria for schizophrenia, dementia, and delirium, as well as for sleep, mood, somatoform, and dissociative disorders. Some reviewers have questioned purchase if libraries already own the *DSM-IV* (4th ed., 1994). Most changes are in "Associated Features and Disorders"; "Specific Culture, Age, and Gender Features"; "Prevalence"; "Course"; and "Familial Pattern" sections of the text. *DSM-IV made easy: The clinician's guide to diagnosis* (Guilford Press, 1995), by James Morrison, is recommended for medical students, psychiatric trainees, professionals in mental health, coders who use *DSM-IV* classification rules, and students and lay readers. Morrison translates the diagnostic criteria of *DSM-IV* into a user-friendly guide for all readers.

215   DSM-IV-TR casebook: A learning companion to the Diagnostic and statistical manual of mental disorders, text revision. Robert L. Spitzer, ed. 576p. American Psychiatric Publishing, 2001. ISBN 9781585620586. $
616.89   RC455.2.C4

Road maps to the *Diagnostic and statistical manual of mental disorders, text revision (DSM)* are apparently still necessary, as evidenced by the continual publication of companions, desk references, and study guides to the *DSM*. In this work, clinical vignettes for illustration and study facilitate the transition from the concepts and terminology to actual clinical situations. Each case is followed by a discussion of the *DSM* diagnostic issues raised.

216   The mental health diagnostic desk reference: Visual guides and more for learning to use the Diagnostic and

Statistical Manual. Carlton E. Munson, ed. 326p. Haworth Press, 2000. ISBN 9780789010766. $

616.89   RC455.2.C4

Provides information on the *DSM-IV* system as well as coverage of the major classes of *DSM-IV* disorders, concise summaries of each class disorder, visual aids, and summaries of treatments.

217   The Oxford companion to the mind. 2nd ed. Richard L. Gregory. 1004p. Oxford Univ. Pr., 2004. ISBN 9780198662242. $

128   BF31

The long-awaited second edition of a classic, this work provides the reader with discussions of concepts like language, memory, and intelligence, side by side with definitions. Added value is provided by three "mini symposia" on consciousness, brain scanning, and artificial intelligence. As with its predecessor, this work is cultural as well as scientific in its approach, and it offers authoritative descriptions and analysis. Weighing in at 1,001 A–Z entries ranging from brief statements to substantial essays on major topics, this book introduces the reader to how philosophers, physiologists, psychologists, and psychiatrists differ in their understanding of what the mind is and how it works.

218   Psychodynamic diagnostic manual (PDM). American Psychoanalytic Association; Alliance of Psychoanalytic Organizations. 857p. Alliance of Psychoanalytic Organizations, 2006. ISBN 0976775824. $

616.89   RC455.2.C4

Intended to expand on the *Diagnostic and statistical manual of mental disorders, text revision* and *International statistical classification of diseases and related health problems* efforts in cataloging the symptoms and behaviors of mental-health patients, this manual opens the door to a fuller understanding of the functioning of the mind and brain and their development. This manual is based on current neuroscience and treatment outcome studies that demonstrate the importance of focusing on the full range and depth of emotional and social functioning. Beginning with a classification of the spectrum of personality patterns and disorders found in individuals and then describing a profile of mental functioning that permits a clinician to look in detail at each of the patient's capacities, the entries include a description of the patient's symptoms with a focus on the patient's internal experiences as well as surface behaviors. The manual comes by way of the Alliance of Psychodynamic Organizations, a collaboration of the major psychoanalytic organizations including the American Psychoanalytic Association, International Psychoanalytical Association, the Division of Psychoanalysis of the American Psychological Association, American Academy of Psychoanalysis, and National Membership Committee on Psychoanalysis in Clinical Social Work.

219   Psychologist's desk reference. 2nd ed. Gerald P. Koocher, John C. Norcross, and Sam S. Hill III. 735p. Oxford Univ. Pr., 2004. ISBN 9780195166064. $

616.89   RC467.2

The second edition of this one-volume handbook features 140 essays, written by subject specialists, covering the entire spectrum of practice issues. Each essay ends with a list of reference and cross-references for related chapters. Difficulty locating topics has been cited as a concern; however, the wealth of orienting information accompanying the entries appears to trump this concern. The suggestion of the well-known *Physician's desk reference* in the work's title is hardly an accident. Koocher, Norcross, and Hill clearly intend their work to set the standard for reference texts aimed at mental-health practitioners, as their peers have done for the medical professionals. A companion website offers a depository of documents, including PowerPoint slide sets. Although many of the documents are password protected, the book reveals the password.

STYLE MANUALS

220   Publication manual of the American Psychological Association. 5th ed. American Psychological Association. 439p. American Psychological Association, 2001. ISBN 1557988102. $ www.apastyle.org.

808   BF76.7

The fifth edition of the American Psychological Association (APA) style manual brings order to the world of electronic communications as well as explanations of a new consensus on presenting statistical data. The foremost guide to writing and publishing in the social sciences, the APA style manual builds on seventy-three years of history and two decades of recognition as a national authority. The manual is now the publication guide for most social sciences and is also used in the human resources, business, and nursing fields. As it has historically, the new volume discusses not only editorial rules but writing style, ways to reduce bias in language, the manuscript acceptance and production processes, and ethical standards for reporting and publishing scientific information. The website helps readers keep up with changes in the manual between editions.

Tests, Measurements, and Questionnaires

221   **Directory of unpublished experimental mental measures, volume 8.** Bert A. Goldman, Paula E. Egelson, and David F. Mitchell. 669p. American Psychological Association, 2003. ISBN 1557989516. $

362   BF431

This directory, number eight in the series, identifies and describes noncommercial experimental mental measures from the fields of psychology, sociology, and education that have been devised by researchers and published in thirty-six top journals. Volume 8 lists tests published in the 1996–2000 issues of those journals. This directory fills an ongoing need for comprehensive information about noncommercial tests, enabling researchers to determine what types of noncommercial experimental test instruments are currently in use. The instruments are not evaluated, but the information given about each test should make it possible for researchers to make a preliminary judgment of its usefulness. Other volumes in the series include the *Directory of unpublished experimental mental measures, volume 7; Directory of unpublished experimental mental measures, volume 6; Directory of unpublished experimental mental measures, volumes 4–5;* and *Directory of unpublished experimental mental measures, volumes 1–3.*

222   **Mental measurements yearbook.** Buros Institute of Mental Measurements.

The seventeenth mental measurements yearbook. Barbara S. Plake and Robert A. Spies, eds. 1100p. 2007. ISBN 9780910674607. $$

The sixteenth mental measurements yearbook. Robert A. Spies and Barbara S. Plake, eds. 1280p. 2005. ISBN 0910674582. $$

The fifteenth mental measurements yearbook. Barbara S. Plake, James C.

Impara, and Robert A. Spies, eds. 1000p. 2003. ISBN 0910674574. $$

The fourteenth mental measurements yearbook. Barbara S. Plake and James C. Impara, eds. 1530p. 2001. ISBN 0910674558. $$

The thirteenth mental measurements yearbook. James C. Impara and Barbara S. Plake, eds. 1322p. 1998. ISBN 091067454X. $$

The twelfth mental measurements yearbook. Jane Close Conoley and James C. Impara, eds. 1259p. 1995. ISBN 091067440X. $$

The eleventh mental measurements yearbook. Jack J. Kramer and Jane Close Conoley, eds. 1183p. 1992. ISBN 0910674337. $$

The tenth mental measurements yearbook. Jane Close Conoley and Jack J. Kramer, eds. 1014p. 1989. ISBN 0910674310. $$

The ninth mental measurement yearbook. James V. Mitchell Jr., ed. 2v., 2002p. 1985. ISBN 0910674299. $$

The eighth mental measurements yearbook. Oscar K. Buros, ed. 2v., 2182p. 1978. ISBN 0910674248. $$

The seventh mental measurements yearbook. Oscar K. Buros, ed. 2v. 1972. ISBN 0910674116. Available on microfiche only. $

The sixth mental measurements yearbook. Oscar K. Buros, ed. 1714p. 1965. ISBN 091067406X. $

The fifth mental measurements yearbook. Oscar K. Buros, ed. 1292p. 1959. ISBN 0803211643. Available on microfiche only. $

The fourth mental measurements yearbook. Oscar K. Buros, ed. 1163p. 1953. ISBN 0910674043. Available on microfiche only. $

The third mental measurements yearbook. Oscar K. Buros, ed. 674p. 1949. ISBN 0910674035. Available on microfiche only. $

The 1940 mental measurements yearbook. Oscar K. Buros, ed. 674p. 1941. ISBN 0910674132. Available on microfiche only. $

The 1938 mental measurements yearbook. Oscar K. Buros, ed. 415p. 1938. ISBN 0910674124. Available on microfiche only. $

016.15   Z5814.P8

The *Mental measurements yearbook* (*MMY*) includes timely, consumer-oriented test reviews, providing evaluative information to promote and encourage informed test selection. It is considered by many to be the major source of critical information on tests in psychology, education, and business. Typical *MMY* test entries include descriptive information of the test and its test scores, publisher, publication date, cost, availability of non-English-language versions of the test, acronym, reliability, validity; one or two professional reviews; reviewer references; and a cross-reference to previous editions of the *MMY* or *Tests in print* that contain relevant information on the test. To be reviewed in the *MMY*, a test must be commercially available, be published in the English language, and be new, revised, or widely used since it last appeared in the *MMY* series. Beginning in *The fourteenth mental measurements yearbook* (2001), tests also must provide sufficient documentation supporting their technical quality to meet criteria for review. The most recent editions include the following indexes: test titles, names (of authors, reviewers, or authors of additional references), acronyms, subject category, and score (the factor, attribute, trait, etc., that is being measured), and publisher. Between the years 1988 and 1999, the Buros Institute of Mental Measurements produced supplements to the ninth through thirteenth *MMY*s. Beginning with the fourteenth yearbook, volumes in the *MMY* series were produced every eighteen to twenty-four months, and the supplements were discontinued. Yearbooks are best used for finding test reviews; finding information on an instrument's validity and reliability; and finding a description of a test. Starting with volume 9, volumes are also available online from Buros Institute (www.unl.edu/buros/).

Websites

223   **American Psychiatric Association.** American Psychiatric Association. www.psych.org.

The American Psychiatric Association is a medical specialty society of psychiatrists recognized worldwide. The site includes information about advocacy, education, ethics, research, psychiatric practice, the organization, careers in the field, and more. A public information component provides visitors with a variety of information and resources on mental health topics.

224   **American Psychoanalytic Association.** American Psychoanalytic Association. www.apsa.org.

Website of the American Psychoanalytic Association. "APsaA, as a professional organization for psychoanalysts, focuses on education, research and membership development." Also lists accredited training institutes and affiliated societies.

225   **American Psychological Association.** American Psychological Association. www.apa.org.

The American Psychological Association is a scientific and professional organization that represents psychology in the United States. It is the largest association of psychologists worldwide. Association information, psychology topics, careers, press, and news are some of the rich resources users will discover here.

226   **Association for Psychological Science.** Association for Psychological Science. www.psychologicalscience.org.

The Association for Psychological Science (previously the American Psychological Society) is a nonprofit organization dedicated to the advancement of scientific psychology and its representation at the national level. Psychology links complement a range of information about the association, teaching psychology, awards and honors, and publications.

227   **Buros Center for Testing.** Buros Institute. www.unl.edu/buros/.

Complete information about the Buros Center for Testing, which contains two institutes focusing on different areas of testing. The Buros Institute of Mental Measurements continues to provide reference materials in print and electronic form that offer valuable information and candidly critical reviews of commercial tests. Reflecting the expanded focus of the center, the Buros Institute for Assessment Consultation and Outreach was created to address evaluation and quality concerns within proprietary testing. Both institutes share a common mission: to improve the science and practice of testing.

228   Classics in the history of psychology—Freud (1914/1917). Christopher D. Green. http://psychclassics.yorku.ca/Freud/History/.

Here is *The history of the psychoanalytic movement,* by Sigmund Freud (1914), translated by A. A. Brill (1917).

229   Historic asylums. Mike Long et al. www.rootsweb.com/~asylums/.

This website is an attempt to catalog and present America's historic psychiatric hospitals (state hospitals, insane asylums) founded mostly in the latter half of the nineteenth century. This site's focus is on architectural preservation; it is not intended in any way to be taken as support of institutionalization in general or as a current or new use for these buildings.

230   Internet mental health. Phillip W. Long. www.mentalhealth.com.

Since 1995 Internet Mental Health has provided information on mental health free of charge. In essence a free encyclopedia, Internet Mental Health was created by a Canadian psychiatrist, Phillip W. Long. Internet Mental Health is for anyone who has an interest in mental health: mental health professionals, patients who want to learn more about their illnesses, friends and families of patients, mental health support groups, students, and members of the general public who want to learn more about mental health.

231   Mental help net. CenterSite. http://mentalhelp.net.

The Mental Help Net website exists to promote mental health and wellness education and advocacy. More specifically, the site seeks to educate the public about mental health and wellness issues; to catalog, review, and make available to everyone useful online mental health and wellness resources as they become available; to promote active communication and collaboration between professionals in all segments of mental health and wellness services development, implementation, and policy and between professionals and consumers of their services; and to advocate for improved access to mental health and wellness services.

232   National Center for Health Statistics. National Center for Health Statistics, Centers for Disease Control and Prevention. www.cdc.gov/nchs/.

The website of the National Center for Health Statistics (NCHS) is a rich source of information about America's health. As the nation's principal health-statistics agency, the NCHS compiles statistical information to guide actions and policies to improve the health of the nation's people. NCHS is a unique public resource for health information—a critical element of public health and health policy. Here are fast stats (A to Z), information about surveys and data, NCHS initiatives, research and development, and more.

233   National Institute of Mental Health. National Institute of Mental Health. www.nimh.nih.gov.

The National Institute of Mental Health (NIMH) is the lead federal agency for research on mental and behavioral disorders. The NIMH is one of twenty-seven components of the National Institutes of Health (NIH), the federal government's principal biomedical and behavioral research agency. NIH is part of the U.S. Department of Health and Human Services. Health information on myriad mental-health topics includes information about signs and symptoms, diagnosis, and treatment.

234   PsychWeb. Russell A. Dewey. www.psywww.com/index.html.

This website contains psychology-related information for students and teachers of psychology.

235   The whole brain atlas. Keith A. Johnson and J. Alex Becker. www.med.harvard.edu/AANLIB/.

This website is a very well-reviewed atlas of the human brain. Sponsored by Harvard Medical School, the Countway Library of Medicine, and the American Academy of Neurology, it presents images "for central nervous system imaging which integrates clinical information with magnetic resonance (MR), X-ray computed tomography (CT), and nuclear medicine images." Sections include the normal brain, cerebrovascular diseases, cancer, and degenerative and inflammatory diseases.

Biographical Sources

236   Biographical dictionary of psychology. Noel Sheehy, Antony J. Chapman, and Wendy A. Conroy. 675p. Routledge, 2002. ISBN 9780415285612. $150   BF109.A1

Clearly, the source of choice for modern psychologists' biographies, this work provides biographical information and critical analysis of the influence, interests, and critical reception of more than 500 individuals who have made a significant contribution to the field of psychology. Written by an international team of contributors, the volume charts the development of the practice of psychology worldwide, from its emergence in the 1850s to the present day. Alphabetically arranged and identically structured entries are followed by indexes of names, interests, institutions, and key terms that facilitate access.

The Occult

237   **A dictionary of superstitions.** Iona Archibald Opie, ed. 494p. Oxford Univ. Pr., 2005. ISBN 9780192806642. $

001.9   BF1775

How many frogs do you need to cure whooping cough? If you aren't sure, are seriously stumped, or are simply curious, then this dictionary will fill the bill. Here are entries on a wide range of spells, omens, rituals, and taboos—the myriad strange and fascinating folk beliefs that form an integral part of our social life. Each entry is arranged alphabetically according to its central idea or object and illustrated with a selection of chronologically ordered quotations that indicate the history and development of each belief.

238   **Dictionary of the esoteric: Over 3,000 entries on the mystical and occult traditions.** Nevill Drury. 344p. Watkins, 2006. ISBN 9781842931080. $

133   BF1407

Mystical and esoteric traditions come to life in this work. Including more than 3,000 cross-referenced entries from the prehistoric to the contemporary, this unique dictionary also features biographies of leading figures in the field, such as astrologer Evangeline Adams and the prophet Zarathustra, and offers a fascinating look at esoteric religious texts, such as *The Egyptian book of the dead, The Dead Sea scrolls,* and the *Zohar,* revealing both human and divine characters from the great legends and myths of the world.

239   **The Element encyclopedia of witchcraft: The complete A–Z for the entire magical world.** Judika Illes. 887p. HarperElement, 2005. ISBN

9780007192939. $

133.4   BF1566

A longtime student of metaphysics and the magical arts, Illes here brings readers a comprehensive celebration and exploration of all facets of witchcraft. This is a reference book that is also a source of entertainment and general interest. Here are entries on the history, folklore, spirituality, and mythology of witchcraft. The work is arranged topically, and there is a helpful index. Individual articles within the topic chapters sometimes have *see* references as well. Chapters cover plants, animals, food and drink, magical beings, famous people in the magical world, the creative arts, witch persecution, and more. Chapters—or sections within the chapters—include A–Z entries that range from a few paragraphs to a few pages. An extensive bibliography and a list of Internet resources complete the work.

240   **The encyclopedia of ghosts and spirits.** 2nd ed. Rosemary Ellen Guiley. 430p. Facts on File, 2000. ISBN 9780816040865. $

133.1   BF1461

A compendium of worldwide paranormal activity from one of the more prolific writers on spirituality and visionary experiences, this work contains alphabetically arranged entries on ghosts, spirits, and related activities. Four-hundred entries are cross-referenced and accompanied by lists of further readings. Do you believe in ghosts? In spirits? Guiley's passion for the subject infuses her work; she is to be credited for avoiding sensationalism and striving for balanced coverage, accuracy, clarity, and brevity.

241   **The encyclopedia of the paranormal.** Gordon Stein. 859p. Prometheus Books, 1996. ISBN 9781573920216. $$

133   BF1025

Topics covered in this encyclopedia include the strictly paranormal, the historical, the philosophical, and work on investigatory photography. Here are ninety subject entries written in short essay form by contributors from diverse fields. Readers will also find entries on notable personages in paranormal phenomena. *Paranormal* is broadly interpreted to include that which cannot be explained by scientific means.

242   **The encyclopedia of vampires, werewolves, and other monsters.** Rosemary Ellen Guiley. 352p. Facts on

File, 2004. ISBN 0816046840. $

133.4   BF1556

Readers interested in vampires and werewolves will delight in Guiley's descriptions. Here, they are in lore and in films, so this book is also great for those who like horror movies. Readers seeking information on werewolves, other shape-shifters and skin walkers, and monsters in general will need to consult another source. Angels, ghosts, spirits, saints, and the otherwise strange, mystical, and unexplained continue to fascinate Guiley; her followers, and those looking for information on vampires, will not be disappointed. Note that Guiley has previously explored this topic. Her work *The complete vampire companion* (Macmillan, 1994) is an examination of the roots of the fascination with vampires, the various popular manifestations of vampires, and what exactly vampires are in the context of contemporary society. Ten years later, she returns to the topic; clearly, the universality of belief in vampires and similar beings has not diminished over time.

243   The encyclopedia of witches and witchcraft. 2nd ed. Rosemary Ellen Guiley. 417p. Facts on File, 1999. ISBN 9780816038480. $

133.4   BF1566

In this A–Z title, Guiley presents a detailed look at witchcraft and its history, from its ancient origins to its modern revival. Coverage of witchcraft practices around the world in different time periods and societies is a particular strength of the work. A total of 500 entries comprise the work; readers should note that the author's focus is primarily on Western tradition and practices, historical and contemporary. Guiley, author of the previous edition and numerous books on the occult and the New Age, continues to set the standard in the growing output of reference works in the occult sciences, insofar as balanced tone and thorough scholarship are concerned.

244   Harper's encyclopedia of mystical and paranormal experience. Rosemary Ellen Guiley. 666p. HarperCollins, 1991. ISBN 9780062503657. $

133   BF1407

Guiley provides 500 cross-referenced entries that emphasize major personalities, mystical techniques and traditions, locations of interest, and mystical and paranormal phenomena. Bibliographic information follows each entry. The need for information on the occult and paranormal seems insatiable, and readers who are mindful of the work's limitations, including scope (coverage is not inclusive); the author's selection of "alternative realities" rather than the occult as her total field; uneven quality of entries; and "air time" given to skeptical literature on a subject will find much here that is useful.

245   The new encyclopedia of the occult. John Michael Greer. 555p. Llewellyn, 2004. ISBN 1567183360. $

133   BF1407

Billed as the most complete occult reference book ever, this work is a comprehensive guide to the history, philosophies, and personalities of Western occultism. The whole range of occult tradition is covered. More than 1,500 entries populate this encyclopedia. Note that Greer intentionally avoids including entries on persons still in the flesh; readers looking for information about authors and leaders still living will need to turn to other sources. Occult scholar and practitioner Greer is here assisted by a cadre of experts, including contributors and reviewers. Readers with a borderline interest in the mystic and the occult; those who have been struggling with terms like *Hermeticism, Rosicrucianism, Tree of Life, Merkabah* (not able to figure out what they were about and, more important, what their connection and inner logic was); and those who are well versed in the material yet seek a neutral and scholarly presentation on the myriad facets of the occult will find this source to be well worth consulting.

246   The spirit book: The encyclopedia of clairvoyance, channeling, and spirit communication. Raymond Buckland. 500p. Visible Ink Press, 2006. ISBN 9780780809222. $

133.9   BF1301

The art and science of spirit communication are the focus of this work, which contains 500 alphabetically arranged and well-written documented entries. Readers interested in mediumship, channeling, and clairvoyance, as well as such topics as automatic writing, electronic voice phenomena, divination, and the Bible, will find much of value here. Added value is provided by a bibliography of print and online resources, 100 black-and-white illustrations, and an index. Wicca Buckland continues to develop his occult oeuvre and to provide readers with a basic, readable encyclopedia that succeeds in filling a niche in popular religion collections.

247   **The ultimate encyclopedia of spells: 88 incantations to entice love, improve a career, increase wealth, restore health, and spread peace.** Michael Johnstone. 200p. Diane Publishing, 2004. ISBN 9780756783235. $

133.4   GR540

In what is essentially a practical workbook, Johnstone provides a comprehensive examination of the long history of spells and gives clear explanations as to their true nature as well as tips on the proper way they should be used. "Ultimate" encyclopedias are increasingly common, and Johnstone has others to his name, including, for example, *The ultimate encyclopedia of fortune telling* (Arcturus, 2004). The extent to which *Spells* is the "ultimate" remains to be seen. Nonetheless, those newly engaged in such practices, as well as more seasoned practitioners, will not be disappointed. Readers might also want to peruse Johnstone's newest entry to the field—the spiral-bound *The book of spells: Positive enchantments to enhance your life* (Book Sales, 2006).

248   **The Watkins dictionary of magic: Over 3,000 entries on the world of magical formulas, secret symbols, and the occult.** Nevill Drury. 328p. Watkins, 2005. ISBN 9781842931523. $

133.4   BF1588

Creatures, spells, and formulas, oh my! The second volume in the Watkins Dictionary series, *The Watkins dictionary of magic,* is filled with explanations for all things magical, including spells, secret rituals, mythical creatures, and more. Featuring more than 3,000 cross-referenced entries, this work serves as a great introduction for neophyte occultists and a useful reference for quick facts and interesting information for seasoned readers. Biographies of leading figures in the field—both well known and obscure—as well as myths and folklore from around the world, are particularly valuable. Drury, well known for his writings and workshops on magic, visionary consciousness, and shamanism, once again serves up a valuable and popular work.

4 Social Sciences, Sociology, and Anthropology

TRACEY A. STIVERS

Because of the broad nature of social sciences, it is no surprise that the number of reference works available in this area is quite vast. However, the number of comprehensive sources that attempt to cover the entire social sciences is still limited. The publication of the twenty-six-volume *International encyclopedia of the social and behavioral sciences,* published in print by Elsevier in 2001 and also available in electronic format, was an enormous accomplishment, but the high cost of this resource prohibited its inclusion in this bibliography. Small and medium-sized libraries with limited budgets may wish to build their collections within specialized subfields of the social sciences instead of acquiring general sources.

Whenever possible, libraries should collect the most recent editions of directories and statistical sources. Local directories of services should also be collected if available.

Most of the titles in this chapter primarily reflect Western culture, yet there is a growing trend to provide international coverage within many of the sources. Every attempt has been made to include international sources for each subfield when available.

Social Sciences (General Sources)

Databases and Indexes

249 **Social sciences index.** H. W. Wilson, 1974–. ISSN 0094-4920. $$$ www.hwwilson.com/Databases/socsci.htm.
016.3   A13

Contains an easy-to-use author-subject index to more than 600 English-language journals. All major social science areas are covered, including anthropology, area studies, criminology, economics, politics, geography, policy studies, psychology, sociology, social work, and urban studies. For information about the print version, please see www.hwwilson.com/sales/printindexes.htm. A CD-ROM version, *Social sciences index/full text,* is available from H. W. Wilson. An online version is available from multiple companies, such as ProQuest's *Social sciences plus text* and H. W. Wilson's *Social sciences full text* via WilsonWeb.

Dictionaries and Encyclopedias

250 **Dictionary of the social sciences.** Craig Calhoun, ed. 563p. Oxford Univ. Pr., 2002. ISBN 0195123719. $
300.3   H41

Provides definitions to more than 1,500 terms from both classic and contemporary topics in the social sciences. Entries are concise (50–500 words) and easy to understand, and many provide references to other helpful articles in the text. Also includes biographies of 275 major influential social scientists and a comprehensive bibliography for further reading and research.

251 Encyclopaedia of the social sciences.
Edwin R. A. Seligman, ed. in chief;
Alvin Saunders Johnson, assoc. ed.
15v. Macmillan, 1930–1935. OP. ISBN
0878273557. $$
303   H41

This classic fifteen-volume resource was the first comprehensive encyclopedia of social sciences. Included are the established disciplines of social science such as political science, economics, sociology, law, anthropology, and social work as well as disciplines with a social aspect, such as ethics, education, biology, and so forth. Volume 1 presents a discussion of the development of social thoughts and institutions as well a discussion of the historical development of social sciences throughout various geographic regions (Great Britain, Latin America, United States, etc.). Also included are 4,000 biographies of deceased individuals whose work has been significant within social sciences. This work complements and is not superseded by the *International encyclopaedia of the social sciences.*

252 International encyclopedia of the social sciences. David L. Sills and Robert King Merton, eds. 17v. Free Press, 1968. OP. Reprint. 17v. in 8v. Macmillan, 1977. OP. Vol. 18, Biographical supplement. 820p. (reprint v. 9) 1979. OP. ISBN 0028956907. $$ Vol. 19, Social science quotations. 437p. 1991. OP. ISBN 0029287510. $$
300   H40

First published in 1968, this classic subject encyclopedia is intended to complement, not supersede, the *Encyclopaedia of the social sciences.* Whereas the previous title took a more historical approach to covering the topic of social sciences, the *International encyclopaedia of the social sciences* reflects the development and expansion of the field in the 1960s. The *Biographical supplement* (volume 18, published in 1979) adds 215 additional biographical sketches to the 600 covered in the previous seventeen volumes. There is very little overlap with the 4,000 biographies covered in the *Encyclopaedia of the social sciences.* The most recent

supplement, *Social science quotations* (volume 19, published in 1991), presents memorable quotes throughout history that make up the "historical core of the social sciences and social thought." For more recent coverage of the topic of social sciences, libraries with larger budgets may want to consider the twenty-six-volume *International encyclopedia of the social and behavioral sciences,* published in print by Elsevier in 2001 and also available in electronic format (the online version is updated regularly). This comprehensive encyclopedia includes 4,000 articles and 150 biographical entries and is the largest work ever published in the social sciences. The cost is quite steep (over $10,000), however, so it might be out of reach for many small or medium-sized libraries.

253 Sage encyclopedia of social science research methods. Michael S. Lewis-Beck, Alan Bryman, and Tim Futing Liao, eds. 3v. Sage, 2004. ISBN 0761923632. $$$
300   H62

This three-volume reference is the first encyclopedia to deal specifically with social science research methods. These topics are essential for users across the various social sciences, including anthropology, communications, education, psychology, sociology, and so forth. Although the material is important for social science students, the entries are written in ordinary English, which makes them accessible to general readers who do not have advanced knowledge of the methods. The encyclopedia includes more than 900 alphabetically arranged entries, which can be divided into two types. The first are short entries that are merely definitions to give the reader a quick explanation of a methodological term. The second type of entries are in-depth essays of varying lengths, which include references and cross-references for additional reading. Each volume includes the same comprehensive bibliography as the appendix, and volume 3 contains an index of subjects and names.

254 Social issues in America: An encyclopedia. James Ciment, ed. 8v. M. E. Sharpe, 2006. ISBN 0765680610. $$
361.973   HN57

Designed for the general reader, this eight-volume encyclopedia provides access to information on a wide range of social issues affecting the United States. Examples of topics covered include academic freedom, consumer debt, homeland security, medical malpractice, stem cell research, and terrorism. Entries are approximately ten pages each and are arranged alphabetically. They include an overview of the topic, a chronology of events related to the topic, bibliographic references including websites, a glossary of important terms, and excerpts from important documents on the topic. Tables and graphs accompany many of the entries. Each volume includes a topic finder, which lists articles under fourteen broad topics, such as educational issues, family issues, and political issues. A cross-reference index is also available near the beginning of each volume listing related topics. Volume 8 is an extensive index to the entire collection.

255   The social science encyclopedia. 3rd ed. Adam Kuper and Jessica Kuper, eds. 2v. Routledge, 2004. ISBN 0415320968. $$
300   H41

Now in its third edition, this two-volume title is an excellent, concise encyclopedia of the social sciences, containing some 600 key concepts and issues. Entries are arranged alphabetically and include cross-references and bibliographic references. In addition to terms such as *race, corruption,* and *marriage,* such prominent individuals as Karl Marx and John Locke are also covered. Volume 1 presents a listing of entries by discipline or subject, such as anthropology, gender, philosophy, and sociology. Several tables and figures are also included. A comprehensive index completes the set.

Bibliographies and Guides

256   Information sources in the social sciences. David Fisher, Sandra P. Price, and Terry Hanstock, eds. 511p. K. G. Saur, 2002. ISBN 3598244398. $
016.3   H61

Published by the German company K. G. Saur, this bibliography presents an international guide to key sources in the social sciences. The intent of this volume is to direct the reader to the most useful materials, which were chosen by subject specialists. The first chapter focuses on general social science sources, while the following chapters deal with various subdisciplines, such as sociology, anthropology, criminology, education, and so forth. Each chapter begins with a discussion of the nature and scope of that topic, followed by the various annotated sources, which are grouped according to their material type. Examples of material types include encyclopedias, bibliographies, websites, journals,

and so forth. A comprehensive index to titles and subjects is available.

257   The social sciences: A cross-disciplinary guide to selected sources. 3rd ed. Nancy L. Herron, ed. 494p. Libraries Unlimited, 2002. ISBN 1563088827 (pbk.). $
016.3   Z7161; H61

This guide contains more than 1,000 annotated citations to resources in the social sciences, selected by subject-specialist librarians. Annotations are organized in four parts: general social sciences; established disciplines, including sociology and economics; disciplines that have acquired a social aspect, such as education and psychology; and related disciplines, like geography and communication. Each chapter contains an essay with an overview of resources in that area, followed by annotations of the various sources organized by type of material (e.g., encyclopedias, handbooks, guides, etc.). Sources include both print, media, and electronic resources. Author, title, and subject indexes are available.

Handbooks

258   Current issues: Macmillan social science library. Macmillan Library Reference USA; Visual Education Corporation. 4v. Macmillan Reference USA, 2003. ISBN 0028657446. $$
306   HN59.2

This four-volume work contains 265 entries of current issues, such as abortion, censorship, pollution, and women's rights. Each article presents an overview of the topic along with relevant background information. Constitutional, environmental, ethical, and social factors related to the topic are also presented. Different points of view on the topic are also offered to provide a balanced presentation, and cross-references at the end of each entry direct users to related topics. Sidebars are often available to provide definitions, quotations, and other information about the topic. Each volume also includes a cumulative table of contents, glossary, cumulative index, and a list of additional resources. This work provides a great starting point for students who need topic ideas for research papers.

259   Reader's guide to the social sciences. Jonathan Michie, ed. 2v. Fitzroy

Dearborn, 2001. ISBN 1579580912. $$
300   H41

Intended as a starting point for research, this two-volume work provides a guide to key literature for various topics within the social sciences. Entries are presented alphabetically and begin with a listing of key resources, followed by a discussion of each resource and its importance for that topic. Each volume includes an alphabetic list of entries and a thematic list of entries by broad categories, such as economics, law, politics, sociology, and so forth. Most of these broad categories are broken down into smaller categories to narrow in on a specific topic, such as elections, gender studies, and urban sociology. Volume 2 presents a book-list index to included books, arranged by author name, along with an extensive general index.

Websites

260   **Fedstats.** Interagency Council on
         Statistical Policy, 2002–. www.fedstats.gov.
         338.973   HC110

This website serves as a gateway to statistics from more than 100 U.S. federal agencies without having to know in advance which agency produces them. Users can browse by an alphabetical list of topics, see profiles of specific geographic areas, or submit a keyword search across agency websites.

261   **H-Net: Humanities and social sciences
         online.** Michigan State Univ., 1995–.
         www.h-net.org.
         300.072; 001.3072;
         370; 378.104; 700.072   H85

This site serves as an international consortium that seeks to enlist participation from academics, students, and scholars on its 100-plus electronic discussion lists. Subscribers to the discussion lists include scholars, teachers, professors, researchers, graduate students, journalists, librarians, and archivists. Messages from each list are archived online and can be searched by the public.

262   **Internet public library social sciences
         subject collection.** Internet Public
         Library. www.ipl.org/div/subject/browse/
         soc00.00.00/.

This site, which is compiled and organized by the University of Michigan, includes a directory of web resources organized by subject categories. The social sciences collection includes sites under the general heading as well as various subheadings, such as anthropology, ethnicity, culture, race, and sociology.

263   **SocioSite.** Albert Benschop, 1996–.
         www.sociosite.net.
         301   HM51

SocioSite, a project based out of the University of Amsterdam, is a multipurpose guide for sociologists with useful links to sites around the world. The site not only serves as a tool kit for social scientists, but also includes great information resources for students. Sites are categorized in various subject areas such as aging, ethnic studies, and terrorism. Biographical information on famous sociologists is also available.

264   **U.S. Census Bureau home page.** U.S.
         Census Bureau. www.census.gov.
         352.7   HA37

The U.S. Census Bureau is the most significant source of demographic information about the population of the United States. The bureau's website provides access to statistical data collected through the American FactFinder, which allows users to search the Economic Census, the American Community Survey, the 1990 Census, Census 2000 and the latest Population Estimates. Other interactive tools on the site include Censtats, QuickFacts, TIGER, US Gazetteer, and DataFerrett.

265   **The WWW virtual library: Social and
         behavioural sciences.** WWW Virtual
         Library. http://vlib.org/SocialSciences/.

Referred to as the "oldest catalogue on the web," this directory of websites was started by web creator Tim Berners-Lee. Each section is maintained by a volunteer who is considered an expert in that particular subject area. The social and behavioral sciences section includes such headings as social sciences, anthropology, archaeology, and sociology. Each broad topic is divided into further subheadings to help find sites specific to certain aspects of a topic (e.g., cultural anthropology or biblical archaeology).

Sociology

Bibliographies and Guides

266   **Sociology: A guide to reference and
         information sources.** 3rd ed. Stephen

H. Aby, James Nalen, and Lori Fielding. 273p. Libraries Unlimited, 2005. ISBN 1563089475. $

016.301   Z7164; HM585

In its third edition, this volume now includes annotations of more than 600 reference sources in sociology and related subdisciplines. Sources include English-language print and electronic materials published from 1997 to early 2004, although some older items of historical value are also listed. This volume is quite expanded from the previous edition due in part to the increased number of websites listed. There are three major parts to the guide: general social science reference sources, sociology, and sociological fields. Within each part, items are divided into subject matter, then material type (except in the case of chapter 1, where general social science sources are divided into material type only). Author/title and subject indexes are provided.

Dictionaries and Encyclopedias

267   **Blackwell dictionary of sociology: A user's guide to sociological language.** 2nd ed. Allan G. Johnson. 413p. Blackwell, 2002. ISBN 0631216812 (pbk.). $

301   HM425

This is a very nice one-volume dictionary of sociological terms. Entries are concise and understandable. Other terms to reference are presented in all caps throughout the definitions, and in many cases, additional reading references are presented at the end of the entry. There is also a separate section for biographical sketches of major figures in sociology, both historical and contemporary. An index of terms and personal names is available.

268   **Dictionary of sociology.** Tony Lawson and Joan Garrod. 273p. Fitzroy Dearborn, 2001. ISBN 1579582915. $

301   HM425

This one-volume, compact dictionary provides a good introduction to the major concepts within the field of sociology. Entries contain a brief definition of the term and, when needed, a more lengthy discussion of the topic along with illustrative examples of the concept. There are cross-references throughout to additional related content within the text.

269   **A dictionary of sociology.** 3rd ed. John Scott and Gordon Marshall, eds. 709p. Oxford Univ. Pr., 2005. ISBN 0198609868. $

301   HM425

The third edition of this work contains more than 2,500 entries in sociology as well as related terms from fields such as psychology, economics, anthropology, philosophy, and political science. Entries have been compiled by an international group of leading experts in sociology. An asterisk placed before a word in a definition indicates that additional relevant information may be found under that term. *See* and *see also* references are also presented throughout. Biographical entries are intermixed with other terms, but coverage of contemporary theorists and researchers is limited to only those who are central to the areas covered in the dictionary.

270   **Encyclopedia of sociology.** 2nd ed. Edgar F. Borgatta, ed. in chief; Rhonda J. V. Montgomery, man. ed. 5v. Macmillan Reference USA, 2000. ISBN 0028648536. $$$

301   HM425

This five-volume set contains more than 400 articles on topics in the field of sociology. The first edition of this work, published in 1992, was the first comprehensive reference to cover sociology as it emerged during the 1960s and 1970s. With all the change that has occurred in the field in recent years, this second edition is a welcome update. Many of the original articles have been updated and expanded, and 60 new articles have been added to the work. Entries are arranged alphabetically, and a nearly 200-page index helps users easily find topics covered.

271   **Sociology basics.** Carl L. Bankston III, consulting ed. 2v. Salem Press, 2000. ISBN 089356205X. $$

301   HM425

This two-volume set extracts articles from *Survey of social sciences: Sociology series* (a five-volume set released in 1995). Ninety of the original 338 articles were selected that cover fundamental topics in sociology. Each entry includes the type of sociology and fields of study to which the topic belongs, followed by a brief summary and principal terms. The body of the articles consists of three sections. First, there is an "Overview" of the topic. Second, the "Applications" section describes how the topic is put into practice. Third, the "Context" section discusses the topic within the field of sociology as a whole. Finally, each entry contains a bibliography and a list of cross-referenced topics.

Handbooks

272   **The international handbook of sociology.** Stella R. Quah and Arnaud Sales, eds. 542p. Sage, 2000. ISBN 0761968881. $$
    301   HM585

The purpose of this book is to evaluate the development of sociology over the last two decades. Unique to this handbook, however, is its decision to focus on specialized fields in sociology instead of general theories. As a result, each of the twenty-three chapters is written by a specialized expert in that field, many of whom are also leaders of research committees of the International Sociological Association. The book is organized into six parts: conceptual perspectives, social and cultural differentiation, changing institutions and collective action, demography, cities, and housing, art and leisure, and social problems. Each chapter presents the full spectrum of research literature on a topic, including opposing traditions of thought and approaches. References are incorporated at the end of each chapter, and comprehensive subject and name indexes are provided at the end of the book.

273   **The Sage handbook of sociology.** Craig Calhoun, Chris Rojek, and Bryan S. Turner, eds. 590p. Sage, 2005. ISBN 0761968210. $$
    301   HM586

This handbook provides an overview of the field of sociology over the last twenty years. The book is broken up into three parts: theory and methods, the axial processes of society, and primary debates. In total, there are thirty-two articles written by sociologists from multiple countries, giving the book an international perspective. Each article contains references for further reading, and there is a comprehensive index at the end of the book.

Abortion

274   **Encyclopedia of abortion in the United States.** Louis J. Palmer Jr. 420p. McFarland, 2002. ISBN 0786413867. $
    363.46   HQ767

Since the 1973 U.S. Supreme Court decision *Roe v. Wade,* abortion has become a very controversial topic in the United States. This encyclopedia presents a nonbiased overview of the history of abortion in the United States. Entries are arranged alphabetically and include many of the political, legal, social, religious, and medical issues associated with abortion. All U.S. Supreme Court opinions on the topic of abortion up to the year 2002 are presented. The abortion laws for each of the fifty states are also listed. Leading abortion organizations on both sides of the issues are also discussed along with many other pressing topics, such as embryonic cloning, assisted reproductive technology, and surrogacy. A bibliography and index are provided.

275   **Reproductive issues in America: A reference handbook.** Janna C. Merrick and Robert H. Blank. 241p. ABC-CLIO, 2003. ISBN 1576078167. $
    616.6   RG133

This handy reference book includes a wide variety of information related to reproductive science and policy. The first two chapters provide an overview of controversial reproductive issues, such as abortion, assisted reproductive technologies, and embryonic research. The third chapter provides a chronology of important events in human reproductive science and policy from 1873 to 2003. Chapter 4 covers biographical sketches of major contributors to human reproductive science, while chapter 5 includes a list of facts and statistics associated with these various issues. Chapter 6 contains a list of organizations and governmental agencies that contribute to clinical research or policy development in the area of reproductive issues. The final chapter provides an annotated bibliography of print and nonprint resources related to reproductive issues, including books, journals, videos, and websites. A glossary and a comprehensive subject index are included.

Aging

276   **Aging in America A to Z.** Adriel Bettelheim. 280p. CQ Press, 2001. ISBN 156802584X. $
    305.26   HQ1064

This encyclopedia of topics concerning older Americans contains more than 250 alphabetically arranged entries. Entries include medical, political, legal, financial, and social issues affecting the elderly. Some examples of topics covered include Alzheimer's disease, Roth IRA, living will, Medicaid, and Medicare. In addition there are brief biographies of people who have made an impact on policy or public attitudes toward aging, including Ronald Reagan and Franklin D. Roosevelt. No bibliography is available, but there is a comprehensive index.

277   Encyclopedia of aging. David J. Ekerdt, ed. in chief. 4v. Macmillan Reference USA, 2002. ISBN 0028654722. $$
305.26   HQ1061

This four-volume work is intended to bring the latest research on aging to the general reader. More than 400 alphabetically arranged entries are individually signed and cover a broad range of topics surrounding aging, including medical, psychological, sociological, public-policy, and biological subjects. In addition to an alphabetical presentation, there is also an outline of contents in volume 1 that lists all articles relating to a particular field or topic. Articles include cross-references and a bibliography for further reading. A comprehensive index is also available.

278   Older Americans: A changing market. 4th ed. 404p. New Strategist, 2001. ISBN 1885070500. $
305.26   HQ1064

The fourth edition of this title (previously titled *Americans 55 and older: A changing market*) presents characteristics, lifestyles, incomes, and spending habits of older Americans, a group that is seeing dramatic changes in recent years due to the influx of the baby boomer generation. The book is divided into nine chapters: "Education," "Health," "Housing," "Income," "Labor Force," "Living Arrangements," "Population," "Spending," and "Wealth." The book contains data on each topic collected by several agencies of the federal government, including the Census Bureau, the Bureau of Labor Statistics, the National Center for Education Statistics, and the Federal Reserve Board. These data have been compiled into tables and graphs to help analyze trends within each area. A glossary, bibliography, and index are included.

Alcoholism and Drug Abuse

279   Alcohol and temperance in modern history: An international encyclopedia. Jack S. Blocker Jr., David M. Fahey, and Ian R. Tyrell, eds. 2v. ABC-CLIO, 2003. ISBN 1576078337. $$
362.292   HV5017

This resource (available in both print and electronic format) presents both the history of alcohol and temperance in one volume. Included are nearly 500 alphabetically arranged entries that discuss the production and use of alcoholic beverages, cultural perceptions, legal issues, temperance movements, research, and treatment. There is a breakdown of entries by geographic area that will assist readers looking for place-specific information. Also included is a chronology of major events in the history of alcohol and temperance movement over the last 500 years. Entries include references and cross-references for additional reading. The appendix includes legal documents, Internet resources, English song themes that deal with alcohol, and a bibliography of tools and reference works. A comprehensive index is also available.

280   Alcoholism sourcebook: Basic consumer health information about the physical and mental consequences of alcohol abuse, including liver disease, pancreatitis, Wernicke-Korsakoff syndrome (alcoholic dementia), fetal alcohol syndrome, heart disease, kidney disorders, gastrointestinal problems, and immune system compromise, and featuring facts about addiction, detoxification, alcohol withdrawal, recovery, and the maintenance of sobriety, along with a glossary and directories of resources for further help and information. Karen Bellenir, ed. 613p. Omnigraphics, 2000. ISBN 0780803256. $
616.86   RC565

This book provides information about alcohol use and abuse, which remains a major problem in the United States with almost 10 percent of adults meeting the diagnostic criteria for alcohol abuse. The book is divided into seven parts. Part 1 includes a discussion on alcohol use and abuse. Part 2 discusses the physical effects of alcohol. Part 3 looks at alcohol and pregnancy. Part 4 is a discussion of the effects of alcohol on the brain. Part 5 presents information about treatment and recovery. Part 6 has information about preventing alcohol abuse. Part 7 lists additional help and information, including a glossary of alcohol-related terms, resources for recovery and support, a directory of information resources, and state substance-abuse agencies. A comprehensive index is also available.

281 Drug abuse sourcebook: Basic consumer health information about illicit substances of abuse and the misuse of prescription and over-the-counter medications, including depressants, hallucinogens, inhalants, marijuana, stimulants, and anabolic steroids; along with facts about related health risks, treatment programs, prevention programs, a glossary of abuse and addiction terms, a glossary of drug-related street terms, and a directory of resources for more information. 2nd ed. Catherine Ginther, ed. 607p. Omnigraphics, 2004. ISBN 0780807405. $

362.29   HV5801

The second edition of this title includes information about the health risks and other effects of drug abuse. Examples of topics covered include depressants, hallucinogens, inhalants, marijuana, stimulants, anabolic steroids, and prescription and over-the-counter medications. The book is divided into seven parts: "Part 1—Introduction to Drug Abuse"; "Part 2—The Nature of Drug Addiction"; "Part 3—Drugs of Abuse"; "Part 4—Recognizing and Treating Drug Abuse"; "Part 5—Health Risks Related to Drug Abuse"; "Part 6—Drug Abuse Prevention"; and "Part 7 Additional Help and Information." The final part includes a glossary of drug-related terms, a directory of resources for assistance, and a comprehensive index.

282 Drug use: A reference handbook. Richard Isralowitz. 269p. ABC-CLIO, 2004. ISBN 157607708X. $

362.29   HV5801

This volume examines the drug-use problem in the United States. The book starts with definitions of such terms as *drug, use, abuse,* and *dependence,* then goes on to define the eleven types of drugs. These include alcohol, amphetamines, caffeine, cannabis, cocaine, hallucinogens, inhalants, nicotine, opiates, phencyclidine, and sedatives, hypnotics, and anxiolytics. In addition, the history, production, and trafficking of drugs are also discussed. Statistical illustrations are presented throughout the text to

further understanding. There is also a chapter of biographical sketches of fifteen individuals who have had a significant influence on drug policy, research, and treatment in the United States. A directory of organizations, associations, and agencies that address drug issues is provided along with a bibliography of additional print and web resources. A glossary of drug terms and a comprehensive index are also available. Available in print and electronic formats.

Encyclopedia of drugs, alcohol, and addictive behavior, see **870**.

283 Tobacco in history and culture: An encyclopedia. Jordan Goodman, ed. in chief. 2v. Thomson Gale, 2005. ISBN 0684314053. $$

394.1   GT3020

This two-volume resource deals with every aspect of tobacco. More than 130 entries discuss the scientific, manufacturing, political, cultural, and religious issues surrounding tobacco. Sidebars include definitions of terminology as well as other interesting pieces of information. Also included are more than 250 graphics, including photos (both color and black and white), charts, graphs, and drawings, that illustrate various advertisements, individuals, or statistics related to tobacco. A timeline of major events in the history of tobacco, starting with 50,000 BC, is incorporated into the second volume along with a comprehensive index. This item is also available as an e-book.

Criminology

284 The American dictionary of criminal justice: Key terms and major court cases. 3rd ed. Dean J. Champion. 513p. Scarecrow, 2005. ISBN 0810854066. $

364   HV7411

As the title indicates, this item provides definitions to more than 5,000 key terms, concepts, and names in criminal justice as well as 125 U.S. Supreme Court cases. The U.S. Supreme Court cases are presented alphabetically, and there is also an index to cases on various topics, which is handy for users who may not know any or all of the cases dealing with a various topic, such as the death penalty or obscenity laws. In the appendixes, there is a directory of PhD programs in criminal justice, a listing of websites relating to criminal justice, a listing of federal and state probation and parole agencies, and a listing of contact information for regional departments of corrections. A bibliography is also available for further reading.

285 Crime in the United States. Federal Bureau of Investigation. http://purl .access.gpo.gov/GPO/LPS3082.
364.973   HV6787

This title is published annually on the Web. The printed publication ceased in 2004. Previously it was titled *Uniform crime reports for the United States*. This essential resource provides detailed statistics on U.S. crime as reported to the Federal Bureau of Investigation by more than 17,000 city, university and college, county, state, tribal, and federal law enforcement agencies. The data are presented in various tables and graphs and cover such topics as offenses reported, persons arrested, and law enforcement personnel.

286 Encyclopedia of capital punishment in the United States. Louis J. Palmer Jr. 606p. McFarland, 2001. ISBN 0786409444. $
364.66   HV8694

The purpose of this encyclopedia is to provide a comprehensive resource to the legal, social, and political history and present status of capital punishment in the United States. Entries include the majority of U.S. Supreme Court decisions relating to capital punishment. Also included is an entry for each state and almost 200 nations that detail current death penalty laws. Other entries include individuals and organizations related to the death penalty as well as various methods of execution, such as lethal injection and hanging. Lots of photographs and graphical illustrations are presented throughout. A comprehensive index and bibliography are also available.

287 Encyclopedia of crime and punishment. David Levinson, ed. 4v. Sage, 2002. ISBN 076192258X. $$$
346   HV6017

Much information has been published dealing with the topic of crime and punishment over the last decade. This four-volume set attempts to give readers a comprehensive overview of the topic by surveying the entire field of criminal justice and presenting information from a variety of sources. As a result, the work includes 439 alphabetically arranged, individually signed articles covering

twelve major themes: crimes, law and justice, policing and forensics, corrections, victimology, punishment, social/cultural context, nations/regions/religions, concepts and theories, studying crime and punishment, organizations and institutions, and special populations. A readers' guide at the beginning of volume 1 lists articles according to these themes to help readers locate articles on related topics. Volume 4 presents four appendixes. Appendix 1 has information about careers in criminal justice. Appendix 2 lists web resources for criminal justice. Appendix 3 is a directory of professional and scholarly associations. Appendix 4 is a selected bibliography. A comprehensive index and a chronology of important events in criminology are also available.

288 Encyclopedia of criminology. Richard A. Wright and J. Mitchell Miller, eds. 3v. Routledge, 2005. ISBN 1579583873. $$
364   HV6017

This three-volume encyclopedia includes more than 525 signed articles on the latest research in the multidisciplinary field of criminology. Entries are arranged alphabetically, and volume 1 also includes a thematic list of articles under broad areas such as "correlates of criminal behavior" (age, gender, etc.) and "types of criminal behavior" (arson, counterfeiting, war crimes, etc.). All entries have references for further reading as well as cross-references. One unique aspect of this title is its inclusion of biographical entries for prominent figures in the field, such as J. Edgar Hoover. A comprehensive index is available.

289 Encyclopedia of terrorism. Harvey W. Kushner. 523p. Sage, 2003. ISBN 0761924086. $$
303.6   HV6431

Though work on this title began more than a year before September 11, 2001, the events of that day spurred an increasing interest in the topic of terrorism. This one-volume title includes more than 300 articles covering terrorist-related events, groups, individuals, methods, activities, and responses. Entries include references and cross-references, and in some cases, photographs are provided as well. Appendix A contains maps of all the continents (minus Antarctica) highlighting locations of terrorist activity. Appendix B lists websites relating to terrorist activity or prevention. Appendix C has a chronology of terrorist attacks in the United States and on U.S. interests abroad beginning in 1865. A comprehensive index and bibliography are also presented.

290   Oxford handbook of criminology.
3rd ed. Mike Maguire, Rodney Morgan, and Robert Reiner, eds. 1227p. Oxford Univ. Pr., 2002. ISBN 0199256098; 0199249377 (pbk.). $$; $ (pbk.)
364   HV6025

In its third edition, this title remains a comprehensive one-volume source of information on the subject of criminology. Though most of the contributors are from the United Kingdom, the material discussed is appropriate for the general study of criminology. The book is divided into 5 parts. Part 1 is entitled "Criminology: History and Theory." Part 2 discusses the "Social Construction of Crime and Crime Control," including topics such as crime statistics and crime representation in the media. Part 3 includes "Dimensions of Crime"; examples include gender and crime and ethnicity in crime. Part 4 presents "Forms of Crime," such as violent crime and white-collar crime. Part 5, "Reactions to Crime," includes discussions about policing and imprisonment. Articles include bibliographic references and, in many cases, illustrations, such as statistical tables. A comprehensive index is available.

291   Terrorism: Assassins to zealots. Sean Anderson and Stephen Sloan. 468p. Scarecrow, 2003. ISBN 081084589X (pbk.). $
303.6   HV6431

This volume is a revised, updated paperback version of the *Historical dictionary of terrorism*. It includes information about major terrorist groups and individuals, significant terrorist events, and weapons used in terrorist attacks. Examples of included entries are "Islamic Jihad" and "Pan Am Flight 103 Bombing." Also included at the beginning of the volume is a listing of acronyms and abbreviations as well as a chronology of important terrorist events from AD 66. A nicely organized bibliography provides additional sources on terrorism.

Death and Dying

292   Death and dying sourcebook. Annemarie Muth, ed. 641p. Omnigraphics, 2000. ISBN 0780802306. $
362.1   R726

The purpose of this book is to provide readers with information on the medical, legal, and ethical issues relating to death and dying. The book is divided into eight parts. Part 1 presents statistics on death and dying in the United States. Part 2 includes information on various attitudes toward death and dying. Part 3 contains information on health-care options for the terminally ill. Part 4 discusses end-of-life medical care issues and innovations. Part 5 looks at the experiences of someone who is approaching death. Part 6 includes information on final arrangements, such as wills and funerals. Part 7 discusses the process of bereavement. Part 8 includes various resources for additional help and information, including a glossary of medical and legal terminology related to death and dying as well as list of agencies and online resources for further assistance. A comprehensive index is available.

293   Encyclopedia of death and dying. Glennys Howarth and Oliver Leaman, eds. 534p. Routledge, 2002. ISBN 0415188253. $$
306.9   HQ1073

Including more than 400 entries, this encyclopedia covers all aspects of death and dying. Each article is individually signed and includes cross-references and references for further reading. Most of the contributors come from Australia or the United Kingdom, which gives the vocabulary of the entries a British emphasis (e.g., *cot death*, not *crib death*). Despite this emphasis, the volume contains many articles on unusual topics, such as "death by chocolate" and "pets." In addition to subject entries, there are also biographical entries, such as "Jack Kevorkian" and "Sylvia Plath." A bibliography and name and subject index are also available.

294   The encyclopedia of death and dying. Dana K. Cassell, Robert C. Salinas, and Peter S. Winn. 369p. Facts on File, 2005. ISBN 0816053766. $
306.9   HQ1073

Although this one-volume work has a title similar to others, there is surprisingly little overlap in the included terms. This encyclopedia contains more than 500 articles explaining the medical, social, religious, and legal concepts surrounding death and dying. Entries present clear, concise definitions of terms and, in many cases, a bibliography for further reading. There are also some interesting inclusions in the appendixes, including a table with odds of dying from various injuries and a list of U.S. wars and the number of resulting deaths. Other useful items in the appendixes include a sample "Advanced Care Plan" document, a checklist for funeral preplanning, and a list of organization and web resources. A comprehensive index and bibliography are also available.

295   Handbook of death and dying. Clifton D. Bryant, ed. in chief. 2v. Sage, 2003. ISBN 0761925147. $$

306.9   HQ1073

This two-volume work presents 103 essays on various topics related to thanatology, the study of death and dying. The first volume, *The presence of death,* contains articles on confronting death, the fear of death, euthanasia, and the dying process. Volume 2 is entitled *The response to death* and includes entries about death ceremonies, body disposition, the bereavement process, and the legalities of death. Articles are individually signed and include bibliographic references for further reading. A comprehensive index is available.

296   Life and death in the United States: Statistics on life expectancies, diseases, and death rates for the twentieth century. Russell O. Wright. 139p. McFarland, 1997. ISBN 0786403209. $

304.6   HB1335

This book contains lots of charts and tables depicting statistics on life expectancy and death rates in the United States in the twentieth century. Most of the data in this book come from *The statistical abstract of the United States,* although some data come from other sources, such as the American Heart Association and the American Cancer Society. The book is divided into five parts. Part 1 deals with life expectancy; part 2, with death rates. Part 3 looks at cardiovascular diseases. Part 4 looks at cancer, and Part 5 discusses the future. There is a listing of tables and figures at the beginning of the book; an index is available at the end.

297   Macmillan encyclopedia of death and dying. Robert Kastenbaum, ed. in chief. 2v. Macmillan Reference USA, 2003. ISBN 002865689X. $$

306.9   HQ1073

This two-volume set presents multidisciplinary coverage of death and dying in society. More than 300 alphabetically arranged articles cover topics such as necrophilia, ghosts, Elvis sightings, and organ donation and transplantation. Also included are entries on various important individuals in the field, such as Elisabeth Kübler-Ross and Socrates. Illustrations, such as tables and photographs, are

included in many of the entries, and a bibliography is available at the end of each article. Volume 2 contains an appendix with information on organizations in the field of death and dying as well as a comprehensive index to both volumes.

Ethnic Studies

298   Dictionary of race, ethnicity and culture. Guido Bolaffi et al., eds. 355p. Sage, 2003. ISBN 0761968997; 0761969004 (pbk.). $$; $ (pbk.)

305.8   GN495

Containing some 200 entries, this one-volume resource covers common terms associated with the areas of race, ethnicity, and culture. Entries range in length from one paragraph to several pages and provide a good introduction for students or others requiring quick definitions of terms. Entries include cross-references and bibliographic references. A subject and name index is also included.

299   Encyclopedia of racism in the United States. Pyong Gap Min, ed. 3v. Greenwood, 2005. ISBN 0313326886. $$

305.8   E184

Focusing on the persistent issue of racism, which has plagued the United States since its inception, this three-volume work contains 447 articles on minority groups, individuals, associations, court cases, concepts, beliefs, and theories. Each of the three volumes includes an introduction on racism in the United States, followed by a chronology of important events regarding race and racism starting in 1790. Each volume also includes a guide to related entries, which lists all articles related to a broad topic, for example, "African Americans" or "Immigration and Immigrants." Entries are individually signed and include cross-references and a bibliography. Some entries also contains photographs or illustrations. Volume 3 also contains text of twenty-six primary or original documents along with a selected bibliography and a comprehensive index.

300   Encyclopedia of the world's minorities. Carl Skutsch, ed.; Martin Ryle, consulting ed. 3v. Routledge, 2005. ISBN 157958392X. $$

305.8   GN495

This three-volume reference contains 562 essays divided into four main categories: topic entries, nations entries, minority-group entries, and bio-graphical entries. Topic entries cover broad ideas, concepts, and concerns surrounding minority issues (e.g., affirmative action and racism). Nations entries include historical background, social con-ditions, and current situation on 173 countries. Groups entries explain the history and current situation of more than 250 minority groups (e.g., Muslims in the Americas, Italians, homosexuality, and minority status). The final category of entries are biographies of significant persons in the his-tory of minority communities. Groups and nations entries include information about location, lan-guage, population, and religion. Entries range in length from 1,000 to 5,000 words and include ref-erences for further reading. A comprehensive index is available.

301   Gale encyclopedia of multicultural America. 2nd ed. Robert Dassanowsky, contributing ed.; Jeffrey Lehman, ed. 3v. Gale, 2000. ISBN 0787639869. $$
305.8   E184

The second edition of this title includes essays on 152 different cultural groups currently resid-ing in the United States. Well-known groups, such as African Americans, Mexican Americans, and Chinese Americans, are covered along with lesser-known groups, such as Acadians, Hopis, and Yupiat. The average length of each entry is 8,000 words, and each covers an overview (e.g., history, settlement, migration, etc.), acculturation and assimilation (traditions, cuisine, music, etc.), language, religion, economic, politics, and so forth. Each chapter concludes with individual and group contributions in various fields such as academia, arts, music, sports, and so forth, along with media outlets (print, radio, etc.), organizations, museums and research centers, and sources for additional study. Volume 3 includes a general bibliography and a comprehensive index.

302   Race relations in the United States: A chronology, 1896–2005. Paul D. Buchanan. 211p. McFarland, 2005. ISBN 0786413875. $
305.8   E184

Starting with the *Plessy v. Ferguson* decision in 1896, this book recounts the chronology of more than 200 significant events affecting race rela-tions in the United States up to 2005. Entries are arranged chronologically, and a bibliography and an index are also available.

303   Racial and ethnic diversity: Asians, blacks, Hispanics, Native Americans, and whites. 4th ed. Cheryl Russell. 974p. New Strategist, 2002. ISBN 1885070454. $
305.8   E184

Based on data collected in the 2000 Census, this one-volume reference presents various statistics related to the many racial and ethnic groups in the United States. The first six chapters cover various ethnic groups, such as American Indians, Asians, blacks, Hispanics, Native Hawaiians, and whites. Chapter 7 presents collective statistics on the total population, and the final chapter looks at attitudes and behaviors, such as perceptions of diversity and immigration. The section entitled "For more information," offers lists of websites, subject specialists departments within fed-eral agencies, census regional offices, and state data centers and industry data centers. Also included are a glossary and a comprehensive index.

304   Racial and ethnic diversity in America: A reference handbook. Adalberto Aguirre. 277p. ABC-CLIO, 2003. ISBN 157607983X. $
305.8   E184

This one-volume work provides a good start-ing point for those interested in racial and ethnic diversity in the United States. Chapter 1 presents a history of immigrants in early America. Chapter 2 discusses the present-day racial and ethnic situa-tion. Chapter 3 discusses the challenges that face a diverse population. Each of the first three chapters contains statistical illustrations and bibliographic references for further reading. Chapter 4 presents a chronology of important events surrounding racial and ethnic diversity. Chapter 5 contains biographical sketches of fourteen selected schol-ars writing and conducting research in the areas of diversity, race, and ethnic relations in the United States. Chapter 6 lists statistics on the racial and ethnic population along with laws and quotations. Chapter 7 is a directory of organizations related to diversity. Chapter 8 lists print resources, while chapter 9 contains nonprint resources. A compre-hensive index is available.

305   Racial and ethnic relations in America. Carl L. Bankston III, ed. 3v. Salem Press, 2000. ISBN 0893566292. $$
305.8   E49

Covering both Canada and the United States, this three-volume set contains close to 900 easy-to-read articles on important topics, events, and issues related to race and ethnicity. Alphabetically arranged entries range in length from 200 words to more than 2,500 words. All entries contains *see also* references, and longer entries also contain a list of core bibliographic resources. Charts, tables, graphs, and photographs are also included with some entries. All three volumes include a categorized list of entries to identify multiple articles under a broad topic. Volume 3 contains short biographic entries of pioneers of intergroup relations organized by ethnic group (e.g., African Americans, Hispanic Americans, etc.). Also included in volume 3 are a timeline of important events, a bibliography, a personage index, and a subject index.

AFRICAN AMERICANS

306   **The African American almanac.** 9th ed. Jeffrey Lehman, ed. 1500p. Gale, 2003. ISBN 0787640204. $$
973   E185

Published every three years, this large one-volume reference (formerly titled *The Negro almanac*) contains a plethora of information on African Americans. The ninth edition is divided into twenty-nine chapters, most of which cover subject areas such as civil rights, politics, education, religion, popular music, and so forth. A typical subject chapter includes an introduction to the topic, followed by a discussion of significant individuals, events, places, or organizations. Illustrations, such as photographs, tables, and graphs, accompany many of the chapters. In addition to subject chapters, other chapters include an extensive chronology, African American firsts, significant documents, and important landmarks in the African American community. An appendix includes listing of African American award recipients of various awards and Olympic medals. A general bibliography and index are also available.

307   **African American lives.** Henry Louis Gates and Evelyn Brooks Higginbotham, eds. 1025p. Oxford Univ. Pr., 2004. ISBN 019516024X. $
920   E185

This book represents a subset of the African American National Biography project. Included in this sampler are some 600 biographies of prominent African Americans, mostly deceased. Some of the entries are pulled from the *American national biography* (Oxford, 1999). Entries are arranged

alphabetically and include a bibliography for further reading. There is also a listing of entries arranged by category or area of renown, such as activism or medicine. Also included is a listing of African American prizewinners, medalists, members of Congress, and judges. An index is also available.

308   **Africana: The encyclopedia of the African and African American experience.** 2nd ed. Anthony Appiah and Henry Louis Gates. 5v. Oxford Univ. Pr., 2005. ISBN 0195170555. $$$
960   DT14

The initial edition of this reference work (published in 1999) was inspired by W. E. B. DuBois's vision to publish a black *Encyclopaedia Britannica*. Now in its second edition, this five-volume set includes more than 4,000 entries on individuals, events, places, ethnic groups, organizations, movements, and countries from America and Africa. Alphabetically arranged entries include cross-references and a bibliography, along with colorful images, maps, charts, and tables. Volume 1 includes a selected chronology of important events in African and African American history. Volume 5 contains a topical outline of selected entries under such broad topics as abolitionism and political and social movements. Also included are a bibliography and a comprehensive index.

309   **Black firsts: 4,000 groundbreaking and pioneering historical events.** 2nd ed. Jessie Carney Smith. 787p. Visible Ink Press, 2003. ISBN 1578591538. $
909   E185

This second edition (previous edition, 1994) includes more than 1,000 new entries of black achievements. Entries are broken up into such categories as arts and entertainment, business, education, and sports. Within each category, entries are listed chronologically. Photographs and tables are included in many entries. Also included are a list of bibliographic sources and a comprehensive index.

310   **Black heritage sites: An African American odyssey and finder's guide.** Nancy C. Curtis. 677p. American Library Association, 1996. ISBN 0838906435. $
973   E159

This guide developed out of a personal quest to reconnect with the author's African American heritage. In writing this resource, the author visited many of the sites herself. The entries are arranged into five regions: South, Northeast, Midwest, Southwest, and West. Each section includes an introduction that highlights the types of structures in that region. Within each region, entries are organized by state, then city. Users may also find entries using the comprehensive index. Although some of the contact, fee, and hours information included in each entry may be outdated, this is still a valuable resource for information about historic African American sites.

311 Black heroes. Jessie Carney Smith. 733p. Visible Ink Press, 2001. ISBN 0780807286. $
920   E185

Including more than 150 alphabetically arranged entries, this book presents biographical profiles of prominent African Americans over the last 100 years. Unlike *African American lives,* most of those covered in this volume are still living. Examples of some included individuals are Maya Angelou, Oprah Winfrey, and Colin Powell. Most entries contain a photograph of the individual, and many entries contain more than one photograph. A comprehensive index is available.

312 Black women in America. 2nd ed. Darlene Clark Hine, ed. in chief. 3v. Oxford Univ. Pr., 2005. ISBN 0195156773. $$
305.48   E185

Now in its second edition, this three-volume reference remains a highly recommended resource for its coverage of the often overlooked contributions of African American women in society. This new edition contains biographical profiles of 325 women (from 1800 to the present) along with entries on various topics related to arts, culture, family, gender, law, occupations, politics, religion, science, and sports, for a total of 560 articles. More than 600 photographs accompany the entries, and a bibliography for further reading is available at the end of each entry. Volume 3 contains a chronology of black women's history starting in 1619, a selected bibliography, and a comprehensive index. Also included is a thematic outline of entries, which lists articles under both topical (culture, business and economics, etc.) and biographical (actors, lawyers, etc.) subjects.

313 Who's who among African Americans. Katherine H. Nemeh and John B. Smith

Sr. Thomson Gale, 1997–. Annual. ISSN 1081-1400. $$
920   E185

Published annually, this title includes short biographies of more than 20,000 prominent African American men and women. Entries are arranged alphabetically, and there is also an index by geography and occupation. Available online through LexisNexis, as part of the Gale Biographies file, and through Gale Group's online database, *Biography resource center.*

ASIAN AMERICANS

314 The Asian databook: Detailed statistics and rankings on the Asian and Pacific Islander population, including 23 ethnic backgrounds from Bangladeshi to Vietnamese for 1,883 U.S. counties and cities. David Garoogian, ed. 2274p. Grey House, 2005. ISBN 1592370446. $$
305.895   E184

This reference provides statistical information about one of the fastest-growing populations in the United States. Statistical data are drawn from the 2000 Census and cover the fifty states plus the District of Columbia, 786 counties (with populations greater than 49,999), and 1,045 cities (with populations greater than 9,999). Section 1 is divided into fourteen topics, such as overall population, median age, languages spoken at home, educational attainment, and so forth. Within these fourteen topics, data are organized by state, then county, then city. Section 2 presents rankings of states and the top 75 counties and the top 75 cities for the same fourteen topics. Also included is a city-finder list, which will assist users in finding a city when the county is unknown. A companion CD-ROM is available at no additional charge to purchasers of the print book and includes the same information as the print edition but for a total of 3,426 locations.

315 Distinguished Asian Americans: A biographical dictionary. Hyung-chan Kim, ed. 430p. Greenwood, 1999. ISBN 0313289026. $
920   E184

This work contains 166 biographical profiles of Asian Americans, both native and foreign born, who have made significant contributions to American society. Entries are arranged alphabetically and include a selected bibliography. In some cases, a picture of the person is also included. Appendix A lists the biographies by fields of professional activity, and appendix B lists entries by ethnic subgroup, such as Chinese American or Japanese American. A comprehensive index is also available.

316   UXL Asian American reference library.
2nd ed. Helen Zia et al., eds. 6v. UXL/
Thomson Gale, 2004. ISBN 0787675997
(set). $$
920   E184

UXL Asian American almanac. 2nd ed.
Irene Natividad and Susan B. Gall, eds.
268p. UXL/Thomson Gale, 2004.
ISBN 0787675989. $
973   E184

UXL Asian American biography.
2nd ed. Helen Zia and Susan B. Gall,
eds. 2v. UXL/Thomson Gale, 2004.
ISBN 0787676012. $$
973   E184

UXL Asian American chronology. 2nd
ed. Maura Malone and Susan B. Gall,
eds. 196p. UXL/Thomson Gale, 2004.
ISBN 0787676047. $
973   E184

UXL Asian American voices. 2nd
ed. Deborah Gillan Straub, ed. 315p.
UXL/Thomson Gale, 2004. ISBN
0787676004. $
973   E184

**UXL Asian American reference
library: Cumulative index.** 2nd ed.
Sonia Benson, ed. 58p. UXL/Thomson
Gale, 2004. ISBN 0787676063. $
973   Z1361; E184

As a set, this resource provides a wealth of information about Asian Americans. The *Almanac* includes various statistics, significant documents, and landmarks as well as information on immigration, civil rights, the legal system, religion, languages, and so forth. The *Biography* has two volumes with profiles of 150 prominent Asian American men and women. The *Chronology* presents significant social, political, economic, cultural, and professional milestones arranged by year, then month and day. *Voices* contains complete and excerpted speeches given by prominent Asian Americans in the twenti-

eth century. Finally, the *Cumulative index* provides greater access to various topics and individuals covered throughout the volumes. All the titles in the set include numerous illustrations, such as photographs and tables. The units can also be purchased separately to meet individual collection needs.

HISPANIC AMERICANS

**317   Encyclopedia of Latino popular
culture.** Cordelia Candelaria, ed. 2v.
Greenwood, 2004. ISBN 0313322155. $$
973   E184

The recent explosion in the Latino population in the United States has undoubtedly impacted popular culture in recent years. This two-volume set covers all aspects of Latino popular culture, including food, art, music, and entertainment along with entries for prominent contemporary Latinos, such as Christina Aguilera and Enrique Iglesias, as well as more historic figures, such as César Chávez and Frida Kahlo. Both volumes include a listing of entries alphabetically and by subject. Biographical entries are listed by field of endeavor and by the person's country of origin or heritage. Each of the approximately 600 individually signed entries contains bibliographic references, and many also include photographs. Volume 2 includes a bibliography by subject, along with a comprehensive index.

318   Great Hispanic Americans. Nicolás
Kanellos, consultant; Robert Rodriguez
and Tamra Orr, contributing writers.
128p. Publications International, 2005.
ISBN 1412711487. $
920   E184

This eye-catching resource provides bibliographic profiles on fifty-five Hispanic Americans from such diverse areas as literature, science, entertainment, and law. Examples of included individuals are Alberto Gonzales, Desi Arnaz, and Joan Baez. Entries are arranged alphabetically, accompanied by color photographs and illustrations, and easy to understand. A comprehensive index is also available.

**319   The Hispanic databook: Detailed
statistics and rankings on the
Hispanic population, including 23
ethnic backgrounds from Argentinian
to Venezuelan, for 1,266 U.S. counties
and cities.** 2nd ed. David Garoogian,
ed. 1920p. Grey House, 2004.

ISBN 159237008X. $$
305.868   E184

Now in its second edition, this title provides important statistical information about the largest minority group in the United States. Statistical data are drawn from the 2000 Census and cover the fifty states plus the District of Columbia, 525 counties (with populations greater than 99,999), and 689 cities (with populations greater than 49,999). Section 1 is divided into fifteen topics, such as overall population, median age, languages spoken at home, educational attainment, and so forth. Within these fifteen topics, data are organized by state, then county, then city. Section 2 presents rankings of states and the top 75 counties and the top 75 cities for the same fifteen topics. Also included is a city-finder list, which will assist users in finding a city when the county is unknown. A companion CD-ROM is available at no additional charge to purchasers of the print book and includes the same information as the print edition but for a total of 5,071 locations.

**320   The Oxford encyclopedia of Latinos
         and Latinas in the United States.**
         Suzanne Oboler and Deena J. González,
         eds. in chief. 4v. Oxford Univ. Pr., 2005.
         ISBN 0195156005. $$$
         973   E184

This four-volume reference covers more than 900 articles of topics related to the often-overlooked historical, intellectual, social, artistic, and political experiences of Latinos and Latinas in the United States. Entries are arranged alphabetically and include cross-references and bibliographic references. More than 400 illustrations, charts, and maps are also included throughout the resource. Volume 4 includes a topical outline of entries in fourteen broad categories, such as society, education, places, and biographies. Included entries cover court cases, specific states, geographic regions (e.g., East Los Angeles), organizations, individuals (e.g., Jennifer Lopez, Anthony Quinn), and so forth. A nearly 200-page index completes the set.

**321   UXL Hispanic American reference
         library.** 2nd ed. 5v. UXL/Thomson Gale,
         2003. ISBN 0787666025 (set). $$
         973.046   E184

UXL Hispanic American almanac. 2nd
ed. Sonia Benson, Nicolás Kanellos, and
Bryan Ryan, eds. 247p. UXL/Thomson
Gale, 2003. ISBN 0787665983. $
973.468   E184

UXL Hispanic American biography.
2nd ed. Sonia Benson, Rob Nagel, and
Sharon Rose, eds. 321p. UXL/Thomson
Gale, 2003. ISBN 0787665991. $
920   E184

UXL Hispanic American chronology.
2nd ed. Sonia Benson, Nicolás
Kanellos, and Bryan Ryan, eds. 216p.
UXL/Thomson Gale, 2003. ISBN
0787666009. $
973   E184

UXL Hispanic American voices. 2nd
ed. Sonia G. Benson and Deborah Gillan
Straub, eds. 294p. UXL/Thomson Gale,
2003. ISBN 0787666033. $
973   E184

**UXL Hispanic American reference
library cumulative index.** 2nd ed.
Carol DeKane Nagel, index coordinator.
50p. UXL/Thomson Gale, 2003. ISBN
0787666017. $
016.973   Z1361; E184

As a set, this resource provides a wealth of information about Hispanic Americans. The *Almanac* presents historical and contemporary information about Hispanic American life and culture. The *Biography* has profiles of 100 prominent Hispanic American men and women. The *Chronology* presents significant social, political, economic, cultural, and professional milestones arranged by year, then month and day. *Voices* contains twenty-one complete and excerpted articles, memoirs, essays, speeches, and letters written by prominent Hispanic Americans. Finally, the *Cumulative index* provides greater access to various topics and individuals covered throughout the volumes. All the titles in the set include numerous illustrations, such as photographs and tables. The units can also be purchased separately to meet individual collection needs.

NATIVE PEOPLES OF NORTH AMERICA

**322   A Native American encyclopedia:
         History, culture, and peoples.** Barry M.
         Pritzker. 591p. Oxford Univ. Pr., 2000.
         ISBN 019513897X; 0195138775 (pbk.). $
         970   E76

This resource provides information about 200-plus North American Indian groups in Canada and the United States. The book is divided into ten regional areas (e.g., Southwest, California, the Arctic, etc.), and tribes are listed alphabetically within each region. Entries begin with the tribal name, translation, origin, and definition. Next, information about the history, location, population, religion, and culture of each tribe is covered. Finally, contemporary information on each group's government, economy, legal status, and land holdings is presented. Appendix 1 is a listing of Alaska native villages by language. Appendix 2 is an alphabetical list of Anca village corporations. A glossary, bibliography, and index are also included.

323   Reference library of Native North America. Duane Champagne, ed. 4v. African American Publications, 2001. ISBN 0787656151. $
970.004   E76.2

This four-volume resource provides broad coverage of Native North America including both the United States and Canada. Volume 1 includes a chronology; directories of sites, landmarks, cultural centers, and so forth; and demographics from pre-1700 to the twentieth century. Volume 2 contains information on a wide range of topics, such as languages, law, environment, religion, arts, health, and education. Volume 4 includes brief biographies on prominent Native North Americans. Access to additional biographies is available through the publisher's website (www.nativepubs.com). In addition to the 400 illustrations throughout the set, each of the four volumes includes an extensive glossary, general bibliography, and a comprehensive index. This title is also published in a single-volume format under the title *The Native North American almanac: A reference work on Native North Americans in the United States and Canada* (Gale, 2001).

324   UXL encyclopedia of Native American tribes. Sharon Malinowski, Anna J. Sheets, and Linda Schmittroth. 4v., 1275p. UXL/Thomson Gale, 1999. ISBN 0787628387. $$
970   E76

This is a great resource for more in-depth information about specific Native American tribes. The four-volume set examines eighty tribes arranged by ten geographic regions. Entries include information about the name, location, population, and language of each group as well as a discussion of its history, religion, government, economy, customs, notable people, and current tribal issues. Entries include interesting sidebar information, such as recipes

or folktales, as well as multiple illustrations and photographs. Each volume includes an alphabetic listing of tribes, a glossary, a timeline of important events, maps of tribe locations, a comprehensive bibliography, and an index.

Family, Marriage, and Divorce

325   Encyclopedia of family life. Carl L. Bankston III, ed.; R. Kent Rasmussen, project ed. 5v. Salem Press, 1999. ISBN 0893569402. $$
306.85   HQ534

Covering both the United States and Canada, this five-volume set discusses the issues, individuals, organizations, court cases, health concerns, and so forth, that affect family life in modern society. The 452 entries begin by identifying relevant family issues and the significance of the subject or individual to family life in general. Entries range in length from 250 words up to 4,000 words. Cross-references are also presented at the end of each article, and photographs, charts, tables, and graphs appear liberally throughout the set. Volume 5 contains a chronology of important legislative and court decisions along with a timeline of changes to the family from 450 BCE. Also presented are a directory of support groups, a glossary, a select bibliography, and a comprehensive index. A listing of entries within twenty-eight broad categories, such as children, religion, and divorce, is also provided.

326   The encyclopedia of marriage, divorce and the family. Margaret DiCanio. 579p. ToExcel, 2000. ISBN 0595000223 (pbk.). $
306.8   HQ9

Originally published in 1989, this reference covers a wide variety of terms related to changing lifestyles in the United States over the last few decades. Alphabetically arranged entries are fairly brief, but cross-references are provided. Examples of included entries are artificial insemination, interracial marriage, and stepfamilies. Multiple appendixes are included, such as a consumer guide to divorce procedures and a sample living-together agreement. An extensive bibliography and general index are also included.

327   Families in America: A reference handbook. Jeffrey S. Turner. 351p. ABC-CLIO, 2002. ISBN

1576076288. $
306.85   HQ536

Available in both print and electronic formats, this compact one-volume reference presents an in-depth examination of the contemporary American family. The text is broken up into nine chapters that explore the history of the American family, diversity, and issues and controversies such as divorce, abuse, and gay and lesbian families. Also presented are a chronology of important events related to the American family, biographical sketches of more than twenty prominent figures in the field, and a chapter with facts and statistics on the topic. There is a directory of family agencies and organizations along with an extensive list of print, media, and electronic resources. A short bibliography and a comprehensive index complete the volume.

328   Handbook of marriage and the family.
2nd ed. Marvin B. Sussman, Suzanne K. Steinmetz, and Gary W. Peterson, eds. 822p. Plenum Press, 1999. ISBN 0306457547. $$
306.8   HQ518

The second edition of this text addresses current trends and analysis of contemporary research regarding family structure and processes. Articles are individually signed and organized into five separate sections. Part 1 deals with family diversity in the past, present, and future. Part 2 covers theories and methods of family studies. Part 3 focuses on the changing family patterns and roles, specifically the effects of age and gender on family structural and relationship changes. Part 4 discusses the family and other institutions, such as religion and work. Part 5 includes articles on conflict and power, communication, family violence, sexuality, and marital therapy. Each chapter includes bibliographic references, and a comprehensive index is also available.

329   International encyclopedia of marriage and family. 2nd ed. James J. Ponzetti Jr., ed. in chief. 4v. Macmillan Reference USA, 2003. ISBN 0028656725. $$$
306.8   HQ9

This work serves as a reference for the diverse marriage and family lifestyles throughout the world. Now in its second edition, this four-volume work has been greatly expanded to include a more international focus, with coverage of fifty individual countries. In addition to articles on specific

countries, topics related to marriage and the family are also covered, for example, birth control, home, infidelity, love, remarriage, wedding rings, and so forth. Entries range in length from about two to six pages and include cross-references, a bibliography, and in some cases, illustrations, such as photographs, tables, or graphs. A comprehensive index is available.

330   Marriage customs of the world: From henna to honeymoons. George Monger. 327p. ABC-CLIO, 2004. ISBN 1576079872. $
392.5   GT2690

This interesting reference explores the many marriage customs in various cultures and religions throughout the world, highlighting both the similarities and differences. There are approximately 200 alphabetically arranged entries that examine such expected topics as arranged marriage and polygyny as well as some truly strange customs, such as marriage to a tree and marriage over the broom. Entries include cross-references and a bibliography, and some pictures are included as well. A comprehensive index is also available.

Gay and Lesbian Studies

331   Encyclopedia of lesbian and gay histories and cultures. George Haggerty and Bonnie Zimmerman, eds. 2v. Garland, 2000. ISBN 0815333544. $$
306.76   HQ75

This work is unique in its presentation of separate volumes for *Lesbian* (v. 1) and *Gay* (v. 2) histories and cultures. Traditionally, more emphasis has been given to gay males, so it's refreshing to see a resource give equal treatment to lesbians. Each volume includes a subject guide to help readers identify multiple articles under a given topic (e.g., AIDS, history, law, etc.). The types of topics covered are broad, including literature, theater, health, geography, and politics. Also covered are biographical entries of prominent figures in gay and lesbian culture. Entries include a bibliography and cross-references. A comprehensive index is also available at the end of each volume.

332   Encyclopedia of lesbian, gay, bisexual, and transgender history in America. Marc Stein, ed. in chief. 3v. Scribner/Thomson Gale, 2004.

ISBN 0684312611. $$

306.76   HQ76

Covering various aspects of lesbian, gay, bisexual, and transgender (LGBT) history, culture, politics, and society in America, this three-volume set contains some 550 articles authored by researchers and academics in the LGBT community. Half of the entries are biographical, while other entries fall under such general topics as culture and the arts, economics, religion, and even profiles of various geographic locations (e.g., New York City). Entries are arranged alphabetically and include cross-references and a bibliography. Also included are some 230 photographs. Volume 1 contains an extensive chronology of U.S. LGBT history, starting in the fifteenth century. The appendix in volume 3 lists repositories with LGBT materials in the United States and Canada. Volume 3 also contains a systematic outline of contents and a detailed index.

333   **The gay and lesbian atlas.** Gary J. Gates and Jason Ost. 232p. Urban Institute Press, 2004. ISBN 0877667217. $

306.76   HQ76

Using information on same-sex partners collected for the first time in the 2000 Census, this title provides a statistical and demographic illustration of gay and lesbian couples in the United States. The first part of the book discusses the reasons for studying gay and lesbian location patterns along with an explanation of the tools used to collect the data. The next few chapters present the data in tables covering such topics as the top ten states, cities, and zip codes for gay and lesbian couples. The majority of the book focuses on the colorful maps, which include a couple of national maps, a map for each of the fifty states, and maps for more than twenty metropolitan areas. The maps show the concentration of gay and lesbian couples within that region. A short bibliography and index are also included.

334   **Reader's guide to lesbian and gay studies.** Timothy F. Murphy. 720p. Fitzroy Dearborn, 2000. ISBN 1579581420. $$

305.90664   HQ75

Although the field of gay and lesbian studies is still quite new, there has been an increase in materials published on the topic in recent years. This volume serves as a guide to the academic literature covering topics of particular interest to gay and lesbian studies. The 470 entries include a list of works (mainly English-language titles), a brief introduction to the topic, and a more detailed overview of the secondary literature. The length of articles is determined by the amount of works published on that topic. Entries are arranged alphabetically, but there is also a thematic index to all the articles, and a book-list index to included books arranged by author name. Cross-references are included throughout, and a general comprehensive index is also available.

335   **Same-sex marriage in the United States: Focus on the facts.** Sean Cahill. 161p. Lexington Books, 2004. ISBN 0739108816; 0739108824 (pbk.). $

306.84   HQ1034

With the recent spotlight on same-sex marriage, this book attempts to break through the rhetoric and provide facts on the issue. Similar to *The gay and lesbian atlas,* this title pulls much of its data from the 2000 Census, but it focuses on the topic of same-sex marriage. The author begins by looking at the legal decisions on same-sex marriage, followed by a discussion of the antigay movement. A brief overview of family policy issues affecting gays and lesbians is presented along with gay rights in the political arena up to spring 2004, shortly before the presidential election. The final chapter presents the case for marriage equality by presenting real-life stories of lesbian and gay couples. Tables, charts, maps, photographs, and sidebars with interesting facts are presented throughout the volume. A select bibliography and index are also included.

336   **Who's who in gay and lesbian history: From antiquity to World War II.** Robert Aldrich and Garry Wotherspoon, eds. 502p. Routledge, 2001. ISBN 0415159822. $

305.90664   HQ75

Who's who in contemporary gay and lesbian history: From World War II to the present day. Robert Aldrich and Garry Wotherspoon, eds. 460p. Routledge, 2001. ISBN 041522974X. $

305.90664   HQ75

As the title suggests, these volumes present biographical, alphabetically arranged entries of prominent men and women in gay and lesbian history. The first volume covers ancient times to World War II. The second volume covers persons from World War II to the early twenty-first century. Each volume contains approximately 500 individuals, included for their impact on gay and lesbian life and not necessarily because they were gay. Many entries include a bibliography. The work does have limitations; most of the entries are from the Western world, and there are a far greater number of male entries. Despite these issues, this resource provides a good starting place for learning about individuals in gay and lesbian history.

337   Youth, education, and sexualities: An international encyclopedia. James T. Sears, ed. 2v. Greenwood, 2005. ISBN 0313327483. $$
371.826   LC192

This two-volume work serves as a valuable resource for those seeking an understanding of lesbian, gay, bisexual, and transgender (LGBT) youth. Included are more than 200 entries on various topics related to LGBT youth, such as bullying, school curriculum, parents, teachers, and so forth. Also included are entries for various prominent individuals, such as Alfred Kinsey and Matthew Shepard. Articles that focus on LGBT youth in various countries, such as South Africa, Australia, China, and so forth, help provide a global perspective on this topic. Entries include a bibliography of print materials as well as websites. Volume 2 contains a general bibliography and a comprehensive index.

Men's Studies

338   American masculinities: A historical encyclopedia. Bret E. Carroll, ed. 562p. Sage, 2003. ISBN 0761925406. $$
305.31   HQ1090

Published shortly before *Men and masculinities: A social, cultural, and historical encyclopedia,* this one-volume resource was the first to cover the growing field of men's studies. Included are more than 250 entries on individuals, organizations, movements, events, political and social issues, and concepts and theories. Entries include related terms, a bibliography of references, and in some cases, illustrations, such as drawings or photographs. An extensive bibliography and a comprehensive index are also included.

339   American men: Who they are and how they live. 2nd ed. New Strategist Publishers, Inc. 330p. New Strategist, 2006. ISBN 1885070721. $
305.31   HQ1090

Now in its second edition, this title presents a wealth of demographic data about the lives of American men. Included are chapters on education, health, income, labor, population, time use, and so forth. Data are drawn from the Current Population Survey (CPS) taken monthly by the U.S. Census Bureau. Tables, graphs, and charts of the data are presented liberally throughout the text. A brief glossary, bibliography, and index complete the reference. The index is fairly comprehensive and a good entry point for researchers looking for specific data. A companion volume, *American women,* is also available.

340   Men and masculinities: A social, cultural, and historical encyclopedia. Michael S. Kimmel and Amy Aronson, eds. 2v. ABC-CLIO, 2004. ISBN 1576077748. $$
305.31   HQ1090

Although some overlap exists with *American masculinities: A historical encyclopedia,* this two-volume encyclopedia has a much broader focus, covering more international (Michelangelo) and contemporary (Sylvester Stallone) figures. In addition to biographical entries, concepts are also covered, such as aging, homosexuality, puberty, technology, and so forth. The 400 entries are arranged alphabetically and include references and cross-references. Black-and-white photographs also accompany some of the entries. A comprehensive index is also available.

341   The new men's studies: A selected and annotated interdisciplinary bibliography. 2nd ed. Ernest R. August. 440p. Libraries Unlimited, 1994. ISBN 1563080842. $
016.30531   Z7164; HQ1090

Though this title is slightly older, it is still a good tool for identifying English-language titles within men's studies. Included are 1,000 annotated entries that are broken down into various sections related to health, divorce, sexuality, psychology, spirituality, and so forth. Each chapter includes cross-references, and there are author/title and subject indexes.

342   Reference library of American men. Jennifer Mossman, ed. 4v. Gale, 2002. ISBN 0787662593. $$ www .americanmenpubs.com.
920.71   CT215

Presents biographical profiles of 650 men who have contributed significantly to human culture and society. Alphabetically arranged entries are pulled from Gale's extensive biographical database and include both contemporary and historic figures from a wide variety of fields. Examples of included individuals are Johnny Carson, Bill Gates, Martin Luther King Jr., and George Washington. Entries average 800 words and include bibliographic references for further reading, and in some cases photographs or illustrations accompany the article. A name index and occupation index are included. Also, purchase of the print volume entitles users to access the online web enhancement for extended coverage of notable individuals covered in the print volume and also coverage of other prominent figures not included in the print publication.

Sex Studies

343   The Continuum complete international encyclopedia of sexuality. Robert T. Francoeur and Raymond J. Noonan, eds.; Beldina OpiyoOmolo et al., assoc. eds. 1419p. Continuum, 2004. ISBN 0826414885. $$
306.7   HQ21

This large one-volume reference comprises the four-volume *International encyclopedia of sexuality* (published 1997–2001), including new and updated content. Sexual attitudes and behaviors for more than sixty countries are presented, including China, India, the United Kingdom, and the United States. Smaller countries, such as Botswana, Ghana, and Nepal, are also presented. Each country article is presented in a similar format for easy comparison and includes demographic information and information on gender roles, heterosexual and homosexual behaviors, contraception, sexually transmitted diseases, and so forth. Maps and statistical tables are also included with many of the entries. An extensive list of bibliographic references is also available with each article. A directory of sexological organizations and a comprehensive index complete the volume.

344   Dating and sexuality in America: A reference handbook. Jeffrey S. Turner. 287p. ABC-CLIO, 2003. ISBN 1851095845. $
306.73   HQ801

This volume presents research-based information on the increasingly complex topic of dating and sexuality. The author begins with a discussion of the history of dating, then moves on to a discussion of such current issues as date rape and Internet romance. Also included is a section covering other parts of the world, including Australia, Latin American, and the United Kingdom. A chronology of important events, biographical sketches of thirty-three prominent individuals in the field, and a chapter with facts and data in the form of tables and charts is also presented. Chapter 7 is a directory of organizations, associations, and agencies related to the study of dating and sexuality. Chapter 8 provides a bibliography of additional resources in print, media, and online resources. A glossary and an index are also included.

345   Encyclopedia of sex. Rev. ed. Ruth K. Westheimer, ed. in chief. 319p. Continuum, 2000. ISBN 0826412408. $
306.7   HQ9

This inexpensive one-volume encyclopedia includes some 250 entries on topics surrounding sexuality. Entries are written in clear, easy-to-understand language and include illustrations and cross-references. A short glossary of sexual terms and a glossary of sexual slang are also included along with a bibliography and an index.

346   Sexuality: The essential glossary. Jo Eadie, ed. 286p. Oxford Univ. Pr., 2004. ISBN 0340806753; 0340806761 (pbk.). $
306.7   HQ9

Including approximately 400 entries, this one-volume reference provides brief discussions for key terms dealing with sexuality. Such traditional terms as *rape* and *kissing* are covered, but so are more contemporary terms, such as *lipstick lesbian* and *plastic sexuality*. Terms include cross-references, and an extensive bibliography is also provided.

Social Service and Philanthropy

347   The Blackwell encyclopaedia of social work. Martin Davies, ed.; Rose Barton, asst. ed. 412p. Blackwell, 2000. ISBN 0631214518. $
361.3   HV12

Although this work's editors are from the United Kingdom, the 400-plus entries in this volume represent universal topics in the practice of social work today. Examples of included topics are alcohol and alcohol problems, domestic violence, and welfare rights. Terms are arranged alphabetically and include a brief bibliography for further reading. There is also a lexicon at the beginning of the volume that lists entries under such broad categories as addiction and problem drug use, family, and theories for social work practice. A list of references and a name and subject index complete the volume.

348   Catalog of federal domestic assistance.
U.S. Office of Management and Budget.
2v. General Services Administration,
1969–. Annual. ISSN 0097-7799. $
www.cfda.gov.
338.973   HC110

Available in print, on CD-ROM, and online, this resource, published by the U.S. government, provides access to federal programs, projects, services, or activities providing assistance or benefits to the public. Entries describe each program, how to apply, and financial resources.

349   Encyclopedia of social work. 19th
ed. Richard L. Edwards. 3v. National
Association of Social Workers, 1965–.
Irreg. (19th ed., 1995.) ISSN 0071-0237;
ISBN 0871012553. $$
361.3   HV35

**Encyclopedia of social work: 1997
supplement.** Richard L. Edwards. 428p.
National Association of Social Workers,
1997. ISBN 0871012774. $
361.3   HV35

**Encyclopedia of social work: 2003
supplement.** Richard A. English. 236p.
National Association of Social Workers,
2003. ISBN 0871013533 (pbk.). $
361.3   HV35

The most comprehensive reference work for the field of social work in the United States. The nineteenth edition, published in 1995, includes three volumes with 290 scholarly articles and 142 biographies. The 1997 supplement adds 30 new entries, and the 2003 supplement adds 17 new entries. Examples of topics covered include bisexuality, family planning, juvenile corrections, and substance abuse. Articles are arranged alphabetically and include subject cross-references and extensive bibliographic references. Users can locate articles using the comprehensive readers' guide, the keywords listed at the end of each article, or the detailed index. Also included in the appendixes are the National Association of Social Workers and

International Federation of Social Workers code of ethics, distinctive dates in social welfare history, acronyms, and a chart showing the evolution of selected organizations. Also available on CD-ROM.

The foundation directory, see **49**.

**350   Notable American philanthropists:
Biographies of giving and
volunteering.** Robert T. Grimm Jr.,
ed. 388p. Greenwood, 2002. ISBN
1573563404. $
361.7   HV27

Contains 78 alphabetically arranged articles on 110 individuals or families that have significantly impacted American life through their voluntary service or charitable donations. Some entries are well-known philanthropists, such as Bill Gates, the Rockefeller family, and Andrew Carnegie, but others cover lesser-known philanthropists, such as Oseola McCarty, a laundress who gave $150,000 to the University of South Mississippi in 1995. Entries include bibliographic references and, in many cases, photographs and/or information about where the individual's papers are located. Also included is a timeline of American philanthropy, a list of videos and children's books, and a comprehensive index.

**351   Philanthropy in America:
A comprehensive historical
encyclopedia.** Dwight Burlingame,
ed. 3v. ABC-CLIO, 2004. ISBN
1576078604. $$
361.7   HV91

This three-volume work is the first encyclopedia on the topic of philanthropy in the United States. Included are more than 200 alphabetically arranged entries that cover individuals, organizations, events, theories, and legislation related to philanthropy. Also included are a timeline of key events and a glossary of philanthropic terms, and volume 3 contains more than seventy-five primary source documents in philanthropy, such as the Poor Laws of 1601 and the Global Sullivan Principles. A comprehensive index completes the reference.

352   The social work dictionary. 5th ed.
Robert L. Barker. 493p. NASW Press,
2003. ISBN 087101355X (pbk.). $
361.3   HV12

Contains brief definitions of nearly 8,000 terms in the increasingly complex field of social work. A total of 2,000 terms are new to this edition. Also included is a list of frequently used acronyms and chronology of milestones in the development of the field.

353 **Social workers' desk reference.** Albert R. Roberts and Gilbert J. Greene, eds. 910p. Oxford Univ. Pr., 2002. ISBN 019514211X. $

361.3   HV40

Compiled by leading practitioners in the field, this resource provides quick, easy-to-read information about various aspects of social work. Included are 146 chapters on such topics as social work ethics, assessment tools, family therapy, crisis management, treatment planning, community practices, and case management. Examples of best practices, program evaluations, step-by-step treatment plans, and validated assessment scales are included within each chapter, along with a list of bibliographic references. A glossary and name and subject index are also available at the end of the text. This volume will not only be useful for social work practitioners but also students, teachers, and others seeking quick, useful information on social work practice.

Statistics and Demography

354 **The American census handbook.** Thomas Jay Kemp. 517p. Scholarly Resources, 2001. ISBN 0842029257. $

016.929   CS49

This handbook is an important, time-saving tool for those doing genealogical research by providing the first comprehensive guide to all census indexes currently available, from federal and other censuses up to and including the 1920 population census. Entries are arranged geographically by state, and then chronologically. Researchers interested in a particular area and timeframe are quickly able to see what records, indexes, and abstracts are available on microfilm, on CD-ROM, on the Web, or published as books and articles. Also included is a small section with indexes that focus on general topics, such as a particular ethnic group, and indexes to current or former military personnel.

355 **America's top-rated cities: A statistical handbook.** 12th ed. David Garoogian, ed. 4v. Grey House, 2005. ISBN 1592370764. $$

307.76   HA214

Now in its twelfth edition, this four-volume reference provides statistical information on 100 cities

considered to be the best for business and living in the United States. The four volumes represent a different geographic region: southern, western, central, and eastern. Within each volume, cities are arranged alphabetically. Each entry includes background and ranking information, followed by statistical data on a variety of topics, such as business ownership, transportation, and taxes. Each volume includes appendixes with area definitions (both historical and current), an extensive section of comparative statistics, and a directory of chambers of commerce and state departments of labor. If smaller libraries do not want to purchase the whole set, they should consider purchasing their regional volume. There is a companion volume, *America's top-rated smaller cities.*

356 **America's top-rated smaller cities: A statistical profile.** 5th ed. David Garoogian, ed. 1729p. Grey House, 2004. ISBN 1592370438. $$

307.76   HT123

A companion volume to *America's top-rated cities: A statistical handbook,* but the focus is on the top 100 U.S. cities with populations between 25,000 and 99,000. Entries are arranged by state (forty-eight states included), then alphabetically by city. Each entry includes background information and rankings, followed by statistical data on a number of different topics, such as income, demographics, and employment. The appendixes include a list of cities by the closest metropolitan area, a list of cities by county, a directory of chambers of commerce and state departments of labor, and a lengthy section of comparative statistics.

Demographics of the U.S., see **426***.*

357 **Encyclopedia of population.** 2nd ed. Paul George Demeny and Geoffrey McNicoll, eds. 2v. Macmillan Reference USA, 2003. ISBN 0028656776. $$

304.6   HB871

Previously titled *International encyclopedia of population* (1982), this new edition presents 336 articles on topics and individuals in the field of population studies. Unlike the previous edition, which was arranged by country, this edition organizes topics alphabetically. Examples of included topics are climate change, famine, immigration trends, population projections, and urbanization. Biographies of sixty individuals prominent in the field, such as Charles Darwin and Karl Marx, are also included. As expected, lots of tables and graphs accompany the articles. Entries include cross-references and bibliographic references. A topical outline to articles and a comprehensive index provide easy access to included topics.

358   Social trends and indicators USA.
Arsen Darnay and Helen S. Fisher.
4v. Thomson Gale, 2003–. ISBN
0787659061. $$$
306   NH60

For libraries requiring more detailed historical statistical data not included in *Demographics of the U.S.: Trends and projections,* this four-volume resource is the answer. Each of the four volumes covers different topics. Volume 1 covers work and leisure, and volume 2 covers community and education. Volume 3 covers health and statistics, and volume 4 covers crime and justice. Although *Demographics of the U.S.: Trends and projections* pulls data primarily from the federal government, this resource pulls data from a variety of sources, including federal and state statistical agencies and nonprofit and commercial sources. Entries include lengthy descriptions of the statistical data, which are presented in tables and graphs. A keyword index (for each volume), along with a cumulative index for the set, is available at the end of each volume.

Urban Studies

359   The dictionary of urbanism. Robert
Cowan. 468p. Streetwise Press, 2005.
ISBN 0954433009. $
711.403   HT108.5

This one-volume reference is the first and only dictionary of urban terms. Included are nearly 7,000 terms dealing with urban design, planning, and regeneration and the culture of cities. Although this title was created and published in the United Kingdom, many of the terms described in the dictionary are used internationally. Entries are arranged alphabetically and include cross-references, and bibliographic references are also available. An online supplement at www.urbanwords.com provides additional and amended entries that will be incorporated into the next printed edition.

**360   Encyclopedia of community: From
the village to the virtual world.** Karen
Christensen and David Levinson, eds. 4v.
Sage, 2003. ISBN 0761925988. $$$
307   HM756

This four-volume reference is the first encyclopedia focusing on the concept of community. Included are 500 articles on such topics as specific community case studies and biographies of prominent individuals in the field as well as articles dealing with aspects of religion, politics, human development, the Internet, and urban and suburban life. Articles include bibliographic references and, in many cases, photographs or interesting sidebar information. Each volume includes appendix 1, which is a resource guide to twenty-one broad subject areas, listing related books, websites, journals, and organizations for those who want to do more in-depth research. Volume 4 contains "Appendix 2: Libraries Build Communities," and appendix 3, which discusses the community in popular culture. Appendix 4 is the master bibliography on community resources. An extensive index completes the set.

361   Encyclopedia of the city. Roger W.
Caves, ed. 564p. Routledge, 2005.
ISBN 0415252253. $$
307.76   HT108.5

With an increase in urban development in recent years, the study of cities has become a hot topic. This title includes more than 500 alphabetically arranged articles on topics and individuals related to urban studies and associated fields. Person entries include a list of key works, and all entries include a bibliography for further reading. A comprehensive index is also available.

**362   Encyclopedia of urban America: The
cities and suburbs.** Neil L. Shumsky,
ed. 2v. ABC-CLIO, 1998. Print OP. ISBN
0874368464. $$
307.76   HT123

Contains 547 alphabetically arranged entries highlighting various issues, individuals, and associations relating to urban and suburban life. Examples of topics covered include African Americans in cities, downtown, homelessness, neighborhood, traffic, and so forth. In addition to articles on general concepts, there are also several entries on specific urban or suburban areas, such as New York, New Orleans, and Clifton, Ohio. Entries include cross-references and bibliographic references. Volume 2 contains a list of entries under sixteen broad categories, such as arts, institutions, recreation and leisure, and transportation. A comprehensive index completes the set.

**363   Encyclopedia of urban cultures: Cities
and cultures around the world.** Melvin

Ember and Carol R. Ember, eds. 4v. Grolier, 2002. ISBN 0717256987. $$

307.76   HT108.5

This four-volume reference focuses on cultures of urban areas, in which 50 percent of the world's population currently resides. Volume 1 begins with sixteen thematic essays that deal with major issues in urban sociology, such as migration and cities, urbanization in the Middle East, and the declining city. Following these general essays are nearly 240 individually signed, A–Z profiles of specific urban areas. Each profile includes various sections, such as orientation (e.g., name of city, location, population, languages, etc.), history, infrastructure (e.g., educational system, transportation system), cultural and social life (e.g., cuisine, family, arts, work, etc.), quality of life, and future of the city. Also included with each profile is a small map, photograph(s), a bibliography, and in some cases, a list of useful websites. Volume 4 includes finding aids to included cities with listings alphabetically, by country, and by region. A list of statistical tables is included, along with selected websites. A comprehensive index completes the set.

Women's Studies

364 American women: Who they are and how they live. 3rd ed. New Strategist. 346p. New Strategist, 2006. ISBN 188507073X. $

305.0973   HQ1421

Now in its third edition, this title presents a wealth of demographic data about the lives of American women. Included are chapters on education, health, income, labor, population, time use, and so forth. Data are drawn from the Current Population Survey (CPS) taken monthly by the U.S. Census Bureau. Tables, graphs, and charts of the data are presented liberally throughout the text. A brief glossary, bibliography, and index complete the reference. The index is fairly comprehensive and a good entry point for researchers looking for specific data. A companion volume, *American men,* is also available.

365 Encyclopedia of women social reformers. Helen Rappaport. 2v. ABC-CLIO, 2001. ISBN 1576071014. $$

303.48   HQ1236

Profiles of more than 400 women social reformers, active from the late eighteenth century to the present in a variety of causes, such as abolition, education, child welfare, reproductive rights, and so forth. Half of the entries cover women from the United States or the United Kingdom, while the rest come from more than sixty other countries. Articles are arranged alphabetically by last name and include cross-references and a short bibliography. Some entries even include a photograph or illustration of the woman being profiled. Volume 2 includes a listing of organizations with founding date and name-change information. A chronology of events, an extensive bibliography, and an index are also included.

366 Reader's guide to women's studies. Eleanor B. Amico, ed. 732p. Fitzroy Dearborn, 1998. ISBN 188496477X. $$

016.3054   Z7961; HQ1180

Although the field of women's studies is still fairly new, there has been a great increase in the amount of literature published on the topic. This book provides the user with a brief discussion of some of the best books on more than 500 topics and individuals in this global, multidisciplinary field. Due to the wide scope of the topic, the book is limited to English-language titles, journal articles are not included, and only secondary literature is covered. Entries are arranged alphabetically, but there are also a thematic index to all the articles and a book-list index to included books arranged by author name. Cross-references are included throughout, and a general comprehensive index is also available.

367 Reference library of American women. Jennifer Mossman, ed. 4v. Gale, 1999. ISBN 0787638641. $

305.4   CT3260

Presents biographical profiles of 650 women who have contributed significantly to human culture and society. Alphabetically arranged entries are pulled from Gale's extensive biographical database and include both contemporary and historic figures from a wide variety of fields and several different countries. Examples of included individuals are Maya Angelou, Joan of Arc, Martina Navratilova, and Rosa Parks. Entries average 800 words and include bibliographic references for further reading, and in some cases, photographs or illustrations accompany the article. Name, nationality, and occupation indexes are included, along with a historical chronology.

368 Routledge international encyclopedia of women: Global women's issues and

knowledge. Cheris Kramarae and Dale Spencer, general eds. 4v. Routledge, 2000. ISBN 0415920884. $$$

305.4   HQ1115

With contributors from various disciplines and languages, and with cultures from more than seventy different countries, this four-volume work provides an international look at women's issues and concerns. Each volume includes an alphabetical list of the 900-plus articles, and volume 1 contains a topical list of articles that presents articles under the following topics: arts and literature; culture and communication; ecology and environment; economy and development; education; health, reproduction, and sexuality; history and philosophy of feminism; households and families; politics and the state; religion and spirituality; science and technology; violence and peace; and women's studies. Entries on individual persons and nations are excluded, although some individuals and countries are covered in the topical entries. Article lengths vary from a paragraph to several pages, and all include cross-references and suggestions for further reading. A very thorough, comprehensive index is included at the end of volume 4.

369   **What American women did, 1789–1920: A year-by-year reference.** Linda Miles Coppens. 259p. McFarland, 2001. ISBN 0786408995. $

305.409   HQ1154

Chronological account of women's accomplishments in the areas of art, education and scholarship, domesticity, work, religion, law and politics, and reform efforts, from 1789 to 1920. In addition to highlighting women, prominent men are also included, both those who supported and opposed women's rights. A good number of illustrations and photographs are included throughout the text. The appendix includes several statistical tables on various topics, such as graduate degrees earned by females, 1895–1920, and females in selected occupations, 1870–1920. A bibliography and index are also included.

370   **Who's who of American women.** Marquis Who's Who, 1971–. Biennial. ISSN 0083-9841. $$ www.marquiswhoswho.com.

920.72   E176

Published biennially, this title includes short biographies of more than 30,000 American women prominent in various professions, such as politics, sports, and entertainment. In addition to the alphabetical listing, entries are also indexed by geography and profession. Biographies are also available online through a subscription to Who's Who on the Web.

371   **Women's issues.** Margaret McFadden, consulting ed. 3v. Salem Press, 1997. ISBN 0893567655. $$

305.4   HQ1115

This three-volume resource contains almost 700 articles on various terms, individuals, associations, historical events, and contemporary issues related to women in the United States and Canada. Entries are arranged alphabetically and range in length from 100 to 4,000 words. Each entry includes dates and locations (where applicable), a list of relevant issues, the topic's significance to women's studies, and cross-references; in many cases, a bibliography and illustrations are also available. A list of entries by fifteen broad categories, such as court cases and legislation, education, marriage and family, and notable women, is included in each volume. Volume 3 contains such useful information as a list of educational institutions with programs in women's studies; a directory of landmarks, monuments, and historic sites; a list of museums, archives, and research centers; significant organizations and societies; significant Supreme Court decisions affecting women; a timeline of important events; a comprehensive bibliography; a filmography; and a name and subject index.

372   **Women's studies: A recommended bibliography.** 3rd ed. Linda A Krikos, Cindy Ingold, and Catherine Loeb. 828p. Libraries Unlimited, 2004. ISBN 1563085666. $$

016.30542   Z7963; HQ1180

Intended as a reference and collection development tool, this one-volume resource covers women's studies literature in nineteen different subject areas (e.g., psychology, sociology, etc.) from 1986 to 1999. Each entry includes an annotation of the resource along with information about its importance to women's studies. Each subject chapter includes a list of core titles, and a section of websites is also included. The appendix lists special issues of journals on various topics within women's studies. Separate author, title, and subject indexes are included.

Youth and Child Development

373   **Child abuse sourcebook.** Dawn D. Matthews, ed. 620p. Omnigraphics,

2004. ISBN 0780807057. $

362.76   HV6626

Covers various forms of child abuse, including physical, sexual, and emotional abuse and neglect. Part 1 defines child abuse and includes chapters on such topics as sibling abuse and crimes against children on the Internet. Part 2 deals with the physical, mental, and emotional effects of child abuse. Consequences and signs of abuse are presented in this section. Part 3 discusses intervention and treatment for child abuse. Part 4 contains research on child abuse and includes discussions of why people abuse children, statistics on abuse, and child fatalities caused by abuse. Part 5 covers child protective services, such as government programs related to child welfare and foster parenting. Part 6 discusses parenting challenges, including steps to more effective parenting and physical discipline. Part 7 contains additional information, such as a glossary of related terms, a list of organizations dealing with child abuse, family violence, and child welfare legal issues. Also included are a directory of state toll-free child abuse reporting numbers and a brief section on how to report child pornography. Indexed.

374   Contemporary youth culture: An international encyclopedia. Shirley R. Steinberg, Priya Parmar, and Birgit Richard, eds. 2v. Greenwood, 2006. ISBN 0313327165. $$

305.23509   HQ796

Despite what the title indicates, this two-volume resource is not a traditional encyclopedia with topics arranged in alphabetic order. Instead, essays on various topics are arranged in five sections: studying youth culture, media culture and youth, youth identities and subcultures, politics and youth activism, and teaching and learning in and out of school. Examples of various essay topics include instant messaging, hip-hop, piercing, skateboarding, and stepfamilies. Each article is individually signed and includes a list of resources for further reading. Indexed.

375   Encyclopedia of children and childhood: In history and society. Paula S. Rass, ed. in chief. 3v. Macmillan Reference USA, 2004. ISBN 0028657144. $$

305.23   HQ767

This three-volume resource contains 445 alphabetically arranged articles on various topics and individuals related to childhood, from birth to adolescence. As the title indicates, childhood in various historical periods is discussed, from ancient Greece and Rome to contemporary times. Entries range in length from 500 to 5,000 words and include cross-references and a bibliography. Photographs and illustrations accompany many of the entries. A topical outline to the articles is available in volume 1, which lists articles under twenty broad categories, such as children in history, psychology, children's literature, and contemporary childhood. Volume 3 contains excerpts from various primary sources, including court cases, correspondence, poetry, and literature. An extensive index is included.

376   National directory of children, youth and families services. National Directory of Children, Youth, and Families Services. Marion L. Peterson, 1979–. Annual. ISSN 1072-902X. $$

362.7   HV741

Published annually, this title includes state listings of social services, health and mental health services, juvenile justice agencies, educational services, and special services geared to children and youth. Part 2 has information about federal government agencies, national organizations, runaway youth centers, grants, and so forth, that assist children, youth, young adults, and their families. Part 3 is a buyers guide and resource section.

Anthropology and Archaeology

Atlases

377   Past worlds: HarperCollins atlas of archaeology. 319p. Borders Press in association with HarperCollins, 2001. ISBN 0723010056. $

912   G1046

This is a reprint of *Past worlds: The Times atlas of archaeology*, originally published in 1988 and last revised in 1991. Despite its age, this is still a very useful reference book. The introductory chapter focuses on understanding archaeological methods and techniques. The atlas covers early human origins, the agricultural revolution, the first cities, empires of the old world, the new world, and the modern world to 1800. Text and photographs enhance understanding of the well-drawn maps. A glossary, bibliography, and a comprehensive index are available.

378   Student atlas of anthropology. John Logan Allen and Audrey Shalinsky. 178p. McGraw-Hill, 2004. ISBN 0072889853. $

301   G1046

Though intended for students, this atlas of anthropology provides information for anyone interested in the topic of anthropology. The atlas is divided into eight sections. Part 1 deals with world patterns or the environmental dimensions of anthropology and provides global views of topics, such as annual precipitation and temperatures. Part 2 covers physical anthropology and includes maps of the evolution of primates and the origins and distribution of Homo sapiens. Part 3 focuses on archaeology, and examples in this section include maps of ancient civilizations and mound-builder sites of eastern North America. Part 4 is titled "Linguistic Anthropology" and contains world languages and languages of various regions. Part 5, "Cultural Anthropology," is the largest section and covers demographics, economy, human society, and political systems. Part 6 covers the changing world and looks at global air pollution, pollution of the oceans, and loss of biodiversity. Part 7 focuses on world regions, including the physical features and political divisions of various geographic areas. Part 8 is a geographic index to approximately 1,500 names of cities, states, countries, rivers, lakes, mountain ranges, oceans, capes, bays, and other geographic features. A list of sources is also available.

Dictionaries and Encyclopedias

379   Biographical dictionary of social and cultural anthropology. Vered Amit. 613p. Routledge, 2004. ISBN 0415223792. $$

301   GN20

Presents biographical information about approximately 600 individuals (most still living) whose work has helped to shape social and cultural anthropology. Entries are arranged alphabetically by last name and include birth and death (if applicable) information, a general overview of the individual's work, educational credentials, fieldwork, and key publications. Most included individuals hail from such English-speaking nations as Britain and the United States; however, a few individuals are from other countries, for example, Mexico, France, and India. Multiple indexes accompany the work, including an index of interests, an index of institutions, an index of names, and an index of concepts.

380   The concise Oxford dictionary of archaeology. Timothy Darvill. 506p. Oxford Univ. Pr., 2003. ISBN 0192800051. $$

930.1   CC70

This one-volume resource contains more than 4,000 brief definitions of archaeological terms. Each term is coded by type, such as artifact, biographical, legal term, slang, and so forth. Also included is a quick reference section with lists of archaeological conventions, a timeline of cultural phases, and a list of Egyptian rulers and Roman empires.

381   Encyclopedia of anthropology. H. James Birx, ed. 5v. Sage, 2006. ISBN 0761930299. $$$

301   GN11

This colorfully illustrated five-volume resource is the first comprehensive international encyclopedia of anthropology. Written in clear, nonscholarly language, this resource includes more than 1,000 alphabetically arranged articles on topics in physical anthropology, archaeology, cultural anthropology, linguistics, and applied anthropology. Each volume includes a chronology of important events in anthropology, a conversion chart, an alphabetical list of entries, and a readers' guide that classifies included articles under broad categories, such as applied anthropology, archaeology, biography, evolution, and so forth. Volume 5 includes an extensive master bibliography and a comprehensive index.

382   Encyclopedia of archaeology: History and discoveries. Tim Murray, ed. 3v. ABC-CLIO, 2001. ISBN 1576071987. $$

930.1   CC100

Companion text to *Encyclopedia of archaeology: The great archaeologists,* this three-volume set covers the history and discoveries of archaeology. Included are approximately 500 articles on sites, events, countries, institutions, and major individuals. Although this title takes a more topical approach to archaeology, more than half of the entries are biographies. Though the same individuals are covered, the biographies that are included are much shorter and contain far few bibliographic references. All entries include cross-references, bibliographic references, and in some cases, such illustrations as maps, photographs, or drawings. Volume 3 includes a glossary and an extensive index.

383 Encyclopedia of archaeology: The great archaeologists. Tim Murray, ed. 2v. ABC-CLIO, 1999. ISBN 1576071995. $$

930.1   CC110

Intended as a companion text to *Encyclopedia of archaeology: History and discoveries,* this two-volume set contains fifty-eight biographies of prominent archaeologists. Though these same biographies are included in the other title, each individual gets greater coverage in this reference. Each entry discusses the life and contributions of the individual, focusing on his or her role in the development of archaeology as a discipline. An extensive list of primary and secondary references is included with each article. Entries are presented chronologically by birth year, starting with William Camden, who was born in 1551. An alphabetically arranged list of individuals is provided in each volume. Volume 2 includes an essay on writing archaeological biography along with a glossary and index. A number of illustrations are included throughout the text.

384 Encyclopedia of historical archaeology. Charles E. Orser, ed. 607p. Routledge, 2002. ISBN 0415215447. $$

930.1   CC77

This volume includes more than 370 articles on topics in historical archaeology, a rapidly growing field within archaeology. The work attempts to balance the two different definitions of historical archaeology, one that focuses on history and another that focuses on anthropology. Entries cover geographic sites, concepts, and issues as well as research methods used in historical archaeology. Most entries include a bibliography for further reading and cross-references. A comprehensive index is also available.

385 Encyclopedia of social and cultural anthropology. Alan Barnard and Jonathan Spencer, eds. 658p. Routledge, 2002. ISBN 0415285585 (pbk.). $

305.8003   GN307

Originally published in 1996, this useful reference (now in paperback) contains more than 230 entries on the major ideas, arguments, and history of social and cultural anthropology. Entries are arranged alphabetically and include cross-references and a bibliography for further reading. Examples of included topics are ancestors, cannibalism, ethnicity, migration, and ritual. Also included is an appendix with biographical profiles of some 200 important figures

in the history of anthropology. A glossary of 600-plus key terms and ideas is also available. Separate name, people and places, and subject indexes provide easy access to included topics.

386 The Greenwood encyclopedia of world folklore and folklife. William M. Clements, ed.; Thomas A. Green, advisory ed. 4v. Greenwood, 2006. ISBN 0313328471. $$

398   GR35

Intended for students, scholars, and general readers, this four-volume work contains more than 200 entries written by an international team of folklorists. Each volume focuses on folklore cultures within a specific geographic area. Volume 1 starts off with 39 short essays on various processes, research tools, social and intellectual movements, and concepts that provide a basis for understanding folklore. Following these essays, volume 1 covers Africa, Australia, and Oceania. Volume 2 covers Southeast Asia, India, Central and East Asia, and the Middle East. Volume 3 includes Europe, and volume 4 covers North and South America. A typical entry contains geography and history, religion and ritual, oral traditions, song, dance, music, arts and crafts, challenges to the modern world, and a list of folklore studies of that region. A bibliography is included with each entry, and many entries include such illustrations as maps, photographs and drawings. Volume 4 contains a glossary of key terms, and a cumulative index is included at the end of each volume.

Handbooks

387 The Oxford companion to archaeology. Brian M. Fagan, ed. in chief; Charlotte Beck et al., eds. 844p. Oxford Univ. Pr., 1996. ISBN 0195076184. $

930.1   CC70

This one-volume resource provides a wealth of information on the topic of archaeology. Included are more than 700 alphabetically arranged entries on various topics ranging from geographic areas, such as Greece, Egypt, China, and so forth, to biographical entries, such as Gertrude Bell and Max Uhle. Interesting topical entries include the Similaun man (aka Ice man), the domestications of the camel, Egyptian hieroglyphics, and the Mayan calendar. Each entry includes cross-references and bibliographic references. Maps, timelines, and a comprehensive index are also included.

5 *Business and Careers*

ERICA COE

The various sources here will be beneficial to students, business professionals, and the general public. This is not intended to stand alone as a core resource guide, but it should provide general guidance for beginning or expanding a collection. New to this edition are encyclopedias covering trade, leadership, and public relations. Trends and changing interests have also been addressed with new and reorganized sections. The growing interest in small businesses needs to be supported by a collection that can be used to answer questions about starting, planning, and managing these endeavors. For academic libraries, there is also a need to support the courses and degrees on entrepreneurship offered by business schools. A new section has been added to provide a few basic resources to support these interests. The previous edition's "Marketing and Sales" section has been extended to "Advertising, Marketing, and Consumer Research" to reflect the increased attention being given to the needs and wants of consumers. Current trends also influencing business include sustainable growth, environmental awareness, and "green" business efforts. Several websites already provide "Green Business" directories at the city,

county, and national levels. Anticipate encyclopedias, dictionaries, and handbooks on these topics as related to business management and also investing.

Although business has an increasingly international perspective, publications out of the United States and United Kingdom were selected for their ready availability. Book entries are for print sources, but libraries interested in e-books will find that many publishers—including Thomson Gale, Greenwood, and Routledge—provide electronic versions as well. Entries include publication information for the most recent edition when available, even if the item is published as a serial.

General Sources

Bibliographies and Guides

388 **Basic business library: Core resources.** 4th ed. R. S. Karp and B. S. Schlessinger, eds. 288p. Greenwood, 2002. ISBN 1573565121. $
016.0276   Z675

Designed for librarians and library students, the completely revised fourth edition provides a core list of "essential business reference tools" and essays on topics related to business reference sources and services. The entries in the core list include citation, authority and scope, and evaluation. For smaller and budget-conscious libraries, recommended entries are noted with an asterisk. To supplement the core list, essays cover databases, periodicals, investment sources, and government information guides, directories, and essential sources. Other essays explore issues and services in business libraries, for example, acquisitions and collection development, practice of organization, reference, and marketing.

389   Encyclopedia of business information sources. 22nd ed. L. D. Hall, ed. 1249p. Thomson Gale, 2007. ISBN 0787683078. $$
016.33   HF5351

This directory provides more than 35,000 citations for business information sources, including directories, periodicals and newsletters, handbooks, abstracts and indexes, bibliographies, biographical sources, databases, almanacs and yearbooks, encyclopedias, dictionaries, financial ratios, trade associations, research centers and institutes, and statistics sources. The main directory is arranged by subject. Publications and databases include publisher, frequency, cost, and basic description. Organizations include address, phone and fax numbers, e-mail and web address, and basic description. Cross-references are provided in the contents outline and within entries. The sources-cited section sorts all entries from the main text alphabetically by publication or organization name and includes complete contact information. The subject organization of this directory makes it valuable for librarians and researchers looking for useful sources for a particular industry, topic, or issue.

390   Industry research using the Economic Census: How to find it, how to use it. J. C. Boettcher and L. M. Gaines. 305p. Greenwood, 2004. ISBN 157356351X. $
338.0973   HC101

This source provides an excellent overview of how to use the Economic Census and the wealth of information available within this generally underutilized work. The Economic Census is published every five years by the U.S. Census Bureau and contains numerous data on business, including products, establishments, companies, industries, gross domestic product estimates, input/output

measures, and price indexes. This guide is divided into three parts: overview, history, and content of the census; examples of industry sectors; and appendixes. The appendixes include acronyms, sample questionnaires, regional federal depository libraries, data center lead agencies, and Census Bureau regional offices. This source will be invaluable to librarians, students, professionals, and the general public.

391   Strauss's handbook of business information: A guide for librarians, students, and researchers. 2nd ed. R. W. Moss. 455p. Libraries Unlimited, 2003. ISBN 1563085208. $
016.33   HF1010; Z7164

This valuable source provides an overview of selected sources, business concepts, and research strategies. There are two parts, the first covering formats and the second covering specific areas. Resource reviews are extensive, and similar resources are often grouped together and compared. Students and researchers will find the concept explanations in part 2 helpful. In the marketing section, a real-world example is provided for the four main marketing activities: product, price, place, and promotion. Appendixes cover acronyms and abbreviations, federal government departments and agencies, federal government corporations and independent agencies, key economic indicators, and selected websites. Indexes are provided for titles and subjects.

Biographical Sources

392   African-American business leaders and entrepreneurs. R. Kranz. 322p. Facts on File, 2004. ISBN 0816051011. $
338.092   HC102.5

Part of the American Biographies series, this work provides more than 155 biographical entries on African American business leaders from colonial times to the present. The A–Z entries begin with birth and death dates, followed by a statement of the person's role, such as cookie company founder. The person's importance is explained further, followed by a chronological telling of his or her life. Suggestions for further reading follow each entry, and a separate bibliography of recommended sources is also included. Entries are also classified by business type and year of birth. The index is fairly comprehensive. This easy-to-read and engaging encyclopedia will be of interest to students, historians, and the general public.

393 **American inventors, entrepreneurs, and business visionaries.** C. W. Carey. 410p. Facts on File, 2002. ISBN 0816045593. $

338.092   CT214

Part of the American Biographies series, this work provides 260 biographical entries on famous and not so famous men and women who illustrate the history of invention and entrepreneurialism in America. The topical introduction discusses how the economy has changed since the seventeenth and eighteenth centuries and highlights some of the individuals who instigated these changes. The A–Z entries begin with birth and death dates, followed by a statement of the person's role, such as inventor of plastic. The person's importance is explained further, followed by a chronological telling of his or her life. Suggestions for further reading follow each entry, and a separate bibliography of recommended sources is also included. Entries are also classified by invention/business type and year of birth. The index is fairly comprehensive. This easy-to-read and engaging encyclopedia will be of interest to students, historians, and the general public.

394 **Who's who in finance and business.** Marquis Who's Who, 2005–. Annual. ISSN 1930-3262. $$

338   HF3023

This title, formerly *Who's who in finance and industry,* provides more than 24,000 entries on business leaders from the United States and more than 100 other nations and territories. Entries are provided for executives of the largest U.S. firms, largest minority-owned businesses, and largest Mexican and Canadian industrial firms. Also included are chairpersons and presidents of North America's stock exchanges, presidents of chambers of commerce, heads of relevant federal departments, and administrators and professors from the top business schools in the United States, Mexico, and Canada. Following the typical Marquis Who's Who format, entries include name, occupation, vital statistics, family information, education and certifications, career history, activities and memberships, political affiliation, religion, and addresses. The professional index is divided by business area, then by country and region and/or city.

Databases

395 **ABI/Inform.** ProQuest. www.proquest .com.

Produced by ProQuest, this database provides articles from major business publications, including newspapers, magazines, journals, and trade publications. Coverage is typically from 1971 to the present. Three versions exist to meet the needs of different libraries, and content varies. The Select version covers 350 core business periodicals, Research covers almost 1,400 North American sources, and Global covers almost 1,800 worldwide business periodicals. See the website for additional details. This database is popular because of its relatively easy search features, some full-text availability, and quality of sources.

396 **Business source premier.** EBSCO. www.epnet.com.

Provided through EBSCOhost, this database provides cover articles, company profiles, case studies, and reports on industries, market research, and countries. Coverage varies by publication, and some full-text journals go back to 1965. Articles are from magazines, newspapers, journals, and trade publications, more than 2,200 of which include full text. The full text of 10,120 company profiles, 5,031 industry reports, 166 case studies, and 426 market-research reports are published by Datamonitor, a well-known provider of industry and market analysis. Some 1,415 full-text country reports are assembled from several sources by major publishers, including *Background notes,* by the U.S. Department of State; *Country monitor,* by Global Insight, *Country profiles,* by Datamonitor; *Country review,* by CountryWatch; *Economic competitiveness,* by ICON Group; and *Political risk yearbook,* by PRS Group. Despite the multidiscipline application, these country reports are not available in other EBSCOhost databases. Two other versions exist, Business Source Elite and Business Source Complete. See the website for details (www.epnet.com). This database is popular because of its relatively easy search and navigation features, availability of full text, and quality and quantity of sources.

397 **Hoover's online.** Hoover's. www .hoovers.com.

This database from Hoover's contains full-text information from the print editions of *American business, World business, Private companies,* and *Emerging companies,* including company and industry profiles, executive biographies, news and press releases, company financials, and SEC reports. Three subscription packages are available, and details are presented on the website. For pricing, contact the publisher. The website also includes some free content with limited information on the company, including overview, key numbers, key people (names only), top competitors with key numbers, SEC filings, news and press releases, interviews with expert analysts and business leaders by industry, and a list of subsidiaries and affiliates. This databases is relatively easy to use, provides full text, and is an excellent source for company information.

Dictionaries and Encyclopedias

398 Business: The ultimate resource. 2nd ed. 1973p. Basic Books, 2006. ISBN 9780465008308. $
658   HD38.15

This "ultimate resource" provides a wealth of information in one well-organized, well-written work. Comprised of seven distinct sections, this work includes best-practice essays from leading writers, management checklists and action lists, a management library with summaries of the most influential books, profiles of business thinkers and management giants, a global dictionary, a business almanac with country and industry profiles, and a guide to best sources. Readers can also use the password in the user's guide to log on to the book's website and sign up for e-mail updates. All collections will find this source useful.

399 Business cycles and depressions: An encyclopedia. D. Glasner, ed. 800p. Garland, 1997. ISBN 0824009444. $$
338.5   HB3711

Written for students, researchers, and laypeople, this encyclopedia includes more than 300 articles on business cycles, recessions, depressions, financial panics, and crises, including theories and the statistical techniques used to study them. Biographical entries are provided for important contributors to the study of business cycles born before 1920. Cross-references and bibliographies are provided for entries. Appendixes include chronologies of classical business cycles since the late eighteenth century and a chronology of growth cycles since 1948. The index is comprehensive.

400 Encyclopedia of African American business history. J. E. K. Walker. 721p.

Greenwood, 1999. ISBN 0313295492. $$
338.6   HD2344.5

This well-written and comprehensive work includes more than 200 entries comprised of biographies and topics related to black business history and surveys of black business participation in select industries. Topics cover enterprises, industries, events, trends, movements, and other activities. Several entries are tied to a specific historical period and are noted in the title or just after the title of the entry. Entries are arranged alphabetically, and the index is substantial. Cross-references are noted with an asterisk indicating that the term or name has its own entry. Selected bibliographies are provided for all entries, and these citations are compiled into a larger bibliography arranged by subject. A chronology of black business history from 1619 to 1999 is also provided.

401 Encyclopedia of American business. W. D. Folsom and R. Boulware, eds. 516p. Facts on File, 2004. ISBN 0816046433. $
338.0973   HF1001

Written in an easy-to-understand style, this encyclopedia is geared toward students and others who need a basic understanding of economic issues, concepts, principles, laws, and institutions. Most entries have further-reading suggestions, and there is a general bibliography at the end. The index is well planned and provides a good starting point for researchers.

402 Encyclopedia of American women in business: From colonial times to the present. C. H. Krismann. 2v., 692p. Greenwood, 2004. ISBN 0313327572. $$
338.092   HD6054.4

This encyclopedia provides a general introduction to the role women have played in American business. The bulk of the work includes more than 300 biographies of important American businesswomen. Additional entries cover such issues facing women as child care, diversity, and education. Women's role in various industries is also explored. Appendixes list the most powerful businesswomen in America, the top women business owners, and women business leaders by ethnic/cultural heritage, historical periods, and professions. Entries include further readings, and there is a separate bibliography at the end of volume 2.

403 Encyclopedia of capitalism. S. B. Hussain, ed. 3v., 1115p. Facts on File,

2004. ISBN 0816052247. $$
330   HB501

This well-written and accessible three-volume set contains 750 entries covering the historical evolution of capitalism on an international scope. Written by scholars and experts, this encyclopedia explores capitalism through definitions, biographies, company profiles, policies of presidential administrations, country profiles, and historical events and social movements. Entries include a bibliography for additional research. A timeline, glossary, and a bibliography of selected sources are also provided. The appendixes provide statistics on international trade by region and sector. The index is comprehensive, with extensive cross-references. This source will be useful to students and researchers at all levels who are interested in economic history.

404   Encyclopedia of leadership. G. R. Goethals, G. J. Sorenson, and J. M. Burns, eds. 4v. Sage, 2004. ISBN 076192597X. $$$
658.4   HD57.7

This encyclopedia serves to cover leadership on an interdisciplinary and global level, with entries on people, leadership characteristics, events, theories, styles, scholarship, and organizations. Leadership has become an increasingly important aspect of business studies in recent years, and this work includes biographies of business leaders, company case studies, and historical entries on several fields of business. This work also includes an examination of leadership issues relating to women and gender. A readers' guide listing entries by topic is available at the front of each volume. Individual entries include further reading, and a bibliography of significant works is provided as an appendix. There are two appendixes covering primary sources: one with presidential speeches on foreign policy and war and one with sacred texts from major religions. A directory of leadership programs is also provided. This work is valuable to multiple user groups, including students, scholars, practitioners, managers, and the general public.

405   Encyclopedia of public relations. R. L. Heath, ed. 2v. Sage, 2005. ISBN 0761927336. $$
659.2   HD59

The goal of this work is to foster a better understanding of public relations (PR)—a much misunderstood area according to the editor. This work delves into the many facets of PR, covering biographies, terminology,

theories, organizations, events, and research methods on an international scope. Entries are written with the general public in mind and include bibliographies. The extensive appendixes include codes of ethics, historical milestones, a report on PR education, sample historical and recent corporate annual reports, a directory of local society chapters, online resources, colleges and universities with PR programs, and a dictionary of PR measurement.

406   Encyclopedia of world trade: From ancient times to present. C. C. Northrup, ed. 4v. M. E. Sharpe, 2005. ISBN 0765680580. $$
382   HF1373

This source provides an excellent introduction to how trade has developed throughout the world. Entries cover biographies, historical events, organizations, countries, and political and social issues. Longer essays explore the connections between trade and religion, war, communication, and other issues. A topic finder supplements the alphabetical arrangement. Maps are provided to illustrate major subjects like "Global Economy, 1600" and "Global Oil Trade, 2004." A brief bibliography accompanies each entry, and a comprehensive bibliography is provided in volume 4. More than sixty primary documents are also included, such as "Code of Hammurabi," "Wealth of Nations," and "Agreement Establishing the World Trade Organization." A chronology of world trade and a glossary are also included. There are three indexes: general, biographical, and geographical.

407   Historical encyclopedia of American labor. R. E. Weir and J. P. Hanlan, eds. 2v. Greenwood, 2004. ISBN 0313318409. $$
331.88   HD8066

Written for students and the general public, this work provides an excellent introduction to important events, legislation, terminology, unions, and union leaders that have had an impact on American labor. Entries are well written and comprehensively cross-referenced. Suggested readings are provided for entries, and a separate bibliography is organized by category. The appendix contains excerpts from primary documents, including organization contracts, mission statements, interviews, poems, songs, and articles from newspapers and magazines.

408   St. James encyclopedia of labor history worldwide: Major events in

labor history and their impact.
N. Schlager, ed. 2v. St. James Press,
2004. ISBN 1558625429. $$
331.8   HD4839

Covering events from 1800 to 2000, this encyclo-
pedia provides an excellent and accessible intro-
duction to labor history on an international level.
There are two topical introductions: one covering
U.S. labor history and one for international labor
history. Entries include a synopsis, timeline, event
and context overview, key players, and a bibliog-
raphy. A glossary, chronology, and reading list
supplement the collection.

Directories

409   **Business organizations, agencies,
      and publications directory.** 19th ed.
      L. D. Hall, ed. 2033p. Thomson Gale,
      2006. ISBN 0787678295. $$$
      061.3   HF3010

The subtitle says it all—a guide to more than
40,000 new and established organizations, agencies, and publications concerned with international and U.S. business, trade, and industry. The
directory is divided into five sections: U.S. and
international organizations, government agencies
and programs, facilities and services, research and
education facilities, and publications and information services. Section descriptions are provided for
users and include content and selection criteria,
arrangement, source, and what entries are indexed
by. A name and keyword index lists all entries in
the directory with entry numbers, not page numbers. Providing a one-stop source for associations,
labor unions, chambers of commerce, federal agencies, diplomatic offices, conference and convention
centers, trade shows, business schools, periodicals
newsletters and more, this directory will be useful for all libraries although the price will likely be
prohibitive for some. *Headquarters USA* provides
similar information and costs less.

410   **Directory of business information
      resources, 2007.** 14th ed. R. Gottlieb,
      ed. 2300p. Grey House, 2006. ISBN
      1592371469. $$
      016.65   HF54.52

This annual directory is organized by industry and
lists associations, newsletters, magazines, journals, magazine special issues, trade shows, directories, databases, websites, and international trade

contacts. For associations, entries include address,
contact numbers, e-mail, website, key executives, descriptions, number of members, and year
founded. Publication entries include contact information, description, frequency, subscription price,
circulation, and scheduled special issues for magazines. Trade-show entries include contact information, description, attendees, and months. Indexes
are provided for entry and publisher.

411   **Headquarters USA: A directory of
      contact information for headquarters
      and other central offices of major
      business and organizations in the
      United States and Canada.** 2v.
      Omnigraphics, 2001–. Annual. ISSN
      1531-2909. $$
      384.6   E154.5

This annual directory provides contact information
for businesses, organizations, agencies, institutions,
and high-profile individuals. Coverage includes
chambers of commerce, colleges and universities,
convention and visitors bureaus, cultural organizations, foundations, libraries, media, military
bases, sports organizations, and United Nations
agencies. Listings are provided alphabetically and
by subject and contain mailing addresses, phone
numbers, toll-free numbers, web addresses, and
stock symbols. A section on conglomerates used
in the directory lists businesses with subsidiaries,
divisions, and/or units. This directory will be useful for all libraries.

412   **National trade and professional
      associations of the United States.**
      C. Colgate and J. J. Russell.
      Columbia Books, 1982–. Annual.
      ISSN 0734-354X. $$
      061.3   HD2425

This directory lists more than 7,600 trade associations, professional societies, labor unions, and
related national groups that support business and
industry. Listings can include address, at least one
contact person, number of members, number of
full-time staff, annual budget, meetings and conferences, and publications. The historical note
can include a description of the history, purpose,
membership, programs, membership fees, political affiliation, and alliances with other associations.
Indexes are provided by subject, geography, budget, executive, and acronym. A roster of association
management firms is also included.

413 **State and regional associations of the United States.** Columbia Books, 1989–. Annual. ISSN 1044-324X. $$
380.1   HD2425

A companion volume to *National trade and professional associations of the United States,* this is arranged by state/region and covers 7,300 associations and professional societies. Listings can include address, at least one contact person, number of members, number of full-time staff, annual budget, meetings and conferences, and publications. A roster of association management firms is also included.

Handbooks, Yearbooks, and Almanacs

414 **Business rankings annual.** Business Library (Brooklyn Public Library). Thomson Gale, 1989–. Annual. ISSN 1043-7908. $$
338.7   HG4050

This annual publication provides lists of companies, products, services, and activities ranked by factors, including assets, sales, revenue, production, employees, market value, and more. This source is arranged by subject and is international in scope. Data have been compiled from a variety of published sources, and each entry provides the source information, including when it is published, for example, annual or semiannual. This makes it easy to search for updated statistics, as many of the results are two to three years old. Having the source information to follow up on also allows libraries to purchase this work every two or three years to save on expenditures for this costly title. The index is fairly comprehensive and provides entry numbers, not page numbers. A separate cumulative index going back to 1989 is provided as part of the set.

415 **Business statistics of the United States: Patterns of economic change, 2006.** 11th ed. C. J. Stawser, ed. 656p. Bernan Press, 2006. ISBN 1598880098. $$
330.021   HC101

Compiled largely from government sources, this book of statistical tables is an excellent starting point for gathering data on the U.S. economy, industry profiles, historical data, and regional and state data. Commonly requested data covered here include gross domestic product, household income distribution, consumer spending, consumer price indexes, and international comparisons and exchange rates. When available, annual data are provided from 1946

to 2004, with the historical data chapter covering selected annual data from 1929 to 1948. The reader is provided with an introductory section on how to use the data, and each chapter includes notes and definitions. Unfortunately, the index is weak and lacks useful cross-references.

416 **Handbook of U.S. labor statistics: Employment, earnings, prices, productivity, and other labor data, 2006.** 9th ed. E. E. Jacobs, ed. 564p. Bernan Press, 2006. ISBN 1598880055. $$
331.0973   HD8064

This updated edition provides recent and historical data on U.S. employment, earnings, prices, consumer expenditures, industries, productivity, living conditions, and related topics. Data were compiled from the Bureau of Labor Statistics and other government and private agencies. Highlights, notes, and definitions supplement the statistical tables. The ninth edition includes new data from the BLS Household and Payroll Surveys and the American Time Use Survey. The index includes cross-references and is a good entry point for researchers.

Accounting

417 **Accountants' handbook.** 10th ed. D. R. Carmichael and P. Rosenfield. 2v. Wiley, 2003. ISBN 047126993X. $$
657   HF5621

This two-volume set provides an extensive review of accounting principles and practices. Volume 1 covers financial accounting and general topics, while volume 2 is focused on special industries and topics. Sources and suggested references are provided for each chapter. Although aimed at accountants and other financial professionals, such sections as Securities and Exchange Commission reporting requirements, analyzing financial statements, and managing shareholders' equity could be useful to students, entrepreneurs, shareholders, and the general public.

418 **Accounting handbook.** 4th ed. J. G. Siegel and J. K. Shim. 993p. Barron's, 2006. ISBN 0764157760. $
657   HF5635

This comprehensive work provides a practical overview of accounting principles and practices, and a dictionary of related terms. Chapters are divided by area, including financial, management/cost, forensic, international, taxation and personal financial planning. Selected readings and relevant websites are provided throughout. An index is provided, but it lacks adequate multiple-entry points and cross-references. The three appendixes cover the Sarbanes-Oxley Act summary; financial reporting differences between the United States, Canada, and Mexico; and selected tables.

419 Dictionary of accounting terms. 4th ed. J. G. Siegel and J. K. Shim. 506p. Barron's, 2005. ISBN 0764128981. $

657   HF5621

This clear, well-written dictionary provides definitions and illustrative examples for more than 2,500 key terms from all areas of accounting and related business fields. Entries for organizations and associations include brief mission statements. Cross-references are indicated with small capitals and italicized *see* and *see also* references. There are two appendixes, covering abbreviations and acronyms and compounded value tables. This dictionary is appropriate for professionals, students, and the general public.

Advertising, Marketing, and Consumer Research

420 The advertising age encyclopedia of advertising. J. McDonough and K. Egolf, eds. 3v., 1873p. Fitzroy Dearborn, 2003. ISBN 1579581722. $$

659.1   HF5803

This comprehensive and fascinating encyclopedia includes biographies, select countries, theories, methods and mediums, cultural issues, agency histories, and histories of advertisers, brands, and markets. Entries on ad agencies include a brief chronology of key dates, a selective list of clients, and a chronologically arranged descriptive history. Illustrations and further-reading lists accompany many entries. The vast amount of information on advertising presented makes this work a standard for all collections serving students, business professionals, and historians. The advertising images and related information will also be of interest to the general public.

421 American generations: Who they are and how they live. 5th ed. S. Mitchell. 501p. New Strategist, 2005. ISBN 1885070691. $

330.973   HC110

This source, now in its fifth edition, provides an excellent starting point for anyone interested in exploring how generations compare when it comes to attitudes and beliefs, wants, and needs. Trends covered are education, health, housing, income, labor force, living arrangements, population, spending, time use, and wealth. Studying generations can be difficult because statistics are often organized by age ranges that do not meet the generational range. This publication extrapolates and approximates data from government sources. When two generations cross one age range, the generation that accounts for the majority of the range is discussed. Charts and tables are provided, with the original data source noted. The index is fairly comprehensive and a good entry point for researchers looking for specific data. This source will prove valuable for libraries serving business professionals, entrepreneurs, and students.

422 American incomes: Demographics of who has money. 5th ed. C. Russell. 396p. New Strategist, 2005. ISBN 1885070683. $

339.2   HC110

This book covers income trends in the following categories: household income, men's income, women's income, discretionary income, wealth, and poverty. Most data are from 2002, with some historical tables dating back to 1980. Household trends are arranged by age, household type, race and ethnicity, education, region, and work status. The men and women sections are arranged by demographics. The wealth section covers assets, debts, and net worth of households, and the poverty section provides a variety of household and demographic data. Many of the data come from government publications although discretionary income is not monitored by any government department. The discretionary income data have been compiled by the New Strategist researchers and, as such, are not available elsewhere, making this book very useful. This source will prove valuable for libraries serving business professionals, entrepreneurs, and students.

423 The American marketplace: Demographics and spending patterns. 7th ed. New Strategist. 524p. New

Strategist, 2005. ISBN 1885070608. $
658.83   HF5415.33

Now in its seventh edition, this source is designed for all users in need of easily accessible lifestyle and demographic data. Data on trends in education, health, housing, income, labor force, living arrangements, population, spending, and wealth are presented in a user-friendly, easy-to-read format. Sample health trends include "Americans eat more and weigh more" and "More than one in five Americans smoke." Each section begins with highlights of the major trends in that area. These trends, and others, are then discussed further and illustrated with charts and tables of statistical data, primarily from the U.S. Census and other government documents. Appendixes include a brief glossary and bibliography. The index is fairly comprehensive and a good entry point for researchers looking for specific data. This source will prove valuable for libraries serving business professionals, entrepreneurs, and students.

American men, see **339**.

American women, see **364**.

424   **The baby boom: Americans born
       1946 to 1964.** 5th ed. C. Russell, ed.
       336p. New Strategist, 2006. ISBN
       188507090X. $
       304   HN60

       **Generation X: Americans born
       1965 to 1976.** 5th ed. New Strategist.
       334p. New Strategist, 2006. ISBN
       1885070896. $
       658.83   HC110

       **The millennials: Americans born
       1977 to 1994.** 3rd ed. New Strategist.
       400p. New Strategist, 2006. ISBN
       1885070888. $
       658.83   HQ796

The increased focus on consumer age groups makes the American Generations series by New Strategist a must for libraries serving business professionals, entrepreneurs, and students. This series provides data on trends in education, health, housing, income, labor force, living arrangements, population, spending, and wealth in a user-friendly, easy-to-read format. Each section begins with highlights of the major trends in that area. These trends, and others, are then discussed further and illustrated with charts and tables of statistical data, primarily from the U.S. Census and other government documents.

425   **Best customers: Demographics of
       consumer demand.** 3rd ed. New
       Strategist. 754p. New Strategist, 2004.
       ISBN 1885070756. $
       568.81   HC79

Based on unpublished data from the Bureau of Labor Statistics Consumer Expenditure Survey, this book is a useful tool for anyone interested in examining American spending patterns. For each spending category, a table of statistics is provided indicating the national average, best customers, and biggest customers (market share) by age, income, household type, race, Hispanic origin, region, and education. Spending categories range from food and drink to entertainment and reading material. Appendixes include an explanation of the Consumer Expenditure Survey with additional statistics and a glossary. The index is fairly comprehensive and a good entry point for researchers looking for specific data. This source will prove valuable for libraries serving business professionals, entrepreneurs, and students.

426   **Demographics of the U.S.: Trends
       and projections.** 2nd ed. C. Russell.
       453p. New Strategist, 2003. ISBN
       1885070489. $
       304.6   HB849.49

The importance of this work lies in its easily accessible coverage of demographic trends, many from 1950 to 2000, with projections to 2010. Categories covered are attitudes and behavior, education, health, housing, income, labor force, living arrangements, population, spending, and wealth. The data, based largely on government statistics, are provided by five-year increments from 1950 to 1980 and in yearly increments after 1980. The 2010 projections of population by age, sex, race, and Hispanic origin were calculated by New Strategist. Sample trends include "More excitement, less happiness" in attitudes and behavior; "In college, women outnumber men" in education; and "People are fatter but fitter" in health. Also included are future projections for such topics as population rates in 2010 for certain racial and age groups. In the section entitled "For More Information," there are lists of websites, subject specialists departments within federal agencies, census regional offices, and state data centers and industry data centers. The index is fairly comprehensive and a good entry point for researchers looking for specific data.

427   **Household spending: Who spends
       how much on what.** 10th ed. New

Strategist. 656p. New Strategist, 2006. ISBN 188507087X. $

339.47   HC100

Now in its tenth edition, this source provides tables of household and detailed spending statistics organized by major product and service category with demographic categories including age, income, household type, race and Hispanic origin, region, and educational attainment. Spending categories include apparel, entertainment, financial products and services, food and alcohol, gifts, health care, housing, personal care, and transportation. Based on unpublished data collected by the Bureau of Labor Statistics Consumer Expenditure Survey, the most recent numbers are from 2003. Using this source, you can find out how much money married couples with the oldest child age six to seventeen spent on fresh fruits versus processed fruits. Appendixes include an explanation of the Consumer Expenditure Survey with additional statistics and a glossary. The index is fairly comprehensive and a good entry point for researchers looking for specific data. Includes CD-ROM.

Older Americans, see **278**.

Banking, Finance, and Investment

428   Barron's finance and investment handbook. 7th ed. J. Downes and J. E. Goodman. 1220p. Barron's, 2007. ISBN 0764159925. $

332.678   HG173

Covering investment opportunities, how to read annual reports and financial pages, terminology, information sources for assistance, historical data, and a directory of public companies, this source will be useful to anyone seeking investment guidance. Appendixes include an annotated bibliography, world currencies, and abbreviations and acronyms.

429   Dictionary of finance and banking. 3rd ed. N. Hand and J. Smullen, eds. 436p. Oxford Univ. Pr., 2005. ISBN 0198607490. $

332   HG151

This dictionary contains more than 5,000 clear and concise definitions of terms relating to banking, financial markets, and public finance on an international scope. Cross-references are identified with asterisks and italicized *see* and *see also* references. This source will be useful for anyone needing to understand banking and investing terminology.

430   Dictionary of finance and investment terms. 7th ed. J. Downes and J. E. Goodman. 832p. Barron's, 2006. ISBN 0764134167. $

332   HG151

This dictionary provides clear, concise definitions for more than 5,000 terms related to stocks, bonds, banking, corporate finance, mutual funds, and tax laws. Charts and graphs are used to illustrate terms. Cross-references are indicated with small capitals and italicized *see* and *see also* references. The appendix covers abbreviations and acronyms. This dictionary is appropriate for professionals, students, and the general public.

431   Encyclopedia of business and finance. 2nd ed. B. S. Kaliski, ed. 2v. Macmillan Reference USA, 2006. ISBN 0028660617. $$

650   HF1001

This completely revised and expanded second edition offers thirty new essays, including e-marketing, identity theft, forensic accounting, and green marketing. Written for the layperson, this well-written and easy-to-understand work covers finance and banking, accounting, marketing, management, and information systems. Special treatment is given to two topics: careers and ethics. Bibliographies are included for each entry. The index is a useful entry point to the topics.

432   Encyclopedia of retirement and finance. L. A. Vitt. 2v. Greenwood, 2003. ISBN 0313324956. $$

305.26   IIQ1064

This encyclopedia includes well-written entries covering financial topics, services, advisors, programs, institutions, products, and social policies. Subheadings, bulleted lists, tables, and charts are used to enhance readability. Entries also include suggested readings and references. Useful cross-referencing is provided throughout. The alphabetical arrangement is supplemented by a "Core Topics" guide. Appendixes include a chronological summary of "Post-ERISA Benefit" legislation, organizations and resources, and types of benefits by tax treatment and function. Written as a tool to educate the general public, especially baby boomers, about retirement issues in an era full of uncertainty, this source will be invaluable to all collections.

433 International encyclopedia of the stock market. M. Sheimo and A. Loizou, eds. 2v., 1320p. Fitzroy Dearborn, 1999. ISBN 1884964354. $$

332.642   HG4551

This two-volume encyclopedia covers terms, biographies, institutions, events, and countries in a well-written and engaging style. Cross-references are provided at the end of entries. Appendixes include an overview of emerging stock markets, a chart of world currency, a directory of organizations, and an annotated bibliography of useful investment books. The index is unfortunately incomplete, but this does not devalue the content. Appropriate for public, corporate, and academic libraries.

434 Mergent's handbook of common stocks. Mergent FIS. ISSN 1547-8343. $$

332   HG4501

This quarterly publication provides reports on 900 stocks that are included in Russell 1000, Standard and Poor's 400 and 500, and Mergent's Dividend Achievers. The reports include capsule stock information, a long-term price chart, valuation analysis, institutional holdings, a business summary, recent developments, prospects, key financials, auditors, and transfer agents. The exceptional items are years as dividend achiever and "Mergent's Price Scores," which measure the stock's performance. Additional features include analysis of stock price movements by company, company rankings by short-term price scores and selected investment criteria, and industry classification. Charts are also provided for Dow Jones Industrial Average and New York Stock Exchange Composite Index. Libraries serving users interested in investing in or studying stocks will find this source useful.

435 Standard and Poor's 500 guide. McGraw-Hill, 2006. ISBN 0071468234. $

338.7   HG4057

This annual publication provides stock information for the 500 companies with an average market capitalization exceeding $20 billion. Reports provide buy, sell, or hold recommendations; a three-year price chart; a business summary; recent developments; sales history; key financials; and the Standard and Poor' ranking (A+ to D). Charts are also provided for A+- and A-ranked earnings and dividends, five consecutive years of earning

increases, rapid-growth stocks, and fast-rising dividends. Libraries will find this an economical choice to assist users interested in investing in or studying stocks.

436 Standard and Poor's stock reports: New York Stock Exchange, American Stock Exchange, NASDAQ Stock Market and regional exchanges. Standard and Poor's. ISSN 1097-4490. $$$$

338.7   HG4905

This quarterly publication provides reports on approximately 3,000 companies traded on the three major U.S. exchanges listed in the title as well as regional exchanges. Reports are listed alphabetically and include a snapshot of the activities, performance, and outlook of the companies. Recommendations to buy or hold, target price, key stock statistics and charts, highlights, investment rationale/risk, qualitative risk assessment, quantitative evaluations, business summary, and company financials are provided for most companies. Funds include a business summary, key financials, risk profile, return measures, capitalization, tax issues and fund performance. This source is valued for its qualitative buy/sell/hold STARS (STock Appreciation Ranking System) rankings. Libraries serving users interested in investing in or studying stocks will find this source useful; however, the price will likely be prohibitive for many. A more affordable alternative, though less comprehensive, is the *Standard and Poor's 500 guide.*

Company and Industry

437 Brands and their companies: Consumer products and their manufacturers with addresses and phone numbers. 28th ed. L. D. Hall. 2v. Thomson Gale, 1995. ISBN 0787689505. $$$$

658.827   T223

This two-volume directory of consumer brand names and their owners or distributors is useful for anyone researching products by the brand or trade name. The first volume provides an alphabetical index for more than 390,000 brands with the product type and the related company. Stars are used to indicate that a brand is out of production. The second volume provides an alphabetical listing of the companies with contact information and web address. Numerical company names are listed in a separate section before the directory. A square icon is used to indicate that a company is out of business. A resource-listing section provides information on trade journals and other important publications that provide trade-name information. This guide is essential to keep track of the vast number of brands available on the ever-changing market today.

438 Companies and their brands: Manufacturers, their addresses, and phone numbers, and the consumer products they produce. 28th ed.
L. D. Hall 2v. Thomson Gale, 2006.
ISBN 0787689610. $$$
658.827   T223

A companion to *Brands and their companies, Companies and their brands* provides an alphabetical directory to manufacturers and distributors, from small businesses to large corporations and from the public sector to the private sector. As the subtitle notes, the listing includes contact information, web address when available, and product names with description. Stars indicate that a brand is out of production, and square icons indicate that a company is out of business. A resource-listing section provides information on trade journals and other important publications that provide trade-name information. This guide is valuable for researchers needing to know all of the brands produced or distributed by a company.

439 Company profiles for students. 3v.
Thomson Gale, 1999–. ISSN 1520-815X. $$
338   HG4057

From Abercrombie and Fitch to Kraft Foods to Walt Disney, this set provides company information for the prominent companies that students study the most. Profiles generally include a company overview, contact information, finances with charts, analysts' opinions, history, strategy, influences, current trends, products, corporate citizenship, global presence, and employment. Sidebars provide a chronology and fast facts, including competitors. A bibliography and website for the annual report are also provided. Industry profiles provide overview, history, finances, significant events, key competitors, projections, global presence, employment, and additional study sources. Volumes 1 and 2 were published in 1999 and cover 280 companies. The third volume was published in 2002 and includes an additional 152

entries. This source is essential for all libraries serving company researchers.

440 D and B business rankings. Dun and Bradstreet. Dun and Bradstreet, 1997–.
Annual. ISSN 0734-2845. $$
380   HG4057

This annual publication provides rankings of public and private businesses by sales volume and employee size. Sections cover rankings by size, within state, and within industry category. There are also two separate sections for public companies and private/foreign-owned companies ranked by size. Symbols used include a triangle for public company, square for public family member, and star for parent company. Industry codes refer to SIC, and the introductory section includes numerical and alphabetical descriptions for this classification scheme. An alphabetical cross-reference index is provided at the front of the book listing company name, state, primary SIC code, employees, sales, and relevant sections. This source is useful for company researchers, whether students, professionals, or the general public.

441 Encyclopedia of corporate names worldwide. A. Room. 585p. McFarland, 2002. ISBN 0786412879. $
929.7   HD69

This handy resource provides the origins and stories behind more than 3,500 commercial names of companies, products, and services. Many of the names originated in the United States or Britain, but some are from other countries, including France, Germany, Italy, and Japan. Entry headings include the name, with the type of product in parentheses, for example, "AT and T (telecommunications)." Here one can read that AstroTurf was first used in the AstroDome by its builder, Roy M. Hofheinz, because the Bermuda grass kept dying. Entries can also include if the product was sold to another company, when a trademark or patent was issued, and the success or failure of the company or product. Supplemental materials include a selection of advertising slogans, the naming of nylon story, and a bibliography.

442 The franchise annual. 36th ed.
T. Dixon. 371p. Info Press, 2005.
ISSN 0318-8752. $
338   HF5429.3

This directory lists franchise opportunities in America, Canada, and overseas by category. Entries generally include company name, contact information, description, established and franchising start dates, number of units, franchise fee, royalties, and total investment. Included is a helpful section on franchising, with information on how to investigate the franchisor, checklists of questions to ask, and state regulations.

443   Hoover's handbook of American business. Reference Press, 1992–.
Annual. ISSN 1055-7202. $$
338   HG4057

This annual publication provides company profiles of the largest and most influential companies in the United States. Profiles include company overview, history, executives, locations, products/operations, competitors, and historical financials. Lists are provided, ranking companies with profiles by largest companies by sales, most profitable companies, most valuable public companies, largest employers, and fastest growing. Indexes cover industry, headquarter location, and executives. Also available as a set for $495 with *World business, Private companies,* and *Emerging companies.* A combined index to the set is included in the back of *Hoover's handbook of emerging companies.* Online profiles are available through Hoover's Online, at www.hoovers.com.

444   Hoover's handbook of emerging companies. Reference Press, 1994–.
Annual. ISSN 1069-7519. $$
338   HG 4057

This annual publication provides company profiles for companies with demonstrated growth and potential for future gains in the United States. Profiles include company overview, history, executives, locations, products/operations, competitors, and historical financials. Lists are provided ranking companies with profiles by growth of sales, income, and employment; market value; profit margin; and stock ratios and appreciation. Lists from *Forbes, Fortune,* and *Business week* are also provided. Indexes cover industry, headquarter location, and executives. Also available as a set for $495 with *American business, World business,* and *Private companies.* A combined index to the set is included in the back of *Hoover's handbook of emerging companies.* Online profiles are available through Hoover's Online, at www.hoovers.com.

445   Hoover's handbook of private companies. Hoover's Business Press, 1997–. Annual. ISSN 1555-3744. $$
338   HG4057

This annual publication provides company profiles for the largest and most influential privately owned companies. Profiles generally include company overview, history, executives, locations, products/operations, competitors, and historical financials. Lists are provided for the largest and fastest-growing private companies. Indexes cover industry, headquarter location, and executives. Also available as a set for $495 with *American business, World business,* and *Emerging companies.* A combined index to the set is included in the back of *Hoover's handbook of emerging companies.* Online profiles are available through Hoover's Online, at www.hoovers.com.

446   Hoover's handbook of world business. Reference Press, 1992–. Annual. ISSN 1055-7199. $$
338.7   HG4009

This annual publication provides company profiles for the world's most influential companies. Profiles include company overview, history, executives, locations, products/operations, competitors, and historical financials. Lists are provided ranking companies with profiles by largest companies by sales, most profitable companies, most valuable public companies, largest employers, and fastest growing. Lists from *Forbes* and *Business week* are also provided. Indexes cover industry, headquarter location, and executives. Also available as a set for $495 with *American business, World business,* and *Emerging companies.* A combined index to the set is included in the back of *Hoover's handbook of emerging companies.* Online profiles are available through Hoover's Online, at www.hoovers.com.

447   Hoover's MasterList of U.S. companies. Hoover's Business Press, 2003–. Annual. ISSN 1549-6457. $$
338.7   HF5035

This source covers public companies, large and important private companies, associations, organizations, foundations, universities, government agencies, and subsidiaries of large corporations. Entries contain contact information, stock exchange and ticker symbol, key executives, company type, description, basic financials, and employees. Company rankings are provided by sales, employees, sales growth, and market value. Indexes cover industry, headquarters location, and stock symbol.

448   LexisNexis corporate affiliations. LexisNexis. LexisNexis, 2002–. Annual.

ISSN 1543-9763. $$$$
658.0025   HG4057

This "who owns whom" directory includes public and private companies in the United States and internationally. Four volumes cover the United States, two cover international, and two provide the master index. The criteria for inclusion is flexible, but generally U.S. companies must exceed $10 million in revenue, have more than 300 employees, or be publicly traded. International companies must exceed $50 million in revenue. Entries are listed under the parent company, with contact information, year founded, basic financials, stock exchange, business description including industry codes, and key personnel followed by similar information for each subsidiary. The master index includes indexes by company name, personnel-arranged corporate responsibilities, geography, and industry codes (SIC and NAICS). Included in each volume are customized user guides to assist the user. This extensive directory will be useful for all libraries.

449   Standard and Poor's register of corporations, directors and executives. Standard and Poor's. 2v. Standard and Poor's, 1973–. Annual. ISSN 0361-3623. $$$$
332.6   HG4057

This annual directory provides corporate listings in volume 1 and biographies of executives in volume 2. Company listings include contact information, key personnel, sales, stock exchange, employees, business description or products, and NAICS industry codes. Subsidiaries are listed individually, with references to the parent company. The director and executive bios include business affiliation, business and residence addresses, birth year and location, college and graduation year, fraternal memberships, and e-mail addresses. Volume 2 also includes indexes for NAICS industry code scheme, company by NAICS, geography, corporate family relation, obituaries, and executives and companies new to the edition. Two supplements are published annually, in April and September. The strength of this work lies in its coverage of personnel.

450   Ward's business directory of U.S. private and public companies. Thomson Gale, 1990–. Annual. ISSN 1048-8707. $$$$
338   HG4057

This annual publication contains company descriptions and rankings. The first three volumes provide

an alphabetical directory for companies. Entries include contact information, import/export designation, company type (public, private, etc.), basic financials, stock exchange, employees, year founded, industry codes, business description, and key personnel. Volume 4 provides a geographic listing for states by zip code and rankings of largest private companies, public companies, and employers. Rankings by sales within SIC industry codes are included nationally in volume 5 and by state in volumes 6 and 7. Volume 8 includes rankings by NAICS industry codes. This standard source is most valuable for its coverage of private companies and rankings, but the cost will be prohibitive for many small libraries.

Economics

451   The American economy: A historical encyclopedia. C. C. Northrup. 2v., 709p. ABC-CLIO, 2003. OP. ISBN 1576078663.
330.973   HC102

This comprehensive resource provides an excellent overview of the role of economic policy in American history. Volume 1 includes more than 500 short entries covering key ideas, initiatives, organizations, people, and events in the history of U.S. economic policy. Volume 2 includes thirty-one in-depth essays on core economic issues and trends and nineteen primary source documents covering legislation, speeches, treaties, and reports. Entries in both volumes often include references, and a separate selected bibliography is also provided. This work is useful for all libraries. Available as an e-book.

452   A dictionary of economics. 2nd ed. J. Black. 507p. Oxford Univ. Pr., 2003. ISBN 9780198607670. $
330   HB61

This dictionary provides clear, concise definitions of more than 2,500 economic terms and related terms from mathematics and statistics. Personal finance terms, including *insurance, pensions,* and *stock market investment,* are also included. Equations and graphs illustrate concepts. Cross-referencing is noted by an asterisk within definitions and *see* and *see also* references at the end. Appendixes cover the Greek alphabet and a list of Nobel Prize winners in economics. This Oxford dictionary will be useful for students and the general public.

453   The new Palgrave: A dictionary of economics. J. Eatwell, M. Milgate, and P. K. Newman. Palgrave, 1998. ISBN 9780333740408 (pbk.). $$
330   HB61

The 1998 paperback edition is a reprint of the original, published in 1987. An updated, six-volume edition of this work is expected for publication in 2008. This dictionary covers the broad scope of economic study, including institutions, theory, techniques, practices, policy, and people. The focus of the work is on England, the United States, and English-speaking colonies. Biographical entries are provided for economists still living in 1987 who were born after January 1, 1916, and wrote primarily in English. Bibliographies are included for many entries. Appendixes include entries by author and a subject index. This work is a continuation of *Palgrave's dictionary of political economy* (A. M. Kelley, 1963), with only fifty original entries reprinted. Cross-referencing is provided throughout the work, and the index is comprehensive. This title is strongly recommended for all economics collections.

454   The Oxford encyclopedia of economic history. J. Mokyr, ed. 5v. Oxford Univ. Pr., 2003. ISBN 0195105079. $$$
330   HC15

This well-written and accessible five-volume set includes nearly 900 entries covering economic history on a global scale from prehistoric times to the present. Entries are arranged alphabetically, but there is a topical outline of articles broken down into eleven categories covering general areas, such as geography and demography, and specific subfields, such as money, banking, and finance. Maps are used to illustrate major topics, for example, world deforestation and oil industry, 2001. Charts, tables, and illustrations help break up the text and provide appropriate examples. Entries include bibliographies with recommended primary sources and useful works in English. The index is comprehensive, covering all topics in the encyclopedia including those not listed as main entries. This source will form the foundation of economic collections.

Entrepreneurship and Small Business

455   Business plans handbook. L. M. Pearce, ed. 459p. Thomson Gale, 2005. ISBN

0787666815. $$
658.4

This handbook provides actual business plans written by entrepreneurs who are seeking funding. Volume 11 presents sample plans for a range of company types, including brewpub, day-care facility, giftware company, homeless shelter, massage therapists, and pizza restaurant. All volumes in this series present plans for retail, service, and manufacturing industries, but unique plans are provided in each. Appendixes provide two fictional business-plan templates; a directory of organizations, agencies, and consultants; and a glossary of small business terms. The cumulative index covers the entire series. This is an excellent source for libraries serving business students, entrepreneurs, and small business owners.

456   Directory of venture capital and private equity firms, domestic and international. 9th ed. 1200p. Grey House, 2006. ISBN 1592371027. $$
332.67   HG4751

The annual publication includes detailed information on more than 3,000 venture capital and private equity firms, including contact information and website addresses for primary and branch locations, mission statements, geographic preferences, fund size, average and minimum investments, investment criteria, industry group preferences, and portfolio companies. Key executives are also listed, with e-mail address; education, with school and degree; and professional background. Descriptive listings are divided into domestic and international, and five indexes cover college and university, executive, geographic, industry preference, and portfolio company. This resource is valuable for any library serving entrepreneurs and small business owners.

457   Encyclopedia of small business. 3rd ed. 2v. Thomson Gale, 2006. ISBN 9780787691127. $$
658.02   HD62.7

This fully revised and expanded third edition provides more than 600 in-depth articles and overviews of key topics related to small business. Topics covered included financing, financial planning, business-plan creation, market analysis, sales strategy, tax planning, human resource issues, and more. Illustrations include tables, graphs, and photographs. Entries include further-reading recommendations. This is an excellent source for libraries serving business students, entrepreneurs, and small business owners.

458 Entrepreneur press. Entrepreneur.com. www.entrepreneurpress.com.
Provides several useful books on new, small, and home businesses and franchises. One series to note is the SmartStart State series, which includes "How to start a business in" guides.

Insurance

459 Complete book of insurance: Understand the coverage you really need. R. Zevnik. 272p. Sphinx, 2004. ISBN 1572483830. $
368   HG8061
This well-written and readable consumer guide provides articles on property and casualty coverage for home owners, autos, tenants, and business owners. The discussion focuses on Insurance Services Office's policies, which are typically used by other insurance agencies. Chapter 1 covers the insurance business, including its economic role, business structure, and marketing and selling. Chapter 2 covers home, and chapter 3 covers auto. Supplemental material includes a glossary and a directory of state insurance commissioners. This source is appropriate for all collections.

460 Dictionary of insurance terms. 4th ed. H. W. Rubin. 573p. Barron's, 2000. ISBN 0764112627. $
368   HG8025
This clear, well-written dictionary provides definitions and illustrative examples for more than 4,200 key terms from all areas of insurance. Organizations and associations are included with a brief mission statement. Important legislation is also covered. Cross-references are indicated with small capitals and with italicized *see* and *see also* references. The appendix covers abbreviations and acronyms. This dictionary is appropriate for professionals, students, and the general public.

Management

461 The Blackwell encyclopedia of management. 2nd ed. C. L. Cooper et al., eds. 12v. Blackwell, 2005.

ISBN 0631233172. $$$$
658   HD30.15
This comprehensive resource on management topics is written for both students and laypeople. Each volume covers a different area of business: accounting, business ethics, entrepreneurship, finance, human-resource management, international management, management information systems, managerial economics, marketing, operations management, organizational behavior, and strategic management. Entries include definitions of terms and extended essays on key topics. Tables, illustrations, and formulas are provided as needed. Bibliographies for each entry are often lengthy, and cross-references are ample. Indexes are provided for each volume, with a comprehensive index in a separate volume. Despite the cost, this is an excellent source for libraries serving business students at all levels.

462 Encyclopedia of management. 5th ed. M. M. Helms. Thomson Gale, 2006. ISBN 0787665568. $$
658   HD30.15
This well-written source covers more than 300 terms, issues, and concepts in management theories and applications. The alphabetical arrangement is supplemented by a "Guide to functional-area readings" arranged by topic. Subheadings, lists, and figures within entries make this easy to read. Cross-references are provided for entries, and these are repeated in the index. Entries also include further-reading suggestions. This is an excellent first-stop source for anyone with a management-related question.

Real Estate

463 Barron's real estate handbook. 6th ed. J. P. Friedman, J. C. Harris, and B. A. Diskin. Barron's, 2005. ISBN 0764157779. $
333.33   HD1375
This comprehensive source includes a glossary of terms; guides for home buyers, sellers, and investors; federal legislation and regulations; careers; tables; and websites. The glossary provides definitions and examples with cross-references. Tables and diagrams are used to illustrate some concepts. Appendixes cover parts of a house, abbreviations, measurement tables, mathematical formulas and forms, and worksheets. This source will be useful to both professionals and the general public.

464   Dearborn real estate education.
REcampus. www.dearborn.com/
recampus/.

Publishes affordable Real Estate Basics guides for
nineteen states that cover licensing, operating business, brokerage relationship, contracts and clos-
ings, license law, specialty topics, and title issues.
Other state resources are also available on practice
and law and exam preparation.

Careers and Vocational Guidance

**465   The career guide: Dun's employment
opportunities directory.** Dun's
Marketing Services. Dun and Bradstreet,
1985–. Annual. ISSN 0740-7289. $$
331.12   HF5382.5

This directory provides company information on
leading U.S. companies that have at least 1,000
employees. Listings are provided alphabetically,
geographically, and by industry classification. Ad-
ditional geographic sections cover employer branch
offices and disciplines hired. Entries include busi-
ness name plus parent/headquarters, contact in-
formation, officers, sales, number of employees,
percentage range of blue- and white-collar em-
ployees, ticker symbol and exchange, SIC industry
classification codes, occupations hired with per-
centage, and other locations. This source will be
useful for all libraries.

**466   Encyclopedia of careers and vocational
guidance.** 13th ed. L. Likoff. 5v.
Ferguson, 2005. ISBN 081606055X. $$
331.7   HF5381

This encyclopedia provides overviews of 93 career
fields and 738 career articles. The career-field overviews provide background; structure of the industry; outlook, including statistics; and sources of
additional information. The career articles cover
occupations and provide overview, history, job

duties, education and training requirements, how
to explore and gain experience with the career,
typical places of employment, how to get a first
job, advancement, earnings, work environment,
outlook, and sources of additional information.
Also included is an introductory section on how to
choose a career, how to find and apply for jobs, and
helpful information for after you are hired, including salary/wages and employment laws. Appendixes
cover career resources and associations for individuals with disabilities and internships, apprentice-
ships, and training programs. Indexes are provided
for organizations and websites and job titles.
There are also indexes based on common government classification systems, including Dictionary
of Occupational Titles, Guide for Occupational
Exploration, National Occupational Classification
System (Canada), and Occupational Information
Network Standard Occupational Classification
Index. This easy-to-read and well-organized source
will be useful for all libraries.

**467   Occupational outlook handbook,
2006–07.** U.S. Department of Labor
staff. U.S. Dept. of Labor, 2006. ISBN
0160729416. $ www.bls.gov/oco/.
331.7   HD8051

This premier source is updated biennially and
presents overviews of professional careers and
careers in the fields of management, service, sales,
administration, farming, construction, installation, production, transportation, and armed forces.
Entries include nature of the work, working conditions, education and training requirements,
employment statistics and industries, job outlook,
earnings, related occupations, and sources of additional information. Supplemental material includes
a general outlook of job opportunities, sources of
career information, and how to find and evaluate a
job offer. One downside to this publication is the
classification of job titles. Fortunately, the index
provides cross-references. The website provides
free access to the entire work.

6   *Political Science and Law*

DONALD ALTSCHILLER

For library users wanting the most up-to-date information on international, national, and local politics or the names of current government officials and political leaders, the Internet has emerged as the essential source. Nevertheless, print literature still serves a vital function in offering a vast range of information on political science and law. Although some books listed below may be out of print (OP), these titles should still be considered when creating a comprehensive reference collection. This chapter includes entries on important print reference volumes and also on the burgeoning web sources now available on these subjects.

Bibliographies and Guides

468   American foreign relations since 1600: A guide to the literature. Robert L. Beisner, ed. 2v. ABC-CLIO, 2003. ISBN 1576070808. $$
016.32773   Z6465; E183

Produced under the auspices of the Society for Historians of American Foreign Relations, this massive two-volume work contains 16,000 annotated entries covering books, journal articles, microforms, and some websites. Each entry includes basic bibliographic information and an evaluative annotation; works listed more than once are cross-referenced to the primary citation. An invaluable literature guide.

469   C-SPAN. National Cable Satellite Corporation. http://c-span.org.

Established by the cable industry in 1979 to provide public-service programming, this cable network has become a vital resource on American politics and government. The site offers free access to its archives and also live streams a wide range of political and public affairs programming.

470   Legal information institute. Cornell Univ. Law School. www.law.cornell.edu/lii.html.

The Cornell Law Library created this site—which it still maintains—in 1992, attracting widespread use by the general public and legal professionals. Known as the "law-not-com" site, it has the most links to law resources on the Web. An essential first stop for library users looking for any type of legal information.

471   Legal research in a nutshell. 8th ed. Morris L. Cohen and Kent C. Olson. 478p. Thomson/West, 2003. ISBN 0314147071. $
340   KF240

First published in 1969, this classic research guide has increasingly incorporated electronic sources, but it still devotes considerable coverage to print materials. The first few chapters introduce the major primary and secondary sources; later sections discuss more specialized topics, including administrative law, international law, and legislative history, among many other topics. Compact in size, this work is a superb source for general readers and both law and nonlaw students.

472   **Members of Congress: A bibliography.** Robert U. Goehlert, Fenton S. Martin, and John R. Sayre. 507p. Congressional Quarterly, 1996. ISBN 0871878658. $$
016.32873   Z7165; JK1030

This unique source provides biographical references to most individuals who served in Congress from 1774 to 1995. The bibliography contains citations to books, journal and magazine articles, and essays within anthologies, covering both the public and private lives of these legislators. This outstanding reference work should particularly help library users wanting to track down hard-to-find biographical information.

473   **Political science resources on the Web.** University of Michigan Documents Center. Documents Center, Univ. of Michigan, 1996–. www.lib.umich.edu/govdocs/polisci.html.
320   JA66

Created by librarians at the University of Michigan library in 1995, this documents center metasite provides quick access to a number of links, including the U.S. and foreign government sites and country and international statistics, among numerous others.

474   **Tapping the government grapevine: The user-friendly guide to U.S. government information sources.** 3rd ed. Judith Schiek Robinson. 286p. Oryx, 1998. ISBN 1573560243. $
025.04   ZA5055

Engagingly written and nicely illustrated, this guide contains excellent information on the plethora of sources for finding information about the federal government. A caveat: much material has become outdated because of the Web. Nevertheless, this work contains useful and hard-to-find information on the history of these reference works.

475   **USA.gov.** Office of Citizen Services and Communication, U.S. General Services and Communications, 2000–. www.usa.gov.
ZA5075

"Whatever you want or need from the U.S. government, it's here" is the seemingly boastful yet probably accurate description of this metasite.

Dictionaries and Encyclopedias

476   **American conservatism: An encyclopedia.** Bruce Frohnen, Jeremy Beer, and Jeffrey O. Nelson. 979p. ISI Books, 2006. ISBN 9781932236439. $
320.520973   JC573

Containing more than 600 entries, this comprehensive encyclopedia surveys the history, personalities, and philosophies of an ideological movement that has transformed U.S. politics for the last several decades.

477   **The American political dictionary.** 10th ed. Jack C. Plano and Milton Greenberg. 702p. Harcourt Brace College Publishers, 1997. ISBN 0030173175 (pbk.). $
320.473   JK9

Arranged alphabetically by broad subject heading (finance and taxation, business and labor, etc.), this work serves as both a dictionary and a study guide. Each entry contains a brief description of the topic and also includes a unique feature—its historical and contemporary "significance." Frequent cross-references and a useful index provide easy access.

478   **Black's law dictionary.** 8th ed. Bryan A. Garner, editor in chief. 1810p. Thomson/West, 2004. ISBN 0314151990. $
340   KF156

Published since 1891, this work is the preeminent reference dictionary on law. Containing more than 25,000 terms, the dictionary also includes thousands of quotations from scholarly works and also pronunciation information. An abridged version and pocket edition are also available.

479   **Brewer's politics: A phrase and fable dictionary.** Nicholas Comfort. 693p. Cassell, 1993. ISBN 0304340855. $
320   JA61

According to the editor, this work "perpetuates the mildly whimsical approach to the selection of entries" in the venerable reference work *Brewer's dictionary of phrase and fable.* Unsurprisingly, this British work devotes much coverage to Great Britain—with the customary delightful wit—but it also contains much political material on the English-speaking Commonwealth countries, the United States, and some other countries. Author Comfort acknowledges that some material and quotations are offensive—reflecting the crude attitudes of some politicians or unsavory political behavior—but he nevertheless disclaims responsibility. Although these selections and the occasional lack of references may compromise the suitability of this work, it is still a browsable, fun work, with some useful reference material.

480 Concise Oxford dictionary of politics.
2nd ed. Iain McLean and Alistair McMillan. 606p. Oxford Univ. Pr., 2003. ISBN 0192802763. $
320   JA61

Compiled by British political-science scholars, this compact dictionary covers political concepts, noteworthy individuals, and institutions. The short, informative, and lucidly written entries make it a superb ready-reference source.

481 Encyclopedia of human rights. 2nd
ed. Edward H. Lawson and Mary Lou Bertucci. 1715p. Taylor and Francis, 1996. ISBN 1560323620. $$$
323.4   JC571

This hefty volume covers UN-related human-rights activities and programs, although it is not an official UN publication. Most topical entries include bibliographic references; organization listings include address and contact information. The appendixes list every international convention or treaty since 1921, including the names of the country signatories for major agreements. A useful ready-reference source, especially for such harder-to-find material as international human-rights documents on sexual orientation and "health as a human right."

**482 Encyclopedia of presidential
campaigns, slogans, issues, and
platforms.** Robert North Roberts and Scott J. Hammond, eds. 395p. Greenwood, 2004. ISBN 0313319731. $
324.973   E176

Primarily aimed at high school and college students, this work is divided into two sections. The first part surveys every presidential campaign from 1789 to 2000; the second section contains famous slogans ("Tippecanoe and Tyler Too"), major personalities, important issues, and political jargon ("swing

voters"). Many entries include useful bibliographical references. A lively and informative work.

483 Encyclopedia of the American Left.
2nd ed. Mari Jo Buhle, Paul Buhle, and Dan Georgakas. Oxford Univ. Pr., 1998. ISBN 0195120884. $$
335   HX86

First published in 1990, this revised and updated one-volume work is the most comprehensive reference encyclopedia on the history and politics of American radicalism since the American Revolution. The book features a wide variety of entries on left-wing activists, organizations, and ideological views. A helpful glossary and an outline of topics provide easy access to the text.

**484 Encyclopedia of the United States
cabinet.** Mark Grossman, ed. 3v. ABC-CLIO, 2000. ISBN 0874369770. $$
352.24   E176

Five Nobel Peace Prize winners and ten individuals who later became presidents have served in U.S. cabinets. This three-volume set contains biographies of the hundred individuals who served as cabinet secretaries from the presidencies of George Washington to Bill Clinton. Compiled over eight years by a remarkably diligent editor, this work fills a noticeable literature gap on this vital component of the executive branch. The book is arranged alphabetically by cabinet departments, and the biographies follow in chronological order.

**485 International encyclopedia of human
rights: Freedoms, abuses, and
remedies.** Robert L. Maddex, ed. 404p. CQ Press, 2000. ISBN 1568024908. $$
323   JC571

A multipurpose work, this encyclopedia contains essays on the key concepts of human rights, summaries of major documents, listings of human-rights intergovernmental and national agencies, and advocacy groups. In addition, the volume also profiles almost fifty prominent activists. The set is superbly designed, with numerous black-and-white illustrations and easy-to-read type, and most entries include a bibliography and cross-references.

**486 Macmillan dictionary of political
quotations.** Lewis D. Eigen and Jonathan P. Siegel, eds. 785p. Macmillan, 1993. ISBN 0026106507. $
082   PN6084

Organized in approximately 100 broad subject headings, this dictionary contains a wide variety of quotations. The topics include campaigns and conventions, freedom and liberty, and foreign policy. Selections were based on "terseness [and] clear statement of an important principle, controversy, humor, surprise," and many other factors. Because a large number of world leaders and political philosophers have been white Christian men, the editors honestly acknowledge an "inevitable" bias in their selections. They also readily declare that there was "no serious attempt to provide balance on issues. If, on a particular issue, one side was more witty, pithy, urbane, and widely published, that is the way it appears in this book." Each entry includes the source reference; an author and concept index provides easy access to the text.

487 Oxford dictionary of political quotations. 3rd ed. Antony Jay, ed. 541p. Oxford Univ. Pr., 2006. ISBN 0192806165. $
320   PN6084

The editor succeeds at his admirable goal: to produce a classic reference work containing the "political quotations [that] are part of the currency of political speeches and writings throughout the English-speaking world." Alphabetically arranged by author, the entries are set in two well-spaced columns—the entry and the source. Because many quotation dictionaries are often printed in small type, with little space between entries, the appealing graphic design enhances the readability of this well-researched reference source.

488 Penguin dictionary of international relations. Graham Evans and Jeffrey Newnham. 623p. Penguin, 1998. ISBN 0140513973 (pbk.). $
327   JZ1161

Published soon after the end of the cold war, this paperback contains more than 700 entries covering ideas, organizations, events, and specialized terms. Frequent cross-references help broaden the understanding of each term.

489 Safire's new political dictionary: The definitive guide to the new language of politics. William Safire. 930p. Random House, 1993. ISBN 0679420681. $
320   JK9

New York Times columnist and former speechwriter Safire has produced this outstanding compilation,

a culmination of more than a quarter century of writing about the language of politics. According to the author, this political dictionary does not define common terms about government or governmental offices, for example, *vice president* or *president;* rather, this work offers the etymology of terms and phrases such as *veep, heartbeat away from the presidency,* and *the loneliest job in the world.* Safire, a very diligent researcher and witty literary stylist, has compiled an essential reference work for most libraries.

Directories

490 Federal regulatory directory. 12th ed. Congressional Quarterly. Congressional Quarterly, 2005. ISBN 1568029756. $$
351.02573   HC110

Known as FRED, this perennial reference work provides detail on more than 100 federal regulatory agencies, brief histories and contact information, legislation purview, and biographies of notable administrators.

491 Public interest group profiles. 12th ed. CQ Press and the Foundation for Public Affairs, 2006. ISBN 0872893448. $$
332.43   JK1118

This hefty reference source features much useful information on selected public advocacy groups, including purpose, funding sources, membership statistics, publications, and media comments about their effectiveness.

492 State and local government on the Net: A Piper Resources guide to government sponsored Internet sites. Piper Resources. Piper Resources, 1998–. www.statelocalgov.net/index.cfm.
973.025   Z1123

This metasite provides easy access to the large number of state and local information sources.

493 United States government Internet manual. Peggy Garvin, ed. Bernan Press, 2004–. Annual. ISSN 1547-2892. $
351   ZA5075

This printed guide to U.S. government Internet sites lists title, sponsoring agency, address, and a description. Useful when working with patrons seeking government information.

494 **U.S. courts.** Administrative Office of the U.S. Courts. www.uscourts.gov.

A metasite providing links to U.S. district and appellate courts.

495 **Washington information directory.** Congressional Quarterly. Congressional Quarterly, 2005. ISSN 0887-8064. $$
975.3   F192

Published for more than 30 years, this directory provides contact information on the vast number of government agencies and congressional committees in the nation's capital. Especially helpful are entries on nongovernmental organizations, which are listed alongside government agencies. Flow charts and easy-to-read entries enhance its usefulness. A superb telephone and in-person ready-reference source.

Handbooks, Yearbooks, and Almanacs

496 **Almanac of American politics, 2006: The senators, the representatives, and the governors; their records and election results, their states and districts.** Michael Barone and Richard E. Cohen. 1907p. National Journal, 2005. ISBN 0892341114. $
328.3   JK1341

This biennial volume contains entries on all 535 members of the current Congress. Arranged alphabetically by state, the entries provide basic biographical information, votes on major issues, ratings by special interest groups, narrative descriptions of their districts, and the political and economic issues influencing local voters. Similar to *Congressional Quarterly's politics in America* (Congressional Quarterly, annual). A superb ready-reference source.

497 **Annenberg political fact check.** Annenberg Public Policy Center. Annenberg Public Policy Center, 2004–. www.factcheck.org.
378.04   JK275

This website received national attention—and also evoked much public snickering—during the 2004 election debates. Vice President Cheney erroneously referred to it as "factcheck.com," which, in fact, was an anti-Bush website. He meant,

of course, to recommend this nonpartisan site, FactCheck.org, which analyzes the accuracy of political speeches, debates, and partisan advertisements since December 2003. Funded by the Annenberg Public Policy Center of the University of Pennsylvania, this superb site has helped raise the level of honesty and accuracy in contentious political contests. An important resource for the informed citizen and voter.

498 **Basic facts about the United Nations.** United Nations Department of Public Information. United Nations, 1947–. ISSN 0067-4419. $
341.23   JX1977

This inexpensive official handbook describes the organization, programs, agencies, and activities of this world body. A superb ready-reference source, this paperback volume contains the full names of all its constituent agencies in addition to charts and maps.

499 **The book of the states.** Council of State Governments. 613p. Council of State Governments, 2006. ISBN 0872928322. $
353.9   JK2403

An almanac-style work covering all fifty states and providing extensive comparative data and also surveys of state legislation.

500 **Congress A to Z.** 4th ed. David R. Tarr and Ann O'Connor. 605p. CQ Press, 2003. ISBN 1568028008. $$
328.73   JK1021

Part of the Congressional Quarterly's American Government A to Z series, this work describes the structure, operation, and history of the U.S. Congress. Entries range from the "Courts and Congress" to "War Powers." Excellent appendixes include reference material and charts on the Speaker of the House, dates of every session since 1789, and party leadership, among other charts.

501 **Congressional Quarterly's desk reference on American government.** 2nd ed. Bruce Wetterau. 344p. CQ Press, 2000. ISBN 1568025491. $
320.473   JK274

Similar in format to the *Desk reference on the presidency,* this volume contains more than 600 questions and answers on the executive, legislative, and judicial branches of the U.S. government.

502 **Congressional Quarterly's desk reference on the presidency.** Bruce Wetterau. 311p. CQ Press, 2000. ISBN 1568025890. $
973   JK516

Containing more than 500 questions and answers, this reference source provides a vast range of information on the lives of presidents and their families and the history and powers of the most powerful position in the world. Frequent cross-references provide easy access to related material. A superb ready-reference source.

503 **Congressional Quarterly's politics in America.** Congressional Quarterly. CQ Press, 2000–. ISSN 1064-6809. $$
328.73   JK1012

Similar to *Almanac of American politics* (Gambit, annual), this biennial work provides biographical and political information on every member of Congress, descriptions of the state and congressional districts, campaign contributions and interest group ratings, among other topics.

504 **Elections A to Z.** 2nd ed. John L. Moore. 614p. CQ Press, 2003. ISBN 1568028016. $$
324.6   JK1976

Complementing *Congress A to Z,* this volume will answer basic questions about U.S. elections and the electoral process. Engagingly written, entries cover a wide variety of topics, including contested elections, the origin of the "whistle stop" campaign appearance, and a delightful section on voter apathy and boredom, aptly titled "ZZZ," for snoozing! Also includes useful charts and reference material.

505 **European political facts of the twentieth century.** 5th ed. Chris Cook and John Paxton. 481p. Palgrave, 2001. ISBN 0333792033. $
320.94   JN12

An excellent compilation covering the changing political history of Europe, including names and dates of prime ministers, election statistics, and short histories of political parties.

506 **Gay and lesbian Americans and political participation: A reference handbook.** Raymond A. Smith and Donald P. Haider-Markel. 339p. ABC-

CLIO, 2002. ISBN 1576072568. $
305.9   HQ76

This work provides useful historical information, important documents, a chronology and an annotated bibliography.

507 **Historical guide to the U.S. government.** George T. Kurian, ed. 741p. Oxford Univ. Pr., 1998. ISBN 0195102304. $
352.3   JK9

This hefty volume surveys the history of federal agencies, departments, and cabinet posts and describes their evolution, growth, and occasional demise. Each alphabetically arranged entry offers a concise history followed by a bibliography. Compiled by historians and government specialists, this work is an outstanding ready-reference source for queries on the history of the U.S. executive branch.

508 **Jews in American politics.** Louis Sandy Maisel et al. 506p. Rowman and Littlefield, 2001. ISBN 0742501817. $
973   E184

This unique reference source contains both historical analysis and much ready-reference material, including biographies and interesting facts and statistics.

509 **Major acts of Congress.** Brian K. Landsberg, editor in chief. 3v. Macmillan Reference USA, 2004. ISBN 0028657497. $$
348.73   KF154

Containing entries on 262 laws passed by Congress since the founding of the nation, this unique reference source provides historical background and assesses the political significance of this major legislation. The entries range from 300 to 2,500 words and include print and web sources. Nicely designed with illustrations and photographs, this work serves as an excellent starting point for researching congressional legislation from 1789 to the USA PATRIOT Act.

510 **Oxford companion to American law.** Kermit L. Hall, editor in chief, and David Scott Clark et al., eds. 912p. Oxford Univ. Pr., 2002. ISBN 0195088786. $
349.73   KF154

Aimed at a diverse audience ranging from general readers to law scholars, this work provides succinct and authoritative entries covering a wide range of legal topics: biographies of law scholars and activists, major constitutional cases, and legal philosophy, to name only some. The contributors—both scholars and practitioners—have produced an easily read work, remarkably devoid of arcane legal jargon.

511   Political handbook of the world.
Arthur S. Banks, Thomas Christian Müller, and William Overstreet. 1620p. CQ Press, 2006. ISBN 1568029527. $$
320.9   D860

First published in 1928 by the Council on Foreign Relations, this classic work contains a wealth of information on more than 200 countries and territories, including political parties and organizations, statistics, names of leaders and cabinet members, and extensive essays on recent government political history. In addition, a section covers regional and international organizations.

512   Project Vote Smart: The most trusted source for political information.
Project Vote Smart. Project Vote Smart, 1992–. www.vote-smart.org.
342.0418; 353.9   JK1968

Similar to the goals of the League of Women Voters, this nonpartisan site aims to help educate an informed electorate. The site provides links to voting records, the stated positions of candidates for public office, and campaign finance information.

513   THOMAS: Legislative information on the Internet. Library of Congress, 1995–. http://thomas.loc.gov.
025   KF1

The preeminent source for finding recent congressional legislation, committee reports, status of pending bills, and the *Congressional record,* among numerous other links.

514   U.S. Department of State. U.S. Dept. of State. www.state.gov.

This website provides links to foreign policy and trade information, among many other issues involving this cabinet department. Also includes full-text versions of the venerable collection *Foreign relations of the United States.*

515   U.S. government manual. Office of the Federal Register, National Archives and Records Administration. Federal

Register, Supt. of Docs., U.S. Govt. Print. Off., 1974–. Annual. ISSN 0092-1904. $
351.973   JK421

An official handbook of the U.S. government, this annual publication provides concise information on the legislative, executive, and judicial branches.

516   Vital statistics on American politics.
Harold W. Stanley and Richard G. Niemi. CQ Press, 1988–. Annual. ISSN 1534-4762. $
324   JK274

This annual volume offers a cornucopia of political and government statistics: campaign finances, elections, public-opinion polling data, Medicare, foreign aid, civil service, employment, television ownership of presidential debates, and so forth. One needn't be a statistics junkie to enjoy this remarkably eclectic work. One learns, for example, that it took only three months from congressional approval until ratification of the Twenty-sixth Amendment to the Constitution; the Twenty-seventh Amendment, however, which sets congressional salaries, took 203 years to enact!

Biographical Sources

517   Almanac of the unelected. Almanac of the Unelected, 1998–. ISSN 1047-0999. $$
328   JK1083

A unique source for biographical information on selected House and Senate committee staff. Arranged by committee name, this work offers interesting background material on influential—yet generally unknown—individuals.

518   Biographical dictionary of congressional women. Karen Foerstel. 300p. Greenwood, 1999. ISBN 0313302901. $
328.73   JK1012

This somewhat dated volume contains short biographies of more than 200 women who served in Congress. This work complements the *Biographical directory of the U.S. Congress.*

519   Biographical directory of the U.S. Congress. United States; Congress; House; Office of the Clerk. U.S. Congress, 2002–. http://bioguide

.congress.gov/biosearch/biosearch.asp.
973.3   JK1010

Provides short biographical information on every member of Congress, from 1774 to the present.

520   Black members of the U.S. Congress. U.S. Senate. www.senate.gov/reference/resources/pdf/RL30378.pdf.

An excellent source listing all African Americans who served in Congress from 1870 to 2005.

521   Chiefs of state and cabinet members of foreign governments. United States; Central Intelligence Agency; Directorate of Intelligence. CIA Directorate of Intelligence, 1900–. https://www.cia.gov/publications/chiefs/index.html.
351.003   JF37

Published by the CIA, this site provides the most up-to-date information on foreign government leaders and cabinet members. The site is updated weekly.

522   Who's who in American politics. 20th ed. Paul A. Theis and Edmund Lee Henshaw. R. R. Bowker, 2005–2006. ISSN 0000-0205. $$
320   E176

This biographical directory lists almost 30,000 "politically influential" Americans. Entries have a similar format to other Marquis biographical directories.

523   Who's who in international affairs, 2005. 4th ed. 560p. Europa, 2005. ISBN 185743272X. $$
327   JZ1242

This directory contains biographical information on more than 5,500 individuals involved in international affairs, diplomacy, law, and economics. Includes listings of country embassies and consular missions around the world.

7 Education

DEBBIE BOGENSHUTZ

As the nature of education has changed over the past several years, so has the nature of education reference tools. The periodic, often annual guides to educational institutions and curriculum resources are still important, but they no longer dominate the reference collection. There are now available some excellent education encyclopedias as well as encyclopedias dealing with special topics and special populations in education. As education receives more popular and legislative attention, reference publishers are responding with more encyclopedic resources.

Bibliographies and Guides

General Sources

524 **Education: A guide to reference and information sources.** 2nd ed. Nancy P. O'Brien and Lois Buttlar. 189p. Libraries Unlimited, 2000. ISBN 1563086263. $
016.37   Z5811; LB15

Concentrating on items published 1990–1998, with older materials included in some circumstances, this bibliography presents almost 500 items, arranged in fourteen categories. Bibliographic information,

price, and short annotations are given. Indexed by author, title, and subject.

Media and Curriculum Materials

525 **Best books for children: Preschool through grade 6.** 8th ed. Catherine Barr and John T. Gillespie. 1783p. Libraries Unlimited, 2006. ISBN 1591580854. $$
011.62   Z1037

More than 25,000 books are presented in this volume, designed to provide recommended recreational reading as well as to support a typical school curriculum. Coverage is from preschool through grade 6. Basic arrangement is by subject, with indexes by author/illustrator, title, and subject/grade level. Entries include publication data, price, and short description. Companion volumes include *Best books for middle school and junior high readers* (2004) and *Best books for senior high readers* (2004). More than one-third of the more than 25,000 titles are new to the eighth edition. Sources consulted include *Booklist, Bulletin for the Center for Children's Books, Horn book, Library media connection,* and *School library journal.* Libraries Unlimited publishes a series of similar titles for different audiences/age groups.

526 **Educational media and technology yearbook.** Michael Orey, Jo McClendon, and Robert Maribe Branch. 431p.

Libraries Unlimited (in cooperation with the Association for Educational Communications and Technology), 1985–. Annual. ISSN 8755-2094. $
371.3   LB1028

Articles by specialists provide state-of-the-art reviews of recent developments and trends, technology updates, and leadership profiles. A significant portion provides directories of media organizations and associations, graduate programs, funding sources, and producers, distributors, and publishers.

527   **Educators guide to free family and consumer education materials.** Educators Progress Service, 2001–. Annual. ISSN 1543-5687 (pbk.). $
016.64   TX1

Educators guide to free films, filmstrips and slides. Educators Progress Service, 1995–. Annual. ISSN 0070-9395 (pbk.). $
371.33   LB1044

Educators guide to free guidance materials. Mary H. Saterstrom. Educators Progress Service, 1962–. Annual. ISSN 0070-9417 (pbk.). $
016.37142   HF5381

Educators guide to free health, physical education, and recreation materials. Foley A. Horkheimer. Educators Progress Service, 1968–. Annual. ISSN 0424-6241 (pbk.). $
011   Z6121

Educators guide to free Internet resources—elementary/middle school edition. Kathleen Suttles Nehmer. Educators Progress Service, 2002–. Annual. ISSN 1548-5234 (pbk.) $
005.3   LB1044

Educators guide to free Internet resources—secondary edition. Kathleen Suttles Nehmer. Educators Progress Service, 2003–. Annual. ISSN 1549-6996 (pbk.). $
005.3   LB1044

Educators guide to free multicultural materials. Educators Progress Service, 1998–. Annual. ISSN 1549-1056 (pbk.). $
016.370   LC1099

Educators guide to free science materials. Educators Progress Service, 1960–. Annual. ISSN 0070-9425 (pbk.). $
507   Q181

Educators guide to free social studies materials. Educators Progress Service, 1961–. Annual. ISSN 0070-9433 (pbk.). $
307   AG600

Educators guide to free videotapes— elementary/middle school edition. Educators Progress Service, 2000–. Annual. ISSN 1068-9206 (pbk.). $
371.3   LB1043

Educators guide to free videotapes— secondary edition. Educators Progress Service, 2000–. Annual. ISSN 1068-9206 (pbk.). $
371   LB1043

Elementary teachers guide to free curriculum materials. Educators Progress Service, 1944–. Annual. ISSN 0070-9980 (pbk.). $
016.372   Z5817

Homeschooler's guide to free teaching aids. Educators Progress Service, 1999–. Annual. ISSN 1546-6337 (pbk.). $
649   LC40

Homeschooler's guide to free videotapes. Educators Progress Service, 1999–. Annual. ISSN 1546-6337 (pbk.). $
649   LC40

Middle school teachers guide to free curriculum materials. Educators Progress Service, 1999–. Annual. ISBN 9780877084495 (pbk.). $
371.33   LB1044

Secondary teachers guide to free curriculum materials. Educators Progress Service, 1998–. Annual. ISBN 0877083290 (pbk.). $
371.33   LB1044

Still standards in the field, these guides give source and acquisition information for a wide variety of resources, many from U.S. government resources.

528   NICEM film and video finder online.
National Information Center for
Educational Media (NICEM), 1996–
2005. $$ www.nicem.com/index.html.

This long standard print resource is now available
online, offering bibliographic information on more
than 630,000 items from the early twentieth cen-
tury to the present. Searchable by title, date, age
level, subject, and media type, this database pro-
vides access not only to films and videos but other
traditional learning media as well. MARC records
can be printed or downloaded into OPACs. Prices
start at $500/year for a single user license.

**529   100 top picks for homeschool
curriculum: Choosing the right
curriculum and approach for your
child's learning style.** Cathy Duffy.
314p. Broadman and Holman, 2005.
ISBN 0805431381. $
371.042   LC40

Decidedly Christian in emphasis, this guide helps
the novice homeschooler explore the many cur-
ricula and course materials available. Does an
excellent job for its target audience, and nothing
comparable exists for a larger audience.

**530   Special educator's complete guide to
109 diagnostic tests.** Roger Pierangelo
and George A. Giuliani. 328p. Jossey-
Bass, 1998. ISBN 087628893X. $
371.9   LC4019

Discusses assessments of intelligence, achievement,
language, and spelling as well as physical and psy-
chological assessments. Provides basic information,
strengths and weaknesses of each test, and infor-
mation about the parents' role in assessment and
individual education plans.

**531   Tests: A comprehensive reference
for assessments in psychology,
education, and business.** 5th ed. Taddy
Maddox, ed. 531p. Pro-Ed, 2003. ISBN
0890799083. $$
150   BF176

"Education Instruments" is the largest section in
this book, which gives descriptive annotations for a
wide variety of tests. Population, purpose, description, format (including time), scoring, and cost are
considered. This volume provides a tremendous
amount of information for the price.

532   Vertical file index. H. W. Wilson. ISSN
0042-4439. $$/year
025.172   Z1231

Published six times per year, this title provides a
subject index to free and low-cost pamphlet mate-
rial, giving ordering information and/or URLs for
downloading PDF files.

Databases and Indexes

**533   Education index: A cumulative author
and subject index to a selected list of
educational periodicals, books, and
pamphlets.** H. W. Wilson, 1932–. ISSN
0013-1385. $$$/year
016.3705   Z5813

Available in print, on CD, and online. Indexes
nearly 700 serial publications. The first index for
education literature and still an essential purchase.
Although only *Education index* is available in print,
additional products *Education abstracts, Education
full-text* (providing full text for about 40 percent
of the titles indexed), and *Education index retrospective: 1929–1983* are also available electronically.
See www.hwwilson.com/databases/educat.htm for
more information and to request pricing.

534   Education research complete. EBSCO,
2006.

EBSCO has entered the field with this online database, which debuted in July 2006. Provides indexing and abstracts for more than 1,500 journals,
more than 100 books, and numerous conference
papers. Full text is provided for articles from more
than 750 journals and some nonbook materials as
well. See www.epnet.com for more details, including a complete title list.

**535   ERIC: Education Resources
Information Center.** U.S. Dept. of
Education, Institute of Education Science
(IES). www.eric.ed.gov.

Once available only through fee-based providers
or through the print *Resources in education,* the
ERIC bibliographic database is now available as a
free Internet resource. The database contains well
more than a million records going back to 1966,
with new resources added weekly. ERIC serves
as an index to education journals and to non-
journal documents, many of which are now provided full text at no fee. The goal of the Institute

of Education Science (IES) is to provide access via ERIC within one month of publication. An online thesaurus, which is searchable or browsable alphabetically or by category, facilitates use. Two search modes are available: Basic (by keyword, title, author, descriptor, or ERIC number) and Advanced (offering Boolean search, and adding search by ISSN/ISBN, source institution, and sponsoring agency, and offering limits by type of publication and date). Now that ERIC is freely available, libraries of all sizes should make it available on their websites.

Dictionaries and Encyclopedias

536 American educators' encyclopedia.
Rev. ed. David E. Kapel, et al. 634p.
Greenwood, 1991. ISBN 0313252696. $$
370   LB15

An older but still available single-volume reference book, providing more than 1,900 alphabetically arranged entries covering all aspects of education. Bibliographical references are included for most entries. Extensive cross-references and index.

537 Concise encyclopedia of special education. 2nd ed. Cecil R. Reynolds and Elaine Fletcher-Janzen, eds. 1062p. Wiley, 2002. ISBN 0471392618; 0471652512 (pbk., 2004). $$; $ (pbk.)
371.9   LC4007

Derived from the three-volume *Encyclopedia of special education* (Wiley, 2000), this one-volume edition will handily fill the need in smaller libraries. It features assessment instruments, teaching methods, legal issues, and more. Designed to give the reader (educator, administrator, or parent) an overview of the subject, including history and current practice.

538 Education and technology: An encyclopedia. Ann Kovalchick and Kara Dawson, eds. 2v. ABC-CLIO, 2004. ISBN 1576073513. $$
371.33   LB1028

An easy-to-read overview of education and technology, from acceptable use policies to wireless networks. Although most entries cover topics, some are devoted to leaders in the field and to professional associations. Also includes a helpful glossary.

539 Encyclopedia of American education.
2nd ed. Harlow G. Unger. 3v., 1350p.
Facts on File, 2001. ISBN 0816043442. $$
370   LB17

An up-to-date and comprehensive encyclopedia, with more than 2,500 highly readable articles covering educational trends and people and defining educational terms. Appendixes give a chronology of American education from the first settlement at Jamestown, significant legislation and court decisions, and an overview of education for the profession. Essential for all education collections.

540 Encyclopedia of education. 2nd ed. James W. Guthrie, editor in chief. 8v. Macmillan Reference USA, 2003. ISBN 002865594X. $$$$
370   LB15

A comprehensive encyclopedia for the field, offering information on individuals, institutions, and concepts, from Plato to No Child Left Behind and from the Brookings Institute to the Girl Scouts of America. Education collections in all types of libraries will want this source.

541 Encyclopedia of educational research.
6th ed. Marvin C. Alkin, ed. 4v.
Macmillan, 1992. ISBN 0029004314. $$
370   LB15

Sponsored by the American Educational Research Association, this standard source presents a critical synthesis and interpretation of reported research in about 250 articles contributed primarily by U.S. scholars. Article topics are broad, for example, "attitude measurement" and "motivation." Extensive bibliographies complete each article. Well indexed and illustrated.

542 The Greenwood dictionary of education. Edited by John William Collins and Nancy P. O'Brien. 431p. Greenwood, 2003. ISBN 0897748603. $
370   LB15

The first comprehensive dictionary of education in more than twenty-five years, this dictionary presents more than 2,600 terms, focusing on contemporary terminology in education, and words from other disciplines defined within an education context. An essential purchase.

543 **Higher education in the United States: An encyclopedia.** James J. F. Forest and Kevin Kinser, eds. 2v. ABC-CLIO, 2002. ISBN 1576072487. $$
378.73   LA225

A highly readable, well-rounded resource on higher education in the United States in approximately 200 articles. Appendixes include an annotated bibliography of important books about higher education and a timeline of significant events.

544 **World education encyclopedia: A survey of educational systems worldwide.** 2nd ed. Rebecca Marlow-Ferguson, ed. 3v. Thomson Gale, 2002. ISBN 0787655775. $$
370   LB15

This encyclopedia, which was totally revised since the previous edition, provides a descriptive survey of 233 worldwide educational systems and is arranged alphabetically. Well-written and easily readable essays cover the history and background of each geographical entity and its constitutional and legal foundations and provide overviews of the educational systems, preprimary and primary education, secondary education, higher education, administrative, finance and educational research, nonformal education, and the status and training of the teaching profession. This set provides an enormous amount of comparative data at a very affordable price.

Directories

545 **AV market place.** R. R. Bowker, 1989–. Annual. ISSN 1044-0445. $$
011; 001   LB1043

This directory lists more than 6,500 companies, supplying more than 1,250 "industry-related products and services" and giving addresses, telephone and fax numbers, and e-mail and website addresses. Indexed by product, and then geographically. Also lists associations, film and television commissions, awards and festivals, a calendar of events, and reference books for the trade.

546 **The directory for exceptional children: A comprehensive listing of special-needs schools, programs and facilities.** 15th ed. 1152p. Porter Sargent, 2004–. Triennial. ISSN 0070-

5012; ISBN 0875581501. $
371.92058   LC4007

Presents basic factual data for 2,500 public and private schools for blind, deaf, diabetes, emotional disturbance, HIV/AIDS, learning disabilities, mental retardation, orthological/neurological disorders, pervasive developmental disorders, and speech impairments. Basic arrangement is alphabetical by name, within alphabetically arranged states. Also lists governmental agencies and private organizations providing additional information and assistance.

547 **Funding sources for K–12 education, 2005.** 7th ed. 448p. Oryx, 2005. ISBN 1573566152. $
379.11; 374.97   LC243

Directory of more than 1,760 funding opportunities in the United States and Canada, offering a total of more than $7 billion. Organized by title of grant program, and indexed by subject, sponsoring organization, program type, and geographically, this volume gives you all the information you need to apply. Introductory material provides a guide to the grant-writing process. Essential for libraries supporting K–12 education.

548 **Guide to summer camps and summer schools, 2006/2007: An objective, comparative reference source for residential summer programs.** 30th ed. Porter Sargent, 2005. ISSN 0072-8705; ISBN 0875581579; 0875581587 (pbk.). $
371.232   GV193

Divided into sections for academic programs, academic programs abroad, academic programs for the learning disabled, academic programs specialized by focus, music and arts programs, special interest (ranging from adventure travel, scuba diving, and wilderness canoeing to chess, community service, and peace studies), travel programs, sports programs, special needs programs (by condition), and religious (by affiliation). Gives descriptions of the programs, enrollment and staffing numbers, fees, and housing information.

549 **Guide to the evaluation of educational experiences in the armed services.** American Council on Education, under contract with the Defense Activity for Non-Traditional Education Support

(DANTES), on behalf of the Defense
Department. 3v. Oryx, 2004. ISBN
1573566071. $$
355   U408.3

Used to evaluate training received in the U.S. armed
service, this volume gives course number, length of
time spent in course, course objectives, and recom-
mends semester hours credit.

**550   Handbook of private schools:
An annual descriptive survey of
independent education.** 86th ed. Porter
Sargent, 1952–. Annual. ISSN 0072-
9884. $
373   L901

Provides information for 1,600 elementary and
secondary schools in the United States. Profiles
include curriculum, student profile, faculty profile,
and financial data. Basic arrangement is by nine
geographical areas, with indexes helping identify
schools with special focus, single sex or coeduca-
tional, and so forth.

**551   Peterson's private secondary schools,
2007.** 27th ed. 1401p. Thomson/
Peterson's, 2006. ISBN 076892152X. $
373.2   L900

Peterson's short term study abroad.
500p. Thomson/Peterson's, 2006. ISBN
0768918952. $
370.116   LB2376

Peterson's study abroad, 2006. 616p.
Thomson/Peterson's, 2006. ISBN
0768918944. $
370.116   LB2376

**Summer opportunities for kids and
teenagers, 2005.** 1590p. Thomson/
Peterson's, 2004. ISBN 0768915473. $
790.19   GV186

Peterson's publishes a host of guides to different
types of educational experiences. Those listed are
but a sampling of some of the most appropriate for
most collections. Buy in accordance with your par-
ticular audience.

**552   Schools abroad of interest to
Americans: A survey of international
primary and preparatory education.**
11th ed. 590p. Porter Sargent, 2006.
Triennial. ISSN 0899-2002; ISBN

9780875581552. $
370.196   L900

Arranged alphabetically by continent, then coun-
try, this directory provides information on 700
elementary and secondary schools. Provides basic
information about curriculum, student life, faculty,
and fees.

553   World of learning. 55th ed. 2v. Allen
and Unwin, 1947–. ISSN 0084-2117.
$$$ www.worldoflearning.com.
060.25   AS2

The standard international directory for the nations
of the world, covering learned societies, research
institutes, libraries, museums and art galleries,
and universities and colleges. Arranged alphabetically by nation and by cultural institution. Includes
address, officers, purpose, foundation date, publications, and so forth, for each institution. A classic
library reference source. Also available as a subscription-based website.

School and College Directories

**554   Accredited institutions of post-
secondary education, 2004–2005:
Includes candidates for accreditation
and accredited programs at other
facilities.** 2004–2005 ed. Kenneth A.
Von Alt, ed. 846p. American Council
on Education, 2005. ISSN 0270-1715;
ISBN 1573566063. $
378.73   L901

Information on accredited degree-granting institutions is readily available, but this volume also
includes non-degree-granting institutions, such as
beauty schools, business schools, and mechanics
institutes.

555   American universities and colleges.
American Council on Education. Walter
de Gruyter, 1928–. Annual. ISSN 0066-
0922. $$
378.73   LA226

Arranged alphabetically by state, and then institu-
tion, this guide gives basic information including
accreditation, calendar, distinctive educational pro-
grams, characteristics of student body and teach-
ing staff. This one-volume work should be in every
library.

556   **Barron's guide to graduate business schools.** 14th ed. Eugene Miler and Neuman F. Pollack, eds. 835p. Barron's, 2005. ISBN 0764131982. $
650.071173   HF1131

After introductory material about choosing and applying to business schools, this guide gives information on more than 600 institutions in the United States and Canada. Basic information is arranged alphabetically by state and includes programs, requirements, admissions, costs, library, research and computer facilities, and information on student body and faculty. Indexed by institution.

557   **Barron's guide to law schools.** 16th ed. 582p. Barron's, 2005. ISSN 1062-2489; ISBN 0764123076. $
340.071173   KF266

After introductory material about choosing and applying to law schools, this guide gives information on approximately 200 law schools in the United States. Basic information is arranged alphabetically by institution and includes programs, calendar, admissions, costs, and information on student body, faculty, and organizations. Indexed by institution.

558   **Barron's guide to medical and dental schools.** 10th ed. Saul Wischnitzer and Edith Wischnitzer, eds. 674p. Barron's, 2003. ISBN 0764120417. $
610   R690

Provides information on medical and dental schools in the United States and Canada and foreign medical schools with significant numbers of American students. Besides factual information about admissions, curriculum, and affiliated hospitals, this volume provides essays about choosing a medical career, preparing for medical school, accessing opportunities for women and minorities, and so forth.

559   **Barron's profiles of American colleges: Description of the colleges.** Barron's. Barron's, 1991–. Biennial. ISSN 1065-5026. $
378.73   L901

Comprehensive guide, with CD-ROM, to accredited four-year colleges in the United States. Profiles include data on admission requirements, application deadlines, housing, campus environment, financial aid, extracurricular activities, and other essential information. Features an "at-a-glance" chart with information on enrollments, costs, and standardized test scores for each college and a comprehensive index of college majors.

560   **Bear's guide to college degrees by mail and Internet: 100 accredited schools that offer associates, bachelor's, master's, doctorates, and law degrees by distance learning.** 10th ed. Mariah Bear. 151p. Ten Speed Press, 2005. ISBN 1580086543. $
374.4025   L901

After some introductory material about the distance-education process and some guides for preparing the admissions application, *Bear's guide* settles into descriptions of 100 programs offering associate's, bachelor's, master's, doctorates, and law degrees that can be completed entirely or almost entirely by distance, in the United States and throughout the English-speaking world. Appendixes cover accreditation concerns and offer a glossary. Additional *Bear's guides* are available.

561   **Black American colleges and universities: Profiles of two year, four year and professional schools.** Levirn Hill, ed. 796p. Gale, 1994. ISBN 081039166X. $
378.73   LC2781

A guide to 118 historically and predominantly black colleges and universities. Entries include contact information, enrollment, admission requirements, accreditation, degrees offered, selectivity, brief history, and descriptions of campus life and activities.

562   **College blue book.** Macmillan Reference USA. ISSN 1082-7064. $$
378.73   L901

Still the standard, the *College blue book* provides data on more than 3,000 two- and four-year institutions in the United States and Canada; 6,500 institutions providing occupational education; more than 4,500 subject areas; and nearly 3,000 distance-learning programs as well as providing background information on this growing field.

563   **The College Board guide to high schools.** 3rd ed. College Entrance Examination Board. 2393p. College Entrance Examination Board, 2001.

ISBN 0874476593. $$

373.73   L901

Guide to private and public schools, giving special emphasis to honors programs and AP offerings.

564 The HEP Higher education directory.
Higher Education Publications, 1983–.
Annual. ISSN 0736-0797. $

378.73   L901

Directory of accredited postsecondary institutions in the United States and its territories. Provides basic information, including addresses, enrollment, Carnegie class, calendar system, and chief officers. Basic arrangement is alphabetical by state, then college. Index of key administrators, accreditation agency, Federal Interagency Committee on Education (FICE) number, and college name.

565 International handbook of universities. 18th ed. International Association of Universities. 3214p. Palgrave Macmillan, 2005. ISBN 1403906882. $$

378   L900

Arranged alphabetically by country, this volume provides information on approximately 17,000 universities, with data provided from the IUA/UNESCO Information Centre on Higher Education database. Information includes contacts, areas of study, and statistics for faculty, students, libraries, and other facilities.

566 Medical school admission requirements (MSAR): The most authoritative guide to all U.S. and Canadian medical schools. Association of American Medical Colleges, 1964–. Annual. ISSN 0066-9423. $

371   R745

Provides address, telephone number, description of the curriculum, entrance requirements, selection factors, financial aid, brief information for minorities, application and acceptance policies for the current first-year class, expenses, and percentages of successful applicants. Introductory chapters discuss a variety of subjects of significance to those considering medical education.

567 Official guide to ABA-approved law schools. Law School Admission Council. Law School Admission Council, 2002–.

Annual. ISSN 1534-3502. $

340.071173   KF273

Most complete information available about the application process at all ABA-approved law schools. Descriptions cover library and physical facilities, program of study and degree requirements, special programs, activities, admissions process and dates, expenses and financial aid, housing, placement, and address and phone number. Data on applicant groups are provided for many programs. Introductory essays discuss the legal profession, becoming a lawyer, applying to law schools, and other topics of interest to aspiring attorneys.

568 Peterson's colleges for students with learning disabilities or ADD. 7th ed. Thomson/Peterson's, 2003–. Irregular. ISSN 1525-3813. $

378   L901

Peterson's 440 colleges for top students, 2007. 26th ed. 536p. Thomson/Peterson's, 2006. ISBN 0768921511. $

378.73   LB2351

Peterson's four-year colleges, 2007. 37th ed. 2922p. Thomson/Peterson's, 2006. ISBN 0768921538. $

378.73; 378.1542029   L901

Peterson's graduate and professional programs. 40th ed. 6v. Thomson/Peterson's, 2006. ISBN 076891907X. $$

378.73   L901

Peterson's graduate schools in the U.S., 2007. 7th ed. 634p. Thomson/Peterson's, 2006. ISBN 0768923034. $

378.1   L901

Peterson's nursing programs, 2007. 12th ed. 633p. Thomson/Peterson's, 2006. ISBN 0768921651. $

610.73   RT79

Peterson's smart choices: Honors programs and colleges. 4th ed. 571p. Thomson/Peterson's, 2005. ISBN 0768921414. $

378.1   LB2364

Peterson's two-year colleges. 37th ed. 712 p. Thomson/Peterson's, 2006. ISBN 0768921546. $

378.154; 378.73; 378.1542029   L901

Peterson's vocational and technical schools—east. 7th ed. 579p. Thomson/Peterson's, 2006. ISBN 0768921392. $
378.73; 374   L903

Peterson's vocational and technical schools—west. 7th ed. 566p. Thomson/Peterson's, 2006. ISBN 0768921406. $
374; 373.246   LC1046

Peterson's publishes a host of guides to different types of educational institutions and experiences. Those listed are but a sampling of some of the most appropriate for most collections. Buy in accordance with your particular audience.

Scholarship and Financial Aid Directories

569   Athletic scholarships: Thousands of grants—and more than $400 million—for college-bound athletes. 4th ed. Andy Clark, Amy Holsappe Clark, and Karen Breslow. 338p. Facts on File, 2000. ISBN 0816043094; 0816043086 (pbk.). $
796   GV351

Listing alphabetically by state, then school, this guide gives contact information on and amounts of financial aid available for both men's and women's sports. Sport-by-sport index and introductory information about the application process.

570   College money handbook. Thomson/Peterson's, 2002–. Annual. ISSN 1541-1591. $
378.3   LB2337

Scholarships, grants and prizes. Thomson/Peterson's, 2002–. Annual. ISSN 1545-0961. $
378.3   LB2337

Peterson's publishes a host of guides to different types of educational institutions and experiences. Those listed are but a sampling of some of the most appropriate for most collections. Buy in accordance with your particular audience.

571   College student's guide to merit and other no-need funding. Reference Service Press, 1998–. Biennial. ISSN 1099-9086. $
378   LB2337

Directory of financial aids for women. Gail Ann Schlachter. Reference Service Press, 1978–. Biennial. ISSN 0732-5215. $
378.3   LB2338

Financial aid for African Americans. Gail Ann Schlachter and R. David Weber. Reference Service Press, 1984–. Biennial. ISSN 0738-4122. $
378   LB2338

Financial aid for Asian Americans. Gail Ann Schlachter. Reference Service Press, 1984–. Biennial. ISSN 0738-4122. $
378   LB2338

Financial aid for Hispanic Americans. Gail Ann Schlachter. Reference Service Press, 1984–. Biennial. ISSN 1099-9078. $
378   LB2338

Financial aid for Native Americans. Gail Ann Schlachter. Reference Service Press, 1984–. Biennial. ISSN 1099-9116. $
378   LB233

Financial aid for the disabled and their families. Gail Ann Schlachter and R. David Weber. Reference Service Press, 1989–. Biennial. ISSN 0898-9222. $
378.3   LB2337.2

Financial aid for veterans, military personnel, and their dependents. Gail Ann Schlachter. Reference Service Press, 1989–. Biennial. ISSN 0896-7792. $
362.8   UB403

The absolute best guides for finding funding for specialized populations. These guides describe scholarships, fellowships, loans, grants, awards, and internships, listing program title, sponsoring organization, geographic location, subject, and filing date in the indexes. Multiple indexes for easy use. Recommended for public and academic libraries of all sizes.

Handbooks, Yearbooks, and Almanacs

572   African American education: A reference handbook. Cynthia L. Jackson. 294p. ABC-CLIO, 2005. ISBN 157607269X. $
379.89   LC2741

Alternative schools: A reference handbook. Brenda Edgerton Conley. 273p. ABC-CLIO, 2002. ISBN 1576074404. $

371.03   LC46

Charter schools: A reference handbook. Danny K. Weil. 211p. ABC-CLIO, 2000. ISBN 1576072452. $

371.01   LB2806

Community colleges: A reference handbook. David L. Levinson. 255p. ABC-CLIO, 2005. ISBN 1576077667. $

378.1   LB2328

Elementary education: A reference handbook. Deborah A. Harmon and Toni Stokes Jones. 261p. ABC-CLIO, 2005. ISBN 1576079422. $

372   LB1555

Historically black colleges and universities: A reference handbook. Cynthia L. Jackson and Eleanor F. Nunn. 253p. ABC-CLIO, 2003. ISBN 1851094229. $

378.73   LC2781

Middle grades education: A reference handbook. Pat Williams Boyd, ed. 465p. ABC-CLIO, 2003. ISBN 1851095101. $

373.236   LB1623

Secondary schools: A reference handbook. Leila E. Villaverde. 255p. ABC-CLIO, 2003. ISBN 1576079813. $

373.73   LA222

Special education: A reference handbook. Arlene Sacks. 235p. ABC-CLIO, 2001. ISBN 1576072746. $

371.9   LC3981

Student rights: A reference handbook. Patricia H. Hinchey. ABC-CLIO, 2001. ISBN 1576072665. $

344.73   KF4150

ABC-CLIO focuses on different areas of education in this handy series of one-volume handbooks that do an excellent job of presenting history, legal and societal influences, and current topics. Most include a glossary; a directory of organizations, associations, and government agencies; and a bibliography of print, nonprint, and online resources.

573 American college regalia: A handbook. Linda Sparks and Bruce Emerton, comps. 380p. Greenwood, 1988. ISBN 0313262667. $

378.73   LB3630

Organized alphabetically by state, then college name, entries provide school nickname, colors, mascot, name of newspaper and yearbook, and the title and text of the alma mater for 469 schools with enrollments of 2,500 or more. Indexed by school name, school colors, and mascot. Dated, but this information isn't handily compiled elsewhere.

574 Baird's manual of American college fraternities. 20th ed. Jack L. Anson and Robert F. Marchesani, eds. Baird's Manual Foundation, 1991. ISBN 0963715909. $

371.85   LJ31

Comprehensive source of information about American college fraternities, sororities, professional fraternities, honor societies, recognition societies, and their campus homes.

575 The educator's desk reference (EDR): A sourcebook of educational information and research. 2nd ed. Melvyn N. Freed, Robert K. Hess, and Joseph M. Ryan. Praeger, 2002. ISBN 1573563595. $

370   LB1028

This useful source for the educator and educational administrator provides a guide to finding additional information needed for the job, descriptions of useful education websites and journals, a guide to publishing in the education field, and an overview of research, sampling, and preparing reports. As the title implies, this belongs not just in the library but on the personal bookshelf of educational administrators.

576 Guide to getting financial aid. College Entrance Examination Board, 2007–. Annual. $

378.73   LB2342

Practical information on financing a college education, including what college costs, how much a family will be expected to pay, tips for obtaining financial aid, sample cases and work sheets, and a glossary of terms. Also provides a detailed listing of expenses and financial aid information for more than 3,100 colleges, universities, and proprietary schools. Previous title was *The college costs and financial aid handbook*.

577 Law of schools, students, and teachers in a nutshell. 3rd ed. Kern Alexander and M. David Alexander. 540p. Thomson/West, 2003. ISBN 0314144617. $

344.73; 347.3047   KF4119

Handy synopsis of U.S. law pertaining to education, including references to court cases. Issues discussed include teacher dismissal, educational taxes, and privacy of student records. Highly recommended for all collections.

578 NEA handbook. National Education Association of the United States. National Education Association of the United States, 1946–. Annual. ISSN 0147-2240. $$

370.6273   L13

Statements on professional practice for K–12 education.

579 Policy documents and reports. 9th ed. American Association of University Professors. 324p. AAUP, 2001. ISBN 0964954818. $

378   LB2331

This source presents the basic principles of higher education in an easy-to-read format.

580 Private colleges and universities. John F. Ohles and Shirley M. Ohles. 2v. Greenwood, 1982. ISSN 0271-9509. $$

378.73   L901

Public colleges and universities. John F. Ohles and Shirley M. Ohles. 1014p. Greenwood, 1986. ISBN 0313232571. $

378.73   L901

These volumes in the Greenwood Encyclopedia of American Institutions series provide histories of all the colleges and universities, private and public, at the time of its writing. Colleges and universities are provided in alphabetical arrangement, but appendixes list them by location and year of founding. Private colleges are listed by religious affiliation.

581 Public schools USA: A comparative guide to school districts. Charles Hampton Harrison. 483p. Peterson's Guides, 1991. ISBN 1560790814. $

317   LA217

Statistical profiles of all K–12 school districts enrolling at least 2,500 students and within twenty-five miles of a major metropolitan area. Appraises school leadership, quality of instruction, and school environment. Charts state-by-state performance.

582 Requirements for certification of teachers, counselors, librarians, administrators for elementary schools and secondary schools. 69th ed. Univ. of Chicago Pr., 1990–. Annual. ISSN 1047-7071. $

370.711   LB1771

The most current and thorough source for initial certification requirements in the public-education field. Arranged by state, then by category. Also provides addresses of state offices of certification.

Statistical Sources

583 Condition of education. National Center for Education Statistics. U.S. Dept. of Education, Office of Educational Research and Improvement, National Center for Education Statistics, 1975–. Annual. ISSN 0098-4752. $

370   L112

Annual data on sixty key education indicators that shed light on the condition of education in the United States. Data include student performance, resources in the schools, student characteristics, special education, and racial and ethnic composition of schools. Introductory text summarizes positive developments and discusses areas of concern. Essential for public and academic collections. Online edition and PDF downloads of publications available at http://nces.ed.gov/programs/coe/.

584 Digest of education statistics. National Center for Education Statistics. U.S. Dept. of Education, 1975–. Annual. ISSN 0502-4102. $ http://nces.ed.gov/programs/digest/.

370   L11

Essential compilation of educational statistics from the U.S. Department of Education, covering preschool through postgraduate, with some information on libraries and educational technology and some international comparisons. Online edition and PDF downloads available.

585   Education state rankings, 2005–2006: Pre K–12 education in the 50 United States. 4th ed. Kathleen O'Leary Morgan and Scott Morgan, eds. Morgan Quitno, 2005. ISBN 0740107364. $
371   LA217

Hundreds of education statistics converted to first to last rankings. Statistics are presented alphabetically by state. Finance, achievement, and safety are among the factors analyzed.

586   National profile of community colleges: Trends and statistics. 4th ed. Kent A. Phillippe and Leila Gonzales Sullivan. Community College Press/American Association of Community Colleges, 2005. ISSN 1083-2882. $
378.73   LB2328

Statistical information presented as charts and graphs on community college enrollment, the social and economic impact of community colleges, staffing and services, and costs and financing. Some charts compare two- and four-year colleges.

587   Projections of educational statistics to 2014. William J. Hussar. http://nces.ed.gov/pubsearch/pubsinfo.asp?pubid=2005074.

The National Center for Education Statistics, part of the Institute of Education Science and the U.S. Department of Education, projects statistics to the future. This is an essential tool for educational planners.

588   State-by-state profiles of community colleges. 6th ed. 132p. Community College Press/American Association of Community Colleges, 2003. ISBN 0871173565. $
378.1543   LB2328

Arranged alphabetically by state, this volume presents basic statistical information about community colleges in that state, demographics, including educational attainment, and workforce information, including highest-paying, fastest-growing, and fastest-declining occupations requiring some college or a community college degree.

Biographical Sources

589   Biographical dictionary of American educators. John F. Ohles, ed. 3v. Greenwood, 1978. ISBN 0837198933. $$
370.973   LA2311

Articles about 1,665 American teachers, reformers, theorists, and administrators, from colonial times to 1976, including many state and regional educators, women, and minorities. Many entries include bibliographical references. Individuals included must have reached the age of sixty, retired, or died by January 1, 1975.

590   A biographical handbook of education: Five hundred contributors to the field. Ann Keith Nauman. 237p. Irvington, 1985. ISBN 0829007229. $
370   LA2301

Short biographical sketches of prominent scholars and educators. Alphabetical entries cite further sources of information.

591   Directory of American scholars. 10th ed. Caryn E. Klebba, ed. 6v. Gale, 2002. ISSN 0070-5101; ISBN 0787650137. $$$
001.202573   LA2311

Profiles more than 30,00 scholars currently active in the United States and Canada. Volumes are by academic discipline: volume 1: history, archaeology, and area studies; volume 2: English, speech, and drama; volume 3: foreign languages, linguistics, and philology; volume 4: philosophy, religion, and law; volume 5: psychology, sociology, and education. Volume 6 provides alphabetical, discipline, institution, and geographic indexes. Alphabetical entries include education, career history, memberships, publications, and contact information.

592   Who's who in American education. Marquis Who's Who, 1989–. Annual. ISSN 1046-7203. $$
370   LA2311

Contains alphabetically arranged sketches describing more than 23,000 prominent contemporary Americans from adult, elementary, secondary, and teacher education. Each entry contains full name, basic biographical information, education, nature of work, areas of practice, professional positions, memberships, awards, publications, research, and home or office address.

8

Words and Language

SCOTT KENNEDY

Encyclopedic reference sources focusing on the study of words and language are still relatively new. However, stylebooks, desk dictionaries, thesauri, and other practical writers' aids have been around for decades and continue to be in great demand: the supply has been robust, and the best products are continually updated and augmented. Principal or unabridged dictionaries, the result of painstaking and time-consuming scholarship, are few and far between in any language; English is fortunate to have several excellent sources to turn to. Though revised on a less-frequent basis than their thematic relatives, they are the sources from which the other products draw their data, and new editions are looked upon as great and significant events. Bilingual foreign-language dictionaries are in a middle ground. The most studied languages—as one might expect—provide the largest market and see the largest number of commercial players. When seeking a small to middle-sized English-based bilingual dictionary for the more popular languages, a visit to the publications lists of Oxford University Press, HarperCollins, and Larousse generally reveals several viable options.

General Sources

Bibliographies and Guides

593 **Linguistics: A guide to the reference literature.** 2nd ed. Anna L. DeMiller. 396p. Libraries Unlimited, 2000. ISBN 1563086190. $

016.41   ZA00; P121

The second edition of this strong annotated guide describes 1,039 linguistics reference sources published between 1957 and 1998. There are three principal divisions to the guide: general sources, including encyclopedias, biographies, core periodicals, periodical indexes and abstracts, and atlases; interdisciplinary and discipline-specific sources, such as anthropological linguistics and sociolinguistics; and sources on individual languages or language groups. The focus is upon publications in English. This new edition also includes websites existing as late as 1999. Author, title, and subject indexes.

Encyclopedias, Companions, and Atlases

594 **The Cambridge encyclopedia of the world's ancient languages.** Roger D. Woodard, ed. 1162p. Cambridge Univ. Pr., 2004. ISBN 0521562562. $$

409   P371

Selected as an outstanding reference title by *Choice,* this encyclopedia of ancient languages contains forty-three chapters prepared by thirty-five internationally recognized scholars. Each chapter describes an individual language or language group; its historical relevance; and its script, grammar, phonology, morphology, syntax, and lexicon and suggests sources for further reading. Indexing by subject, grammar, linguistic law or principle, and language.

595   Compendium of the world's languages.
2nd ed. George L. Campbell. 2v.
Routledge, 2000. ISBN 0415202981. $$
403   P371

This second edition of the *Compendium*, first published in 1992, was designated an outstanding reference title by *Choice*. Considerably expanded and reworked, this new edition follows the general structure of the first. Entries for several hundred languages, ancient and modern, are arranged alphabetically; descriptions range from four to ten pages in length. Each entry provides information about the language's script, phonology, morphology, and syntax; sample texts are provided as is a bibliography. Scholarly yet readable, this is an excellent resource for any library.

596   Dictionary of languages: The definitive reference to more than 400 languages.
Andrew Dalby. 734p. Columbia Univ.
Pr., 2004. ISBN 0231115695 (pbk.). $
403   P371

This work was designated an outstanding reference source by the American Library Association when it first appeared, in 1999. Its aim is to categorize and describe the 400 major languages of the twentieth century, providing a historical, social, and geopolitical context as well as information about the language's origin, dialects, number of speakers, characteristics, and alphabet. Illustrative specimens include anecdotes and literary quotations. Includes maps, extensive cross-references, glossary, and index.

597   Ethnologue: Languages of the world.
15th ed. Raymond G. Gordon Jr. and
Barbara F. Grimes, eds. 1272p. SIL
International, 2005. ISBN 155671159X.
$ www.sil.org/ethnologue/.
410   P371

Produced by the Summer Institute of Linguistics, a Christian organization based in Dallas, *Ethnologue*'s aim is to catalog "all the languages known to be spoken in the world today." Started more than fifty years ago, the fifteenth edition of *Ethnologue*

includes descriptive entries for 6,912 known living languages, organized by content and country. Entries include name of language, alternate names, estimated population of speakers, region where the language is spoken, dialects, availability of dictionaries, and the linguistic classification. A total of 208 color maps display the location and distribution of languages. The free web version provides the same content as the print in an easily searchable database format.

598   International encyclopedia of linguistics. 2nd ed. William Frawley, ed.
4v., 2142p. Oxford Univ. Pr., 2003.
ISBN 0195139771. $$$
410.3   P29

This second edition, appearing ten years after the first, highly acclaimed original, was designated an outstanding title by *Choice*. An excellent purchase for all libraries, it is especially appropriate for those unable to afford the fourteen-volume *Encyclopedia of language and linguistics* (Elsevier, 2006). Arranged alphabetically and signed, the entries in this four-volume set range from broad topical articles, such as "Sociolinguistics," to concepts such as cognitive grammar, to descriptions of individual languages, to biographical essays. With contributions from 600 scholars, this work is authoritative, easy to use, accessible, up-to-date, well illustrated, and expertly indexed.

English Language

Bibliographies and Guides

599   Kister's best dictionaries for adults and young people: A comparative guide. Kenneth F. Kister. 438p. Oryx,
1992. ISBN 0897741919. $
423   PE1611

Kister's pragmatic evaluation and comparison of 300 English-language dictionaries, 132 for adults and 168 for children, is now fourteen years old and, as such, is less relevant today than when it first appeared to such great acclaim. Kister provides citation, purpose, scope, and authority for each source reviewed. In evaluating the merit of each work, he often quotes from relevant reviewer commentary. Of particular note is the sixty-one-page opening section on "Questions and Answers about Dictionaries," which discusses lexicography, how dictionaries are compiled, types of dictionaries, and so forth. There are five appendixes: a list of dictionary and language-related associations; a list of publications that regularly review dictionaries; an annotated bibliography of books and articles on dictionaries; an annotated list of materials dealing with language and linguistics; and a directory of dictionary publishers and distributors. Indexing is by author, title, and subject.

Encyclopedias and Companions

600 Cambridge encyclopedia of the English language. 2nd ed. David Crystal. 499p. Cambridge Univ. Pr., 2003. ISBN 052182348X; 0521530334 (pbk.) $

420   PE1072

Crystal is a widely published authority on the English language. This work is divided into twenty-five chapters covering the history of the English language, English vocabulary, English grammar, spoken and written English, English usage, and learning English. This edition adds a chapter on English online. The attractive layout and generous use of illustrative materials, including photographs, maps, graphs, and diagrams, enhance its readability and appeal for the generalist as well as for students who are beginning their study of languages and linguistics and wish a general overview of the primary discoveries and issues. Appendixes include a glossary of terms, a key to symbols and abbreviations, and references. The bibliography is extensive and up-to-date, and there are indexes for names, items, and topics.

601 Oxford companion to the English language. Tom McArthur, ed. 1184p. Oxford Univ. Pr., 1992. ISBN 019214183X. $

420   PE31

This work aims to provide an "interim report on the nature and use of the English language in our contemporary world." Part dictionary, part usage guide, part style manual, part grammar, this delightful companion serves as an authoritative, comprehensive, and highly readable sourcebook that illustrates—by means of more than 5,000 alphabetical entries prepared by some 100 scholars—the current state of the English language and its many vernaculars.

Dictionaries

PRINCIPAL ENGLISH-LANGUAGE DICTIONARIES

602 Oxford English dictionary. 2nd ed. J. A. Simpson and E. S. C. Weiner. 20v. Oxford Univ. Pr., 1989. ISBN 0198611862. $$$

423   PE1625

Oxford English dictionary: Additions series. J. A. Simpson, E. S. C. Weiner, and Michael Proffitt, eds. 329p. (v. 1); 336p. (v. 2); 406p. (v. 3). Oxford Univ. Pr., 1993–1997. ISBN 0198612923 (v. 1); 0198612990 (v. 2); 0198600275 (v. 3). $$/set; $/v.

423   PE1625

The preeminent dictionary of the English language. A complete revision of the monumental dictionary first published in 1933, the second edition integrates the text of the first edition published in twelve volumes, the four-volume supplement (1972–1986), and approximately 5,000 new words or new senses of existing words. This edition contains general revisions and presents an alphabetical list of words in the English vocabulary from the time of Chaucer to the present day, with all the relevant facts concerning their form, history, pronunciation, and etymology. Also valuable for the 2,400,000 quotations that explain the definitions and provide examples of usage over time. Spellings are British, with American spellings listed as variants. The volumes in the *Additions series* offer definitions of approximately 3,000 new words each, incorporating illustrative quotations from around the world. Smaller libraries may consider the *Shorter Oxford English dictionary on historical principles.*

603 Oxford English dictionary online. Oxford Univ. Pr. www.oed.com.

Designated an outstanding title by *Choice,* the *Oxford English dictionary online* (*OED online*) is, by everyone's estimation, a triumphant success. Comprehensive and up-to-date, this online version of the greatest language reference work every compiled includes the contents of the earlier editions and the *Additions series* and adds new entries and revises older ones at a rate of some 5,000 per year. It is easy to search and a wonderful tool for exploring the richness of English words, their meanings, their usage, their pronunciation, their etymology, and their spellings. The more than 2.5 million quotations are searchable by year as well as by author or source. Tracing the meaning and usage history of more than 600,000 English-language words, the *OED online* is an inexhaustible treasure. The third edition of the *OED* is being developed and will appear in the online version first.

604 **Random House Webster's unabridged dictionary.** 2nd ed. 2230p. Random House Reference, 2001. ISBN 0375425993. $
423   PE1625

The smallest and youngest of the unabridged dictionaries, this revised second edition of *Random House dictionary,* originally published in 1966, keeps the work up-to-date. The second edition contains many new entries and new definitions, bringing the total number of entries to 315,000. Adhering to a descriptive approach, *Random House* emphasizes words in current use, including new scientific and technical terms, idiomatic phrases, slang and colloquialisms, and proper names. Stylistic labels employ such restrictive tags as "slang," "offensive," "vulgar," and "informal," and the most frequently used meaning is given first. Many entries also note the date of a word's first appearance in the language. Features include extensive biographical and geographical entries as well as numerous black-and-white illustrations. Although not as comprehensive as *Webster's third,* this is an easy-to-use and authoritative unabridged dictionary for contemporary English.

605 **Webster's third new international dictionary of the English language.** Rev. ed. Philip Babcock Gove. 2662p. Merriam-Webster, 2002. ISBN 0877792011. $$ http://unabridged .merriamwebster.com.
423   PE1625

The largest and most prestigious dictionary published in the United States, *Webster's third* was first published in 1961, covering English language in use since 1755. An addendum of new words is added to each subsequent printing (e.g., eight pages of new words appeared in the 1966 printing, sixteen pages in 1971, thirty-eight in 1976, forty-eight in 1981, fifty-six in 1988, and so on). *Webster's third* excludes biographical and geographical names and is much less prescriptive regarding usage than *Webster's second.* Clear, accurate definitions are given in historical order. Outstanding for its numerous illustrative quotations, impeccable authority, and etymologies, *Webster's third* is regarded as the most reliable, comprehensive one-volume unabridged dictionary. Libraries owning *Webster's second* will want to retain it for its prescriptive usage

labels and biographical and geographical names. The online version, *Merriam-Webster Unabridged,* incorporates entries from other Merriam-Webster dictionaries and adds audio pronunciations for some 100,000 words as well as additional quotations and extensive cross-references.

DESK DICTIONARIES

606 **The American Heritage dictionary of the English language.** 4th ed. 2112p. Houghton Mifflin, 2000. ISBN 0395825172. $
423   PE1628

The most practical and comprehensive of the desk dictionaries, the *American Heritage* contains more than 200,000 entries; its bright, clear, easy-to-read definitions; numerous illustrations along the sidebars; and extensive illustrative quotations make this one of the most pragmatic tools in the collection. Entries for words, abbreviations, biographical names, and geographic names are interfiled. The fourth edition adds 10,000 new words and 4,000 full-color illustrations and is an excellent selection for the home or the ready-reference collection.

607 **New Oxford American dictionary.** 2nd ed. Erin McKean. 2051p. Oxford Univ. Pr., 2005. ISBN 0195170776. $
423   PE1628

Hardly more than a decade old, this major new dictionary from Oxford is already in its second edition. It is the most up-to-date and perhaps the most pragmatic American English dictionary on the market. Its distinguishing feature is that it provides the most common meaning of each of its 250,000 entry words first. By linking meaning to modern usage norms, it precludes the confusion that exhaustive multiple meanings often engender. The dictionary provides definitions for more than 12,000 proper names and incorporates several handy features that have been dropped from some competitor dictionaries of late, including a history of the language, a grammar usage guide, a punctuation guide, presidents of the United States, the Constitution and Declaration of Independence, chemical elements, weights and measures, and so forth.

608 **Shorter Oxford English dictionary on historical principles.** 5th ed. William R. Trumble, Angus Stevenson, and Lesley Brown, eds. 2v., 3984p. Oxford Univ. Pr., 2002. Thumb indexed.

ISBN 0198604572. $$

423   PE1625

Part abridgement of the *OED* and part entirely new work, this two-volume dictionary (A–M, N–Z) brings the scholarship and authority of the *OED* to the general reader and smaller library. Some 300,000 words are described, defined, and explicated. It prefers British pronunciation and usage but remains international in scope, listing words from all parts of the English-speaking world, including South Africa, Australia, and the Caribbean. Like the *OED* it traces every word back to the first documented use and makes extensive use of quotation to illustrate meaning. It is the most literate and scholarly of the desk dictionaries.

Abbreviations and Acronyms

609   Abbreviations dictionary. 10th ed. Dean Stahl, Karen Kerchelich, and Ralph De Sola. 1529p. CRC Press, 2001. ISBN 0849390036. $

423.1   PE1693

This edition of a standard reference work now boasts 300,000 entries, including abbreviations, acronyms, contractions, geographical equivalents, initials, nicknames, short forms, signs, symbols, and lists of specialized terms. Entries are arranged alphabetically and numerically. Also included are lengthy lists of items frequently abbreviated or standing for something else, such as airlines, airports, eponyms, birthstones, nicknames, signs and symbols, and winds and rains of the world. Although there is some overlap with the *Acronyms, initialisms, and abbreviations dictionary,* larger ready-reference collections will want both.

610   Acronyms, initialisms, and abbreviations dictionary: A guide to acronyms, abbreviations, contractions, alphabetic symbols, and similar condensed appellations. 37th ed. 4v. Thomson Gale, 2007. ISSN 0270-4404; ISBN 078767821X. $$$$

423.1   P365

Now in its thirty-seventh edition and contained in four hefty volumes, this standard Gale annual expands 800,000 entries—acronyms, initialisms, abbreviations, and similar contractions—so that their full context is apparent. Entries are arranged alphabetically and often provide descriptive information, such as language source or sponsoring

organization. With the growing sophistication of Internet searching, and the advent of such free tools as Acronym Finder (www.acronymfinder.com), an annual purchase is no longer requisite.

Crossword Puzzle Dictionaries

611   American Heritage crossword puzzle dictionary. 885p. Houghton Mifflin, 2003. ISBN 0618280537. $

793.73   GV1507

Based upon the *Chambers concise crossword dictionary,* this new iteration offers 230,000 puzzle answers intended to serve both classic and modern crossword puzzle styles. It includes 15,000 proper names and arranges all entries alphabetically by subject. This edition includes numerous reference lists such as poets, countries, and capital cities.

612   The million word crossword dictionary. Stanley Newman and Daniel Stark. 1268p. HarperCollins, 2004. ISBN 0060517565; 0060517573 (pbk.). $

793.73   GV1507

Claiming to be the first all-new crossword puzzle dictionary in twenty years, this source offers more than 1,000,000 answers to 250,000 clues. Included are 3,000 literary works, 5,000 film titles, 20,000 famous people; lists of Oscar winners, Nobel laureates, popes, auto makes; and more than 75,000 fill-in-the-blank clues. This is probably the most complete crossword dictionary on the market.

613   Random House Webster's crossword puzzle dictionary. 4th ed. Stephen Elliot. 870p. Random House, 2006. ISBN 0375426086. $

793.73   GV1507

The fourth edition of this crossword puzzle standard features 700,000 clues and answers and includes thousands of new words from pop culture. All answer words are grouped by their number of letters for easy review. This is the most recently published of the three dictionaries noted here.

Etymology and Word and Phrase Origins

Brewer's dictionary of phrase and fable, see **1405.**

614   Chambers dictionary of etymology. Robert K. Barnhart and Sol Steinmetz.

1284p. Chambers, 1999. ISBN 0550142304. $

422   PE1580

Originally published in 1988 as the *Barnhart dictionary of etymology,* this etymological dictionary focuses on words used in contemporary American English and words of American origin and incorporates current American scholarship. Entries give spelling variations, pronunciation for difficult words, part of speech, definition, and information on word origins. Written for a wide audience, this is a very attractive, readable work suited for most library users.

615   **The Facts on File encyclopedia of word and phrase origins.** 3rd ed. Robert Hendrickson. 822p. Facts on File, 2004. ISBN 0816048134; 0816059926 (pbk.). $

422   PE1689

This popular, highly readable, often humorous, comprehensive etymological dictionary covers some 12,500 words and phrases. Entries range from one line to about a page in length. It includes an alphabetical index and numerous *see* and *see also* references, and authoritative sources are cited. Written in a nonacademic style, this work will appeal to the general reader curious about the origins of words or expressions used in everyday speech.

616   **Oxford dictionary of English etymology.** C. T. Onions et al., eds. 1024p. Clarendon Press, 1992. ISBN 0198611129. $

422   PE1580

This authoritative work by one of the giants of English lexicography is now in its fifth printing. Tracing the history of common English words back to their roots, this etymological dictionary provides the pronunciation, definition, century of origin, and first recording of more than 38,000 English words. It is the most complete and reliable of the etymological dictionaries.

Foreign Words and Phrases

617   **The Facts on File dictionary of foreign words and phrases.** Martin H. Manser and David Pickering. 432p. Facts on File, 2002. ISBN 0816044589; 0816044597 (pbk.). $

422   PE1670

This delightful dictionary defines and describes some 4,000 foreign words and phrases, from *Abacus* to *Zombie*. Entries include everyday expressions, technical terms, and familiar phrases. For each word or phrase, information on the pronunciation in American English, language of origin, and original meaning is provided. Sample quotations illustrate contemporary usage of the word or phrase. An index by language of origin helps one to visualize the variety, richness, and scope of foreign expressions naturalized into modern English usage.

618   **The Oxford dictionary of foreign words and phrases.** Jennifer Speake. 512p. Oxford Univ. Pr., 1997. ISBN 0198631596; 0198610513 (pbk.). $

422.4   PE1582

This dictionary aims to provide a comprehensive record and explanation of foreign expressions currently used by speakers of the English language. Included are more than 8,000 foreign words and phrases from forty different languages. Each entry defines the word or phrase, indicates common pronunciation, provides examples of usage, and indicates its language of origin. Changes in meaning are traced over time. An appendix provides a listing by language and century of origin of all words included.

Handbooks

619   **The writer's market.** F and W, 1922–. ISSN 0084-2729. $

800   PN161

Very useful information for aspiring and established authors, for example, a listing of fifty literary agents or sample rates for advertising, copywriting, and public relations. Chapters include interviews, the business of writing, literary agents, book publishers, Canadian and international book publishers, small presses, consumer magazines, trade journals, contests and awards, a glossary, and indexes. Each listing includes name and address of the publication or company, its editorial needs, and its rate of payment.

Idioms and Usage Dictionaries

620   **American Heritage dictionary of idioms.** Christine Ammer. 729p. Houghton Mifflin, 1997. ISBN

039572774X; 0618249532 (pbk.). $
423.1   PE2839

This authoritative dictionary includes nearly 10,000 figures of speech, phrases, clichés, and colloquialisms; entries are listed alphabetically in boldface. For each entry there is a clear definition, an example of use, and an indication of historical origin. Variant definitions are numbered and ordered by frequency of use.

621   Cambridge guide to English usage.
Pam Peters. 608p. Cambridge Univ. Pr., 2004. ISBN 052162181X. $
423.1   PE1464

This work does not aim to target a particular language community but rather to address the broad international population of English speakers. Drawing upon the latest research, it offers two kinds of entries: specific words and phrases and general topics on language and writing. The 4,000 short entries are arranged in A–Z format and provide authoritative information on spelling, punctuation, grammar, and style. The longer entries offer analytical discussions of contemporary grammar, speech, and language rules. For those interested in the precise and effective use of the English language, this is a superb source.

622   Columbia guide to standard American English. Kenneth G. Wilson. 482p. Columbia Univ. Pr., 1993. ISBN 023106988X; 0231069898 (pbk.). $
428.0097   PE2835

This is a superb addition to our English-language usage tools. Wilson, without being overly prescriptive, still advocates linguistic good manners. He presents 6,500 entries, primarily American expressions, explaining appropriate uses, pointing out some of the finer nuances between words (e.g., *naked* and *nude*), clearly differentiating troublesome pairs (such as *disinterested* and *uninterested*), and generally setting the record straight in a delightful, easy, and familiar style. This guide to current American usage is accessible, authoritative, and eminently pragmatic.

623   Fowler's modern English usage. 3rd ed. H. W. Fowler and R. W. Burchfield, eds. 896p. Oxford Univ. Pr., 2004. ISBN 0198610211. $
428.2   PE1628

The title of the modern version of this usage classic (first published in 1926) appears to morph from year to year; however, the purpose remains pretty much the same. Fowler's original work, revised by Gowers in 1965, has again been revised for a new generation of English speakers. Burchfield, a distinguished lexicographer, has in fact produced a recognizably new work, adding numerous entries that discuss recent foibles and perversities of usage. The new *Fowler's* provides comprehensive and clear advice on the correct use of the complex communication tool we call the English language. Libraries owning the earlier editions will want to obtain this one as well.

624   Garner's modern American usage. 2nd ed. Bryan A. Garner. 879p. Oxford Univ. Pr., 2003. ISBN 0195161912. $
423.1   PE2827

Originally titled *A dictionary of modern American usage,* this guide offers advice on American English usage through individual word entries as well as short essays on usage and style. Each of the 7,000 short entries provides an example of the usage of the word, an illustrative quotation, and an appropriate citation. The short essays address topics such as abbreviations, alliteration, etymology, and pronouns. Sometimes referred to as the American Fowler, Garner addresses common American English usage issues, including grammar, syntax, spelling, word choice, and capitalization. The illustrative quotations are drawn from contemporary sources, such as newspapers and speeches. The first edition of this work was designated an outstanding reference title by both ALA's Reference Sources Committee and *Choice.*

Pronunciation Dictionaries

625   NBC handbook of pronunciation.
4th ed. Eugene Ehrlich, Raymond Hand Jr., and James F. Bender, eds. 539p. HarperPerennial, 1991. ISBN 0062730568. $
423   PE1137

This standard pronunciation reference tool for "general American speech" was originally compiled by James F. Bender in 1943. Listings for each of the 21,000 entries provide spelling and a simplified phonetic respelling to indicate pronunciation. Included are common words frequently mispronounced or difficult to pronounce plus numerous geographical and personal names.

626 Pronouncing dictionary of proper names. 2nd ed. John K. Bollard, ed. 1097p. Omnigraphics, 1998. ISBN 0780800982. $

423   PE1137

This dictionary aims to present the proper pronunciation for more than 23,000 proper names "selected for currency, frequency, or difficulty of pronunciation." Each entry includes an identification or definition of the proper name entry and two representations of its pronunciation: the first is based on a simplified respelling, and the second on the symbols and conventions of the International Phonetic Alphabet. With its focus upon proper names, including company and product names, this is a particularly useful addition to the reference collection.

Rhyming Dictionaries

627 The complete rhyming dictionary: Including the poet's craft book. Clement Wood; rev. by Ronald J. Bogus. 627p. Doubleday, 1991. ISBN 0385413505. $

808.1   PE1519

This expanded and updated edition of the classic 1936 rhyming dictionary is both authoritative and comprehensive. It includes more than 60,000 entries, including one-, two-, and three-syllable rhymes. Within each section, words are arranged by vowel sound and then alphabetically.

628 Oxford rhyming dictionary. Clive Upton and Eben Upton. 659p. Oxford Univ. Pr., 2004. ISBN 0192801155. $

423.1   PE1519

Based upon British English pronunciations, this rhyming dictionary does not require the user to discover rhymes by phonetics or vowel sound; instead, one looks up the word in question in a standard alphabetized index, and one is then referred to the appropriate section, where similar-sounding words are grouped by end, double, and triple syllable rhymes. Some 90,000 words are listed, including proper nouns, names, places, brands, slang words, colloquialisms, and commonly used foreign words.

629 Words to rhyme with: A rhyming dictionary; Including a primer of prosody, a list of more than 80,000

words that rhyme, a glossary defining 9,000 of the more eccentric rhyming words, and a variety of exemplary verses, one of which does not rhyme at all. 3rd ed. Willard R. Espy; updated by Orin Hargraves. 683p. Facts on File, 2006. ISBN 0816063036. $

423.1   PE1519

The third edition of this very popular rhyming dictionary has just appeared. Like its predecessors, entries are arranged by rhyming sound rather than by spelling. The approximately 100,000 words listed are divided into single, double, and triple rhymes. Included is a glossary where 9,000 of the more obscure words listed are defined. A 100-page "Primer of Prosody" introduces poetic techniques, making ample use of sample illustrations. This third edition has added many new trademark words, common acronyms and abbreviations, and new technological terms. Its subtitle notwithstanding, this most comprehensive and playful of the rhyming dictionaries is for all word lovers.

Sign Language Dictionaries

630 The American sign language handshape dictionary. Richard A. Tennant and Marianne Gluszak Brown. 407p. Clerc Books and Gallaudet Univ. Pr., 1998. ISBN 1563680432. $

419   HV2475

As the title implies, this dictionary organizes signs by hand shape rather than by alphabet. Some 1,600 signs are included, those most prevalent in sign conversation. The hand-shape approach allows the learner to progress from sign to word rather than vice versa. Each sign is clearly illustrated and explained in terms of five parameters: configuration, location, movement, orientation, and nonmanual markers. There is a brief history of sign language in the United States that points out the fundamental grammatical differences between American Sign Language and American English. An index of English glosses at the end allows one to progress from English words to the appropriate hand shape, for those who wish to take that route.

631 Gallaudet dictionary of American sign language. 558p. Gallaudet Univ. Pr., 2005. ISBN 1563682826. $

419   HV2475

Produced under the auspices of Gallaudet University, this most recent of the sign dictionaries presents some 3,000 alphabetically arranged illustrated entries. The illustrations are clear and easy to interpret. Listings of English synonyms throughout help to clarify usage. Of particular value, this dictionary comes with a DVD that offers a clear demonstration of each sign. These video illustrations can be played at normal, reduced, or accelerated speed or set to play frame by frame.

632   Random House American Sign Language dictionary. Elaine Costello and Lois Lenderman. 1067p. Random House, 1994. ISBN 0394585801. $
419.03   HV2475

This compendium of more than 5,600 words and signs was prepared by the then director and editor in chief of Gallaudet University Press. Used as the primary communication vehicle by some 500,000 Americans, the American Sign Language is among our most common languages. This dictionary includes a detailed introduction to the language that clearly explains its origins, its use, and its structure. It provides full torso illustrations and includes separate sections on geographical signs and how numbers are signed. This most comprehensive of the signing dictionaries includes more than 3,000 cross-references.

Similes, Metaphors, and Clichés

633   The Facts on File dictionary of clichés. 2nd ed. Christine Ammer. 488p. Facts on File, 2006. ISBN 081606279X. $
423   PE1689

This phrase dictionary traces the origins, explains the meanings, and illustrates the use of some 3,500 clichés commonly found in American English. Originally published in 1999 as *Have a Nice Day—No Problem!* this delightful and engaging work is not as scholarly as Eric Partridge's *Dictionary of clichés* (Routledge, 1978) but is more intriguing and more fun. Entries are arranged alphabetically by the first major word in the phrase; a detailed index and numerous cross-references add to its usefulness.

634   Metaphors dictionary. Elyse Sommer and Dorrie Weiss, eds. 883p. Gale, 1995. ISBN 081039149X. $
081   PE1689

This dictionary collects and elucidates some 6,500 metaphoric comparisons, from ancient times to the present, organized in 500 alphabetically arranged thematic sequences. An introduction discusses the various types of metaphor (mixed, extended, personification, etc.). There are separate listings for the most common metaphors and metaphors from Shakespeare. The work includes author/speaker and subject indexes and a bibliography of sources.

635   Similes dictionary. Elyse Sommer and Mike Sommer, eds. 950p. Gale, 1988. ISBN 0810343614. $
082   PN6084

This dictionary arranges more than 16,000 similes alphabetically under some 500 thematic categories. Authors of similes are given, but not sources. Covering a wide range of materials from classical literature to film and television, this work is a rarity. An author index is included.

Slang and Euphemisms

636   Dictionary of American slang. 3rd ed. Robert L. Chapman, Harold Wentworth, and Barbara Ann Kipfer, eds. 617p. HarperCollins, 1995. ISBN 006270107X. $
427   PE2846

This is a revised edition of a standard work, *Dictionary of American slang* (Crowell, 1975). This version includes many slang expressions from the original work along with hundreds of new words from the intervening years. Notations include pronunciations, appropriate classification and dating labels, illustrative phrases, and numerous cross-references.

637   Encyclopedia of swearing: The social history of oaths, profanity, foul language, and ethnic slurs in the English-speaking world. Geoffrey I. Hughes, ed. 573p. M. E. Sharpe, 2006. ISBN 0765612313. $$
427   PE3724

This is a new work that aims to provide a social history of foul language. Although focusing on American and British English, examples from all corners of the English-speaking world are included. The several hundred topical entries are arranged alphabetically; there are entries on historical periods, specific authors, and ethnic groups; sample topics include "Anatomical Insults," "Anglo-Saxon

Terms," "Whore and Whoreson," and "Zounds!" A chronology, bibliography, and index are provided.

638 **How not to say what you mean: A dictionary of euphemisms.** 4th ed. R. W. Holder. 384p. Oxford Univ. Pr., 2007. ISBN 9780199208395. $
428   PE1449

This is a straightforward A–Z listing and translation of common euphemisms. Entries are accurate and succinct and accompanied by illustrative quotations. A separate thematic index directs the user to appropriate euphemisms for several of the most commonly avoided spades, such as death, obesity, and urination.

639 **The new Partridge dictionary of slang and unconventional English.** 9th ed. Eric Partridge; rev. by Tom Dalzell and Terry Victor. 2v. Routledge, 2006. ISBN 0415212588. $$
427.09   PE3721

Marketed as "the successor to *The dictionary of slang and unconventional English* by Eric Partridge," which first appeared in 1937, this new work contains 65,000 entries, from *A* to *Zymy,* in two volumes. Although this new dictionary focuses upon post–World War II British and American slang, it is truly international in scope, incorporating entries from English-speaking nations around the world. Entries list the term, identify the part of speech, elucidate its meaning, indicate the country of origin, and provide quotations to illustrate usage. Published sources are given for most entries.

640 **NTC's dictionary of American slang and colloquial expressions.** 3rd ed. Richard A. Spears. 560p. NTC, 2000. ISBN 0844204617. $
427.973   PE2846

Spears has been monitoring American slang for almost thirty years. His latest offering is a straightforward dictionary with headwords listed alphabetically. Some 10,000 words and phrases are simply defined and simply illustrated. The value of this dictionary is that it focuses on our contemporary world and includes numerous terms from popular culture, pop technology, the Internet, and Generation X.

641 **Random House historical dictionary of American slang.** 4v. Random House, 1994–. ISBN 0394544277 (v. 1);

067943464X (v. 2). $
427   PE2846

A monumental work, scrupulously researched, this is the first historical dictionary to be devoted exclusively to American slang. Each entry is followed by a succinct definition and illustrative quotations that give life and form to the words. The quotations are drawn from both oral and written tradition and range in time from the seventeenth century to the present day. A complete list of the 8,000 sources cited in the dictionary will appear in a later volume; however, as of early 2008, neither volume 3 (P–S) nor volume 4 (T–Z) have been published. This is a work of such substance that, when completed, it will be received with great acclaim by all libraries.

Thesauri: Synonyms, Antonyms, and Homonyms

642 **Homophones and homographs: An American dictionary.** 4th ed. James B. Hobbs, comp. McFarland, 2006. ISBN 0786424885. $
423   PE2833

New editions of this extraordinary work have been appearing about every six years since 1986, and each new edition is more useful and more comprehensive than the last. Homophones are words that sound alike but have different spellings and meanings (*bear* and *bare*); homographs are spelled the same, but have different meanings and pronounced differently (*bass* and *bass*). This new edition contains 9,040 homophones and 2,133 homographs. The work concludes with an extensive annotated bibliography. This American dictionary recognizes, celebrates, and expertly explicates that rather narrow range of vocabulary that initially confuses and ultimately delights.

643 **Merriam-Webster's dictionary of synonyms: A dictionary of discriminated synonyms with antonyms and analogous and contrasted words.** 909p. Merriam-Webster, 1984. ISBN 0877793417. $
423.1   PE1591

Although not revised since 1968, this remains the preferred synonym dictionary because it quite clearly and expertly explains the differences between similar words. A total of 8,500 main entries are treated. Antonyms and analogous and contrasted words are noted. Included are more than 17,000 illustrative quotes from Merriam-Webster's large citation file. Introductory pages survey the history of synonymy and explore the meanings of *synonym, antonym,* and analogous words. The work is alphabetically arranged with ample cross-references; an appendix provides a listing of all the authors quoted.

644 **Oxford American writer's thesaurus.**
Christine A. Lindberg, comp. 1088p. Oxford Univ. Pr., 2004. ISBN 0195170768. $
423   PE1591

This new thesaurus from Oxford claims to be "the first to be developed by writers for writers." Included are the expected 30,000 synonyms and 10,000 antonyms, but what makes this thesaurus particularly interesting is the use of some 200 word banks, where collections of related nouns are grouped together under broad headings (e.g., under *bread* one might find, not synonyms, but *rye, pita, croissant, baguette,* or other specific examples) and the use of word spectrums, lists of 30 or more related words and phrases that run the incremental gamut from, for example, *begin* to *end* or *lucky* to *unlucky.* Both these features are designed to help writers discover the perfect word for their particular context. Included also are short essays by members of the editorial board; these are brief thought excursions by notable writers on specific words that they find particularly intriguing, puzzling, or disturbing.

645 **Random House Webster's word menu.**
Rev. ed. Stephen Glazier. 800p. Random House, 1998. ISBN 0375700838. $
423   PE1680

The *Word menu* classifies some 65,000 words into relevant categories and subcategories. Though unclassifiable itself, the *Word menu* can be used by anyone seeking to find related terms, equivalent terms, or just interesting words that are common to certain fields of endeavor. You won't find help with pronunciation, etymology, or usage; it is the richness of the relationships presented that is unique. Anyone who crafts with words or who loves words will find this work a longtime companion.

646 **Roget's international thesaurus.** 6th ed. Barbara Ann Kipfer and Robert L. Chapman, eds. 1248p. HarperResource, 2001. ISBN 0060185759. $
423   PE1591

Thoroughly revised and updated, the sixth edition reflects contemporary vocabulary, including slang, technical terms, and idiomatic expressions. This is a true thesaurus, based on the principles of Peter Mark Roget, arranged topically with an alphabetical index to the 330,000 entries. There are 1,075 categories in this edition; within each category, words are grouped by part of speech in the following order: nouns, verb, adjectives, adverbs, prepositions, conjunctions, and interjections. Most important or most commonly used terms are indicated by boldface type. After almost 150 years, Roget's fundamental structure remains as useful as ever.

Style Manuals

647 **American Medical Association manual of style: A guide for authors and editors.** 9th ed. Cheryl Iverson, ed. 660p. Williams and Wilkins, 1998. ISBN 0683402064. $
808   R119

To promote "clarity, organization, and style," the principal American Medical Association publications editors have prepared these guidelines for authors and editors engaged in writing and preparing articles for publication in the medical field. From style, usage, and nomenclature to advice on grammar and nonsexist language, the manual is vigilant in promoting clear, readable, reliable, and authoritative writing. The manual is divided into five sections—preparing an article, style, terminology, measurement and quantification, and technical information—and is completed by a comprehensive index.

648 **The Associated Press stylebook and briefing on media law.** 39th ed. Norm Goldstein, ed. 378p. Basic Books, 2004. ISBN 0465004881. $
808.06607   PN4783

Called the "journalist's bible," the *Associated Press stylebook* is a dictionary, handbook, and style guide, all in one. The 3,000 plus alphabetically arranged entries lay out the Associated Press rules on grammar, spelling, punctuation, and usage. Updated every two years, the guide also provides practical advice on libel, right to privacy, and copyright as well as details about proofreader's marks and the Associated Press Agency.

649 **The bluebook: A uniform system of citation.** 18th ed. 415p. Harvard

Law Review Association, 2005. ISSN
1062-9971. $
348.73; 347.30847   KF245

**Prince's Bieber dictionary of legal
citations: Reference guide for
attorneys, legal secretaries, paralegals,
and law students.** 6th ed. Mary Miles
Prince and Doris M. Bieber. 391p. W. S.
Hein, 2001. ISBN 1575886693. $
349.73   KF246

The *Bluebook* is compiled by the editors of the
Harvard law review in conjunction with the editors of the Columbia law review, the University of
Pennsylvania law review, and the Yale law journal
and serves as the standard source for style formats
in U.S. law journals. *Bieber dictionary* is a companion to the *Bluebook* and is meant to serve as a helpful interpretive tool when using that source. In this
edition of *Bieber,* an exact reproduction of the seventeenth edition of the *Bluebook* is appended.

650   The Chicago manual of style. 15th ed.
956p. Univ. of Chicago Pr., 2003. ISBN
0226104036. $
808   Z253

The fifteenth edition of this standard style manual
reflects the latest technological developments, discusses the new copyright laws, and provides more
sample citations of footnotes and bibliographic
entries and more guidance on the basics of style,
including proper pronunciation, quotation, and
abbreviation. A reference staple since 1906, the
current edition fully incorporates the electronic
revolution while still providing expert advice on
the fundamentals of manuscript preparation, punctuation, and spelling.

651   The Columbia guide to online style.
2nd ed. Janice R. Walker and Todd W.
Tyler. 218p. Columbia Univ. Pr., 2006.
ISBN 0231132107; 0231132115
(pbk.). $
808   PN171

Providing rules for electronic citation, guidelines
for formatting documents for online publication,
and tips on preparing texts electronically for print
publication, the first edition (1998) of the *Columbia
guide* quickly became the definitive guide to online
style.

652   The elements of legal style. Bryan A.
Garner. 268p. Oxford Univ. Pr., 2002.

ISBN 0195141628. $
808   KF250

This is a practical guide for those who engage in
legal writing and editing by one of the foremost
authorities in the field. On the assumption that
"legal writing shouldn't be lethal reading," Garner
provides clear advice on such matters as punctuation, word choice, grammar and syntax, principles
of legal writing, rhetorical figures, exposition and
argument, and speaking. Although the focus is
upon legal writing, anyone interested in strong,
healthy prose will benefit from consulting this
work.

**653   A manual for writers of term papers,
theses, and dissertations.** 6th ed. Kate
L. Turabian; rev. and expanded by John
Grossman and Alice Bennet. 308p. Univ.
of Chicago Pr., 1996. ISBN 0226816265;
0226816273 (pbk.). $
808.02   LB2369

This is the standard guide for students preparing
formal papers, including term papers, theses, and
dissertations, in both scientific and nonscientific
fields. The manual offers practical advice on the
mechanics of writing (e.g., punctuation, spelling,
capitalization) as well as information on such matters as the parts of the paper, preparing and refer-
ring to tables and illustrations, and preparing a
manuscript for submission. The citation practice of
this edition conforms to the *Chicago manual of style*
(14th ed.).

**654   MLA handbook for writers of research
papers.** 6th ed. Joseph Gibaldi. 332p.
Modern Language Association of
America, 2003. ISBN 0873529758;
0873529863 (pbk.). $
808.027   LB2369

Based on the 1951 *Modern Language Association
style sheet* as revised in 1970, 1977, and 1988,
this handbook contains style rules covering such
matters as abbreviations, footnotes, and bibliographies. In addition it discusses the mechanics of
the research paper, including such issues as how to
choose a term-paper topic, how to make effective
use of the library, and the process of composing the
research paper. This edition provides a new chapter
on plagiarism and appropriately devotes consider-
able attention to citing electronic publications.

655   The Oxford style manual. R. M. Ritter,
ed. 1033p. Oxford Univ. Pr., 2003.

ISBN 0198605641. $

808.027   PN147

This seeming newcomer to the community of style is actually a conjoining and reworking of two classic works, the *Oxford dictionary for writers and editors* and *Hart's rules*. Part 1, titled "Oxford Guide to Style," provides guidance on mechanics of writing, such as grammar, punctuation, abbreviation, and quotation, as well as advice on larger matters, for example, copyright and the proper treatment of notes, references, and illustrations. Part 2, titled "Oxford Dictionary for Writers and Editors," provides alphabetical entries on words that frequently prove problematic to writers.

Publication manual of the American Psychological Association, see **220**.

656 **Scientific style and format: The CSE manual for authors, editors, and publishers.** 7th ed. Style manual committee, Council of Science Editors. 658p. Council of Science Editors, 2006. ISBN 097796650X. $

808   T11

Previously published as the *CBE manual* (Council of Biology Editors), the new name and new edition reflect a broader scope. Described as the "authoritative reference for authors, editors, publishers, students, and translators in all areas of science," the manual covers both American and British styles. This edition is divided into four parts: publishing fundamentals, general style conventions, special scientific conventions, and technical elements of publication. There are new chapters on the responsibility of authors, editors, and peer reviewers and on copyright; a thirty-page index completes the book.

Foreign-Language Dictionaries

Bibliographies and Guides

657 **Guide to world language dictionaries.** Arnold Dalby, ed. 470p. Fitzroy Dearborn, 1998. ISBN 1579580696. $$

016.413   P361

Organized in alphabetical order by language, from Abkhaz to Zulu, this guide appraises the general and historical dictionaries of the world's 275 main written languages. Entries provide a description of the language, language family, geographic region

where spoken, number of speakers, and alphabet. For major languages, dictionaries are listed under subheadings that differentiate historical dictionaries, modern standard dictionaries, regional dictionaries, slang dictionaries, and so forth. Also included are a history of dictionaries and an explanation of the International Phonetic Alphabet. The index lists personal names and book titles.

Arabic

658 **Arabic-English lexicon.** Edward William Lane and Stanley Lane-Poole, eds. 2v., 3064p. Islamic Texts Society, 1984. ISBN 0946621039. $$

492.7   PJ6640

This is the standard dictionary for classical Arabic, particularly useful for those studying and translating Islamic texts. The work of nineteenth-century scholars, it carefully references literary sources when known. A CD version is also available.

659 **Elias Modern dictionary: English-Arabic.** 32nd ed. Elias A. Elias and Edward E. Elias. 912p. Elias Modern Publishing House, 1993. ISBN 9775028299 $

492.732   PJ6640

This standard modern Arabic dictionary covers about 48,000 entries. First published in the 1920s, it includes both classical and modern Arabic vocabulary and usage. Entries are arranged alphabetically according to their root, with all derivatives subsumed under the root entry.

Chinese

660 **ABC Chinese-English dictionary.** John DeFrancis, ed. 1439p. Univ. of Hawai'i Pr., 2003. ISBN 082482766X. $

495.1   PL1455

Unlike most Chinese-English dictionaries, which arrange entries by character, this dictionary took advantage of computer technology to list words in strict alphabetical sequence using Pinyin orthography. This updated edition includes more than 196,000 entries and is particularly useful when looking up a term whose pronunciation is known. There are charts to help locate characters whose pronunciation is not known; conversion tables for Pinyin, Wade-Giles, and other orthographies;

and much relevant information about the Chinese language.

661 Oxford Chinese dictionary: English-Chinese, Chinese-English = [Ying Han, Han Ying]. Martin H. Manser, Zhu Yuan, and Wang Liangbi, eds. 1168p. Oxford Univ. Pr., 2003. ISBN 0195964594. $

495.1321   PL1455

This new dictionary of 88,000 words and phrases claims to be up-to-date and practical. It is accompanied by a CD-ROM that is searchable in Chinese or English and offers audio pronunciations in Mandarin Chinese.

662 The Pinyin Chinese-English dictionary. Wu Chingjung, ed. 976p. Commercial Press and Pitman Advanced Pub. Program, 1979. ISBN 0471275573; 0471867969 (pbk.). $$; $ (pbk.)

495.103   PL1455

Compiled by a staff of more than fifty Chinese and English linguistic specialists, the 125,000 entries are divided into single and compound characters. It reflects the straightforward presentation of Chinese characters adopted by the Pinyin system of English transliteration.

French

663 Collins Robert comprehensive French-English, English-French dictionary and thesaurus. 2nd ed. 2v. HarperCollins, 2000. ISBN 000472433X (v. 1); 0004724313 (v. 2). $

443.21   PC2640

This two-volume set is the result of a collaborative effort of the Collins staff with Paul Robert and the Société Nouveau Littré. Designed to meet the needs of students, teachers, businesspeople, and the general reader, it includes about 280,000 headwords and compounds, and approximately the same number of current phrases and idioms, providing 490,000 translations in all.

664 Harrap's new standard French and English dictionary. Rev. ed. R. P. L. Ledésert and Margaret Ledésert; J. E. Mansion, ed. 4v. Harrap, 1972–1980. ISBN 0245509720 (v. 1); 0245509739 (v. 2); 0245518592 (v. 3); 0245518606

(v. 4). $$/set

443.21   PC2640

This is a monumental work, exceptionally thorough, reliable, and accurate—indispensable to student and specialist alike. It is considered by many to be the most comprehensive and authoritative of the French-English bilingual dictionaries.

665 The Oxford-Hachette French dictionary: French-English, English-French. 3rd ed. MarieHélène Corréard and Valerie Grundy, eds. 1986p. Oxford Univ. Pr., 2001. ISBN 0198603630. $

443.21   PC2640

With more than 350,000 entries and 530,000 translations, this is a superb one-volume dictionary of contemporary French. Usage examples are drawn from the everyday world of newspapers and advertising. Also included is a lengthy guide to effective communication in French, including correspondence, telephone, and e-mail.

666 Le Robert and Collins senior. 7th ed. Daphne Day, ed. HarperCollins, 2005. ISBN 9780060748937. $

443.21   PC2640

As the title implies, the HarperCollins *Robert* is a collaboration between HarperCollins and the French publisher Robert. Updated about every two years and with more than 850,000 entries, it aims to provide the most complete coverage of contemporary French of any one-volume language dictionary; included are the latest terms from business, technology, politics, and culture.

German

667 Collins German-English, English-German dictionary: Unabridged. 5th ed. Peter Terrell, ed. 2108p. HarperCollins, 2004. ISBN 0060733810.

433.21   PF3640

Now in its fifth edition, this popular one-volume dictionary aims to be up-to-date with the latest business, political, and technical terms. With its emphasis on colloquial usage, the *Collins* dictionary is particularly useful for language students.

668 Langenscheidt's new Muret-Sanders encyclopedic dictionary of the English and German languages: Based on the

original work. E. Muret and D. Sanders; Otto Springer and Eduard Muret, eds. 2 pts. in 4v. Langenscheidt, 1962–1974. ISBN 3468011245. $$

433.2   PF3640

This is the largest German and English dictionary. The German-English section of some 200,000 headwords is particularly valuable and has useful appendixes, including abbreviations, biographies, a gazetteer, and a table of mathematical equivalents.

669   Oxford-Duden German dictionary: German-English, English-German. 3rd ed. M. Clark, O. Thyen, and Werner Scholze-Stubenrecht, eds. 1751p. Oxford Univ. Pr., 2005. Thumb indexed. ISBN 0198609744. $

433.21   PF3640

The third edition includes 320,000 entries and incorporates the use of color to enhance layout. The addition of usage boxes makes this a practical dictionary for learners; however, British English is favored. Other features include cultural notes and advice on e-mailing and text messaging,

Greek

670   A Greek-English lexicon. 9th ed. Henry George Liddell, Robert Scott, and Henry Stuart Jones, eds. 2042p. Clarendon Press, 1968. ISBN 0198642148.

483   PA445

Greek-English lexicon: A supplement. Rev. ed. Henry George Liddell, Robert Scott, and Henry Stuart Jones, eds. 153p. Clarendon Press, 1968. ISBN 0198642237. $$/set

483   PA445

Frequently reprinted (a 1996 printing is now available with the 1996 revised supplement bound in), this is the standard Greek and English lexicon, covering the language to about AD 600, omitting Patristic and Byzantine Greek.

671   The Oxford dictionary of modern Greek: Greek-English, English-Greek. J. T. Pring, ed. 380p. Clarendon Press and Oxford Univ. Pr., 1986. ISBN 0198641370; 0198641486 (pbk.). $

489.33   PA1139

This is a concise dictionary of about 20,000 words, emphasizing modern conversational and written Greek.

Hebrew

672   The complete Hebrew-English dictionary. R. Alcalay, ed. 2v. Chemed Books/Yedioth Ahronoth, 1996. ISBN 0875592120. $

492.43   PJ4833

Considered by many to be the most complete and authoritative Hebrew-English dictionary, it is particularly useful for textual study.

673   NTC's Hebrew and English dictionary. 671p. Arié Comay and Naomi Tsur. NTC, 2000. ISBN 0658000659. $

492.4   PJ4833

This is a straightforward bilingual dictionary with about 100,000 entries. It focuses on contemporary usage, excluding archaisms and poetic forms, using one-word translations. Included is a review of both English and Hebrew grammar.

674   The Oxford English-Hebrew dictionary. N. S. Doniach and Ahuvia Kahane, eds. 1091p. Oxford Univ. Pr., 1998. ISBN 0198601727. $

492.432   PJ4833

This dictionary has been prepared for those studying the Hebrew of the twentieth century. It contains more than 50,000 entries and includes current idioms and phrases, slang, colloquialisms, and technical terminology.

Italian

675   The Cambridge Italian dictionary. Barbara Reynolds, ed. 2v. Penguin, 1962–1981. ISBN 0521060591. $

453.2   PC1640

This is regarded as an excellent translator's dictionary. It provides word equivalents rather than definitions, emphasizing usage and idiom. It generously includes proper names, Tuscan words, technical terms, and colloquialisms and includes both contemporary and obsolete words, with a good representation of specialties, such as economics, sociology, and philosophy.

676   English-Italian, Italian-English.
2409p. Rizzolli Larousse, 2003.
ISBN 9788852500251. $
453.21   PC1640

This is a comprehensive contemporary Italian dictionary with 900,000 entries, incorporating current technical, political, and business terms.

677   Oxford Paravia il dizionario inglese-italiano, italiano-inglese.
2651p. Oxford Univ. Pr., 2001.
ISBN 0198604378. $
453.21   PC1640

Oxford, in collaboration with one of the foremost publishers in Italy, has produced a new unabridged dictionary of Italian. Included are definitions of more than 700,000 words; illustrative sentences demonstrate contemporary usage, and text boxes explain points of grammar.

Japanese

678   Kenkyusha's new English-Japanese dictionary. 6th ed. Shigeru Takebayashi, ed. 2886p. Kenkyusha, 2002. ISBN 4767410266. $$
495.6321   PL679

Kenkyusha's new Japanese-English dictionary. 5th ed. Watanabe Toshiro and Edmund R. Skrzypczak, eds. 2827p. Kenkyusha, 2003. ISBN 4767420164. $$
495.6321   PL697

The fullest Japanese-English and English-Japanese dictionaries; romanized Japanese entries are alphabetized in transliterated form, followed by Japanese characters and their English equivalents.

Latin

679   Cassell's Latin dictionary: Latin-English, English-Latin. Donald Penistan Simpson, ed. 883p. Cassell and Macmillan, 1977. Thumb indexed. ISBN 0025225804. $
473   PA2365

This is an authoritative and durable favorite, first published in 1854. It has been frequently revised for new generations. The first part is designed to

assist the reader; the second part, the writer of Latin.

680   Oxford Latin dictionary. P. G. W. Glare, ed. 2126p. Clarendon Press, 1996. ISBN 0198642245. $$
473.21   PA2365

This standard work was originally published in eight fascicles between 1968 and 1982; it became available as a single bound volume in 1983. Based on fifty years of scholarship and an entirely fresh reading of original Latin sources, this comprehensive and authoritative dictionary follows the principles of the OED. It covers classical Latin from the earliest recorded words to the end of the second century AD and presents entries for approximately 40,000 words drawn from a collection of more than one million quotations. Included are proper names and major Latin suffixes. Quotes appear chronologically within each entry, showing whenever possible the earliest known instance of a particular usage.

Russian

681   English-Russian, Russian-English dictionary. Rev. ed. Kenneth Katzner. 1098p. Wiley, 1984. ISBN 0471056774; 0471017078 (pbk.). $
491.73   PG2640

This one-volume bilingual dictionary was compiled and published in the United States for American English speakers. There are 26,000 English entries and 40,000 Russian entries. It describes Russian parts of speech, grammar, usage, synonyms, and colloquial and idiomatic expressions and provides a glossary of geographical and personal names.

682   The Oxford Russian dictionary.
3rd ed. Marcus Wheeler et al., eds. 1293p. Oxford Univ. Pr., 2000. ISBN 0198601603. $
491.73   PG2640

This is an excellent, up-to-date, comprehensive one-volume bilingual dictionary compiled and published in the United Kingdom for English speakers. Now in its third edition, it contains 185,000 headwords and phrases, provides numerous illustrative examples, and claims to emphasize "modern idioms and colloquial language." Abbreviations and acronyms are included.

Spanish

683   The American Heritage Spanish dictionary: Spanish/English, Inglés/ Español. 2nd ed. 1103p. Houghton Mifflin, 2001. ISBN 0618127704. $

463.21   PC4640

This bilingual dictionary emphasizes American English and Latin American Spanish. The second edition defines more than 120,000 words and phrases and includes contemporary popular and technical vocabulary. Useful features include grammar and usage notes, irregular verbs, abbreviations, pronunciation guides, and synonyms to distinguish meanings.

684   Collins Spanish dictionary. 8th ed. Jeremy Butterfield, ed. 2141p. HarperCollins, 2005. ISBN 0007183747. $

463.21   PC4640

Now in its eighth edition, this respected unabridged dictionary is updated about every two years to include the latest popular, business, and technical terms. The current edition explores some 230,000 headwords; definitions focus on contemporary usage; more than 1,000 sidebars provide readers with illustrations of life and culture in Spanish-speaking countries.

685   The Oxford Spanish dictionary: Spanish-English/English-Spanish. 3rd ed. Beatriz Galimberti Jarman, Roy Russell, and Carol Styles Carvajal, eds. 1977p. Oxford Univ. Pr., 2003. ISBN 0198604750. $

463.21   PC4640

The Oxford dictionary aims to cover Spanish as it is spoken throughout the entire Spanish-speaking world, and, as such, usage examples explicate meanings for specific geographic locations. There are more than 300,000 main entries, colorized for easy searching. This expanded edition includes the terms from twenty-first-century life and technology; informative cultural notes are interspersed throughout the volume.

9

Science and Technology

JACK O'GORMAN

In *The creation: An appeal to save life on Earth,* renowned biologist E. O. Wilson states that "the ongoing explosive growth of knowledge, especially in the sciences, has resulted in a convergence of disciplines and created the reality, not just the rhetoric, of interdisciplinary studies" (W. W. Norton, 2006, 135). This chapter reflects the interdisciplinary and convergent aspects of scientific and technical information. An example of this is the *Encyclopedia of bioethics.* The history of science is also included for the first time.

Speculating about the future of scientific reference sources, I believe the obvious trend is more materials available online. Access Science is a useful online product and a good example of electronic publishing. Science and technology will continue to be areas where authoritative, accurate information is essential to practitioners and thus will continue to be essential components of reference collections for libraries of all sizes.

Bibliographies and Guides

686 **Information sources in science and technology.** 2nd ed. C. D. Hurt.

450p. Libraries Unlimited, 1997. ISBN 1563085283. $
016.5   Q158.5

Covers information sources in eighteen major scientific disciplines, providing short and descriptive annotations along with recommendations for audience. The second edition is reorganized by broad subject areas; computer science now is included as a separate discipline. Author, title, and subject indexes.

687 **Reference sources in science, engineering, medicine, and agriculture.** H. Robert Malinowsky, ed. 368p. Oryx, 1994. ISBN 0897747429; 0897747453 (pbk.). $; $
026.6   Q158.5

Malinowsky is a well-known author in science and technology literature. This work is a bibliographic guide to 2,400 titles in science, engineering, medicine, and agriculture. Part 1 contains three short chapters on issues facing sci-tech librarians; part 2 is a selective bibliography in each discipline. This book will be useful for librarians doing collection development, library science students, and researchers looking for information in one of these fields.

Databases and Indexes

688 **Applied science and technology abstracts.** H. W. Wilson, 1958–.

ISSN 0003-6986.

620.5   Z7913

This practical database cumulates English-language periodicals in the fields of engineering, science, computers, chemistry, energy, and so forth. Covers 750 journals, some back to 1983. Half of the journals are peer reviewed. Abstracts are written by the H. W. Wilson staff and use subject thesaurus developed by H. W. Wilson. or this product. Includes quality indexing and abstracting and library holdings indicator. Available on CD and online.

689   General science index. H. W. Wilson, 1978–. ISSN 0162-1963.

016.5   Z7401

Cumulative subject index to English-language science journals covering 190 periodicals. Nonspecialist subject headings have cross-references from technical terms or chemical designations to more common terms. Coverage includes atmospheric and earth sciences, conservation, food and nutrition, and biology. Its accessible subject headings, broad coverage, and identification of articles on current topics in widely owned periodicals are helpful for high school and college students and public library patrons alike.

690   NTIS. National Technical Information Service. www.ntis.gov.

The National Technical Information Service (NTIS) is run by the U.S. Department of Commerce and acts as a clearinghouse for U.S.-government-funded research in science, technology, and business. Site contains more than 600,000 products from more than 200 federal agencies. Includes items in the news, new products, and NTIS best sellers. It is part of the NTIS mission to support economic growth by providing access to "information that stimulates innovation and discovery."

691   Web of science. Thomson Scientific. http://isiwebofknowledge.com.

The Web of Science is a broad multidisciplinary database that includes the *Science citation index, Social sciences citation index,* and the *Arts and humanities citation index.* The interface is called the Web of Knowledge, and the database products are called the Web of Science. Other databases include ISI HighlyCited .com, BiologyBrowser, Index to Organism Names, in-cites, and ScienceWatch.com. Coverage includes about 8,700 journals, extending, in some cases, back to 1945. Using the cited reference-search feature, users can move forward toward the research front or

backward to the seminal papers in an area. System is OpenURL link enabled so that users can navigate to full-text articles.

Dictionaries and Encyclopedias

692   AccessScience @ McGraw-Hill: The online encyclopedia of science and technology. McGraw-Hill, 2000–. www.AccessScience.com.

McGraw-Hill concise encyclopedia of science and technology. 5th ed. 2651p. McGraw-Hill, 2005. ISBN 0071429573. $$

503   Q121

McGraw-Hill encyclopedia of science and technology. 10th ed. 20v. McGraw-Hill, 2007. ISBN 9780071441438. $$$$

503   Q121

The choice for these sources is a function of size, activity, and how much demand electronic reference sources have at your library. Smaller libraries may want only the *McGraw-Hill concise encyclopedia of science and technology.* Medium-sized libraries may want to subscribe to AccessScience, which is the electronic version of the *McGraw-Hill encyclopedia of science and technology.* This encyclopedia is indispensable in answering scientific reference questions. In either format, it provides authoritative, clear information without being too technical. McGraw-Hill has also produced other titles based upon this title in chemistry, astronomy, engineering, environmental science, and physics.

693   American Heritage science dictionary. 695p. Houghton Mifflin, 2005. ISBN 0618455043. $

503   Q123

This award winning science dictionary belongs on the reference shelf of small and medium-sized libraries. Defines 8,500 terms and includes "Closer Look" for certain terms as well as biographies and usage definitions.

694   Cool stuff and how it works. Chris Woodford. 256p. Dorling Kindersley, 2005. ISBN 0756614651. $

600   T48

How does a refrigerator work, and how do video games work? This title presents a visual description of the inner workings of modern technology. Appendixes include timelines, groundbreakers, technological terms, and an index.

695   Encyclopedia of science, technology, and ethics. Carl Mitcham, ed. Macmillan Reference USA, 2005. ISBN 0028658310. $$
503   Q175.35

Useful for those studying ethics in a modern context. Introductory essays on topics such as technologies of humility, ethics and technology, and research ethics. Entries range from 200 to 5,000 words and include books, journals, and websites. Access is via the subject index, list of articles, a topical outline, and cross-references. Appendixes include an annotated bibliography, Internet resources, glossary, chronology, and codes of ethics from various engineering and scientific organizations.

696   The handy science answer book. Compiled by the Science and Technology Department of the Carnegie Library of Pittsburgh; James E. Bobick and Naomi E. Balaban, eds. Visible Ink Press, 2003. ISBN 1578591406. $
500   Q173

What is the difference between a rock and a mineral? What color is lightning? Are there any multiple Nobel Prize winners? This source is the perfect place to turn to answer questions like these. Arranged by broad categories like space, energy, the animal world, and health and medicine, it is also fun for browsing. The indexing is even more critical for this work than for other reference books. Other titles include *The handy biology answer book* and *The handy physics answer book.*

697   McGraw-Hill dictionary of scientific and technical terms. 7th ed. 2380p. McGraw-Hill, 2003. ISBN 007042313X. $$
503   Q123

"The language of science and technology is expanding not only in its role in our culture; it is growing in its breadth and depth as scientific disciplines mature and whole new technologies, such as nanotechnology and genomics, arise." This seventh edition contains 110,000 terms, including 3,000 illustrations, and brief biographical listings for about 1,600 scientists. Synonyms, acronyms, and abbreviations are given within definitions as well as in alphabetical sequence as separate entries.

Entries include pronunciation guide, U.S. and SI (metric) units, and an indication of the subject field. Contains appendixes on the SI system, table of the chemical elements, chemical nomenclature, mathematical notation, and other symbols.

698   Oxford dictionary of scientific quotations. W. F. Bynum and Roy Porter. 712p. Oxford Univ. Pr., 2005. ISBN 0198584091. $
503   Q173

Scientists, poets, novelists, and theologians talk about the craft of science. This source is like the *Oxford dictionary of quotations* (Oxford, 2005) with a scientific focus. Entries are alphabetical by author and include birth and death dates. Quotations are in chronological order, with original spelling and capitalization. The most important word of the quotation is indexed with an abbreviation of the author's name and page and quote number. A thoroughly researched and easily browsed volume.

699   Sizes: The illustrated encyclopedia. John Lord. 374p. HarperPerennial, 1995. ISBN 0062732285. $
530.8   QC82

A very readable guide to measurement. Just what is a pennyweight, and what does octane mean, and what is a bond rating? Charts, illustrations, and a clear layout help the reader decipher measuring units. Entries include the origin of a unit, how it is used, and cross-references. Includes graphical conversion charts and a subject index.

700   Van Nostrand's scientific encyclopedia. 9th ed. Glenn D. Considine and Peter H. Kulik. 2v. Wiley-Interscience, 2002. ISBN 0471332305. $$
503   Q121

Van Nostrand's concise encyclopedia of science. Christopher Gordon De Pree and Alan Axelrod. 821p. Wiley, 2003. ISBN 0471363316. $
503   Q121

The ninth edition continues a long tradition as a comprehensive source of scientific and technical information. The authors have endeavored to keep pace with the rapidly expanding basis of scientific knowledge. Entries are arranged alphabetically by subject and cover earth sciences, life sciences, energy and the environment, materials science, physics, chemistry, and mathematics. Valuable for libraries of all sizes. Smaller libraries may wish to consider *Van Nostrand's concise encyclopedia of science* (Wiley, 2003).

Handbooks, Yearbooks, and Almanacs

701 General information concerning patents: A brief introduction to patent matters. U.S. Patent and Trademark Office. www.uspto.gov/web/offices/pac/doc/general/.

A classic booklet, now available as a website. Your library may want to include this site in the catalog to refer patrons to authoritative patent information. Contains general information on the application for and the granting of patents, expressed in non-technical language for the layperson. It is expressly intended for inventors, prospective applicants, and students. This site answers the most commonly asked question about the operations of the U.S. Patent and Trademark Office. Similar to this is *Basic facts about trademarks,* at www.uspto.gov/go/tac/doc/basic/.

702 Science and technology desk reference: 1,700 answers to frequently-asked or difficult-to-answer questions. 2nd ed. The Carnegie Library of Pittsburgh Science and Technology Department staff. 795p. Gale, 1996. OP. ISBN 0810391767. $
  500   Q173

Compiled from other reference sources, this title provides brief entries with some illustrations. It originated in the quick-reference file of the Science and Technology Department in the Carnegie Library in Pittsburgh. A one-volume sci-tech ready-reference tool, useful for smaller libraries without extensive science collections.

Biographical Sources

703 American men and women of science: A biographical directory of today's leaders in physical, biological and related sciences. 22nd ed. 8v. R. R. Bowker, 1906–. ISSN 0000-1287. $$$$
  509.2   Q141

Brief biographical sketches of about 133,000 scientists and engineers active in the United States and Canada. About 4,000 of them are listed for the first time in the twenty-second edition. Arranged alphabetically, with the discipline index using headings from the National Science Foundation's *Standard taxonomy of degree and employment specialties.* Useful in all libraries for biographical information on scientists. Also available online.

704 Concise dictionary of scientific biography. American Council of Learned Societies. 1097p. Scribner, 2000. ISBN 0684806312. $$
  509.2   Q141

The *Dictionary of scientific biography* is a substantial biographical work for American scientists. Libraries owning the 1990 edition may want to keep it in reference for historical questions about scientists. However, smaller libraries may want to consider purchasing the *Concise dictionary of scientific biography* if they do not own the larger work. Covers scientists who died before 1981. "What this one volume abridgement offers is the essential facts from all entries, set forth briefly and clearly and in significant proportion to the scope of the original articles."

705 Notable twentieth-century scientists. Emily J. McMurray, Jane Kelly Kosek, and Roger M. Valade. 4v. Gale Research, 1995. ISBN 0810391813. $$
  509.2   Q141

The four-volume 1995 edition and 1998 supplement present the biographies of 1,600 scientists active in the last century. The international coverage includes the supplement, which has additional coverage of women and minority scientists. Major award winners, discoverers, and well-known figures are included. Entries include basic biographical information, an essay of between 400 and 2,500 words, writings by the biographee, and further readings. Contains subject, field, nationality, and gender indexes.

Astronomy

Dictionaries and Encyclopedias

706 National Geographic encyclopedia of space. Linda K. Glover et al. 400p. National Geographic, 2005. ISBN

0792273192. $
629.4   TL787.5

As one might expect from the National Geographic Society, this source is a colorful and visual representation of space and space travel. Deep space, the solar system, maneuvering in space, human spacecraft, the Earth and space commerce, and military uses of space are chapters in the book. As a special feature, experts on space have written short essays on such topics as a space elevator or a flight to Saturn. Browsable, informative, and fun.

Handbooks, Yearbooks, and Almanacs

707   The astronomical almanac online. U.S. Nautical Almanac Office (USNO) and Her Majesty's Nautical Almanac Office (HMNAO). http://asa.usno.navy.mil/index.html.

This publication, available as a depository item and from the G.P.O., is published jointly by the U.S. Nautical Almanac Office and Her Majesty's Nautical Almanac Office in the United Kingdom. Contains "precise ephemeredes of the Sun, Moon, planets, and satellites, data for eclipses and other astronomical phenomena for a given year, and serves as a world-wide standard for such information." Online version publishes data for several years ahead. In the 2006 edition, models from the International Astronomical Union (IAU) are used.

708   Encyclopedia of the solar system. Paul Weissman, Lucy-Ann McFadden, and Torrence Johnson, eds. 794p. Academic Press, 1998. ISBN 0122268059. $
523.2   QB501

The encyclopedia offers forty thematically organized chapters, further subdivided into authoritative articles written by more than fifty scientists. The work incorporates information gathered through the planetary explorations of *Voyagers 1* and *2, Magellan, Galileo, Pathfinder,* and the Hubble orbiting telescope. Includes references to related studies, a glossary, and clear contents tables for each chapter. Well illustrated with magnificent color images, figures, and tables.

709   Facts on File dictionary of astronomy. 4th ed. Valerie Illingworth, ed. 528p. Facts on File, 2000. ISBN 0816042837. $
520.3   QB14

Clear and concise definitions make this work an excellent choice as a good basic dictionary of astronomy. Numerous cross-references, line drawings, and tables enhance its reference value.

710   Firefly encyclopedia of astronomy. Paul Murdin and Margaret Penston. 472p. Firefly Books, 2004. ISBN 1552977978. $
520   QB14

According to the preface, "There are few sciences where professionals work so closely with amateurs, and this encyclopedia is evidence of that proximity." This work is drawn from professional astronomical literature, but the intended audience is the amateur astronomer, astronomy students, and interested readers. Entries are clearly written and include colorful photos and cross-references but no bibliography. Dictionary-style entries, so no subject index.

711   Night sky atlas. Robin Scagell. 96p. DK, 2004. ISBN 075660284X. $
522   QB63

The audience for this title may be younger children, but adults can also use it to find constellations in the sky. Plastic overlay sheets identify the stars and show the shape of the constellations. As can be expected from DK, colorful photos throughout.

Chemistry

Bibliographies and Guides

712   The literature of chemistry: Recommended titles for undergraduate chemistry library collections. Judith A. Douville. 191p. Association of College and Research Libraries, American Library Association, 2004. ISBN 0838983081. $
016.54   Z675

Useful as a collection development tool for undergraduate chemistry collections. Basic chemistry, applied science, and analytical, inorganic, organic, and biological chemistry are all covered in this guide. Most of the 1,000 entries have annotations.

Dictionaries and Encyclopedias

713   Chemistry: Foundations and applications. J. J. Lagowski. 4v., 1246p.

Macmillan Reference USA, 2004. ISBN 0028657217. $$

540   QD4

This four-volume set was an ALA Outstanding Reference Source in 2005. Its more than 500 articles cover a broad range of chemical topics, including nanochemistry, biochemistry, energy, and medical applications. Terms used in the entries are defined in the margins. Entries are written in nontechnical language, usable by high school or college chemistry students. Charts, photos, bibliographies, and, of course, some equations are included in the entries. A valuable addition to the science collections of libraries of all size.

714   Encyclopedia of the elements: Technical data, history, processing, applications. Per Enghag. 1243p. Wiley-VCH, 2004. ISBN 3527306668. $$

546   QD466

More of a university reference book than that for a public library. Developed under the auspices of the Swedish National Committee for Chemistry and was translated into English. Gives properties, uses, and the environmental impact of the elements, including the transuranic elements. For example, one chapter covers sodium and potassium. It includes facts about them; physical, thermodynamic, and nuclear properties; their discovery; the origin of the names; and uses.

715   The Facts on File dictionary of chemistry. John Daintith. 310p. Facts on File, 2005. ISBN 0816056498. $

540   QD5

Oxford dictionary of chemistry. John Daintith. 602p. Oxford Univ. Pr., 2004. ISBN 0198609183. $

540.3   QD5

Your library needs an inexpensive chemical dictionary. Either of these titles will fit the bill. Because they are inexpensive, why not buy both? *The Facts on File dictionary* contains more than 3,000 entries and includes appendixes. There is a companion volume, *The Facts on File dictionary of organic chemistry*. The *Oxford dictionary* is derived from the *Concise science dictionary*, retitled the *Dictionary of science* for the 1999 edition. Included physical chemical and biochemical terms. All units are expressed in SI (metric) units.

716   McGraw-Hill concise encyclopedia of chemistry. 663p. McGraw-Hill, 2004.

ISBN 0071439536. $

540   QD4

This one-volume paperback makes a good student guide as students study chemistry. Entries are taken from the *McGraw-Hill encyclopedia of science and technology*. Of the 700 alphabetically arranged topics, many have graphics or charts accompanying the text. United States and SI (metric) units are used, and the work includes a subject index.

717   Van Nostrand's encyclopedia of chemistry. 5th ed. Glenn D. Considine. 1831p. Wiley-Interscience, 2005. ISBN 0471615250. $$

540   QD4

The fifth edition of this title represents "75% new text." Entries have increased from about 1,250 to 2,750 topics. Cross-references, graphics, and the index have been redone from the previous edition. The author has focused on the following areas: process, raw materials, metals, energy, waste and pollution, instrumentation chemicals in foods, materials, plans, and biotechnology. The result is a useful source for practicing chemists and chemistry students. *The Facts on File encyclopedia of chemistry* (Facts on File, 2005) might be a better choice for a high school audience.

Handbooks, Yearbooks, and Almanacs

718   CRC handbook of chemistry and physics: A ready-reference book of chemical and physical data. 86th ed. David R. Lide, ed. CRC Press, 1913–. ISSN 0147-6262. $$ www.crcnetbase.com.

540   QD65

The standard source for libraries to provide chemical information. The eighty-sixth edition has a larger size, increasing readability. The scope of this work is "to provide broad coverage of all types of data commonly encountered by physical scientists and engineers, with as much depth as can be accommodated in a one-volume format." The index is particularly useful in getting to the data. Also available online via CRCnetBASE.

719   Lange's handbook of chemistry. 16th ed. Norbert Adolph Lange and J. G. Speight. 1000p. McGraw-Hill, 2005. ISBN 0071432205. $$

540   QD65

General reference source for chemists, chemical engineers, and college students. It is divided into four major sections; inorganic chemistry, organic chemistry, spectroscopy, and general information with conversion tables. Chemical properties like solubility, conductivity, enthalpies, and entropies are presented in the first two sections.

720   The Merck index: An encyclopedia of chemicals, drugs, and biologicals. 14th ed. Maryadele J. O'Neil et al., eds. 1756p. Merck, 2006. ISBN 9780911910001. $$
615   RS51

A source of basic information on chemical substances. Entries give physical properties, chemical structure, and synonyms. To reflect the growing interdependence of chemistry, biology, and medicine, the work incorporates information on biochemistry, pharmacology, toxicology, and agriculture and the environment: "10,250 monographs describe significant chemical, drugs, and biological substances." CAS Registry Numbers have been added with this edition. This standard reference source is also available online. Visit http://scistore.cambridgesoft.com for more information.

721   Sax's dangerous properties of industrial materials. 11th ed. Richard J. Lewis Sr. and N. Irving Sax. 3v. Wiley, 2004. ISBN 0471476625. $$$
604.7   T55.3

Information is the key to safe handling of chemicals. With that in mind, this title is useful in libraries where clientele are handling industrial chemicals. Two-thirds of the almost 26,000 entries were revised for the eleventh edition. Entries include DOT hazard codes, physical properties, toxicity, OSHA and other standards and recommendations, CAS Registry Numbers, safety profiles, NIOSH analytical methods, and cited references. Consensus reports indicate inclusion on EPA extremely hazardous substances list, EPA genetic toxicity program, and community right-to-know lists and other toxicity lists. Volume 1 contains extensive indexing, while data are presented in volumes 2 and 3.

Computer Science

Bibliographies and Guides

722   ACM guide to computing literature and ACM digital. Association for

Computing Machinery. http://portal.acm.org/guide.cfm; Digital Library, www.acm.org/dl/.

"The *Guide* is a collection of bibliographic citations and abstracts of works published by ACM and other publishers." Includes more than 750,000 citations from more than 3,000 publishers, including the Association for Computing Machinery (ACM). Contents include books, articles, conference proceedings, dissertations, theses, and technical reports. "The Digital Library is the full-text repository of papers published by ACM and by other publishers that have co-publishing or co-marketing agreements with ACM." Basic search and browse features are freely available to libraries and their patrons.

Dictionaries and Encyclopedias

723   Berkshire encyclopedia of human-computer interaction. William Sims Bainbridge. 958p. Berkshire, 2004. ISBN 0974309125. $$
004   QA76.9

This new encyclopedia covers an emerging area of computer science. It focuses on applications, approaches, breakthroughs, challenges, interfaces, and social implications of human-computer interaction (HCI). Entries show a multidisciplinary approach to HCI. Special features include sidebars, illustrations, glossary, bibliography of HCI books and journals, and a pop-culture appendix.

724   The computer glossary: The complete illustrated dictionary. 9th ed. Alan Freedman. 465p. AMACOM, 2001. ISBN 0814470947. $
004   QA76.15

This important computer glossary provides plain definitions for complex terms. Now in its ninth edition, it continues to improve. The 6,000 terms and 175 illustrations and photographs define hardware, software, PCs, mainframes, and networking terms. This dictionary will be useful to everyone from computer neophyte to computer guru and should be in every library, large or small.

725   Computer sciences. Roger R. Flynn. 4v. Macmillan, 2002. ISBN 0028655664. $$
004   QA76

The audience for this work is high school students, undergraduates, and general readers. As such, it is well suited for public and academic libraries. Volume 1 discusses the foundations of computer science, while volume 2 covers hardware and software. Volume 3 emphasizes the social dimension, and volume 4 is on networks. Contains 286 entries from 125 contributors coming from universities, industries, and private practice. Graphic design and layout make it easy to read, and frequent photos enliven the text.

726   Dictionary of computer and Internet words: An A to Z guide to hardware, software, and cyberspace.
298p. Houghton Mifflin, 2001. ISBN 0618101373. $
004   QA76.15

Just what is a macro virus, or a GIF, or a kluge? This inexpensive dictionary will be a welcome addition to your library's computer science reference shelf. From the editors of *American Heritage* dictionaries, the definitions are clear and understandable. *See* references refer the reader from acronyms to terms. Contains some illustrations.

727   The dictionary of multimedia: Terms and acronyms. 4th ed. Brad Hansen.
611p. Franklin, Beedle and Associates, 2005. ISBN 1887902732. $
004   QA76.15

Already in its fourth edition, this source has kept up with the rapidly changing terminology of multimedia. JPEG, plug and play, and Chernobyl packets are representative of the more than 5,000 entries. "Programming, graphics, digital publishing, audio, video, telecommunications, networking, and Internet development" terms are defined.

728   Encyclopedia of computer science and technology. Harry Henderson. 450p.
Facts on File, 2003. ISBN 0816043736. $
004   QA76.15

The one- or two-page entries with bibliographies provide an overview of computer science topics. Reading level is appropriate for high school or college computer science students. Cross-references are indicated in the text, with subject index in the back. Entries give the background and usage on topics like Fortran, mathematics of computing, and data abstraction.

729   Encyclopedia of computers and computer history. Raúl Rojas. 2v., 930p. Fitzroy Dearborn, 2001. ISBN

1579582354. $$
004   QA76.15

When studying computer science, it is easy to lose sight of the tremendous growth in such a short time. This source chronicles that growth with entries like BIOS, data encryption, and biographies (John von Neumann, Bill Joy, etc.). Cross-references are in bold, and entries include selected writings for individuals and further readings. Topical bibliography and index included. Very useful for students of computer science.

730   Gale directory of databases. Alan Hedblad and Martha E. Williams.
2v. Thomson Gale, 2004. ISBN 078766409X. $$
004.25   Z699.22

This two-volume guide lists 10,400 databases of all types. Volume 1 covers online products, and volume 2 covers CD-ROMs, DVDs, diskettes, tapes, handheld computers, and batch-access databases. Word-oriented databases, number-oriented databases, image/video, audio files, electronic services, and software databases are included. Typical entries include database name, address, contact, alternative names, content, subject listings, years of availability, updating frequency, and other formats. Alphabetical arrangement with four indexes, including producers, online services, and subject and a master index. Also available as part of Gale's Ready Reference Shelf.

731   A glossary of netspeak and textspeak. David Crystal. 197p. Edinburgh Univ. Pr., 2004. ISBN 0748619828. $
004.678   QA76.15

Just what are the young people saying online and in text messages? This source presents an up-to-date A–Z glossary of netspeak, emoticons, textspeak, and Internet domain names. Netspeak section includes quick cross-references.

732   1001 computer words you need to know. Jerry Pournelle. 240p. Oxford Univ. Pr., 2004. ISBN 0195167759. $
004   QA76.5

This guide is more than just a computer dictionary. It also has short sections on dealing with spam and "the ten best tools and peripherals you didn't know about." Dictionary-style entries with syllables, pronunciations, and usage examples.

733   World of computer science.
Brigham Narins. 2v. Gale, 2002.
ISBN 0787649600. $$
004   QA76.15

Contains almost 800 entries on computer sci-
ence and technology. This source is written for
students in a clear, understandable language.
Entries have an alphabetical arrangement with
cross-references. Bibliography not included at the
end of the entries, but a sources-consulted list at
the back of volume 2 can provide the reader with
further information. Includes chronology and
subject index.

History of Science

Bibliographies and Guides

**734   Reader's guide to the history of
science.** Arne Hessenbruch, ed.
934p. Fitzroy Dearborn, 2000.
ISBN 188496429X. $$
509   Q125

Essays on 500 topics in the history of science.
Entries deal with individuals, disciplines, and
institutions on topics like ecology or materials sciences. Emphasis is on books, not articles,
and coverage of the secondary literature of science. Contains thematic list, booklist, and general
index.

Dictionaries and Encyclopedias

735   A dictionary of the history of science.
Anton Sebastian. 373p. Parthenon,
2001. ISBN 185070418X. $
503   Q124.8

"The aim of this book is to give a brief historical
understanding of the world around us on a scientific basis, so that we can relate to and appreciate
it." Scientific terms from ancient to modern times
are defined. Includes frequent cross-references
from scientists who invented or discovered the
item listed, and from other terms. For instance, the
listing for *continental drift* refers the reader to *tec-
tonic theory.*

**736   Encyclopedia of the Scientific
Revolution: From Copernicus to
Newton.** Wilbur Applebaum. 741p.

Garland, 2000. ISBN 0815315031. $$
509.4   Q125

The social and cultural context of the scientific
revolution is considered in this source. The 441
articles track the progress of Copernicus, Galileo,
Descartes, and their contemporaries. Developments
over the sixteenth and seventeenth centuries in
mathematics, astronomy, medicine, and even
alchemy and astrology are chronicled. An impor-
tant work for libraries of all sizes.

**737   Science and its times: Understanding
the social significance of scientific
discovery.** Neil Schlager and Josh
Lauer, eds. 7v. Gale, 2000/01. ISBN
078763932X. $$$
509   Q175.46

This title divides the history of science into seven
eras, one volume per time period. Ancient and
medieval science, the scientific revolution, and
modern science are all covered. Includes chronologies, overviews, topical essays, biographies,
and bibliographies. Sample topics include fractal
theory, "new math" in the schools, the measure of
time, and crop rotation.

Handbooks, Yearbooks, and Almanacs

**738   History of modern science and mathe-
matics.** Brian S. Baigrie. 4v. Scribner,
2002. ISBN 0684806363. $$
509   Q125

Topical essays on the history of science and math-
ematics with twenty-three disciplines represented.
Well indexed with books and websites in the bibli-
ography. Useful for advanced high school, college
students, and general adult readers.

**739   The Oxford companion to the history
of modern science.** J. L. Heilbron.
941p. Oxford Univ. Pr., 2003. ISBN
0195112296. $$
509   Q125

This guide will help the reader browse through the
history of science. Contains 609 signed entries with
bibliographies, of which about 100 are biographical. Includes some black-and-white photos, ample
cross-references and indexing. For medium-sized
and larger public and academic libraries.

Internet

740 **Extreme searcher's Internet handbook.** 2nd ed. Randolph Hock. 326p. CyberAge Books, 2007. ISBN 9780910965767. $

025.04   ZA4230

OK, so a book about Internet searching is a little bit anachronistic, but this guide can get the casual searcher up to speed and searching like an information scientist. Contains chapters on searching basics, portals, specialized directories, search engines, mailing lists, and creating an Internet reference shelf. Sights and sounds, news, online shopping, and Internet publishing round out this source.

741 **The Internet: A historical encyclopedia.** Hilary W. Poole et. al. 3v. ABC-CLIO, 2005. ISBN 1851096590. $$

004.67   TK5105.875

The three volumes of this source contain biographies, a chronology, and Internet issues. Forty-four leaders are chronicled in the biography section; most are still living and working in their fields. Sample issues include content filtering, the digital divide, and spam. The index is done volume by volume. Because this resource is appropriate for high school, college, and general readers, it will be useful in libraries of all sizes. Also available online.

Earth Sciences

Bibliographies and Guides

742 **Earth science resources in the electronic age.** Judith Bazler. 303p. Greenwood, 2003. ISBN 1573563811. $

025.06   QE48.87

This title presents earth sciences on the Internet. The first chapter covers the basics of finding information. The second one reviews quality websites. Other chapters include supplies, museums and summer programs, and career information in earth sciences. A handy guide.

Dictionaries and Encyclopedias

743 **Encyclopedia of earth and physical sciences.** 13v. Marshall Cavendish,

2005. ISBN 0761475834. $$$

500.2   QE5

High school and public library readers will appreciate the coverage, layout, and design of this resource. Entries include colorful photos, definitions, "core facts," and short bibliographies. Sidebars include "A Closer Look," history of science, looking to the future, and science and society. Volume 13 includes conversion charts, a periodic table, a geologic timeline, Nobel Prize winners, a glossary, and an index.

Databases and Indexes

744 **Georef.** American Geological Institute. www.agiweb.org/georef/.

Produced by the American Geological Institute, this database contains more than 2.5 million citations in the geosciences. Available through a variety of vendors, including CSA, Dialog, EBSCO, OCLC, Ovid, and STN. Essential for geology researchers.

Geology

745 **The Audubon Society field guide to North American rocks and minerals.** Charles W. Chesterman. 850p. Knopf, 1978. ISBN 0394502698. $

552.097   QE443

Although older, this title has retained its usefulness and remained in print. It is designed to be used in three ways: "as a tool for identifying minerals, as a guide to identifying rocks, and as a convenient reference source for mineral collecting in the field." The small format, designed to be carried into the field, contains full-color plates identifying rocks and minerals and text describing color, hardness, occurrence, and other information. Indexes are by name and location.

746 **Encyclopedia of geology.** Richard C. Selley, L. R. M. Cocks, and I. R. Plimer. 5v. Elsevier Academic, 2005. ISBN 0126363803. $$$$

551.03   QE5

This new work is solid, both from the weight of the pages and the depth of scholarship, and forms the cornerstone of a geology reference collection. Other branches of earth sciences are covered by the *Encyclopedia of the solar system, Encyclopedia of ocean sciences, Encyclopedia of atmospheric sciences,* and the

Encyclopedia of soils in the environment, also from the same publisher. Entries, written by experts from around the world, include graphs and maps, some in color; cross-references; and bibliographies. The reading level is that of the professional geologist or geology student. As such, it may be best suited for an academic library supporting a program in geology.

747 Firefly guide to gems. Cally Oldershaw. 224p. Firefly Books, 2003. ISBN 1552978141. $
553.8 QE392

As you might expect, this guide is colorful and full of information on gems. Text describes the gems, and sidebars present technical specs for them. For example, color, refractive index, hardness, luster, and transparency are a few ways that gems are described. Stunning examples of finished and raw gems and diagrams of how they are cut enhance the entries.

748 Volcanoes. Mauro Rosi. 335p. Firefly Books, 2003. ISBN 1552976831. $
551.21 QE522

One hundred well-known active volcanoes are described in this brief yet visually appealing guide. In addition to stunning photos, a description and type of the volcano are given. Latitude, longitude, and altitude are given, in addition to a global view locating the mountain. This inexpensive title is a welcome addition to the reference shelf of libraries of all sizes.

Oceanography

749 Oceans: A visual guide. S. Hutchinson and Lawrence E. Hawkins. 303p. Firefly Books, 2005. ISBN 1554070694. $
551.46 GC21

This reference book could double as a coffee-table book. Full of colorful aquatic photos, it covers all aspects of the oceans, including exploration, ocean life, human impact, and a fact line. Appropriate for libraries both big and small.

Climatology

750 Encyclopedia of global change: Environmental change and human society. Andrew Goudie. 2v. Oxford Univ. Pr., 2002. ISBN 0195108256. $$
363.7 GE149

This well-written encyclopedia can be given to students with confidence that their papers on global warming, acid rain, or the carbon cycle will receive excellent coverage. Global change encompasses climate change, atmospheric changes, land-use changes, marine and artic changes, and changes in natural systems. Both anthropogenic and Earth's natural changes are considered. Charts, graphs, and bibliographies accompany the text, and it includes an index.

751 Encyclopedia of weather and climate. Michael Allaby. 672p. Facts on File, 2002. ISBN 0816040710. $$
551.6 QC854

Encyclopedia of world climatology. John E. Oliver. 854p. Springer, 2005. ISBN 1402032641. $$
551.503 QC854

Audience determines which of these titles your library should own. Academic libraries and larger public libraries should consider the *Encyclopedia of world climatology,* while high school and smaller public libraries should purchase the *Encyclopedia of weather and climate.* The Springer title uses more illustrations and charts and has extensive bibliographies. The Facts on File title does not have further readings. Both cover climate topics but to a varying depth.

Engineering

Bibliographies and Guides

752 Guide to information sources in engineering. Charles R. Lord. 345p. Libraries Unlimited, 2000. ISBN 1563086999. $
025.066 T10.7

A very thorough bibliography on engineering information. Organized by type of material (reference books, trade journals, etc.) and then by discipline. Lists more than 1,600 annotated entries. Features a chapter on how engineers use information.

Dictionaries and Encyclopedias

753 Macmillan encyclopedia of energy. John Zumerchik, ed. 3v., 1270p. Macmillan Reference USA, 2001.

ISBN 0028650212. $$

621.042   TJ163.28

Understanding energy and its environmental and social cost is certainly a twenty-first-century issue. "The encyclopedia includes 253 alphabetically arranged entries written by 170 authors. The text is supplemented with more than 600 photographs, illustrations, sidebars, and maps." Timeline and subject index included in volume 3.

Standards

754 IHS/Global. IHS. http://global.ihs.com.

Occasionally, libraries will receive questions about standards. Only specialized libraries can afford to subscribe to standards from standards-issuing agencies like ASTM, IEEE, or the U.S. government. IHS/Global has 800,000 new and historical standards for sale, with more than one-half million available as PDF files. Libraries can refer patrons to this site or, if they choose, purchase the standards the patron is looking for. According to its website, "IHS/Global is the world's most comprehensive source of hardcopy technical industry standards and government and military standards."

Electronics and Electrical Engineering

755 The ARRL handbook for the radio amateur. American Radio Relay League, 1991–. Annual. ISSN 0890-3565. $

621.3841   TK6550

The bible for hams, this handbook contains a wealth of information on equipment, operations, and regulations. It also explains concepts, from basic theories and principles, and provides instructions for advanced projects. This handbook is also valuable for the amateur who wishes to obtain a license.

756 National electrical code: 2005. 772p. National Fire Protection Association, 2004. ISBN 0877656231. $

621.319   KF5704

The National Fire Protection Association (NFPA) began publishing this well-known title in 1911. The newest edition has been approved as a national standard by the American National Standards Association (ANSI) and supersedes all previous editions. The purpose of the code is the practical

safeguarding of persons and property from hazards arising from the use of electricity. Coverage includes electrical equipment in homes, businesses, public buildings, and other structures, such as mobile homes, recreational vehicles, and industrial substations. Recommended for all libraries.

757 Wiley electrical and electronics engineering dictionary. Steven M. Kaplan. 885p. IEEE Press and Wiley-Interscience, 2004. ISBN 0471402249. $

621.3   TK9

Defines 35,000 electronics and electrical engineering terms. Sponsored by the IEEE, this exhaustive dictionary will support computer scientist, networking professionals, and electrical engineers and students in those fields.

Manufacturing Engineering

758 Dictionary of engineering materials. Harald Keller and Uwe Erb. 1314p. Wiley, 2004. ISBN 0471444367. $$

620.1   TA402

What is it? What is it made of? How is it used? These are question this dictionary can be used to answer. Almost 40,000 terms for both proprietary and common engineering materials are defined. *Rebar* and *laminate* are two terms defined here. Useful in materials science, engineering, and construction.

759 ThomasNet. Thomas Industrial Network. www.thomasnet.com.

Do you remember that big green set that used to take up lots of reference shelf space? This old friend has morphed onto the Web as ThomasNet, as the site says "powered by *Thomas Register* and *Thomas Regional*." Provides names and addresses of manufacturers, producers, importers, and other sources of supply in all lines and in all regions of the United States. Acts as a portal to company websites. Very handy for locating a manufacturing firm.

Vehicle Maintenance and Repair

760 Auto repair reference center. EBSCO. www.ebscohost.com.

Cars have become increasingly complicated, and patrons still rely upon the library for information on automobile home maintenance and repair. The Auto Repair Reference Center is produced in partnership with Point 5 Technologies, the former publisher of the Chilton automotive series, and the Delphi Integrated Service Solutions. It "contains information on most major manufacturers of domestic and imported vehicles, with repair information for most vintage makes starting as far back as 1945." Covers almost 30,000 vehicles, with about 190,000 drawings and step-by-step instructions; 72,000 service bulletins; and 114,000 wiring diagrams. Content in the resource has been created by ASE-certified technicians.

761   NADA official used car guide. National Automobile Dealers Association, 1992–. Quarterly. ISSN 1061-9054. $
629   HD9710

One of several National Automobile Dealers Association (NADA) value guides, this ubiquitous book is prized by car dealers, shoppers, and traders. The latest edition lists seven years of used-car values. Should be in every library serving patrons old enough to drive. Edmunds.com provides detailed reports about car values, so it can function as an alternative or second opinion to the NADA guide.

Life Sciences

Biology

BIBLIOGRAPHIES AND GUIDES

762   Biology resources in the electronic age. Judith Bazler. 286p. Greenwood, 2003. ISBN 1573563803. $
025.06   QH303.5

This resource is a solid guide to the Internet for biologists. Includes resources in biology, biology supplies online, museums, science centers, and summer programs and career information for biology students. Entries describe the site, indicate grade level, state which search engine you will find it through, and give a lengthy review of the site.

763   The Internet for cell and molecular biologists. 2nd ed. Andrea Cabibbo, Richard P. Grant, and Manuela Helmer-Citterich. 452p. Horizon Bioscience, 2004. ISBN 0954523202. $
025.065716   QH585.5

Designed for the practicing biologist and bio students, this guide is more than a traditional guide to the literature. It is intended as a guide to

understanding how to practically use the computer and Internet in a biological framework. In addition to chapters on setting up websites and using e-mail and newsgroups, it also covers protein sequence analysis, protein structure prediction, and genomics and bioinformatics.

764   Using the biological literature: A practical guide. 3rd ed. Diane Schmidt, Elisabeth B. Davis, and Pamela F. Jacobs. 474p. Marcel Dekker, 2002. ISBN 0824706676. $ www.library.uiuc.edu/bix/biologicalliterature/.
570.   QH303.6

A comprehensive bibliography of the biological literature. Includes biochemistry, molecular biology, genetics, microbiology, ecology, evolution, plant biology, anatomy, and zoology. The third edition incorporates more Internet resources. The website allows readers to keep up-to-date.

DATABASES AND INDEXES

765   Biological abstracts. Thomson Scientific. http://scientific.thomson.com/products/ba/.

Biological Abstracts is the major database in the biological sciences. Produced by Thomson Scientific, it is available from multiple vendors. Containing more than 9 million records, it features BIOSIS indexing, MESH medical disease terms, and CAS Registry Numbers. "Essential for all life sciences researchers."

766   Biological and agricultural index. H. W. Wilson, 1964–. ISSN 0006-3177; ISBN 068522239X (1964–1989); 0315564505 (1989–1994). $$$
016.63   S1

A detailed alphabetical subject index to more than 200 English-language periodicals. Useful for periodical articles in the fields of agriculture, biology, microbiology, ecology, veterinary medicine, and related fields. Available on CD and online.

DICTIONARIES AND ENCYCLOPEDIAS

767   The counter-creationism handbook. Mark Isaak. 330p. Greenwood, 2005. ISBN 031333305X. $ www.talkorigins.org/indexcc/.
231.7   BS651

From school boards to the classroom, this issue will not go away any time soon. This source may be used as a counter to pseudoscientific claims that creationists may put forth. Topically organized, with a subject index. A claim is stated and then refuted. For example, "CB360.1: The human appendix is functional, not vestigial." Then the refutation includes reference, related claims, and sources cited. Full references are given in a bibliography near the back of the book. There is also a website for more information.

768   A dictionary of biology. 5th ed. Robert Hine and Elizabeth Martin. 698p. Oxford Univ. Pr., 2004. ISBN 0198609175 (pbk.). $
570   QH302.5

More than 5,000 biological terms are defined in this one-volume paperback, with 300 new entries for this edition. Its low cost; clear, well-written definitions; and occasional illustrations make this source a recommended title for libraries of all sizes.

769   A dictionary of genetics. 7th ed. Robert C. King and William D. Stansfield. 530p. Oxford Univ. Pr., 2006. ISBN 0195143248. $
576.5   QH427

The seventh edition of this dictionary reflects the rapidly growing nature of genetics. Contains almost 7,000 definitions, of which 20 percent are new for this edition. Entries are filed using a letter-by-letter alphabetization. Appendixes include classification, domesticated species, chronology, periodical names and addresses, Internet sites, genome sizes, and gene numbers.

770   Encyclopedia of biodiversity. Simon A. Levin, ed. 5v. Academic Press, 2000. ISBN 0122268652. $$$$
333.95   QH541.15

This important encyclopedia establishes a basis for research in this field. With 313 longer articles, it is well suited for researchers, students, and interested general readers. Entries include outline, glossary, body of the article, charts and graphs, cross-references, and bibliography. Volume 5 contains an extensive subject index, list of contributors, and glossary of key terms.

771   Encyclopedia of bioethics. 3rd ed. Stephen Garrard Post. 5v. Macmillan Reference USA, 2004.

ISBN 0028657748. $$$
174   QH332

This encyclopedia appeared about the time that genes were first being spliced. The first edition was a Dartmouth Award winner. The third edition continues that tradition of excellence. Now in five volumes, it contains 450 entries, of which 110 are new. Emerging topics like cloning, stem cell research, and antiaging interventions are included. Most of the articles have new bibliographies. Volume 5 has appendixes that include primary documents. This source was the inspiration for the *Encyclopedia of science, technology and ethics.* Also available online.

772   Encyclopedia of biology. Don Rittner and Timothy Lee McCabe. 400p. Facts on File, 2004. ISBN 0816048592. $
570   QH309.2

A practical one-volume encyclopedic guide to biology. Audience is high school, undergraduate, and general readers. Contains 800 entries on topics like cloning, Krebs cycle, and the pH scale. Clear illustrations and photos.

773   Encyclopedia of evolution. Mark D. Pagel, ed. 2v., 1205p. Oxford Univ. Pr., 2002. ISBN 0195122003. $$
576.8   QH360.2

This encyclopedia belongs in high school, public, and university libraries of all sizes. With the controversy surrounding the teaching of evolution, an articulate and well-documented encyclopedia can keep the study of evolutionary biology in the curriculum. Offers 365 alphabetically arranged articles from 330 contributors. Bibliographies at the end of the entries and a subject index add to its utility.

774   Encyclopedia of genetics. Eric C. R. Reeve, ed. 952p. Fitzroy Dearborn, 2001. ISBN 1884964346. $$
576; 576.503   QH427

There are two encyclopedias with this title. This one, edited by Reeve, was an ALA Outstanding Reference Source in 2002. The other is a two-volume set from Salem Press published in 1999. "This encyclopedia is a collection of articles of varying length on a great variety of genetic topics, supported by plenty of references that show how each topic built upon many strands of research." Entries include author's name and affiliation, the text, references, and glossary terms. There is a longer glossary in the back near the subject index.

775   Facts on File dictionary of biology.
Robert Hine. 406p. Facts on File, 2005.
ISBN 0816056471. $
570   QH302.5

Contains 3,700 entries that define biological terms.
Appropriate for high school, university, and public libraries. Includes pronunciation guide, cross-
references, and illustrations for important entries.

**776   The Facts on File dictionary of
cell and molecular biology.** Robert
Hine. 248p. Facts on File, 2003. ISBN
0816049122. $
571.6   QH575

Defines terms around cellular structure, metabo-
lism, physiology, and molecular biology. Also contains brief biographic entries for major names in
the field. Includes chronology, bibliography, and
a list of websites. The intended audience is undergraduate biology students and advanced high
school students.

777   Grzimek's animal life encyclopedia.
2nd ed. Bernhard Grzimek, Neil Schlager,
and Donna Olendorf. 17v., 9609p. Gale,
2003. ISBN 0787653624. $$$$
590   QL7

The second edition of this comprehensive animal
encyclopedia was very well received. Entries are
arranged taxonomically and include photographs,
range maps, and detailed information about many
species of animals. Because of the emphasis on
scientific names, it is critical to use the index. An
expensive source for libraries, but necessary for a
life sciences reference collection.

Botany and Agriculture

778   AGRICOLA. National Agricultural
Library, U.S. Dept. of Agriculture.
http://agricola.nal.usda.gov.

AGRICOLA has two collections. One is the catalog of the National Agricultural Library. The other
is a database of agricultural citations that includes
journal articles, book chapters, and other reports.
"The records describe publications and resources
encompassing all aspects of agriculture and allied
disciplines, including animal and veterinary sciences, entomology, plant sciences, forestry, aqua-
culture and fisheries, farming and farming systems,
agricultural economics, extension and education,

food and human nutrition, and earth and environmental sciences." Patrons will have to use their
local libraries to locate the resources.

779   Agricultural statistics. U.S. Department
of Agriculture. U.S. Govt. Print. Off.,
1936–. Annual. ISSN 0082-9714. $
www.usda.gov/nass/pubs/agstats.htm.
630   HD1751

Agricultural statistics is published each year in both
print and web formats. The USDA home page is
also useful to visit (www.usda.gov/wps/portal/usda
home/.) It is a "reference book on agricultural production, supplies, consumption, facilities, costs, and
returns." Tables on national and state data arranged
by topic usually contain annual statistics for three to
ten years and occasionally give foreign data for comparison. Prior to 1936, data were issued as part of
the *United States Department of Agriculture yearbook.*

**780   Encyclopedia of North American
trees.** Sam Benvie. 304p. Firefly Books,
2000. ISBN 1552094081. $
582.16   QK110

Your library needs to have at least one book on
trees, and this is a very good choice. Arranged by
scientific name, entries include color photo, common name, and description of the tree's growth
and habitat. Some trees have sidebars with key features. Appendixes include tree hardiness zones, a
glossary, organizations, and an index.

**781   Magill's encyclopedia of science: Plant
life.** Bryan D. Ness. 4v. Salem Press,
2003. ISBN 1587650843. $$
580   QK7

Just as *Grzimek's animal life encyclopedia* is a schol-
arly source for animals, *Magill's encyclopedia of sci-
ence: Plant life* is an authoritative source for plant
information. Entries include categorization and a
one-sentence summary. Photos, cross-references,
and bibliographies enhance the text. Appendixes
include common to scientific and scientific to com-
mon indexes, a timeline, a glossary, a bibliography,
websites, a categorized index, and a general subject
index. Appropriate for smaller and larger public
and academic libraries.

**782   Pesticides: An international guide to
1,800 pest control chemicals.** George
W. A. Milne. 609p. Ashgate, 2004. ISBN
0566085429. $$
631.8   SB951

A total of 1,800 chemicals, including herbicides, bactericides, insecticides, and fungicides, that have been used in agriculture and public health are chronicled in this source. Entries include chemical name, formula, CAS Registry number, European Inventory of Existing Commercial Chemical Substances (EINECS) number, and monograph number from the thirteenth edition of the *Merck index*. Synonyms, usage, toxicity, physical properties, and manufacturers are listed. Indexes for CAS Registry number, EINECS number, and names and synonyms are included.

783   Plant. Janet Marinelli. 512p. DK, 2005. ISBN 075660589X. $

580   QK45.2

The cover describes this text as "The ultimate visual reference to plants and flowers of the world." About 2,000 various plants are described, with photos. Habitat, origins, and the conditions for survival are covered. Sample topics include classifying plants, redefining the weed, and identifying invasive plants from around the world. Includes glossary, index, and photo credits.

Gardening

784   The American Horticulture Society A–Z encyclopedia of garden plants. Rev. U.S. ed. Christopher Brickell and Judith D. Zuk, eds. 1092p. Dorling Kindersley, 2004. ISBN 0756606160. $

635.9   SB403.2

A comprehensive dictionary describing more than 15,000 ornamental plants, with nearly 6,000 full-color illustrations, prepared by a team of 100 horticultural experts. Alphabetically arranged by botanical name, each description includes information on garden use, cultivation, propagation, pests, and diseases. The most authoritative single-volume reference source available.

785   Hortus third: A concise dictionary of plants cultivated in the United States and Canada. Liberty Hyde Bailey. 1290p. Macmillan, 1976. ISBN 0025054708. $$

582   SB45

The goal of this "Bible of nurserymen" is to provide an inventory of accurately described and named plants of ornamental and economic importance in continental America north of Mexico, including

Puerto Rico and Hawaii. Brief directions for use, propagation, and culture of more than 20,000 species are included. Index lists more than 10,000 common plant names.

786   The National Arboretum book of outstanding garden plants: The authoritative guide to selecting and growing the most beautiful, durable, and care-free garden plants in North America. Jacqueline Hériteau. 292p. Simon and Schuster, 1990. ISBN 0671669575. $

635.9   SB407

A directory of more than 1,700 flowers, herbs, trees, and other proven plants selected by the National Arboretum as the most beautiful, durable, and carefree plants of their kind to grow in North America. Entries include plant description, growing information, gardening tips, and many color photographs. Gardeners will enjoy this title.

787   10,000 garden questions answered by 20 experts. 4th ed. Marjorie J. Dietz, ed. 1057p. Random House Value, 1995. ISBN 051712226X. $

635   SB453

A well-known garden guide, with botanical names revised in the fourth edition to conform to *Hortus third*. Each chapter begins with introductory material in which questions with answers by specialists are grouped by subject (e.g., soils and fertilizers, perennials, houseplants). A good all-purpose garden book, particularly appropriate for public library collections. Indexed.

Paleontology

788   The Dinosaur Society's dinosaur encyclopedia. Don Lessem et al., eds. 533p. Random House, 1993. ISBN 0679417702. $

567.9   QE862

The Dinosaur Society has compiled a compendium of most of the species that have been formally named, including some of doubtful validity. Each entry includes species name, pronunciation, what is known about the dinosaur, and an illustration of its skeleton or a drawing of what it may have looked like. Dinosaurs are arranged alphabetically by genus (e.g., *Tyrannosaurus rex* is listed under

Tyrannosaurus). A period index and geographic indexes are included. There is also a listing of extinct animals that are not considered dinosaurs and, thus, are not included in the main text.

789 **The dinosauria.** 2nd ed. David B Weishampel, Peter Dodson, and Halszka Osmólska. 861p. Univ. of California Pr., 2004. ISBN 0520242092. $

567.9   QE861.4

The second edition reflects the growth in dinosaur scholarship in the more than one decade since the last edition was published. Increased dinosaur diversity, taxonomic revision, and the phylogenetic analysis have all been taken into account. Taxonomic chapters with the cladistic analysis are also provided at www.dinosauria.ucpress.edu. Professional-level text with an eighty-nine-page bibliography.

790 **Dinosaurs: The encyclopedia.** Donald F. Glut. 1088p. McFarland, 1997. ISBN 0899509177. $$

567.9   QE862

Presents the most current information available on dinosaurs and their world. Appeals to both the scholar and the educated lay reader. Describes the origins of dinosaurs and current theories on their extinction; provides thorough systematics, listing all known species as well as doubtful and no longer substantiated genera. Includes more than 1,400 illustrations. Exhaustive index and massive bibliography.

791 **Encyclopedia of dinosaurs.** Phillip J. Currie and Kevin Padlan, eds. 870p. Academic Press, 1997. ISBN 0122268105. $$

567.91   QE862

An award-winning work with alphabetically arranged, signed entries and detailed bibliographies. Added features include a classified list of dinosaur genera, a list of further readings, a glossary, and a chronology of events related to the study of prehistoric life.

792 **Encyclopedia of paleontology.** Ronald Singer, ed. 2v. Fitzroy Dearborn, 1999. ISBN 1884964966. $$

560   QE703

Scholarly and award winning, this important work in paleobiology covers all major fossil groups.

Coverage of prehistoric life in this source encompasses so much more than dinosaurs. For example, there are articles on sponges and bats. A typical entry includes text, charts, graphs, and an extensive bibliography. Includes taxonomic and subject indexes.

Zoology

793 **The encyclopedia of animals: A complete visual guide.** F. Cooke and Jenni Bruce. 608p. Univ. of California Pr., 2004. ISBN 0520244060. $

590   QL7

The University of California Press has produced a visually delightful resource on the animal kingdom. Habitat, classification, color illustrations, conservation status, and other details are presented for birds, mammals, reptiles, amphibians, fish, and invertebrates. Glossary included, and a general index with genus special and common names.

794 **Encyclopedia of cryptozoology: A global guide to hidden animals and their pursuers.** Michael Newton. 584p. McFarland, 2005. ISBN 0786420367. $

001.944   QL88.3

This topic can fire the imagination of young readers and encourage them to learn more about science. It can also lead to the forests of the Pacific Northwest or the highlands of Scotland in search of "monsters." Much that is written about cryptids, or unknown species, is speculative, combining folklore and what little documentation is available. Entries include giant rabbits, relict species, and now-extinct subspecies. There are illustrations but, unfortunately, few photos.

795 **Encyclopedia of the world's zoos.** Catharine E. Bell. 3v., 1577p. Fitzroy Dearborn, 2001. ISBN 1579581749. $$

590   QL76

"The goal of the *Encyclopedia of the world's zoos* is to provide an overview of the institutions, individuals, species, and subjects that have shaped both the historical and modern day zoological community." Entries for zoos include address, description, photos, awards, and bibliography. Species entries describe that species in relation to zoos, including breeding and preservation programs. Subject index provides access to the 400 entries.

796 Oxford dictionary of zoology. Michael Allaby. 597p. Oxford Univ. Pr., 2003. ISBN 019860758X (pbk.). $

590   QL9

Part of the Oxford Paperback Reference series, it contains more than 5,000 zoological terms. A few of the areas covered include animal behavior, ecology, cytology, and zoogeography. Audience is high school, college, and general interested readers.

Mathematics

Bibliographies and Guides

797 Guide to information sources in mathematics and statistics. Martha A. Tucker and Nancy D. Anderson. 348p. Libraries Unlimited, 2004. ISBN 1563087014. $

016.51   QA41.7

Bibliography for math and statistical information, with publication dates of items from the 1800s to the present. Electronic resources and paper resources included. Codes indicate whether items are for undergraduates, and it includes bibliographic, electronic, statistical, and translated resources.

Databases and Indexes

798 MathSciNet. American Mathematical Society. www.ams.org/mathscinet/.

MathSciNet is a subscription-based database sponsored by the American Mathematical Society. Offers "access to a carefully maintained and easily searchable database of reviews, abstracts and bibliographic information for much of the mathematical sciences literature." Grew out of the printed *Mathematical reviews* and contains more than 2 million articles back to 1864. The place for mathematical journal articles.

Dictionaries and Encyclopedias

799 The concise Oxford dictionary of mathematics. 3rd ed. Christopher Clapham. 320p. Oxford Univ. Pr., 2004. ISBN 0198607423. $

510   QA5

This dictionary defines terms that high school and undergraduate mathematics students are likely to encounter in their studies. Alphabetical arrangement, boldface cross-references, formulas and graphs, and seven appendixes.

800 Encyclopedic dictionary of mathematics. 2nd ed. Ito Kiyosi, ed. 2v. MIT Press, 1993. ISBN 0262590204 (pbk.). $$

510   QA5

Under the auspices of the Mathematical Society of Japan, with assistance from the American Mathematical Society, MIT Press has published the most important mathematical encyclopedia in English—a concise, up-to-date collection of significant results in pure and applied mathematics. It has boldface cross-references and a lengthy subject index. Specialized libraries may also want to consider the *Encyclopedia of mathematics,* a 1988 translation of a Soviet mathematical encyclopedia. The publication of the paperback edition should make the *Encyclopedic dictionary of mathematics* more affordable to libraries.

801 The words of mathematics: An etymological dictionary of mathematical terms used in English. Steven Schwartzman. 262p. Mathematical Association of America, 1994. ISBN 0883855119 (pbk.). $

510   QA5

This title is an etymological guide to 1,500 common mathematical terms, defined not in a technical sense but rather by their origins and literal meanings. As mathematics developed, words were borrowed and minted from Greek, Latin, Arabic, and English. Entries are arranged alphabetically, some with line drawings, and include forms and origins of terms with their modern meaning. Useful for students and teachers of mathematics.

Websites

802 Math forum: Internet mathematics library. Drexel Univ. http://mathforum.org/library/.

"The Math Forum's Internet Mathematics Library is an annotated catalog of mathematics and mathematics education websites." Sponsored by Drexel University.

Biographical Sources

803 **Biographies of women mathematicians.** Agnes Scott College. www .agnesscott.edu/Lriddle/women/.

Sponsored by Agnes Scott College, a women's college in Atlanta, this site presents biographies of notable women mathematicians. A useful site that can encourage young women to enter into the mathematics profession.

804 **Notable mathematicians: From ancient times to the present.** Robyn V. Young and Zoran Minderovic. 612p. Gale, 1998. ISBN 0787630713. $$
510   QA28

The key number for this title is 303. That's how many noted mathematicians are featured. Other numbers include 50 women, 15 minority mathematicians, and 30 scholars from outside the United States. Entries range from 450 to 1,000 words and include selected writings and further readings. A timeline, math awards, and a bibliography are also included, along with a subject index.

Physics

Dictionaries and Encyclopedias

805 **AIP physics desk reference.** 3rd ed. E. Richard Cohen, David R. Lide, and George I. Trigg. 888p. Springer, 2003. ISBN 0387989730. $
530   QC61

This source functions as a handy physics handbook. The first edition was originally inspired by the Italian physicist Enrico Fermi. This third edition is "a concise volume of essential definitions, equations, and data from all the fields of physics." Useful in libraries of all sizes.

806 **A dictionary of physics.** 4th ed. Alan Isaacs. 546p. Oxford Univ. Pr., 2000. OP. ISBN 0192801031. $
530   QC5

With more than 3,500 physics terms, like group theory, particle beams, and harmonics, this title is an ideal low-cost, high-value physics dictionary. A practical purchase for libraries big and small.

807 **The Facts on File physics handbook.** 272p. Facts on File, 2006. ISBN 0816058806. $
530   QC61

This one-volume source is useful for students of high school physics. Well laid out, with black-and-white sketches for biographees, and simple diagrams and definitions. Includes chronology, glossary, and formulas.

808 **Macmillan encyclopedia of physics.** John S. Rigden. 4v. Simon and Schuster Macmillan, 1996. ISBN 0028973593. $$$
530   QC5

Building blocks of matter: A supplement to the Macmillan encyclopedia of physics. John S. Rigden. 530p. Macmillan, 2003. ISBN 0028657039. $$
539.7   QC793.2

These 900 articles, arranged alphabetically, offer clear explanations of the concepts, laws, and phenomena of physics as they relate to topics ranging from rainbows to earthquakes. These accessible essays do much to open the world and work of physics to the general reader. Includes numerous biographical entries, tables, and an index. Supplemented by the 2003 publication *Building blocks of matter.*

Weapons and Warfare

809 **Americans at war: Society, culture, and the homefront.** John P. Resch, ed. 4v. Macmillan, 2005. ISBN 002865806X. $$
973   E181

Four volumes covering the impact of war on American society, from the discovery of the New World to the present. The 395 articles were written for undergraduate students and general readers. Primary source documents are included in appendixes. A useful and informative encyclopedia.

810 **PDR guide to terrorism response: A resource for physicians, nurses, emergency medical services, law enforcement, firefighters.** John G. Bartlett and Michael I. Greenberg. 341p. Thomson, 2005. ISBN 156363550X. $
       RA645.5

This new source from Thomson PDR needs to be in the reference collection of libraries of all sizes and, hopefully, read before a disaster occurs. Covers terrorism incident management, signs and symptoms, terrorism agents in brief, and biological and chemical agents. Medical management in explosive, incendiary, and nuclear attacks are also included. Drugs for terrorism response, such as treating anthrax, cholera, or cyanide, are listed. Personally, this is one reference source that I hope gathers dust. However, wide dissemination of this information may save lives.

10 *Health and Medicine*

BARBARA M. BIBEL

Because health-science information changes rapidly, it is important to maintain a current collection. Works listed here were the latest available editions at the time, but many are updated regularly. When ordering, always request the latest edition.

General Sources

Databases and Indexes

811 Consumer health complete. EBSCO. www.ebscohost.com.

This database contains full text for 176 health reference books and encyclopedias as well as 5,781 serials and 4,300 health reports featuring evidence-based information. Medical images and videos are also available. It also has Salud en español for Spanish-language information.

812 Health and wellness resource center. Gale. www.gale.com/HealthRC/.

The Health and Wellness Resource Center provides access to full-text periodical articles, drug information, web links, and Gale reference products, such as *The Gale encyclopedia of medicine.* Optional modules cover alternative medicine and health statistics.

813 PubMed. National Center for Biotechnology Information (NCBI) at the National Library of Medicine. http://pubmed.gov.

PubMed contains approximately 16 million bibliographic citations from clinical and academic biomedical journals. The coverage is international and dates back to the 1950s. Free full text is available for the articles in the PubMedCentral subset. There are links to participating publisher's websites for others. PubMed uses the Medical Subject Headings (MESH) for classification. All articles have English-language abstracts. The My NCBI feature allows users to store searches and articles. The site has links to other NCBI databases as well. This is the world's principal index for the biomedical literature.

Dictionaries and Encyclopedias

814 The American Heritage Stedman's medical dictionary. 2nd ed. 944p. Houghton Mifflin, 2004. ISBN 0618428992. $

610.3   R121

A desk dictionary for lay readers that contains more than 45,000 entries, including biographical information about important scientists and physicians. There are charts and tables of anatomy, weights and measures, and recommended daily allowances of nutrients. Illustrated with line drawings.

815 Cecil textbook of medicine. 22nd ed. Lee Goldman and Dennis Ausiello,

146

eds. 2656p. Saunders, 2003. ISBN
072169652X; 0721696538 (2v. ed.). $$;
$$ (2v. ed.)
616   RC46

**Harrison's principles of internal
medicine.** 16th ed. Dennis L. Kasper
et al. 2607p. McGraw-Hill, 2004.
ISBN 0071402357. $$
616.22   RC46

These standard medical textbooks offer detailed information about the diagnosis and treatment of diseases affecting all the systems of the human body. Although they are technical, lay readers use them, often with a medical dictionary, to learn more about various conditions and illnesses. Libraries should consider purchasing one of these.

**816 Concise dictionary of modern
medicine.** J. C. Segen, comp. and
ed. 1300p. McGraw-Hill, 2005.
ISBN 0838515355. $
610.3   R121

A sourcebook of 20,000 currently used medical expressions, jargon, and technical terms. There are many words here that are not included in more traditional medical dictionaries. Some abbreviations are defined.

**817 Dorland's illustrated medical
dictionary.** 30th ed. W. A. Newman
Dorland. 1940p. Saunders, 2003. ISBN
0721601464. $
610.3   R121

The new edition of *Dorland's illustrated,* for professional and educated lay users, contains 125,000 entries, and 3,000 are new. Some 800 terms are related to complementary and alternative medicine. Improvements include full-color, three-dimensional anatomy drawings as well as color photographs and diagnostic and pathologic images, a better typeface. Appendixes include medical abbreviations; weight, measure, dosage, and temperature conversion; and reference laboratory values. This is the standard professional source and the authority for the Medical Subject Headings (MESH).

**818 Encyclopedia of medical devices and
instrumentation.** 2nd ed. John G.
Webster, ed. in chief. 6v. Wiley, 2006.
ISBN 0471263583. $$$$
610.28   R856

A unique encyclopedia that explains the structure and function of medical instruments and devices. It contains articles on everything from dialysis machines to CAT and MRI scanners. The language is somewhat technical but accessible to most readers.

819 Gale encyclopedia of medicine. 3rd ed.
Jacqueline L. Longe, ed. 5v. Gale, 2006.
ISBN 1414403682. $$$
610.3   RC41

Compiled by experienced medical writers, this encyclopedia has become a mainstay of the medical reference collection. It describes the most common medical disorders, conditions, tests, and treatments with both authority and thoroughness. The text and its language are aimed at the general reader, and the author provides definitions and illustrations to enhance comprehension. This fills the gap that exists between single-volume medical encyclopedias and medical textbooks.

**820 International dictionary of medicine
and biology.** E. Lovell Becker, Sidney I.
Landau, Alexandre Manuila, eds.
3v., 3200p. Wiley, 1986. ISBN
047101849X. $$
610.3   R121

An unabridged dictionary of the biomedical sciences containing more than 150,000 terms and 159,000 definitions. It is written for professionals, but informed lay readers will be able to use it.

**821 Melloni's illustrated medical
dictionary.** 4th ed. Ida G. Dox et al.,
eds. 778p. Taylor and Francis, 2001.
ISBN 185070094X. $
610.3   R121

The outstanding feature of this dictionary is the use of illustration as an integral part of the definitions. There are more than 3,000 high-quality line drawings sharing equal space with the text of the 30,000 entries. The definitions are written for lay readers. The new edition has increased coverage of medical abbreviations.

**822 Mosby's dictionary of medicine,
nursing and health professions.** 7th ed.
Tamara Myers. 2304p. Elsevier, 2006.
ISBN 9780323035620. $
610.3   R121

This dictionary for paraprofessional and lay readers has been updated with the addition of 56,000 new entries, 2,450 full-color illustrations, and many tables. The appendixes contain diagnostic and procedural information, abbreviations, and anatomical classifications. A CD-ROM includes a spell-checker, audio pronunciations, and an English-Spanish phrase translator. An excellent general medical dictionary.

823   The Oxford dictionary of sports science and medicine. 3rd ed. Michael Kent, ed. 612p. Oxford Univ. Pr., 2006. ISBN 9780199210893 (pbk.). $
617.1   RC1206

Growing interest in sports and fitness makes this dictionary timely as well as useful. It contains 8,000 entries with brief definitions of terms used in sports science and medicine, reflecting the new technologies used in sports training and the importance of sports nutrition.

824   The Oxford illustrated companion to medicine. Stephen Lock et al., eds. 924p. Oxford Univ. Pr., 2001. ISBN 0192629506. $
610.3   R121

The new edition of this classic reference has been reduced to one volume and written for anyone with an interest in medicine. It is a cross between a dictionary and a one-volume encyclopedia, with articles on medical fields and broad topics, such as "Art and Medicine," as well as 500 illustrations. Libraries owning the old two-volume edition will want to retain it because it contains useful material not found in the new version. The new edition also has material not in the old one.

825   Stedman's abbreviations, acronyms, and symbols. 883p. Williams and Wilkins, 2005. ISBN 0781760518. $
610.14   R123

Definitions of more than 75,000 terms and symbols. There is an alphabetical section for letter abbreviations and a separate visual section for symbols organized by type: arrow, statistical symbols, genetic symbols, Greek alphabet, and so forth. Slang terms are included.

826   Stedman's medical dictionary. 28th ed. Thomas Lathrop Stedman. 2100p. Williams and Wilkins, 2005. ISBN 9780781733908. $
610.3   R121

A standard dictionary for health professionals. The new edition has 107,000 entries and full-color illustrations; 5,000 entries are new. The definitions are concise and accurate. A total of 45 consultants from various medical specialties reviewed the text.

Directories

827   AHA guide to the healthcare field. American Hospital Association, 1945–. Annual. ISSN 0094-8969. $$
362.1   RA977

Geographical listing of accredited hospitals; health-care systems, networks, and alliances; health-care agencies, organizations, and other providers; and American military hospitals. Codes designate available services and facilities. A companion volume, *Hospital statistics* (annual), supplies data on utilization, expenses, revenues, and personnel. Available free on MedlinePlus.

828   American dental directory. American Dental Association. http://medlineplus .gov.

No longer available in print, but there is free access via MedlinePlus. It lists licensed dentists and dental specialists in the United States. Searchable geographically and by name.

829   Directory of physicians in the United States. 39th ed. 4v. American Medical Association, 2006. ISBN 1579476325. $$$
610.69   R712

Licensed physicians and doctors of osteopathy who are members of the American Medical Association. There are alphabetical and geographic indexes. Numerical codes indicate medical schools attended, residencies, and type of practice for each physician. More than 875,000 physicians are included. Also available as a CD-ROM.

830   National directory of chiropractic. National Directory of Chiropractic. Free. www.chirodirectory.com.
617.58   RZ233

Lists more than 65,000 licensed chiropractors in the United States. Searchable by name and geographic location. MedlinePlus also has a directory of chiropractors from the American Chiropractic Association.

831 The official ABMS directory of board certified medical specialists. 39th ed. 4v. Saunders, 2007. ISBN 9781416037385. $$$

610.25   R712

Information about board-certified medical specialists is organized by specialty and geographically within each specialty. There are instructions for use and a list of abbreviations in each volume. Lists of state medical boards, certifying boards, tables of numbers of specialists, and a master name index are included. More than 600,000 profiles of board-certified medical specialists are included.

Handbooks, Statistics, and Diagnosis

832 The American College of Physicians complete home medical guide. 2nd. ed. David R. Goldmann, ed. 1104p. DK, 2003. ISBN 0788496739. $

616   RC81

This lavishly illustrated lay medical guide offers current basic medical information. It uses flowcharts to guide users through self-diagnosis and treatment decisions. A first-aid guide, glossary, list of websites, and index complete the work. A good source for unsophisticated readers.

833 The American Medical Association complete medical encyclopedia. Jerrold B. Leikin and Martin S. Lipsky eds. 1408p. Random House, 2003. ISBN 0812991001. $

610   RC81

This single-volume encyclopedia includes symptom charts, an anatomy atlas, an essay on twenty-first-century medicine, and an alphabetical encyclopedia with more than 5,000 entries and 1,750 illustrations. It also has sample legal forms for health-care advance directives, a list of self-help organizations, and information about the Health Insurance Portability and Accountability Act (HIPAA).

834 Conn's current therapy. Robert E. Rakel, ed. Saunders, 1982–. Annual. ISSN 8755-8823. $

615.5   RM101

Each year this book provides an overview of the latest developments in treating diseases and chronic conditions. It is written for physicians, but lay readers will also find it useful.

835 Current medical diagnosis and treatment. 45th ed. Lawrence M. Tierney et al., eds. 1884p. McGraw-Hill, 1961–. Annual. ISSN 0092-8682. $

616.075   RC71

Current obstetric and gynecological diagnosis and treatment. 9th ed. Alan H. DeCherney and Lauren Nathan. 1230p. McGraw-Hill, 2002. ISBN 0838514014. $

618   RG101

Current pediatric diagnosis and treatment. 17th ed. William W. Hay. 1490p. McGraw-Hill, 2004. ISBN 0071429603. $

618.92   RJ50

Current surgical diagnosis and treatment. 12th ed. Gerard M. Doherty and Lawrence W. Way. 1426p. McGraw-Hill, 2005. ISBN 007142315X. $

617   RD31

The Current Diagnosis and Treatment series keeps medical practitioners informed about the latest developments in their fields. Librarians and their patrons use them as ready-reference sources for current medical information. The medical volume is annual. The others are revised on an irregular schedule.

836 Dictionary of medical syndromes. 4th ed. Sabina C. Magalini and Sergio I. Magalini. 976p. Lippincott Williams and Wilkins, 1996. ISBN 9780397584185. $$

616   RC69

This dictionary presents concise but complete information on all known syndromes. This edition includes 200 new entries. Entries begin with the patient's complaint and include signs, symptoms, and known treatments.

837 **Health, United States.** U.S. Department of Health and Human Resources. National Center for Health Statistics, 1975–. Annual. ISSN 0361-4468. $ www.cdc.gov/nchs/hus.htm.

362.1   RA407.3

Information about the general health of Americans. *Health, United States* covers trends in disease prevalence and health determinants, with racial and ethnic detail, utilization of health resources, and expenditures. Every third year a prevention profile is included. Available free online.

838 **The home health guide to poisons and antidotes.** Carol Turkington. 372p. Diane Publishing, 2002. ISBN 9780756755881. $
615.9   RA1216

Covers poisonous snakes, spiders, plants, chemicals, drugs, and agricultural chemicals. It also deals with food poisoning. Symptoms, treatments, and descriptions are given for each of the substances. There are directories of poison-control centers, hotlines, organizations, and sources of educational materials. Indexes of toxicity ratings and poisons by symptoms complete the book.

839 **Injury facts.** Statistics Department, National Safety Council staff, comps. National Safety Council, 1921–. Annual. ISSN 1538-5337. $
363.1021   HA217

An annual compendium providing a wealth of statistical information on different types of accidents in the United States. The majority are transportation related, but occupational and home accidents are also included. A bargain that belongs in all collections.

840 **Johns Hopkins symptoms and remedies: The complete home medical reference.** Rev. ed. Simeon Margolis, ed. 704p. Rebus, 2003. ISBN 0929661796. $
616.02   RC81

This book explains symptoms and their possible causes. It has two sections. The first is in chart format, showing symptoms with diagnostic possibilities. The second is a list of diseases with symptoms, diagnosis, treatment, prevention, and information on when to call a physician.

841 **Mayo Clinic family health book.** 3rd ed. Scott C Litin. HarperCollins, 2003. ISBN 0060002506. $
613   RC81

An excellent general overview of human anatomy and physiology, diseases, symptoms, and treatments. It has good coverage of nutrition and the aging process.

842 **Merck manual of medical information.** 2nd home ed. Mark H. Beers, ed. 1905p.

Merck, 2003. ISBN 0911910352. $
616   RC81

The Merck manual of diagnosis and therapy. 18th ed. 3000p. Merck, 2006. ISBN 0911910182. $
615.5   RM127

The Merck manual of health and aging: The comprehensive guide to the changes and challenges of aging for older adults and those who care for them. 992p. Random House, 2005. ISBN 0345482743. $ www.merckmanuals.com.
613   RA777.5

These Merck manuals offer a wealth of information for both professional and lay readers. The eighteenth edition of the classic *Merck manual* now includes color illustrations and new disease summaries and clinical approaches. The home edition has comprehensive information on diseases, wellness, and alternative therapies in lay language. The manual of health and aging focuses on seniors and the conditions that affect them. All are available free online. The *Merck manual* and the home edition are available in other languages (Spanish, Chinese, Portuguese, and French), also.

843 **The Mount Sinai Medical Center family health guide to dental health.** Jack Klatell et al. 304p. Macmillan, 1991. OP. ISBN 0025636758.
617.6   RK61

This guide explains oral anatomy, basic dental health, and dental treatments, including orthodontia and implants, in lay language. It is the only current source on this subject.

844 **The perfect smile: The complete guide to cosmetic dentistry from tooth whitening and bleaching to veneers and implants.** James Doundoulakis and Warren Strugatch. 160p. Healthy Living Books, 2005. ISBN 9781578260959. $
617.6   RK 60.7

This book covers all dental treatments and products currently available. It discusses the cost, the durability, the effectiveness, and the risks involved in each procedure and includes information about insurance coverage.

845 **National Organization for Rare Disorders.** National Organization for Rare Disorders. www.rarediseases.org.

Access to the database is free, with a small fee for ordering reports. Institutional subscription with full access has a per-year price plus an extra fee for IP access. This database provides information on more than 1,150 rare diseases. Abstracts are available online, but there is a fee for full reports if one is not a subscriber. It also offers information about organizations and support groups for patients and families dealing with rare diseases.

846   The surgery book: An illustrated guide to seventy-three of the most common operations. Robert M. Youngson. 448p. St. Martin's, 1997. ISBN 0312152183. $
617   RD31.3

This book explains preparation for surgery, operating-room procedures, the specifics of common operations, and the advantages and disadvantages of outpatient and inpatient treatment. It also offers advice about choosing practitioners and facilities. Line drawings show surgical procedures.

847   Toxics A to Z. John Harte. 576p. Univ. of California Pr., 1991. ISBN 0520072243 (pbk.). $
615.9   RA1213

This book provides an overview of toxic substances and pollution at home and in the workplace, the environmental implications of their use, methods of exposure, management, and regulation. There is an alphabetical listing of common toxics with their characteristics and how to prevent exposure and protect oneself and a bibliography.

848   Understanding your medical laboratory tests and surgical biopsy reports: A patient's guide. Robert W. Christie. 366p. Xlibris, 2005. ISBN 9781413447309. $
616.07   RB38.2

Describes in detail the most common diagnostic procedures currently in use. A welcome addition to the health collection of any public library.

AIDS and STDs

849   AIDS sourcebook. 3rd ed. Dawn D Matthews. 664p. Omnigraphics, 2003. ISBN 078080631X. $
362.1   RC606.64

Provides for the lay reader clear and direct information about AIDS and HIV infection; includes historical and statistical data, current research, prevention measures, and special topics of interest for persons living with AIDS. Sources for further assistance are listed for each topic.

850   Encyclopedia of sexually transmitted diseases. Jennifer Shoquist and Diane Stafford. 352p. Facts on File, 2003. ISBN 0816048819. $
616.95   RC200.1

More than 600 alphabetical entries cover specific diseases, their treatment, diagnosis, and prevention. A series of appendixes offer statistics, resource lists, and a bibliography.

851   Sexually transmitted diseases sourcebook. 3rd ed. Amy L. Sutton. 629p. Omnigraphics, 2006. ISBN 078080824X. $
616.95   RC200.2

This book offers the most current information about the types of sexually transmitted diseases; their diagnosis, treatment, and prevention; and current research on new therapies and vaccines.

Anatomy and Physiology

852   Atlas of human anatomy. 4th ed. Frank H. Netter, ed. 640p. Saunders, 2006. ISBN 1416033858. $
611.0022   QM25

Grant's atlas of anatomy. 11th ed. Anne M. R. Agur and Arthur F. Dalley. 848p. Lippincott Williams and Wilkins, 2004. ISBN 0781742552. $
611   QM25

Human body on file. Diagram Group staff. 2v., loose-leaf. Facts on File, 2003. ISBN 0816051054. $$
611   QM25

Basic anatomy atlases are heavily used in both public and academic libraries. Netter and *Grant's* atlases provide very detailed coverage of the whole body by organ system and in layers, starting from the outside and working inward. But because these books are bound and in color, their illustrations are not easy to reproduce. *Human body on file* offers clear black-and-white line drawings in a loose-leaf format, which makes photocopying easy.

853   Gray's anatomy: The anatomical basis of clinical practice. 39th ed. Susan Standring. 1600p. Churchill Livingstone, 2004. ISBN 0443071683. $$

611   QM23.2

The classic text and standard reference tool for human anatomy. The new edition is organized by body region and has many more color illustrations. For a small fee, one may have a CD-ROM and online access, which offers three-dimensional, interactive anatomical models.

854   Human body. Martyn Page and Ann Baggaley, eds. 448p. Dorling Kindersley, 2001. ISBN 0789479885. $

611   QM25

A basic introduction, written in lay language and profusely illustrated with drawings, photographs, X-rays, and scans. It is organized by organ system and includes a section on the human life cycle and genetics. A glossary and an index complete the book.

855   Textbook of medical physiology. 11th ed. Arthur C. Guyton and John E. Hall. 1104p. Saunders, 2005. ISBN 0721602401. $$

612   QP34.5

A classic textbook and standard reference source. It is written in technical language, but educated lay readers will be able to understand it. Functions of all human organs and systems are explained in great detail. The new edition has a full-color layout with many charts, tables, and clinical vignettes. It also has access to online text and supplemental information via Student Consult (a medical website) and is downloadable to PDAs.

Cancer

856   Everyone's guide to cancer supportive care: A comprehensive handbook for patients and their families. Ernest H. Rosenbaum and Isadora Rosenbaum. 600p. Andrews McMeel, 2005. ISBN 0740750410. $

616.99   RC271

An oncologist and a medical assistant at the University of California San Francisco Comprehensive

Cancer Center have written a book that goes beyond the basics of diagnosis and treatment, looking at the roles of spirituality, fitness, nutrition, and the will to live as factors in surviving and maintaining quality of life while fighting cancer.

857   Everyone's guide to cancer therapy. 4th ed. Malin Dollinger et al. 848p. Andrews McMeel, 2002. ISBN 0704718568. $

616.99   RC263

This book explains various cancer treatments in common use, how they work, and their side effects, risks, and benefits. It is a useful, reassuring source accessible to all users.

858   The Gale encyclopedia of cancer: A guide to cancer and its treatments. 2nd ed. Jacqueline L. Longe, ed. 2v. Gale, 2005. ISBN 1414403623. $$

616.99   RC254.5

This set provides the latest information on cancer diagnosis and treatment, including alternative therapies. It has information about rare cancers not found in other sources. It has a list of Comprehensive Cancer Center locations, support groups, government agencies, and research groups in the United States.

859   Informed decisions: The complete book of cancer diagnosis, treatment, and recovery. 2nd ed. Harmon J. Eyre et al. 784p. American Cancer Society, 2001. ISBN 0944235271. $

616.99   RC263

A good overview of cancer: biology, diagnosis, treatment, rehabilitation, and prevention. It includes lists of agencies, organizations, and regional cancer centers for referral. The new edition has information on coping with fatigue and the financial aspects of cancer treatment.

Children's Health

860   Baby and child health. Jennifer Shu and Jane Collins, eds. 352p. DK, 2004. ISBN 9780756604547. $

618.92   RJ61

An excellent overview of child development, childhood illness, and basic parenting skills from the American Academy of Pediatrics. It covers mental and emotional as well as physical development and includes a valuable section on "Making Sense of Health Information" that discusses evaluating what one may find on the Web. It also has a resource list of organizations and agencies.

861   The Gale encyclopedia of children's health: Infancy through adolescence. Kristine M. Krapp and Jeffrey Wilson, eds. 4v. Gale, 2005. ISBN 1787692417. $$$

618.92   RJ26

This new encyclopedia from Gale has more than 600 alphabetical articles about children, from conception through eighteen years of age. It covers physical, psychosocial, and emotional development; diseases and disorders; and family life. Color illustrations enhance the text. A glossary, children's growth charts, and information about pediatric medications appear in appendixes.

862   Smart medicine for a healthier child: A practical A-to-Z reference to natural and conventional treatments for infants and children. 2nd ed. Janet Zand, Bob Roundtree, and Rachel Walton. 576p. Avery, 2003. ISBN 9781583331392 (pbk.). $

618.92   RJ61

A unique text on children's health written by a physician, a registered nurse, and a naturopath, this book assumes that conventional medicine and alternative treatments can complement each other. The book has three sections: an explanation of the various therapies, an alphabetical listing of diseases and conditions with suggested treatments, and illustrated instructions for applying the treatments. A glossary, bibliography, referral list of hotlines and organizations, and list of suppliers of alternative health products complete the book.

Complementary and Alternative Medicine

863   Alternative medicine: The definitive guide. 2nd ed. Larry Trivieri and John W. Anderson. 1233p. Celestial Arts, 2002. ISBN 1587611414. $

615.5   R733

A classic source on alternative therapies, this book contains an interesting essay on the future of medicine, a section on symptoms, and articles on forty-three alternative treatments with contributions by 380 doctors who use them. Some are physicians who incorporate complementary therapies, and others are naturopaths, doctors of Oriental medicine, and so forth.

864   Encyclopedia of natural medicine. 2nd ed. Michael Murray and Joseph Pizzorno. 960p. Three Rivers Press, 1997. ISBN 0761511571 (pbk.). $

615.5   RZ433

Written by two naturopaths, this encyclopedia provides detailed information about alternative therapy for common illnesses and chronic conditions. The authors are careful to indicate when the services of a traditional physician are needed (appendicitis, fractures, etc.).

865   The Gale encyclopedia of alternative medicine. 2nd ed. Jacqueline L. Longe, ed. 4v. Gale, 2005. ISBN 0787674249. $$

615.5   R733

This encyclopedia has more than 800 articles covering 150 therapies, 275 diseases and conditions, and 300 herbs. It includes information on the efficacy of the treatments based on research done at the National Institute of Complementary and Alternative Medicine and other institutions. These evidence-based data make it a valuable resource.

866   Tyler's herbs of choice: The therapeutic use of phytomedicinals. 2nd ed. James E. Robbers and Varro E. Tyler. 287p. Haworth Press, 1999. ISBN 9780789001597. $

615.3   RM666

This new edition provides current information on herbs and phytomedicinals from the clinical research literature. There are brief monographs with references on those of herbs for treating more than 100 ailments. The chapter "Herbal Regulations" explains that herbal remedies are not subject to the testing that is done for prescription drugs.

Drugs

867   The complete guide to prescription and nonprescription drugs. Rev. ed.

H. Winter Griffith and Stephen
Moore. 1120p. Penguin, 2006. ISBN
0399532080 (pbk.). $

615.1   RM671

A useful source containing the latest information
about prescription and nonprescription drugs. It
includes information on taking medicine properly
and safely, drug interactions with foods and other
drugs, and adverse effects.

868   **The complete guide to psychiatric
drugs.** Rev. ed. Edward H. Drummond.
341p. Wiley, 2006. ISBN 047175062X
(pbk.). $

615.788   RM315

This book provides the latest information on the
diagnosis and treatment of mental illness and the
drugs that may be prescribed. The author includes
information on the use of these drugs to treat
women, minorities, seniors, and children and the
increased risk of adverse affects in these groups. He
also discusses alternative treatments.

869   **The consumer drug reference.** 1752p.
Consumer Reports Books, 1980–.
Annual. ISSN 1543-754X. $

615   RS51

Objective information about prescription and nonprescription drugs. It includes detailed instructions about the proper way to take medication and
a color drug-identification guide. It is written in lay
language and is easy to use.

870   **Encyclopedia of drugs, alcohol, and
addictive behavior.** 2nd ed. Rosalyn
Carson-Dewitt, ed. 4v. Macmillan, 2000.
ISBN 0028655419. $$$

362.29   HV5804

The second edition of this four-volume work (pre-
viously titled *Encyclopedia of drugs and alcohol*) has
been revised and expanded. In addition to address-
ing information on substance abuse, the title also
presents issues surrounding the new field of addic-
tion studies, which includes such topics as gam-
bling and eating disorders. Volume 1 lists included
articles along with their respective authors, who
come from a variety of government, educational,
and medical settings. Although articles address
the political, economic, legal, social, mental, and
physical issues surrounding addiction, they are
written in language that is accessible to lay read-
ers. A bibliography for further reading is included

with each entry. Volume 4 provides five appen-
dixes: appendix 1 is a list of poison-control centers.
Appendix 2 presents a U.S. and state government
drug-resources directory. Appendix 3 has a state-
by-state directory of treatment and prevention
programs. Appendix 4 presents information from
the Bureau of Justice Statistics. Appendix 5 is the
schedules of controlled substances, as outlined in
the Controlled Substances Act of 1970. A compre-
hensive index is available.

871   **Encyclopedia of herbal medicine.** Rev.
ed. Andrew Chevallier. 366p. DK, 2000.
ISBN 9780789467836. $

615.321   RS164

A comprehensive reference guide to 550 herbs
and their use as remedies for common ailments. It
includes current scientific research as well as infor-
mation about the major herbal traditions in various
world cultures. Color illustrations and instruc-
tions for preparing herbal medicines complete the
work.

872   **Physicians' desk reference.** Thomson,
1947–. Annual. ISSN 0093-4461. $

615.1   RS75

**Physicians' desk reference for
nonprescription drugs and dietary
supplements.** Thomson, 1980–.
Annual. ISSN 1525-3678. $

615.1   RM671

These sources provide detailed drug information.
The *PDR* contains package insert data from phar-
maceutical companies. The *PDR for nonprescription
drugs and dietary supplements* covers over-the-
counter medications, vitamins, and herbal prepara-
tions. Both have color identification guides and are
available online.

Nutrition and Diet

*Bowes and Church's food values of portions
commonly used,* see **952**.

873   **The encyclopedia of nutrition and
good health.** 2nd ed. Robert Ronzio.
736p. Facts on File, 2003. ISBN
0816049661. $

613.2   RA784

More than 2,500 alphabetical entries cover
such topics as vitamins, processed foods, health

disorders related to nutrition, allergies, and eating disorders. Approximately one-third of the material in this edition is new.

874   **Wellness foods A to Z: An indispensable guide for health-conscious food lovers.** Sheldon Margen. 640p. Rebus, 2002. ISBN 0929661702. $

613.2   RA784

This is a fine guide to maintaining health by eating properly. The author, a professor of nutrition at the University of California, Berkeley, takes readers from the market to the kitchen and, finally, to the table, showing them how to select, store, and prepare fresh foods in a healthy, appetizing manner.

Physical Impairments

875   **The encyclopedia of blindness and vision impairment.** 2nd ed. Jill Sardegna. 352p. Facts on File, 2002. ISBN 0816042802. $

362.4103   RE91

This book provides an overview of vision impairment. Entries cover medical, historical, and psychosocial subjects. There is a bibliography as well as a list of agencies for referral.

876   **The encyclopedia of deafness and hearing disorders.** 2nd ed. Carol Turkington and Allen E. Sussman. 304p. Facts on File, 2004. ISBN 0816056153. $

617.8   RF290

An overview of hearing impairment. Medical, historical, and psychosocial subjects are covered. There is a bibliography and a list of agencies for referral.

877   **Encyclopedia of disability.** Gary L. Albrecht. 5v. Sage, 2005. ISBN 0761925651. $$$

362.4   HV1568

An outstanding multidisciplinary resource that looks at all aspects of disability. Some 500 international scholars wrote more than 1,000 entries covering disability issues in law, medicine economics, education, art, religion, and other fields. Volume 5 contains primary source material. There are 200 biographies of disabled people and a large section devoted to the "experience of disability."

878   **Making life more livable: A practical guide to more than 1,000 products and resources for living well in the mature years.** Ellen Lederman. 384p. Fireside/Simon and Schuster, 1994. ISBN 9780671875312 (pbk.). $

646.7   HQ1064

This book contains information on products for low-vision and hearing- and mobility-impaired people. It also contains listings of books, pamphlets, and organizations that help people live with these problems. It has a very good index.

Women's and Men's Health

879   **Conception, pregnancy, and birth.** 2nd ed. Miriam Stoppard. 376p. DK, 2005. ISBN 0756609569. $

618.2   RG525

Mayo Clinic book of pregnancy and baby's first year. Robert V. Johnson. 768p. Morrow, 1994. ISBN 0688117619. $

618.2   RG525

Two excellent illustrated sources in lay language explaining conception, fetal development, labor, childbirth, and care of the newborn. The Mayo Clinic book offers more depth and coverage of the first year of life along with parenting information, advice on returning to work after giving birth, and grandparenting.

880   **Contraceptive technology.** 18th ed. Robert A. Hatcher et al. 908p. Ardent Media, 2004. ISBN 9780966490268. $

613.94   RG136

This book offers the latest information on contraception, sexuality, sexually transmitted diseases, and family planning. It is frequently revised.

881   **The encyclopedia of men's health.** Glenn S. Rothfeld and Deborah S. Romaine. 400p. Facts on File, 2005. ISBN 9780816051779. $

613   RA777.8

A physician trained in both traditional and alternative medicine and a medical writer have produced an encyclopedia with more than 600 alphabetical entries covering all aspects of men's health. They examine the medical, scientific, social, and lifestyle issues that have an impact on men. Entries cover

anatomy and physiology, diseases, nutrition, fitness, and stress reduction. The book has a glossary,
a bibliography, and resource lists.

882   The encyclopedia of women's health.
5th ed. Christine Ammer. 448p. Facts on
File, 2005. ISBN 0816057907. $
613   RA778

A concise encyclopedia of women's health, arranged alphabetically. It includes both traditional
and alternative treatment information. There are
line drawings to illustrate anatomy and charts to
summarize some information. Appendixes contain
resource lists and a bibliography.

**883   Harvard Medical School guide to
men's health: Lessons from the
Harvard men's health studies.**
Harvey B. Simon. 485p. Free Press,
2004. ISBN 0684871823. $
613.0423   RA777.8

A physician looks at data from the Harvard men's
health studies and provides recommendations to
help men improve their health. He examines diet,
stress, and fitness and answers frequently asked
questions about such issues as alcohol consumption and PSA tests to screen for prostate cancer.

**884   The new Harvard guide to women's
health.** Karen J. Carlson et al. 768p.
Harvard Univ. Pr., 2004. ISBN
0674012828; 0674013433 (pbk.).
$; $ (pbk.)
616   RA778

A comprehensive, thoughtful, clearly written encyclopedia covering more than 300 topics of special
concern to women, from coffee and cancer to cos-
metics and mental health. Well-depicted illustrations enhance the text. Suggestions for further
information include websites, videos, and organizations. Highly recommended.

**885   Our bodies, ourselves: A new
edition for a new era.** Rev. ed. Boston
Women's Health Book Collective.
832p. Simon and Schuster, 2005.
ISBN 0743256115. $
613   RA778

Our bodies, ourselves offers in-depth coverage of
women's health, addressing political and psychosocial issues as well as medical problems. It includes
notes at the end of each chapter, a resource list, and
an extensive bibliography.

886   Our bodies, ourselves: Menopause.
Boston Women's Health Book Collective.
352p. Simon and Schuster, 2006. ISBN
0743274873. $
618.1   RG186

The producers of *Our bodies, ourselves* take an in-
depth look at menopause. They treat it as a natural
part of life and offer both scientific and psychosocial information as well as narrative testimony from
diverse women to provide the tools that women
need to make informed decisions about handling
this transition.

11

Households

SUE POLANKA AND TERESE DESIMIO

Many of the works in this chapter are appropriate not only for the reference collection but also for the circulating collection and for the home library. From beer to pets, this chapter supports the varying interests of a broad spectrum of readers.

Beverages

887 **The bartender's best friend: A complete guide to cocktails, martinis, and mixed drinks.** Mardee Haidin Regan. 376p. Wiley, 2003. ISBN 0471227218. $
641.8   TX951

More than 850 recipes for cocktails, nonalcoholic drinks, punches, shooters, and participatory drinks are alphabetically arranged in this guide to mixed drinks. The first fifty pages discuss the equipment, ingredients, glassware, and techniques of bartending. Bartending tips, a glossary, a bibliography, and an index are also included, with a waterproof cover and a place-keeping ribbon. Unfortunately, no photos or illustrations are included. Also available electronically.

888 **Drinks.** 1st American ed. Vincent Gasnier. 512p. DK, 2005. ISBN 075661323X. $
641.8   TP505

Drinks is a colorfully illustrated guide to wines, beers, cocktails, spirits, and liqueurs of the world.

Entries include descriptions of color; aroma or taste for wine, spirits, liquor, and beer; and ingredients and recipes for cocktails. Photos of nearly every bottle or cocktail add value to this useful encyclopedic resource. A glossary and index are included.

889 **Great beer guide.** 1st American ed. Michael Jackson. 544p. Dorling Kindersley, 2000. ISBN 0789451565. $
663   TP577

Jackson, known as "Beer Hunter" on Discovery Channel and PBS, has included in this shopper's guide 500 one-page articles on beer varieties. They are organized alphabetically by beer name. Each article includes a large photo of the bottle, the beer decanted into a glass, a descriptive paragraph and bullet points to demonstrate the region of origin, style, alcohol content, and ideal serving temperature of each beer. Additional content includes user guides for pouring and tasting beer, a lexicon of flavors and aromas, and cooking and pairing beer with food; a glossary; useful addresses: world organizations, festivals, publications, retailers, and websites; and an index.

890 **Larousse encyclopedia of wine.** Rev. ed. Christopher Foulkes. 624p. Larousse, 2001. ISBN 2035850134. $
641.2   TP548

Foulkes, an award-winning author and editor of wine books, gathers contributions from twenty wine experts for this updated version. The first 100 pages provide wine history, keeping, and serving information. The remainder of the encyclopedia details the wine lands of the world, including France; Germany, Switzerland, and Austria; Italy and the Mediterranean; Spain and Portugal; the Danube and Black Sea areas; North America; Central and South America; Australia and New Zealand; and the rest of the world. A reference section provides insight on reading wine labels, wine quality regulations, vintage charts, and wine zones and statistics and includes both a glossary and index. Charts, graphs, maps, tables, sidebars, and beautiful color photographs and illustrations are strewn throughout. The *Larousse encyclopedia of wine* is listed in *American reference books annual*.

891 **Mr. Boston official bartender's and party guide.** Anthony Giglio. 244p. Wiley, 2006. ISBN 0764597329. $

641.8   TX951

Anyone needing information on the tools, equipment, glassware, drink ingredients, and party planning need look no further. *Mr. Boston* includes information about the various liquors used in drink making and features recipe sections for shooters, frozen drinks, hot drinks, eggnogs and punches, wine in mixed drinks, and nonalcoholic drinks. Although a compact book with tiny text, it is packed with facts and includes a few color photos in the center section.

892 **The Oxford companion to wine.** 3rd ed. Jancis Robinson, ed. 813p. Oxford Univ. Pr., 2006. ISBN 0198609906. $

641.2   TP548

This is the third edition of a classic encyclopedia-dictionary of wine. Nearly one half of the original entries were revised, and more than 500 new entries were added. Arranged alphabetically, it includes more than 3,500 entries. Cross-references, illustrations, color photos, charts, and graphs are included in the text. Appendixes include a list of wine varieties officially allowed in the world's controlled wine appellations and statistics on vineyard acreage and wine consumption and investment worldwide.

893 **Party punches: Punch recipes from around the world.** Tim Page, Marianne Page Smith, and Amy Charlene Reed. 200p. Overmountain Press, 2004. ISBN 1570722331. $

641.8   TX815

Page has researched the historical record of punches and party beverages for fifty years. With the assistance of his coauthors, he has gathered recipes from nearly every country in the world and chosen the best 300 to feature in this book. He also states that some recipes included have never been published before. All recipes are alcohol-free. Introductory material includes a measurement equivalence chart, top-ten all-time favorites, and secrets to a perfect punch. Chapters feature punches from around the world including fruit, slushy, spiced, and minted punches. Also included are ciders, cocoa and milk-based drinks, coffee, eggnog, lemonade, tea, and vegetable drinks. Disappointing is the lack of pictures, but otherwise it's easy to use with the simple directions. *Party punches* is a great reference for nonalcoholic beverages.

894 **Premium beer drinker's guide.** Stephen Beaumont. Firefly Books, 2000. OP. ISBN 155209510X.

641.2   TP577

Beaumont, a beer aficionado, includes an introduction to beer, beer ingredients, and a guide to beers from the common to the unusual. Brewery addresses (no URLs) and an index are available as well as a glossary of beer terms. Some 150 of 224 pages feature one- to three-page articles about the individual beers and include photos. Each article includes icons that demonstrate the relative cost compared to domestic beer, freshness and durability, and availability. Photos from both the inside and outside of international breweries and pubs are included.

895 **Raising the bar: Better drinks, better entertaining.** Nick Mautone, Marah Stets, and Mette Randem. 287p. Artisan, 2004. ISBN 1579652603. $

641.8   TX951

Raising the bar is a comprehensive collection of recipes, including cocktails; bubblies; "Nogs, grogs, and other holiday warmers"; punches; and drinks to soothe the morning-after ails ("morning glories" and "tonics to cure what ails you"). Plenty of attractive color photos complement the recipes for drinks, snacks, and hors d'oeuvres. Each recipe begins with recommended serving times and appropriate accompanying meal types. Introductory material includes basic home bar equipment and ingredients to keep on hand. A bibliography and index are also available.

896 **The Running Press pocket guide to beer: The connoisseur's companion to more than 2,000 beers of the world.**

7th ed. Michael Jackson. 208p. Running Press, 2000. ISBN 0762408855. $

641.2   TP577

Tiny and *pocket-size* describe perfectly this guide to more than 2,000 beers of the world. The bulk of the book contains articles on beer and breweries of the world arranged by selected countries where "beer-brewing is an important tradition." Each country includes an overview of local beer and suggestions on where to drink it, listing breweries and the beers served for each country. Jackson provides a short description and a star rating (one to four) for each beer. Stars include "typical to country and style," "above average," "worth seeking out," and, finally, a "world classic." Beers similar in nature include facts on density, original gravity, and percent alcohol by weight in order to make distinctions. A beer and brewery index, short introduction, and glossary are included.

897   The Sotheby's wine encyclopedia.
4th ed. Tom Stevenson. 664p. Dorling Kindersley, 2005. ISBN 0756613248. $

641.2   TP548

The wines of countries and regions of the world are listed with a description of the wine, the region grown, and the variety of grapes used. Colorful maps, illustrations, charts, and graphs complement the text. Introductory material includes assessing wine, a glossary of grape varieties and grape synonyms, storing and serving wine, and selecting wine to complement food. Extensive glossary and index, wine tasting chart, and troubleshooting guide are also included.

898   Wine: An introduction. 1st American ed. Joanna Simon. 224p. DK, 2001. ISBN 0789480638. $

641.2   TP548

Simon provides a beautifully illustrated guide to wine, including wine styles, grape varieties, wine tasting, and a general guide to the world's wines. Interesting features include the "if you like" "then try" section and the wine pronunciation and label-reading guides. This title is perfect for beginners as it includes just enough information.

899   Wines of the world. 1st American ed. 672p. Dorling Kindersley, 2004. ISBN 0756605172. $

641.22   TP548

This is an oversized pocket guide to the wines of the world. Thirteen color-coded country chapters focus on the major wine-producing countries. Each chapter begins with a history of wine production in each country, highlighting wine regions and grape varieties. For each wine region a directory of winemakers, with types of wine, history of the maker, and contact information, is included. Color photos, maps, charts, and graphs complement the text. Introductory material includes a history of wine, grape varieties and wine styles, overview of *terroir* (soil), and overviews of the vineyard and winery production processes.

Calendars

900   The American book of days. 4th ed. Stephen G. Christianson and Jane M. Hatch. 945p. H. W. Wilson, 2000. ISBN 0824209540. $$

394.26973   GT4803

A classic since 1937, *The American book of days* provides a look at American history, day-by-day, 366 days a year (includes February 29). Arranged by month and day, the history of events that shaped America is described and includes such occasions as significant birthdates and anniversaries, festivals, feasts, natural disasters, and even the premiers of television shows. Important historical documents such as the Constitution, Declaration of Independence, and Articles of Confederation are included in the appendixes.

901   Chase's calendar of events, 2006.
751p. McGraw-Hill, 2006. ISBN 0071461108. $

394.26   D11.5

A classic in every reference collection, *Chase's* is the place to begin for holidays, anniversaries, or events on a particular date or topic. Arranged in a day-by-day fashion, each day includes well-known birthdays and known international and national events. Supplementary material includes information about U.S. government leaders, North American state and country facts, daylight standards, perpetual calendars, and more. An extensive index, black-and-white illustrations, and a fully searchable CD are included.

902   The international book of days.
Stephen G. Christianson et al. 889p. H. W. Wilson, 2004. ISBN 0824209753. $$

394.26973   GT4803

This is a guide to the international events and world historical events occurring on each of the 366 days of the year (includes February 29). Content emphasis is on anniversaries of significant historical events, religious and secular holidays, and some birth/death dates of individuals. Distinctive appendix material includes an overview of the calendar, the era, days of the week, the UN Charter, the Universal Declaration of Human Rights, and the North Atlantic Treaty. Cross-referencing and an extensive index are included.

Consumer Affairs

903 **The bargain buyer's guide 2005: The consumer's bible to big savings online and by mail.** Elizabeth Cline. 659p. Print Project, 2005. ISBN 0965175065. $
381.142   HF5465.5

The twenty-seventh edition, formerly called *Wholesale by mail and online,* claims that consumers can save 20–90 percent on everything offered by the "best of the best" 500 vendors reviewed. Chapters on a variety of topics, from animals and pets to the wacky, weird, and wonderful, include an alphabetical listing of vendors who sell products in the various categories. Each vendor report includes the name, address, phone, URL, print/online catalog, payment accepted, items for sale, store and/or virtual presence, hours, and a review that includes "special factors." At almost 700 pages, this guide is comprehensive and current.

904 **Bargain hunter's secrets to online shopping.** Michael Miller. 320p. Que, 2004. ISBN 0789732017. $
658.8   TX335

Online shopping secrets, money-saving secrets, and an online shopping directory for the bargain hunter are included in this guide.

905 **Consumer Reports buying guide: Best buys.** Consumers Union of United States. Consumers Union, 1942–. Annual. ISSN 1555-2357 $
381.33   TX335

Published every year by Consumers Union, the largest independent, nonprofit testing and information organization in the world, the *Buying guide* is a cumulative list of the year's best buys, a cumulative index of all products reviewed since 1998, and a staple in most libraries. Introductory material includes advice on protecting one's identity and shopping strate-

gies for great values. Arranged by general categories ranging from home entertainment to automobiles, each article includes ratings charts for the products evaluated, which are cross-referenced to a later section called "Product Ratings and Reliability."

906 **Consumer sourcebook: A subject guide to more than 23,500 federal, state, and local government agencies and offices, national, regional, and grassroots associations and organizations, information centers, clearinghouses, publications, Internet resources, multimedia resources, media contacts, corporate contacts and related consumer resources.** 18th ed. Matthew Miskelly, ed. 1415p. Thomson Gale, 2006. ISBN 0787671053. $$
381.33   HC110

A directory of resources for consumers including contact information and descriptions of organizations, government offices, media contacts, multimedia sources, and publications to assist consumers. More than 23,000 entries are arranged in seventeen subject chapters, such as credit and personal finance, food and drugs, and employment. Within each chapter, entries are arranged by type of resource or organization. All entries are numbered, and an extensive index, both alphabetic and subject, refers to the entry number.

907 **The Shopping Bags: Tips, tricks, and inside information to make you a savvy shopper.** Anna Wallner and Kristina Matisic. 243p. Dutton, 2005. ISBN 0525948872. $
640   TX335

Wallner and Matisic, of the TV show *The Shopping Bags,* include in this book the topics of fashion, food, furnishings, and more. All topics included have bullet-pointed informational tips and a glossary if necessary. The "Ten Shopping Commandments," rules that can be applied to every shopping experience, make a nice introduction. This could be especially valuable to those newly independent or new to the United States.

908 **2005 online shopping directory for dummies.** Barbara Kasser and Frank Fiore. 652p. Wiley, 2004. ISBN 0764574957 (pbk.). $
658.8   TX335

Kasser, an "avid online shopper and author of several books about the Internet and Internet shopping," and Fiore, an "online shopping guru for About.com," provide online-shopping insight in a variety of areas: secure shopping, product and merchant reviews, finding the best prices, and more. Twenty chapters of the book provide information on shopping for particular products, from antiques to zany fun. A directory and keyword index are both available. Each website included has symbols representing recommended, price, selection, convenience, service, and security.

909 2006 consumer action handbook.
Federal Citizen Information Center
(U.S.). U.S. General Services Admin.,
GSA Office of Communications, Federal
Citizen Information Center, 2005. $
www.consumeraction.gov.
381.3402   HC110

Available in print or online, this handbook provides detailed consumer information in three major areas: being a savvy consumer, filing complaints, and a directory of consumer-assistance organizations. The index and table of contents provide the best access to the contents, which are loosely arranged with tips and quick facts. The handbook includes timely information on spam, the telemarketing "do not call" list, and payday loans.

Construction

910 The big book of home plans.
Creative Homeowner Press. 592p.
Creative Homeowner, 2005. OP.
ISBN 1580112498.
728   NA7205

This big book includes almost 600 pages of home plans for traditional, luxury, farmhouse, contemporary, southwest, vacation, and country homes. Smaller sections on trim details, baths, window treatments, decks, and landscaping are also included. Large colorful photos and illustrations provide inspiration and ideas.

911 The big book of home plans: 500+ home designs in every style—plus landscape plans. Hanley Wood. 463p. Hanley Wood, 2005. ISBN 1931131368. $
728.370222   NA7205

The big book is an idea book for home designs organized by home size—seven different sizes are included. Each plan featured shows a color photograph or drawing of the completed house, small drawings of the blueprints, and a chart listing sizes and specs for the homes. All styles appear very current and stylish. Blueprints, not included, cost between $450 and $1,775.

912 Building an affordable house: Trade secrets to high-value, low-cost construction. Fernando Pages Ruiz.
202p. Taunton Press, 2005. ISBN
1561585963. $
690   TH4815.8

Ruiz, who spent thirty years designing and building affordable homes, discusses the steps involved in building a home, including the design, foundation, plumbing, wiring, and more. Appendixes provide further guidelines concerning the cost per square foot for various shaped foundations; recommended heating, ventilation, air-conditioning, and insulation; and a joist-span table. Colorful pictures, illustrations, sidebars like "Trade Secrets," and tables of data add clarifying details.

913 Building your own home for dummies.
Kevin Daum, Janice Brewster, and Peter
Economy. 364p. Wiley, 2005. ISBN
0764557092. $
690.8   TH148; NA7115

Organized in typical "dummies" fashion, this guide includes tips and information on building plans and financing, the construction process, common mistakes and how to avoid them, and ideas for making a home "green."

914 Habitat for Humanity: How to build a house. Larry Haun, Vincent Laurence, and Tim Snyder. 282p. Taunton Press, 2002. ISBN 1561585327. $
690   TH4815

With help from Laurence and Snyder, Haun, a carpenter with forty years' experience and builder of Habitat for Humanity Homes, provides an overview of the home-building process. Site planning, preparation, and finishing touches are included, but plumbing, heating, and wiring are excluded. Well-labeled black-and-white illustrations complement the text and add detail.

915 How to plan, contract, and build your own home. 4th ed. Richard M. Scutella and Dave Heberle. 793p. McGraw-Hill, 2005. ISBN 0071448853. $

690   TH4815

Scutella and Heberle, builders and authors of home-building books, provide the answers to the basic questions of who, what, when, where, and how in building a home. A detailed index helps readers navigate the comprehensive articles, which contain plenty of black-and-white and well-labeled illustrations, options with advantages and disadvantages, "points to ponder" that reiterate important considerations at the end of each chapter, and frequent checklists.

916   Means illustrated construction dictionary. 2nd ed. 567p. Reed Construction Data, 2003. ISBN 0876296975. $

624   TH9

Workers, hobbyists, and home builders will discover more than 13,000 brief, nontechnical definitions in this valuable guide to the specialized and changing vocabulary of the construction industry. Black-and-white sketches, abbreviations at the beginning of each letter section, and the inclusion of some slang and regionalisms add to an already useful package. Includes practical tables of weights, measures, conversions, size determinations, and symbols as well as a list of professional associations concerned with the construction industry.

917   New house/more house: Solving the residential construction project puzzle. Richard Preves. 237p. Portico, 2001. ISBN 0971104409. $

690   TH4815

Preves, a licensed architect, provides a great resource for those careful planners with no prior building experience. It covers what you need to know when building, from working with design and construction professionals to choosing interior and exterior finishes. Appendixes include sample documents and an index. Ideally read before starting a construction or renovation project, this book could help a home owner administer the project effectively through checklists, sample contracts, and examples of how to keep records concerning the project.

918   350 small home plans: Up to 2,500 square feet. 384p. Hanley Wood, 2005. ISBN 1931131422. $

728   NA7205

This idea book for small homes includes 350 plans for actual houses, landscapes, and outdoor projects. Each house has one page that includes a photo, small blueprint drawings, a description, and a chart with basic building sizes and specs. The designs look current and attractive, and although they are not included, information on how to order them, with prices, is included. Prices range from $450 to $1,775 for blueprints.

Cooking

919   The all new Good Housekeeping cook book. 831p. Hearst Books, 2001. OP. ISBN 1588160408.

641.5   TX714

Organized in a traditional cookbook fashion, the contents include basics, appetizers, meats and other protein sources, pastas, vegetables and fruits, breads, desserts, beverages, and canning and freezing. A lengthy index and food and measuring equivalence charts are included. Each chapter is color coded and includes sidebars, color photographs, charts, and well-labeled illustrations and diagrams. Each chapter also begins with a few pages of introductory material: description and background of topic and purchasing, cooking, and storing guidance. Recipes include a brief description, preparation and cooking time estimates, ingredients list, enumerated preparation steps, and nutritional and calorie content per serving.

920   Classic home cooking. Rev. ed. Mary Berry and Marlena Spieler. 544p. DK, 2003. ISBN 0789496747. $

641.5   TX652

This revised edition includes hundreds of recipes for a multicultural palette using modern guidelines for less fat, sugar, and salt. Recipes, organized by course, include ingredients, step-by-step instructions, healthy options, servings, and color photos of the completed dish. Several cooking techniques, like preparing a rack of lamb, cutting vegetables, and making a yeast dough, are pictorially described. An index includes cooking terms as well as recipes. Introductory material includes sections on freezing, flavoring, using kitchen equipment, and safe and healthy cooking.

921   The cook's essential kitchen dictionary: A complete culinary resource. Jacques Rolland. 413p.

R. Rose, 2004. ISBN 0778800989. $
641; 641.3   TX349

This resource is an A–Z dictionary of more than 4,000 culinary terms ranging from *abalone* to *zymurgy*. Definitions include some brief history or origin of items. Occasional charts and black-and-white illustrations complement the text. Both food and beverage terms are included. Although not essential in every kitchen, it is essential in any reference collection.

922   The essential kitchen: Basic tools, recipes, and tips for a complete kitchen. Christine McFadden. 144p. Rizzoli, 2000. ISBN 084782263X. $
683   TX656

McFadden, a "successful food writer and kitchen designer," has included in her book recipes, tips, and tools for a variety of kitchen tasks, including cutting, grinding, mixing, sieving, and numerous cooking techniques. Colorful pictures of kitchen equipment and food entice the reader, with recipes scattered throughout. Occasional pages fold out for extensive coverage on a topic.

923   The food substitutions bible: More than 5,000 substitutions for ingredients, equipment and techniques. David Joachim. 621p. R. Rose, 2005. ISBN 0778801195. $
641.5   TX652

Arranged in alphabetical order, this is a guide to a wide range of substitutions for ingredients, equipment, and techniques used in today's kitchens. A brief definition is listed for each item, and references are included. Excellent ingredient guides and measurement equivalents are compiled in easy-to-use charts and graphs. Also includes an extensive bibliography.

924   The *Gourmet* cookbook: More than 1000 recipes. Ruth Reichl. 1040p. Houghton Mifflin, 2004. ISBN 0618374086. $
641.59   TX651

A classic name in a cookbook with more than 1,000 recipes for anything you'd ever want, from simple meals for two to parties of fifty. Exotic foods, everyday foods, and classic and modern recipes, most compiled from more than sixty years of *Gourmet* magazine, are included. Cooking tips and techniques, a glossary, a directory of sources, and an

extensive index are included. Unfortunately, there are no photographs.

925   The guide to cooking schools. Shaw Associates, 1989–2005. ISSN 1040-2616.
641.5   TX661

Published annually, this is a directory of culinary programs around the world. It is arranged by career and professional programs, recreational programs, wine courses, and food/wine organizations. Entries include the program sponsor (school or professional chef), courses, faculty, cost, location, and contact information. Appendixes include a list of accredited programs arranged geographically and a cooking-school index. This source was discontinued in 2005, so libraries may want to hold on to their latest edition until the information becomes too dated.

926   Herbs and spices. 1st American ed. Jill Norman. 336p. DK, 2002. ISBN 0789489392. $
641.6   TX406

This is a beautiful color encyclopedia of herbs and spices organized by aroma and flavor. Entries provide an overview of each herb or spice, culinary uses, tasting notes, parts used, buying and storing tips, and harvesting. Supplementary chapters include material on preparing spices, recipes, a bibliography, herb and spice sources, and an index.

927   How to break an egg: 1,453 kitchen tips, food fixes, emergency substitutions, and handy techniques. By the editors, contributors, and readers of *Fine cooking* magazine. 394p. Taunton Press, 2005. ISBN 1561587982. $
641.5   TX651

Written in Q and A format, *How to break an egg* provides answers to common cooking-tip questions. The index is critical, and recommended, for finding information by topic. The chapters include cookware, appliances, ingredient tips, serving, storage, and kitchen safety, among others, and within each chapter, the questions and answers are not in any particular order. Most pages have violet and blue-green graphics and page highlights. "Handy Kitchen Techniques" is the only chapter with color pictures, and this is appropriate and helpful in demonstrating techniques.

928   Joy of cooking. Irma von Starkloff Rombauer et al. 1136p. Scribner, 1997.

ISBN 9780684818702. $
641.5973   TX715

A classic cooking title since 1931, the *Joy of cooking* provides thirty-nine chapters of recipes and cooking tips for every item imaginable. Several black-and-white illustrations are used to clarify ingredients or techniques but may be difficult for the novice to interpret. All measurements are in English units, but a conversion chart is included. Text includes cross-referencing, and occasional sidebars called "Rules" offer tips. Whether for breads, meats, sauces, or stews, the *Joy of cooking* is sure to offer a recipe.

929   Julia's kitchen wisdom: Essential techniques and recipes from a lifetime of cooking. Julia Child and David Nussbaum. 127p. Knopf, 2000. ISBN 0375411518. $
641.5   TX651

Even though Julia Child died in 2001, her cookbooks are still classics. This one contains the following: soups and two mother sauces; salads and their dressings; vegetables; meats, poultry, and fish; egg cookery; breads, crepes, and tarts; and cakes and cookies. Several photo spreads of Julia in action are included. Many recipes have a "Variations" section with alternate ingredient lists. Detailed charts for vegetables include the name of vegetable, preparation, cooking, and finishing techniques. Cross-referencing throughout and tip boxes highlighted in light red add to the ease of use. Child and Nussbaum's is a very succinct reference book.

930   Larousse gastronomique. Rev. ed. Joël Robuchon et al. 1350p. Clarkson Potter, 2001. ISBN 0609609718. $
641.3   TX349

Begun in 1938, *Larousse gastronomique* is the ultimate reference work for culinary professionals. Arranged alphabetically from *abaisse* (a sheet of rolled pastry) to *zuppa inglese* (a dessert invented by Neapolitan pastry cooks and ice-cream makers in the nineteenth century), it is an encyclopedic dictionary containing the history and culture of culinary items from around the world. Recipes, color photos, and graphs are scattered throughout the text. Both a general and a recipe index are included.

931   The new American Heart Association cookbook. 7th ed. American Heart Association. 700p. Clarkson Potter,

2004. ISBN 1400048265. $
641.5   RC684

For thirty years *The American Heart Association cookbook* has concentrated on the taste of its recipes. The seventh edition is no exception and introduces 150 new recipes. Introductory material includes dietary guidelines and overviews of several food groups and additives, including carbs, proteins, fats, dairy, sodium, and salt. Each recipe includes servings, ingredients, directions, and serving analysis. Cooks' tips are strewn throughout, with convenience and storing suggestions. Appendixes include information on healthy shopping and cooking, menu planning, and equivalents and substitutions. The cookbook also includes an extensive index.

932   The new best recipe. 2nd ed. John Burgoyne, Carl Tremblay, and Daniel Van Ackere. 1028p. America's Test Kitchen, 2004. ISBN 0936184744. $
641.5   TX715

America's Test Kitchen tests between ten and fifty variations of a recipe and selects the best one. This cookbook, from the editors of *Cook's illustrated* magazine and affiliated with America's Test Kitchen, includes 1,000 of these recipes in twenty-two chapters. Informative sidebars like "Science" provide stories behind some cooking phenomena and include data tables, special techniques, hints about ingredients, and food safety. A few black-and-white photos and illustrations are included. Recipes requiring special equipment include a description of the equipment, such as tart pans, fine mesh strainers, torches, and ice-cream makers. The authors also provide evaluations and recommendations of some brand-name equipment. Extensive cross-referencing is used throughout.

933   The new complete book of herbs, spices, and condiments. Carol Ann Rinzler. 422p. Checkmark Books, 2000. ISBN 0816041520. $
641.3   TX406

Those interested in the nutritional and medicinal value of plants will find this source useful. Arranged like an encyclopedia, each article provides the chemical name, common name, USDA rating, medicinal properties, and uses of various herbs, spices, and condiments. Includes no pictures or illustrations, but a lengthy bibliography, with online resources, is included. An appendix lists items that are used in pharmaceuticals, many of which are hazardous.

934   The organic cook's bible: How to select and cook the best ingredients on the market. Jeff Cox. 546p. Wiley, 2006. ISBN 0471445789. $

641.5   TX741

Cox provides a guide to selecting and preparing more than 150 organically grown foods from fruits and vegetables to meat, dairy, and eggs. Arranged by general food categories, each entry includes a description of the ingredient history, varieties available, nutritional benefits, seasonality, preparation, and uses. One recipe is included for each organic item. Supplemental materials include sections on varieties of organic produce, a recipes index by category, sources of organic food, a bibliography, and an index.

935   Vegan planet: 400 irresistible recipes with fantastic flavors from home and around the world. Robin Robertson. 576p. Harvard Common Press, 2003. ISBN 1558322108. $

641.5   TX837

Robertson, a former chef and vegetarian-cooking instructor, provides twenty chapters of vegetarian recipes ranging from beverages to breads and sauces to sandwiches. A lengthy list of resources (with URLs) and an index are available, but no pictures. Highlighted tip articles and "Did You Know" sidebars provide additional information in easy-to-read format. The recipes appear both practical and tasty and should work for the beginner or novice. A "Vegan Basics" chapter with nutritional information provides a nice introduction.

936   Vegetables from amaranth to zucchini: The essential reference; 500 recipes and 275 photographs. Elizabeth Schneider. 777p. Morrow, 2001. ISBN 0688152600. $

641.6   TX801

Schneider, a prolific author of books and articles about food, features more than 500 recipes and 275 photographs for soups, sauces, and hundreds of vegetables, from amaranth to zucchini. Each vegetable has its own article containing the description, basic use, selection, storage, preparation, and a recipe(s). Caution: this source is not a vegetarian cookbook; many dishes include meat. Also includes a bibliography, recipe ideas, and indexes for recipes and vegetables by their common and botanical names.

937   Vegetables, herbs and fruit: An illustrated encyclopedia. Matthew Biggs, Bob Flowerdew, and Jekka McVicar. 640p. Firefly Books, 2006. ISBN 1554071267. $

635   SB320.9

This is a beautifully illustrated guide to vegetables, herbs, and fruits. Arranged in such manner, each entry includes several color photographs in various forms—seed, plant, raw item, and cooked item. Varieties, cultivation, companion planting, medicinal, and culinary uses of each item are discussed. Supplementary material includes types of gardening—herb, greenhouse, and more; an extensive glossary; a bibliography; seed sources; and an index.

Etiquette

938   Behave yourself! The essential guide to international etiquette. Michael Powell. 141p. Globe Pequot Press, 2005. ISBN 0762736720. $

395   BJ2137

Sleek and small, this guide to international etiquette is ideal for the traveler. Organized by country, each chapter includes tips for meeting and greeting, conversing, eating and drinking, being out and about, dressing, and giving gifts and tips. Color photos and flags of the countries are included. Forty-five countries from around the globe are included.

939   Emily Post's etiquette. 17th ed. Peggy Post. 876p. HarperCollins, 2004. ISBN 0066209579. $

395   BJ1853

Peggy Post, a descendant of Emily Post and "today's recognized leading authority on etiquette," has provided a completely rewritten and revised edition to a classic. In addition to the standard advice on entertainment and social gatherings, the seventeenth edition also covers netiquette, road rage, online dating, cell-phone courtesy, and travel post–September 11. Includes an extensive index, and chapters have page cutouts for quick access. The main piece of advice is in boldface, followed by a description.

940   Emily Post's wedding etiquette. 5th ed. Peggy Post. 405p. HarperCollins, 2006. ISBN 0060745045. $

395.2   BJ2051

Post provides a premiere guide to wedding etiquette from the engagement through the anniversary celebrations. New material includes same-sex ceremonies, the use of technology in wedding planning, and destination weddings.

How to be a perfect stranger, see **115**.

941 **International business etiquette: Asia and the Pacific Rim.** Ann Marie Sabath. 223p. ASJA Press, 2002. ISBN 0595248012. $
395.5209   HF5389.3

International business etiquette: Europe. Ann Marie Sabath. 255p. Choice Press, 2004. ISBN 0595323316. $
395.52094   HF5389.3; E87

International business etiquette: Latin America. Ann Marie Sabath. 221p. Career Press, 2000. ISBN 1564144291. $
395.5   HF5389.3

In this series, Sabath, an author and speaker on the topic of business etiquette, provides an overview of conducting business internationally and of the cultures of hundreds of countries in Asia and the Pacific Rim, Europe, and Latin America. For each country, demographic details and cultural differences are discussed, including dining, gestures, greetings, decision making, punctuality, tipping, and women in business. General statistics and travel information on each country are also provided. Of particular interest is the "Whatever You Do (Don't Do This)" section in each book that highlights the absolute unacceptable business behavior in each country.

942 **Miss Manners' guide to excruciatingly correct behavior.** Rev. ed. Judith Martin. 858p. W. W. Norton, 2005. ISBN 0393058743. $
395   BJ1853

A reference classic, *Miss Manners' guide* provides a humorous question-and-answer discussion of the appropriate behavior for any occasion. Ranging from birth to death and marriage to children, each section begins with an introduction and is followed by the question-and-answer format.

943 **The new basic black: Home training for modern times.** Rev. ed. Karen Grigsby Bates and Karen E. Hudson. 523p. Doubleday, 2006. ISBN

0385516266. $
395   BJ1854

Bates, an NPR correspondent, *Time* magazine columnist, and author, and Hudson, a columnist for Wave Newspaper Group, author, and speaker, have created a revision of the 1996 edition. Contents include communication, life lessons, dating, race in the workplace, and holidays. The intended audience is African Americans, but most of the advice applies to all humans.

Festivals and Holidays

944 **Encyclopedia of American holidays and national days.** Len Travers. 2v. Greenwood, 2006. ISBN 0313331308. $$
394.26973   GT4803

An in-depth look at thirty-six of America's holidays and national days, including several nontraditional entries, like Earth Day, Gay Pride, Halloween, Election Day, Super Bowl Sunday, and Father's Day. Traditional national and religious events, like Easter, Passover, Thanksgiving, Christmas, Kwanzaa, and Hanukkah, are included as well. Entries are several pages in length and discuss the origin, development, and changes in each celebration. Black-and-white photos and a bulleted list of facts and statistics of each event are listed. An extensive index and a bibliography are also included.

945 **Encyclopedia of holidays and celebrations: A country-by-country guide.** Matthew Dennis. 3v. Facts on File, 2006. ISBN 0816062358. $$
394.26   GT3930

Holidays and celebrations from Afghanistan to Zimbabwe and 204 other countries in between are highlighted in this three-volume set. The first two volumes are organized alphabetically by country and include a country fact file with statistics and cultural description of the country, a historical introduction, short entries for various holidays and celebrations, and further readings. Volume 3 contains longer overview entries, alphabetically, on major holidays and world religions. Detailed appendixes include maps of the world, calendar systems, holidays by country, and various indexes. Fun fonts, graphics, and illustrations bring the pages to life.

946 **Holiday symbols and customs.** 3rd ed. Sue Ellen Thompson.

895p. Omnigraphics, 2003. ISBN
0780805011. $
394.26 GT3930

This is an international guide to the religious, calendar, and national festivals of hundreds of nations. The entries are arranged alphabetically, and each entry includes the type of holiday, date of observance, location where celebrated, symbols and customs, related holidays, origins, further reading, and websites.

947 Holidays and anniversaries of the world: A comprehensive catalog containing detailed information on every month and day of the year, with coverage of more than 26,000 holidays, anniversaries, fasts and feasts, holy days of the saints, the blesseds, and other days of religious significance, birthdays of the famous, important dates in history, and special events and their sponsors. 3rd ed. Beth A. Baker. 1184p. Gale, 1999. ISBN 0810354772. $$
394.26 CE76

The third edition includes more than 26,000 entries on regional, national, and international holidays; birthdates of prominent individuals; and historical events. Arranged daily, including February 29, each day begins with international holidays, religious calendar events, and birthdates and ends with historical events. Each month is highlighted with the history, holidays, and special events of the month. A 100-page index of names, terms, and events is included.

948 Holidays, festivals, and celebrations of the world dictionary: Detailing nearly 2,500 observances from all 50 states and more than 100 nations; A compendious reference guide to popular, ethnic, religious, national, and ancient holidays. 3rd ed. Helene Henderson. 906p. Omnigraphics, 2005. ISBN 0780804228. $$
394.26 GT3925

The third edition of this classic collection contains nearly 2,500 observances from the United States and more than 100 nations. New content includes more than 400 brand-new entries including independence and national days around the world; religious holidays from the Muslim, Sikh,

Jain, and Zoroastrian denominations; Native North American Indian celebrations; an expanded section on calendar systems; and a perpetual calendar. The dictionary is arranged alphabetically by the name of the celebration and ranges from Aban Parab, at entry number 0001, to the Zydeco Music Festival, at number 2496. Entries include the name of the celebration, time period, a brief description, contact information, and sources consulted.

949 Traditional festivals: A multicultural encyclopedia. Christian Roy. 2v. ABC-CLIO, 2005. ISBN 1576070891. $$
394.26 GT3925

More than 150 traditional festivals from around the world are described at great length. The festivals include the major feasts of all world religions and religious groups—Christianity, Judaism, Hinduism, Sikhism, Buddhism, Voodoo, Baha'ism, Islam, ancient Greek and Roman, Native American, and several African tribes. With an alphabetical arrangement, each article is titled and includes *see also* references and recommended readings.

950 United States holidays and observances: By date, jurisdiction, and subject, fully indexed. Steve Rajtar. 165p. McFarland, 2003. ISBN 0786414464. $
394.26973 GT4803

Arranged by month and day, this source lists and describes holidays in the United States. Federal, state, and religious holidays are included for the fifty states and U.S. territories. A subject index, name index, and list of holidays by jurisdiction (state and territory) are included.

Foods

951 An A–Z of food and drink. John Ayto. 375p. Oxford Univ. Pr., 2002. ISBN 0192803522. $
641.03 TX349

First published in 1990 as *The glutton's glossary,* then in 1993 as *The diner's dictionary.* Here, Oxford provides the origin and description of hundreds of culinary terms, from *abundance* (a firm cheese) to *zwieback* (a biscuit). The definitions range from a few sentences to paragraphs and do not include pronunciation. This title is also available electronically.

952 Bowes and Church's food values of portions commonly used. 18th ed. Jean A. Thompson Pennington and Judith Spungen Douglass. 452p. Lippincott Williams and Wilkins, 2005. ISBN 0781744296. $

613.2   TX551

A niche book, this contains tables of the nutritional content of foods, from infant formula, to fast food, to the usual categories of food consumed by humans. Each entry includes common name and serving size and thirty-two other associated nutritional values. Charts include common name versus Latin name and food name versus synonym. Brand names are provided to help identify foods. Items listed include calories, fats, carbohydrates, fiber, vitamins, minerals, and amino acids in an average portion. More than 8,500 foods are listed. This will be a valuable reference for anyone with special dietary concerns.

953 The Cambridge world history of food. Kenneth F. Kiple and Kriemhild Coneè Ornelas. 2v., 2200p. Cambridge Univ. Pr., 2000. ISBN 0521402166. $$

641.3   TX353

A two-volume encyclopedia, *Cambridge* provides a comprehensive look at the history of world food, including staple foods, food-related disorders, food and drinks from around the world, nutrients and deficiencies, and much more. Supplementary materials include sources consulted, a name and Latin name index, and a very extensive subject index. Several black-and-white photos and illustrations and charts and tables appear throughout the volumes, each 1,100 pages in length.

954 Encyclopedia of food and culture. Solomon H. Katz and William Woys Weaver. 3v. Scribner, 2003. ISBN 0684805685. $$

394.1   GT2850

This informative and delightful encyclopedia includes more than 600 scholarly articles about food and culture in society, with an international focus. Articles range from 250 to 10,000 words and include a bibliography. Three volumes cover topics ranging from wedding cakes to pancakes and Baha'i to bento box. More than 400 photos, sidebars, menus, and recipes are scattered throughout; includes an index.

955 Food and Nutrition Information Center. Food and Nutrition Information Center, United States Dept. of Agriculture, National Agricultural Library. www.nal.usda.gov/fnic/.

A freely accessible website from the Department of Agriculture, the Food and Nutrition Information Center has provided information on food and nutrition for more than thirty-five years. It is searchable by keyword, browsable in a number of ways, and provides access to specialized databases. Information is thorough, current, and true to the quoted claim.

956 The foodlover's atlas of the world. Martha Rose Shulman. 288p. Firefly Books, 2002. ISBN 1552975711. $

641.3   TX641

Covering Europe, Africa and the Middle East, Asia and Australia, and the Americas, this atlas includes recipes, beautiful photographs, history, staple foods, and other specialties of the region. Sidebars include signature dishes and traditional ingredients of various countries and regions. Further readings and an index are included.

957 The Oxford book of health foods. J. G. Vaughan and Patricia A. Judd. 188p. Oxford Univ. Pr., 2003. ISBN 0198504594. $

641.3   TX369

This health-food book is arranged in encyclopedic fashion with entries from *alfalfa* to *yarrow*. Each entry features a color illustration (sometimes a color photo) of the item, the origin and cultivation, description, culinary and nutritional value, folklore, and evidence. Supplementary material includes recommended reading, glossary, and index.

958 The Oxford companion to food. 2nd ed. Alan Davidson and Tom Jaine. 907p. Oxford Univ. Pr., 2006. ISBN 0192806815. $

641.3003   TX349

More than 2,600 articles on everyday staple foods from around the world are included, from aardvark (tastes like pork) to *zuppa inglese* (tastes like a sponge cake). Arranged alphabetically, the entries are generally one-third page and discuss the origin and history of particular foods and food-related issues. Cross-references, highlighted in green text, stand out in each entry, along with the occasional black-and-white illustration. Entries were included if they fit into one of four broader categories—food plants, animals, cooked foods and prepared beverages, and the larger aspect of culture, regional dishes, diet, and meals. The impact of globalization on food availability and the impact of television cooking shows also receive discussion. Maps detailing food globalization are included as well as a selective index to terms.

959   The Oxford encyclopedia of food and drink in America. Andrew F. Smith. 2v. Oxford Univ. Pr., 2004. ISBN 0195154371. $$
641.3   TX349

In two volumes, more than 700 entries describe the history of American food. Arranged alphabetically, the encyclopedia includes articles on food items, regional and cultural cooking, and holidays. Entries are signed and include a bibliography. Extensive index, bibliography, food festivals, libraries, and museums are included in supplementary material.

Home Improvement

960   Additions: How to expand your home. Larry Johnston. 175p. Meredith Books, 2005. ISBN 0696225441. $
643.7   TH4816.2

Chapters cover the steps from assessing your current home to planning and building your addition. Only 175 pages, but this slim book seems to cover the topic well and also includes a glossary, an index, color-coded chapters, and sidebars. Each article features plenty of color photographs and illustrations. *Additions* appears to focus on covering available options for home owners interested in building an addition themselves.

961   Complete home improvement and repair. 2nd ed. Donald W. Vandervort and Lowe's. 560p. Sunset, 2005. ISBN 0376009225. $
643.7   TH4816

Color-coded chapters discuss planning and options, interior and outdoor finishes, and mechanical systems. Each chapter starts with a guide to each system, tools needed, any special techniques required, and installation and maintenance issues. Adding detail are the plentiful and colorful photos, charts, well-labeled parts diagrams, sidebars for additional details and tips, and an index. Unusual words are defined in context, and project steps are enumerated, concise, and clear.

962   The complete photo guide to home improvement: 300 projects and 2000 photos. Rev. ed. Black and Decker. 598p. Creative Pub. International, 2005. ISBN 1589232127. $
643   TH4816

This comprehensive guide is organized in two parts. The first part focuses on planning and infrastructure: basic carpentry, plumbing, and wiring techniques. The second part focuses on details, like remodeling projects for doors and windows, walls and ceilings, floor finishes, basements and attics, and kitchens and bathrooms. An abundance of photographs with parts labeled as well as many well-labeled black-and-white illustrations provide additional detail. Each article has sidebars at the beginning listing tools and materials required and sidebars scattered throughout with special notes and techniques. Reference charts and tables, a glossary, and an index are also included.

963   The complete photo guide to outdoor home improvement: More than 150 projects. Black and Decker. 502p. Creative Pub. International, 2002. ISBN 1589230434. $
643   TH4816

Using text, photographs, and step-by-step instructions, this guide highlights more than 150 outdoor projects, including fences, walls, decks, porches, sheds, and outdoor accessories. Entries average four pages in length and include the tools and materials needed, written steps, and photos of techniques, perfect for photocopying. An index is also available.

964   Home improvement 101: Everyday care and repair made easy. Jerri Farris and Thomas G. Lemmer. 270p. Creative Pub. International, 2005. ISBN 1589231805. $
643   TH4817.3

A Black and Decker publication, *Home improvement 101* provides tips for the care and repair of everyday household problems like plumbing; heating, ventilation, air-conditioning, and insulation; appliances; and walls. Each chapter starts with a description of the way things should work, with well-labeled illustrations of all significant structural parts, then an FAQ-like article. Articles include sidebars like "Call a Pro!" when a job requires more than a home owner can realistically do and lots of colorful photos and illustrations. Cutaways and exploded views add valuable detail. Repair steps are numbered and brief, including most common household repairs and maintenance but not the less-common or difficult ones. A glossary, conversion charts, and an index are also available.

965   **Renovation.** 3rd ed. Michael W. Litchfield. 534p. Taunton Press, 2005. ISBN 1561585882. $

643   TH4816

Litchfield, who has thirty years of home-renovation experience, provides a comprehensive guide to home improvement. The twenty chapters cover assessing, planning, building, and finishing. Also includes a glossary; lots of good, colorful, and well-labeled photos and illustrations; sidebars; and tables. At more than 500 pages, *Renovation* is detailed without being too technical for the average home owner.

Housekeeping

966   **Cleaning: Plain and simple.** Donna Smallin. 307p. Storey Books, 2006. ISBN 1580176070. $

648   TX324

Smallin, a "recognized expert on efficient ways to clear clutter and simplify life" and author of *Organizing: Plain and simple,* discusses room-by-room and everyday challenges and solutions. It contains no color pictures, but it is still attractive and includes sidebars offering tips on keeping it simple, making it yourself, saving money, and recognizing safety issues. Comprehensive coverage also features laundry solutions, lists of further resources with URLs, tables, charts, and a detailed index.

967   **The complete household handbook: The best ways to clean, maintain and organize your home.** Good Housekeeping Institute. 400p. Hearst Books, 2005. ISBN 1588164039. $

640   TX301

This handbook would be great for the newly independent or new to the United States because all aspects of basic housekeeping are covered: cleaning, laundry and clothing care, food and the kitchen, decorating, storage, maintenance and repair, home finances, and safety. Also features lots of colorful illustrations, charts, detailed special instructions,

sidebars, conversion charts, an index, and cross-references throughout.

968   **Household safety sourcebook.** Dawn D. Matthews. 606p. Omnigraphics, 2002. ISBN 0780803388. $

613.6   TX150

One of the ninety-three books included in the Health Reference Series, this basic consumer-health information guide tells how to avoid or minimize the potential dangers in poisons, chemicals, and fire. It includes information on water hazards, safe use of home maintenance equipment, choosing toys and nursery furniture, and holiday and recreation safety. Although no pictures are included, it does feature plenty of bullet-pointed information, instructions, and checklists as well as a glossary and lists of additional resources.

969   **How to clean and care for practically anything.** The Editors of Consumer Reports. 280p. Consumer Reports Special Publications, 2002. ISBN 0890439656. $

348.5   TX324

All articles are A–Z style and include cleaning agents, appliances, tools, laundry, and flooring. Special topics include stain removal, fire and flood damage, and homemade cleaning products. An index, helpful-hints sidebars, tables, and charts add detail. Although it seems up-to-date and includes current fabric names like viscose and lyocell, it has poor-quality paper that is already browning and outdated-looking clip art.

970   **How to organize just about everything: More than 500 step-by-step instructions for everything from organizing your closets to planning a wedding to creating a flawless filing system.** Peter Walsh. 501p. Free Press, 2004. ISBN 0743254945. $

640   TX147

Walsh, a professional organizer and host of the Learning Channel TV show *Clean Sweep,* provides a thorough guide to getting organized, with chapters covering the small to large organizational challenges of living plus chapters like "Travel and Adventure," "The Unexpected," and "In Your Dreams" (how to win an Academy Award, become an Olympian, etc.). Sidebars include "Tips," "Warning," and "Who knew." Chapters have unique page-corner icons for easy browsing. A big index and cross-references throughout provide easy access to specific information. No photographs or illustrations, but it does have lots of charts and tables and guidelines broken down into enumerated steps.

Interior Decoration

971   **The pocket decorator.** Leslie Banker and Pamela Banker. 216p. Universe, 2004. ISBN 0789310570. $

747   NK2115

Leslie Banker, a leading interior decorator with thirty years' experience whose work has appeared in *Architectural digest, House and garden,* and *Town and country,* along with her daughter, has created a pocket-size reference featuring the principles of design, architectural elements, fabrics, furniture, hardware, lighting, motifs, trimmings, and wall, window, and floor treatments. Although no specific interior-decorating advice is given, the various elements of interior decoration are explained.

972   **The ultimate house book.** Terence Conran and Elizabeth Wilhide. 272p. Conran Octopus, 2003. ISBN 1840912863. $

747   NK2115

Wilhide and Conran, "one of the world's leading designers," illustrate the concepts behind good home architecture and interior decorating rather than providing lots of examples of good ideas, focusing mostly on modern, minimalist design theory. Part 1 covers how to plan, build, and decorate living spaces, while part 2 provides guides to home improvements, buying a first home, and working with contractors and architects. Supplementary materials include an interior-decorating and architectural-materials directory and an index.

Maintenance and Repair

973   **Big book of home how-to.** 928p. Meredith Books, 2003. ISBN 0696217287. $

643   TH4817.3

The publishers of *Better homes and gardens* magazine have produced a more than 900-page bargain costing only $25. Contents include basic and advanced repair and installation guides for all household systems. Also included are a glossary, an index, charts,

and many clear, colorful, and well-labeled illustrations. Each chapter begins with a detailed table of contents, and each has informative sidebars, enumerated steps, and cross-referencing.

974   **Carpentry and trimwork step-by-step.** Larry Johnston. 160p. Meredith Books, 2004. ISBN 0696221101. $

694.6   TH5607

Color-coded chapters include safety, tools, materials, techniques, and projects. Each project has a "you'll need" sidebar detailing time, skill, and tool requirements. Instructions are clear, and steps are numbered. Cross-references throughout, lots of color photographs, tables and charts, a glossary, and an index add value. Features good photographs of proper tool usage.

975   **Complete do-it-yourself manual.** Rev ed. *Family Handyman* editors. 528p. Reader's Digest, 2005. ISBN 0762105798. $

643   TH4817.3

From the editors of *Family handyman* magazine, this revised edition includes hand and power tools, fasteners and adhesives, and repair and improvement guidelines for all major household systems. Additional chapters cover furniture repair, healthy homes, emergency repair, and storage projects. Lots of well-labeled colorful pictures, illustrations, and cutaway views provide detail. Chapters are color coded, have sidebars and charts, and show tools in use by men and women. An index and resource section are also available.

976   **The complete guide to home plumbing.** 3rd ed. Black and Decker and Creative Publishing. 302p. Creative Pub. International, 2005. ISBN 1589232011. $

696   TH6124

The steps necessary in planning and installing new plumbing to replacing and repairing old plumbing are detailed in this guide. Exploded and cutaway views make information very clear, and lots of colorful pictures and illustrations, with parts clearly labeled, add more detail. Additional materials are conversion charts, resources, and an index.

977   **The complete guide to home wiring: Including information on home electronics and wireless technology.** Rev. ed. Andrew Karre. 334p. Creative Pub. International, 2005. ISBN

1589232135. $

621.319   TK3285

This big, attractive book has its contents broken down into two broad sections: basic electrical repairs and advanced wiring projects, which includes outdoor wiring, home automation, and networking. Lots of colorful pictures with parts clearly labeled as necessary and photographs showing typical problem areas to aid in troubleshooting add detail. More detail is provided by charts, diagrams, and sidebars, including "Everything You Need" and "See Inspector's Notebook" sections, cross-references, a resource list, and an index. All states' building codes are not covered, but a center section describes common electrical code requirements.

978   Complete trimwork and carpentry. Stanley Works. 240p. Meredith Books, 2004. ISBN 0696221144. $

694   TH5695

Primarily discussing remodeling, this book covers planning, employing basic techniques, customizing ideas, and choosing tools and materials. More detail is provided in sidebars with checklists and tips, color photographs and illustrations, conversion charts, a glossary, a resource guide, and an index.

979   The home plumbing handbook. Charles McConnell. 177p. Delmar/ Thomson Learning, 2004. ISBN 140185625X. $

696   TH6124

McConnell, a journeyman and master plumber, says he wrote this book for the do-it-yourselfer, but he usually writes for professionals. The twenty-four chapters cover common plumbing replacements and repairs and include sidebars detailing materials and tools needed. Additional material details fittings, calculations, building-code resources, and parts.

980   Plumbing: Basic, intermediate and advanced projects. Merle Henkenius. 271p. Creative Homeowner, 2002. ISBN 1580110851. $

696   TH6124

Plumbing changes and additions; drains, vents, and traps; repairs and installations of toilets, sinks, bathtubs, and showers; water heaters, filters, and softeners; and sump pumps, septic systems, and wells are discussed in this home-owner's guide. Each how-to article lists required tools and materials and time needed and includes sidebars. Steps are numbered

and simple. Has lots of colorful pictures and multicolored, well-labeled illustrations. Cutaway and exploded views add more information, as do the glossary and index, but this is not as thorough coverage as *The complete guide to home plumbing.*

981   Popular Mechanics complete home how-to. Albert Jackson and David Day. 514p. Hearst Books, 2004. ISBN 1588163024. $

643   TH4817.3

This book discusses plans, decorations, repairs, improvements, security, and tools using well-labeled, colorful pictures and illustrations, sidebar tips, cutaway views, and comparison tables to add detail. It includes a glossary and a detailed index, and the chapters are color coded. Bonus material includes inside-front-cover and back-cover sizing guides and conversion charts.

982   The ultimate home and property maintenance manual. Joe Beck. 350p. McGraw-Hill, 2005. ISBN 0071439307. $

643   TH4817.3

Beck, an "expert contractor/landscaper with years of experience caring for prestigious homes," covers everything from tools and all household elements to pools and yards. Additional materials include climate and geographic considerations and such special problems as radon, asbestos, and floods. Each repair task is identified as being from "Easy: 1–2 hours" to "Very Difficult: 7–10 hours" and features sidebars and black-and-white photographs, which are somewhat outdated in appearance. The times given are for a beginner with proper tools. Coverage is expansive, and articles are informative yet succinct, but the listed costs of tools and materials could become outdated quickly.

Parenting

983   Caring for your baby and young child: Birth to age 5. 4th ed. Steven P. Shelov and American Academy of Pediatrics. 752p. Bantam Books, 2004. ISBN 055338290X. $

649   RJ61

In the biggest book published by the American Academy of Pediatrics, the more than 750 pages cover topics like preparation for the new baby, birth, basic infant care, and feeding, and chapters cover the first days, first month, and so forth. It also covers emergencies, various bodily systems, and environmental concerns. Comprehensive coverage with cross-references, charts, bullet-pointed highlighted information, and sidebars.

984 Caring for your school-age child: Ages 5 to 12. Rev. ed. Edward L. Schor and American Academy of Pediatrics. 624p. Bantam Books, 1999. ISBN 0553379925. $
649   HQ772

The more than 600 pages discuss topics like health and normal development, behavior and discipline, emotional problems and behavior disorders, chronic health problems, and common medical problems. Includes an index, charts, and enumerated or bullet-pointed important information detailed with sidebars.

985 Caring for your teenager: The complete and authoritative guide. Donald E. Greydanus and Philip Bashe. 606p. Bantam Books, 2003. ISBN 0553379968. $
305.235   HQ799.15

The more than 600 pages and comprehensive coverage feature topics from adolescent change; teens at home, school, and in the world; and good health for teens. An index, charts, enumerated or bullet-pointed important information, and sidebars add valuable information.

Encyclopedia of children and childhood, see **375.**

986 The family in America: An encyclopedia. Joseph M. Hawes and Elizabeth F. Shores. 2v. ABC-CLIO, 2001. ISBN 1576072320. $$
306.85   HQ536

Hawes, a professor of history, and Shores take an "incisive, multidisciplinary look at the American family over the past 200 years. Important coverage includes: public policies, organizations and programs, health and social issues, the family constellation, research and theorists, family customs and pastimes." This two-volume set, similar in layout to *Parenthood in America,* is also one of the six titles making up the American Family series. Topics are arranged alphabetically, have encyclopedia-like entries, include cross-references, and have a list of references. Provides a few black-and-white photos and a huge index.

International encyclopedia of marriage and family, see **329.**

987 Parenthood in America: An encyclopedia. Lawrence Balter. 2v. ABC-CLIO, 2000. ISBN 1576072134. $$
306.85   HQ755.8

Balter, a professor of applied psychology at New York University and a "nationally known expert in child development and parenting," is editor for these two volumes totaling more than 700 pages written by more than 180 contributors. It is similar in layout to *The family in America* and is also one of the six titles making up the American Family series. Topics are arranged alphabetically, have encyclopedia-like entries, include cross-references, and have a list of references. Provides a few black-and-white photos and a huge index.

988 A parent's guide to first aid. Roxanne Nelson. 208p. Parent's Guide Press, 2002. ISBN 1931199205. $
618.9200252   RJ370

Nelson has written an easy-to-use first-aid manual for parents. Topics are arranged alphabetically and include minor first aid through the emergency. Articles have sidebars indicating important information and severity of a problem and bullet-pointed information with alternating shading for sections of lengthy text to make for easier reading and place keeping. The back of the book has an index and blank pages for parents' notes and emergency phone numbers.

989 Toy tips: A parent's essential guide to smart toy choices. Marianne M. Szymanski and Ellen Neuborne. 242p. Jossey-Bass, 2004. ISBN 0787974366. $
649   GV1218.5

Toys for babies through adolescents are discussed in this guide. Shopping for toys, educational toys, family toys, classics, and modern videos and DVDs are included. Very few brand names are given, and toys are arranged by function, with paragraphs titled "Benefits," "Timing," "Warning," and "Conclusion." Articles have sidebars and work sheets, and some have a "Tales from the Toy Tips Lab" anecdote.

Pets

990 The complete home veterinary guide. Chris C. Pinney. 819p. McGraw-Hill,

2004. ISBN 0071412727. $

636.089   SF981

Pinney, a veterinarian, includes detailed home veterinary care for every pet imaginable, the exception—horses. Cats, dogs, fish, birds, rabbits, potbellied pigs, reptiles, amphibians, and invertebrates are just part of what is covered. If that isn't enough, Pinney also covers injured and orphaned wildlife, geriatric pets, unusual diseases, and holistic pet care. Also available electronically.

991 Encyclopedia of pets and pet care: The essential family reference guide to pet breeds and pet care. David Alderton. 512p. Lorenz Books, 2004. ISBN 0754813967. $

636.0887   SF416

Published as a compilation of three older pet-care books—*Cats, cat breeds and cat care,* by Alan Edwards (1999); *Complete dog book,* by Peter Larkin and Mike Stockman (2001); and *The ultimate encyclopedia of small pets and pet care* (a U.S. publication called *Exotic pet handbook*), by David Alderton and Yolanda Heersma (2001)—this encyclopedia includes information on the care of cats, dogs, birds, fish, herptiles and invertebrates, and other small animals. Similar in layout to a DK title, it includes many color photos and illustrations.

992 The Merck veterinary manual. 9th ed. Cynthia M. Kahn, ed. 2712p. Merck, 2005. ISBN 0911910506. $

636.089   SF745

With a much greater emphasis on veterinary medicine and animal health, the fiftieth anniversary edition of this manual includes current concerns such as West Nile virus and chronic wasting disease. Included are horses, cattle, swine, sheep, goats, chickens, dogs, and cats, with a special section on exotic and laboratory animals. Bodily systems from circulatory to urinary, behavior, pathology, and emergency medicine are all discussed. *Merck veterinary* is very comprehensive.

Birds

993 The complete pet bird owner's handbook. 3rd ed. Gary A. Gallerstein and Julie R. Mancini. 441p. Avian, 2003. ISBN 1895270251. $

636.6   SF461

Gallerstein, a veterinarian, and Mancini have written an informative guide to owning a bird. Bird selection, characteristics, and care are discussed and illustrated. Bird clubs and shows, breeding and anatomy, and veterinary care are also discussed. Appendixes include national bird clubs, websites, a brief history of birds, and a lengthy general index.

994 The ultimate encyclopedia of caged and aviary birds: A practical family reference guide to keeping pet birds, with expert advice on buying, understanding, breeding and exhibiting birds. David Alderton. 256p. Southwater, 2005. ISBN 1844761606. $

636.6   SF460.6

In his simply written guide to birds, Alderton discusses choosing the equipment, giving basic care, buying, showing, and breeding of birds. Bird groups are discussed as well, each describing various characteristics of the birds. Each bird included gets several paragraphs of coverage, one color picture (more if male and female have different coloring), and a "breed box" listing length, incubation period, fledging period, and clutch size.

Cats

995 ASPCA complete cat care manual. A. T. B. Edney. 192p. Dorling Kindersley, 2006. ISBN 0756617421. $

636.8   SF447

Edney, a veterinarian, provides care, feeding, grooming, and health information for cats of all types. Many illustrations demonstrate various training techniques in steps and stages, including bathing a cat! Color photos, a glossary, a cat-care health record, an index, and resources for more information are also included.

996 The Cat Fanciers' Association complete cat book. Mordecai Siegal. 495p. HarperResource, 2004. ISBN 0062702335. $

636.8   SF442

After a brief history of the Cat Fanciers' Association and pedigreed cats, the majority of this book highlights hundreds of cat breeds in alphabetical order. Each breed has several pages of coverage, including a photo, introduction and physical description, personality information, grooming requirements, origin and history, and standard grading sheet.

Additional material discusses selecting a cat, cat and kitten behavior, and a veterinary guide. A color photo spread is found in the center of the book.

997   Cat owner's manual. Bruce Fogle. 288p. DK, 2003. ISBN 0789493209. $
636.8   SF447

Cat breeds of all types are discussed and described in this owner's manual. General cat anatomy, behavior, and a veterinary guide are also discussed. Each cat breed features several color photos, a description, and a history of the breed. A sidebar for each breed contains the key facts and standards for the breed.

998   Essential cat: The ultimate guide to caring for your cat. Caroline Davis. 192p. Reader's Digest, 2005. ISBN 0762104961. $
636.8   SF447

This general guide to choosing a cat highlights cat behavior, cat care, and general health-care and reproductive information. Information is presented with fast facts, questions and answers, and "Did You Know" sidebars. Color photos, illustrations, and charts and graphs add value to material.

999   The new encyclopedia of the cat. Bruce Fogle. 288p. DK, 2001. ISBN 0789480212. $
636.8   SF442.2

The history of felines, their relationships with humans, and typical feline anatomy and behavior are discussed in this encyclopedia. The majority of the book focuses on domestic cat breeds, with each breed charting the characteristics of sociability, activity level, grooming, vocal abilities, and registries for the breed. Includes a short veterinary guide, a glossary, and an index as well.

Dogs

1000   ASPCA complete dog care manual. Bruce Fogle. 192p. Dorling Kindersley, 2006. ISBN 075661743X. $
636.70887   SF427

Arranged in typical DK fashion, this source includes lots of photos, charts, and graphs for the care and training of dogs. Feeding, grooming, training, and health-care information are discussed as well as breeding and showing dogs. A glossary, index, dog-care record, and further-information resources are listed as well.

1001   The complete dog book. 20th ed. American Kennel Club. 858p. Ballantine, 2006. ISBN 0345476263. $
636.7   SF426

Arranged by type of dog—sporting, hound, working, terrier, toy, and nonsporting—this is a guide to hundreds of dog breeds. Each entry includes a slightly outdated photo, history, and official standards of the breed. Additional information includes tips for living with your dog, canine health and first aid, a glossary, and an index.

1002   Dogs: The ultimate dictionary of over 1,000 dog breeds. Desmond Morris. 752p. Trafalgar Square, 2002. ISBN 1570762198. $
636.7   SF422

A quick reference guide to dog breeds, *Dogs* is organized by type of breeds—sporting, livestock, and service dogs. Each entry includes a black-and-white illustration and an overview of the history and origin of dog breeds. Brief descriptions of physical characteristics are included as well. The focus of this book is the history of the dog breed.

1003   Encyclopedia of dog breeds. 2nd ed. D. Caroline Coile. 352p. Barron's, 2005. ISBN 0764157000. $
636.7   SF422

This encyclopedia covers as many breeds as AKC's 2006 book, with larger pages and lots of colorful pictures. It covers the history, temperament, upkeep, health, form and function of the various breeds. Charts for each breed highlight the energy level, temperament, ease of training, grooming, and ideal conditions for the dogs. Definitions of medical conditions, canine genetic health resources, a glossary, and dog anatomy are also included.

1004   New complete dog training manual. 1st American ed. Bruce Fogle et al. 176p. DK, 2002. ISBN 078948398X. $
636.7   SF431

Fogle, a veterinarian, presents training and behavioral techniques for dogs, from basic commands of come, sit, and stay to advanced techniques of retrieving and agility training. The color photos, step-by-step instructions with illustrations, and ease of reading make this a great book for new dog owners. When not in use, it will sit nicely on the coffee table.

1005 The original dog bible: The definitive source for all things dog. Kristin Mehus-Roe. 750p. BowTie Press, 2005. ISBN 1931993343. $

636.7   SF426

This source discusses the history of dogs, choosing the right dog, health and care, breeds, training, and behavioral characteristics. Individual breed entries include the history, description with general physical characteristics, temperament, special needs and possible health concerns, and recommendations for the best owner. Supplemental material includes top show dogs, dog-activity titles, a glossary, an index, and additional resources.

Fish

1006 Complete encyclopedia of the freshwater aquarium. John Dawes. 304p. Firefly Books, 2001. ISBN 1552975444. $

639.34   SF456.5

Hundreds of freshwater fish are discussed, described, and illustrated in this encyclopedia. Each fish entry contains the family, color and description, distribution, size, behavior, diet, ideal conditions, and breeding. The care and selection of aquarium plants are also discussed.

1007 Complete encyclopedia of the saltwater aquarium. Nick Dakin. 400p. Firefly Books, 2003. ISBN 1552978176. $

639.34   SF457.1

The complete care of saltwater aquariums is discussed, including maintaining the aquarium and caring for fish and invertebrates. For each fish, the distribution, length, diet and feeding, aquarium behavior, invertebrate compatibility, and a short description are provided. Lots of beautiful and appropriate color pictures complement the text.

1008 Encyclopedia of aquarium and pond fish. 1st American ed. David Alderton. 400p. Dorling Kindersley, 2005. ISBN 0756609410. $

639.3403   SF456.5; SF457

With hundreds of color photos and illustrations, the care of freshwater fish is discussed and described. Setting up and maintaining the tank, selecting and caring for fish, and breeding are

discussed. Additional material includes a glossary, useful websites, an index of common and scientific names, and a general index.

Horses

1009 Complete horse care manual. 2nd American ed. Colin Vogel. 216p. DK, 2003. ISBN 0789496410. $

636.1   SF285.3

Vogel, a British veterinarian, provides information about horse anatomy, general care, outdoor versus stabled horses, equipment needed, and other hints and tips. Featuring beautiful and plentiful photographs, it also includes useful North American horse industry and organization addresses, with URLs. The coverage seems broad but shallow. An index and a glossary are provided.

1010 The encyclopedia of horses and ponies. Tamsin Pickeral. 384p. Parragon, 1999. ISBN 0752582771. $

636.1   SF285

Pickeral, an equestrian and competitor, includes topics like the basics of the history of horsemanship, anatomy, care, equipment, riding, training, and competition. Almost half of this more than 380-page book is an extensive breed index. The breeds are listed alphabetically within the categories of "Ponies," "Heavy Horses," and "Light Horses." Each breed features a chart listing name, height, colors, and origin; sidebars with icons representing blood temperature, uses, and temperament; one-half to a full page of history and description; and color photographs. Useful addresses, a bibliography and further-reading section, a glossary, and an index are also included. This title has been reprinted many times.

1011 The new encyclopedia of the horse. Rev. American ed. Elwyn Hartley Edwards. 464p. Dorling Kindersley, 2000. ISBN 0789471817. $

636.1   SF285

Chapters discuss equine history and contributions to civilization, more than 150 of the major horse and pony breeds, training, equipment, basic care, and more. It features lots of big, beautiful, and colorful photographs and an "origins" sidebar for each breed included. A glossary and index are available.

1012 Storey's horse-lover's encyclopedia: An English and western A-to-Z guide.

Deborah Burns. 471p. Storey Books, 2001. ISBN 1580173179. $

636.1   SF278

Coverage in this dictionary-like book is broad but relatively shallow, with most articles being a paragraph or two in length. It includes black-and-white photos, lots of illustrations, sidebars, some charts and checklists, and cross-referencing throughout. This seems comprehensive—but a horse owner's manual or handbook might be more useful to a horse owner in practical matters—and also seems current, covering the newer concern of West Nile virus.

Unusual Pets

1013   The exotic pet handbook: A guide to caring for caged and aviary birds, reptiles, amphibians, invertebrates and fish. David Alderton. 160p. Southwater, 2003. ISBN 1842157558. $

636.0887   SF411.5

Alderton, an "internationally recognized best-selling authority on pets and their care," covers a variety of exotic pets, from birds to snakes. Presented with beautiful color photos and illustrations, each section includes an introduction, a list of species, housing, feeding, general care, and breeding. Information is brief for each species.

1014   Reptiles and amphibians. 1st American ed. Mark O'Shea and Tim Halliday. 256p. Dorling Kindersley, 2002. ISBN 0789493934. $

597.9   QL644

This is a catalog of reptiles, each with color photo, map of origin, and a description of the species with length, diet, and activity levels. Introductory material describes the reptile and amphibian species,

their reproductive processes, and feeding habits. A unique feature—an identification key—helps to identify the main families of reptiles and amphibians. Also includes an index and a glossary.

Tools

1015   The homeowner's ultimate tool guide: Choosing the right tool for every home improvement job. Sandor Nagyszalanczy. 282p. Taunton Press, 2003. ISBN 1561585823. $

643   TH4816

Nagyszalanczy, a professional woodworker and consultant, features in this book tool kits for various purposes. These include tool kits for home maintenance and repair, the automobile, sharpening, flooring, and more. After this, the individual tools are organized by function and described. Lots of big colorful pictures showing tools in use by men and women, charts, sidebars, and an index are included. Each chapter has a table of contents–like chart, and the top of every page has easy browsing labels.

1016   Tools: A tool-by-tool guide to choosing and using 150 home essentials. Steve Dodds. 224p. Firefly Books, 2005. ISBN 1554070600. $

621.9   TJ1195

Contents include guides on tool kits for variety of purposes: apartment, auto, home, plumbing, electrical, craft, and more. Each tool featured has a description of proper use and a visual guide for relative cost, necessity, and skill level required for proper use. This small book has nice photos and layout of text and includes a glossary and an index, but it has no photographs of tools in use, and some of the text is very small.

12 Visual Arts

SHEILA NASH

The visual arts are nonverbal in nature. They communicate through symbols, on two-dimensional surfaces, by three-dimensional objects, or through architecture, clothing, or furniture. This chapter presents information sources for such arts as architecture, photography, costumes, and comics. The changes to art information since the last edition obviously include Internet sources. Yet there is still a role for classic printed reference sources. This chapter covers everything from eBay to the *Dictionary of art,* published by Oxford University Press in 2003.

Databases and Indexes

1017   **Art full text.** H. W. Wilson, 1984–.
ISSN 1092-146X. www.hwwilson.com/
sales/printindexes.htm.
016.7   Z5937

Some 475 international and domestic periodicals are indexed in this online database. It includes titles about architecture, graphic arts, pottery, textiles, antiques, landscape architecture, and many other disciplines. Full-text articles are available for 150 journals as far back as 1997, and additional journals are added over time. A Wilson subject thesaurus is used as well as name authority. In the citations of some articles, there are links

to websites. Simultaneous searching is available for this file and the AMICO (Art Museum Image Consortium) Library, which provides access to more than 100,000 works of art that are cleared for educational use. For information about the online or CD-ROM version, see the website.

1018   **Art index retrospective.** H. W. Wilson,
1929–1984. ISSN 1529-9767. www
.hwwilson.com/sales/printindexes.htm.
016.7   Z5937

This is an index to fifty-five years of nearly 600 periodicals in the fine, decorative, and commercial arts. The titles are in French, Italian, Spanish, German, Dutch, and English. A Wilson subject thesaurus is used along with uniform name authority. There are direct links to websites that are cited in articles. The database can be searched along with other Wilson titles. Available in print, CD, and online.

1019   **Art museum image gallery.** H. W.
Wilson. www.hwwilson.com/databases/
artmuseum.htm.

This database can be searched alone or with other Wilson databases. There are high-resolution images in the fine and decorative arts of almost 100,000 images that include full descriptions, with provenance, multiple views, and details. It is worldwide in scope, with images from 3,000 BC to the present. The art images in rich digital resolution are cleared for educational use to illustrate items such as papers, assignments, lectures, and websites. For information about the online version, see www.hwwilson

.com/sales/printindexes.htm. Contact publisher for pricing information.

1020 Avery index to architectural periodicals. CSA, 1934–. ISSN 1085-2875. www.csa.com/contactus/index.php.
720   Z5945

This online index provides access to more than 2,500 American and international journals. Three-fourths of these journals are not indexed in any other source. Coverage is from 1934 to the present, with select coverage back to 1741. The periodicals include titles for landscape architecture, city planning, interior design and decoration, and historic preservation. There are more than 550,000 entries, including more than 13,000 obituaries going back to the 1800s. The ten-volume *Burnham index,* from the Art Institute of Chicago, with a midwestern emphasis is also included. Contact publisher for pricing information.

1021 Design and applied arts index (DAAI). CSA, 1973–. ISSN 1352-1298. $$$$
016.7   NK1160

This online index includes abstracts and bibliographic records for more than 500 design and applied-arts periodicals covering such diverse areas as advertising, vehicle design, product design, theater, web design, computer-aided design, animation, and fashion, from 1973 to the present. It includes more than 150,000 records, and approximately 1,200 more are added each month. For information about the online and CD-ROM versions, see www.csa.com/contactus/index.php.

1022 Grove art online. Oxford Univ. Pr. www.groveart.com/grove-owned/art/subscribe.html.

Grove art online, the online version of the *Dictionary of art,* edited by Jane Turner, provides easy access to 45,000 articles using keyword searching. More than 3,000 art images and drawings are available, and in addition there are links to image databases and worldwide museum and gallery websites. A What's New page includes updates, new articles, and new links to images. Contact publisher for pricing information.

Websites

1023 Art history resources on the Web. Christopher L. C. E. Witcombe. http://witcombe.sbc.edu/ARTHLinks.html.

Designed in 1995 by Christopher L. C. E. Witcombe, a professor at Sweet Briar College in Virginia, this metasite is a directory of art history resources on the Web. It is arranged by movements and periods.

1024 Artcyclopedia: The fine art search engine. John Malyon/Artcyclopedia. www.artcyclopedia.com.

This is a guide to museum-quality fine art that is found on the Internet. More than 2,300 sites are indexed, and it has more than 8,500 artists. Access is provided to more than 150,000 works of art, and it can be searched by name, subject, nationality, and medium. Links open directly to images. Website started in 1996.

1025 Artfact: Find, price and research antiques and fine art. Artfact. www.artfact.com.

The material in this great database is gathered from more than 500 fine auction houses throughout the world. The results include 10 million antiques, collectibles, and fine art. A variety of information may be included, such as abridged auction results and year, house, titles, description, estimated value, the selling price, provenance, photos, and other information. It is used by everyone from librarians to gallery owners. It is free to register, but purchasers must subscribe.

1026 ArtLex art dictionary. Michael Delahunt. www.artlex.com.

This dictionary includes definitions of more than 3,600 terms dealing with styles, genres, techniques, and media. In addition there are more than 50,000 links and thousands of images. Artists are only included if they are a part of a definition.

1027 ArtSource. Interactive Learning Paradigms. www.ilpi.com/artsource/welcome.html.

Networked resources on art and architecture with original material submitted by librarians, artists, and art historians. It has museum information, general resources, electronic exhibitions, organizations, online journals, libraries, and more. In this site it mentions that the "*BEST* source of information is your local librarian."

1028 AskART. AskART. www.askart.com/AskART/index.aspx.

AskART began in 1998 and has more than 42,000 American artists from the early sixteenth century to the present. Entries may include biographical information, references to books and periodical articles, auction records, images, and museum and gallery references. The auction results start in 1987. This very useful site also includes links to museum websites and a discussion board. It is used by gallery owners, researchers, artists, librarians, collectors, and insurers.

1029 The costume page. Julie Zetterberg Sardo. www.costumepage.org.

Started in 1995 and still maintained by Julie Zetterberg Sardo. This site includes her personal library of costumes as well as costuming-related links. The links are to more than 2,000 websites organized in sections such as historical, theatrical, ethnic, and making costumes.

1030 The costumer's manifesto: Your free one-stop site for costume information and images. Tara Maginnis. www .costumes.org.

All the pages in this site may be used for nonprofit educational uses. Started in 1996 by Tara Maginnis, professor at the University of Alaska, Fairbanks, and underwritten by OnlineCostumeStore.com.

1031 eBay: The world's online marketplace. eBay. www.ebay.com.

According to the website, "eBay's mission is to provide a global trading platform where practically anyone can trade practically anything." There are chat rooms, discussion boards, eBay blogs, eBay wiki, eBay groups, and a suggestion box. It is easy to use, and the photographs and information provided can be useful for a variety of reference needs.

1032 Jacques-Edouard Berger Foundation: World art treasures. Ecole Polytechnique Fédérale de Lausanne— Mouvement pour l'Art. www .bergerfoundation.ch/index.html.

There are more than 125,000 slides available here belonging to the Jacques-Edouard Berger Foundation that were gathered by Berger for lectures that he had given. Berger had been a curator at the Museum of Fine Arts in Lausanne. The site began in 1994.

1033 Mother of all art and art history links page. School of Art and Design, Univ. of Michigan. http://art-design.umich .edu/mother/.

An online resource guide managed and produced by the School of Art and Design at the University of Michigan. It includes schools of fine arts, online exhibitions, art museums, databases, library catalogs, research resources in art history, and more.

1034 NYPL digital. New York Public Library, Astor, Lenox and Tilden Foundations. http://digitalgallery.nypl.org/nypldigital/.

There are more than 450,000 images here from the holdings of the New York Public Library. Included are maps, posters, prints, photographs, illustrated books, illuminated manuscripts, ephemera, and more. Keyword and advanced search options are available. Many views may be available, and images may be downloaded for personal research and study purposes only. Named "Best Research Site" by Museums and the Web, 2006.

1035 Timeline of art history: The Metropolitan Museum of Art. Metropolitan Museum of Art. www .metmuseum.org/toah/splash.htm.

This site is a chronological, geographical, and thematic timeline of the history of world art that is illustrated mostly with images of the holdings in the Metropolitan Museum. Students, educators, and scholars seeking information from prehistoric art to the present day use it. There are charts of time periods, regional maps, an overview, and a list of key events. Users are able to compare art from around the world during any time period. There are links to other areas of the Metropolitan website as well as external sites. Copyrighted in 2000, and was named "Best Research Site" by Museums and the Web, 2005.

Architecture

1036 African American architects: A biographical dictionary, 1845–1945. Dreck Spurlock Wilson, ed. 550p. Routledge, 2004. ISBN 9780415929592. $$
720   NA736

A total of 168 alphabetical entries ranging from 250 to 4,000 words are cross-referenced and include photographs of the architects. Each entry includes a list of buildings with address at time of construction, date built, and, when possible, a selected bibliography. An appendix lists buildings by state. The format is modeled on *Concise dictionary of*

American biography and includes the input of 100 contributors. This title is recommended for general readers, students, preservationists, historians, and architects.

1037 American architecture: An illustrated encyclopedia. Cyril M. Harris. 384p. W. W. Norton, 2003. ISBN 9780393731033. $
720   NA705

More than 2,500 definitions describe construction materials and techniques, landscaping features, and the decorative arts and help in identifying nearly 200 styles that cover precolonial times to the present. Almost 1,000 illustrations are included.

1038 American shelter: An illustrated encyclopedia of the American home. Rev. ed. Lester Walker. 336p. Overlook Press, 1998. ISBN 9780879518714. $
728.37   NA7205

This encyclopedic history includes floor plans and exploded diagrams along with text that describes all styles of American housing. It begins with early Native American structures and goes through post-modernism and includes the manner in which each style developed. A bibliography, glossary, and an index to architects round out this tool.

1039 Contemporary architects. 3rd ed. Muriel Emanuel, ed. 1125p. St. James Press, 1994. ISBN 9781558621824. $$
720   NA680

This edition has added 40 architects for a total of more than 580. There are new illustrations in many entries, and it is 100 pages longer than the first edition, in 1980. Some architects who were not active prior to World War II were removed. Entries vary from minor to thorough coverage.

1040 Dictionary of architecture and construction. 4th ed. Cyril M. Harris. 1040p. McGraw-Hill Professional, 2005. ISBN 0071452373. $
720   NA31

Almost 25,000 definitions, more than 2,500 new, are included in this updated and expanded edition along with 200 new illustrations. This is a classic reference tool for students, librarians, researchers, historians, and practitioners, compiled by a well-known editor along with fifty expert contributors.

1041 Dictionary of architecture and landscape architecture. 2nd ed. James Stevens Curl. 992p. Oxford Univ. Pr., 2006. ISBN 9780192806307. $
720.3   NA31

Now up-to-date, this fully revised and expanded edition includes landscape terminology and biographies of modern architects. This source covers all of Western architectural history with more than 5,000 entries and more than 250 illustrations, over 50 of them new. All entries include a bibliography providing suggestions for further reading. Good for students, professionals, and the general reader.

1042 The elements of style: An encyclopedia of domestic architectural detail. 3rd ed. Stephen Calloway and Elizabeth Cromley, eds. 592p. Firefly Books, 2005. ISBN 9781554070794. $
728   NA2850

More than 500 years of architectural style, both American and British, are covered in this well-illustrated "visual survey." It is organized by period, then style feature. Supplier directories for Britain and North America have been updated, and glossaries are provided in American and British vernacular. With the input of many experts, Calloway, a curator at the Victoria and Albert, and Cromley edited this encyclopedia.

1043 Encyclopedia of interior design. Joanna Banham, ed. 2v., 1450p. Fitzroy Dearborn, 1997. ISBN 9781884964190. $$
747   NK1165

This two-volume set covers ancient Greece through the mid- to late 1990s. There are more than 500 black-and-white illustrated individual entries and longer articles. The individual entries include designers, architects, furniture styles, types of rooms, decorative objects, patrons, and critics, and the longer articles are surveys of countries, periods, and styles. This work focuses on American and European secular design of the nineteenth and twentieth centuries. All entries include a signed essay, a list of collections, cross-references, and a bibliography of major works. An impressive list of more than 300 advisors and contributors helped in publishing this reference set, which won at least four reference book awards.

1044 Encyclopedia of 20th-century architecture. R. Stephen Sennott, ed.

3v., 1568p. Fitzroy Dearborn, 2003. ISBN 9781579582432. $$$
724   NA680

This three-volume set includes more than 700 cross-referenced articles, ranging from 1,000 to 4,000 words, and covers all regions of the world. Bibliographies, photographs, and drawings support the articles. Categories include architects, firms, cities and countries, building types, movements, and styles. More than 300 writers contributed to this title, designed for the general public as well as students.

1045   A history of architecture. 20th ed. Banister Fletcher; Dan Cruickshank, ed. 1794p. Architectural Press, 1996. ISBN 9780750622677. $$
720.9   NA200

Sir Banister Fletcher's 100-year-old classic work has now been updated, chapters expanded, and new chapters added. One-third of the book is new. This standard one-volume history of architecture includes new chapters on twentieth-century architecture in the Middle East, Asia, India, and the Soviet Union. Coverage of twentieth-century western Europe has changed dramatically, and there is now detailed coverage of pre-1900 Latin America and the Caribbean. Under Cruickshank's excellent editorship, these changes and others have been made. Half of this wonderful work is filled with more than 2,000 photographs and illustrations.

1046   Illustrated dictionary of architecture. 2nd ed. Ernest E. Burden. 400p. McGraw-Hill Professional, 2001. ISBN 9780071375290. $
720   NA31

A highly visual resource that focuses mostly on design and includes almost 4,000 definitions and more than 3,000 illustrations. It is a good ready-reference tool that covers styles, details building elements and systems, and also includes biographies and examples of the works of more than 300 architects.

1047   The Penguin dictionary of architecture and landscape architecture. 5th ed. Nikolaus Pevsner, John Fleming, and Hugh Honour. 656p. Penguin, 2000. ISBN 9780140513233. $
720   NA31

This basic reference with biographies, movements, styles, and terminology has been revised and expanded. There are also many new entries for landscape architecture, and it includes more American architects and architecture. Entries are as long as several pages and include cross-references and reading lists. Good for student assignments.

1048   The Phaidon atlas of contemporary world architecture. Phaidon Press editors. 824p. Phaidon Press, 2004. ISBN 9780714843124. $$
724.7   NA680

The most outstanding world architecture in approximately seventy-five countries built between 1998 and 2002 is examined in this survey. It illustrates 1,052 buildings and is organized geographically. The atlas has more than 5,000 illustrations, 2,000 line drawings, 4,500 color images, and 60 maps. A committee of seven along with 150 international jurors helped to narrow down the list of 4,000 buildings.

1049   The Phaidon atlas of contemporary world architecture: Travel edition. Phaidon Press editors. 440p. Phaidon Press, 2005. ISBN 9780714844503. $
724.7   NA687

This condensed edition of the above title covers the most outstanding world architecture in approximately seventy-five countries built between 1998 and 2002. It includes the same buildings as the original but has only one illustration and a short description for each. It also includes forty-one regional maps and twenty-eight city orientations. This condensed edition includes the same buildings as the original, but the book is very portable and would be useful as a circulating item.

1050   The visual dictionary of American domestic architecture. Rachel Carley. 272p. Owl Books/Henry Holt, 1997. ISBN 9780805045635. $
728   NA7205

With more than 500 annotated illustrations, this book spans history from indigenous Native American structures to homes of the 1990s. Each chapter includes a description of a style, a period, or a type of architecture. There are many interior and exterior views of chosen dwellings and details of houses, such as doors, windows, and stairs. All entries are very well illustrated and labeled. An LJ Best Reference of 1995.

1051   A visual dictionary of architecture.
Francis D. K. Ching. 320p. Wiley, 1995.
ISBN 9780471284512. $
720.3   NA31

This source is a series of illustrations along with definitions, and in this manner more than 5,000 architectural terms are defined. The terms are organized in sixty-eight groups and then defined with line drawings. Next to the drawings are brief definitions. Additional access is provided through an alphabetical index.

Art

Dictionaries and Encyclopedias

1052   Artist's illustrated encyclopedia.
Phil Metzger. 512p. North Light
Books/F and W, 2001. OP. ISBN
9781581800234.
702   N8510

More than 1,000 cross-referenced terms used by the art student or artist are defined here. Materials, techniques, and some product names are included, and no attempt is made to explain how to use them. Phonetics is used for words that are hard to pronounce. Most entries are a few sentences long. This reference includes hundreds of illustrations.

**1053   The concise Oxford dictionary of
art and artists.** 3rd ed. Ian Chilvers.
672p. Oxford Univ. Pr., 2003. ISBN
9780198604778. $
703   N33

This concise dictionary, based on the Oxford *Dictionary of art*, has more than 2,500 entries and is a useful source for anyone interested in art. There are approximately 1,000 fewer entries than the unabridged edition, but those items remaining are virtually identical. Areas including artists, major works of art, techniques, patrons, museums, and materials are covered. Entries range from a few sentences to several pages in length. Circulating copies will be useful, as this edition is intended to be more portable. There are items from ancient times through the present, but artists born after 1965 are not included.

**1054   The concise Oxford dictionary of art
terms.** Michael Clarke. 272p. Oxford
Univ. Pr., 2001. ISBN 9780192800435. $
703   N33

More than 1,800 terms used in the visual arts are described briefly in this dictionary. Periods and styles throughout time are well represented. This title explains materials, techniques, and foreign and philosophical terms.

1055   The design encyclopedia. 2nd ed. Mel
Byars. 832p. Museum of Modern Art,
2004. ISBN 9780870700125. $
745.2   NK1370

The last 130 years of design described in more than 3,600 entries. The decorative arts, crafts, and industrial design comprise the areas covered. Biographies of major designers comprise the greater part of the entries and include works, exhibitions, and bibliographies. Author Byars compiled information gathered by design experts from many sources, but the 700-plus color reproductions are mostly from the Museum of Modern Art's collection.

1056   Dictionary of art. Jane Turner, ed.
32600p. Oxford Univ. Pr., 2002. ISBN
9780195170689. $$$ www.groveart
.com.
703   N31

Also known as "Grove's Dictionary of Art," this highly acclaimed thirty-four-volume encyclopedia is global in scope and includes all aspects of the visual arts throughout time. There are more than 41,000 signed articles by 6,000 contributors from 120 countries. The index has 670,000 entries and may be purchased separately. The longest biographies are up to thirty pages in length (Michelangelo). In deciding whether to purchase this title, need, cost, and space limitations must be considered. Many in-depth reviews are available online to help with this decision. This title is also available online by subscription, and thousands of partial biographies are available for free at www.artnet.com.

1057   Dictionary of Christian art. Linda
Murray and Peter Murray, eds. 658p.
Oxford Univ. Pr., 2004. OP. ISBN
9780198609667.
704.9   N7825

A total of 1,700 entries explore art and architecture influenced by Christian history, stories, and principles. Includes stained glass, manuscripts, and churches and other art inspired by Christian belief and tradition. There are major essays on styles and periods of art with hundreds of specific examples of works and where they can be located. It is an excellent work that concludes with a glossary of architectural terms and an expansive bibliography.

1058   A dictionary of modern design.
Rev. ed. Jonathan M. Woodham.
544p. Oxford Univ. Pr., 2006. ISBN
9780192806390 (pbk.). $
745.403   NK1165

A well-designed concise history as well as a dictionary that spans the mid-nineteenth to the end of the twentieth century. There are more than 2,000 entries on movements and individuals. Ceramics, furniture, graphics and designers, manufacturers, movements, and museums are included. Each alphabetical section begins with an example of design. No other illustrations are included. The dictionary section is followed by a topical bibliography, timelines, and a name index.

1059   Dictionary of symbols in Western art.
Sarah Carr-Gomm. 240p. Facts on File,
1995. ISBN 9780816033010. $
704.9   N7740

This dictionary includes symbols that appear in Western sculpture and paintings since the Renaissance. Included are symbols from Greek and Roman mythology, religion, astrology, and flowers. It is well illustrated with more than 175 drawings. It also has cross-references, footnotes in the margins, and descriptive panels. Good for students and teachers.

**1060   Encyclopedia of American
folk art.** Gerard C. Wertkin, ed.
704p. Routledge, 2003. ISBN
9780415929868. $$
745   NK805

More than three centuries of folk art are surveyed in this source. Folk art is only one name used; others are outsider art, vernacular art, visionary art, and self-taught art. A total of 92 specialists along with individuals at the American Folk Art Museum have included approximately 600 cross-referenced and indexed articles and bibliographies. Categories covered are artists, materials, and movements and range in length from one paragraph to one page. There are 100 black-and-white photos throughout as well as eight sixteen-page full-color inserts.

**1061   Museum of American folk art
encyclopedia of twentieth-century
American folk art and artists.**
Chuck Rosenak and Jan Rosenak.

416p. Abbeville Press, 1991. ISBN
9781558590410. $
709   NK808

This was published as a companion to an exhibit at the Museum of American Folk Art. It includes biographies of more than 250 self-taught painters, sculptors, potters, and creators of environments and is alphabetically arranged. Biographies include background, descriptions of the work, and materials and techniques. Included is at least one color plate for each artist. It is filled with color photographs. In the back is a list of major exhibitions from 1924 through 1990, an extensive bibliography, and an index.

1062   The Oxford companion to Western art.
Hugh Brigstocke. 888p. Oxford Univ. Pr.,
2001. ISBN 9780198662037. $
703   N33

This title has been almost completely rewritten since the 1970 edition. There are more than 2,600 alphabetical entries of artists, works of art, styles, forms, and movements. Entries range in length from 100 to 1,000 words. It covers classical times through the twentieth century but concerns itself with topics and individuals pre–World War I. The edition dropped architecture and non-Western subjects.

1063   The Oxford dictionary of art. 3rd ed.
Ian Chilvers, ed. 864p. Oxford Univ.
Pr., 2004. ISBN 9780198604761. $
703   N33

With 200 more pages, this edition has been thoroughly revised and expanded and includes approximately 3,500 entries on painting, sculpture, drawing, and the applied arts. About two-thirds of the entries are for artists. Architects, photographers, and applied artists do not have a main entry unless they are also well known as painters, sculptors, or printmakers. There are more than 200 new entries on contemporary artists, but no artists born after 1965 have their own heading. The time period is from classical times to the twenty-first century. It includes an updated chronology of major works and a directory of museums and galleries around the world.

**1064   The Penguin concise dictionary of art
history.** Nancy Frazier. 784p. Penguin,
2001. OP. ISBN 9780140514209.
709.003   N5300

This dictionary has more than 1,500 entries for artists and architects from ancient times to the present.

Biographical entries include medium, style, and school of art. There are entries included also for movements, styles, and works. Entries range in length from one sentence to several pages.

1065 Prestel dictionary of art and artists. Wieland Schmied and Frank Whitford. 384p. Prestel, 2000. ISBN 9783791323251. $

709   N33

This dictionary of twentieth-century art and artists has more than 1,300 entries and more than 500 illustrations, many in full color. The entries are concise and deal with artists, movements, techniques, and styles and have a short bibliography at the end of each entry. Biographical entries include information on exhibitions. It is international in scope, but the emphasis is on western European and U.S. artists.

1066 Self-taught, outsider and folk art: A guide to American artists, locations and resources. Betty-Carol Sellen and Cynthia J. Johanson. 334p. McFarland, 1999. ISBN 078640745X. $

745   NK805

This title is in two parts. The first is a state-by-state guide to galleries, auctions, festivals, museums, organizations, and other resources for outsider art. The second part is alphabetical and has information on hundreds of artists. Each entry has style, techniques, and personal information. Contact information and the information in the first section may be out of date because of the 1999 publication date, but it is still a useful tool.

1067 Thames and Hudson dictionary of art terms. 2nd ed. Edward Lucie-Smith. 240p. Thames and Hudson, 2003. ISBN 9780500203651. $

703   N33

Redesigned and revised, this dictionary has more than 2,000 terms used in the arts. There are 400 illustrations and diagrams of architectural terms. It defines words and phrases throughout the world and throughout history. It now includes terms connected with computer technology.

Directories

1068 Art across America: A comprehensive guide to American art museums
and exhibition galleries. John J. Russell and Thomas S. Spencer, eds. 898p. Friar's Lantern, 2000. ISBN 9780966714418. $

708.13   N510

In alphabetical order state-by-state and city-by-city, this guide includes almost 1,700 galleries and museums. Unlike *The official museum directory* (American Association of Museums, annual), this title is unique in its focus on the visual arts. Each gallery or museum entry is filled with practical data and including when available a URL to get updated information and facts about current exhibitions.

1069 Artists communities: A directory of residences that offer time and space for creativity. 3rd ed. Alliance of Artists' Communities staff. 336p. Allworth Press, 2005. ISBN 9781581154047. $

700   NX110

This book is organized in such a way that the interested artist can navigate through the detailed profiles for 95 leading communities in the United States and more than 350 programs throughout the world and make an informed choice.

1070 2007 artist's and graphic designer's market. Mary Cox, ed. 650p. Writer's Digest Books/F and W, 2006. ISBN 1582974292. $

741.60688; 706   N8600

More than 2,500 listings are in this serial publication geared toward amateur and professional artists and graphic designers and filled with marketing information. There are ten sections, from greeting card companies to record labels. A total of 600 listings are new this year.

Histories

1071 Art in the modern era: A guide to styles, schools, and movements. Amy Dempsey. 304p. Harry N. Abrams, 2002. ISBN 9780810941724. $

709   N6490

Some 300 schools and movements are organized chronologically beginning with impressionism and ending with a few movements in the twenty-first century. Two hundred secondary entries are cross-referenced to the 100 main entries. The main entries are one to three pages in length and include key collections and book lists for further study. Many illustrations support the text. There is also helpful supplemental material, including a foldout timeline and an in-depth index.

1072 Atlas of world art. John Onians, ed. 352p. Oxford Univ. Pr., 2004. ISBN 9780195215830. $$
709   N7425

Onians has compiled and edited the work of more than sixty art historians, archaeologists, and others to track world art throughout time, from prehistory to the present The atlas is arranged chronologically and then regionally and includes roughly 150 double-page spreads. More than 300 color maps are included. Color reproductions are spread throughout as well as lengthy captions when necessary.

1073 The Collins big book of art: From cave art to pop art. Ian Zaczek and David G. Wilkins. 528p Collins Design, 2005. ISBN 9780060832858. $
709   N5300

This history of European art is supplemented by the art of women, people of color, and non-Western civilizations. The first section of this book is a chronology that covers art from cave paintings through the sixties and is well illustrated with more than 1,200 works of art. A timeline is located across the top of this section. The second section expounds on themes in art and shows how art has illustrated those themes. The lengthy reference section includes many indexes. The way in which the book is arranged allows people to access information according to interest. The book is informative and can be enjoyed on many levels.

1074 History of art. 7th ed. Anthony Janson; Penelope J. E. Davies et al., eds. 1200p. Prentice Hall, 2006. ISBN 9780131934788. $$
709   N5300

The following comes from the press release about the seventh edition. "The six new author experts infuse their individual chapters with current perspectives, methodologies, and contexts, all for the purpose of communicating the power and meaning of art to the reader" in the same narrative style. All chapters have been revised and reorganized "to reflect a context-based, rather than formalist, discussion of style." The focus continues to be on the

Western tradition, with a new chapter on Islamic art and its relationship to Western art.

1075 The queer encyclopedia of the visual arts. Claude J. Summers, ed. 400p. Cleis Press, 2004. ISBN 9781573441919. $
704   N72

There are more than 200 alphabetically arranged entries that place the achievements of gay, lesbian, bisexual, transgender, and queer artists into the appropriate areas of art history. Their portrayal in the various arts is studied. Articles vary in length, are written and signed by accomplished scholars in their fields, and end with a brief bibliography. Indexes, illustrations, and cross-references also help the researcher.

Biographical Sources

1076 A to Z of American women in the visual arts. Carol Kort and Liz Sonneborn. 272p. Facts on File, 2002. ISBN 9780816043972. $
704   N6505

Some 130 American women artists from the eighteenth century through the time of publication are included in this title. The artists work in a wide variety of visual arts, including painting, crafts, folk arts, performance art, and earth art. There are approximately fifty photographs of the artists. Works of art only appear if they are in the photo of the artist. The artist entries range in length from one to three pages and include a reading list of a few specific titles. There are four indexes: by medium, style, and year of birth and a general index. Twenty-four artists do not appear in *North American women artists of the twentieth century*.

1077 African American art and artists. 3rd ed. Samella S. Lewis. 360p. Univ. of California Pr., 2003. ISBN 9780520239357 (pbk.). $
704.03   N6538

This classic work now surveys the works and lives of artists from the eighteenth century to 2003. A new introduction by Mary Jane Hewitt includes a lot of information about the author, Samella S. Lewis. A new section describes 1990–2002; the other five sections are much the same. There is also an expanded conclusion and bibliography.

1078 **American women sculptors: A history of women working in three dimensions.** Charlotte S. Rubinstein. 600p. G. K. Hall, 1990. ISBN 9780816187324. $

730   NB236

This title starts with early Native American women artists and includes women active through the 1980s. Basketry, textiles, ceramics, and other three-dimensional artists are documented along with traditional sculptors. The volume is well illustrated with black-and-white images.

1079 **Artists from Latin American cultures: A biographical dictionary.** Kristin G. Congdon and Kara Kelley Hallmark. 344p. Greenwood, 2002. ISBN 9780313315442. $

709   N6502.5

Approximately seventy-five Latin American artists from the United States, Central America, South America, and the Caribbean are listed in this dictionary. There are artists working in many areas, including installation artists and performance artists. Includes biographical material, information on artists' works, and places to view their works. There are many photographs in color and black and white.

1080 **Artists: From Michelangelo to Maya Lin.** 2nd ed. Aimee G. Ergas. 500p. UXL/Thomson Gale, 2001. ISBN 9780787653637. $$

709   N40

This set (volume 3 and volume 4) has ten updated entries and fifty new entries from the 1995 set (volume 1 and volume 2). Volume 1 and volume 2 include approximately sixty entries. A sampling of new entries are Yoko Ono, Norman Rockwell, and Julia Margaret Cameron. Each entry averages seven pages in length, and most include an artwork in black and white and a photograph of the artist. Aimed at a young adult audience, these books are a good starting point for reports. Recommended for libraries that already have the first set.

1081 **Contemporary artists.** 5th ed. Sara Pendergast and Tom Pendergast. 2v., 1340p. St. James Press, 2001. ISBN 1558624074. $$

709   N6490

This title has been completely revised and is now in two volumes. It examines 850 artists and has approximately 600 black-and-white photos of the artists and representative works. Entries contain a statement by the artist, biographies, and information regarding collections, public installations, and exhibitions. It is international in scope and includes artists in all areas not just visual artists, for example, Laurie Anderson and John Cage.

1082 **Contemporary designers.** 3rd ed. Sara Pendergast. 981p. St. James Press, 1997. OP. ISBN 1558621849.

745.2   NK1390

This edition explores the work of more than 650 international designers. Included are graphic designers, industrial designers, fashion designers, interior designers, architects, and others in a variety of fields. Living artists contributed a statement on their work or on contemporary design. Entries include biographical information and material regarding their works and bibliographies. Several dozen artists were removed from the last edition, and about seventy-five were added.

1083 **Dictionary of women artists.** Delia Gaze, ed. 1512p. Fitzroy Dearborn, 1997. ISBN 9781884964213. $$

709.2   N8354

More than 550 women artists, including painters, sculptors, photographers, and applied artists from medieval times to the present and born before 1945, are included in this dictionary. All entries are illustrated and include biographical information, an exhibition list, primary and secondary bibliographies, and a signed essay by one of several hundred art historians. This is the most comprehensive work on women artists working in the Western tradition.

1084 **Encyclopedia of artists.** William Vaughn, ed. 6v., 576p. Oxford Univ. Pr., 2001. ISBN 9780195215724. $$

709   N31

This compact six-volume set aimed at young adults includes more than 200 artists and more than 400 full-color images. The artists, from the Middle Ages to the present, are in alphabetical order in the first five volumes. Each volume starts with a timeline. The entries are two pages long and include a short essay, a biography in a sidebar, a box with the artist's style, and up to two color reproductions. The last volume covers major movements and schools of art and an index, a glossary, and suggestions for further reading.

1085   **North American women artists of the twentieth century: A biographical dictionary.** Jules Heller and Nancy G. Heller, eds. 736p. Garland, 1997. ISBN 9780815325840. $
709   N40

Approximately 1,500 women artists from Canada, the United States, and Mexico are in this dictionary. Twentieth-century artists born before 1960 and working in a broad range of fields are included. Entries average 330 words and include background, media, exhibitions, awards, and brief bibliographies. There are 100 black-and-white photos.

Cartoons and Comics

1086   **Comic book encyclopedia: The ultimate guide to characters, graphic novels, writers and artists in the comic book universe.** Ron Goulart. 384p. Harper Entertainment, 2004. ISBN 9780060538163. $
741.5   PN6707

Covering the 1930s to the publication date, this book includes characters, artists, writers, and the history of comic books, strips, and graphic novels. The reproductions are in color where appropriate and are excellent in quality. The superhero is emphasized and gets more in-depth coverage, but also included are some independent comic characters as well as some children's characters. If your library can only get one title, this might be a good choice, as Marvel, DC, and others are all included.

1087   **The DC Comics encyclopedia: The definitive guide to the characters of DC World.** Phil Jimenez and Dorling Kindersley Publishing staff. 352p. Dorling Kindersley, 2004. ISBN 9780756605926. $
741.5   PN6725

Beginning with DC Comics inception in the 1930s through the early 2000s, this encyclopedia features more than 1,000 characters. It is well illustrated and includes the date of first appearance, category (hero, villain, techno-sorcerers, etc.), and personal information about each character and includes many cross-references.

1088   **The Marvel encyclopedia.** DK Publishing staff. 352p.

Dorling Kindersley, 2006. ISBN 9780756623586 (v. 1). $
741.5   PN6725

Marvel published the *Fantastic four* in 1961 and has continued to create one classic after another. This illustrated volume includes more than 1,000 characters with essential facts and full details, including allies, enemies, and powers. Five additional volumes featuring the X-Men, the Hulk, Spider-Man, Marvel Knights, and the Fantastic Four have been published. These volumes go into more detail than the encyclopedia and feature all friends and foes.

1089   **World encyclopedia of comics.** 2nd ed. Maurice Horn, ed. 7v., 1061p. Chelsea House, 1999. ISBN 9780791048542. $$
741.5   PN6710

This source attempts to cover all aspects of comics in most areas of the world, making this useful in a very different way than the titles listed above. It begins with a very large section on the history of comics. Approximately half of the 1,200 original entries have been revised in this new edition, and approximately 200 new entries have been added. There are black-and-white illustrations throughout, and approximately one-half of the third volume is filled with color images. There are seven special indexes that provide access by name, title, location, and subject as well as other useful information in the last volume.

Costume and Fashion

1090   **Accessories of dress: An illustrated encyclopedia.** Katherine Lester and Bess Viola Oerke. 608p. Dover, 2004. ISBN 9780486433783. $
391.4   GT2050

This is an unabridged republication of the 1940 title *An illustrated history of those frills and furbelows of fashion which have come to be known as: Accessories of dress*. It describes the personal accessories that men and women have used throughout time. More than 600 figures and fifty plates from magazines, books, and paintings illustrate such items as shoes, hats, and wigs.

1091   **The complete fashion sourcebook.** John Peacock. 424p. Thames and Hudson, 2006. ISBN 9780500285725. $
391.00904   GT596

The well-known drawings of Peacock illustrating fashion from the 1920s through the 1980s are now in one rather than seven volumes. The year-by-year format includes day and evening wear, sports and leisure wear, accessories, underwear, and wedding attire, and each garment is described. There is a chart showing how shapes and styles evolved, biographies of well-known designers, and a bibliography. It is a very useful tool for reference and circulation.

1092   The complete history of costume and fashion: From ancient Egypt to the present day. Bronwyn Cosgrave. 256p. Checkmark Books, 2001. ISBN 9780816045747. $
391   GT375

This is a thorough guide to the history of clothing and fashion. It is organized by time period covering nearly 5,000 years, beginning in ancient Egypt and Rome and ending with haute couture in the twentieth century. It covers the evolution of style for men and women. Fashion is shown as it reflects history and the influences of culture, stature, professions, and individual style. It is extensively illustrated in color and is recommended for circulation but not as a reference tool.

1093   Contemporary fashion. 2nd ed. Taryn Benbow-Pfalzgraf. 700p. St. James Press, 2002. ISBN 9781558623484. $$
746.9   TT505

Revised edition of the 1995 title covers more than 400 designers and companies from the forties through 2002. There are approximately fifty new entries in this edition and double the photographs; all are black and white. Each entry is alphabetically arranged, and after a short biography or history, there is a bibliography and a signed article or essay. The more than seventy contributors are critics or scholars in fashion and costume. Not recommended for small libraries unless there is an institution nearby with a fashion curriculum.

1094   Costume and fashion: A concise history. 4th ed. James Laver. 304p. Thames and Hudson, 2002. ISBN 9780500203484. $
391   GT511

Laver's 1965 guide to the most important markers in the history of costume, beginning in ancient times, is much the same except for the last chapter, which covers 1940–2001. This chapter was originally written by Amy de la Haye of the Victoria and

Albert Museum and has been revised by Andrew Tucker to include the 1990s. It is a good introductory tool that is highly pictorial. This source has a slight British bias and sometimes uses different terminology from other fashion reference tools. Good for an overview or as a circulating item.

1095   A dictionary of costume and fashion: Historic and modern. Unabridged. Mary Brooks Picken. 446p. Dover, 1998. ISBN 9780486402949. $
746.9   TT503

Defining more than 10,000 words and including more than 700 detailed illustrations, this lexicon provides current and historic usage. The terms are arranged alphabetically or in categories such as elements of dress, parts of dress, design, or style. Great ready-reference tool for finding definitions of fashion and dress.

1096   Encyclopedia of clothing and fashion. Rev. ed. Valerie Steele. 3v., 1600p. Scribner, 2004. ISBN 9780684313948. $$
391   GT507

Culture and fashion throughout history are covered in this set. There are more than 600 alphabetically arranged articles, almost 600 black-and-white illustrations, and some color plates. Each article has a brief bibliography and may cover the history of clothing and textiles, periods, styles, trends, designers, and fashion houses. Articles range from one-half page to several pages. Steele, of the Fashion Institute of Technology Museum, and more than 300 contributors have composed this resource. At the back of volume 3 there is a timeline, outline of topics, and a detailed index. These volumes will be useful to students from high school through college and the general public.

1097   Fashion in costume, 1200–2000. 2nd ed. Joan Nunn. 288p. New Amsterdam Books/Ivan R. Dee, 2000. ISBN 9781566632799. $
391   GT580

Costumes of the Western world are covered in this title. Each chapter covers a particular period and includes an introduction and descriptions of accessories and dress worn by men, women, and children. This is an illustrated reference book that includes more than 800 line drawings by the author. The last two decades are covered in this edition. It is a good tool for the general reader, those interested in designing costumes, and students of fashion, the arts, and culture.

1098   **Fashions of a decade.** Facts on File staff. 8v. Facts on File, 1998. ISBN 9780816024643. $$
391   GT596

This set of eight books covering the 1920s through the 1990s is geared to young adults. Each decade is well illustrated with ads, other graphics, and photographs from the times. Each book has a summary that includes trends in the arts and sciences, lifestyles, politics of the decade, and changes in fashion. The next section in each is divided into eight topics, each four pages long. There is a glossary, bibliography, and chart in each.

1099   **The illustrated encyclopedia of costume and fashion: From 1066 to the present.** Jack Cassin-Scott. 192p. Cassell, 2006. ISBN 9781844034833. $
391   GT730

This source follows the content of the 1994 edition, adding 500 years of coverage. While the 1994 edition covered 1066–1550, this edition covers 1066 to the present. Organized by period, with plates that include notes at the bottom, this is a good visual source for students, artists, historians, wardrobe designers, and others.

1100   **In an influential fashion: An encyclopedia of 19th and 20th century fashion designers and retailers who transformed dress.** Ann T. Kellogg et al. 392p. Greenwood, 2002. ISBN 9780313312205. $
391   TT505

More than 160 designers and companies are featured in this book. An emphasis was placed on those who influenced current society or the fashion industry and with a focus on the United States. Where appropriate this source includes the economic side of fashion, with items such as licensing agreements and innovations in marketing. All entries range in length from one to two pages and are followed by a short reading list. Black-and-white illustrations were created specifically for this title. Appendixes include a chart of designers and the period they were active, designers by country and specialty, college and design programs, and costume collections.

1101   **Shoes: The complete sourcebook.** John Peacock. 168p. Thames and Hudson,

2005. ISBN 9780500512128. $
391.41309   GT2130

This is a very useful pictorial source featuring more than 2,000 color illustrations. There are examples of shoes for men and women from all eras arranged chronologically and including descriptions of materials, details, and styles. There is a time chart showing development throughout history, biographies of leading designers and manufacturers, and a bibliography. Peacock is an experienced costume and fashion designer.

1102   **Twentieth-century fashion.** John Peacock. 240p. Thames and Hudson, 1993. ISBN 9780500015643. $
391.009   GT596

Arranged by decade, this is another useful reference work by Peacock. Each chapter illustrates fashion by starting with the work of well-known designers and then shows clothing worn in leisure, day, and evening; wedding attire; and accessories and underwear. There are more than 1,000 full-color illustrations. This tool also has a time chart, biographies of leading designers, and a bibliography.

Decorative Arts and Antiques

1103   **Dictionary of furniture.** 2nd ed. Charles Boyce. 378p. Diane Publishing, 2001. ISBN 9780756767075 (pbk.). $
749   NK2205

In addition to new entries and new illustrations, many other useful new sections have been added in this edition. The main section has approximately 2,000 entries and covers styles, time periods, manufacturers, artists, definitions, and more. The text is the more useful part of this book. The new sections that have been included are a history of furniture, a guide for purchasing, a directory of major collections, a bibliography, and an index.

1104   **The elements of design: A practical encyclopedia of the decorative arts from the Renaissance to the present.** Noel Riley and Patricia Bayer, eds. 544p. Free Press, 2003. ISBN 9780743222297. $
745.4   NK750

The chapters of this very visual survey are organized by time period. Each period covers a variety of objects, such as furniture, textiles, silver, glass, and ceramics. More than 3,000 images help to illuminate the periods. Also included are biographies and information regarding conservation. Different individuals authored the various sections. This source provides a good overview of the time periods covered.

1105 An illustrated dictionary of ceramics.
Harold Newman and George Savage.
320p. Thames and Hudson, 2000.
ISBN 9780500273807. $
738   NK3770

More than 3,000 words or phrases describing styles, materials, patterns, and ceramic processes are explained. There is also a list of English and European factories, including dates, marks, and people. It includes many illustrations that are well labeled. This is the same edition as the 1985 paperback edition.

1106 Illustrated dictionary of practical pottery. 4th ed. Robert Fournier. 368p. Krause, 2000. ISBN 9780873419055. $
738.1   TT919.5

This is a new edition of a reference tool first published in 1973. Included are more than 1,000 terms describing glazes, techniques, equipment, recipes, charts, and firing methods. This title now includes health issues and concerns.

1107 The illustrated history of antiques: The essential reference for all antique lovers and collectors. Huon Mallalieu, ed. 640p. Diane Publishing, 2002. ISBN 9780756760809. $
745.1   NK1125

With everything from maps to coins, this source is divided into chapters that cover such items as costumes, rugs, arms and armor, jewelry, books, and most all areas of antiques. Every chapter has an introduction that puts the items into a historic and cultural context. Some terms are defined, and a glossary and bibliography are included in each chapter. There are more than 800 color photos that include descriptions, and where appropriate, there may be diagrams or charts. Expert contributors helped compile this useful reference book.

1108 Maloney's antiques and collectibles resource directory. David J. Maloney. Wallace-Homestead, 1995–2003. OP.
ISSN 1083-8449. $
745.1   NK1127

This is an excellent book for finding collectors, dealers, clubs and associations, experts, museums and libraries, periodicals, and Internet sources for antiques and collectibles. An extensive index provides cross-references to the main alphabetical section. With more than 900 pages, this reference book was previously described by *Library journal* as "one of the best reference books." The seventh edition of this title, published in 2003, is the last for the time being. The former publisher is working to bring it back in print and online format.

1109 Materials and techniques in the decorative arts: An illustrated dictionary. Lucy Trench, ed. 576p. Univ. of Chicago Pr., 2000. ISBN 9780226812007. $
745   NK30

As the title states, this dictionary describes the materials and techniques used in the decorative arts. The main materials are ceramics, glass, paints, stone, wood, metals, textiles, and paper, but many additional materials are included. There are *see* references and cross-references that help users to navigate easily. It is a good source for collectors, decorators, curators, and others. The contributors come from many areas of specialty, including art historians and scientists. The bibliography includes items arranged by materials in addition to general titles.

Graphic Design and Illustration

1110 The illustrator in America, 1860–2000. 3rd ed. Walt Reed. 464p. Harper Design International, 2003. ISBN 9780060554880. $
745.1   NK1127

Organized in chapters by decade, this edition now includes more than 600 illustrators from 1860 to 2000. There is a timeline at the start of the book and an introductory section at the beginning of each chapter. In addition to the coverage of 1980–2000, new artists have been added to each decade. The biographies are from a couple of paragraphs in length to a couple of pages and are accompanied by a characteristic color illustration.

1111 The Thames and Hudson dictionary of graphic design and designers. 2nd ed. Alan Livingston and Isabella Livingston. 240p. Thames and Hudson,

2003. ISBN 9780500203538. $

741.603   NC997

This book includes all areas of graphic design from 1840 to the present as well as developments in the field as far back as the first use of typography and printing presses. Movements, styles, techniques, artists, designers, and printers are defined or described. More than 450 illustrations, a chronological chart, and cross-references are included, and this new edition has more than 150 new entries.

Photography

1112   The Abrams encyclopedia of photography. Quentin Bajac and Christian Caujolle. 288p. Harry N. Abrams, 2004. ISBN 9780810956094. $

770   TR9

In four sections, this volume surveys the nearly 200 years of the history of photography. Prior to the sections is a list of important dates in photographic history. The first three sections are chronologically divided, and the last section includes biographies. The most coverage that a photographer receives is nearly two pages. The various themes that recur in photographs, such as landscapes, photojournalism, fashion, and nudes, are examined. There are more than 200 photographs included. It is recommended for communities that have larger art collections or that serve students involved in the visual arts.

1113   Contemporary photographers. 4th ed. Colin Naylor. 837p. St. James Press, 2004. ISBN 9781558623187. $$

770   TR139

Detailed information on more than 600 photographers with an international reputation is given, with coverage of all aspects of the field: studio art, commercial portraiture, journalism, and adverting. Entries consist of biographic information, a photograph from the person's work, a list of shows and exhibitions, a bibliography, critical information, and, in many cases, a statement by the photographer about his or her work.

1114   Encyclopedia of twentieth-century photography. Lynne Warren. 3v. Routledge, 2005. ISBN 9781579583934. $$$

770   TR642

This three-volume set examines the last 100 years of photography. Six sections cover areas such as history, equipment, terminology, processes, and people. Each volume contains more than 100 black-and-white photos, a color insert, and a glossary of terms. There are some articles written by experts that average five pages.

1115   A history of women photographers. 2nd ed. Naomi Rosenblum. 400p. Abbeville Press, 2000. ISBN 9780789206589. $

770   TR139

This history is a necessary edition for chronicling the accomplishments of women throughout the entire history of photography. Arranged chronologically, more than 250 photographers are examined, and examples of their works are included. The biographies are very detailed and include annotated bibliographies. This work has become a standard and a vital acquisition for any library that has an interest in art history or photography.

1116   The Oxford companion to the photograph. Rev. ed. Robin Lenman, ed. 800p. Oxford Univ. Pr., 2005. ISBN 9780198662716. $

770.3   TR9

This alphabetical source of approximately 1,600 items, half dealing with individuals connected with photography, details the international history and theory of photography. Articles range in size from one paragraph to several pages in length. The initials of one of the 180 contributors appear at the end of each article. Other useful features are a list of key websites arranged by country and type of site, a chronology, and an index of individuals and companies. This tool is similar in coverage to *The photography encyclopedia*.

1117   The photography encyclopedia. Fred W. McDarrah and Gloria S. McDarrah. 689p. Schirmer Books, 1998. ISBN 9780028650258. $$

770.3   TR9

This title is useful for biography, vocabulary, photographic processes, and history and is arranged alphabetically. Biographies range in length from a few paragraphs to almost one page. Other entries are much briefer. Following the main section are lists that include films by photographers and about photographers, galleries, and museums; Pulitzer Prize winners through 1998; a chronology; and a bibliography. In addition to hundreds of photographs, there are almost 100 portraits of photographers taken by the authors. The authors' intended audience was young adults, but it is effective for all levels of researchers.

1118 **2006 photographer's market.** Donna Poehner and Erika Kruse O'Connell, eds. 631p. Writer's Digest Books/F and W, 2005. ISBN 9781582973951. $

770.688   TR12

This is a serial publication that provides marketing information for amateur and professional photographers. There are articles on primary issues affecting photographers and interviews with professional photographers. More than 2,000 opportunities are listed, with contacts, needed items, and guidelines for submission.

13 *Performing Arts*

CAROLYN M. MULAC

Unlike the visual arts, which only need to be seen, performing arts require public performance to be appreciated. The performing arts included here are dance; film and video; television, radio, and telecommunications; and theater. Because of the large number of reference books in the field, music is treated separately, in the next chapter.

General Sources

Bibliographies and Guides

1119 **The performing arts: A guide to the reference literature.** Linda K. Simons. 244p. Libraries Unlimited, 1994. ISBN 9780340741917. $
016.791   Z6935

An annotated bibliography of more than 700 reference sources on theater, dance and musicals, but not film or television. Most sources listed are in English and have been published since the mid-1960s. Includes bibliographies, indexes, encyclopedias, core periodicals, libraries and archives and professional organizations. Author-title and subject indexes.

Databases and Indexes

1120 **A guide to critical reviews.** James M. Salem.

Part 1: American drama, 1908–1982.
3rd ed. 669p. Scarecrow, 1984. ISBN 9780810816909. $
016.8092   Z5781; PN2266

Part 2: The musical, 1909–1989.
3rd ed. 828p. Scarecrow, 1991. ISBN 9780810823877. $
016.8092   ML128

Part 3: Foreign drama, 1909–1977.
2nd ed. Scarecrow, 1979. OP.

Part 4: The screenplay from *The Jazz Singer* to *Dr. Strangelove*.
2034p. Scarecrow, 1971. ISBN 9780810803671. $$
809.2   PN1995

Part 4, supplement 1: The screenplay, 1963–1980. 708p. Scarecrow, 1982. ISBN 9780810815537. $
016.8092   PN2266

These volumes supply citations to reviews in general periodicals and the *New York Times*, with some coverage of regional and specialty periodicals. The reviews are of particular productions rather than general literary criticism. Each volume includes a number of special lists of awards, long runs, and so forth, as well as several indexes.

Directories

1121 **Dance annual directory.** Macfadden Dance Magazine, 2004–. Annual.

ISSN 1529-9570. $

791   GV1580

Contains listings for U.S., Canadian, and international dance companies, theaters, schools, individual artists, choreographers, opera companies, symphony orchestras, stage directors, theater companies, and more. A second section includes listings of performing arts resources and services. Index to advertisers.

1122   Musical America: International directory of the performing arts. 2006 ed. Commonwealth Business Media, 2005. ISBN 9781891131943. $$

780.25   ML12

An international directory of the performing arts with yearly highlights of dance, music, opera, and concerts. Entries include those for dance and opera companies, orchestras, music publishers, booking organizations, and periodicals and newspapers. Festivals and performing arts activities in the United States and around the world are also listed. The online version includes an archives featuring newspapers, directories, and magazines from 1905 on as well as daily news updates and a calendar of events. Online version available at www.musicalamerica.com.

1123   SIBMAS: International directory of performing arts collections and institutions. International Association of Libraries and Museums of the Performing Arts. www.sibmas.org.

From the Société Internationale des Bibliothèques et des Musées des Arts du Spectacle (SIBMAS), a listing of several thousand institutions around the world describing their collections in the areas of radio, television, cabaret, ballet, opera, music, circus, film, pantomime, and theater. May be browsed by name, collection, or location.

Biographical Sources

1124   African Americans in the performing arts. Steven Otfinoski. 276p. Facts on File, 2003. ISBN 081604807X. $

791.089   PN2286

Offers nearly 200 one- or two-page biographies of prominent African Americans in the performing arts from the early twentieth century through 2002. Includes an index, suggestions for further reading, and listings by year of birth and area of activity.

1125   Contemporary theatre, film, and television. Thomson Gale, 1984–. ISSN 0749-064X. $$

791   PN2285

A comprehensive biographical guide continuing the coverage of the seventeen editions of *Who's who in the theatre* (1912–1981) and expanding it to include choreographers, composers, critics, dancers, designers, executives, producers, and technicians along with theater, film, and television performers. Starting with volume 3, there are cumulative indexes in each volume that also index *Who's who in the theatre* and *Who was who in the theatre* (Gale, 1978).

Awards

1126   Academy of Motion Picture Arts and Sciences. Academy of Motion Picture Arts and Sciences. www.oscars.org.

Oscar's searchable home in cyberspace, this is the official website of the Academy of Motion Pictures Arts and Sciences. Includes history of the academy, press releases, and access to the Margaret Herrick Library.

1127   Academy of Television Arts and Sciences. Academy of Television Arts and Sciences. www.emmys.com.

The official cyber home of the Emmy and the Academy of Television Arts and Sciences. According to its website, "The mission of the Academy of Television Arts and Sciences is to promote creativity, diversity, innovation and excellence through recognition, education and leadership in the advancement of the telecommunications arts and sciences."

1128   Entertainment awards: A music, cinema, theatre and broadcasting guide, 1928. 3rd ed. Don Franks. 623p. McFarland, 2004. ISBN 9780786417988. $

792   PN2270

The third edition of a complete listing of major performance awards through 2003, including Oscars, Tonys, Obies, Emmys, Peabodys, and more.

1129   Tony awards. League of American Theatres and Producers and the American Theatre Wing. www.tonyawards.com.

The American Theatre Wing's repository of theater excellence on the Web. Includes a video library, press releases, events calendar, and other information about the theater awards.

Dance

Bibliographies and Guides

1130 **CyberDance: Ballet on the Net.** Rose Ann Willenbrink. www.cyberdance.org.

"An extensive Internet dance database containing thousands of links to classical ballet and modern dance resources on the Internet."

Dictionaries and Encyclopedias

1131 **American Ballet Theatre's online ballet dictionary.** Ballet Theatre Foundation. www.abt.org/education/dictionary/index.html.

American Ballet Theatre Company dancers demonstrate terms from the *Technical manual and dictionary of classical ballet* (Dover, 1982). A total of 170 ballet terms are demonstrated on this site.

1132 **Concise Oxford dictionary of ballet.** 2nd ed. Horst Koegler, ed. 503p. Oxford Univ. Pr., 1984. OP.
792.803   GV1585

Provides short entries on all aspects of ballet, including people, companies, and technical terms as well as modern, ethnic, and ballroom dance. Originally translated and adapted from Friedrich's *Ballett lexicon von A–Z* (1972), this is an update of the second edition, published in 1982.

1133 **International dictionary of ballet.** 2nd ed. Martha Bremser, ed. 2v. St. James Press, 2005. ISBN 9781558622319. $$
792.8   GV1585

More than 700 entries on dancers, choreographers, designers, teachers, ballet companies, and ballets accompanied by lists of related publications and signed, critical essays. Includes black-and-white photographs and other illustrations and indexes to professions, institutions, and nationalities.

1134 **International dictionary of modern dance.** Taryn Benbow-Pfalzgraf, ed. 900p. St. James Press, 1998. ISBN 9781558623590. $
792.803   GV1585

More than 400 signed entries about choreographers, companies, dancers, teachers, schools, works, trends, and more accompanied by black-and-white photographs. Includes a chronology of developments in modern dance and a bibliography.

1135 **International encyclopedia of dance.** Selma Jeanne Cohen, ed. 6v., 4048p. Oxford Univ. Pr., 2004. ISBN 9780195173697 (pbk.). $$
792.6   GV1585

A slipcased paperback edition of a classic work of dance scholarship first published in 1998. More than 2,000 articles by 600 scholars cover virtually every kind of dance, dance production, and dance company from every country, culture, and period of world history. Enhanced by more than 2,300 photographs, drawings, and other illustrations.

1136 **Oxford dictionary of dance.** Debra Craine and Judith Mackrell. 544p. Oxford Univ. Pr., 2005. ISBN 9780198607656. $
792.803   GV1580

Offers a comprehensive treatment of many aspects of dance in more than 2,500 articles. Traditional and modern forms of dance, dance company histories, and technical terms are among the topics covered.

Directories

1137 **Balletcompanies.com.** Dick Heuff. www.balletcompanies.com.

More than 3,000 links to ballet and dance companies around the world. This ballet search engine will help ballet fans find performances in their areas.

Handbooks

1138 **The dance handbook.** Allen Robertson and Donald Hutera. 278p. Macmillan, 1990. ISBN 9780816118298. $
792.8   GV1601

Comprised of entries on 200 major dancers, dance companies, choreographers, and dances that include critical commentary as well as factual information. A brief glossary of terms and a bibliography are included along with a directory of magazines, companies, and festivals.

1139 **One hundred one stories of the great ballets.** George Balanchine and Francis

Mason. 560p. Doubleday, 1975.
ISBN 9780385033985. $
792.8   MT95

Based on Balanchine's *Complete stories of the great ballets* (Doubleday, 1977), this handbook includes old favorites and newer works up to 1975. Concise, detailed stories are accompanied by production information, for example, the date and place of premiere, choreographer, principal dancers, designers, and music.

Film and Video

Bibliographies and Guides

1140   **Film and television: A guide to the reference literature.** Mark Emmons. 384p. Libraries Unlimited, 2006. ISBN 1563089149. $
016.791   Z5784

A comprehensive annotated bibliography supplying for television and film research what Simons does in *The performing arts: A guide to the literature for research.*

Databases and Indexes

1141   **All movie guide.** All Media Guide. www.allmovie.com.

Offers descriptions and ratings of more than 220,000 feature films and documentaries. An impressive site that librarians may wish to add to their lists of websites.

1142   **Internet movie database.** Internet Movie Database. www.imdb.com.

Complete details on more than 470,000 films, including made-for-television movies and series. Reviews by readers as well as professional film critics, box office grosses, trivia, and much more. This site is well known and heavily used by film fans.

Dictionaries and Encyclopedias

1143   **Dictionary of film terms: The aesthetic companion to film art.** Frank E. Beaver. 363p. Peter Lang, 2005. ISBN 9780820472980. $
791.43   PN1993.45

An updated version of a 1984 publication concentrating on aesthetics rather than technology. Current films are used as examples in many of the entries.

1144   **Film cartoons: A guide to 20th century American animated features and shorts.** Douglas L. McCall. 267p. McFarland, 2005. ISBN 9780786424504. $
016.791   NC1766

An alphabetically arranged listing of some 1,614 animated films, including synopses, credits, and voices. Offers extended discussions of 180 full-length features. A paperback reprint of the 1998 hardcover edition.

1145   **The film encyclopedia.** 5th ed. Ephraim Katz. 1552p. HarperCollins, 2005. ISBN 9780060742140. $
791.43   PN1993.45

The fifth edition of a well-respected reference work offering thousands of entries on stars, directors, producers, screenwriters, cinematographers, studios, styles, genres, and schools of filmmaking. Definitions of film terms and jargon are included.

1146   **Film studies dictionary.** Steve Blandford, Barry K. Grant, and Jim Hillier. 296p. Oxford Univ. Pr., 2001. ISBN 9780340741900; 9780340741917 (pbk.). $
791.43   PN1993.45

Approximately 1,000 film terms and concepts are explained in a work intended for film and media students.

1147   **Glossary of film terms.** Joel Schlemowitz. http://homepage. newschool.edu/~schlemoj/film_courses/ glossary_of_film_terms/.

A supplement to a film production course, this is a "glossary of the nomenclature of filmmaking." May be printed out for personal use only.

1148   **International dictionary of films and filmmakers.** 4th ed. Tom Pendergast and Sara Pendergast, eds. 4v., 1552p. St. James Press, 2000. ISBN 9781558624498. $$$/set; $$/v. Vol. 1, Films. ISBN 9781558624504. Vol. 2, Directors. ISBN 9781558624771. Vol. 3, Actors and actresses. ISBN

9781558624528. Vol. 4, Writers and production artists. ISBN 9781558624535.

791.43   PN1997.8

Provides detailed and authoritative information on films and their makers that "represent[s] the current concerns of North American, British, and West European film scholarship and criticism." Entries include those on films, directors, actors and actresses, writers, and production artists.

1149   The literary filmography: 6,200 adaptations of books, short stories and other nondramatic works. Leonard Mustazza. 2v. McFarland, 2006. ISBN 9780786424719. $

016.791   Z5784

Extensive list of English-language literary works adapted as theatrical and television films. Entries indicate directors, screenwriters, casts, and availability in DVD or VHS. Includes a selected bibliography and index of persons.

1150   Magill's cinema annual. Thomson Gale, 1983–. Annual. ISSN 0739-2141. $$/v.

791.43   PN1993.3

A yearly retrospective offering synopses on contemporary English- and foreign-language films released in the United States during the year. Includes critical reviews, credits, awards, and Motion Picture Association of America ratings.

1151   The motion picture guide, 1927–1984. Jay Robert Nash and Stanley Ralph Ross. 12v. Cinebooks, 1985–1987. ISBN 9780933997004. $$$/set

791.43   PN1993

The motion picture guide annual. Jay Robert Nash, Stanley Ralph Ross, and Robert B. Conelly, eds. Cinebooks, 1985–. Annual. ISBN 9780933997431. $$

791.43   PN1993

A major reference source for casual to in-depth questions about film. The first nine volumes cover every movie made in English as well as notable foreign films. Volume 10 covers silent films, and volumes 11 and 12 cover major film awards, title changes, and film series. Each entry supplies detailed production credits, casts, a synopsis, other facts, and critical commentary. *The motion picture guide annual* updates the original set and contains indexes to awards, names, and country of film

origin. The latest volume is *The motion picture guide annual, 1999.*

1152   New historical dictionary of the American film industry. Anthony Slide. 256p. Scarecrow, 2001. ISBN 9780810839571. $

384   PN1993.5

An updated version of the author's *The American film industry: A historical dictionary* (Greenwood, 1986) containing a third more entries than its predecessor. Includes descriptions of film techniques and genres, definitions of industry terms, information on film companies and organizations, and more.

1153   The New York Times film reviews. Times Books, 1968–2000. Biennial. ISSN 0362-3688. $$

791.43   PN1995

Reviews of films by critics of the *New York Times,* arranged by their date of publication in the newspaper. Series runs from 1968 to 2000. Older volumes are available back to 1913. The reviews are also indexed in *The New York Times index.* A handy source for older film reviews.

1154   RogerEbert.com. rogerebert.com. http://rogerebert.suntimes.com.

Thousands of movie reviews; hundreds of essays, interviews, and articles; and a number of special features—all by Ebert, "the best-known and most widely read film critic in the world." Edited by Jim Emerson.

Directories

1155   An actor's guide to the talkies: A comprehensive listing of 8,000 feature-length films from January, 1949, until December, 1964. Richard B. Dimmitt. 2v., 771p. Scarecrow, 1967. OP.

An actor's guide to the talkies, 1965 through 1974. Andrew A. Aros. Scarecrow, 1977. ISBN 9780810810525. $

016.79   PN1998

A title guide to the talkies: A comprehensive listing of 16,000 feature-length films from October, 1927, until December, 1963. Richard

B. Dimmitt. 2v. Scarecrow, 1965. OP.
016.79   PN1998

A title guide to the talkies, 1964 through 1974. Andrew A. Aros.
336p. Scarecrow, 1977. ISBN 9780810809765. $
016.79   PN1998

A title guide to the talkies, 1975 through 1984. Andrew A. Aros.
347p. Scarecrow, 1986. ISBN 9780810818682. $
016.79   PN1998

The volumes on actors list U.S. and foreign films, arranged by title, with the name of the studio and producer, year of release, and complete cast. The volumes on titles serve as a source for finding the novel, play, or nonfiction work that served as the basis of the film.

1156   Bowker's complete video directory.
4v. R. R. Bowker, 2006. ISBN 9780835247993. $$
016.29143   PN1992.95

Now in four volumes, this comprehensive directory offers 250,000 entries for entertainment, educational, and special-interest videos in a variety of formats. Indexes include those by title, genre, cast/ director, and more.

1157   CineMedia: The Internet's largest film and media directory. CineMedia and Dan Harries. www.cinemedia.org.

More than 25,000 links to film and media sites, including those for television, cinema, actors, directors, radio, studios, organizations, schools, and much more.

1158   DVD and video guide, 2007.
Mick Martin and Marsha Porter. 1664p. Bantam Books, 2006. ISBN 9780345493316. $
791.43   PN1992.93

Includes television programs, B westerns, and made-for-television movies along with a great variety of films. There are indexes by director and star and a list of Academy Award winners. Entries include summaries, commentaries, and MPAA ratings as well as full cast, credits, and year of release.

1159   Halliwell's film, video and DVD guide, 2006. John Walker, ed.

1315p. HarperCollins, 2006. ISBN 9780007205509. $
791   PN1993.45

A long-running guide to thousands of movies, packed with a variety of features, including plot synopses, available formats, and soundtrack availability along with full cast and credits and interesting film trivia.

1160   Leonard Maltin's movie guide, 2007.
Leonard Maltin. 1664p. Penguin, 2006. ISBN 9780452287563. $
791.43   PN1992.8

Television film critic's take on thousands of movies; detailed entries indicate availability on video or DVD.

1161   VideoHound's golden movie retriever: 2007. Jim Craddock. 1692p. Thomson Gale, 2006. ISBN 9780787689803. $
791.43   PN1992.5

More than 27,000 films are reviewed in this perennial favorite, which rates the best and worst among them. Indexes by writers, cast, director, and so forth.

Handbooks

1162   International motion picture almanac. Quigley, 1956–. Annual. ISSN 0895-2213. $$
791.43   PN1993.3

Provides biographical sketches of movie personalities, lists of services, distributors, film corporations, companies, theaters, suppliers, organizations, markets, and government agencies, primarily in the United States. Lists films of the previous decade and reviews the previous year in film awards, polls, and festivals.

1163   Screen world. John Willis. Applause, 1949–. Annual. ISSN 0080-8288. $
791.43   PN1993.3

Each volume supplies release date, running time, rating, full cast and partial production credits, brief plot synopses, and stills from major domestic and foreign films released in the United States in the previous year. Includes lists of the past year's Academy Award nominations and previous years' winners, box-office statistics, and brief bios of more than 2,000 performers.

Biographical Sources

1164 **Character actors: The names you don't remember, the faces you can't forget.** Dave Mazor. www.what-a-character.com.

Created and maintained by Dave Mazor, this site offers a number of ways to search (name, film, television program) for those ubiquitous character actors. Information provided includes biographies and photos.

1165 **Halliwell's who's who in the movies.** 4th ed. John Walker, ed. 656p. HarperCollins, 2006. ISBN 9780007169573. $
791.43   PN1993.45

The latest edition of a popular encyclopedia that covers film people as thoroughly as *Halliwell's film, video and DVD guide* covers films. Includes entries on actors, actresses, directors, producers, and other film personnel.

1166 **The new biographical dictionary of film.** David Thomson. 1008p. Knopf, 2004. ISBN 9780375709401. $
920   PN1998.2

An update of a reliable source of information on the lives and careers of actors and actresses, directors, writers, and producers important in the history of cinema.

1167 **Who was who on the screen.** Evelyn Mack Truitt. R. R. Bowker, 1984. OP.
791.43   PN1998

An authoritative and unfortunately out-of-print biographical directory of 13,000 screen personalities who died between 1905 and 1981. Entries include original and screen names, birth and death dates and places, cause of death, screen credits, and more.

Television, Radio, and Telecommunications

Dictionaries and Encyclopedias

1168 **Broadcast communications dictionary.** 3rd ed. Lincoln Diamant, ed. 266p. Greenwood, 1989. ISBN 9780313265020. $
384.54   PN1990

Several thousand common technical and slang terms from radio and television programming and production, network and cable operations, and audio- and videotape production.

1169 **Children's television, 1947–1990: Over 200 series, game and variety shows, cartoons, educational programs and specials.** Jeffrey Davis. 295p. McFarland, 1995. ISBN 9780899509112. $
791.45   PN1992.8

A select encyclopedia covering children's programming. Entries are alphabetically arranged under broad categories such as "Cartoon Shows," "Kindly Hosts and Hostesses," "Puppets, Marionettes and Dummies," and more. Appendixes include a chronology and a list of awards.

1170 **Complete directory to prime-time network and cable TV shows, 1946–present.** 8th ed. Tim Brooks and Earle Marsh. 1616p. Ballantine, 2003. ISBN 9780345455420. $
791.45   PN1992.18

The latest edition of one of the most useful reference works on television programs. Covers thousands of series on commercial networks in entries that include type of show, broadcast history, cast, plot or format, and spin-offs. Appendixes list each season's prime-time schedules, Emmy Award winners, and more.

1171 **Encyclopedia of radio.** Christopher H. Sterling. 3v., 1920p. Routledge, 2003. ISBN 9781579582494. $$
791.4475   TK6544

Produced in association with the Museum of Broadcast Communications in Chicago, this comprehensive set offers in-depth articles about all aspects of radio: its history and development and its roles in advertising, entertainment, popular media and propaganda, and more.

1172 **Encyclopedia of television.** 2nd ed. Horace Newcomb, ed. 4v., 2697p. Fitzroy Dearborn, 2005. ISBN 1579583946 $$$
384.55; 791.45   PN1992.18

Commissioned by the Museum of Broadcast Communications in Chicago, and drawing heavily on its archives, the second edition of this comprehensive work provides an excellent starting point for investigating almost any aspect of television or the television industry. The entire first edition of this landmark work is also available online at no charge at www.museum.tv/archives/etv/index.html.

1173 Movies made for television, 1964–2004. Alvin H. Marill. 5v., 2168p. Scarecrow, 2005. ISBN 9780810851740 $$
791.45   PN1992.8

The first four volumes consist of an exhaustive list of several thousand made-for-TV movies arranged alphabetically within each of four time periods (1964–1979, 1980–1989, 1990–1999, 2000–2004) and offering detailed information about each included film. The fifth volume is a comprehensive index.

1174 The Museum of Broadcast Communications. Museum of Broadcast Communications. www.museum.tv.

The online home of one of the three broadcast-history museums in the United States. The Museum of Broadcast Communications, in Chicago, is also home to the Radio Hall of Fame. Search the archives catalog and view or listen to television and radio programs online.

1175 On the air: The encyclopedia of old-time radio. John Dunning. 840p. Oxford Univ. Pr., 1998. ISBN 9780195076783. $
791.44   PN1991.3

This one-volume encyclopedia is an amplified and reorganized version of the author's *Tune in yesterday* (Prentice-Hall, 1976), covering some 1,500 programs from radio's golden age. Features include broadcast details and behind-the-scenes information.

1176 Television cartoon shows: An illustrated encyclopedia, 1949 through 2003. 2nd ed. Hal Erickson. 2v., 1054p. McFarland, 2005. ISBN 9780786420995. $
791.453   PN1992.8

The second edition of a comprehensive source in which coverage has increased by ten years. Entries include show titles, network, studio, producer, voice credits, and a critical essay with plot description, commentary, and other information.

1177 Television production handbook. Roger Inman and Greg Smith. 1980–2006. www.tv-handbook.com.

Originally intended as a guide for people using public and government access cable television channels, this site introduces the basics of television production (i.e., composition, lighting, and basic audio and video). Although it may not be duplicated or distributed, a hard-copy version is available for purchase.

Directories

1178 Broadcasting and cable yearbook. 2v. R. R. Bowker, 1993–. Annual. ISSN 0000-1511. $$
384.54   HE8689

The most comprehensive directory for the broadcasting and cable industries. Includes listings for U.S. and Canadian radio and television stations, satellite services, programming and production services, advertising and marketing services, and much more.

1179 Television and cable factbook: The authoritative reference for the television, cable and electronics industries. 4v. Warren, 1983–. Annual. ISSN 0732-8648. $$$
384.55   TK6540

Now in four volumes, two each for TV stations and cable systems, a comprehensive source of information for TV, cable, and related industries. Among the kinds of data provided are directory and statistical information, maps of broadcast areas, station and system ownership, revenues, and advertising figures.

Handbooks

1180 International television and video almanac. Quigley, 1987–. Annual. ISSN 0539-0761. $$
384.55   HE8700

Lists TV and cable industry personnel and personalities, services, distributors, press contacts, shows, series, movies, stations, publications, equipment, expenses and advertising, TV households, and more.

1181   World radio TV handbook. Billboard, 1961–. Annual. ISSN 0144-7750. $
621.3811   TK6540

Listings of long-, medium-, and shortwave television and radio broadcast frequencies, operating times, and addresses for every country in the world. Lists English-language and world satellite broadcasts. Maps of principal transmitter sites.

Theater

Bibliographies and Guides

1182   Basic catalog of plays and musicals. Samuel French. www.samuelfrench.com/store/.

Basic catalogs and supplements available for downloading. According to its website, "Samuel French seeks out the world's best plays and makes them available to the widest range of producing groups. Sources of Samuel French's plays range from Broadway and England's West End to publication of unsolicited scripts submitted by unpublished authors."

1183   Complete catalogue of plays, 2005– 2006. Dramatists Play Service, 2005. www.dramatists.com/text/catalogues .html.

Downloadable catalog published in odd years and supplement published in even years. Its website states it is "representing the American theatre by publishing and licensing the works of new and established playwrights."

Databases and Indexes

1184   Index to children's plays in collections. 2nd ed. Scarecrow, 1977. OP.

Index to children's plays in collections, 1975–1984. 3rd ed. 124p. Scarecrow, 1986. ISBN 9780810818934. $
016.8   PN1627

Some 950 plays from sixty-two collections have been added to the first edition (1972). The 1986 edition extends access by indexing 540 plays from forty-eight collections published between 1975 and 1984, to bring the series total to 1,990 plays.

1185   An index to one-act plays, for stage, radio and television. Hannah Logasa and Winifred Ver Nooy, comps. Faxon, 1924–1966. OP.
016.8082.   Z5781

Title, author, and subject indexes to one-act plays in collections and separately published editions. Radio plays begin to be indexed in the third supplement, and television plays start to appear in the fourth supplement. This title and its five supplements are all out of print.

1186   Index to plays, 1800–1926. Reprint. Ina Ten Eyck Firkins, comp. AMS Press, 1971. ISBN 9780404023867. $

Index to plays, supplement, 1927–34. Ina Ten Eyck Firkins, comp. 140p. H. W. Wilson, 1935. OP.
016.80882   Z7581

A comprehensive index of 7,872 plays by 2,203 authors, and in the supplement, of 3,284 plays by 1,335 authors, indicating where the text of each play can be found in anthologies or other sources. Title and subject index. This predecessor to *Play index* is useful for older plays.

1187   Index to plays in periodicals. 2nd ed. Dean H. Keller. 836p. Scarecrow, 1979. ISBN 9780810812086. $
016.8082   PN1721

Index to plays in periodicals, 1977– 1987. Dean H. Keller. 399p. Scarecrow, 1990. ISBN 9780810822887. $
016.8082   PN1721

The 1979 volume contains references to more than 9,500 entries found in 267 periodicals through 1976. The 1990 volume has 4,605 plays from 104 periodicals. Both volumes are arranged by author and contain citations to plays, an indication to the number of acts, and language if not English. Both contain title indexes.

1188   Ottemiller's index to plays in collections: An author and title index to plays appearing in collections published between 1900 and 1985. 7th ed. Billie M. Connor and Helene Mochedlover. 576p. Scarecrow, 1988. ISBN 9780810820814. $
016.8082   PN1655

A standard work for locating plays in collections, providing locations of more than 10,000 copies of more than 4,000 different plays by 2,000 different authors as found in about 2,000 anthologies. Includes full-length plays from all periods and literatures. One-act plays and radio and television dramas are included when found in anthologies of full-length plays.

1189 Play index. 10v. H. W. Wilson, 1952–. ISSN 0554-3037. $–$$
016.812   PN1627

Index of full-length, one-act, radio, television and Broadway plays; plays for amateurs, children, young adults, and adults. Arrangement is by author, title, and subject in one index, with such information as number of acts and scenes, size of cast, number of sets, bibliographic information, and a brief synopsis. Includes a list of plays by type of cast and number of players, a list of collections indexed, and a directory of publishers and distributors. The ten volumes are also available online on WilsonWeb.

1190 Plays for children and young adults: An evaluative index and guide. Rashelle S. Karp and June H. Schlessinger. Garland, 1991. OP.

Plays for children and young adults: An evaluative index and guide, supplement 1, 1989–1994. Rashelle S. Karp, June H. Schlessinger, and Bernard S. Schlessinger. 384p. Garland, 1996. ISBN 9780815314936. $$
016.812   PN1627

Alphabetically arranged entries for 3,560 plays published between 1975 and 1989 indicate bibliographic citation, audience grade level, cast number and gender required for production, number of acts, production time, setting, plot summary, royalty, and source. The supplement describes and evaluates some 2,000 additional plays published between 1989 and 1994 that are appropriate for young people to produce.

Dictionaries and Encyclopedias

1191 American musical theater: A chronicle. 3rd ed. Gerald Bordman. 917p. Oxford Univ. Pr., 2001. ISBN 9780195130744. $
782.1   ML1711

A comprehensive history covering influences on American musical theater prior to its birth in 1866 through the 1999–2000 Broadway season. The book moves year by year to describe every musical, citing opening date, theater, plot synopsis, and notable performers, directors, producers, and musicians. Three indexes cover shows and sources, songs, and people.

1192 American plays and musicals on screen: 650 stage productions and their film and television adaptations. Thomas S. Hischak. 351p. McFarland, 2004. ISBN 9780786420032. $
791.43   PS338

A guide to film and television versions of hundreds of stage productions. Entries supply full credits for both stage and film versions. Critical commentaries assess the success of transitions from stage to screen.

1193 Broadway musicals, 1943–2004. John Stewart. 1050p. McFarland, 2006. ISBN 0786422440. $$
782.14   ML102

More than 750 entries providing detailed information on musicals produced on Broadway. Includes pre-, post-, and Broadway runs; casts; awards; theaters; songs; and more. Song title and personnel indexes are appended.

1194 The Cambridge guide to American theatre. 2nd ed. Don B. Wilmeth and Tice L. Miller. 477p. Cambridge Univ. Pr., 1996. ISBN 9780521564441. $
792.0973   PN2221

The U.S.-related entries from *The Cambridge guide to world theatre* (1988) were revised and updated for this source, which includes signed entries on people, shows, and theaters as well as such topics as vaudeville, burlesque, circus, and off-off Broadway; African American, Asian American, and Hispanic theater; a select bibliography; a biographical index; and some 170 black-and-white illustrations.

1195 The Cambridge guide to theatre. 2nd ed. Martin Banham. 1247p. Cambridge Univ. Pr., 1995. ISBN 9780521434379. $
792.09   PN2035

A revised edition of the successor to *The Cambridge guide to world theatre* (1988) covering the history and current practice of theater throughout the world, broadly interpreted to include other popular staged entertainment, such as puppetry and the circus.

1196   The encyclopedia of the musical theatre. 2nd ed. Kurt Ganzl. 3v., 2274p. Thomson Gale, 2001. ISBN 9780028649702. $$
782.1403   ML102

First published in 1994, this substantial source has grown to three volumes packed with interesting, accessible articles spanning two centuries of musical theater history. Color photographs and black-and-white illustrations accent the detailed entries.

1197   The New York Times theater reviews. Publisher varies. 1870–2000. ISSN 0160-0583 (ceased); ISBN 9780405066641 (1870–1919, set); 9780824075538 (1912–1919, v. 5); 0824075684 (1977–1978); $$$ 0824075730 (1987–1988); 0815306431 (1991–1992, v. 27); 081530644X (1993–1994); 0815306458 (1995–1996); 0815333412 (1997–1998); 0415936977 (1999–2000).
792.973   PN2266

Reprints of all the theater reviews that have appeared in the *New York Times* in the order in which they appeared in the newspaper. Includes title, production company, and personal name indexing. Gives a complete citation for all reviews and biographical information about the critics who wrote the reviews. The reviews are also indexed in the *New York Times index.*

1198   The Oxford companion to American theatre. 3rd. ed. Gerald Bordman and Thomas S. Hischak. 696p. Oxford Univ. Pr., 2004. ISBN 9780195169867. $
792.0973   PN2220

Latest edition of a standard work in which older entries have been condensed rather than eliminated to make room for new material. Alphabetical listing of major American plays, long-running foreign plays, and theatrical notables, such as actors, authors, producers, and others. Numerous cross-references.

1199   Stage it with music: An encyclopedic guide to the American musical theatre. Thomas S. Hischak. 328p. Greenwood, 1993. ISBN 9780313287084. $
792.60973   ML102

A comprehensive one-volume source providing nearly 900 entries spanning 1866 to 1992. Individual shows, actors, directors, producers, composers, choreographers, and other theater people are presented, as are articles on musical series, genres, and other subjects. Includes combined index by subject, name, show, and song title.

1200   Two hundred years of the American circus: From Aba-Daba to the Zoppe-Zauatta Troupe. Tom Ogden. 416p. Facts on File, 1993. ISBN 9780816026111. $
791.303   GV1815

Entries cover performers, types of acts, animals, circus jargon, history, and related subjects. Cross-references, black-and-white illustrations, a bibliography, and an index to names, places, and subjects.

Handbooks

1201   The best plays theater yearbook. Limelight Editions, 2004–. Annual. ISSN 1071-6971. $
792   PN6112

Annual chronicle of the theater season on, off-, and off-off Broadway and around the country. "Ten Best Plays" provides a synopsis of the story and actual dialogue from key scenes. Complete credits for each play produced in New York each year are supplied, as are statistics of runs, lists of awards, and more. Published since 1899 under different titles by various publishers and annually since 1920. The preceding title is *The best plays of 2003*, also published by Limelight Editions since 1993.

1202   Theatre world. John Willis, ed. Applause, 1945–. Annual. ISSN 1088-4564. $
792   PN2277

Long-running publication that provides a record of performances, casts, and other production information for New York and American regional theater. Includes photographs and a listing of actors and actresses with brief biographical information.

14 *Music*

EMILY HICKS

Music reference sources continue to evolve, in part because of technological developments and a broadening interest in nonclassical genres, including world music. A few classic works were removed from the list because they are no longer widely available. Others have been subsumed by new print or electronic works. General sources are listed first, followed by sources specific to one or two genres of music. Major categories include blues and jazz, classical, country and gospel, rock and popular, and world music. Works encompassing more than two genres of music are included in the "General Sources" section. Several select online databases are included, and web links to related sources have been inserted into the narrative, as appropriate.

General Sources

Bibliographies and Discographies

1203 **A basic music library: Essential scores and sound recordings.** 3rd ed. Elizabeth A. Davis, ed. 665p. American Library Association, 1997. ISBN 0838934617. $$
016.78026   ML113

This selection and buying guide continues to be an important tool for building and evaluating music collections of all sizes. In addition to the more than 3,000 musical scores, the third edition includes, for the first time, more than 7,000 sound recordings of worldwide scope. A three-tiered ranking system identifies resources suitable for small, medium-sized, or large libraries. Part 1, "Scores," is organized by type of score (e.g., score anthologies, orchestral music, chamber music, vocal music, solo performance), and each entry contains composer, uniform title/title, publisher, language(s), and price. Although price and publisher information are outdated, the relevance of the work to library collections remains. Part 2, "Sound Recordings," is organized within the broad topics of "Western Classical Music," "Traditional and Popular Musics of the Americas and Europe," and "Musics of the Non-Western World." Entries include author, title, publisher, physical format, and recording date. Although availability of the listed sound recordings, particularly in relation to physical format, may have changed since publication, the lists are still valuable as a starting point for collection development.

1204 **Music reference and research materials: An annotated bibliography.** 5th ed. Vincent H. Duckles, Ida Reed, and Michael A. Keller, eds. 812p. Schirmer Books, 1997. ISBN 0028708210. $
016.78   ML113

This guide contains annotations of more than 3,500 significant music reference sources, including more than 1,100 new titles in this fifth edition. Material is organized by category of publication, including guides, bibliographies, catalogs, directories, electronic resources, dictionaries, and encyclopedias. Many entries include citations of published reviews. A single, more user-friendly index has replaced the previous edition's four indexes. Although the section on electronic information resources is understandably out-of-date, this text continues to be an important tool for music research.

1205   Song sheets to software: A guide to print music, software, and websites for musicians. 2nd ed. Elizabeth C. Axford. 267p. Scarecrow, 2004. ISBN 0810850273. $

780.26   ML74.7

Now in its second edition, this unique guide lists song sheets in print, music software, instructional media, and music-related websites for use by music educators or anyone wanting to learn more about music. New to this edition is the inclusion of instructional DVDs and CD sets covering a range of topics, including scoring and notation programs, composition and songwriting software, digital recording and editing, computer-aided instruction, and music theory. The volume also includes a brief history of printed music, essays on music royalties and copyright laws, a list of technical terms, and a bibliography.

Databases and Indexes

1206   Alexander Street Press music online. Alexander Street Press. www .alexanderstreet.com/products/muso.htm.

Alexander Street Press Music Online delivers more than 160,000 tracks of diverse music from a variety of genres, including classical, world, blues, and jazz. This unique online resource incorporates the music and liner notes from Classical Music Library, Smithsonian Global Sound for Libraries, African American Song, American Song, and other online music-listening databases as available into one online music library. Music Online is available on the Web through annual subscription. The service allows the creation of password-protected, custom playlists and course folders with static URLs. Includes *Baker's student encyclopedia of music* and *Baker's biographical dictionary of musicians.*

1207   The music index: A subject-author guide to music periodical literature. Harmonie Park Press, 1949–. ISSN 0027-4348. $$$$ www.hppmusicindex.com.

016.78   ML118

The music index provides citations for approximately 775 international music periodicals covering all musical styles and genres. A subject list organizes topical and geographic headings about classical and popular music. News and articles about music, performers, and the industry are included. Reviews of books, recordings, and performances are also indexed. First performances and obituaries are noted. *The music index* provides access to the indexes from 1976 to the present and is available either as a stand-alone product or bundled with the print version. The online version supports OpenURL and full-text links to JSTOR participants.

Dictionaries and Encyclopedias

1208   Baker's student encyclopedia of music. Laura Diane Kuhn, comp. 3v. Schirmer Books, 1999. ISBN 0028653157. $$

780   ML100

This three-volume comprehensive encyclopedia provides more than 5,500 concise entries on a broad range of music, musicians, composers, conductors, musical terms, and musical styles aimed at the junior high school level and up. These easy-to-read volumes include timelines for major historical figures, icons denoting entries for people or instruments, sidebars, and illustrations. Each volume contains an index and a full-color insert featuring a musical topic, such as popular performers and music around the world. Coverage includes classical, rock, rap, jazz, reggae, hip-hop, country, folk, popular, world, and New Age music. This resource is also part of the Alexander Street Press Classical Music Reference Library (www.alexander street.com/products/bakr.htm). This online database with approximately 30,000 pages is available either by annual subscription or through one-time purchase of perpetual rights, with prices scaled to budget and size of staff.

1209   The Billboard illustrated encyclopedia of music. Paul Du Noyer. 448p. Billboard Books, 2003. ISBN 0823078698. $

780.3   ML100

This visually appealing volume contains general overviews of the popular music genres of the last century, with an emphasis on recent styles. The work categorizes rock, pop, jazz, folk, blues, country, classical, electronic, dance, reggae, gospel, hip-hop and rap, soul and R&B, world and traditional, soundtracks and theater, and popular and novelty. These sections are further subdivided into subcategories such as fifties pop, Latin jazz, and alternative music. Each section contains a definition of the style, illustrations, a representative example of music, a glossary of instruments and terms, a list of leading exponents of style, and an alphabetical list of performers, composers, producers, and songwriters, with cross-references to relevant music styles.

1210   The book of world-famous music: Classical, popular, and folk. 5th ed. James J. Fuld. 718p. Dover, 2000. ISBN 0486414752. $
016.78   ML113

First published in 1966, this useful resource compiles historical information for nearly 1,000 of the world's most famous songs, including origins, composers, first lines of music, and copyright dates. Now in its fifth edition, the text has been updated and expanded to include new biographical and bibliographical data. Supplementary information includes first performers, performance dates, and recordings. A broad range of musical compositions are covered, including "Happy Birthday to You," "Greensleeves," "My Old Kentucky Home," and Beethoven's Symphony no. 5. The volume includes an extensive introduction to the work, an index, and selected illustrations.

1211   The concise Oxford dictionary of music. 4th ed. Michael Kennedy and Joyce Bourne Kennedy, eds. 815p. Oxford Univ. Pr., 2004. ISBN 0198608845. $
780   ML100

Derived from the *Oxford dictionary of music* (1994), this affordable concise edition provides more than 10,000 entries on musical terms, works, composers, musical instruments, and performers. Entries are alphabetical with cross-references. Entries for composers include work lists. Although some entries have been excluded or compressed for this edition, entries for major composers have not been abridged. A list of abbreviations used is included. Written for general readers as well as professionals, this volume is an authoritative reference work. Also available through Oxford Reference Online.

1212   The Harvard dictionary of music. 4th ed. Don Michael Randel, ed. 978p. Belknap Press, 2003. ISBN 0674011635. $
780   ML100

The fourth edition of this classic music reference work is often referred to as the essential single-volume music dictionary. The work has reverted back to its original title, dropping the word *new* that was added to the previous edition. Although the focus is still Western classical music, many existing entries have been updated and new entries added, giving greater attention to world and popular music and reflecting new developments in musical scholarship. Entries range from one or two words to encyclopedia length. The volume includes a list of contributors, bibliographical abbreviations, drawings, and musical examples. Unlike other single-volume music references, this work does not include biographical entries.

1213   Music since 1900. 6th ed. Laura Diane Kuhn and Nicolas Slonimsky. 1174p. Schirmer Reference, 2001. OP. ISBN 0028647874. $$
780   ML197

This sixth edition, the first published since famed musicologist Nicolas Slonimsky died in 1995, retains his unique mark while updating entries to reflect the end of the twentieth century. This detailed reference chronologically records significant events in the history of music during the entire twentieth century, including deaths, performances, festivals, publishing milestones, and music-related documents from around the world. Entries provide pertinent details in a single sentence. Some entries contain further information from letters and other documents as well as Slonimsky's own insights. The volume includes a list of letters and documents, a dictionary of terms, and an index. This entertaining work provides a wealth of information about classical music, composers, and musicians. This edition has more than 1,500 new entries.

1214   National anthems of the world. 11th ed. M. J. Bristow, ed. 629p. Weidenfeld and Nicolson, 2006. ISBN 9780304368266. $
784.4   ML1627

Compiled in cooperation with embassies and governments, this book is the definitive international authority on the national anthems. Entries are arranged alphabetically and include the musical score and lyrics when available. Words are presented in the original language and English, with a transliterated phonetic version if necessary. The eleventh edition features the words and music for 198 countries, including the new anthems for Afghanistan, Bosnia-Herzegovina, Georgia, Iraq, Rwanda, Somalia, and Timor-Leste.

1215 The new Grove dictionary of music and musicians. 2nd ed. Stanley Sadie and John Tyrrell, eds. 29v. Grove, 2001. ISBN 0195170679. $$$ www .grovemusic.com.
780.3   ML100

The second edition of this indispensable reference work arrived simultaneously in print and online in 2001. Even grander in size and scope than the laudable twenty-volume 1980 edition, this edition expands to twenty-nine volumes, with entire volumes devoted to the appendixes and the index. With the addition of 6,500 new articles now totaling 29,000, this edition expands its coverage of non-Western music, such as Latin American and African music, and covers the developments in musicology during the last twenty years. Although Grove Music Online began as the online version of *The new Grove dictionary of music and musicians,* regular updates and editions to the content have been continuous. Now Grove Music Online also includes *The new Grove dictionary of opera* and the second edition of *The new Grove dictionary of jazz.* Grove Music Online has full-text searching and links to related sites, including more than 500 musical examples. Overall, this is still the definitive source for music scholars. Although the price may seem high, consider that the volumes cost less than $100 each, and history has shown that new editions do not arrive frequently.

1216 The Oxford companion to music. Rev. ed. Alison Latham, ed. 1434p. Oxford Univ. Pr., 2002. ISBN 0198662122. $
780   ML100

This new edition of the classic reference work replaces the single-volume *Oxford companion to music* (Scholes, 1938) and the subsequent two-volume *New Oxford companion to music* (Arnold, 1983). This single-volume work provides entries on a broad range of topics, including biographies of composers and musicians, instruments, works, musical genres, and areas of current research. Western classical music is treated comprehensively although jazz and popular music are included as

well. Alphabetical entries range from short definitions of musical terms to extensive articles on musical forms and styles. Tables and examples of notation are included, but portraits and other illustrations included in previous editions are omitted. More than 1,000 new entries have been added on topics such as music on the Internet and politics and music. The volume includes a list of contributors, abbreviations, cross-references, further readings, and an index of people referred to in the text but who do not have separate entries. This reasonably priced title is a useful reference work for general readers. Also available through Oxford Reference Online.

1217 The Oxford dictionary of musical terms. Alison Latham, ed. Oxford Univ. Pr., 2004. ISBN 0198606982. $
780   ML108

This affordable A–Z listing provides succinct definitions of more than 2,500 musical terms commonly used in Western music, including jazz and popular music genres. Based on *The Oxford companion to music,* this dictionary encompasses a broad range of subjects, including genres, musical periods, scales, pitch, rhythm, and tempo. Entries provide etymologies and cross-references. Some entries include music examples and tables. This book is ideal for students, teachers, musicians, concertgoers, and anyone wanting a quick reference guide to musical terms.

Directories

1218 Songwriter's market. 29th ed. Writer's Digest Books/F and W, 1979–. Annual. ISSN 0161-5971. $
338.4   MT67

This guide to where and how to market songs is now in its twenty-ninth edition. The annual directory contains hundreds of listings for record companies, music publishers, music producers, booking agents, and others connected to the industry. The resource also includes interviews with music professionals, articles about songwriting and the music business, and a "quick-start" guide for those new to the music business. Music company entries include contacts, addresses, submission instructions, and musical genres of interest. The guide indicates new listings, companies accepting submissions from beginners, awards, changes to contact information, and firms that put music in films or television shows. Multiple indexes, lists of related websites and publications, and information about contests, awards, grants, workshops, and conferences are also included.

Handbooks

1219 **This business of music: The definitive guide to the music industry.**
9th ed. M. William Krasilovsky, Sidney Schemel, and John M. Gross. 526p. Billboard Books, 2003. ISBN 0823077284. $

338.4   ML3790

Now in its ninth edition, this resource continues to be an authoritative reference to the legal, economic, and financial issues of the music industry, addressing such topics as the implications of MP3, copyright revisions, antibootlegging initiatives, public domain, and more. The resource contains an updated directory of websites for music business information and research sources. An index and appendixes with excerpts from the Copyright Act, a list of music industry organizations, and contract checklists are also included.

Biographical Sources

1220 **Baker's biographical dictionary of musicians.** 9th ed. Nicolas Slonimsky and Laura Diane Kuhn, eds. 6v. Schirmer Books, 2001. ISBN 0028655257. $$$

780   ML105

This classic reference work celebrates its 100-year mark with an expanded centennial edition. Also called the ninth edition, this publication is the first since the death of editor Nicolas Slonimsky, in 1995. The six-volume set contains almost 2,000 new entries on rock, popular, jazz, and country music that had not been extensively covered in previous editions. Coverage of the nonclassical genres continues to be selective. Existing classical entries have been revised and more than 1,000 new classical entries added for a total number of entries in excess of 15,000. Signed entries are alphabetical and range in length from one paragraph to multiple pages. Works or discographies are included as appropriate. Indexes for genre, nationality, and women composers and musicians are included. This resource is available as part of the Alexander Street Press Classical Music Reference Library

(www.alexanderstreet.com/products/bakr.htm). This online database with approximately 30,000 pages is available either by annual subscription or through one-time purchase of perpetual rights, with prices scaled to budget and size of staff.

Blues and Jazz

Bibliographies and Discographies

1221 **The Penguin guide to jazz recordings.** 8th ed. Brian Morton and Richard Cook. 1534p. Penguin, 2006. ISBN 9780141023274. $

781.65   ML156.4

This substantial work continues to be a comprehensive compilation of jazz recordings. Entries are alphabetical by artist with brief biographical information and chronological disc reviews. A four-star rating system is used, and a crown symbol indicates the authors' personal favorites. The "Core Collection" designation, new in the seventh edition, identifies approximately 200 recordings that the authors consider essential to any jazz library. With the 2006 edition, it will be published biennially.

Dictionaries and Encyclopedias

1222 **The Billboard illustrated encyclopedia of jazz and blues.** Ted Drozdowski, Howard Mandel, and John Scofield. 352p. Billboard Books, 2005. ISBN 0823082660. $

781.6503   ML102

This one-volume illustrated encyclopedia spans 100 years of music and provides a basic overview of jazz and blues music and artists. Each chapter covers one decade and contains separate sections for each genre, noting important artists, themes, and styles. Key tracks of music demonstrating an artists' overall sound are examined, and popular melodies characterizing the music style of the time period are highlighted. The work contains lists of artists in each genre and instruments and equipment used to play jazz and blues. Internet links to sound files, a users' guide, a glossary, an index, and cross-references are also included.

1223 **The new Grove dictionary of jazz.** 2nd ed. Barry Dean Kernfeld, ed. 3v. Grove, 2002. ISBN 1561592846. $$

www.grovemusic.com.

781.65   ML102

This second edition builds upon the impressive first edition (1988), expanding to three volumes and adding 2,750 new entries, including 1,500 on musicians who emerged in the 1980s and 1990s. This one-stop resource to all things jazz provides alphabetical entries for composers, performers, instruments, terms, record labels, venues, and more. Many entries include bibliographies and selected recordings when applicable. The work includes illustrations, listings of abbreviations, a comprehensive bibliography of resources on jazz, a calendar of births and deaths, and list of contributors. This work is now available online along with *The new Grove dictionary of music and musicians* and *The new Grove dictionary of opera,* making regular updates and editions to the content easy. Grove Music Online has full-text searching and links to related sites, including more than 500 musical examples.

Biographical Sources

1224   The big book of blues: A biographical encyclopedia. Robert Santelli. 559p. Penguin, 2001. ISBN 0141001453. $

781.643   ML102

This concise biographical encyclopedia is the revised and updated edition of a work first published in 1993. This edition profiles more than 650 blues artists, discussing each artist's career, style, musical contribution, and essential recordings. The author's broad definition of the blues includes early rock, soul, swing, and boogie-woogie, allowing the inclusion of more artists and a more extensive view of the genre. A bibliography and index are included.

Classical Music

Bibliographies and Discographies

1225   Classical music: The listener's companion. Alexander J. Morin, ed. 1201p. Backbeat Books, 2002. ISBN 0879306386. $

781.6   ML156.9

This guide to classical recordings provides reviews and recommendations to help users decide which CDs to buy to suit their individual tastes. The scope encompasses 500 composers over nearly 500 years.

The book is divided into three parts and is indexed. Part 1 contains articles that discuss the important works of a composer, listed alphabetically by last name. Entries include brief information about the composer's work, historical significance, and recordings. Part 2 provides articles and recommendations organized by genre, such as Christmas music, film music, and Eastern chant. Part 3 contains articles and recommendations organized by musical instrument and artist. Although this work has not been updated since 2002, it is still a good United States–centric companion to *The Penguin guide.*

1226   The Penguin guide to compact discs and DVDs. 2005–06 ed. Ivan March, Edward Greenfield, and Robert Layton. 1520p. Penguin, 2005. ISBN 0141022620. $

780.266   ML156.9

The Penguin guide, now in its thirtieth-anniversary edition, continues to be an important resource for collectors of significant classical recordings. Although the work displays a bias toward British composers and recordings, it lists an impressive number of recordings. A rating system of one to three stars is used, with rosettes arbitrarily awarded to reviewers' favorites. Recommendations are included for the best new classical recordings and "must-have" recordings of classical music. The guide also includes limited super audio CDs and DVD recordings of musical performances. Entries are alphabetical by composer, with brief biographical data, notes about recordings, and price.

1227   The rough guide to classical music. 4th ed. Joe Staines and Duncan Clark, eds. 642p. Rough Guides, 2005. ISBN 1843532476. $

780.92   MT90

This fourth edition includes more than 200 alphabetical entries of significant classical composers, with brief biographical information, a discussion of important works, and reviews of recommended recordings. Essays featuring musical topics are interspersed among the composer listings. The work does not try to be a comprehensive guide to composers or their works. Instead, *The rough guide* provides an overview of mainstream classical music and selected CD recommendations. A chronology of composers, a glossary, and an index are also included.

Databases and Indexes

1228 **Naxos music library.** Naxos Digital
Services. www.naxosmusiclibrary.com.

The Naxos label is known for its high quality, budget-priced classical CDs. This affordable database contains more than 150,000 tracks of streaming audio from Naxos, Marco Polo, and nearly two-dozen other labels. In addition to covering the full range of the classical repertoire, the collection includes jazz, New Age, world, folk, and Chinese music. Access is through annual subscription. Subscribers have access to new material as it is released, typically more than 200 CDs per year. Users can read notes on the works being played as well as biographical information on composers or artists. Features include custom playlists, static URLs, near-CD quality sound, and extensive searching capability by composer, artist, period, year of composition, instrument, or genre. MARC records are available for purchase. Subscribers can add the Naxos Music Library Jazz, featuring the Fantasy label; the Naxos Spoken Word Library, containing classic literary works; and the SheetMusicNow collection of scores for relatively modest additional fees.

Dictionaries and Encyclopedias

1229 **The Billboard illustrated
encyclopedia of opera.** Stanley
Sadie and Jane Bellingham, eds.
320p. Billboard Books, 2004.
ISBN 0823077217. $
782.1   ML102

This beautifully illustrated volume examines the history of opera from its roots in the musical theater of ancient Greece through the twentieth century. Chapters are organized chronologically and include an introductory essay, discussion of prevalent operatic genres and styles, a list of key composers, and other prominent figures, such as librettists and singers. Synopses of operas, recommended recordings, a glossary, a bibliography, and indexes are also included. Color-coded themes highlight the history of opera, including developments in composition and vocal techniques; the most celebrated opera houses and performance companies; how composers tailored works to showcase the abilities of prominent performers; and how operas were performed and staged during a particular time period.

1230 **The new Grove dictionary of
opera.** Stanley Sadie, ed. 4v. Grove's
Dictionaries of Music, 1992. ISBN
0935859926; 0195221869 (pbk.). $$$;
$$ (pbk.). www.grovemusic.com.
782.1   ML102

This core reference source for opera is now available in paperback, making it much more affordable. Covering virtually every aspect of Western opera from composers, conductors, performers, and directors to genres, costumes, terminology, and venues, this work is now available online along with *The new Grove dictionary of music and musicians* and *The new Grove dictionary of jazz.* Grove Music Online has full-text searching and links to related sites, including more than 500 musical examples. For those preferring print, this four-volume set contains signed articles, organized alphabetically with cross-references and bibliographies. Biographical entries include vital statistics and lists of operatic works. Volume 4 contains an index of roles, an index of first lines, and a list of contributors.

1231 **The new Penguin opera guide.** Rev.
ed. Amanda Holden. 1142p. Penguin,
2001. ISBN 0140514759 (pbk.). $
782.1   ML102

The Penguin concise guide to opera.
Amanda Holden. 593p. Penguin, 2005.
ISBN 0141016825. $
782.1   ML102

The new Penguin opera guide, first published in 1993 as *The Viking opera guide,* is a comprehensive, one-volume encyclopedia of composers and works from the sixteenth century through the twentieth century. In total, the volume includes almost 2,000 works by 850 composers, covering all forms of opera and a wide-range of composers, from Mozart and Wagner to contemporary composers Holliger and Tan Dun. Alphabetical by composer's surname, articles summarize the composer's operatic career and contribution to the field with entries for major works listing title, background, plot synopses, libretto, duration, premiere information, cast, orchestra, and musical analysis. Brief bibliographies and selected recordings are included. A glossary, list of contributors, index of librettists, and index of opera titles conclude the volume. *The Penguin concise guide to opera* includes the most popular composers and frequently performed works from the full version. Critics have deemed it "irreplaceable," "superb," and "marvelous."

1232   The Oxford dictionary of musical works. Alison Latham, ed. 213p. Oxford Univ. Pr., 2004. ISBN 0198610203. $
780   ML100

This inexpensive, accessible dictionary, based on *The Oxford companion to music,* provides brief entries of more than 2,000 musical works, encompassing a wide range of genres, including opera, ballet, choral music, orchestral pieces, chamber ensembles, hymns, national anthems, and traditional melodies. Entries provide the genre, composer, librettist, number of movements or acts, scoring, historical context, and important dates, such as composition date or first performance. An appendix lists the composers included in the volume. This handy quick-reference work provides essential details about frequently performed and recorded works and is ideal for anyone wanting more information about the music he or she listens to or performs.

Biographical Sources

1233   Dictionary of American classical composers. 2nd ed. Neil Butterworth. 548p. Routledge, 2005. ISBN 0415938481. $$
780   ML106

This volume provides synopses of more than 650 composers active in the United States from the eighteenth to the twenty-first century. Alphabetical entries include biographical data, work lists, and critical examination of key works and influence. Many entries have been checked for accuracy by the composers. A selective list of American composers and their students is provided. Illustrations, a bibliography, and an author index are also included. Unfortunately, the index is not searchable by topic or musical composition.

1234   The lives and times of the great composers. Michael Steen. 984p. Oxford Univ. Pr., 2004. ISBN 0195222180. $
780   ML390

This volume presents fifty notable composers of classical music within the social, cultural, musical, and political contexts of their times. Beginning with Handel and Bach, this work encompasses 350 years of European history. Each narrative chapter presents a series of sketches from the lives of one or more composers. Readers desiring full biographical

accounts or in-depth analysis of individual musical works should look elsewhere. The usefulness of this text is the insights into when, where, and how the composer lived. The volume includes color plates, a map of composers' birthplaces, bibliographical references, and an index.

Country and Gospel Music

Bibliographies and Discographies

1235   Joel Whitburn's top country songs, 1944–2005, Billboard. 6th ed. Joel Whitburn. 621p. Record Research, 2005. ISBN 0898201659. $
016.781642   ML156

This sixth edition lists more than 2,300 artists and 17,800 songs that debuted on Billboard's country singles charts from January 8, 1944, through June 25, 2005. Entries are alphabetical by artist and include brief biographical information, song title, date song debuted on the chart, peak chart position, number of weeks on the chart, and record label. New features of this edition include songwriters' name, major music award winners, and artists' hit songs prior to 1944. A special recordholders section lists top artist and record achievements, including peak chart position of songs and a chronological list of number-one hits. The illustrated, easy-to-use volume provides quick access to country music trivia.

Dictionaries and Encyclopedias

1236   Encyclopedia of American gospel music. W. K. McNeil, ed. 489p. Routledge, 2005. ISBN 0415941792. $$
782.25   ML102

This encyclopedia defines American gospel music as "songs reflecting the personal religious experience of people" and covers both the African American and white gospel traditions. Significant events, musical instruments, musical styles, radio stations, record labels, publications, societies, and biographical profiles of performers, composers, and writers are included. The influence of gospel music on other genres of music and culture is examined. Entries are alphabetical and include selected bibliographies, Internet sites, and discographies. The volume also includes illustrations, end-of-article cross-references, and an index.

1237   **The encyclopedia of country music: The ultimate guide to the music.** Paul Kingsbury, ed.; The Country Music Foundation, comp. 634p. Oxford Univ. Pr., 2004. ISBN 0195176081. $

781.642   ML102

This work, first published in 1998, includes nearly 1,300 concise alphabetical entries on the singers, songwriters, record companies, and industry insiders that have made country music one of the most popular musical genres in North America today. Compiled by the Country Music Foundation, this guide presents eighty years of country music history, from the earliest "hillbilly" recordings in the 1920s to the mainstream success of Garth Brooks in the 1990s. Entries include biographical data, professional milestones, representative recordings, and cross-references. Black-and-white photographs are included along with 16 pages of color album art. The volume includes lists of best-selling albums, award winners, Country Music Hall of Fame members, and Grand Ole Opry members. An index is not included.

Rock and Popular Music

Bibliographies and Discographies

1238   **All music guide: The definitive guide to popular music.** 4th ed. Vladimir Bogdanov, Stephen Thomas Erlewine, and Chris Woodstra, eds. 1491p. Backbeat Books/All Media Guide, 2001. ISBN 0879306270. $ www.allmusic.com.

016.78026   ML156.9

This expansive guide to popular music is divided into sixteen major genres of music, including rock, blues, rap, gospel, country, bluegrass, folk, and jazz. Entries include artist name, a brief biography, a discussion of musical style, album reviews, lists of essential recordings, and suggested first purchases. More than 20,000 albums are reviewed and rated, including compilations, box sets, collections, and reissues. The volume also includes essays on musical topics and music maps highlighting the evolution of musical style and influential performers. The volume's index has been updated online to correct significant errors (www .backbeatbooks.com/pdfs/0879306270_index .pdf). All music guides have also been published for the following genres: classical, country, electronica, hip-hop, jazz, rock, soul, and blues. For the most up-to-date, comprehensive coverage, consult the website.

1239   **The Billboard book of top 40 hits.** 8th ed. Joel Whitburn. 852p. Billboard Books, 2004. ISBN 0823074994. $

016.78164   ML156.4

Now in its eighth edition, *The Billboard book of top 40 hits* features America's most popular songs and artists from the beginning of the rock era through 2003. This work lists every song that charted in the top 40 on Billboard's pop-singles charts from January 1, 1955, through December 27, 2003, alphabetically listed both by artist and song title. Artist entries include biographical information, chart information, and original label name and catalog number. A special record-holders section lists top artist and record achievements, including the top 100 hits of the rock era, the top 25 number-one hits by decade, the top 100 artists from 1955 through 2003, the top 25 artists by decade, and the number-one singles listed chronologically from 1955 through 2003. The illustrated volume provides quick access to top 40s trivia.

1240   **The Billboard book of top 40 R and B and hip-hop hits.** Joel Whitburn. 813p. Billboard Books, 2006. ISBN 0823082830. $

016.781643   ML156.4

This first edition lists top 40 music-chart information for the most popular rhythm and blues (R&B) and hip-hop songs and artists from October 24, 1942, through December 25, 2004. In 1942 Billboard magazine created the "Harlem Hit Parade," which charted the musical genre that would become R&B. By 1963, in the wake of rock and roll, the R&B and pop charts were so similar that the R&B chart was discontinued until 1965. Chart research from *Cash box* magazine is included for this time period. Billboard's R&B chart was revived in 1965 and featured hits by James Brown, Aretha Franklin, and the Supremes. Rap music entered the charts in 1979 with "Rapper's Delight" by the Sugarhill Gang and was popularized in the following decades by Run-D.M.C., LL Cool J, and others. Today the music of hip-hop artists such as Usher, Jay-Z, and OutKast is considered "mainstream." Entries are alphabetical by artist or group name and include brief biographical data, date of song debut in the top 40, highest chart position achieved, total weeks in the top 40, and original record label information. The volume also includes an alphabetical song list and lists of top artist and record achievements.

1241   The Green book of songs by subject: The thematic guide to popular music. 5th ed. Jeff Green. 1659p. Professional Desk References, 2002. ISBN 0939735105; 0939735202 (pbk.). $
016.78242164   ML156.4

Now in its fifth edition, *The Green book of songs by subject* organizes more than 35,000 songs into nearly 1,800 themes, such as desire, sadness, marriage, politics, animals, cars, and love. Entries span 100 years and cover all genres of popular music, including rock, country, R&B, rap, hip-hop, jazz, oldies, contemporary hits, popular standards, television themes, and advertising jingles. Compiled over twenty-five years by a music-industry professional, this thematic guide lists songs, artists, selected discographies, and record labels. This fifth edition includes 4,000 search terms and keywords in an expanded index with cross-references.

Databases and Indexes

1242   The children's song index, 1978–1993. Kay Laughlin et al., comps. 153p. Libraries Unlimited, 1996. ISBN 1563083329. $
016.78242   ML128

This reference tool compiles 2,654 children's songs found in 77 American songbooks listed in the *Cumulative book index, 1977–1994,* under the subject heading "Children's songs." The work contains a list of songbooks included, a song-title index, an index of first lines, and a subject index with subject thesaurus.

1243   Popular song index. Patricia Pate Havlice. 933p. Scarecrow, 1975. ISBN 081080820X. $

First supplement. 386p. 1978. ISBN 0810810999. $

Second supplement. 530p. 1984. ISBN 0810816423. $

Third supplement. 875p. 1989. ISBN 0810822024. $
016.784   ML128

Fourth supplement, 1988–2002. 2005. ISBN 0810852608. $$
016.78242164   ML128

The fourth supplement of the indispensable resource indexes 333 collections of popular songs

published from 1988 to 2002 in different genres, including rock, folk, country, blues, show tunes, children's songs, and movie soundtracks. Songs are listed by title, first line, and first line of the chorus, with an index of composers and lyricists. The original volume indexes 301 song collections published between 1940 and 1972. The first three supplements reference collections published primarily between 1970 and 1987.

1244   SongCite: An index to popular songs. William D. Goodfellow. 433p. Garland, 1995. ISBN 9780815320593. $
016.78242164   ML128

Supplement 1. William D. Goodfellow. 400p. Garland, 1999. ISBN 081533298X. $
016.78242164   ML128

Building on the venerable *Song index,* by Minnie Sears (1926; repr., Shoe String Press, 1966), and the *Popular song index,* by Patricia Pate Havlice, the original edition indexes more than 7,000 compositions from 248 collections of popular songs published between 1988 and 1994. Criteria for inclusion include publication date, the popular appeal of songs, and the lack of indexing in a similar work. A variety of popular music genres are represented, including rock, country, show tunes, jazz, folk, gospel, and holiday music. The resource contains a bibliography of indexed collections with corresponding codes, an index of titles and first lines, an index of composers, and an index of works from musicals, films, and television. The supplement indexes 6,500 popular songs published in 201 collections between 1990 and 1996. The inclusion of first lines as well as titles makes this resource particularly useful.

Dictionaries and Encyclopedias

1245   The American songbook: The singers, songwriters and the songs. Ken Bloom. 320p. Black Dog and Leventhal, 2005. ISBN 1579124488. $
782.4216409730904   ML3477

This visually striking volume presents an illustrated history of twentieth century American popular song and the 200 most prominent performers and songwriters of the era, including Louis Armstrong, Bing Crosby, Rosemary Clooney, Ella Fitzgerald, Stephen Foster, Richard Rodgers, Duke Ellington, and Cole Porter. Each entry contains information about the artist's life and career, famous songs, important contributions, record covers, anecdotes, quotes, and photographs. Hundreds of songs and related topics are featured throughout the book. Coverage is not comprehensive, but is a good overview, particularly of Tin Pan Alley artists. The volume includes song lists, capsule biographies, and index.

1246   The encyclopedia of popular music.
3rd ed. Colin Larkin, ed. 8v. Muze, 1998. ISBN 1561592374. $$$
781.64   ML102

The third edition of this monumental work expands upon its predecessor, the *Guinness encyclopedia of popular music* (Guinness, 1995), by adding 4,500 new entries and two more volumes for a total of 18,500 entries in eight volumes. Coverage includes the popular music of the United States and United Kingdom in the twentieth century, including rock, pop, country, jazz, soul, blues, reggae, show tunes, and rap. Entries vary in length from a paragraph to several pages and cover individuals, bands, recordings, musical theater, films, record labels, and topics. Volume 1 contains an essay on popular music. Volume 8 contains bibliographies by artist and subject, a list of selected fanzines, song title index, general index, and quick reference guide. A useful album rating system has been added to this edition, ranking albums from outstanding (five stars) to poor (one star). This work does have minor problems—the entries are unsigned and the general index does not list the volume with the page number—but overall, this work's comprehensive nature makes it a worthy addition to library collections.

1247   Encyclopedia of rap and hip hop culture. Yvonne Bynoe. 449p. Greenwood, 2006. ISBN 0313330581. $
782.421649   ML102

This comprehensive work covers the four components of hip-hop—MCing (or rapping), B-boying (or break dancing), DJing, and aerosol art or graffiti—providing a much-needed reference source about the thirty-year-old genre. The A–Z listing includes artists such as Dr. Dre, the Beastie Boys, Eminem, and the Sugar Hill Gang, who released the first commercially successful rap record, "Rapper's Delight," in 1979. Also included are entries for subjects (gangsta rap, censorship); record labels (Def Jam Recordings, Death Row Records); films (*Boyz n the Hood*, blaxploitation); and musical techniques (scratching, beatboxing). Entries range from a paragraph to several pages, with cross-references and select illustrations. The volume includes a well-written introduction on the history of hip-

hop, a selected discography of rap, a selected bibliography, an index, and the Hip Hop Declaration of Peace, presented to the United Nations in 2002.

1248   Rock and roll year by year. Luke Crampton and Dafydd Rees. 599p. DK, 2005. ISBN 0756613345 (pbk.). $
781.66   ML3534

This volume records the history of rock and roll with day-by-day entries and lavish photographs marking milestones of musical trends, artists' careers, recordings, and prominent industry insiders. The chronicle begins with the opening of Sam Phillips' Memphis Recording Service on January 1, 1950, and ends with the death of punk icon and Clash cofounder Joe Strummer, in December 2002. Each chapter covers one decade with almost daily entries and includes lists of each year's chart-topping singles in the United States and the United Kingdom. Brief "Roots" sections highlight the beginning steps of some of rock's most legendary stars. Written in association with the Rock and Roll Hall of Fame and Museum, the book includes photographs of rock memorabilia from the museum's collection. An index is also included.

1249   The Rolling Stone encyclopedia of rock and roll: Revised and updated for the 21st century. 3rd ed. Patricia Romanowksi Bashe, Holly George-Warren, and John Pareles, eds. 1114p. Fireside/Simon and Schuster, 2001. ISBN 0743201205. $
781.66   ML102

Now in its third edition, this authoritative encyclopedia covers rock-and-roll artists from the 1950s to the twenty-first century. The scope of this work is broad and includes artists as diverse as Elvis, Britney Spears, Eminem, and 'N Sync. The new edition includes revisions to the 1,800 existing entries and more than 100 new entries. Alphabetical entries contain vital statistics, discography, and critical essays detailing the performer's career and contribution to the field. Considered the premier guide to the history of rock and roll, this work is the official source of information for the Rock and Roll Hall of Fame and Museum.

Biographical Sources

1250   Baker's biographical dictionary of popular musicians since 1990.

2v. Schirmer Reference, 2004. ISBN 0028657993. $$

781.64   ML102

This excellent companion to Baker's biographical dictionary of musicians focuses on artists impacting the popular music scene since 1990. In contrast to Baker's biographical dictionary of musicians which emphasizes classical composers and their works, this dictionary focuses on the musical recordings of the included artists. Written for the general audience, the entries provide an overview of each artist's career with birth and death data, genre, best-selling recordings since 1990, and selected discography. The majority of the almost 600 artists included are from the rock/pop, rap, hip-hop, and rhythm and blues genres, although country, classical, jazz, world, and Latin artists are also included. Some artists such as Britney Spears and the Backstreet Boys are included for their commercial success, while others, like the Beatles and Nirvana, are included for their innovation and influence. The London Symphony Orchestra is included because of its prolific recordings—it released almost 100 albums in the 1990s alone. It has a long history of recording movie soundtracks, including Superman, Raiders of the Lost Ark and Star Wars and has accompanied a long list of popular artists. The appendix provides historical context with essays on grunge music, rap music, the transformation of commercial radio, and the music industry. A glossary, genre index, and general index are also included.

World Music

Bibliographies and Discographies

1251 The rough guide to world music, vol. 1: Africa, Europe and the Middle East. 3rd ed. Simon Broughton, Mark Ellingham, and Jon Lusk. 898p. Rough Guides, 2006. ISBN 1843535513. $
780.9   ML102

The rough guide to world music, vol. 2: Latin and North America, the Caribbean, Asia and the Pacific. 2nd ed. Simon Broughton, Mark Ellingham, and James McConnachie. 673p. Rough

Guides, 2000. ISBN 1858286360. $
780.9   ML102

First published in 1994, *The rough guide to world music* became the authoritative source for world music. Volume 1, covering the music of Africa, Europe, and the Middle East, is now in its third edition. Volume 2, covering the Americas, the Caribbean, India, Asia, and the Pacific region, is in its second edition. Features include articles on the popular and roots music of more than sixty countries, complete with discographies, biographical notes, music reviews, playlists for iPod or MP3 players, and photographs.

Databases and Indexes

1252 Smithsonian global sound for libraries. Smithsonian Global Sound. www.smithsonianglobalsound.org.

This database is available on the web through annual subscription and contains more than 35,000 tracks of music, spoken word, and other sounds, including the Smithsonian Folkways collection, founded by Moses Asch. The variety of recordings is immense, from a frog being eaten by a snake to classical violin instruction. The virtual encyclopedia also includes readings of plays, poetry, and other literary works, some spoken by the authors themselves. The children's collection includes songs, games, stories, and sing-alongs from around the world. The majority of the recordings are North American in origin. Controlled vocabularies enable users to browse by a variety of fields, including country, cultural group, genre, or instrument. The service allows the creation of password-protected, custom playlists and course folders with static URLs. The publisher also offers two subsets—Smithsonian Global Sound for Libraries—North America, with 19,000 tracks, and Smithsonian Folkways Recordings Online, covering approximately 325 CDs from the Folkways collection. The Alexander Street Press Music Online Subscription (available at www.alexanderstreet.com/index.html) also includes the Classical Music Library, African American Song, and American Song databases.

15 *Crafts and Hobbies*

CAROLE DYAL

Works published for crafters and hobbyists can be wonderfully entertaining. Although they may not be as scholarly or academic as other reference materials, they must be well organized and easy to use. Instructions must be clear but also inspirational for the enthusiast. Many of the works in this chapter are appropriate not only for the reference collection but also for the circulating collection. A rich source for any crafter or hobbyist is the Internet. A keyword search will produce unlimited websites with extraordinary amounts of information, ideas, and guidance for any hobby or craft; indeed, many of the publishers of the guides noted below produce elaborate websites with much additional information. The Internet, however, does not often supply the kind of overview and general context that crafters and hobbyists need to grasp the essence of their field of interest, nor does it provide the portability that hard copy allows.

Handbooks

1253   **Artist beware: The hazards in working with all art and craft materials and the precautions every artist and craftsperson should take.** 3rd ed. Michael McCann. 608p. Globe Pequot Press, 2005. ISBN 9781592285921 (pbk.). $

363.1   RC963.6

Supplies commonly used by artists and crafters are often highly toxic. This guide describes the relationship of such toxic materials to specific diseases and gives the threshold limit values for many common chemicals used in art and hobby materials, including raw materials, pigments and dyes, solvents, and plastics. Safe substitutes for toxic materials are listed. Precautions are clearly articulated, including protective equipment and proper disposal of materials. Organizations and published works of relevance are described.

1254   **Favorite hobbies and pastimes: A sourcebook of leisure pursuits.** Robert S. Munson. 366p. American Library Association, 1994. ISBN 0838906389 (pbk.). $

790.13   GV1201.5

A book of descriptions and information sources for eighty-four hobbies and pastimes. Entries are arranged alphabetically and range from three to six pages with an overview of the pastime or hobby that often includes a brief history as well as specifics detailing rules and equipment or tools needed. Entries close with a brief bibliography that includes reference books, periodicals, and associations for the hobbyist. For those who like to browse library shelves, a listing of library classification call numbers is given, and a subject index provides a further subdivision of the various entries.

Crafts

Beading

1255 **The bead directory: The complete guide to choosing and using more than 600 beautiful beads.** Elise Mann. 256p. Interweave Press, 2006. ISBN 9781596680029. $
745.582   TT860

Chapters are arranged by bead composition, including glass, stones, wood, and ceramics for more than 600 individual beads. Beads are pictured from all angles to allow foolproof identifications. Descriptions include dimensions, possible colors, weight, possible uses, and special care. Suppliers are listed both in store locations and websites. Well indexed.

1256 **Beadwork: A world guide.** Caroline Crabtree and Pam Stallebrass. 208p. Rizzoli, 2002. OP. ISBN 9780847825134.
745.582   NK3650

This volume is beautifully illustrated with beading techniques and beading examples from cultures around the world. A history of beading is followed by various manufacturing centers and historical trading patterns. Examples of beadwork from four main geographical areas (Africa, America, Asia, Europe) make up the majority of the book. There is a bibliography by country as well as listings of beading collections. Tips for collecting and for the proper storage of beads are included. The section on construction and techniques is appropriate for the more experienced beader, but beaders of all levels will be inspired by the wide-ranging and diverse examples of beadwork from around the world. The extensive index is by country and also by technique.

1257 **The encyclopedia of beading techniques: A step-by-step visual guide, with an inspirational gallery of finished works.** Sara Withers and Stephanie Burnham. 160p. Running Press, 2005. ISBN 9780762420438. $
745.582   TT860

This is a true step-by-step visual guide to beading. The first section focuses on tools and materials, including how to identify and select beads, threads, and tools. Small color photographs are shown with detail explaining each item. In the second section, various techniques, including traditional and contemporary methods, are well illustrated with step-by-step instructions. Section 3 will serve as an inspiration to beaders, with more than thirty pages of finished works of each type of beading illustrated in the second section. A short list of resources, including societies, suppliers, and websites, is included. Well indexed.

Knitting

1258 **Big book of knitting stitch patterns.** Sterling Publishing Company staff. 288p. Sterling, 2005. ISBN 9781402727634. $
746.432042   TT820

This book contains more than 550 knitting patterns made from nearly 150 different stitches. Basic stitches and patterns are covered extensively; other patterns are presented two per page. A black-and-white knitting chart as well as a color photograph of each pattern is included. Patterns are presented alphabetically within traditional categories. In addition to basic, classic, crossovers, creative, lace, textured, and slipstitches are multicolored and jacquard patterns.

1259 **Knitter's handbook: A comprehensive guide to the principles and techniques of handknitting.** Montse Stanley. 318p. Reader's Digest, 1999. ISBN 9780762102488. $
746.432   TT820

A truly comprehensive compendium of knitting techniques. At once clearly written and remarkably detailed, this work will appeal to both beginners and advanced students. Includes gauge charts and pattern instructions. Extra detail for finishing touches, including buttonholing and edging, is provided. Also included is a "Help" section that helps diagnose and remedy common knitting problems. All techniques discussed are well illustrated.

1260 **A treasury of knitting patterns.** Reprint. Barbara G. Walker. 320p. Simon and Schuster, 1981. ISBN 068417314X (pbk.). $
746.432   TT820

A second treasury of knitting patterns. Barbara G. Walker. 433p. Schoolhouse Press, 1998. ISBN 0942018176 (pbk.). $

746.4   TT820

Charted knitting designs: A third treasury of knitting patterns. Barbara G. Walker. 304p. Scribner, 1986. ISBN 0684125668; 0684174626 (pbk.). $

746.432043   TT820

A fourth treasury of knitting patterns. Barbara G. Walker. 241p. Schoolhouse Press, 2001. ISBN 9780942018202. $

746.432041   TT820

These are classic knitting stitch pattern compendia illustrated with close-up photographs of stitches along with explicit directions on how to knit more than 500 patterns. Includes simple knit-purl combinations, ribbings, color-change patterns, slip-stitch patterns, twist-stitch patterns, fancy texture patterns, patterns made with yarn-over stitches, eyelet patterns, lace, cables, and cable-stitch patterns. Includes information on the origin and use of patterns. Indexed.

1261   Vogue knitting: The ultimate knitting book. Vogue Knitting editors. 280p. Sixth and Spring Books, 2002. ISBN 9781931543163. $

746.43   TT820

A basic encyclopedia of knitting that is clearly written and easy to comprehend. Includes a history of knitting and a stitch dictionary that illustrates more than 120 popular stitches. Describes knitting supplies and basic techniques, including how to design garments. Includes 1,600 full-color illustrations.

Needlework

1262   The complete encyclopedia of needlework. 4th ed. Thérèse de Dillmont. 704p. Running Press, 2002. ISBN 9780762413188. $

746.4   TT705

Originally published in France in the nineteenth century, this work offers a very traditional approach to stitchery, describing needlework ranging from linen and silk embroidery to tapestry. Provides directions for both simple and advanced

techniques of every kind of needlework, including sewing and knitting.

1263   The complete encyclopedia of stitchery. Mildred Graves Ryan. 689p. Sterling, 2005. ISBN 9781402719486. $

746.403   TT760

Includes sections on crocheting, embroidering, knitting, rug making, sewing, and tatting. Entries are arranged alphabetically by stitch. Provides black-and-white block illustrations and step-by-step instructions that are clear and easy to follow.

1264   The complete illustrated stitch encyclopedia. Crafter's Choice staff. 320p. Sterling, 2004. ISBN 9781402713804. $

746.44   TT778.C3

This encyclopedia is very well illustrated with easy-to-follow directions for more than 250 hand stitches. Each technique is demonstrated and explained in full. The introduction includes a fabric guide and describes the particular language of the various stitches. The stitches are then presented by type, from embroidery to needlepoint to special techniques to finishing, which includes tassels and fringes. Examples and finished projects are pictured after each section. The index is easy to use.

1265   The needlepoint book: A complete update of the classic guide. 2nd ed. Jo Ippolito Christensen. 428p. Simon and Schuster, 1999. ISBN 9780684832302. $

746.44   TT778.C3

Originally published in 1976, this resource is a complete guide to the craft of needlepoint. A sixteen-page section of projects photographed in color are inspirational. Updates include new fabrics and fibers and how to work with them. More than 1,300 illustrations are shown with more than 370 stitches. Common errors with suggestions of how to avoid them are discussed. A true classic.

1266   Stitch sampler. Lucinda Ganderton. 160p. Dorling Kindersley, 2006. ISBN 9780756619008. $

746.44   TT770

A total of 234 stitches are illustrated in a "gallery of stitches." The small color photographs in the gallery magnify each stitch, list the name, and refer the sewer to the exact page for instructions. The instructions are two to a page and give alternative names for the stitches, level of expertise required, various uses for the stitch, and what the method of stitch is as well as step-by-step instructions with simple and clear color photographs. Technique variations are often provided, as are appropriate materials. The introduction gives an overview of materials, tools, and equipment needed.

Quilting

1267   Complete guide to quilting.
American Patchwork and Quilting.
320p. Meredith Books, 2002. ISBN
9780696215124. $
746.46   TT835

The complete quilting course. Gail
Lawther. 176p. New Line Books, 2001.
ISBN 9781577172215. $
746.46   TT835

The quilter's companion.
Katherine Guerrier. 256p. Creative
Pub. International, 2003. ISBN
9781589232433. $
646.25   TT835

Quilter's complete guide. 2nd
ed. Marianne Fons and Liz Porter.
272p. Oxmoor House, 2003. ISBN
9780848724665. $
746.9   TT835

All the above are excellent comprehensive guides to quilting, describing requisite equipment and supplies and introducing quilting skills in an accessible how-to approach. Layouts and quilt planning with yardage charts are given. In each case, several examples are included as well as practical projects are given.

**1268   Encyclopedia of pieced quilt
patterns.** Barbara Ann Brackman,
comp. 551p. American Quilter's Society,
1993. ISBN 0891458158. $
746.46   TT835

Spanning the years 1830–1980, this encyclopedia presents the most complete index to published American quilt designs in existence. A simple black-and-white graphic illustration is provided for each pattern indexed. Designs are presented in twenty-five clearly differentiated categories (one patch, strip, four patch, wheels, fans, etc.), each

with several subdivisions. Provides the original publication source of reference for each pattern. This is both a practical tool and a historical catalog. A masterpiece. Extensive bibliography.

1269   5,500 quilt block designs. Maggie
Malone. 448p. Sterling, 2005. ISBN
9781402720475. $
746.46   TT835

This is a visual feast for quilters of all levels. The color line drawings are clearly organized by pattern type, from traditional nine patch patterns to more elaborate twenty-four patch patterns. Circles and curves patches are included as well as octagons and stars and alphabets. International signal flags are also shown. Each section begins with a grid that can be used to create the pattern. The color illustrations very clearly display each pattern. Alternative names for patterns are given, and a key at the beginning of the book reveals when the pattern first appeared and in what publication. Not as comprehensive for research as the *Encyclopedia of pieced quilt patterns* but a wonderful addition to any quilting collection. The index is by pattern name.

Scrapbooking

**1270   Creating keepsakes: Encyclopedia
of scrapbooking.** 320p. Leisure Arts,
2005. ISBN 9781574864984. $
745.593   TR645

From the editors of *Creating keepsakes scrapbook magazine,* this a principal guide for scrapbooking. A brief history of scrapbooks in America going back to the mid-1800s begins this volume. Basics, from a tool guide to advanced embellishments, are discussed and illustrated. The table of contents is quite thorough and can be used as an alternative to an index. Appendixes cover archiving tips as well as computer applications. A list of resources, a glossary, and an index complete this useful book.

**1271   Designer scrapbooks with Mrs.
Grossman.** Andrea Grossman. 144p.
Sterling, 2004. ISBN 9781402710582. $
745.593   TR465

This book does include directions for how to make scrapbooks, but what sets it apart from other scrapbook efforts is the personal narrative of the author. Page after page is filled with inspirational ideas for scrapbooking as well as the thoughts behind why scrapbooks have such meaning for the crafter. Mrs.

Grossman is well known as a designer and manufacturer of decorative stickers. This volume will inspire scrapbookers of all levels.

1272   The encyclopedia of scrapbooking tools and techniques. Susan Pickering Rothamel. 320p. Sterling, 2005. ISBN 9781402710315. $

745.593   TR645

This encyclopedia begins with a history timeline of scrapbooks that goes back further than the *Creating keepsakes* volume. From John Locke's 1705 *New method of making commonplace books* to the late 1980s, scrapbooking has a fun history. Topics are arranged alphabetically, with generous color illustrations. Every essential scrapbooking tool or technique is described in this thorough reference work. Section on storage tips and photograph preservation are included. The acknowledgments include many websites for additional information as well as companies, including telephone numbers, for supplies. Scrapbooking publications and magazines are listed. In addition to a regular index, a twelve-page project index provides quick reference to the multitude of projects and ideas presented.

Sewing

1273   Claire Shaeffer's fabric sewing guide. 2nd ed. Claire B. Shaeffer. 544p. KP Books, 1997. ISBN 9780801986284 (pbk.). $

646.4   TT557

This is the most comprehensive guide to the selection, wear, care, and sewing of all fabrics. Part 1 describes fiber content, including natural fibers, man-made fibers, leathers, synthetic suedes, vinyls, furs, and feathers. Part 2 discusses fabric structure: woven fabrics, knits, and stretch-woven fabrics. Part 3 discusses all manner of fabric surface characteristics, including special-occasion fabrics, such as satin and taffeta, sequined and beaded fabrics, lace and net; napped and pile fabrics; felt and felted fabrics; reversible fabrics; quilted fabrics; and fabrics with designs, such as plaids, stripes, and prints. Part 4 discusses linings and interfacings. Part 5 describes sewing techniques, such as seams, hems, edge finishes, closures, and hand stitches. Part 6 is a fabric and fiber dictionary. There are several useful appendixes, a glossary, a bibliography, and an index.

1274   Complete book of sewing: A practical step-by-step guide to every technique. Jeffery Chris. 320p. Dorling Kindersley, 2003. ISBN 9780789496584. $

646.2   TT705

Complete photo guide to sewing: 1100 full-color how-to photos. Creative Publishing International staff. 320p. Creative Pub. International, 2005. ISBN 9781589232266 (pbk.). $

646.2   TT713

New complete guide to sewing: Step-by-step techniques for making clothes and home accessories. Reader's Digest Editors. 416p. Reader's Digest, 2002. ISBN 9780762104208. $

646.2   TT705

These basic sewing guides complement each other well. The Dorling Kindersley volume is fully illustrated with color photographs, color drawings, and charts. Chapters begin with an easy-to-follow guide to the sections and techniques that follow. Tools, patterns, notions, fabrics, and general and professional techniques, including finishing and tailoring, are included. A small section on mending is useful. The glossary and index are extensive. The *Complete photo guide* is a step-by-step guide to sewing. Each step is illustrated with a color photograph that clearly demonstrates each component. Chapters begin with a text overview, followed by specific directions. The Reader's Digest volume contains more color line drawings than the Dorling Kindersley volume and is very easy to follow. Projects are included for each section that well illustrate the particular techniques described. It also contains a section on tailoring for men, lacking in the others. The sections on sewing supplies and fabric selection are in color, and the fabric guide is quite useful. Because each book is slightly different in approach, sewers may want to compare illustrations and directions from each volume for an exceptionally thorough understanding of each technique.

1275   Encyclopedia of sewing machine techniques. Nancy Bednar and Joanne Pugh-Gannon. 336p. Sterling, 2007. ISBN 9781402742934 (pbk.). $

646.2   TT713

This volume illustrates how to use a sewing machine to its fullest potential. An overview of how to use a machine (any brand) is given as well as generic maintenance tips. The guide to selecting from all the available needles and thread is straightforward. Every presser foot imaginable is detailed with a photograph and then an illustration of the final product the particular foot creates. This is followed by specific tips for each foot. The next section details creative techniques, followed by indispensable, or standard, techniques. A list of manufacturers and contacts is included. The index is thorough and includes a separate index for the many tips.

1276   **The Fairchild dictionary of fashion.**
        3rd ed. Charlotte Mankey Calasibetta,
        Phyllis G. Tortora, and Bina Abling,
        eds. 522p. Fairchild, 2003. ISBN
        1563672359. $
        391.003   TT503

Entries have been organized into categories that make this dictionary easy to use. For example, footwear contains all shoes, boots, sandals, and slippers. More than 15,000 terms are detailed with more than 800 new drawings for this edition. Numerous cross-references eliminate many of the overlapping categories found in the previous editions. The appendix of fashion designers has been shortened to a briefer, biographical note. What is missing in this new edition are the black-and-white photographs found in the second edition that illustrate examples of well-known designers and trends.

1277   **The Vogue/Butterick step-by-step**
        guide to sewing techniques. 3rd ed.
        Vogue/Butterick Patterns editors. 428p.
        Butterick, 1999. ISBN 9781573890045
        (pbk.). $
        646.2   TT705

Demonstrates more than 500 of the 2,000 dress-making procedures regularly used in Vogue and Butterick patterns. The alphabetical organization makes this easy to use, and the illustrations are well placed. This is a fundamental reference for any sewer. The index is thorough. The vocabulary list is linked to page numbers. A total of forty-seven sections focus on specific garment pieces or specific techniques (e.g., appliqués, basting, buttonholes, collars, linings, marking, and ruffles).

Woodworking

1278   **The complete illustrated guide to**
        furniture and cabinet construction.

Andy Rae. 320p. Taunton Press, 2005.
ISBN 9781561584024 (pbk.). $
684.104   TT195

The complete illustrated guide to joinery. Gary Rogowski. 390p. Taunton Press, 2002. ISBN 9781561584017. $
684.1   TT185

Taunton's complete illustrated guide to box making. Doug Stowe. 160p. Taunton Press, 2004. ISBN 9781561585939 (pbk.). $
684.08   TT200

Taunton's complete illustrated guide to choosing and installing hardware. Robert J. Settich. 224p. Taunton Press, 2003. ISBN 9781561585618 (pbk.). $
684.1   TT186

Taunton's complete illustrated guide to finishing. Jeff Jewitt. 302p. Taunton Press, 2004. ISBN 9781561585922. $
684.1   TT199

Taunton's complete illustrated guide to sharpening. Thomas Lie-Nielsen. 224p. Taunton Press, 2004. ISBN 9781561586578. $
684.08   TT186

Taunton's complete illustrated guide to using woodworking tools. Lonnie Bird. 288p. Taunton Press, 2004. ISBN 9781561585977. $
684.08   TT186

Taunton's complete illustrated guide to working with wood. Andy Rae. 288p. Taunton Press, 2005. ISBN 9781561586837. $
684.08   TT180

Taunton Press has provided a truly comprehensive set of reference materials for the woodworker at any level of experience. Each volume is filled with explicit, very high-quality photographs. An easy-to-use visual map at the beginning of each section guides one to details or essays for specific operations. In addition, each section begins with a thorough overview: the visual guide allows those who want to skip the overview to go directly to specific techniques. The step-by-step instructions are accompanied by illustrations that are mostly photographs but with some drawings. Included are tips, multiple variations on techniques and processes, and safety concerns. Within each essay, or set of instructions, are cross-references to related operations. An extensive index, suggested further readings, suppliers, and lists of organizations and other groups complete each volume in this useful set.

1279 Hand tools: Their ways and workings. Aldren A. Watson. 416p. W. W. Norton, 2002. ISBN 9780393322767. $
684.082   TJ1195

How to identify and use hand woodworking tools. More than 450 drawings detail how each tool is properly used and what it can be used for. Includes suggested workbench plans and hand-tool shop inventories. The text is straightforward, with good woodworking hints. Step-by-step instructions are provided. The index is by name of individual tools.

1280 How to design and build your ideal woodshop. 2nd ed. Bill Stankus. 128p. F and W, 2001. ISBN 9781558705876. $
684.08   TT152

A thoughtful, practical guide for the home woodshop. Much space is devoted to creating and realizing a vision of a practical and efficient home shop, whether current attic, closet, or garage will be altered or if a dedicated outbuilding will be used. Various floor plans, which maximize space, are offered. Chapters include ensuring safe electrical power, with lighting guides as well as discussions of safety concerns. Color photographs illustrate sample shops for different types of woodworking (e.g., furniture restoration, cabinetmaking, etc.). Also included is a list of resources for locating machinery and tools. The index is straightforward.

1281 The real wood bible: The complete illustrated guide to choosing and using 100 decorative woods. Nick Gibbs. 256p. Firefly Books, 2005. ISBN 9781554070336. $
684.08   TT180

This handy book is a straightforward guide to woods most commonly used by woodworkers. Also included are woods that are less available but still appropriate for woodworking. The introduction gives an overview of the transformation of trees into boards. Endangered species are listed to be avoided. Various methods of cutting lumber, dry rates, common defects, and storage tips are included. The guide begins with a thumbnail photograph directing one to the appropriate page

for a detailed description. A clear true-to-size photograph to show grain and figure accompanies each one-page overview. Strengths, weaknesses, key characteristics, and key uses are given for each wood. A small section on special effects of grain, figuring, burls, and identifying quartersawn surfaces precedes the glossary and index.

1282 Taunton's complete illustrated guide to woodworking. Lonnie Bird, Jeff Jewitt, and Thomas Lie-Nielsen. 320p. Taunton Press, 2005. ISBN 9781561587698. $
684.082   TT180

This book is a concise version of the first six volumes of Taunton's Complete Illustrated Guide series. It combines in one volume basic and essential information for any woodworker. The format is the same as for the larger series: high-quality photographs, well-designed step-by-step instructions, and numerous cross-references. The appendix includes further readings, sources for materials, organizations, and a quick guide to wood types.

1283 Woodshop dust control: A complete guide to setting up your own system. 2nd ed. Sandor Nagyszalanczy. 208p. Taunton Press, 2002. ISBN 9781561584994. $
684.08   TT180

This comprehensive work addresses the sometimes overlooked personal and environmental hazards of working with wood dust. Color photographs, drawings, charts, and specific instructions detail how to design systems for dust control and dust collection. The author describes various examples of shop systems, from vacuums to respirators to actual installation of ventilation devices. An important safety guide.

Hobbies

Antiques and Collectibles

1284 Antique trader antiques and collectibles price guide, 2006. Kyle Husfloen, ed. 1072p. KP Books, 2005. ISBN 9780873499897 (pbk.). $
745.1   NK805

With more than 1,000 pages, this is the biggest of the antiques and collectibles price guides. This edition has more than 5,000 color photographs and more than 18,000 entries in 160 category types. Prices are for items in good condition. Descriptive information accompanies each illustration, which helps to ensure more accurate identification of items. The table of contents lists the categories, while the index contains many other entries with cross-references.

1285   Kovels' antiques and collectibles price list, 39th ed., 2007. 39th ed. Terry Kovel. 853p. Knopf, 2006. ISBN 9780375721854. $
745.1   NK805

Prices listed are asking prices for the American market: what costs what and when. Listings are by category and then by object, followed by a description. There are more than 45,000 entries in more than 500 categories along with more than 500 color photographs in this edition. Product logos as well as tips about care and identification of collectibles are included. A sixteen-page report details items that sold for unusually high prices over the past year. The alphabetical listing is easy to use. The index contains many cross-references.

1286   Warman's antiques and collectibles price guide: The essential field guide to the antiques and collectibles marketplace. 41st ed. Ellen T. Schroy, ed. 768p. Krause, 2007. ISBN 9780896894976. $
745.1   NK1133

This edition is the first in full color for this title. Objects made between 1700 and the present are included. Lists more than 50,000 objects alphabetically by category, providing a capsule history of the object, bibliographic references, periodicals, clubs, museums, photographs, and marks. Within each category, objects that are actively being sold in the antiques market are listed with clear descriptions and asking prices from auctions and dealers. Prices tend to be for items in very good condition. Well indexed.

Coins and Paper Money

1287   The coin atlas handbook: A comprehensive view of the coins of the world throughout history. Joe Cribb et al. 224p. Book Sales, 2004. ISBN 9780785818540. $
737.494   CJ59

This historical atlas of coinage provides a political history of each country's coinage through text along with more than 400 photographs. A total of 100 maps indicate location of mints and general circulation of coins. Includes a glossary, a selective bibliography, and an index of persons, places, events, metals, and minting processes.

1288   Coin world almanac: Millennium edition. 7th ed. Beth Deisher and William T. Gibbs, eds. 700p. Coin World, 2000. ISBN 9780944945346 (pbk.). $
737.4   CJ1

This work contains "the essential facts which form the permanent record of numismatics." Twenty-two chapters record this information through essays, tables, statistics, and directories. Topics covered include coin collecting, investing, paper money, counterfeits, rarities, and coin design. Lists museums, societies, and organizations of interest to collectors.

1289   Coins and currency: An historical encyclopedia. Mary Ellen Snodgrass. 572p. McFarland, 2003. ISBN 9780786414505. $
737.4   HG231

With more than 250 entries, this volume is an encyclopedia of the use of money throughout history. Included is a timeline of important events in monetary history from 3,500 BC (Sumerian coin shell money) to AD 2002 (introduction of the Euro). Black-and-white photographs throughout highlight various entries. The entries are listed in the beginning followed by numerous *see* references. A chart lists world currencies by symbol, name of currency, and nation or geographical area for the currency. A glossary lists monetary terms used throughout the encyclopedia and is followed by an extensive bibliography. The index has main entries in boldface and illustrations in brackets for easy reference.

1290   The official blackbook price guide to U.S. coins. 46th ed. Thomas E. Hudgeons. 640p. Random House, 2007. ISBN 9780375721663 (pbk.). $
737.4   CJ1735

2007 standard catalog of world coins, 1901–2000. 34th ed. Colin R. Bruce II and Thomas Michael. 2022p. Krause,

2006. ISBN 9780896893658 (pbk.). $
737.4   CJ1751

**Standard catalog of world coins:
Seventeenth century, 1601–1700.**
3rd ed. Chester Krause and Clifford
Mishler. 1366p. KP Books, 2003. ISBN
9780873496667 (pbk.). $
737.4   CJ1751

**Standard catalog of world coins:
Eighteenth century, 1701–1800.** 3rd
ed. Chester L. Krause and Clifford
Mishler. 1272p. KP Books, 2002. OP.
ISBN 9780873494694.
737.4   CJ1751

**Standard directory of world coins:
Nineteenth century, 1801–1900.** 4th
ed. Chester L. Krause, Clifford Mishler,
and Colin R. Bruce II. 1280p. KP
Books, 2004. ISBN 9780873497985
(pbk.). $
737.4   CJ1751

The purpose of these catalogs is to help collectors
identify coins and to list the market prices for coins
in various conditions. The world coins volumes
contain detailed descriptions of international calendars and dating systems with lengthy explanations
for identification. They generally provide a history
of each coin, date of minting, size, and identification marks. There is also a variety of supplementary data in each book, depending on the particular
specialty that is being covered. Each volume also
includes sections on caring for coins.

1291   **The official blackbook price guide
       to U.S. paper money.** 39th ed. Marc
       Hudgeons. 384p. House of Collectibles,
       2007. ISBN 9780375721519 (pbk.). $
       769.55   HG591

**Standard catalog of U.S. paper
money.** 24th ed. Chester Krause and
Robert F. Lemke, eds. 240p. KP Books,
2004. ISBN 9780873497954. $
769.5   HG591

**Standard catalog of world paper
money, vol. I: Specialized issues.**
10th ed. George Cuhaj. 1200p. KP
Books, 2005. ISBN 9780896891615
(pbk.). $
769.5   HG353

**Standard catalog of world paper
money, vol. II: General issues.**
10th ed. Colin R. Bruce. 1176p.
KP Books, 2003. OP. ISBN
9780873497046.
769.5   HG353

**Standard catalog of world paper
money, vol. III: Modern issues.** 12th
ed. George Cuhaj. 1064p. KP Books,
2006. ISBN 9780896893566 (pbk.). $
769.5   HG353

These catalogs describe paper money, the use of
which dates as far back as the fourteenth century.
They provide listings of prices for paper money in
various conditions. There is also a variety of supplementary data in each book, depending on the particular specialty that is being covered. Bank notes
issued by states, municipalities, and companies
are covered in the U.S. volumes. Nearly 300 past
and current governments are covered in the world
volumes. Each volume also includes general collections care guidelines. All have extensive black-and-
white illustrations with pricing information along
with currency-grading guidelines adopted by the
Grading Committee of the International Bank Note
Society.

1292   **Walter Breen's complete encyclopedia
       of U.S. and colonial coins.** Walter
       Breen. 768p. Doubleday, 1988. OP.
       ISBN 9780385142076.
       737.4   CJ1830

A comprehensive history describing the more than
8,000 coins, with more than 4,000 illustrations,
that have been used in the United States. A definitive reference guide.

Stamps

1293   **Linn's world stamp almanac: A
       handbook for stamp collectors.** 6th
       ed. Donna O'Keefe. 756p. Linn's Stamp
       News, 2000. ISBN 9780940403857. $
       769.56   HE6194

Essential facts on philately intended to aid both
research and hobby activities. Historical and directory information, biographical and bibliographical material, stamp production, law, and postal
administration are some of the features of this useful tool.

1294   The Micarelli identification guide to U.S. stamps: Regular issues, 1847–1934. Rev. ed. Charles Micarelli. 168p. Scott, 2001. ISBN 9780894872822. $

769.56973   HE6204

A manual and identification guide to regular issues from 1847 to 1934. Clear illustrations and well-designed tables.

1295   The official blackbook price guide of U.S. postage stamps. House of Collectibles, 1970–. Annual. ISSN 0195-3559. $

769.56   HE6185

Easy-to-use basic guidebook with valuations of more than 20,000 stamps. How to buy, sell, and care for stamps. Many color photographs.

1296   Scott 2007 specialized catalogue of United States stamps and covers. James E. Kloetzel, ed. 960p. Scott, 2006. ISBN 9780894873812. $

769.56973075   HE6185

Scott's standard postage stamp catalogue. 6v. Scott, 1923–. Annual. $/v.

769.56   HE6226

Scott provides the most comprehensive catalog of stamps printed in the United States. Gives minute details, such as date of issue, design, denomination, color, perforation, and watermark, on all stamps issued. Most of the stamps are given a valuation. Volume 1 covers United States and affiliated territories, United Nations, Canada, and British America; volumes 2 through 6 cover the rest of the world. Extensively illustrated.

1297   U.S. first day cover catalogue and checklist. Michael A. Mellone. Scott, 1984–. Annual. ISSN 0747-5381; ISBN 0894873946. $

769.565   HE6184

First day covers are "commemorative covers with stamps, cancellations, and cachets from the first day that a stamp is issued." Explains the process of producing and the reasons for collecting first day covers. Includes prices. The authoritative guide.

1298   World encyclopedia of stamps and stamp collecting: The ultimate illustrated reference to more than 3,000 of the world's best stamps and a professional guide to starting and perfecting a spectacular collection. James MacKay. 256p. Anness, 2005. ISBN 9780754815303. $

769.5603   HE6196

With more than 3,000 color photographs, this is a comprehensive guide for the stamp enthusiast at any level. A history of stamp and postal services, from Roman mail coaches to modern airmail, is given along with notorious anecdotes from the world of stamp collecting and collectors. Step-by-step instructions are detailed with information on how best to mount and preserve stamps. Additional sources, including Internet auction sites, are given.

16 Games and Sports

MAUREEN BARRY

Many factors have contributed to the increasing popularity of sports and leisure in society. Recently, for example, the popularity of extreme sports has grown dramatically. As a result, sport and leisure are growing as academic fields of study, and reference publishing in this area is flourishing.

This chapter includes general works, at least one reference work devoted to each of a wide variety of major sports, and reference resources addressing sport's impact on and connection to societies or cultures.

Small and medium-sized libraries should collect reference works covering the rules and particulars of sports that are locally and regionally popular, like lacrosse. This consideration, along with limited library budgets, means that some sports were excluded from this chapter. Libraries can purchase the recommended sources as needed.

Official rule books have not been listed in previous editions. Since the last edition, national associations for most major sports have begun publishing official rule books along with some statistics on the Internet. URLs for these have been listed as libraries now have an economical option of "owning" official rule books. For consistency's

sake, some print rule books for billiards and chess have been included.

Bibliographies and Guides

1299 **Sports, exercise and fitness: A guide to reference and information sources.** Mary Beth Allen. 287p. Libraries Unlimited, 2005. ISBN 1563088193. $
016.796   GV704

Chapters divided into activity categories, such as Olympic, racquet, precision and accuracy, combat, aquatic, and health and wellness. Most entries contain resources for reference, instruction, and Internet sources. Comprehensive guide of sources with annotations.

Almanacs

1300 **ESPN sports almanac: The definitive sports reference book.** ESPN Books/ Hyperion, 2004–. Annual. ISSN 1555-8304. $
796.05   GV561

This almanac compiles the most recent year's statistics for professional and amateur levels of the following sports: baseball, football, basketball, hockey, other intercollegiate sports, international sports, Olympic games, soccer, bowling, tennis, horse racing, golf, auto racing, and boxing. Also includes halls of fame and awards, who's who, ball-parks and arenas, business, deaths, updates, and a bibliography. Winningest teams, coaches, athletes, conference and national champions, and some historical statistics are also included.

Chronologies

1301 **This day in sports.** Ernie Gross. 386p. McFarland, 2000. ISBN 0786408030 (pbk.). $
796   GV571

Organized chronologically by the calendar year, this title highlights landmark accomplishments, events, and tragedies in sports. Contains limited historical coverage dating back to the 1700s along with more extensive recent coverage through 1998.

Dictionaries and Encyclopedias

1302 **Berkshire encyclopedia of world sport.** David Levinson and Karen Christensen. 1816p. Berkshire, 2005. ISBN 0974309117. $$
796.03   GV567

More than 400 narrative entries focus on a wide array of topics relating to the interdisciplinary nature of sport. This edition updates the *Encyclopedia of world sport: From ancient times to the present.* It includes country or region profiles. Readers' guide helps users navigate to topics and subtopics relating to college sports, media, health and fitness, sports industry, sports in society, sporting events, venues, youth sports, and sport culture. Also includes impact of sports on society, global social issues, culture, industry, and history. Bibliographies, cross-references, index.

1303 **The dictionary of sports: The complete guide for TV viewers, spectators and players.** Gerry Cox. 400p. Carlton Books, 1999. ISBN 1858688000. $
796.03   GV567

Entries in this resource are divided into categories (such as stadium team sports, court games, motor sports, etc.) and then listed alphabetically by sport. Each activity has a glossary of popular terms to provide an overview for novices. Contains some photographs and an index.

1304 **Encyclopedia of international games.** Daniel Bell. 591p. McFarland, 2003. ISBN 0786410264. $
796   GV721

International multisport competitions dating back to 1896 and ranging from World Scholar Athlete Games to X Games are summarized. Most entries include brief contest history and by year, the contest site, sports, dates, and medals awarded. Appendixes include games by year, nation, and host city; largest games by number of participants; and nations and sports.

1305 **The encyclopedia of North American sports history.** 2nd ed. Ralph Hickok. 594p. Facts on File, 2002. ISBN 0816046603; 0816050716 (pbk.). $
796   GV567

This second edition is enhanced with 150 new entries and updates or expansions to the originals. More than 16,000 entries focus on the history of sports, events, athletes, venues, or awards important to professional sports, widely, in North America. Statistics and lists of award winners are present.

1306 **Sport in American culture: From Ali to X-Games.** Joyce Duncan. 479p. ABC-CLIO, 2004. ISBN 1576070247. $
306.4   GV706

Each entry focuses on the impact of that specific sports figure, sport, event, or idea on American culture. Topics include sports, activities, athletes, and organizations at all levels, including youth, recreational, amateur, and professional. Includes extensive bibliography, helpful cross-references, and an index.

1307 **Sports culture: An A–Z guide.** Ernest Cashmore. 482p. Routledge, 2002. ISBN 0415285550. $
306.4   GV706

Topics such as globalization, technological innovations, books with sports themes, and other controversies are covered in this resource. Each of the 174 entries is discussed with regard to its impact on cultures worldwide.

1308 **The ultimate dictionary of sports quotations.** Carlo DeVito. 332p. Facts on File, 2001. ISBN 0816039801; 081603981X (pbk.). $
796   GV707

Notable quotes by authors, athletes, coaches, journalists, scholars, and administrators are presented. Entries are organized alphabetically by sport, athlete, or other broad sport-related topics. Includes selected bibliography and index.

Directories

1309 Disability sport and recreation resources. 3rd ed. Michael J. Paciorek and Jeffery A. Jones. 312p. Cooper, 2001. ISBN 1884125751. $

796.0196   GV709

This title is organized by sport. Includes national and international governing bodies of sport and disabled sport organizations. Sport overviews, equipment required, directory of equipment suppliers, and additional resources, including recommended websites. Also has photographs and a bibliography.

1310 Sports museums and halls of fame worldwide. Victor J. Danilov. 226p. McFarland, 2005. ISBN 0786419636 (pbk.). $

796   GV571

Directory of museums and halls of fame organized by country and by sport. Other sections are organized by athletes or sports personnel; high school sports; collegiate sports; local, state, and regional halls of fame; and sports art and media. Facility's contents, history, and contact information are included.

Biographical Sources

1311 A to Z of American women in sports. Paula Edelson. 278p. Facts on File, 2002. ISBN 0816045658. $

796   GV697

Highlights record-setting and trailblazing American female athletes. Entries contain brief biographical entries covering personal background along with career information. Bibliography of "Recommended Sources on American Women in Sports" includes books and websites.

1312 African Americans in sports. David Kenneth Wiggins. 2v. Sharpe Reference, 2004. ISBN 0765680556 (pbk.). $$

796   GV583

Gives brief biographical information about African American athletes. Also covers African American athletes' impact on and participation in major sports. Other entries discuss social issues, institutions and organizations, such key personnel as coaches or sportswriters, and cultural themes. Contains nearly 450 entries, with further reading suggested for each entry.

1313 Encyclopedia of women and sport in America. Carole A. Oglesby and Doreen L. Greenberg. 360p. Oryx, 1998. ISBN 0897749936. $

796   GV706

Features 140 brief biographies of American female athletes. Those who influenced public perception are highlighted. Fitness, specific sports or activities, halls of fame, and many other topics are discussed as they relate to female athletes. Selected bibliography and index.

1314 International encyclopedia of women and sports. Karen Christensen, Allen Guttmann, and Gertrud Pfister. 3v. Macmillan Reference USA, 2001. ISBN 0028649540; 0028649516 (v. 1); 0028649524 (v. 2); 0028649532 (v. 3). $$/set

796   GV709

Within each entry, major topics are discussed as they pertain to women in sports on an international scale. The concepts of histories, failed attempts, the future, rules, and play are organized with subheadings. Text boxes feature chronologies, interesting stories and facts, document texts, and the like. The readers' guide is categorized by biographies, events, countries and regions, issues, medicine and health, and organizations. Includes an index, bibliographies, and cross-references.

1315 Native Americans in sports. C. Richard King. 2v. Sharpe Reference, 2004. ISBN 0765680548. $$

796   GV583

This title follows the same format as *African Americans in sports* with brief biographical information about Native American athletes and social and cultural topics, such as mascot controversies. Further reading is suggested for each entry, and a chronology of notable events is presented. Includes bibliography and index.

1316 The Scribner encyclopedia of American lives: Sports figures. Arnie

Markoe. 2v. Scribner, 2002. ISBN
0684806657. $$

796   GV997

Covers 614 figures, living and dead, important to
the history of sport in the United States. Further
recommended reading in nearly every entry.
Narrative about each athlete offers personal and
professional background, influences, and accom-
plishments. Index sorts athletes alphabetically and
by sport with which they were involved.

**1317   Sports nicknames: 20,000
professionals worldwide.** Terry W.
Pruyne. 423p. McFarland, 2002. ISBN
0786410647. $

79   GV706

Part 1 is arranged by sport, such as baseball, foot-
ball, basketball, and hockey, then listed by given
name. Include athlete's position, team or teams,
nickname, and origin of nickname. Part 2 is orga-
nized by nickname and provides for each athlete
the sport played and the given name.

Auto Racing

1318   NASCAR encyclopedia. 2nd ed. Peter
Golenbock and Greg Fielden. 1009p.
MBI, 2003. ISBN 076031571X. $

796.72   GV1029

The introduction provides a short history of stock-
car racing. This title is divided into these statistically
comprehensive sections: records, year by year (1949
through 2002), drivers, owners, tracks, and races.
Records include the top thirty drivers for catego-
ries such as winnings, top ten and top five finishes,
laps led, and more. This second edition updates the
previous *The stock car racing encyclopedia* and covers
every driver who has competed in a race.

Backpacking

**1319   The backpacker's field manual: A
comprehensive guide to mastering
backcountry skills.** Rev. ed. Rick
Curtis. 440p. Three Rivers Press, 2005.
ISBN 1400053099. $

796.51   GV199

Arranged by topics such as trip planning, equip-
ment, cooking and nutrition, hygiene and water

purification, safety and emergency procedures, and
so forth. Includes helpful diagrams and an appendix
that features equipment lists, expense and emer-
gency information forms, and logistics and menu-
planning work sheets. Includes bibliography of print
and electronic resources and an index.

Baseball

**1320   The All-American Girls Professional
Baseball League record book:
Comprehensive hitting, fielding and
pitching statistics.** W. C. Madden.
294p. McFarland, 1999. ISBN
078640597X. $

796.357   GV875

As the title suggests, comprehensive hitting, fielding,
and pitching statistics. A complete record highlight-
ing stars of the league, individual records, season
records, play-off records, players' statistics, pitchers'
statistics, league personnel, and playing schedule.

**1321   Baseball: An encyclopedia of popular
culture.** Edward J. Reilly. 371p. ABC-
CLIO, 2000. ISBN 1576071030. $

796.357   GV867

A–Z entries featuring notable players and person-
nel, leagues, concepts, ballparks, and their impact
on society. Includes cross-references, additional
recommended readings, and an index.

**1322   Baseball America directory, 2006:
Your definitive guide to the game.**
23rd ed. Baseball America. 391p.
Baseball America, 2006. ISBN
1932391118. $

796.357   GV875

Contact information and broadcast and stadium
details are included along with schedules for pro-
fessional, international, college, amateur, and
youth levels. Details association information for
organizations concerned with scouting, players
unions, alumni, umpires, and more. Includes local
and national media information as well as driving
directions to major league stadiums.

1323   Baseball America's Almanac. Baseball
America. Baseball America, 1990–.
Annual. $

796.357   GV861

This almanac of American baseball presents a "comprehensive review of the season, featuring statistics and commentary." Provides team statistics and commentary for major leagues, minor leagues, independent leagues, international leagues, and college and high school baseball teams. Also contains draft information, such as the top 100 picks, and top draft picks. The appendix includes previous year's obituaries.

1324   The baseball bibliography. 2nd ed.
Myron J. Smith. 4v. McFarland, 2006.
ISBN 0786424087; 0786415312
(pbk.). $; $$ (pbk.)
016.796357   Z7514; GV863

Completely updates the first edition, which was published in 1986. Includes articles, books, theses, dissertations, yearbooks, programs, fiction, poetry, and government documents.

1325   Baseball desk reference. 1st American ed. Lawrence T. Lorimer. 608p. DK, 2004. ISBN 0789483920. $
796.357   GV863

This reference source is arranged by history; big leagues (teams, histories, statistics, business of baseball, manager profiles, records); levels of the game (international, college, youth, women, Negro Leagues); and lore and lingo (media, song, museums, language, film, books and collectibles). Includes overviews and brief statistics, color illustrations, field dimensions, and an index.

1326   The baseball timeline: In association with Major League Baseball. 1st American ed. Burt Solomon. 1216p. Dorling Kindersley, 2001. ISBN 0789471329. $
796.357   GV863

This reference covers the years 1778–2000. Each annual section is divided into preseason, season, regular season wrap-up, and postseason. Each year features major news headlines to explain context of world affairs and current events. Sidebars emphasize notable facts. "Best of" column highlights best hitters (batting average, slugging average, runs batted in, home runs, hits) and pitchers (earned run average, winning percentage, saves, wins, strikeouts). Includes bibliography and index.

1327   The cultural encyclopedia of baseball. 2nd ed. Jonathan Fraser Light. 1105p. McFarland, 2005.

ISBN 0786420871. $
796.357   GV862

Covers topics from all aspects of the game, for example, night games, grand slams, Hemingway, and collective-bargaining agreements. Includes entries for every club that played in defunct and present leagues: National Association, National League (NL), American Association, Union Association, Players League, American League (AL), and Federal League. Each NL and AL team has subheadings of origins, first game, key owners, nicknames, key seasons, key players, key managers, ballparks, key broadcasters, and books about the team. Boldface words indicate separate entries. Index includes headings and mentions. Coverage is through 2004 postseason.

1328   Diamonds around the globe: The encyclopedia of international baseball. Peter C. Bjarkman. 607p. Greenwood, 2005. ISBN 0313322686. $
796.357   GV862

Organized by country, this encyclopedia focuses on baseball outside the United States. Each entry includes capsule histories of major and minor league baseball teams, selected statistics, notes and bibliographies, and major players. Appendix A includes greatest moments in world baseball history. Index and annotated bibliography close the book.

1329   Encyclopedia of Major League Baseball clubs. Steven A Riess. 2v. Greenwood, 2006. ISBN 0313329915; 0313329923 (v. 1); 0313329931 (v. 2). $$/set
796.357   GV875

In addition to important players and managers in each team's history, essays pay special attention to social and economic histories of all Major League teams. Gambling, liquor sales, ethnic background of players and fans, media coverage, and labor issues are representative concepts as they relate to each team. Includes suggested readings, bibliography, and index.

1330   The ESPN baseball encyclopedia. Peter Palmer and Gary Gillette. Sterling, 2005–. Annual. ISBN 1402736258. $
796.357   GV877

Team-by-team rosters organized alphabetically by year dating back to 1871. All-star games. This source highlights great performances, such as no-hitters, most consecutive hits, or consecutive games. Contains descriptions of big league ballparks. Also contains some coverage of international baseball, including Australia, South Korea, and Latin America.

1331 Major League Baseball official rules. MCB Advanced Media. http://mlb.mlb .com/NASApp/mlb/mlb/official_info/ official_rules/foreword.jsp.

Includes objectives of the game, definition of terms, game preliminaries starting and ending game, putting the ball in play, the batter, the runner, the pitcher, the umpire, and the official scorer. A useful site on the rules of baseball.

1332 The new Bill James historical baseball abstract. Bill James. 998p. Free Press, 2001. ISBN 0684806975. $
796.357   GV863

Part 1 covers the game by decade. Each decade features who played the game, where the game was played, new stadiums, nicknames, and how the game was played. Part 2 includes player ratings and comments organized by position. Part 3 is a reference section that shows win shares of individuals and selected teams and win share team comparison. The comprehensive historical coverage and index make this a valuable baseball compendium.

1333 The team by team encyclopedia of Major League Baseball. Dennis Purdy. 1166p. Workman, 2006. ISBN 0761139435. $
796.357   GV862

Anecdotal stories included in each team's coverage, along with records, standings, attendance, starting lineups, won-loss records versus all opponents, retired uniforms, and awards. Some photographs are included.

1334 Total baseball: The ultimate baseball encyclopedia. 8th ed. John Thorn. 2676p. Sport Media, 2004. ISBN 189496327X. $
796.357   GV863

This source is a narrative and statistical encyclopedia. Player, pitcher, and postseason registers are presented. Player register is alphabetical by name. Sections include biographies and team histories broken down by the following categories: early days, 1901–1945; golden era, 1946–1968; and modern game, 1969–2003. The international arena

is also covered. The appendix gives major league attendance, amateur free-agent draft, evolution of baseball records, all-time leaders (lifetime and single season), manager and umpire rosters, and a glossary of statistical terms.

1335 The women of the All-American Girls Professional Baseball League: A biographical dictionary. W. C. Madden. 288p. McFarland, 1997. ISBN 0786403047. $
796.357   GV875

This dictionary is arranged alphabetically by name. Biographical information on more than 600 of the league's players is included. Entries state statistical information (batting, pitching, and fielding) for those players who participated in more than ten games. Contains some photographs, and a brief history of the league. There is also a key of abbreviations used in statistics.

Basketball

1336 Biographical directory of professional basketball coaches. Jeff Marcus. 443p. Scarecrow, 2003. ISBN 0810840073. $
796.323   GV884

Coaches are listed alphabetically. Entries include college attended, birth and death dates, brief paragraphs with career highlights, and regular season and play-off coaching record. Begins with 1925 American Basketball League and goes through 2001 National Basketball Association season.

1337 College basketball's national championships: The complete record of every tournament ever played. Morgan G. Brenner. 1036p. Scarecrow, 1999. ISBN 081083474X. $$
793.323   GV885

Chronicling major association national championship tournaments, this source includes the National Collegiate Athletic Association (NCAA), League of Christian Colleges, and Association for Intercollegiate Athletics for Women tournaments. Lists association national champions, nonassociation national championship tournaments, and school tournament participation history. Appendixes include school information, school names, tournament site and dates, NCAA vacated tournament teams, and tournament trivia.

1338   **The official NBA encyclopedia.** 3rd
ed. Michael Jordan, David J. Stern, and
Jan Hubbard. 911p. Doubleday, 2000.
ISBN 0385501307. $
796.323   GV885

Various contributors write essays about modern
and early icons of the National Basketball Association (NBA), early professional leagues, NBA pio-
neers, and expansion teams. Topics also covered
include dynasties, rules, coaches, referees, seasons,
Women's National Basketball Association, and
NBA timeline. Includes index.

1339   **Official NBA guide, 2004–2005.**
Corrie Anderson and Rob Reheuser.
750p. Sporting News Books, 2004–
2005. ISBN 0892047429. $
796.32   GV885

Team-by-team review of the 2004–2005 season
as well as National Basketball Association (NBA)
directories, NBA schedule, games on television
and radio, National Basketball Development
League and Women's National Basketball Association. Histories by team, award winners, all-
star games, hall of fame, and memorable games
are also covered. The regular season, play-offs,
finals, and all-star game records are all in this
guide. Lastly, contains year-by-year reviews
beginning with the 1946–1947 season, including final standings.

1340   **Official rules of the National
Basketball Association.** NBA Media
Ventures. www.nba.com/analysis/rules
_index.html.

In addition to the league's official rules, court
dimensions, and referee signals, the site also contains sections explaining the most misunderstood
rules and player dress code.

1341   **Official rules of the NCAA
(basketball).** NCAA. www2.ncaa.org/
portal/media_and_events/ncaa
_publications/playing_rules/.

Complete playing rules of men's and women's
National Collegiate Athletic Association basketball
in PDF format.

1342   **Official rules of the Women's
National Basketball Association.**
WNBA Enterprises. www.wnba.com/
analysis/wnba_rules_regulations.html.

Rulebook can be downloaded in PDF format;
includes definitions, official rules, court dimensions, and referee signals.

1343   **Official WNBA guide and register.**
Sporting News Books, 1997–. Annual.
ISBN 0892047739. $
796.323082   GV885

Presents team-by-team regular season and play-off
reviews and records, with schedules, rosters, and
broadcast and ticket information. Alphabetical listing
of each player in the league features brief biographical information and career statistics. Includes official
Women's National Basketball Association rules.

Bicycling

1344   **A basic guide to cycling.** United States
Olympic Committee. 151p. Griffin,
2001. ISBN 0836827953; 1580000711
(pbk.). $
796.6   GV1043

A concise source that provides useful information
about safety and first aid, tips for buying a bicycle,
international course markings, maintenance, and
accessories. Also includes biographical information about the United States Cycling team. Readers
should use the table of contents in lieu of an index.

1345   **The ultimate mountain bike book:
The definitive illustrated guide to
bikes, components, techniques,
thrills, and trails.** 3rd ed. Nicky
Crowther. 181p. Firefly Books, 2002.
ISBN 155297653X. $
796.6   GV1056

This fully revised and updated third edition includes history, nutrition, maintenance and repair,
technique, jargon, mountain bike fitting, and trails.
Glossary, illustrations, and index are helpful tools.

Billiards and Pool

1346   **Billiards: The official rules and
records book.** Billiard Congress of
America. Billiard Congress of America,
2004. ISBN 1878493140. $
794.72   GV891

Complete playing rules of the Billiard Congress of
America.

1347 **The new illustrated encyclopedia of billiards.** Rev. ed. Michael Ian Shamos. 320p. Lyons Press, 2002. ISBN 1585746851. $

794.7203   GV891

Entries explain billiards terminology and techniques. Helpful illustrations, diagrams, and figures add value. Appendix A explains important numerical values in billiards. Appendix B lists billiard games. Appendix C gives billiard organizations, and appendix D is an index of names.

Card Games

1348 **The A–Z of card games.** 2nd ed. David Sidney Parlett. 441p. Oxford Univ. Pr., 2004. ISBN 0198608705. $

795.4   GV1243

Previous edition was published in 1992 as *A dictionary of card games.* This source is a guide to popular card games like hearts, bridge, and poker.

Chess

1349 **The Oxford companion to chess.** 2nd ed. David Hooper and Ken Whyld. 483p. Oxford Univ. Pr., 1996. ISBN 0192800493. $

794.1   GV1445

This guide is suitable for both experts and nonexperts. Diagrams are included. Biographical information about contemporary players is added. Terminology, tournaments, influential chess players. Glossary and helpful citations suggesting further reading complete the work.

1350 **U.S. Chess Federation's official rules of chess.** 5th ed. Tim Just and Daniel B. Burg. 370p. Random House Puzzles and Games, 2003. ISBN 0812935594. $

794.1   GV1457

Comprehensive coverage of the U.S. Chess Federation's official rules. Rules of play including tournament play, equipment standards, players' rights and responsibilities, code of ethics, rating system, chess notation, Internet chess rules, and conduct. Also has World Chess Federation laws.

Exercise

1351 **The encyclopedia of exercise, sport, and health.** Peter Brukner, Karim Khan, and John Kron. 501p. Allen and Unwin, 2004. ISBN 1741140587 (pbk.). $

617.1   RC1206

This encyclopedia applies to males or females of all ages who are competitive or noncompetitive athletes. More than 1,500 entries covering exercises, sports, health, injuries, anatomy, steroids, supplements, and so forth. Includes helpful diagrams and charts, cross-references, and an index.

Figure Skating

1352 **The encyclopedia of figure skating.** John Williams Malone. 264p. Facts on File, 1998. ISBN 0816032262; 0816037965 (pbk.). $

796.91   GV849

Entries offer brief biographies of figure skaters and descriptions of figure-skating techniques (jumps, spins, lifts, etc.) and important competitions. Appendixes list U.S., World, and Olympic championship medalists.

Fishing

1353 **Ken Schultz's fishing encyclopedia: Worldwide angling guide.** Ken Schultz. 1916p. IDG Books Worldwide, 2000. ISBN 0028620577. $

799.1   SH411

This guide to fishing contains more than 2,000 entries. Comprehensive coverage ranges from fishing techniques, accessories, and safety to scientific and common names, identification characteristics, size, distribution, habitat, life history, behavior, food, and angling information for more than 500 fish species. This source is easily navigable without a glossary or index.

1354 **The new encyclopedia of fishing.** 1st American ed. John Bailey. 288p. DK, 2001. ISBN 0789483998. $

799.1   SH411

This source is arranged topically by tackle, bait, fly, species (freshwater, saltwater), and techniques (freshwater fishing, fly fishing and saltwater fishing). Numerous color illustrations and photographs. Appendixes feature a glossary and an index of scientific names.

Football

1355 **ESPN college football encyclopedia.** ESPN. 1629p. ESPN, 2003. ISBN 1401337031. $

796.33264   GV956

A sample of the essays includes a history of recruiting, integration of college football, and college football in the movies. Division 1-A schools are listed alphabetically, with profiles of best coaches, games, and players, biggest upsets, key data about university and football history, distinguished alumni, and fight-song lyrics. Bar charts also illustrate schools' winning percentage. The annual review gives history of polls and ratings. Year-by-year overviews, 1869–2004, present leading rushers, Heisman trophy vote counts, and more. Also includes a history of current and defunct bowl games.

1356 **NFL rules digest.** NFL Enterprises. www.nfl.com/fans/rules/.

This digest of rules is not intended to replace the official rule book. Includes glossary, summary of penalties, timekeeping, position of players at snap, and more.

1357 **Official 2005 National Football League record and fact book.** Time Inc. Home Entertainment, 2005. http://nfl.com/history/randf/.

This site contains records for individuals, teams, and history, organized by decade.

1358 **Pro football guide.** Corrie Anderson and Dave Sloan. 447p. Sporting News Books, 2005. ISBN 0892047755. $

796.332   GV955

Summary of previous National Football League seasons are compiled with team-by-team histories, week-by-week schedules, team rosters, and directories. This source also previews the upcoming season.

1359 **Total football: The official encyclopedia of the National Football League.** Bob Carroll.

1812p. HarperCollins, 1999. ISBN 0062701746. $

796.332   GV955

Pre-National Football League (NFL) history and history of the league, team histories, defunct franchises, and the origins of the Super Bowl are described in the resource. Includes biographical entries for the greatest 300 players, greatest thirty coaches, and other notable personnel. Awards are chronicled, including the Pro Football Hall of Fame, the Pro Bowl, and All-Pro selections. Talks about the evolution of strategy, the playbook, and more. Also describes other leagues, such as the early American Football League, All American Football Conference, U.S. Football League, and NFL Europe. Appendixes highlight famous pro-football firsts; game scores from 1920 to 1988 (by year and date, who won, where the game was played, and attendance figures); and football quotations.

1360 **The ultimate guide to college football: Rankings, records, and scores of the major teams and conferences.** James P. Quirk. 491p. Univ. of Illinois Pr., 2006. ISBN 025207226X. $

796.332   GV956

This guide is a historical summary of college football. Records of Division 1-A football teams, other major teams, and service teams during World War II are included. Lists major conferences, bowl game records, All-American teams (1883–2003), individual awards, and national rankings. Rules changes are also presented.

Gambling

1361 **Gambling in America: An encyclopedia of history, issues, and society.** William Norman Thompson. 509p. ABC-CLIO, 2001. ISBN 1576071596. $

795   GV1301

Entries cover gambling behaviors, issues relating to gambling, economics, games, individuals associated with gambling, and associations. Chronology of gambling events provided. Appendixes consist of articles and major cases. Includes a glossary and index.

Games

1362   The Oxford history of board games.
David Sidney Parlett. 386p. Oxford
Univ. Pr., 1999. ISBN 0192129988. $
794.09   GV1312

Thematically classifies early and modern board
games. Offers variations on traditional games, such
as dice games and board games, including chess.
Other variations are offered for modern games of
risk, fantasy, war, crime, and more.

1363   Sports and games of the ancients.
Reprint. Steve Craig. 271p. Greenwood,
2005. ISBN 0313316007 (pbk.). $
796   GV17

Offers a history of traditional, indigenous games
worldwide. With each continent or region, there
is an introduction, an explanation, and history of
sports played and developed, with suggestions
for modern play and sources listed for further
consultation.

**1364   Unique games and sports around
the world: A reference guide.** Doris
Corbett, John Cheffers, and Eileen
Crowley Sullivan. 407p. Greenwood,
2001. ISBN 0313297789. $
790.1   GV1201

Organized geographically, this source lists characteristics of players (age, sex); object of game;
number of players; apparel or equipment required;
venue required; length of game; symbolism of
game; and rules of play, including scoring. Also, it
offers a sociological and anthropological perspective. The appendix features a guide for educators
in selecting appropriate games. Includes index and
bibliography.

Golf

1365   Golf Digest's best places to play. 7th
ed. Golf Digest. 849p. Fodor's Travel,
2006. ISBN 1400016290. $
796.3520687   GV981

Directory of the best courses to play throughout the
United States, Canada, Mexico, and the Caribbean.
Resource includes a geographical directory by town
or city. Entries are listed alphabetically by course
name and has metro area index by town. Entries
include opening date, architect, yards, par, course

rating, slope, green fee, cart fee, discounts, walk-
ability, and other notes. Includes star ratings, with
explanation and brief lists featuring "best NEW
courses" and "best service courses."

1366   The illustrated golf rules dictionary.
Rev. ed. Hadyn Rutter. 384p. Triumph
Books, 2004. ISBN 1572436239. $
796.35202022   GV971

Explains rules or techniques with definitions,
basic rules, procedures, penalties, and exceptions.
Includes many color photos and diagrams.

1367   The new encyclopedia of golf. 3rd
American ed. Malcolm Campbell. 384p.
DK, 2001. ISBN 0789480360. $
796.352   GV965

Introduces early and modern games and describes
major players, equipment, course design, championship courses worldwide, hall of fame, records,
and reference. Contains numerous pictures, diagrams, a glossary, and an index.

1368   United States Golf Association rules.
United States Golf Association. www
.usga.org/playing/rules/rules.html.

Site contains rule book, including etiquette and
definitions. Link provided to 2006 new and revised
decisions.

Hockey

1369   The concise encyclopedia of hockey.
M. R. Carroll, Andrew Podnieks, and
Michael Harling. 244p. Greystone
Books, 2001. ISBN 155054845X. $
796.962   GV847

Topics arranged alphabetically include commentary concerning notable players, coaches, concepts,
jargon, leagues, teams, and techniques. Appendixes include Stanley Cup winners 1893–2001,
Memorial Cup winners 1919–2001, National Collegiate Athletic Association champions 1948–2001,
and Men's and Women's Olympic and World
Champion medalists through 2001.

1370   National Hockey League rule book.
National Hockey League. www.nhl.com/
hockeyu/rulebook/.

Alphabetical rule index and site index both
included. The National Hockey League provides

such features as a summary of rule changes and rink and face-off configuration diagrams.

1371 Official guide and record book.
National Hockey League. Triumph Books, 1985–. Annual. ISSN 0828-6647. $
796.962   GV847

This source presents final statistics of previous season, along with team-by-team records, rosters, and management. All-star selections and game results and records, Stanley Cup guide and record book, and player and goaltender registers are included.

1372 Total hockey: The official encyclopedia of the National Hockey League. 2nd ed. Dan Diamond. 1974p. Total Sports, 2000. ISBN 189212985X. $
796.962   GV847

This encyclopedia discusses everything hockey. Data include National Hockey League attendance 1960–2000; Canadian, American, European, and women's hockey; Stanley Cup winners 1917–2000; and a short history of the league broken down by year. International coverage includes the 2002 Olympics, World and European championships, and World Junior championships. Other facets of the game covered include the hall of fame, equipment, safety, hockey and TV, and hockey video games and the Internet. Finally, contains statistical and biographical registers.

Martial Arts

1373 Martial arts of the world: An encyclopedia. Thomas A Green. 2v., 894p. ABC-CLIO, 2001. ISBN 1576071502. $$
796.8   GV1101

Includes regional martial arts forms, such as Okinawan, Japanese, and Chinese. Resource contains a chronology of martial arts history and helpful photographs demonstrating techniques. Folklore and social issues, such as women in martial arts, are covered. Contains a select bibliography, index, and references with most sections.

1374 The practical encyclopedia of martial arts. Fay Goodman. 256p. Lorenz Books, 2004. ISBN 0754814688. $
796.81503   GV1112

The introductions to tae kwon do, karate, aikido, ju-jitsu, judo, kung fu, tai chi chuan, kendo, iaido, and Shinto ryu are enhanced with illustrations. Each chapter includes history and philosophy, apparel, equipment, etiquette, exercises, and techniques. Contains brief biographies of best martial artists for each discipline.

Olympics

1375 Encyclopedia of the modern Olympic movement. John E. Findling and Kimberly D Pelle. 602p. Greenwood, 2004. ISBN 0313322783; 0275976599 (pbk.). $
796.48   GV721

This source presents a history of each Olympic Game (summer and winter) through 2008 and 2010, including bibliographical essays. Appendixes highlight International Olympic Committee members, U.S. Olympic Committee, Olympic Games and television, Olympic feature films, and Internet sources on Olympism.

1376 Historical dictionary of the Olympic movement. Bill Mallion and Ian Buchanan. 411p. Scarecrow, 2006. ISBN 0810855747. $
796.48   GV721

This resource presents a chronology of the Olympic movement and of the summer and winter Olympic Games. It contains an alphabetic listing of concepts, people, events, and sports, with particular attention paid to politics and historical events during the Olympic movement. Appendixes feature presidents of the International Olympic Committee, sites, dates, nations and athletes of Olympiads, and information about positive drug tests at the Olympics.

Outdoors

1377 Complete outdoors encyclopedia. Rev. ed. Vin T. Sparano. 830p. St. Martin's, 1998. ISBN 0312191901. $
799   SK33

Hunting and shooting, game animals and birds, fishing, game fish, camping, and survival are covered in this source. Other topics include boating, archery, hunting dogs, and first aid for choking. Includes helpful diagrams and figures.

1378   **Encyclopedia of outdoor and wilderness skills.** Chris Townsend and Annie Aggens. 434p. Rugged Mountain Press/McGraw-Hill, 2003. ISBN 0071384065. $
796   GV191

Nearly 450 outdoor and wilderness-related entries. Brief commentary intended to supply knowledge about hiking, backpacking, rock climbing, skiing, kayaking, and other activities. Diagrams and photographs. Includes bibliography and index.

Recreation

1379   **Americans at play: Demographics of outdoor recreation and travel.** Alison Stein Wellner. 367p. New Strategist, 1997. ISBN 188507011X. $
790   GV191

Brief overviews complemented by tables filled with numerical data illustrating rankings of participation in and spending on outdoor activities, sports, entertainment, and other recreational activities. Other tables focus on high school and college sports participation by sport, sex, or geographical area.

1380   **Encyclopedia of recreation and leisure in America.** Gary S. Cross. 2v. Scribner, 2004. ISBN 0684312654 (set); 0684312662 (v. 1); 0684312670 (v. 2). $$/set
790   GV53

Topics range from caving or dining out to amusement parks and fashion. Lengthy bibliographies close each entry. Commercialization, popularity, criticism, analysis, and sociological perspective are among the examples covered in the content of each entry.

1381   **Fun and games in twentieth-century America: A historical guide to leisure.** Ralph G. Giordano. 304p. Greenwood, 2003. ISBN 0313322163. $
790   GV53

Organized chronologically by era, each chapter covers public interest, lifestyles, entertainment, music and theater, sports and games, transportation, and vacation. Bibliography and index are included.

1382   **Recreation: Leisure in American society.** Frank Uhle. 117p. Thomson Gale, 2005. ISBN 0787690805. $
790.01   AG6

Chapters include narration and tables and figures detailing how Americans spend their time, the cost of having fun, outdoor recreation, arts and media, football, baseball, and other popular sports. Gambling in America, vacations and travel, and the role of recreation in American society are also covered. Key names and addresses are provided and resources are recommended in appendixes.

Running

1383   **Running encyclopedia.** Richard Benyo and Joe Henderson. 417p. Human Kinetics, 2002. ISBN 0736037349. $
796.42   GV1061

This encyclopedia highlights records, races, record setters, well-known figures, and important running resources. Supplemental index includes names of those that do not have separate entries and cross-references. Jargon and technique are also covered.

Rules

1384   **NCAA playing rules.** NCAA. www2 .ncaa.org/portal/media_and_events/ ncaa_publications/playing_rules/.

Rulebooks for sixteen varsity intercollegiate sports. Many are retrospectively archived to 2000 or 2001.

1385   **Sports: The complete visual reference.** François Fortin. 372p. Firefly Books, 2000. ISBN 1552095401. $
796   GV704

Descriptions and illustrations of playing surface, techniques, competition, equipment, and athlete profile (in terms of ability, muscles used) by sport. Most sports are further classified by event (track—100, 200, 400, relay, etc.).

1386   **The sports rules book.** 2nd ed. Thomas W. Hanlon. 315p. Human Kinetics, 2004. ISBN 0736048804. $
796   GV731

This resource is suitable for fans, athletes, or coaches. Arranged by sport, entries include an overview, terms, equipment, officials, rules, modifications (for children), scoring, and organizations that govern professional and amateur levels. Useful as both a circulating and reference book.

Sailing

1387   The language of sailing. Richard
Mayne. 369p. Fitzroy Dearborn, 2000.
ISBN 1579582788. $
797.124   GV811

Comprehensive dictionary of sailing, with nautical and boating terms, including etymology and evolution.

1388   New complete sailing manual. Rev.
ed. Steve Sleight. 448p. DK, 2005.
ISBN 0756609445. $
797.1   GV811

This sailing guide is organized into an introduction, first principles, small boat sailing, advanced small boat sailing, cruiser sailing, navigation, weather, practical boat care, and staying safe. Includes illustrations, figures and diagrams, and a glossary and index.

Soccer

**1389   The encyclopedia of American soccer
history.** Roger Allaway, Colin Jose, and
David Litterer. 454p. Scarecrow, 2001.
ISBN 0810839806. $
796.334   GV944

Entries focus on individuals, countries, associations, coaches, and stadiums important to the history of all levels of soccer in the United States. Appendixes include statistics and records, memorable games, and a bibliography. Covers U.S. soccer at all levels.

**1390   The ultimate encyclopedia of soccer:
The definitive illustrated guide to
world soccer.** 10th ed. Keir Radnedge
and Gary Lineker. 256p. Carlton Books,
2004. ISBN 1844427420 (pbk.). $
796.334   GV943

This source has good international coverage. It covers early and modern games, major competitions, and great soccer moments by country, great clubs,

legends, great players, great matches, stadiums, business, rules and tactics, equipment, soccer culture, scandals, soccer chronology, and major soccer awards. Also includes chapter about "football" in Great Britain and Ireland and many photos.

**1391   United States Soccer Federation laws
of the game.** U.S. Soccer Federation.
www.ussoccer.com/laws/index.jsp.html.

Interested readers can download the PDF format of laws of the game. This page also links to International Laws of the Game.

Swimming

**1392   The complete swimming pool
reference.** 2nd ed. Tom Griffiths. 472p.
Sagamore, 2003. ISBN 157167523X. $
797.2   RA606

Gives basic pool characteristics along with mechanical information, water chemistry, specialty pools (hot tubs and spas) and safety, supervision, and risk management. Suitable for the needs of novice swimmers, home owners with swimming pools, and staff of public pools. Appendixes include work sheets for emergency phone numbers, pool profile, pool capacity, service technician's record form, problem log, evaluations, lifeguard applications, energy and water conservation checklists, and pool chemistry tests and summaries. Includes diagrams of signage for public pools.

Tennis

**1393   Total tennis: The ultimate tennis
encyclopedia.** Bud Collins. 938p. Sports
Media, 2003. ISBN 0973144343. $
796.34203   GV992

Section 1 through 3 cover 1874–2002. The roots of the game, annual summaries from 1919 to 2002, and detailed essays about tennis pioneers are presented. Section 4 covers major championships, such as the Grand Slam, Australian Open, French Open, Wimbledon, and U.S. Open. Section 5 details international play, like the Davis Cup, Fed Cup, Olympics, and Wightman Cup. Biographies of notable players and registers make up sections 6 and 7. The appendix contains information about the hall of fame, world rankings dating back to 1913 for men and 1921 for women, ATP, Women's

Tennis Association, other men's and women's professional tours, U.S. Pro Championships, London and French Pro Championships, and World Team Tennis.

1394   USTA rules. United States Tennis Association. www.usta.com/rules/.

This page lists code for unofficiated matches. U.S. Tennis Association rules follow International Tennis Federation rules, which can be found at http://dps.usta.com/usta_master/usta/doc/content/doc_13_4198.pdf. Includes official's code of conduct, rules update, umpire directory, referee manual, and ball-person's training manual.

17 *Literature*

CAROLYN M. MULAC

There is no shortage of reference sources on almost any aspect of literature. New, updated, or revised reference sources in this area seem to appear almost daily, as do new areas of literary scholarship. In updating this chapter, particular attention has been paid to expanding the "Special Interest" section, mainly, the literature of several American ethnic and social groups; and the section on literature genres, especially children's literature. The "National and Regional Literatures" section has been enlarged to represent more countries than in the previous edition.

General Sources

Bibliographies and Guides

1395 **The Cambridge guide to literature in English.** 3rd ed. Dominic Head. 1208p. Cambridge Univ. Pr., 2006. ISBN 9780521831796. $
820.90   PR85

A one-volume reference guide covering the literature of Great Britain and the United States as well as the English-language literature of Canada, Africa, Australia, New Zealand, Ireland, India, and the Caribbean. Includes authors, titles, characters,

literary terms, genres, movements, and critical concepts.

1396 **Literary research guide: An annotated listing of reference sources in English literary studies.** 4th ed. James L. Harner. 820p. Modern Language Association, 2002. ISBN 9780873529839. $
016.82   Z2011

Using the same format as previous editions, this annotated guide includes more than 6,000 entries for reference works on English and American literature as well as works relating to particular national literatures (Irish, English, etc.) and related literary topics.

1397 **Reference works in British and American literature.** 2nd ed. James K. Bracken. 727p. Libraries Unlimited, 1998. ISBN 9781563085185. $$
016.8   Z2011

A one-volume revision providing descriptive annotations to important and useful general reference works in British and American literature for the novice scholar as well as the more sophisticated literary researcher. Includes reference works devoted to some 1,500 individual authors.

Databases and Indexes

1398 **MLA international bibliography of books and articles on modern**

language and literature. Harrison T. Meserole, comp. 2v. Modern Language Association, 1921–. Annual. $$$
016.8   Z7006

Classified entries cover literatures in English, literatures in other languages, linguistics, general literature and related topics, and folklore, followed by an index to authors and editors of articles and books. A second volume provides a list of subject terms referring to the classified entries. Contact publisher for availability of the online version.

Dictionaries and Encyclopedias

1399   Benét's reader's encyclopedia.
4th ed. Bruce Murphy, ed. 1168p. HarperCollins, 1996. ISBN 9780062701107. $
809   PN41

A completely revised edition of a basic reference book offering entries on authors, titles, plots, characters, allusions, literary terms and movements, historical events, and other relevant topics.

1400   Encyclopedia of medieval literature.
Jay Ruud. 752p. Facts on File, 2005. ISBN 9780816054978. $
809.02   PN669

A one-volume work covering the authors and literary works, terms, and concepts of western Europe, India, China, Japan, and the Islamic world from 500 to 1500 CE in concise articles that often include bibliographies.

1401   Encyclopedia of Renaissance literature. James Wyatt Cook. 624p. Facts on File, 2005. ISBN 9780816056248. $
809   PN721

Covers the literature of England, France, Germany, Spain, China, India, and the Islamic and New Worlds from 1500 to 1700 CE in one volume. The articles encompass a wide variety of topics and include bibliographies.

Digests

1402   Magill's literary annual. John D. Wilson and Steven G. Kellman, eds. 2v. Salem Press, 1977–. Annual.

ISBN 9781587653728. $$
803   PN44

Two annual volumes provide essay reviews of 200 fiction and nonfiction books of the previous year. The articles are arranged alphabetically by title, range in length from three to five pages, and include bibliographic information, a plot summary, criticism, and sources for further information. Provides an update to Magill's *Masterplots*.

1403   Masterplots. 2nd ed. Frank N. Magill, ed. 12v., 7492p. Salem Press, 1996. ISBN 9780893560843. $$$
808.8   PN44

Entries consist of plot synopses and critical evaluations followed by ready-reference data on the author, type of work, setting, and principal characters. A chronology and author, title, and geographic indexes are located at the end of volume 12. Updated by *Magill's literary annual* and the various Masterplots II series, this is a standard work.

Handbooks

1404   Brewer's dictionary of modern phrase and fable. 2nd ed. Adrian Room. 806p. Cassell, 2002. ISBN 9780304358717. $
423.1   PE1460

Words, phrases, acronyms, slogans, slang expressions, fictional characters, and the titles of songs, books, films, television programs, and more from the past 100 years are explained in this companion to *Brewer's dictionary of phrase and fable.*

1405   Brewer's dictionary of phrase and fable. 17th ed. John Ayto. 1326p. HarperCollins, 2006. ISBN 9780061121203. $
803   PN43

This title is derived from one of the longest-lived reference books. When it was first published, in 1870, Brewer called his dictionary "an almsbasket of words." This compendium of enduring trivia provides the meaning and origin of thousands of proper names in history, fiction, myth, and folklore as well as explanations of numerous curious words and phrases. The current edition also provides lists of such things as the cries of animals (e.g., donkeys bray, turkeys gobble) and animals used in symbolism. Because of the numerous revisions over the years, earlier editions should be retained for their historical value.

1406 A glossary of literary terms. 8th ed. M. H. Abrams and Geoffrey G. Harpham. 384p. Heinle, 2004. ISBN 9781413002188. $
803   PN41

Essay-length entries on the terms used in the study of American, British, foreign, and comparative literature are provided in this excellent guide.

1407 A handbook to literature. 10th ed. William Harmon. 704p. Prentice Hall, 2005. ISBN 9780131344426. $
803   PN41

A standard reference work that includes more than 2,000 entries defining literary terms and topics and provides outlines of English and American literary history and lists of Nobel Prize winners for literature and Pulitzer Prize winners for fiction, poetry, and drama.

1408 The Johns Hopkins guide to literary theory and criticism. 2nd ed. Michael Groden, Martin Kreiswirth, and Imre Szeman, eds. 1008p. Johns Hopkins Univ. Pr., 2004. ISBN 9780801880100. $
801.95   PN81

The second edition of a comprehensive survey of ideas and persons who have made their mark in the world of literary theory. The alphabetically arranged, signed entries on literary critics, theorists, schools, and movements are substantive, and most include bibliographies.

Literary Characters

1409 Cyclopedia of literary characters. 2nd ed. Frank N. Magill and A. J. Sobczak, eds. 5v., 2208p. Salem Press, 1998. ISBN 9780893564384. $$
809   PN44

Describes and identifies more than 29,000 characters drawn from more than 1,400 novels, dramas, and epics of world literature. Arrangement is alphabetical by the title of the work in which the characters appear. Ready-reference use is facilitated by title, author, and character indexes and a pronunciation guide.

1410 Dictionary of fictional characters. William Freeman. Yestermorrow, 1999.

ISBN 9781567231540. $
820.3   PN56

Identifies thousands of characters taken from more than 3,000 works created by some 800 authors. Spans six centuries of British, Commonwealth, and American literature and covers novels, short stories, plays, and poems.

Literary Prizes

1411 Book awards. R. R. Bowker. www.bookwire.com/bookwire/otherbooks/Book-Awards.html.

From Bookwire, a list of links to award sites from the Academy of American Poets: Awards and Prizes to the Shamus Awards. Other sites included are the National Book Award, the Nobel Prize Internet Archive, and the SFWA Nebula Awards.

1412 Pulitzer prizes. Pulitzer Prize. www.pulitzer.org.

Offers resources, a searchable archive of winners and nominated finalists, a history of the awards, and guidelines and entry forms.

Multivolume Criticism

1413 Contemporary literary criticism. Thomson Gale, 1977–. ISSN 0091-3421. $$/v.
809.04   PN771

This multivolume, ongoing series offers contemporary criticism on authors who are now living or who have died since December 31, 1959. More than 200 volumes are now available. Each one provides criticism on some six to eight literary figures, including novelists, playwrights, short story writers, scriptwriters, and other creative writers.

1414 Literature criticism from 1400 to 1800. Thomson Gale, 1984–. ISBN 0787699022. $$/v.
809.03   PN86

Each volume provides criticism on some ten to twenty literary figures from the late Middle Ages, the Renaissance, and the Restoration. More than 100 volumes are now available. Entries are arranged alphabetically by author and include a biographical and critical essay followed by a chronological list of the author's main works.

1415 **Nineteenth-century literature criticism.** Thomson Gale, 1978–. ISSN 0732-1864. $$/v.
809.034   PN761

Excerpts from nineteenth- and twentieth-century criticism in English on writers of all nationalities and genres who died between 1800 and 1900. More than 100 volumes are now available. Each volume covers four to eight authors, and every fourth volume covers topics such as literary movements or trends.

1416 **Twentieth-century literary criticism.** Thomson Gale, 1978–. ISSN 0276-8178. $$/v.
809.04   PN771

A companion series to Thomson Gale's *Contemporary literary criticism,* this set offers criticism on notable literary figures from 1900 to 1999. There are now more than 100 volumes available. Each volume covers some four to eight authors, and every fourth volume covers topics such as literary trends or movements.

Proverbs

1417 **Dictionary of American proverbs.** Wolfgang Mieder, Stewart A. Kingsbury, and Kelsie B. Harder, eds. 736p. Oxford Univ. Pr., 1991. ISBN 9780195053999. $
398.9   PN6426

The result of many years of scholarship, this dictionary includes 15,000 proverbs currently in use in the United States and Canada. Arrangement is alphabetical by key word. Includes variants.

1418 **The Macmillan book of proverbs, maxims and famous phrases.** Burton Egbert Stevenson. 2976p. Macmillan, 1987. ISBN 9780026145008. $
082   PN6405

Formerly titled *The home book of proverbs, maxims, and familiar phrases,* this work follows the pattern of the author's *Home book of quotations.* Contains more than 73,000 sayings arranged by subject and indexed in great detail and includes foreign phrases with English translations.

1419 **The multicultural dictionary of proverbs: Over 20,000 adages from more than 120 languages, nationalities and ethnic groups.** Reprint. Harold V. Cordry. 416p. McFarland, 2005. ISBN 9780786422623 (pbk.). $
082   PN6405

A collection of more than 20,000 proverbs derived from the traditions of more than 120 languages, nationalities, and ethnic groups. Includes subject and keyword indexes and a bibliography.

Quotations

1420 **Bartlett's familiar quotations.** 17th ed. John Bartlett and Justin Kaplan. 1488p. Little, Brown, 2002. ISBN 9780316084604. $
808.88   PN6081

This edition of the gold standard for quotation collections contains 25,000 citations by 2,500 authors arranged chronologically and indexed by author and keyword. Because each new edition necessarily omits some material from its predecessor, retention of every edition is recommended.

1421 **Contemporary quotations in black.** Anita King, ed. 312p Greenwood, 1997. ISBN 9780313291227. $
081   E184

Taking her *Quotations in black* (Greenwood, 1981) into the 1980s and 1990s, King includes more than 1,000 quotations from notable African Americans and black Africans. Entries are arranged alphabetically by author, and then chronologically for each person quoted.

1422 **The home book of quotations, classical and modern.** 10th ed. Burton Egbert Stevenson. 2816p. Dodd, Mead, 1967. OP.
808.88   PN6081

Although unfortunately out of print, this is still one of the most comprehensive and useful collections of quotations. More than 50,000 quotations are arranged by subject, and there is a very detailed index.

1423 **The Oxford dictionary of American quotations.** 2nd ed. Hugh Rawson and Margaret Miner. 912p. Oxford Univ. Pr., 2005. ISBN 9780195168235. $
081.03   PN6081

This is a revision of the authors' *American Heritage dictionary of American quotations* (1996) and includes nearly 6,000 quotations categorized under more than 500 topics and arranged chronologically within those topics.

1424   Oxford dictionary of modern quotations. 2nd ed. Elizabeth Knowles, ed. 512p. Oxford Univ. Pr., 2007. ISBN 9780198609513 (pbk.). $
080   PN6080

More than 5,000 quotations illustrating popular culture and modern history are arranged by author and indexed by keyword and theme.

1425   Oxford dictionary of quotations. 6th ed. Elizabeth Knowles, ed. 168p. Oxford Univ. Pr., 2004. ISBN 9780198607205. $
082   PN6080

The latest edition of a reliable reference work summarizes the wit and wisdom of the ages in more than 20,000 quotations arranged by author and indexed by theme and keyword.

1426   The quotable woman: The first 5,000 years. 2nd ed. Elaine T. Partnow. 992p. Facts on File, 2001. ISBN 9780816040124. $
305.4   PN6081.5

This edition provides more than 18,000 quotations by more than 3,600 women throughout history arranged in chronological order by the speaker's year of birth. Indexes by name, occupation, and nationality or ethnicity are included.

Biographical Sources

1427   Contemporary authors. Thomson Gale, 1962–. $$/v.
810.9   PN451

In this series, brief, factual articles provide bio-bibliographical information on more than 120,000 creative writers in a variety of fields, including literature, journalism, television, and film. More than 200 volumes are now available. Beginning with volume 187, coverage was expanded to include more international authors.

1428   Contemporary authors autobiography series. Gale, 1984–1998. $$/v.
809   PN453

Autobiographical essays by contemporary writers provide unique insights into their life and work. Each of the thirty volumes available covers about twenty writers. The series has been discontinued, but the publisher's website states that new autobiographical essays will appear from time to time in the Contemporary Authors series.

1429   Cyclopedia of world authors. 4th ed. Frank N. Magill and Tracy Irons-Georges, eds. 5v., 3432p. Salem Press, 2003. ISBN 9781587651229. $$
809   PN451

Most of the 2,403 authors included here are represented in various Masterplots series. The alphabetically arranged articles are about 1,000 words in length. All entries from the previous edition have been updated, and more than 300 have been added.

1430   Dictionary of literary biography. Thomson Gale, 1978–. $$/v.
810.9   PS21

An excellent multivolume series, currently in more than 300 volumes, covering the lives and works of those who have contributed to the greatness of literature in America, England, and elsewhere. Each volume examines a particular group of writers organized by topic, period, or genre. *Dictionary of literary biography* is updated by the *Dictionary of literary biography yearbook* (Thomson Gale, 1981–), which reviews the year in literature and includes obituaries and tributes.

1431   Encyclopedia of world writers: Beginnings to the 20th century. Thierry Boucquey and Marie Josephine Diamond, eds. 3v. Facts on File, 2005. ISBN 9780816061433. $$
809   PN451

Three volumes of alphabetically arranged entries offer an array of authors not always represented in standard reference sources. Volume 1 is subtitled *Beginnings through the 13th century*, volume 2 covers the fourteenth through the eighteenth centuries, and volume 3 deals with the nineteenth and twentieth centuries.

1432   Great world writers: Twentieth century. Patrick M. O'Neil, ed. 13v., 1848p. Marshall Cavendish, 2004. ISBN 9780761474685. $$
809   PN771

Signed articles on the lives and work of ninety-three authors from forty-two countries. Alphabetically arranged entries range from ten to twenty-five pages in length and include a photograph, a list of published works, critical evaluations of two or more works, and a bibliography. Volume 13 includes a number of indexes and a glossary.

1433 **Popular contemporary writers.**
Michael D. Sharp, ed. 11v., 1568p.
Marshall Cavendish, 2005. ISBN
9780761476016. $$
810.9   PS228

Ninety-six popular contemporary writers are discussed in this set of alphabetically arranged signed articles. The profiles are approximately fifteen pages in length and include a photograph, biographical essay, critical analyses, and a bibliography. Volume 11 consists of several indexes and a glossary.

Special Interest

African American Literature

1434 **African-American dramatists: An A to Z guide.** Emmanuel S. Nelson, ed. 544p. Greenwood, 2004. ISBN 9780313322334. $
812   PS338

Some sixty-one writers from the last 150 years are profiled in signed articles ranging in length from four to more than twenty pages. Each entry includes biographical information, an overview of the entrant's most important works, a bibliography, and more.

1435 **The Columbia guide to contemporary African American fiction.** Darryl Dickson-Carr. 280p. Columbia Univ. Pr., 2005. ISBN 9780231124720. $
813.5   PS374

Part of the Columbia Guides to Literature since 1945 series, this work includes an overview of the subject, an alphabetical listing of contemporary African American writers of fiction, and a selected bibliography.

1436 **Contemporary black American playwrights and their plays: A biographical directory and dramatic index.** Bernard L. Peterson Jr.

651p. Greenwood, 1988. ISBN
9780313251900. $$
812.5   PS153

Provides information on more than 700 contemporary dramatists, screenwriters, and scriptwriters. Entries include brief biographies and annotated lists of dramatic works. Title index and a selective general index to names, organizations, and awards.

1437 **The Greenwood encyclopedia of African American literature.** Hans Ostrom and J. David Macey, eds. 5v., 2120p. Greenwood, 2005. ISBN 9780313329722. $$
810.9   PS153

A comprehensive work supplying more than 1,000 articles by more than 200 scholars. Writers from colonial times to the present and literary genres from folktales to slave narratives to prison literature to blues poetry are all set in historical and cultural contexts. Among its notable features are a ten-page bibliography and a ten-page chronology.

1438 **Notable African American writers.** Salem Press editors. 3v., 1350p. Salem Press, 2006. ISBN 9781587652721. $$
810.9   PS153

Consists of eighty essays, ranging in length from four to eight pages, on important African American writers, including poets, playwrights, novelists, and more. There are four overview essays on specific literature genres, a bibliography, chronological list of authors, and four indexes.

Asian American Literature

1439 **Asian American short story writers: An A-to-Z guide.** Guiyou Huang, ed. 359p. Greenwood, 2003. ISBN 9780313322297. $$
813   PS153

Contains signed profiles, ranging in length from three to five pages, of forty-nine Asian American short story writers. Entries include a biography, discussions of the entrant's work and its critical reception, and bibliographies of primary and secondary sources. There is also a lengthy introductory essay on the Asian American short story.

1440 **The Columbia guide to Asian American literature since 1945.**

Guiyou Huang. 272p. Columbia Univ. Pr., 2006. ISBN 9780231126205. $
813.5   PS153

Part of the Columbia Guides to Literature since 1945 series, an examination of the work of U.S. and Canadian writers with origins in Asia and South and Southeast Asia. More than 100 authors are covered in entries that include a brief biography, a discussion of major works, and a short bibliography of criticism.

Gay and Lesbian Literature

1441 Contemporary gay American novelists: A bio-bibliographical critical sourcebook. Emmanuel S. Nelson, ed. 456p. Greenwood, 1993. ISBN 9780313280191. $$
813.5   PS374

Fifty-seven writers, from Steve Abbott to Donald Windham, are represented in entries comprised of biographical information, a summary of major works and a discussion of their critical reception, and bibliographies of primary and secondary sources.

1442 Contemporary gay American poets and playwrights: An A-to-Z guide. Emmanuel S. Nelson, ed. 496p. Greenwood, 2003. ISBN 9780313322327. $$
812.5   PS325

Sixty-two writers are profiled in entries consisting of biographical information, a summary of major works and a discussion of their critical reception, and bibliographies of primary and secondary sources.

1443 Contemporary lesbian writers of the United States: A bio-bibliographical critical sourcebook. Sandra Pollock and Denise D. Knight, eds. 688p. Greenwood, 1993. ISBN 9780313282157. $$
810.9   PS153

One hundred writers, from Donna Allegra to Jacqueline Woodson, are represented in entries that include a biography, an analysis of major works and an overview of their critical reception, and bibliographies of primary and secondary sources. There is also an introductory essay as well as an extensive general bibliography.

1444 Gay and lesbian literary heritage: A reader's companion to the writers and their works, from antiquity to the present. 2nd ed. Claude J. Summers, ed. 864p. Routledge, 2002. ISBN 9780415929264. $
809.8   PN56

This revised edition of the 1995 work presents some 400 alphabetically arranged essays by 175 scholars. New to this edition are articles on Tony Kushner, Sarah Waters, and Terrence McNally and essays on literary topics such as autobiography and comedy of manners. All entries conclude with bibliographic information.

1445 Gay and lesbian literature. 2nd ed. Sharon Malinowski, ed. 2v. St. James Press, 1993–1997. ISBN 9781558621749 (v. 1); 9781558623507. $$
809.9   PN56

Each volume presents authoritative biographies, bibliographies, and criticism of more than 200 internationally renowned gay or lesbian authors. Entries include those for James Baldwin, C. P. Cavafy, Tennessee Williams, and Virginia Woolf.

Latino Literature

1446 Chicano literature: A reference guide. Julio A. Martinez and Francisco A. Lomeli, eds. 492p. Greenwood, 1985. ISBN 9780313236914. $$
809.8   PS153

Signed critical essays on the life and works of Chicano authors and on other topics relevant to the history and development of Chicano literature, including articles on the novel, poetry, theater, children's literature, and Chicano philosophy. Selected bibliographies; brief index.

1447 Hispanic literature of the United States: A comprehensive reference. Nicolás Kanellos. 328p. Greenwood, 2003. ISBN 9781573565585. $
810.9   PS153

Features include a "Who's Who of Hispanic Authors of the United States," made up of articles about 100 authors; an overview and chronology of Hispanic literature of the United States; a list of "100 Essential Hispanic Literary Works"; an overview of Hispanic drama; a bibliography; and title and subject indexes.

1448 **Latino and Latina writers.** Alan West-Duran, ed. 2v., 1100p. Scribner, 2003. ISBN 9780684312934. $$
810.9   PS153

Opens with several introductory essays, including "Chicana Feminist Criticism" and "Historical Origins of U.S. Latino Literature," and provides signed articles about Chicano and Chicana authors, Cuban and Cuban American authors, and Dominican and Puerto Rican authors.

1449 **Notable Latino writers.** 3v., 900p. Salem Press, 2005. ISBN 9781587652431. $$
810.9   PS153

Drawn from Salem's *Cyclopedia of world authors,* fourth edition, this set features 122 essays on poets, playwrights, novelists, and short story writers. Each entry includes a biographical sketch, a chronological list of the author's works, and an annotated bibliography.

Native American Literature

1450 **The Cambridge companion to Native American literature.** Kenneth M. Roemer and Joy Porter, eds. 365p. Cambridge Univ. Pr., 2005. ISBN 9780521822831. $
810.9   PS153

Part of the Cambridge Companion series, *The Cambridge companion to Native American literature* examines the work of American Indian writers from 1770 to the present and includes essays on literary genres and their historical and cultural contexts as well as articles on eight individual authors.

1451 **Dictionary of Native American literature.** Andrew Wiget, ed. 616p. Garland, 1994. ISBN 9780815315605. $$
897   PM155

Discusses the oral traditions of individual tribes as well as a number of cultural and historical topics. Includes articles that examine several literary topics, including the teaching of Native American literature as well as biocritical essays on more than forty writers.

Women's Literature

1452 **American women writers: From colonial times to the present; A critical reference guide.** 2nd ed. Taryn Benbow-Pfalzgraf. 3v., 1300p. St. James Press, 1999. ISBN 9781558624295. $$$
810.9   PS147

Of the 1,300 entries in this edition, 100 are new. Articles range in length from one to four pages and include women writing in the fields of anthropology, psychology, history, and religion as well as literature. Biographical details and bibliographies are provided for each entrant, and there are indexes by author and title.

1453 **Encyclopedia of feminist literary theory.** Elizabeth Kowaleski-Wallace 472p. Garland, 1996. ISBN 9780815308249. $$
801.9   PN98

Provides definitions of critical terms, summaries of the work of feminist literary critics, and descriptions of the development of the feminist perspective over time. Entries emphasize American and British views since 1970.

1454 **Encyclopedia of feminist literature.** Kathy J. Whitson. 300p. Greenwood, 2004. ISBN 9780313327315. $
809   PN471

Although focused on English and American authors, a number of the writers represented are from other countries, and all those included (nearly seventy) span the centuries from 1400 to the present. Entries include biographical as well as critical information and suggestions for further reading.

1455 **Feminist writers.** Pamela Kester-Shelton. 641p. St. James Press, 1996. ISBN 9781558622173. $$
809   PN451

Alphabetically arranged entries provide biographical, bio-bibliographical, and critical information on more than 300 feminist writers. There are indexes by author, title, nationality, genre, and subject.

1456 **Irish women writers: An A-to-Z guide.** Alexander G. Gonzalez, ed. 360p. Greenwood, 2005. ISBN 9780313328831. $
820.9   PR8733

Some seventy-five Irish women writers are represented in articles consisting of a short biography, an examination of major works and their critical reception, and bibliographies of primary and secondary sources. There is also a selected general bibliography at the end of the work.

1457 Masterpieces of women's literature.
Frank N. Magill. 608p. HarperCollins, 1996. OP. ISBN 9780062701381.
809.8   PS147

Supplies summaries and evaluations of the principal works of women's literature from *Adam Bede* and *The bell jar* to *Sexual politics* and *The wide Sargasso Sea.* Each of the 175 entries includes a section on the form and content of the work, critical analysis, the literary and social context, and sources for further study.

1458 Modern American women writers.
Elaine Showalter, A. Walton Litz, and Lea Baechler, eds. 1196p. Thomson Gale, 1993. ISBN 9780684190570. $$
810.9   PS151

Forty-one essays on twentieth-century women writers from Maya Angelou to Edith Wharton. Includes a chronology of American women's history from 1640 to 1990 and bibliographies and recommendations for further reading.

1459 Modern British women writers: An A-to-Z guide. Vicki Janik and Del Ivan Janik, eds. 448p. Greenwood, 2003. ISBN 9780312310300. $$
820.9   PR116

Offers entries on fifty-eight British women writers of the twentieth century consisting of biographical information, critical analyses, and bibliographies of primary and secondary sources. A selected general bibliography completes the work.

1460 Nineteenth-century British women writers: A bio-bibliographical critical sourcebook. Abigail Burnham Bloom, ed. 472p. Greenwood, 2000. ISBN 9780313304394. $$
820.9   PR115

More than ninety British women writers of the nineteenth century are profiled in articles comprised of biographical and critical information and analysis supplemented by bibliographies of primary and secondary sources. A selected bibliography of anthologies and critical studies is included.

Specific Genres

Children's Literature

1461 A to zoo: Subject access to children's picture books. 7th ed. Carolyn W. Lima and John A. Lima. 1728p. Libraries Unlimited, 2005. ISBN 9781591582328. $
011   Z1037

A standard reference work on fiction and nonfiction picture books for children organized into five sections: a list of 1,350 subject headings, a subject guide that classifies books under those headings, a bibliographic guide that lists books by author and supplies full bibliographic information, and title and illustrator indexes. Nearly 28,000 in-print and out-of-print titles are covered.

1462 The children's and young adult literature handbook: A research and reference guide. John T. Gillespie. 404p. Libraries Unlimited, 2005. ISBN 9781563089497. $
011.62   Z1037

Evaluates more than 1,000 publications from general background sources and retrospective bibliographies to current American reviewing tools and annual bibliographies, author and illustrator biographies, multicultural sources, special collections and resources, and the Internet and other nonprint resources.

1463 Children's literature: A guide to the criticism. Linnea Hendrickson. 696p. Macmillan, 1987. ISBN 9780816186709. $
011.62   Z2014.5

An annotated bibliography of criticism arranged in two parts: by authors, illustrators, and their works; and by subjects, themes and genres. Works considered range from the picture book to the young adult novel. The major emphasis is on twentieth-century children's literature although some earlier classics are included.

1464 Children's literature review. Gale, 1976–. ISSN 0362-4145. $$/v.
028.52   PN1009

This continuing series presents excerpts from criticism on some 600 authors and illustrators of books for children and young adults. Each volume examines about

15 authors in entries consisting of listings of major works and awards, commentaries by the authors, and excerpts from reviews and criticism. To date, 120 volumes have been published. Includes cumulative indexes to authors, nationalities, and titles.

1465 **Companion to American children's picture books.** Connie Ann Kirk. 440p. Greenwood, 2005. ISBN 9780313322877. $
011.62   Z1033

A rich resource for the study and appreciation of this special category of children's books. Essays discuss the definition and evaluation of a picture book. A total of 400 A–Z entries cover authors, illustrators, works, and special topics. Several appendixes list award-winning picture books, review periodicals, collections of materials on picture books and their creators, and more.

1466 **Dictionary of American children's fiction, 1859–1959: Books of recognized merit.** Alethea K. Helbig and Agnes R. Perkins. 666p. Greenwood, 1985. OP. ISBN 9780313225901.
813   PS374

Dictionary of American children's fiction, 1960–1984: Recent books of recognized merit. Alethea K. Helbig and Agnes R. Perkins. 930p. Greenwood, 1986. ISBN 9780313252334. $$
813.5   PS374

Dictionary of American children's fiction, 1985–1989: Books of recognized merit. Alethea K. Helbig and Agnes R. Perkins. 320p. Greenwood, 1993. ISBN 9780313277191. $
813.5   PS374

Dictionary of American children's fiction, 1990–1994: Books of recognized merit. Alethea K. Helbig and Agnes R. Perkins. 490p. Greenwood, 1996. ISBN 9780313287633. $$
813.5   PS490

Dictionary of American children's fiction, 1995–1999: Books of

recognized merit. Alethea K. Helbig and Agnes R. Perkins. 632p. Greenwood, 2001. ISBN 9780313303890. $$
813.5   PS374

Dictionary of American young adult fiction, 1997–2001: Books of recognized merit. Alethea K. Helbig and Agnes R. Perkins. 584p. Greenwood, 2004. ISBN 9780313324307. $
813.5   PS374

These volumes give brief biographical and bibliographical information as well as plot summaries for American children's fiction written between 1859 and 1999 and for American young adult fiction written between 1997 and 2001. Entries are provided for titles, authors, characters, significant settings, and other elements. A detailed index provides access to all main entries, to major characters for whom there are no separate entries, and to settings, themes, topics, pseudonyms, illustrators, and genres.

1467 **The essential guide to children's books and their creators.** Anita Silvey, ed. 560p. Houghton Mifflin, 2002. ISBN 9780618190836. $
810.9   Z1232

Drawn from the author's *Children's books and their creators* (Houghton, 1995), this is an overview of the best in children's literature from the last 100 years. More than 475 entries, including reading lists; essays on genres, multicultural themes, and perspectives; and personal reflections by writers, illustrators, and critics.

1468 **Index to fairy tales, myths, and legends.** 2nd ed. Mary H. Eastman. 610p. Faxon, 1926. OP.
398.2   GR550

Index to fairy tales, myths, and legends: Supplement. Mary H. Eastman. 566p. Faxon, 1937. OP.
398.2   GR550

Index to fairy tales, myths, and legends: 2nd supplement. Mary H. Eastman. 370p. Faxon, 1952. OP.
398.2   GR550

Index to fairy tales, 1949–1972, 3rd supplement: Including folklore,

legends, and myths in collections.
Reprint. Norma O. Ireland, comp.
741p. Scarecrow, 1988. ISBN
9780810820111. $
398.2   GR550

Index to fairy tales, 1973–1977:
Including folklore, legends, and
myths in collections. Reprint. Norma
O. Ireland, comp. 259p. Scarecrow,
1986. OP. ISBN 9780810818552. $.
398.2   GR550

Index to fairy tales, 1978–1986,
5th supplement: Including folklore,
legends, and myths in collections.
Norma O. Ireland and Joseph W. Sprug,
comps. 575p. Scarecrow, 1989. ISBN
9780810821941. $
398.2   GR550

Index to fairy tales, 1987–1992:
Including 310 collections of fairy
tales, folktales, myths, and legends
with significant pre-1987 titles not
previously indexed. Joseph W. Sprug,
ed. 602p. Scarecrow, 1994. ISBN
9780810827509. $
398.2   GR550

An essential reference providing a valuable source
for the location of folklore and fairy-tale material.
Versions of material suitable for small children are
indicated. Recent supplements include folklore,
legends, and myths in collections; subject index
to stories.

1469   Junior book of authors. 2nd ed.
        309p. H. W. Wilson, 1951. ISBN
        0823200284. $
        809.89   PN1009

Junior authors. 235p. H. W.
Wilson, 1963. ISBN 0824200365. $
809.89   PN1009

Third book of junior authors. H. W.
Wilson, 1972. ISBN 0824204085. $
809.89   PN1009

Fourth book of junior authors and
illustrators. 370p. H. W. Wilson, 1978.
ISBN 0824205685. $
809.89   PN1009

Fifth book of junior authors and
illustrators. 357p. H. W. Wilson, 1983.

ISBN 0824206940. $
809.89   PN1009

Sixth book of junior authors and
illustrators. 356p. H. W. Wilson, 1989.
ISBN 0824207777. $
809.89   PN1009

Seventh book of junior authors and
illustrators. 371p. H. W. Wilson, 1996.
ISBN 0824208749. $
809.89   PN1009

Eighth book of junior authors and
illustrators. Connie G. Rockman,
ed. 592p. H. W. Wilson, 2000. ISBN
0824209680. $$
809.89   PN1009

Ninth book of junior authors and
illustrators. Connie G. Rockman,
ed. 600p. H. W. Wilson, 2005. ISBN
0824210433. $$
809.89   PN1009

A standard work in children's literature collections
since 1951, this series continues to provide author
and illustrator profiles, portraits, bibliographies,
lists of major awards and citations, and a comprehensive index to all volumes.

1470   The Norton anthology of children's
        literature: The traditions in English.
        Lissa Paul et al., eds. 2200p. W. W.
        Norton, 2006. ISBN 9780393327762. $
        820.8   PZ5

A comprehensive collection drawn from 350 years
of literature for children. Nineteen genres are covered, and some 170 authors and illustrators are
represented. Features numerous excerpts and the
full texts of approximately eighty works. Sixty of
the 400 illustrations are reproduced in color.

1471   The Oxford companion to children's
        literature. Humphrey Carpenter and
        Mari Prichard. 600p. Oxford Univ. Pr.,
        1999. ISBN 9780198602286. $
        809.8   PN1008.5

This one-volume handbook contains nearly 2,000
entries for authors, titles, characters, literary terms
and genres, and a variety of topics associated with the
study of children's literature. Emphasis is on British
and American literature, with brief summaries of the
state of children's literature in other countries.

1472   The Oxford dictionary of nursery rhymes. 2nd ed. Iona Opie and Peter Opie. 592p. Oxford Univ. Pr., 1998. ISBN 9780198600886. $

398.8   PZ8.3

A scholarly collection of nursery rhymes, songs, nonsense jingles, and lullabies, with notes and explanations concerning history, literary associations, social uses, and possible portrayal of real people. Both standard and earliest recorded versions (where available) are included. Indexes for "notable figures" and first lines. Eighty-five illustrations.

1473   The Oxford encyclopedia of children's literature. Jack Zipes, ed. 4v., 1824p. Oxford Univ. Pr., 2006. ISBN 9780195146561. $$

809   PN1008.5

Extensive coverage of children's literature in more than 3,000 signed entries covering authors, illustrators, genres, titles, countries, regions, organizations, trends, awards and award winners, research collections, and more. Many of the articles include short bibliographies. The fourth volume includes a selected bibliography, topical outline of the entries, and a comprehensive index.

1474   Something about the author: Autobiography series. Gale, 1986–1998. Series discontinued. ISSN 0885-6842. $$/v.

028.5   PN497

A companion series to *Something about the author: Facts and pictures about contemporary authors* and *Illustrators of books for young people,* these twenty-six volumes contain autobiographical essays by prominent authors and illustrators of books for children and young adults.

1475   Something about the author: Facts and pictures about contemporary authors and illustrators of books for young people. Anne Commire, ed. Gale, 1971–. ISSN 0276-816X. $$/v.

028.5   PN451

A continuing series of illustrated biographical sketches of authors and illustrators of children's books. Cumulative indexes to characters, illustrations, and authors. One hundred and eighty-three volumes available.

PRIZES AND AWARDS

1476   Children's book prizes: An evaluation and history of major awards for children's books in the English-speaking world. Ruth Allen. 250p. Ashgate, 1998. ISBN 9781859282373. $

820.9   Z1037

An evaluation and history of nearly forty different children's book awards.

1477   Children's books: Awards and prizes. Children's Book Council. 576p. Children's Book Council, 2005. ISBN 9780933633070. $$.

809   PN1009

The most complete cumulative listing of the winning titles of extant awards programs, listed in four sections: "United States Awards Selected by Adults"; "United States Awards Selected by Young Readers"; "Australian, Canadian, New Zealand and United Kingdom Awards"; and "Selected International and Multinational Awards." A subscription to Awards and Prizes Online (www.awardsandprizes.cbcbooks .org), a fully searchable database, is available for an additional $50 with the print subscription.

1478   The Newbery and Caldecott awards: A guide to the medal and honor books. Association for Library Service to Children. American Library Association, 1988–. Annual. ISBN 9780838935651. $

011.62   Z1037

An annotated annual list of all the medal and honor books since the inception of the awards. Indexed by author, illustrator, and title.

1479   Newbery and Caldecott medalists and honor book winners: Bibliographies and resource material through 1991. 2nd ed. Muriel Brown and Rita S. Foudray 530p. Neal-Schuman, 1992. ISBN 9781555701185. $

011.62   Z1037

Arranged by author or illustrator, this work provides biographical information on the 325 authors and illustrators who have received recognition as medalists and Honor Book winners and bibliographic data for the works for which they were recognized.

Drama

1480 **Contemporary dramatists.** 6th ed. Thomas Riggs. 891p. St. James Press, 1999. ISBN 9781558623712. $$
822.9   PN1625

Signed critical essays and bibliographies of published works for some 300 living playwrights writing in English. Supplemental sections cover screenwriters, radio writers, television writers, musical librettists, and theater groups. Comprehensive title index.

1481 **Inter-play: An online index to plays in collections, anthologies and periodicals.** Portland State Univ. www .lib.pdx.edu/systems/interplay/.

Maintained by librarians from Portland State University; provides citations to thousands of plays searchable by author or title of work.

1482 **Notable playwrights.** Carl E. Rollyson, ed. 1131p. Salem Press, 2004. ISBN 9781587651953. $$
809.2   PN1625

These 106 alphabetically arranged entries are drawn from the *Critical survey of drama, revised edition* (Salem Press, 2003). Articles are about twelve pages in length and include a bibliography and an illustration of the playwright.

1483 **The Oxford dictionary of plays.** Michael Patterson. 544p. Oxford Univ. Pr., 2005. ISBN 9780198604174. $
809.2   PN1625

One thousand of the most notable plays in the history of the theater are described in entries that contain dates of writing, first performance, and first publication as well as a synopsis, setting, cast composition, commentary, and more. Special features include an index of characters and a select bibliography.

1484 **Playdatabase.com.** Playdatabase.com. www.playdatabase.com.

A free database of plays and monologues, offering 12,498 plays by 5,638 authors as well as 356 monologues. Searchable by author, title, cast size, synopsis, length, and more.

Fantasy

1485 **The encyclopedia of fantasy.** John Clute and John Grant, eds. 1049p. St.

Martin's, 1997. ISBN 9780312145941. $
809.3   PN3435

A comprehensive survey of fantasy in all its forms, including texts, film, art, opera, myth, comic books, authors, characters, and places. Specific authors include E. T. A. Hoffmann, E. A. Poe, George MacDonald, William Morris, Lewis Carroll, J. R. R. Tolkien, C. S. Lewis, the Grimm brothers, Cervantes, Chaucer, and Dante.

1486 **Supernatural fiction writers: Contemporary fantasy and horror.** 2nd ed. Richard Bleiler. 2v., 760p. Scribner, 2002. ISBN 9780684312507. $$
809.3   PN3435

Analyzes 116 contemporary writers of fantasy and horror fiction in essays ranging in length from seven to twelve pages. Entries include bibliographies of primary and secondary sources and lists of book reviews and interviews. Emphasizing contemporary authors, this work supplements *Supernatural fiction writers: Fantasy and horror.*

1487 **Supernatural literature of the world: An encyclopedia.** S. T. Joshi and Stefan Dziemianowicz, eds. 3v., 1556p. Greenwood, 2005. ISBN 9780313327742. $$
809.9337   PN56.S8

Nearly 1,000 alphabetically arranged, signed entries ranging in length from 250 to 3,000 words, on authors, themes, and topics from ancient times to the present provide comprehensive coverage of the subject. Includes indexes to characters and motifs and a general bibliography.

Fiction

1488 **Fiction catalog.** 15th ed. John Greenfieldt. 1317p. H. W. Wilson, 2006. ISBN 0824210557. $$
016.80883   Z5916

A standard annotated bibliography of more than 8,000 works of classic and contemporary fiction. Entries, arranged alphabetically by author, contain full bibliographic information, brief descriptive summaries, and excerpts from critical reviews. Indexed by title and subject. New editions are published every five years; each edition includes four annual paperbound supplements. Online version available; contact publisher for pricing.

1489 Genreflecting: A guide to popular reading interests. 6th ed. Diana Tixier Herald and Wayne A. Wiegand. 584p. Libraries Unlimited, 2005. ISBN 9781591582243. $

016.813009   PS374.P63

A classic readers' advisory tool with reading recommendations for a variety of genres and subgenres of fiction. Includes more than 5,000 titles and three new essays: "The Social Nature of Reading," "The Readers' Advisory Interview," and "A Brief History of Readers' Advisory."

Gothic

1490 Encyclopedia of gothic literature. Mary Ellen Snodgrass. 496p. Facts on File, 2004. ISBN 9780816055289. $

809.911   PN3435

Part of Facts on File's Literary Movements series, this A–Z guide to the genre offers more than 400 entries on genres, literary terms, characters, people, places, books, stories, and more. Each entry includes a brief bibliography.

1491 St. James guide to horror, ghost and gothic writers. David Pringle, ed. 746p. St. James Press, 1997. ISBN 9781558622067. $$

809.3   Z5917

Covers more than 400 historic and contemporary horror, ghost, and gothic writers. Entries feature a biography, a complete list of the author's publications, selected critical and biographical studies, a critical essay by an expert in the field, and, when available, comments by the entrant.

Historical

1492 Dickinson's American historical fiction. 5th ed. Virginia B. Gerhardstein. 368p. Scarecrow, 1986. ISBN 9780810818675. $

016.80883   PS374

First published in 1956, *Dickinson's American historical fiction* classifies, under chronological periods from colonial days to the 1970s, 3,048 historical novels published largely between 1917 and 1984. Selective classics of historical fiction published earlier are also included. Brief annotations place

works in historical perspective. Author-title and subject indexes.

1493 Historical fiction: A guide to the genre. Sarah L. Johnston. 836p. Libraries Unlimited, 2005. ISBN 9781591581291. $

813.8109   PS374

A useful tool for readers' advisory on historical fiction, covering sagas, western historical novels, literary historical novels, Christian historical fiction, and other subgenres. Includes reading lists by plot, pattern, or theme as well as a list of award-winning historical novels.

Mystery

1494 A catalogue of crime. Rev. ed. Jacques Barzun and Wendell H. Taylor. 864p. HarperCollins, 1989. ISBN 9780060102630. $

016.80883   Z5917

This revised, enlarged edition of Barzun's comprehensive bibliography of crime and detective fiction provides bibliographic information and brief plot summaries. Arrangement is alphabetical by author and then by title, with indexes to authors, titles, and names.

1495 Crime fiction II: A comprehensive bibliography, 1749–1990. Rev. ed. Allen J. Hubin. 2v., 1608p. Garland, 1994. ISBN 9780824068912. $$

016.823   Z2014

A revised and updated edition of Hubin's 1984 bibliography and 1988 supplement dealing with mystery, detective, thriller, spy, suspense, and gothic fiction. Cites more than 81,000 novels, plays, and short stories in which crime or the threat of crime is a major plot element. Entries are arranged alphabetically by author, with access provided by title, settings, series, series character, author pseudonyms, and film adaptation.

1496 Mystery and suspense writers: The literature of crime, detection, and espionage. Robin W. Winks. 2v., 1296p. Gale, 1998. ISBN 9780684805214. $$

823   PR830

These two volumes offer in-depth narrative essays on sixty-nine mystery and suspense writers, from

Margery Allingham to Edgar Wallace. Essays are written by noted experts in the field and range in length from 5,000 to 12,000 words. Includes studies of themes and subgenres. Indexed.

1497   Reference and research guide to mystery and detective fiction.
2nd ed. Richard J. Bleiler. 848p. Libraries Unlimited, 2004. ISBN 9781563089244. $
016.80883   Z5917

Provides evaluative reviews and complete bibliographic information for approximately 1,000 reference works on mystery and detective fiction.

1498   Twentieth-century crime and mystery writers. 3rd ed. Lesley Henderson, ed. 1294p. St. James Press, 1991. ISBN 9781558620315. $$
823   PR888

Covers about 600 English-language writers in entries including a brief biography, an evaluative essay, and a bibliography of the author's crime publications and other works. Appendixes include selective representations of earlier mystery writers and foreign-language authors whose books are well known in English translations.

Novel

1499   The contemporary novel: A checklist of critical literature on the English language novel since 1945. 2nd ed. Irving Adelman and Rita Dworkin. 696p. Scarecrow, 1997. ISBN 9780810831032. $$
016.8   Z1231; PS379

A selective bibliography of critical literature on the contemporary English-language novel. For the second edition, the scope was enlarged to include English-language writers outside Britain and America. All of the works of each qualified author are entered, followed by citations to journals and books rather than book reviews.

1500   Contemporary novelists. 7th ed. Susan W. Brown, ed. 1166p. St. James Press, 2000. ISBN 9781558624085. $$
823.9   PR881

Covers approximately 650 English-language contemporary novelists. Provides a biographical sketch,

an address, a bibliography of works published, a signed scholarly essay on each of the writers covered, and, in many cases, a comment by the novelist.

1501   Sequels: An annotated guide to novels in series. 3rd ed. Janet Husband and Jonathan F. Husband. 688p. American Library Association, 1997. ISBN 9780838906965. $
016.8   Z5917

A selective, annotated list of the best, most enduring, and most popular novels in series. Short stories and children's books are excluded; classics, mysteries, and science fiction are included. Arranged by author, with a title and subject index.

1502   To be continued: An annotated guide to sequels. Merle L. Jacob and Hope Apple. 488p. Greenwood, 2000. ISBN 9781573561556. $
016.8   Z6514

Listings by author of English-language fictional sequels and books in series representing a variety of genres, excluding mysteries. Indexed by title, genre, subject, time, and place. Includes a list of additional sources.

Poetry

1503   The Columbia Granger's index to poetry in anthologies. 13th ed. Tessa Kale. 2416p. Columbia Univ. Pr., 2007. ISBN 9780231139885. $$
016.8   PN1022

The standard work, once known as *Granger's index to poetry,* for locating poems in anthologies. Some 85,000 poems by 12,000 poets are indexed by title, first line, last line, author, and subject. Collections of poetry translated from other languages are represented and, for the first time in this edition, include poems in French, Spanish, and Vietnamese. All previous editions should be retained.

1504   The Columbia Granger's index to poetry in collected and selected works. 2nd ed. Keith Newton. 1152p. Edinburgh Univ. Pr., 2004. ISBN 9780231125284. $$
016.80881   PN1022

Indexes more than 50,000 poems by 251 leading poets that appear in 315 selected and collected works. Indexing is by author, title, first line, last line, and subject. Complements *The Columbia Granger's index to poetry in anthologies.* As is the case with that title, all previous editions should be retained because material is sometimes dropped from new editions.

1505 The Columbia Granger's world of poetry online. Columbia Univ. Pr. www.columbiagrangers.org.

Provides full-text versions of 210,000 poems. Contact publisher for subscription price.

1506 Contemporary poets. 7th ed. Thomas Riggs, ed. 1443p. St. James Press, 2000. ISBN 9781558623491. $$
821.9109   PR603

A biographical handbook of contemporary poets featuring alphabetically arranged entries consisting of a short biography, full bibliography, comments by many of the poets, and a signed critical essay.

1507 Guide to British poetry explication. Nancy C. Martinez and Joseph G. Martinez. 4v. Macmillan, 1991–1995. Vol. 1, Old English–medieval. 225p. ISBN 9780816189212. $ Vol. 2, Renaissance. 540p. ISBN 9780816189205. $ Vol. 3, Restoration–Romantic. 576p. ISBN 9780816119974. $ Vol. 4, Victorian–contemporary. 720p. ISBN 9780816189885. $
016.821009   Z2014

A successor to the Joseph Kuntz and Nancy C. Martinez *Poetry explication* (1980), this expanded and completely revised series indexes poetry explication found in books, journal articles, anthologies, and dissertations. Entries are arranged alphabetically by name of the poet, followed by an alphabetical list of titles, with citations to criticisms listed below each title.

1508 Guide to poetry explication: American poetry. 2v. Macmillan, 1989. Vol. 1 by James Ruppert. 225p. ISBN 9780816189199. $ Vol. 2 by John R. Leo. 459p. ISBN 9780816189182. $
016.811   Z1231

A successor to the Joseph Kuntz and Nancy C. Martinez *Poetry explication* (1980), this expanded and completely revised series provides a comprehensive

index to American poetry explication published from 1925 through 1987, incorporating all appropriate entries from the three earlier editions of *Poetry explication.* Entries are arranged alphabetically by name of the poet, followed by an alphabetical list of titles, with citations to criticisms listed below each title.

1509 Last lines: An index to the last lines of poetry. Victoria Kline. 2v., 2880p. Facts on File, 1991. ISBN 9780816012657. $$
016.80881   PN1022

Covers more than 174,000 poems written in or translated into English. Indexes each poem by title, last line, author, and keyword.

1510 New Princeton encyclopedia of poetry and poetics. 3rd ed. Alex Preminger. 1434p. Princeton Univ. Pr., 1993. ISBN 9780691021232. $
808.103   PN1021

The authoritative, scholarly encyclopedia of poetics and poetry. Provides surveys of the poetry of 106 nations, descriptions of poetic genres and forms, explanations of prosody and rhetoric, discussions of major schools and movements, and discussions on the use and place of poetry in the broader context of civilization.

1511 Poetry criticism. Thomson Gale, 1991–. ISBN 9780787698751. $$/v.
809.1   PN1010

Each volume in this series contains biographical and critical information on four to eight poets from various countries and time periods. Entries include a portrait of the author, and most of the critical essays provided are full text. Cumulative indexes by author and nationality are provided as well as volume-specific title indexes. Seventy-five volumes are currently in print.

1512 Poetry handbook: A dictionary of terms. 4th ed. Reprint. Babette Deutsch. 274p. HarperCollins, 1982. ISBN 9780064635486. $
808.1   PN44.5

Definitions are clear and concise and cover terminology and poetic forms as well as broader topics, such as romanticism and nonsense verse. Entries are in alphabetical order and include many illustrative examples from literature. Cross-references. Also includes an index of poets cited in the body of the work.

Romance

1513 **Twentieth-century romance and historical writers.** 2nd ed. Lesley Henderson, ed. 856p. St. James Press, 1990. ISBN 9780912289977. $$
823.08509   PR888

This bibliography of 540 twentieth-century writers of romance and historical fiction is similar in format and appearance to other works in the Twentieth-Century Writers series. Brief biographical information is followed by a bibliography covering the author's total work. Title index.

Science Fiction

1514 **Anatomy of wonder: A critical guide to science fiction.** 5th ed. Neil Barron, ed. 1016p. Libraries Unlimited, 2004. ISBN 9781591581710. $
016.80883   Z5917

The latest edition of a selective annotated bibliography featuring 2,100 works of science fiction. Among the 800 research aids included are publications on history and criticism, science fiction magazines, and science fiction on film and television. There is also a checklist for a core collection.

1515 **Encyclopedia of science fiction.** John Clute and Peter Nicholls. 1386p. St. Martin's, 1995. ISBN 9780312134860. $
809.3876203   PN3433.4

A companion to the *Encyclopedia of fantasy,* this monumental work includes more than 4,300 alphabetically arranged entries offering authoritative information on authors, themes, terminology, films, television, magazines, comics, illustrators, publishers, awards, and more.

1516 **Greenwood encyclopedia of science fiction and fantasy: Themes, works, and wonders.** Gary Westfahl. 3v., 1612p. Greenwood, 2005. ISBN 9780313329500. $$
813.0876203   PS374

A comprehensive treatment of the subject by some 150 experts. The first two volumes examine 400 themes found in science fiction, such as androids, imaginary and lost worlds, and mad scientists; the third volume discusses 200 classic works of science fiction and fantasy.

1517 **Reference guide to science fiction, fantasy and horror.** 2nd ed. Michael Burgess and Lisa R. Bartle. 598p. Libraries Unlimited, 2002. ISBN 9781563085482. $
016.8093   Z5917

An update of the 1992 edition offers 700 detailed annotations on reference sources in the field from standard reference sources, such as bibliographies, encyclopedias, and dictionaries, to fan publications and periodicals. Includes core collection recommendations.

1518 **St. James guide to science fiction writers.** 4th ed. Jay P. Pederson. 1175p. St. James Press, 1995. ISBN 9781558621794. $$
016.813   PS374

Formerly titled *Twentieth-century science fiction writers,* includes more than 600 authors from H. G. Wells to the present in entries consisting of a biography, a bibliography of works, and a signed critical essay.

Short Story

1519 **The Columbia companion to the twentieth-century American short story.** Blanche H. Gelfant, ed. 952p. Columbia Univ. Pr., 2004. ISBN 9780231110983. $
813.010905   PS374

Comprises 11 thematic essays that examine common themes in stories and 113 biographical essays on individual short story writers. Each entry is accompanied by a concise bibliography.

1520 **The Facts on File companion to the American short story.** Abby H. P. Werlock. 560p. Facts on File, 2000. ISBN 9780816031641. $
813.0103   PS374

Supplies 675 entries on authors, characters, literary terms, themes, motifs, and more. Provides analyses and synopses of significant stories. Includes a selected bibliography, lists of award winners and their stories, and a thematic and topical list of short stories.

1521 **The Facts on File companion to the British short story.** Andrew Maunder. 448p. Facts on File, 2007. ISBN

9780816059904. $

823.0109   PR829

Offers some 450 entries on authors (born in Great Britain, Ireland, and British Commonwealth countries); literary movements; notable short story collections; concepts; and more. Includes a bibliography and numerous cross-references.

1522   **Reference guide to short fiction.** 2nd ed. Thomas Riggs, ed. 1197p. St. James Press, 1998. ISBN 9781558622227. $$

809.31   PN3373

Provides detailed information on 375 writers and 400 works of short fiction published in the nineteenth and twentieth centuries. Entries cover both writers and works and average about 1,000 words in length. Author entries include biographical and bibliographical information. The individual works discussed are all considered classics in the genre and include everything from "A Christmas Carol" to "The Marquise of O."

1523   **Short story criticism: Excerpts from criticism of the works of short fiction writers.** Gale, 1988–. ISSN 0895-439. $$/v.

809.31   PN3373

Presents significant critical excerpts on the most important short story writers of all eras and nationalities. Entries give biographical and critical overviews, lists of principal works, excerpts of criticism, and selected bibliographies. Each volume includes indexes by author and nationality as well as one for that specific issue. Ninety-six volumes are currently in print.

1524   **Short story index.** H. W. Wilson, 1900–. ISSN 0360-774. $$

016   Z5917

Published since 1900, a standard reference tool for locating short stories. Five-year cumulations are also issued, for example, 1999–2004. Annual subscription includes an index volume for the year.

1525   **Short story index: An index to 60,000 stories in 4,320 collections.** Dorothy E. Cook and Isabel S. Monro, comps. 1533p. H. W. Wilson, 1953. OP.

808.83   PN3373

Covers stories published in collections from 1900 to 1949.

1526   **Short story index: Collections indexed 1900–1978.** Juliette Yaakov. 349p. H. W. Wilson, 1979. ISBN 0824206436. $$

808.808831   PN3451

Author and title index to the 8,400 story collections indexed in the cumulative volumes of *Short story index* from 1900 to 1978.

1527   **Twentieth-century short story explication: An index to the third edition and its five supplements, 1961–1991.** Warren S. Walker and Barbara K. Walker. 254p. Shoe String Press, 1992. ISBN 9780208023209. $

Twentieth-century short story explication: Interpretations, 1900–1975, of short fiction since 1800. 3rd ed. Warren S. Walker, comp. 880p. Shoe String Press, 1977. ISBN 9780208015709. $

Supplement 1 to 3rd ed. 257p. 1980. ISBN 9780208018137. $

Supplement 2 to 3rd ed. 348p. 1984. ISBN 9780208020055. $

Supplement 3 to 3rd ed. 486p. 1987. ISBN 9780208021229. $

Supplement 4 to 3rd ed. 342p. 1989. ISBN 9780208021885. $

Supplement 5 to 3rd ed. 408p. 1991. ISBN 9780208022998. $

Twentieth-century short story explication, new series. Shoe String Press, 1989–. ISBN 9780208023407 (v. 1, 1989–1990); 9780208023704 (v. 2, 1991–1992); 9780208024190 (v. 3, 1993–1994); 9780208024930 (v. 4, $/v. 1995–1996); 9780208025081 (v. 5, 1997–1998); 9780208025197 (v. 6, 1999–2000).

809.3   PN3373

More than 2,000 authors from around the world are represented in this index to critical analyses of short stories published in books and periodicals since 1900. Arranged by authors and then by stories. The five supplements cover new authors and extend coverage through the 1980s. The new series continues the coverage into the 1990s. Includes checklists of books and journals used and an index of short story writers.

Speech and Rhetoric

1528   Encyclopedia of rhetoric and composition: Communication from ancient times to the information age. Theresa Enos. 832p. Garland, 1996. ISBN 9780824072001. $$
808.003   PN172

Provides an overview of rhetoric and its role in contemporary life. Discusses the application of rhetoric and illustrates its practical benefits. Among the 467 signed entries are articles on major rhetoricians from all time periods.

1529   **Encyclopedia of the essay.** Tracy Chevalier, ed. 1024p. Fitzroy Dearborn, 1997. ISBN 9781884964305. $$
809.4003   PN4500

The heart of this work is a collection of biographical entries for 400 noted essayists, such as Montaigne, Addison, Hazlitt, Woolf, Edmund Wilson, and Susan Sontag. Entries such as the "French Essay" and the "German Essay" supply geographic and historical surveys. Critical bibliographies and suggestions for further reading are provided for the articles on individual writers.

1530   **Speech index: An index to 259 collections of world famous orations and speeches for various occasions.** 4th ed. Roberta Briggs Sutton. 947p. Scarecrow, 1966. ISBN 9780810801387. $
016   AI3

Speech index: An index to collections of world famous orations and speeches for various occasions. Supplement, 1966–1980. 4th ed. Charity Mitchell. 484p. Scarecrow, 1982. ISBN 9780810815186. $
808.85   PN6122

The fourth edition of *Speech index* incorporates all the materials in the three previous editions: 1935, 1935–1955, and 1956–1962, with additional titles in this field published from 1900 through 1965. The supplement cumulates the 1966–1970 and 1971–1975 supplements to the fourth edition and adds titles from 1976 to 1980. Speeches are indexed by orator, type of speech, and subject, with a selected list of titles given in the appendix.

National and Regional Literatures

American

1531   **American drama criticism: Interpretations, 1890–1977.** 2nd ed. Floyd E. Eddleman, ed. 488p. Shoe String Press, 1979. ISBN 9780208017130. $
016.812   PS332

American drama criticism: Supplement I to the 2nd ed. Floyd E. Eddleman, ed. 256p. Shoe String Press, 1984. ISBN 9780208019783. $
016.812   PS332

American drama criticism: Supplement II to the 2nd ed. Floyd E. Eddleman, ed. 240p. Shoe String Press, 1989. ISBN 9780208021380. $
016.812   PS332

American drama criticism: Supplement III to the 2nd ed. Floyd E. Eddleman, ed. 436p. Shoe String Press, 1992. ISBN 9780208022707. $
016.812   PS332

American drama criticism: Supplement IV to the 2nd ed. LaNelle Daniel, ed. 239p. Shoe String Press, 1996. ISBN 9780208023933. $
016.813009   PS332

This revised edition of the 1967 bibliography, together with its supplements, lists interpretations of American plays published primarily between 1890 and 1995. Entries are arranged by playwright and then by title. The work concludes with a "List of Books Indexed" and a "List of Journals Indexed," followed by indexes for critics, adapted authors and works, titles, and playwrights.

1532   **American nature writers.** John E. Elder, ed. 2v., 1210p. Thomson Gale, 1996. ISBN 9780684196923. $$
810.936   PS163

Seventy writers are feature in this biographical-critical set, including Emerson, Thoreau, Muir, Leopold, Carsons, Matthiessen, and Lewis Thomas. Sixty-four scholars participated in this effort to describe the contributions of writer-naturalists who have contributed significantly to the way we interpret the world around us.

1533 American writers. Elizabeth H. Oakes. 448p. Facts on File, 2004. ISBN 9780816051588. $

810.90003   PS129

Profiles more than 250 American writers from colonial times to the present. Novelists, poets, short story writers, essayists, and playwrights are represented in articles that include a biography, criticism, and a bibliography. The entries are indexed by literary movement, genre, and year of birth. There is a general bibliography as well as a list of suggested titles for further reading.

1534 American writers: A collection of literary biographies. 4v. with 17 supplements. Thomson Gale, 1974–. $$$$; $$/supplement

810.9   PS129

A series containing biographical and critical articles on American authors from the seventeenth century to the present. Following each essay is a selected bibliography of the author's work and a list of studies for further reading. The original set is made up of four volumes published by Scribner. There are now seventeen supplemental volumes, which are available from Thomson Gale.

1535 The Facts on File companion to the American novel. Abby H. P. Werlock, ed. 3v., 1519p. Facts on File, 2006. ISBN 9780816045280. $$

813.003   PS371

More than 900 alphabetically arranged entries include articles on authors and novels and extended essays on such topics as the African American novel and the Latino novel. Articles on authors include selected bibliographies and suggestions for further study. There are also lists of six major literary award winners.

1536 Great American writers: Twentieth century. R. Baird Shuman, ed. 3v. Marshall Cavendish, 2002. ISBN 9780761472407. $$$

810.9   PS221

Profiles of ninety authors in articles ranging from four to thirty pages in length accompanied by numerous sidebars and modern art illustrations. The set includes a volume containing a list of writers grouped by genre, a glossary of terms, and lists of literary award winners. There are a number of indexes, including those by writer, work, character, and location.

1537 The Greenwood encyclopedia of American poets and poetry. Jeffrey Gray, ed. 5v., 2012p. Greenwood, 2005. ISBN 9780313323812. $$$

811.00903   PS303

Covering nearly 400 years of poetry and more than 800 writers, this set also discusses poetic terms, movements, theories, genres, and much more. Articles on individual poets include biographical as well as critical information and suggestions for further reading. There is also a general bibliography with an array of citations to anthologies, reference works, critical studies, and more.

1538 The Greenwood encyclopedia of multiethnic American literature. Emmanuel S. Nelson, ed. 5v., 2483p. Greenwood, 2005. ISBN 9780313330605. $$

810.9   PS153

Offers more than 1,100 alphabetically arranged signed entries by some 300 contributors. About 1,000 of those entries are devoted to individual authors; the rest discuss a variety of topics, such as assimilation, bilingualism, immigration, identity, literary genres, ethnic stereotypes, and more. Includes a selected general bibliography.

1539 The HarperCollins reader's encyclopedia of American literature. 2nd ed. George Perkins and Barbara Perkins. 1136p. HarperCollins, 2002. ISBN 9780060198152. $

810.9003   PN41

The second edition of a work based on *Benét's reader's encyclopedia of American literature* (HarperCollins, 1991) consists of more than 6,000 entries on poets, playwrights, novelists, critics, literary terms, genres and movements, and more. Articles on individual works of literature often provide plot synopses. More than 300 writers have been added since the last edition.

1540 The Oxford companion to American literature. 6th ed. James D. Hart and Phillip Leininger. 800p. Oxford Univ. Pr., 1995. ISBN 9780195065480. $

810.9   PS21

This handbook to American literature includes short biographies of American authors, brief bibliographies, plot summaries of novels and plays, and entries on literary schools and movements. Arranged by specific subject in dictionary format, with numerous cross-references. Chronological index.

1541 Reference guide to American literature. 4th ed. Thomas Riggs, ed. 1319p. St. James Press, 1999. ISBN 9781558624177. $$
810.9   PS129

Provides an authoritative bibliography and commentary for American literature. Presents writers and relevant topics alphabetically. Each personal entry lists biographical data, publications, and critical studies and presents a signed scholarly essay on the author's contributions to literature. Includes an exhaustive chronology.

1542 Southern writers: A new biographical dictionary. Joseph M. Flora, Amber Vogel, and Bryan Albion Giemza, eds. 616p. Louisiana State Univ. Pr., 2006. ISBN 9780807131237. $
810.9   PS261

More than 600 southern writers from the colonial period to today are represented by biographical sketches and lists of published works. Poets, playwrights, novelists, short story writers, and other literary artists with either personal or literary connections to the South are included.

Arabic

1543 Encyclopedia of Arabic literature. Paul Starkey and Julie S. Meisami, eds. 2v., 896p. Routledge, 1998. ISBN 9780415068086. $$$
892.70903   PJ7510

Thirteen-hundred signed entries provide information on a variety of topics covering Arabic literature from the classical period to the twentieth century, including authors and their works, literary genres, terms, concepts, and issues. Sources for further reading are provided for most entries. A comprehensive index and a glossary are also included.

British

1544 British writers. 11v. Thomson Gale, 1992–. ISBN 9780684805871. $$$$; $$/supplement
820.9   PR85

A companion to Thomson Gale's American Writers series, this work presents articles by distinguished contributors on major British writers from the fourteenth century to the present. The biographical sketch that opens each entry is followed by a survey of the author's principal works, a critical evaluation, and an updated bibliography. Indexed. Twelve supplements are now available.

1545 Encyclopedia of British writers, 16th to 20th centuries. Alan Hager et. al. 4v., 1712p. Facts on File, 2005. ISBN 9780816061426. $$
820.9   PR421

These four comprehensive volumes cover some 1,400 British novelists, poets, essayists, and playwrights in articles consisting of a concise biography, summary of the entrant's major works, and a brief bibliography.

1546 English novel explication: Criticisms to 1972. Helen H. Palmer and Anne Jane Dyson, comps. 329p. Shoe String Press, 1973. ISBN 9780208013224. $
016.823   PR821

English novel explication: Supplement I. Peter L. Abernethey et al., comps. 305p. Shoe String Press, 1976. ISBN 9780208014641. $
016.823   PR821

English novel explication: Supplement II. Christian J. Kloesel, comp. 326p. Shoe String Press, 1980. ISBN 9780208017093. $
016.823   PR821

English novel explication: Supplement III. Christian J. Kloesel, comp. 533p. Shoe String Press, 1986. ISBN 9780208020925. $
016.823   PR821

English novel explication: Supplement IV. Christian J. Kloesel, comp. 351p. Shoe String Press, 1990. ISBN 9780208022318. $
016.823   PR821

English novel explication: Supplement V. Christian J. Kloesel, comp. 431p. Shoe String Press, 1994. ISBN 9780208023087. $
016.823   PR821

English novel explication: Supplement VI. Christian J. Kloesel, comp. 483p. Shoe String Press, 1998. ISBN 9780208024183. $

016.823   PR821

English novel explication: Supplement VII. Christian J. Kloesel, comp. 478p. Shoe String Press, 2002. ISBN 9780208024886. $

016.823   PR821

Continuing the work begun by Inglis Bell and Donald Baird, the present series provides a checklist of interpretive criticism on the English novel, beginning with 1957. Includes an index of authors and titles and a list of books indexed.

1547 The Oxford companion to English literature. 6th ed. Margaret Drabble, ed. 1184p. Oxford Univ. Pr., 2006. ISBN 9780198614531. $

820.9   PR19

The latest edition of the standard handbook to English literature, first compiled by Sir Paul Harvey in 1932. Contains brief articles on authors, titles, characters, literary allusions, and related literary topics.

1548 The Oxford encyclopedia of British literature. David Scott Kastan, ed. 5v., 2800p. Oxford Univ. Pr., 2006. ISBN 9780195169218. $$$

820.3   PR19

A comprehensive work covering British literature from the seventh century to the present in some 509 alphabetically arranged entries, most of which are dedicated to individual writers and historical figures. Other articles discuss related topics, such as literary criticism, theory and genre, censorship, serialization, and much more. Selected annotated bibliographies of primary and secondary sources are part of every entry.

SHAKESPEARE

1549 The Columbia dictionary of Shakespeare quotations. Mary Foakes and Reginald Foakes, eds. 528p. Columbia Univ. Pr., 1998. ISBN 9780231104340. $

822.3   PR2892

Shakespearean quotations on some 600 subjects are arranged topically in entries that supply play title, speaker, act, scene, and line number (using *The Riverside Shakespeare*) as well as place the excerpt in context.

1550 The essential Shakespeare: An annotated bibliography of major modern studies. 2nd ed. Larry S. Champion. 200p. G. K. Hall, 1993. ISBN 9780816173327. $

822.3   PR2894

A convenient annotated checklist of the most significant Shakespeare scholarship in English from 1900. Some 2,000 entries are arranged under general studies or under individual works.

1551 The Harvard concordance to Shakespeare. Marvin Spevack. 1600p. Olms Verlag AG, 1973. ISBN 9783487048529. $$

822.3   PR2892

A computer-produced concordance based on volumes 4 through 6 of the author's *A complete and systematic concordance to Shakespeare* (Georg Olms, 1968–1970). A thorough piece of scholarship: 29,000 words, statistics on the number of occurrences of words in verse and prose passages, and their relative frequency.

1552 Internet editions. Univ. of Victoria and the Social Science and Humanities Research Council of Canada. http://ise.uvic.ca/index.html.

Provides "scholarly, fully annotated texts of Shakespeare's plays, multimedia explorations of the context of Shakespeare's life and works, and records of his plays in performance." The Internet Shakespeare Editions (ISE) is a nonprofit corporation affiliated with the University of Victoria in Victoria, British Columbia, Canada.

1553 The quotable Shakespeare: A topical dictionary. Charles DeLoach. 568p. McFarland, 1998. ISBN 9780786405718. $

822.3   PR2892

Arranges 6,516 quotations under some 1,000 topics. Includes title, character, and topical indexes.

1554 The reader's encyclopedia of Shakespeare. Reprint. Oscar James Campbell and Edward G. Quinn, eds. 1014p. MJF Fine Books, 1998. ISBN

9781567362577. $

822.3   PR2892

Criticism and information on all aspects of Shakespeare's works. Sources are given at the end of many articles. Among the appendixes are a chronology of events related to the life and works of Shakespeare, transcripts of documents, genealogical table of the Houses of York and Lancaster, and a thirty-page selected bibliography.

1555   **Shakespeare A to Z: The essential reference to his plays, his poems, his life and times, and more.** Charles Boyce. 752p. Facts on File, 1990. ISBN 9780816018055. $

822.3   PR2892

Presents a scene-by-scene synopsis of each play, a critical commentary, a discussion of the play's sources, a history of the text, and the play's theatrical history. Includes entries on all the major characters, Shakespeare's contemporaries, theatrical terms, Shakespearean actors, producers and directors, and Shakespeare's nondramatic poetry.

1556   **A Shakespeare glossary.** 3rd ed. Charles T. Onions and Robert D. Eagleson. 360p. Oxford Univ. Pr., 1986. ISBN 9780198125211. $

822.3   PR2892

Gives definitions of words or senses of words now obsolete, as well as explanations for unfamiliar allusions and for proper names. Illustrative citations from Shakespeare are included for each definition.

1557   **Shakespeare on screen: An international filmography and videography.** Kenneth S. Rockwell and Annabelle H. Meltzer. 407p. Neal-Schuman, 1990. ISBN 9781555700492. $

822.3   PR3093

The principal work on film adaptations of Shakespeare. Includes entries on more than 750 film and video versions made from 1899 through 1989.

1558   **Shakespearean criticism: Excerpts from the criticism of William Shakespeare's plays and poetry, from the first published appraisals to current evaluations.** Thomson Gale, 1984–. ISBN 9780787688455. $$/v.

822.3   PR2965

An ongoing series that provides comprehensive coverage of Shakespearean critiques through the years. Most of the critical essays included are full text. Cumulative indexes to topics and critics.

1559   **Treasures in full: Shakespeare in Quarto.** British Library. www.bl.uk/ treasures/shakespeare/homepage.html.

"On this site you will find the British Library's 93 copies of the 21 plays by William Shakespeare printed in quarto before the theatres were closed in 1642."

1560   **William Shakespeare: His world, his work, his influence.** John F. Andrews, ed. 3v., 940p. Thomson Gale, 1985. ISBN 9780684178516. $$

822.3   PR2976

This set offers a multifaceted view of Shakespeare and his world. Sixty critical essays by British and American scholars examine Shakespeare's life and works, the historical and cultural aspects of the era in which he wrote, and his subsequent influence on literature, theater, and popular culture. Index to names and titles in volume 3.

Classical

1561   **Ancient writers: Greece and Rome.** T. James Luce, ed. 2v., 1148p. Thomson Gale, 1982. ISBN 9780684165950. $$

880.09   PA3009

The forty-seven articles found in this handbook of Greek and Roman literature were written by noted classicists and vary in length from ten to fifty pages. Arranged chronologically, they primarily treat individual authors, although some cover groups of authors. Each article consists of biographical information, a critical analysis of the author's works, and a selective bibliography of primary and secondary sources.

1562   **The classic epic: An annotated bibliography.** Thomas J. Sienkewicz. 265p. Scarecrow, 1991. ISBN 9780810828117. $

883   PA3022

A bibliography "directed toward the first time reader of Classical epics in English translation." Targeting easily accessible materials, the bibliography describes items that discuss social conditions, geographical conditions, composition techniques, translations, characters, and influence of the great classical epics.

1563 Classical and medieval literature criticism: Excerpts from criticism of the works of world authors, from classical antiquity through the fourteenth century, from the first appraisals to current evaluations. Thomson Gale, 1988–. ISBN 9780787680336. $$/v.

809 PN681

Following the pattern of other Thomson Gale series on literature criticism, this work provides an introduction to literary works from antiquity to the fourteenth century. Each entry contains a historical and critical introduction, a list of principal English translations, and excerpts from major critical writings. Cumulative index. A total of eighty-seven volumes published so far.

1564 Classical Greek and Roman drama: An annotated bibliography. Robert J. Forman. 239p. Scarecrow, 1989. ISBN 9780810828094. $

882.01 PA3024

An annotated bibliography of translations and commentaries and accessible English-language criticism of works by Aeschylus, Aristophanes, Ennius, Euripides Menander, Plautus, Seneca, Sophocles, and Terence.

1565 Classical studies: A guide to the reference literature. 2nd ed. Fred W. Jenkins. 424p. Libraries Unlimited, 2006. ISBN 9781591581192. $

016.48 PA91

A variety of reference works on classical studies, such as bibliographies, dictionaries, handbooks, biographical and geographical sources, directories, and Internet resources, are featured in this second edition. Here they are arranged by subject rather than by format, as in the first edition. More than 1,000 entries are included.

1566 The Facts on File companion to classical drama. John E. Thorburn Jr. 688p. Facts on File, 2005. ISBN 9780816052028. $

880.09 PA3024

Features some 400 alphabetically arranged entries on authors, characters, dramas, settings, historical

figures, themes, concepts, genres, and theatrical terms. Covers the major authors of the period, for example, Aeschylus, Euripides, and Plautus, as well as the eighty surviving dramatic works of the classical period, for example, *Antigone, Oedipus Rex,* and *Agamemnon.*

1567 Greek and Latin authors: 800 B.C. to A.D. 1000. Michael Grant. 492p. H. W. Wilson, 1980. ISBN 9780824206406. $$

880.9; 920 PA31

An expert on the ancient world, Grant supplies in each entry the pronunciation of the author's name, biographical background, an overview of major works with critical commentary, and, where relevant, a brief discussion of the influence of the author's works on later literature. A bibliography completes each sketch.

The Oxford classical dictionary, see **1618**.

1568 The Oxford companion to classical literature. 2nd ed. Margaret Howatson. 640p. Oxford Univ. Pr., 1989. ISBN 9780198661214. $

880.9 PA31

A revised edition of Sir Paul Harvey's 1937 standard handbook to classical antiquity. A valuable resource for identifying geographical, historical, mythological, and political backgrounds relevant to the study and understanding of the literature of Greece and Rome. Appendixes include maps and a chronology.

African

1569 African writers. C. Brian Cox. 2v., 936p. Thomson Gale, 1996. ISBN 9780684196510. $$

896 PL8010

The sixty-five writers featured here came from or spent critical periods of their lives on the African continent during the nineteenth or twentieth centuries. Among them are Chinua Achebe, Albert Camus, Doris Lessing, Naguib Mahfouz, Alan Paton, and Wole Soyinka. Entries include a biography, critical analysis, and an extensive bibliography.

Australian

1570 The Cambridge companion to Australian literature. Elizabeth Webby, ed. 348p. Cambridge Univ. Pr., 2000. ISBN 9780521651226. $

820.9   PR9604.3

Covers indigenous narratives, writers from the colonial period, fiction from 1900 to 1970, poetry from the 1890s to 1970, theatre from 1788 to the 1960s, contemporary fiction, poetry and theatre, and more.

Canadian

1571 Canadian fiction: A guide to reading interests. Sharron Smith and Maureen O'Connor. 448p. Libraries Unlimited, 2005. ISBN 9781591581666. $

016.8   Z1277

An addition to the Genreflecting advisory series that provides an overview of Canadian works published from 1990 to 2004 and a variety of helpful features, such as categorizing titles by primary appeal (language, setting, character, story) or classifying them by genre and subgenre. Appendixes list Canadian literary awards, resources, and websites and Canadian publishers.

1572 The Oxford companion to Canadian literature. 2nd ed. Eugene Benson, and William Toye, eds. 1168p. Oxford Univ. Pr., 1998. ISBN 9780195411676. $

810.9   PR9180.2

This comprehensive dictionary consists of more than 1,100 entries on English-language and French Canadian literature. Entries, contributed by more than 300 scholars, cover ethnic and regional literatures as well as other topics and aspects of Canadian literary culture.

Caribbean

1573 Encyclopedia of Caribbean literature. D. H. Figueredo, ed. 2v., 1016p. Greenwood, 2005. ISBN 9780313327421. $$

809.89   PN849

More than 700 alphabetically arranged entries cover a variety of topics, from authors, works, and genres to cultural and historical figures. Immigrant literature, surrealism, feminism in Caribbean literature, and the various historical, cultural, and political contexts in which the literature is created

are among the many topics discussed. Includes an extensive bibliography.

1574 Twentieth-century Caribbean and black African writers. Bernth Linffors and Reinhard W. Sander. 406p. Thomson Gale, 1992. ISBN 9780810375949. $$

810.99   PR9205

Profiles thirty-one authors in articles that consist of biographical and critical sketches, lists of published works, and brief bibliographies. Entries include photos and reproductions of book jackets.

Chinese

1575 The Indiana companion to traditional Chinese literature. William H. Nienhauser Jr. et al., eds. 2v. Indiana Univ. Pr., 1986–1998 ISBN 9780253329837 (v. 1); 9780253334565 (v. 2). $/v.

895.1   Z3108

The original volume was compiled by more than 170 scholars of Chinese literature and covers Chinese literature through 1911. Consists of some 500 signed entries on authors, schools, movements, and genres. Includes, for each entry, a bibliography of editions, translations, and criticism. The first half of volume 2 presents 63 newly researched entries, many of which offer information on general topics such as the printing and circulation of texts, children's literature, and literary Chinese; the second half of volume 2 presents updated bibliographies for the entries found in the original volume. Both volumes provide name, title, and subject indexes.

East Asian

1576 The Columbia companion to modern East Asian literature. Joshua S. Mostow, ed. 700p. Columbia Univ. Pr., 2003. ISBN 9780231113144. $$

895   PL493

Covers the literature of Japan, China, and Korea in more than 100 entries, including thematic essays providing historical overviews and examinations of persistent themes as well as articles on individual authors, works, and schools.

Eastern European

1577 The Columbia guide to the literatures of Eastern Europe since 1945. Harold B. Segel. 776p. Columbia Univ. Pr., 2003. ISBN 9780231114042. $$
809.89   Z2483

Features nearly 700 writers from Albania and Kosovo, Bosnia-Herzegovina, Bulgaria, Croatia, the Czech Republic, the German Democratic Republic, Hungary, Macedonia, Poland, Romania, Serbia and Montenegro, Slovakia, and Slovenia. Includes playwrights, novelists, and poets in articles that include a biography, list of published works, English translations of those works, and citations to criticism.

French

1578 Guide to French literature: 1789 to the present. Anthony Levi. 2v., 900p. St. James Press, 1994. ISBN 9781558623200. $$
840   PQ226

In an A–Z format, provides biographical, critical, and scholarly information on principal figures in French literature and discusses topics, issues, schools, and movements in lengthy essays. Includes a thorough bibliography for each author discussed.

1579 The new Oxford companion to literature in French. Peter France, ed. 926p. Oxford Univ. Pr., 1995. ISBN 9780198661252. $
840.9   PQ41

Discusses cultural and literary movements and those who participated in them. Includes entries for authors, titles of works, literary terms, festivals, literary movements, and historical events with relevance to literature in French.

German

1580 The Oxford companion to German literature. 3rd ed. Henry Garland and Mary Garland. 968p. Oxford Univ. Pr., 1997. ISBN 9780198158967. $$
830.3   PT41

This new revision of a standard work presents entries of varying lengths pertinent to German culture and literature. Includes entries for authors, titles of works, literary terms, festivals, literary movements, and historical events with relevance to German literature.

Indian

1581 History of Indian literature in English. Arvind Krishna Mehrotra, ed. 320p. Columbia Univ. Pr., 2003. ISBN 9780231128100. $
820.9   PR9489.6

Surveys 200 years of Indian literature written in English in chronologically arranged essays on single authors, groups of authors, or genres. Novelists, playwrights, and poets as well as anthropologists, scientists, and social reformers are among the writers represented.

Irish

1582 Dictionary of Irish literature. Rev. ed. Robert Hogan, ed. 2v., 1472p. Greenwood, 1996. ISBN 9780313291722. $$
820.9   PR8706

Supplies more than 500 biocritical sketches about important Irish literary figures that include bibliographies of primary and secondary sources as well as articles on significant related subjects and institutions. There is a chronology that relates political and literary events from the years 432 to the present, an extensive general bibliography, and an index by name, title, and subject.

1583 Modern Irish writers: A bio-critical sourcebook. Alexander G. Gonzalez, ed. 480p. Greenwood, 1997. ISBN 9780313295577. $$
820.9   PR8727

Provides alphabetically arranged entries on more than seventy Irish writers from 1885 to the present, including Joyce, Yeats, Heaney, and Beckett. Entries include biographical information, a discussion of each writer's work, its critical reception, and a bibliography of primary and secondary sources. Publisher's website states that this title is not available online.

1584 The Oxford companion to Irish literature. Robert Welch and Bruce

Stewart. 648p. Oxford Univ. Pr., 1996.
ISBN 9780198661580. $
820.9   PR8706

Covers sixteen centuries of literature from the Emerald Isle. Alphabetically arranged entries provide a comprehensive guide to the evolution and history of Irish literature framed within the context of the unique culture that is Ireland.

Italian

1585   Dictionary of Italian literature.
2nd ed. Peter C. Bonadella, Julia R. Bonadella, and Jody R. Shiffman, eds. 736p. Greenwood, 1996. ISBN 9780313277450. $$
850   PQ4006

Introduces authors, genres, schools, and movements of Italian literature from the twelfth century to the present. The 362 alphabetically arranged entries are thoroughly cross-referenced and indexed. Bibliographies include English translations of primary texts as well as critical studies in various languages.

1586   The Oxford companion to Italian literature. Peter Hainsworth.
692p. Oxford Univ. Pr., 2002. ISBN 9780198183327. $$
850.9   PQ4006

More than 2,400 signed entries on Italian literature from the early thirteenth century to the present. Articles cover a number of topics, from individual authors and their works to literary genres, theories, criticism, and more and are thoroughly cross-referenced.

Japanese

1587   The Princeton companion to classical Japanese literature. Reprint. Earl Miner, Hiroko Odagiri, and Robert E. Morrell. 296p. Princeton Univ. Pr., 1988. ISBN 9780691008257. $
895.6   PL726

Opens with a section that provides a historical context for the text, followed by a chronology, a description of major authors and their works, and entries on literary terms, theaters, reference tools, literary symbols, relevant geographical information, and costumes.

Latin American

1588   Encyclopedia of Latin American literature. Verity Smith. 950p. Fitzroy Dearborn, 1997. ISBN 9781884964183. $$
860   PQ7081

Alphabetically arranged articles supply a guide to authors, works, and issues relevant to the literary culture of Latin America. Most of the 500 entries are about 1,500 words long, but survey articles on individual countries may be as long as 10,000 words.

1589   Handbook of Latin American literature. 2nd ed. David W. Foster, ed. 799p. Garland, 1992. ISBN 9780815303435. $$
809.8   PQ7081

Provides scholarly essays on all Latin American countries as well as Latino writing in the United States and includes a separate essay on literature and film. Discusses literary movements and issues, principal figures, and major works from the colonial period to the present. Each essay concludes with an annotated bibliography. Indexed.

1590   Latin American mystery writers: An A to Z guide. Darrell B. Lockhart, ed. 264p. Greenwood, 2004. ISBN 9780313305542. $
863   PQ7082

After an introductory essay on the genre, traces the development of mystery writing in Latin America over the last century and provides biocritical articles on some fifty-four mystery writers, each of which include bibliographies of primary and secondary sources. Includes authors from countries where Spanish or Portuguese is spoken but omits Latino writers from the United States.

1591   Latin American science fiction writers: An A to Z guide. Darrell B. Lockhart, ed. 248p. Greenwood, 2004. ISBN 9780313305535. $
863   PQ7082

Identical in format to the entry above, this provides biocritical articles on some seventy Latin American science fiction writers. Includes bibliographies of primary and secondary sources. Omits Latino writers from the United States but includes authors from countries where Spanish or Portuguese is spoken.

1592   Latin American writers—Supplement
I. Carlos A. Sole Jr., ed. 500p. Thomson
Gale, 2001. ISBN 9780684805993. $$
860.9   PQ7081

Supplements the three-volume set published in 1989
and offers eight revised essays and twenty-eight new
ones. Covers twentieth-century writers from coun-
tries where Spanish or Portuguese is spoken in arti-
cles that average fifteen pages in length and feature
bibliographies of primary and secondary sources.

Russian

1593   Handbook of Russian literature.
Reprint. Victor Terras, ed. 578p. Yale
Univ. Pr., 1985. ISBN 9780300048681
(pbk.). $
891.7   PG2940

This well-researched companion to Russian litera-
ture covers authors, critics, genres, literary move-
ments, journals, newspapers, institutions, and
other topics of literary interest. Most of the nearly
1,000 articles include bibliographies of secondary
studies; author entries also provide a list of major
works and important translations.

South Asian

**1594   Modern South Asian literature
in English.** Paul Brians. 264p.
Greenwood, 2003. ISBN

9780313320118. $
820.9954   PR9484

Fifteen chapters introduce writers from India,
Pakistan, and Sri Lanka. There are discussions
of works from 1915 to the present. Background
information is supplied as well as a selective
bibliography.

**1595   South Asian literature in English:
An encyclopedia.** Jaina C. Sanga,
ed. 392p. Greenwood, 2004. ISBN
9780313327009. $
820.9   PR9570

Includes writers from India, Pakistan, Sri Lanka,
and Bangladesh and a variety of related literary
topics, such as literary theorists and film adapta-
tions of novels in articles of about one to two pages
in length. Entries include suggestions for further
reading, and there is also a general selected bibliog-
raphy at the end of the volume.

**1596   South Asian novelists in English:
An A to Z guide.** Jaina C. Sanga,
ed. 328p. Greenwood, 2003. ISBN
9780313318856. $
820.9   PR9496

Covers more than fifty writers from Bangladesh,
India, Pakistan, and Sri Lanka in articles that
include a biography, a discussion of major works,
a summary of their critical reception, and a bibli-
ography of primary and secondary sources. There
is also a general selected bibliography at the end of
the work.

18 *History*

TOM WEITZEL

Internationalization, the global economy, and war in the Middle East have produced a greater interest in historical events, and not just in western Europe and North America. This chapter includes more world coverage, chronologies, popular culture, and important new works in American and world history. One change since the last edition is the appearance of primary source materials. Documenting scholarship will continue in this important area for reference collections.

Bibliographies and Guides

1597   **The American Historical Association's guide to historical literature.** 3rd ed. Mary Beth Norton, ed. 2v. Oxford Univ. Pr., 1995. OP. ISBN 9780195057270.
016.9   Z6201

The American Historical Association's guide to historical literature is a selective and annotated bibliography of the most "useful" historical books and articles published primarily between 1961 and 1992. The majority of the cited works are in English and limited to printed works. World historical literature is divided into forty-eight broad subject categories, each of which contain an introductory essay, a guide

to the contents, and an annotated bibliography. There are author and subject indexes included.

1598   **Harvard guide to American history.** Rev. ed. Frank Freidel and Richard K. Showman. 2v., 1352p. Belknap Press, 1974. ISBN 9780674375602. $$
016.973   Z1236

This is an old standard bibliographic guide to books and articles on American history published prior to 1970. It complements *United States history: A multicultural, interdisciplinary guide to information sources* by providing coverage from earlier sources. Volume 1's bibliographies appear under topical headings, such as individual biographies, business, area histories, and the presidency. It also includes a section on historical research methods. Volume 2 is arranged chronologically, with emphasis on political and diplomatic history. It includes both a personal name index and a subject index.

1599   **State names, seals, flags, and symbols: A historical guide.** 3rd ed. Benjamin F. Shearer and Barbara S. Shearer. Greenwood, 2002. ISBN 9780313315343. $
929.9   E155

This is an essential reference source for libraries. In addition to the information promised in the title, this guide provides information on state and territory mottoes, capitols, legal holidays and observances, license plates, postage stamps, fairs and festivals, universities, governors, and professional sports teams. There is even a chapter on "miscellaneous official state and territory designations" that includes things like official fossil, vegetable, dance, and more. It provides full illustrations of seals, flags, flowers, trees, birds, stamps, and license plates. It also contains a selected bibliography of state and territory histories and a general index.

1600 **United States history: A multicultural, interdisciplinary guide to information sources.** 2nd ed. Anna M. Perrault and Ron Blazek. Libraries Unlimited, 2003. ISBN 9781563088742. $

016.973   Z1236

A guide to 1,250 major entries, it describes and evaluates U.S. history books, online databases, websites, and CD-ROM titles. This bibliography covers traditional historical topics as well as recognizing the importance of multicultural and interdisciplinary fields that are vital to the study of history. Most of the titles were published after 1980.

Chronologies

1601 **Cassell's chronology of world history: Dates, events and ideas that made history.** Hywel Williams. 767p. Cassell, 2005. ISBN 9780304357307. $

909   D11

There are yearly entries, and within each yearly entry, historical events are listed under regional and thematic subheadings such as "Economy and Society," "Science and Technology," and "Arts and Humanities." Items are listed in chronological order under each subheading. Additional information and historical context are provided in essays that consider key themes or turning points in the history of the period under consideration. Short biographical profiles of key thinkers of world history are also interspersed within the text. The comprehensive index provides access to the people, the events, and the themes in history.

1602 **Fitzhenry and Whiteside book of Canadian facts and dates.** 3rd ed. Jay Myers and James Musson; Richard W. Pound, ed. 988p. Fitzhenry and Whiteside, 2005. ISBN 9781550411713. $

971   F1006

This is a chronology of Canadian history from the geologic formation of the land to the year 2003. It has more than 10,000 individual entries of Canadian facts, dates, people, places, events, and lore. The *Fitzhenry and Whiteside book of Canadian facts and dates* has a comprehensive index of persons and places for quick access to needed information.

1603 **This day in American history.** 2nd ed. Ernie Gross. 342p. McFarland, 2001. ISBN 7980786408542. $

973   E174.5

Although not strictly a chronology, *This day in American history* gives a list of all the significant events that occurred on each day of the year. Events for each day of the year are listed in chronological order and give the year and a single-sentence explanation of what took place.

1604 **The timetables of history: A horizontal linkage of people and events.** 4th ed. Bernard Grun and Eva Simpson. 835p. Simon and Schuster, 2005. ISBN 9780743270038. $

902   D11

A translation of *Kulturfahrplan,* by Werner Stein, this work is a reliable and authoritative world chronology of human events of the last 7,000 years. Information is listed by year and is categorized and presented in seven columns—"History, Politics"; "Literature, Theater"; "Religion, Philosophy, Learning"; "Visual Arts"; "Music"; "Science, Technology, Growth"; and "Daily Life." The subject-column format makes it easy to follow trends over the years or to place events within historical context. Each entry is very short, but it can be used as a starting point for further reading or research. This bargain-priced chronology is very well indexed for easy use.

Databases and Indexes

1605 **American history and life.** ABC-CLIO. ISSN 1528-3437. www.abc-clio.com.

American history and life is an annotated bibliography of the history and culture of the United States and Canada from prehistory to the present. This is an essential reference tool for most college libraries. Journal coverage is retrospective to 1964. It contains English-language abstracts of scholarly literature appearing in more than 1,700 journals and includes citations to book reviews, media reviews, and dissertations.

1606 **Historical abstracts.** ABC-CLIO. ISSN 1528-3445. www.abc-clio.com.

Historical abstracts covers the history of the world (excluding the United States and Canada) from 1450 to the present. This is an annotated bibliography of more than 2,000 journals of history and specific titles in the humanities and the social sciences that would be useful to history students and researchers. *Historical abstracts* also cites new books reviewed in key English-language history and review journals. Relevant dissertation citations are also included. This is probably an essential database for most college libraries. Journals in more than forty languages are included although all abstracts are in English.

Dictionaries and Encyclopedias

1607 **Bowling, beatniks, and bell-bottoms: Pop culture of 20th-century America.** Sara Pendergast and Tom Pendergast, eds. 5v. UXL/Thomson Gale, 2002. ISBN 9780787656751. $$
306   E169.1

This illustrated five-volume guide to the twentieth-century's American pop culture is both fun and informative and aimed at both the general reader and the student. The information is arranged chronologically by decades, and within each decade, the entries are divided into nine major topical categories: "Commerce"; "Fashion"; "Film and Theater"; "Food and Drink"; "Music"; "Print Culture"; "Sports and Games"; "Television and Radio"; and "The Way We Lived." Articles are generally one page long, and many have a helpful "For More Information" section added. It includes many black-and-white illustrations. Each volume contains a complete index, table of contents, a list of entries in alphabetical order, and a timeline of American pop culture.

1608 **China: A cultural and historical dictionary.** Michael Dillon, ed. 391p. Curzon, 1998. ISBN 9780700704392. $$
951   DS733

This reference covers Chinese culture and history from antiquity to the twentieth century, with entries selected for their interest to the general and specialist reader. It covers the personalities, events, and ideas from art, archaeology, philosophy, politics, and ethnicity important for an understanding of Chinese culture and history.

1609 **Dictionary of American history.** 3rd ed. Stanley I. Kutler, ed. 10v. Thomson Gale, 2002. ISBN 9780684805337. $$$$/set
973   E174

The third edition of this classic work has been substantially revised to reflect a new historical interest in social and cultural diversity beyond the traditional emphasis on political, military, and economic topics. Photographs have been added in this new edition. Articles have cross-references and have short bibliographies. The ninth volume contains an archive of historical maps, with explanatory text and historical documents. Volume 10 contains a learning guide and a comprehensive index. Note that this set does not include any biographies. This is an authoritative starting point for both casual and academic history questions.

1610 **Dictionary of historic documents.** Rev. ed. George Childs Kohn, ed. 646p. Facts on File, 2003. ISBN 9780816047727. $
016.90908   D9

This is a list of historically significant documents in Western civilization, from ancient times to the late twentieth century. Each entry includes a description of the document that details its origins, content, and impact. The text of the documents themselves is not included. A timetable of documents puts them in their historic context. A bibliography and index are included.

1611 **Encyclopedia of African history.** Kevin Shillington, ed. 3v. Fitzroy Dearborn, 2005. ISBN 9781579582456. $$/set
960   DT20

The *Encyclopedia of African history* is a uniquely rich resource on the history, culture, geography, economics, and politics of the entire continent of Africa. The signed articles are about 1,000 words in length and provide a list for further reading and helpful cross-references. Longer articles are included on major topics and regional surveys. Illustrations and maps offer additional information. A comprehensive index is also provided.

1612 **Encyclopedia of ancient Asian civilizations.** Charles Higham. 440p. Facts on File, 2004. ISBN 9780816046409. $
959   DS12

Encyclopedia of ancient Egypt. Rev. ed. Margaret R. Bunson. 462p. Facts on File, 2002. ISBN 9780816045631. $
932   DT58

Encyclopedia of the ancient Greek world. Rev. ed. David Sacks. 412p. Facts on File, 2005. ISBN 9780816057221. $
938   DF16

Encyclopedia of the Roman Empire. Rev. ed. Matthew Bunson. 636p. Facts on File, 2002. ISBN 9780816045624. $
937   DG270

This series covers ancient Asian, ancient Egyptian, ancient Greek, and ancient Roman civilizations. Volumes discuss people, places, events, and ideas from these times. Maps and illustrations complement the text. Volumes contain chronologies of main events, glossaries, and bibliographies. The index in each volume is helpful.

1613   Encyclopedia of Latin American history and culture. Barbara A. Tenenbaum and Georgette M. Dorn, eds. 5v. Thomson Gale, 1995. ISBN 9780684192536. $$$/set
980   F1460

More than 5,000 articles cover the history, culture, and people of Latin America. National topics are often clustered by country. There are cross-references in the text and *see also* references at the end of many entries. There is a comprehensive index in the fifth volume. All articles are signed, and illustrations and maps complement many of the entries.

1614   Encyclopedia of Russian history. James R. Millar, ed. 4v. Macmillan Reference USA, 2003. ISBN 9780028656939. $$$$/set
947   DK14

Although perhaps not the military or political colossus of the Soviet era, Russia remains a geographic giant straddling Europe and Asia. This four-volume set covers more than 1,000 years of Russian history and culture, from the ancient Rus to post-Soviet Russia. Each entry is signed and has cross-references and a bibliography of print and Internet sources. Each volume has black-and-white and some color photographs to illustrate the text or to highlight some important aspect of

Russian history. A comprehensive index is found in the fourth volume.

1615   Encyclopedia of the American Civil War: A political, social, and military history. David S. Heidler and Jeanne T. Heidler, eds. 2733p. W. W. Norton, 2002. ISBN 9780393047585. $
973.7   E468

Originally published as a five-volume work by another publisher, this single volume is an outstanding and comprehensive source of information on all aspects of the Civil War era in the United States. Articles are signed and have cross-references and short bibliographies for further reading. Illustrations and maps add further information to the more than 1,600 articles. It is a good source of information for both the casual reader and student, and a complete index is included.

1616   Historical dictionary of the Civil War and Reconstruction. William L. Richter. 915p. Scarecrow, 2004. ISBN 9780810845848. $
973.7   E468

The *Historical dictionary of the Civil War and Reconstruction* defines and explains the political, judicial, economic, social, and military people and events that shaped these two landmark historical eras. It also contains a select chronology of these two periods and has a lengthy bibliography on each.

1617   Mexico: An encyclopedia of contemporary culture and history. Don M. Coerver, Suzanne B. Pasztor, and Robert Buffington. 621p. ABC-CLIO, 2004. ISBN 9781576071328. $
972.08   F1234

This work is primarily a history of twentieth-century Mexican politics, economics, culture, diplomacy, military affairs, religion, and society. Some entries are extended into the early twenty-first century. Other articles may also provide pre-twentieth-century background. There is a chronology of key events in Mexican history from 1901 to 2004. All entries are signed and include cross-references and suggestions for further reading. An extensive bibliography and an index are also included. Online version also available.

1618   Oxford classical dictionary. 3rd ed. Simon Hornblower and Antony

Spawforth, eds. 1640p. Oxford Univ. Pr., 2003. ISBN 9780198606413. $$

938   DE5

The *Oxford classical dictionary* covers all aspects of the Greco-Roman world. It provides authoritative information on the literature, art, philosophy, law, mythology, science, daily life, and history of the people, places, and events of the classical period. The signed articles may be only a few sentences or extend to a page or more. There are many cross-references but no index, illustrations, or maps. This is an excellent source to begin any inquiry concerning the classical period.

1619   Oxford companion to American military history. John Whiteclay Chambers, ed. 916p. Oxford Univ. Pr., 2000. ISBN 9780195071986. $

355   E181

The *Oxford companion to American military history* provides more than 1,000 signed articles on relevant individuals and topics in American military history from the colonial period to mid-1990. Articles are arranged alphabetically with cross-references and a very good index. Many articles are followed by short bibliographies. Another similar useful title on world military history is *The Oxford companion to military history* (2003).

1620   Oxford companion to British history. Rev. ed. John Cannon, ed. 1042p. Oxford Univ. Pr., 2003. ISBN 9780198605140. $

941.003   DA34

With Britain's impact on so much of American history and culture, this inexpensive yet authoritative and readily accessible source of information is a necessary addition to the reference collection. It explains and defines the social, political, economic, scientific, cultural, and military aspects of British history, from Roman times up to the year 2002. Articles are arranged alphabetically and are brief and usually signed. It includes several black-and-white maps and charts of the kings and queens of England and Great Britain. There is a subject index by headwords rather than page numbers.

1621   Oxford companion to United States history. Paul S. Boyer, ed. 940p. Oxford Univ. Pr., 2001. ISBN 9780195082098. $

973   E174

This single volume has more than 1,400 entries on the people, events, and ideas that have shaped U.S. history. Each entry is arranged alphabetically, and most are followed by a short bibliography. There are numerous cross-references, and the index is extensive. This is a very good starting point for quick information on U.S. history questions. Other useful titles include *Oxford companion to Australian history, Oxford companion to Irish history,* and *Oxford companion to Scottish history.*

1622   World encyclopedia of flags: The definitive guide to international flags, banners, standards, and ensigns. Alfred Znamierowski. 256p. Lorenz Books, 1999. ISBN 9780754801672. $

929.92   CR191

The first section of this book deals with the origin and development of flags; flags in history; military, government, and naval flags; and ensigns. The second section arranges contemporary flags by continent and then by country. It also includes international flags and regional and local flags. The flags are illustrated in color.

Handbooks, Yearbooks, and Almanacs

1623   Famous first facts: A record of first happenings, discoveries, and inventions in American history. 5th ed. Joseph Nathan Kane, Steven Anzovin, and Janet Podell. 1122p. H. W. Wilson, 1997. ISBN 0824209303. $$

031.02   AG5

First facts from American history are arranged by subject categories in chronological order of their occurrence. Information can be found easily by using one of the five indexes—subject index, index by years, index by days, names index, and geographical index. Each entry has a four-digit index number, which makes finding an individual entry on a page very easy. Short entries explain the historical importance of events. The lack of cross-references in the text may make the use of the subject index essential in many cases.

1624   Handbook of American women's history. 2nd ed. Angela Howard and Frances M. Kavenik, eds. 724p. Sage, 2000. ISBN 9780761916352. $$

305.4   HQ1410

The *Handbook of American women's history* provides short, signed articles on the key people, events, and ideas that have shaped the history of American women from the colonial period to today. Articles are arranged in alphabetical order, and each article is followed by a short bibliography. A detailed index is provided.

1625   **National Geographic almanac**
   of American history. James
   Miller and John Thompson. 384p.
   National Geographic, 2006. ISBN
   9780792283683. $
   973   E178

Unsurprisingly, this survey of American history begins with an overview of America's geologic makeup and its effect on our history and development. The next section contains twelve essays on topics that were crucial in shaping American society. The body of the book is divided into eleven historical eras that cover the major themes and people of the time. Each chapter ends with a "World Survey" addressing how major events elsewhere in the world were linked to America. Outstanding photographs, art, and maps provide a visual complement to the text. An appendix has the text of some great American documents, and an index provides easy access to the text.

1626   **Notable last facts: A compendium of**
   endings, conclusions, terminations
   and final events throughout history.
   William Bernard Brahms. 834p.
   Reference Desk Press, 2005. ISBN
   9780976532507. $$
   031.02   AG105

This work covers more than 16,000 facts about the ends of any historically significant event, person, place, or thing. Entries are arranged by subject and are easily accessible through an expanded table of contents and a detailed index. Each entry gives a short summary of each ending and provides a historical date or age. A bibliography of print and web sources is also provided.

1627   **The value of a dollar: The colonial**
   era to the Civil War, 1600–1865.
   Scott Derks and Tony Smith.
   436p. Grey House, 2005. ISBN
   9781592370948. $$
   338.5   HB235

Focuses on what things cost and how much workers made. Each chapter covers a historical era by

providing a historical snapshot of key economic and historical data of the era, selected incomes, services and fees, financial rates and exchanges, the slave trade, commodities, selected prices, and miscellany. Each chapter has a currency-conversion table for approximate price equivalents in 2002 dollars. An index and bibliography are included.

1628   **The value of a dollar: 1860–2004.**
   3rd ed. Scott Derks. 664p. Grey House,
   2004. ISBN 9781592370740. $$
   338.5   HB235

Like its companion volume, this reference book tracks the cost of everyday items and people's income in historical dollars with a chart for comparisons to the 2003 dollar. Each chapter covers a historical period and gives historical and economic data in five-year subchapters. A new section on pricing trends from 1900 to 2000 gives the reader a 100-year view of price trends for specific goods and services.

Historical Atlases

1629   **Atlas of American history.** Gary B.
   Nash and Carter Smith. 346p. Facts on
   File, 2006. ISBN 9780816059522. $
   911   E179.5

Presents more than 200 color maps and many photos charts and graphs of important events in American history. Coverage includes Native America, European, and African heritages; colonization; westward expansion; and the twentieth century to the present. Typically, charts and illustrations are one-half to one-quarter page. Sample entries include economic life in the British Colonies and foreign policy in the Reagan years. Useful for libraries of all sizes.

1630   **Complete atlas of world history.** John
   Haywood. 3v. M. E. Sharpe, 1997. ISBN
   9781563248542. $$
   911   G1030

Each volume covers a large period of history (volume 1 covers from 4 million years ago to AD 600; volume 2 covers AD 600 to 1783; and volume 3 covers 1783 to the present). Each volume begins with an explanation of how to use the set and a volume index. A series index can be found in the third volume. World map spreads show the level of social complexity as each time period is presented. Regional map spreads give more specific illustrations of historical developments and events. Each map spread includes a timeline arranged in thematic or geographic sections. The text provides an explanation of the historical period under consideration. This is an outstanding visual presentation of historical information.

1631 **Historical atlas of the American Revolution.** Ian Barnes.
223p. Routledge, 2000. ISBN 9780415922432. $
973.3   E208

Text, full-color maps, and illustrations detail the history of the colonies, the American Revolution, and the early American Republic. The atlas includes a chronology of American history from 1584 to 1820. It also provides a short biographical sketch of the main participants of the War of Independence and a bibliography. This atlas is well indexed for easy use.

1632 **Historical maps on file.** Rev. ed.
Facts on File and Martin Greenwald Associates. 2v. Facts on File, 2006. ISBN 9780816058976. $$
911   G1030

Presents more than 400 black-and-white outline maps in two volumes without any added text. The first volume covers ancient civilizations and European and U.S. history. The second volume covers the western hemisphere, Africa and the Middle East, Asia, and Australia and the Pacific Islands. The maps are of obvious value to both children and adults who are looking for simple, easy-to-read maps for school assignments or simply for answering historical questions. The loose-leaf binding makes reproduction of these maps easy.

1633 **National Geographic historical atlas of the United States.** Ronald Fisher.
240p. National Geographic, 2004. ISBN 9780792261315. $
911   G1201

This historical atlas contains more than 75 detailed maps and 100 photographs providing a visual of American history from 1400 to the present. Arranged chronologically, the five chapters each begin with a timeline and an essay on important moments in U.S. history. It includes at the end several informative tables on the presidents, electoral college votes, state flags, and an index. This is a beautiful and useful reference tool for both researchers and the general reader.

1634 **Routledge historical atlas of religion in America.** Bret E. Carroll.
144p. Routledge, 2000. ISBN 9780415921312. $
200.9   G1201

The *Routledge historical atlas of religion in America* traces the history of religion in America from the prehistoric indigenous people to today. It uses full-color maps and charts, illustrations, and text to track the diversity of the American religious experience and its relationship to the American experience. It provides a short bibliography for further reading and an index.

Primary Sources

1635 **American decades primary sources.**
Cynthia Rose, ed. 10v. Gale, 2003. ISBN 9780787665876. $$$$
973.91   E169.1

American decades primary sources is a ten-volume set spanning the twentieth century. Each volume covers a single decade by including approximately 200 full or excerpted primary resources in 160–1,709 entries from the period. Included are chapters on the arts, medicine and health, media, education, world events, religion, business and the economy, and sports. Each primary source is structured to include key facts about it, an introduction to the historical background, its significance to contemporaries and historically, the primary source itself, and a list of further resources.

1636 **Encyclopedia of American historical documents.** Susan C. Rosenfeld, ed. 3v. Facts on File, 2004. ISBN 9780816049950. $$
973   E173

The *Encyclopedia of American historical documents* contains the significant documents in American history from the period of European exploration of North America to the twenty-first century. It divides this history into ten eras. Each era examines critical documents related to five basic themes of American history, such as diversity of people, American democracy, the environment, the economy, and intellectual and popular culture. Each entry includes an introduction that places the document in historical perspective, the document itself (either in entirety or excerpted), and the source. Each volume is indexed, and there is a list of suggested readings. Although it does not include every significant historical document, it does provide a good starting point for historical research for the student or interested reader.

19

Geography, Area Studies, and Travel

SUE POLANKA AND JACK O'GORMAN

In the previous edition, the titles listed in this chapter were all print resources. Libraries still need print atlases, and travel guides have retained their popularity, but online sources are also prominent here. In the travel section, the intent is to highlight classic print and new classic online travel products as well as introduce several niche titles. Some niche titles from the previous edition were dated so were not included in this edition.

Atlases

World Atlases

1637   **AAA Europe road atlas.** 6th ed.
Instituto geografico de Agostini. 124p.
Automobile Association Developments,
2004. ISBN 1595080252. $
912   G1797.21

This atlas covers forty European countries and includes thirty district maps. Maps include cities, highways, toll roads (booth shown), tunnels, and distances in kilometers. Additional points of interest, such as castles, ruins, caves, and panoramic views, are shown. The index, including more than 30,000 towns, indicates the city, country, page, and grid location. A distance chart, in kilometers, is available for nearly 60 major European cities.

1638   **Atlas of the world.** 13th ed. 448p.
Oxford Univ. Pr., 2006. ISBN
0195313216. $
912   G1021

An excellent resource, this work features sections on the universe and solar system, climate, geology, landscape, environment, demography, agriculture, and manufacturing and trade. A selection of sixty-six city maps is also included. The 2005 deluxe edition includes cartography by Philips.

1639   **Book of the world.** Kartographisches
Institut Bertelsmann. 533p. Macmillan,
1999. ISBN 0028649664. $$
912   G1021

A large, heavy, and utterly fascinating atlas that offers 264 pages of superb maps and 24 pages of stunning satellite pictures of natural landmarks, such as the Grand Canyon and Mount Kilimanjaro. An object beautiful in itself.

1640   **Goode's world atlas.** 21st ed. J.
Paul Goode and Howard Veregin.
371p. Rand McNally, 2005. ISBN
0528853392. $
912   G1019

Updated and republished on a regular schedule, *Goode's* is an excellent small desk atlas at a reasonable price. Popular with students, it is frequently used to illustrate reports. A large variety of thematic and regional maps are included. Newer ones include HIV infection, military power, women's rights, food aid, and telecommunications. An extensive pronunciation index includes page references as well as latitude and longitude.

1641 Google Earth. Google. http://earth
.google.com.

A really cool feature from Google, Google Earth is an atlas for the Internet age. Uses maps, satellite imagery, and even three-dimensional buildings to show Earth. Everybody flies to his or her own house, but it can also be used to locate landmarks, schools, or parks. Expansions include Google Earth Plus for $20 and Google Earth Pro for $400. Additional features include depth of printing images, spreadsheet data import, and technical support. Next stop is Google Moon (http://moon.google.com).

1642 Mappy road guide. Mappy SA.
www.mappy.com.

Mappy is a web-based multimedia service for maps, itineraries, and travel bookings. Similar to MapQuest, Mappy covers all of Europe and provides service in thirteen different languages. Roads, the tube, and districts are included as well as aerial photos of popular destinations.

1643 MapQuest. MapQuest. www.mapquest
.com.

This site allows you to get directions and a map to places within the United States and Canada. Includes general world coverage. The company began by producing free road maps for gas stations, launched its website in 1996, and is now owned by American Online. New products include MapQuest Mobile, MapQuest Traffic, and MapQuest FindMe. A well-known site for directions.

1644 Maps on file. Facts on File, 1981–.
Annual. ISSN 0275-8083. $$
912   G1021

Single-page maps of the world are arranged in these spiral notebooks for easy removal and photocopying. Arranged alphabetically by continent, maps are included for countries, regions, provinces, and states. Maps are black and white and include boundaries, major roads, railways, airports, capitols, seaports, mountains, and oil fields.

**1645 National Geographic atlas of the
world.** 8th ed. National Geographic
Society. 134p. National Geographic,
2005. ISBN 079227542X; 0792275438

(deluxe ed.). $$
912   G1021

A total of 72 maps of the world and physical, political, thematic, and city maps are illustrated in this world atlas. Maps of space, ocean floors, and the poles are also included. Additionally, 192 nations and territories are summarized and include brief statistics, flag, location on globe, and a description. An index includes the plate and grid locations. Those who purchase also receive access to the online interactive version of the plate maps.

1646 Oxford atlas of world history. Patrick
Karl O'Brien. 368p. Oxford Univ. Pr.,
2002. ISBN 0195215672. $
911   G1030

This new work reflects how the "demand for an unbiased overview of world history has steadily grown in schools, colleges, and universities, and among the general reading public." This atlas covers not just traditional military or political topics but also ecological concerns, health and welfare of populations, and other issues. Covers the ancient world, medieval and early modern times, the age of revolution, and the twentieth century, including the status of states of the former Soviet Union. A valuable addition to reference collections.

North American Atlases

1647 The atlas of Canada. Natural
Resources Canada. http://atlas.nrcan.gc
.ca/site/english/.

The sixth edition of this classic map is now online in a multimedia environment. Included are maps of people, environment, climate, health, and the economy of Canada. The previous five editions of the atlas are also available on the site. Zoom, download, and printing features are available.

1648 Atlas of the United States. H. J. de
Blij, ed. 208p. Oxford Univ. Pr., 2006.
ISBN 0195220447. $
912.73   G1200

A precise and beautifully illustrated atlas, it includes U.S. and North American statistics; thematic maps, charts, and diagrams on North American geography; maps of the fifty U.S. states; thirty-four U.S. city maps; and summaries of each of the fifty states, with photos, maps, flags, and statistics. An index of 30,000 place-names includes letter/figure grid references and latitude and longitude. New digital cartographic map techniques make the maps appear three-dimensional.

1649   Canadian atlas online. Canadian Geographic Enterprises. www .canadiangeographic.ca/atlas/.

Produced by the Royal Canadian Geographical Society, this online atlas "brings cartography to life with exciting graphics and animation." Maps zoom in to a range of 20 km. Includes themes, games, and a learning center. Available in English or French.

1650   National atlas of the United States of America. U.S. Geological Survey. U.S. Geological Survey, 1998. www .nationalatlas.gov.

912   GA1200

This first appeared in 1970 as the *National atlas of the United States,* published by the U.S. Geological Survey. In addition to demographic, economic, and sociocultural maps that equal in cartographic skill those of any other atlas, it contains a unique section of "administrative" maps reflecting changing configurations of governmental districts, functions, and regions. Subject and place-name indexes. Though somewhat out-of-date, and difficult to obtain, it remains a landmark work. The 1970 edition is a version that libraries should keep.

1651   Rand McNally commercial atlas and marketing guide. Rand McNally and Company. Rand McNally, 1876–. Annual. ISSN 0361-9923. $$

912   G1019

Primarily an atlas of the United States, with large, detailed, clear maps. Includes many statistical tables of population, business and manufacturers, agriculture, and other commercial features, such as indicators of market potential.

1652   The road atlas: United States, Canada and Mexico. Rand McNally and Company. Rand McNally, 1924–. Annual. ISSN 0361-6509 (pbk.). $

912.7   G1201

A classic road atlas for libraries and automobiles alike, the Rand McNally atlas offers road maps of each state in the United States, each province in Canada, and a general map of Mexico. Cities, highways, toll roads, airports, points of interest, hospitals, rest areas, and service areas are included. An

index of place-names and mileage/minute charts are included. Large-print version is available.

Dictionaries, Encyclopedias, and Gazetteers

1653   The Cambridge gazetteer of the United States and Canada: A dictionary of places. Archie Hobson, ed. 743p. Cambridge Univ. Pr., 1995. ISBN 0521415799. $

917.3   E154

Includes all incorporated municipalities of more than 10,000 (United States) or 8,000 (Canada) people; this work was, in the words of the preface, "written to be read." After locating each place, the entries give qualitative information that might be of interest. Extensive cross-referencing.

1654   The Columbia gazetteer of the world. Saul B. Cohen, ed. 3v. Columbia Univ. Pr., 1998. ISBN 0231110405. $$$

910.3   G103.5

This three-volume set replaces the classic *Columbia Lippincott gazetteer of the world* (1952), long a standard in many ready-reference collections. It includes more than 160,000 entries, 30,000 of which are new to this edition. Entries include a pronunciation guide and latitude and longitude. Also available online.

1655   Concise dictionary of world place-names. John Everett-Heath. 595p. Oxford Univ. Pr., 2005. ISBN 0198605374. $

910   G103.5

More than 8,000 names from around the world, including countries, regions, deserts, bodies of water, islands, and ruins, are included. Names are followed by the location—country, state, region—and include alternate spellings and a brief description of the history and origin of the place. Place-names with multiple locations, like Victoria, are numerically listed within the entry. Pronunciations are not included; a glossary is.

1656   The concise geography encyclopedia. Clive Gifford 320p. Kingfisher, 2005. ISBN 0753458454. $

910   G63

Written and illustrated with children in mind, this encyclopedia is beautifully illustrated with color photographs, flags, and maps of the countries of the world. It is arranged by world regions and then by country. Each highlighted geographic area receives one page, which includes basic geographic, population, and government information; a description of the area; and color illustrations. An index, world map, and Earth statistics are also included.

1657 Countries of the world and their leaders yearbook. Gale, 1980–. ISSN 0196-2809; ISBN 0787681032. $$
909.82   G1

This source is complied from 2006 State Department reports. Travelers may want to go directly to www .state.gov for updated information before they go overseas. This work has four sections; status of the world's nations, "Background Notes," international treaty organizations, and foreign travel. An excellent source of international information.

1658 A dictionary of geography. 3rd ed. Susan Mayhew. 543p. Oxford Univ. Pr., 2004. ISBN 0198606737. $
910   G63

More than 6,300 definitions for human and physical geography terms are included, many unique from other dictionaries. Black-and-white illustrations and a country fact finder with basic demographic data for forty countries are included. Cross-references are noted with an asterisk within entries.

1659 Encyclopedia of world geography. R. W. McColl, ed. 3v. Checkmark Books, 2005. ISBN 0816057869. $$
910   G63

This encyclopedia takes a worldview on geographic and geopolitical topics. Locations, like the Mekong River; topics, like desertification; and concepts, like human geography, are covered. Suitable for public, school, and university libraries.

1660 Firefly geography dictionary. 256p. Firefly Books, 2003. ISBN 1552978389. $
910   G63

More than 1,500 entries on geography are listed, with cross-references in bold print and *see also* references. Color illustrations, diagrams, and charts explain and add to the content in addition to being aesthetically pleasing.

1661 Historical gazetteer of the United States. Paul T. Hellman. 865p. Routledge, 2005. ISBN 0415939488. $$
911   E154

This source states its goal to be "aggregating American history by place." Entries are arranged alphabetically by state and then by location within a state. Covers historical events that happened in towns and cities, including every county seat in the United States. Consideration for inclusion is by how historical a town is, rather than by its population.

1662 Longman dictionary of geography: Human and physical. Audrey N. Clark. 724p. Longman, 1985. ISBN 0582352614 (pbk.). $
910   G63

Where previous works separated the fields of human and physical geography, Clark has done a fine job of combining the two related fields. The 10,000 entries can easily be understood by nonspecialists. The appendix includes Greek and Latin roots and conversion charts. Not illustrated. The most robust of geography dictionaries.

1663 Merriam-Webster's geographical dictionary. 3rd ed. 1376p. Merriam-Webster, 2001. ISBN 0877795460. $
910   G103.5

This inexpensive dictionary is perfect for the small reference collection. Covers 54,000 entries with 250 maps. Includes continents, countries, and regions and a pronunciation guide. Libraries that own the 1997 edition may not need to upgrade to the 2001 edition.

1664 Nicknames and sobriquets of U.S. cities, states, and counties. 3rd ed. Joseph Nathan Kane and Gerard L. Alexander. 429p. Scarecrow, 2003. ISBN 081081255X. $
917.3   E155

This fun source lists cities and their nicknames. Comprehensive listing of nicknames of cities, counties, and states. Indexed geographically by city and state and alphabetically by nickname. Just where is the Gem of the Cascades, or the Desert Babylon?

1665 The Penguin dictionary of geography. 3rd ed. Audrey N. Clark. 467p. Penguin, 2003. ISBN 0140515054. $
910   G63

Thousands of definitions for terms used by geographers, including physical and human geography, are included. Cross-references appear in all caps within entries, and several black-and-white illustrations are included. There are many distinctive entries compared to other geography dictionaries.

1666   The World Book encyclopedia of people and places. World Book. 6v. World Book, 2004. ISBN 9780716637509. $
031.02   AE5

In six volumes, each nation of the world, from Afghanistan to Zimbabwe, is described and illustrated. Each article includes a description of the history, people, culture, and political situation in each nation, with color photos, maps, and charts with essential facts. This is a great resource for middle and high school students.

1667   Worldmark encyclopedia of the nations. 11th ed. Gale Group. 5v. Gale, 2004. ISBN 0787673307. $$
910.3   G63

Factual and statistical information on the countries of the world, exhibited in uniform format under such rubrics as topography, population, public finance, language, and ethnic composition. Country articles appear in volumes 2 through 5, arranged geographically by continent. Volume 1 is devoted to the United Nations and its affiliated agencies. Illustrations and maps. Brief index of countries and territories.

1668   Worldmark encyclopedia of the states. 6th ed. Gale Group. 956p. Gale, 2004. ISBN 0787673382. $$
973.003; 973.03   E156

This convenient source for accurate and reliable information on each of the fifty U.S. states and on U.S. dependencies is similar in format to the *Worldmark encyclopedia of the nations.* Each state is presented with facts arranged under fifty uniform subheadings. The sections on state and local government, environmental protection, ethnic groups, and languages will be especially useful.

Handbooks, Yearbooks, and Almanacs

1669   Africa. Charles H. Cutter. Stryker-Post, 1966–. Annual. ISSN 0084-2281. $
916   DT1

Canada. Wayne C. Thompson. Stryker-Post, 1985–. Annual. ISSN 0883-8135. $
971   F1001

East and Southeast Asia. Steven A. Leibo. Stryker-Post, 2005–. Annual. ISSN 1043-2140. $
950   DS502

Latin America. Robert T. Buckman. Stryker-Post, 1967–. Annual. ISSN 0092-4148. $
980   F1401

The Middle East and South Asia. Malcolm B. Russell. Stryker-Post, 1967–. Annual. ISSN 0084-2311 $
915   DS44

Nordic, Central and Southeastern Europe. Wayne C. Thompson. Stryker-Post, 2001–. Annual. ISSN 1535-8224. $
940   DL1

Russia and the Commonwealth of Independent States. Merle Wesley Shoemaker. Stryker-Post, 2001–. Annual. ISSN 1062-3574. $
947   DJK1

The USA and the world. Stryker-Post, 2005–. Annual. ISSN 1554-7809. $
327   E183.7

Western Europe. Wayne C. Thompson. Stryker-Post, 1982–. Annual. ISSN 0084-2338. $
940   D901

Updated annually, titles in the World Today series provide historical, political, and economic insight into countries and regions of the world. Each title includes extensive articles on historical periods, various political systems and elections, foreign and defense policies, and the people and culture in the various regions. Maps, multiple black-and-white photos, illustrations, charts of demographic data, and an extensive bibliography are included in each title. The series is not indexed. This series is an inexpensive way to keep your library up-to-date with recent world events.

1670   The American counties: Origins of county names, dates of creation and population data, 1950–2000. 5th ed. Joseph Nathan Kane and Charles Curry Aiken. 528p. Scarecrow, 2005. ISBN

0810850362. $$
917.3   E180

This is an alphabetic listing of each county, state by state, giving statistical census data and brief information on the person, tribe, or feature for which it is named. Following are tables of counties that include county seats, date created, and state act creating them. Also mentions county histories, if available.

America's top-rated cities, see **355**.

1671   Background notes. Bureau of Public Affairs, U.S. Dept. of State. www.state .gov/r/pa/ei/bgn/.

This searchable and A–Z list of *Background notes* provides information on the people, history, government, economy, and tourism of more than 200 countries. Statistical data on geography, people, government, and the economy are listed first, followed by short narratives about the people, culture, political conditions, and foreign relations. Travel information is also included. Hyperlinks to other economic, government, and travel information sites make this resource even more useful.

1672   Central Europe profiled: Essential facts on society, business, and politics in Central Europe. Barry Turner. 307p. St. Martin's, 2000. ISBN 0312229941. $
943   DAW1009

China profiled: Essential facts on society, business, and politics in China. Barry Turner. 178p. St. Martin's, 1999. ISBN 0312227256. $
951.05   DS779.26

France profiled: Essential facts on society, business, and politics in France. Barry Turner. 219p. St. Martin's, 1999. ISBN 031222723X. $
944.081   DC33.7

Germany profiled: Essential facts on society, business, and politics in Germany. Barry Turner. 291p. St. Martin's, 1999. ISBN 0312227264. $
943   DD290.26

Italy profiled: Essential facts on society, business, and politics in Italy. Barry Turner. 187p. St. Martin's, 1999. ISBN 0312227248. $
945   DG441

Latin America profiled: Essential facts on society, business, and politics in Latin America. Barry Turner. 293p. St. Martin's, 2000. ISBN 031222995X. $
918   F1408

Scandinavia profiled: Essential facts on society, business, and politics in Scandinavia. Barry Turner. 312p. St. Martin's, 2000. ISBN 0312229933. $
948   DL5

Southern Africa profiled: Essential facts on society, business, and politics in Southern Africa. Barry Turner. 306p. St. Martin's, 2000. ISBN 0312229968. $
968   DT1719

UK today: Essential facts in an ever changing world. Barry Turner. 544p. St. Martin's, 2000. ISBN 0312229925. $
941   DA27.5

The world today, 2000: Essential facts in an ever changing world. Barry Turner. 1097p. St. Martin's, 2000. ISBN 0312227140. $
320.9   D31

Titles in the SYB Factbook series contain an economic, cultural, and historical view of the country or region. Each title includes chapters on the territory and population, historical events (with chronology), cultural activities, and landmarks and travel information for major cities. Color maps of the country and major cities are included in the centerfold area. There is no index available; however, an extensive table of contents and logical layout will direct users to appropriate information.

1673   Country study series. Foreign Area Studies, American University. U.S. Govt. Print. Off., Dates vary. $ http:// lcweb2.loc.gov/frd/cs/.

Formerly *Area handbooks,* this classic series includes books on individual countries with basic facts about social, economic, political, and military conditions. They include extensive bibliographies and contain a wealth of information at a very affordable price. Although many print titles are dated, updated versions are becoming available online via the Federal Research Division of the Library of Congress.

1674   Europa world yearbook. 2v. Europa, 1959–. Annual. ISSN 0956-2273.
391.184   JN1

The best annual directory of the nations of the world (formerly *Europa yearbook*). For each country it includes demographic and economic statistics and facts about constitution and government, political parties, press, trade and industry, publishers, and so forth. Also incorporates a substantive section with listings and information about international organizations.

Travel Guides

1675   The complete guide to bed and breakfasts, inns and guesthouses in the United States, Canada, and worldwide. Pamela Lanier. Ten Speed Press, 1997–. Annual. ISBN 1580087035. $
917.3   TX907.2

More than 4,500 bed-and-breakfasts in the United States and Canada are included in this annual compilation. Arranged by state, each entry contains the name and contact information (e-mail/web); room information (including children, pets, smoking, and accessible conditions); and a description of the breakfast and other amenities. Special accommodations like hot tubs, weddings, themed dinners, games, community areas, and other events are included.

1676   Expedia. Expedia. www.expedia.com.

The Internet has been a boon to travelers looking for discounts. Places to stay and ways to get there are available through this site. Build your trip, plan your trip, and, of course, go shopping on your trip. Other travel sites include Travelocity (www.travelocity.com) and Orbitz (www.orbitz.com).

1677   Gay travel A to Z. Ferrari International, 1996–. Annual. ISSN 1094-1770. $
306.766   HQ75.25

A world travel guide featuring tour companies, cruises, hotels, restaurants, bars, dance clubs, and other destinations that cater to gays and lesbians. A trip and events calendar highlights international gay and lesbian events with dates and locations.

1678   Globetrotting pets: An international travel guide. David J. Forsythe. 413p.

Island, 2003. ISBN 0972415602. $
636.088   SF415.45

Compiled in one location are the international regulations for importing pets into the countries of the world. Forsythe includes the regulations, contact information, and useful websites for each country. Additional information includes pet travel supplies, forms and health information, and exotic pet travel.

1679   Mobil travel guides. 17v. Fodor's Travel, 1960–. Annual. ISSN Canada 1550-2260 (pbk.); Coastal Southeast 1550-5456 (pbk.); Florida 1096-7788 (pbk.); Great Plains 1550-5448 (pbk.); Hawaii $/v. ISBN 076273924X (2006, pbk.); MidAtlantic 1090-6975 (pbk.); New England 1549-5647 (pbk.); New York 1550-1892 (pbk.); Northern California 1550-0969 (pbk.); Northern Great Lakes 1550-0977 (pbk.); Northern Plains 1550-5626 (pbk.); Northwest and Alaska 1550-0276 (pbk.); Southern California 1096-7786 (pbk.); South 1550-1930 (pbk.); Southern Great Lakes 1550-0063 (pbk.); Southwest 1550-0284 (pbk.); Texas 1550-1094 (pbk.). http://mobiltravelguide.com.

Seventeen regional guides to the United States and Canada that contain information about points of interest, annual or seasonal events, restaurant and lodging facilities (with ratings), and suggested auto tours. Organized by state and city, each provides a good starting point for travel reference collections. Also see the online interactive Mobil Travel Guide (http://mobiltravelguide.howstuffworks.com), which includes ratings and guides to hotels, restaurants, and attractions.

1680   Parks directory of the United States. Darren L Smith and Penny J. Hoffman. 999p. Omnigraphics, 2004. ISBN 0780806638. $$
917.30025   E160

State parks can be hidden jewels. But how can your readers find them? This directory lists national parks, wildlife refuges, and recreational areas, including state parks and parks in Canada. Entries include facilities, activities, and accommodations. Contact information and websites are included.

1681 **Traveling with your pet: The AAA Pet Book; The AAA guide to more than 10,000 pet-friendly, AAA-rated lodgings across the United States and Canada.** 8th ed. 720p. AAA, 2006. ISBN 1595080937. $

917.3

More than 13,000 pet-friendly AAA-rated lodgings and campgrounds in the United States and Canada are listed alphabetically by state and city in this pet travel guide. Entries include the name and contact information, AAA star rating, and amenity icons. A pet-friendly place section includes information on dog parks, animal clinics, service-animal policies, attractions with pet amenities, and national public lands.

1682 **Ultimate guide to the world's best wedding and honeymoon destinations: A comprehensive guide designed to assist you in choosing the perfect destination, whether it be for the most romantic wedding ceremony, or for an unforgettable honeymoon.** Elizabeth Lluch and Alex Lluch. 300p. Wedding Solutions, 2004. ISBN 1887169350. $

910.202   GT2798

This guide provides a description and color photographs of more than 150 wedding and honeymoon resorts around the world. The resort information includes contact information, room rates, romantic features, attractions, facilities, and wedding services offered. Additional travel tips including entry requirements and marriage licenses are discussed.

1683 **Woodall's North America campground directory: The complete guide to campgrounds, RV parks, service centers and attractions.** Woodall, 1967–. Annual. ISSN 1547-6340. $

917.59   GV198.56

Comprehensive directory is divided geographically into eastern and western sections that include Canada and Mexico. Road maps of each state and province show location of each site listed. Brief descriptions are accompanied by evaluative ratings of facilities and recreation. Alphabetical index of sites. Also available in eastern, western, and other regional editions.

Biography

JACK O'GORMAN AND SUE POLANKA

The development of extensive online biographical resources has been a big change since the last edition. Marquis Who's Who on the Web, Biography Reference Bank, and other sources have changed biographical information from a largely print collection into an electronic one.

Databases and Indexes

1684 **American national biography online.** American Council of Learned Societies and Oxford Univ. Pr. www.anb.org/articles/home.html.

Oxford University Press and the American Council of Learned Societies published this source in 1999 as both a print and electronic resource. Includes 19,000 biographies of men and women from colonial times to the present. Entries are for deceased individuals only and include bibliography, cross-references, and some photos. Online version includes the *Oxford companion to United States history* and links to *Oxford dictionary of national biography*.

1685 **Biography and genealogy master index.** Gale. www.gale.com.

Originally a print product, this source functions very well as a database (with subscription access only). Searchable by multiple entry points, including name, dates, portrait, and source. More than

15 million biographies are included from ninety sources. An essential biographical resource.

1686 **Biography reference bank.** H. W. Wilson. www.hwwilson.com/databases/BioBank.htm.

Covers the lives of one-half million people, with images, photos, and text of their lives. Includes *Biography index,* from 1983 forward; *Biography plus illustrated; Current biography;* and the Junior Authors and Illustrator series. Other works, like the *American national biography,* are included. Results display a small photo access to additional articles and books about the biographee. This database has broad biographical coverage.

1687 **The Cambridge biographical encyclopedia.** 2nd ed. David Crystal. 1179p. Cambridge Univ. Pr., 1998. ISBN 0521630991. $
920   CT103

Presents an arrangement of 16,000 entries for ready-reference biography. Includes 150 pages of lists, such as popes, kings, and Nobel Prize winners. Good cross-referencing; includes pronunciation guide.

1688 **Current biography yearbook.** H. W. Wilson, 1955–. Annual. ISSN 0084-9499. $$
920   CT100

Current biography yearbook is a compilation of the monthly *Current biography.* Cumulated index covers back to 1940. This is an excellent place for newly famous people or for little-known information about famous people. For instance, in the 1956 yearbook, Martin Luther King Jr. talks about his love of baseball. The publisher strives for "objective, accurate, and well-documented biographical articles about living leaders in all fields of human accomplishment." Biographees are given the opportunity to review their entry in the monthly journal before inclusion in the yearbook. Obituary notices are included in the yearbook for each person who is listed in the publication. Informative and well written. Included in the Biography Reference Bank.

1689   Encyclopedia of world biography. 2nd ed. Gale, 1998–. ISBN 0787622214; 1414400977 (2006 supplement). $$$$; $$ supplement

920   CT103

This well-known biographical source includes 7,000 biographies of world leaders. For smaller libraries, the *UXL encyclopedia of world biography* covers 750 entries pulled from the larger set. Entries include portrait, biography, and bibliography. Biographies were chosen "for their contributions to human culture and society [and] reputations that stand the test of time." There is a 2006 supplement.

1690   Marquis who's who on the Web. Marquis Who's Who. www .marquiswhoswho.com.

Includes 1.3 million entries of biographees who have been listed in any Marquis publication since 1985. This comprehensive resource includes birth and death dates, background, education, and career of its biographees and is updated daily.

1691   Merriam-Webster's biographical dictionary. 1170p. Merriam-Webster, 1995. ISBN 0877797439. $

920.02   CT103

This title is somewhat dated, but its coverage and readable format make it helpful. This edition has increased coverage from Asia, Africa, and Latin America. Very brief biographical information for about 30,000 world figures. Source only includes those that have died. A new edition of this title would be very useful.

1692   Naked in cyberspace: How to find personal information online. 2nd ed. Carole A. Lane. 587p. CyberAge Books,

2002. ISBN 0910965501. $

001.4   JK2445

Ordinary people and the information trail they create on the Internet are the topic of this resource. OK, famous people are also included. Personal records, job searching, and telephone and professional directories, as well as genealogical, criminal justice, and consumer credit records, are some of the topics covered. Includes a foreword by the founder and director of the Privacy Rights Clearinghouse, who states that individuals need to be aware, be assertive, and be an advocate to take control of information about themselves. This title is a first step in those directions.

1693   Oxford dictionary of national biography. Oxford Univ. Pr. www .oxforddnb.com.

Oxford University Press has also published this source as both a print and electronic resource. It has a more British focus but in a very broad sense. For instance, the entry on George Washington is different than many American accounts of his life. Contains 55,000 biographies. Entries include portraits, cross-references, and bibliographies. The bibliography has a feature that searches local library catalogs.

1694   Who's who in the twentieth century. Asa Briggs, ed. 629p. Oxford Univ. Pr., 1999. ISBN 0192800914. $

920   CT120

Who's who in the twentieth century is one of the titles in Oxford Reference Online. This title is an abridged and updated version of the 1992 *A dictionary of twentieth-century world biography,* also from Oxford. It contains 2,000 entries of important twentieth-century figures. Abridged and updated edition available via Oxford Reference Online.

1695   The who's who of Nobel Prize winners, 1901–2000. 2nd ed. Louise S. Sherby and Wilhelm Odelberg, eds. 277p. Oryx, 2002. ISBN 1573564141. $

001.4   AS911

Brief biographical information about Nobel Prize winners from the inception of the prize to 2000 are presented. Entries include name, prize given, and birth and death dates, where appropriate. Parents, nationality, religion, education, and family information are presented. Also included are career, other awards, and a selected bibliography.

INDEX

Numbers in bold refer to entry numbers. Numbers in roman type refer to mentions in annotations of other works.

A

A to Z of American women in sports, **1311**

A to Z of American women in the visual arts, **1076**

A to zoo, **1461**

AA to Z: Addictionary to the 12-step culture, **190**

AAA Europe road atlas, **1637**

Abbreviations dictionary, **609**

ABC Chinese-English dictionary, **660**

ABC-CLIO's History Reference Online, **57,** 62

Abernethey, Peter L., **1546**

ABI/Inform, **395**

Abling, Bina, **1276**

Abrams, M. H., **1406**

The Abrams encyclopedia of photography, **1112**

Aby, Stephen H., **266**

Academy of American Poets: Awards and Prizes, **1411**

Academy of Motion Picture Arts and Sciences, **1126**

Academy of Television Arts and Sciences, **1127**

Accessories of dress, **1090**

AccessScience @ McGraw-Hill, **692**

Accountants' handbook, **417**

Accounting handbook, **418**

Accredited institutions of post-secondary education, **554**

Achtemeier, Paul J., **99**

Ackere, Daniel Van, **932**

ACM guide to computing literature and ACM Digital, **722**

Acronyms, initialisms, and abbreviations dictionary, **610**

An actor's guide to the talkies, **1155**

Adamec, Christine, **197**

Additions: How to expand your home, **960**

Adelman, Irving, **1499**

Administration of the small public library, **66**

The advertising age encyclopedia of advertising, **420**

Africa, **1669**

The African American almanac, **306**

African American architects, **1036**

African American art and artists, **1077**

African-American business leaders and entrepreneurs, **392**

African-American dramatists, **1434**

African American education, **572**

African American lives, **307,** 311

African Americans in sports, **1312**

African Americans in the performing arts, **1124**

African writers, **1569**

Africana, **308**

Aggens, Annie, **1378**

Aging in America A to Z, **276**

AGRICOLA, **778**

Agricultural statistics, **779**

Aguirre, Adalberto, **304**

Agur, Anne M. R., **852**

AHA guide to the healthcare field, **827**

Aharoni, Yohanan, **90**

AIDS sourcebook, **849**

Aiken, Charles Curry, **1670**

AIP physics desk reference, **805**

Albrecht, Gary L., **877**

Alcalay, R., **672**

Alcohol and temperance in modern history, **279**

Alcoholism sourcebook, **280**

Alderton, David, **991, 994, 1008, 1013**

Aldrich, Robert, **336**

Alexander, Gerard L., **1664**

Alexander, Kern, **577**

Alexander, M. David, **577**

Alexander Street Press, 1220

Alexander Street Press Music Online, **1206**

Alibris, 23

Alkin, Marvin C., **541**

All movie guide, **1141**

All music guide, **1238**

The all new Good Housekeeping cook book, **919**

Allaby, Michael, **751, 796**

*The All-American Girls Professional Baseball
    League record book,* **1320**

Allaway, Roger, **1389**

Allen, John Logan, **378**

Allen, Mary Beth, **1299**

Allen, Ruth, **1476**

Alles, Gregory D., **114**

Alliance of Artists' Communities, **1069**

Alliance of Psychoanalytic Organizations, **218**

Almanac of American politics, **496**

Almanac of the unelected, **517**

Alternative medicine, **863**

Alternative schools, **572**

Altman, Ellen, **71**

Amazon.com, 24

America the beautiful, 43

American Academy of Pediatrics, **983, 984**

American architecture, **1037**

American Association of University Professors,
    579

American Automobile Association, **1681**

American Ballet Theatre's online ballet dictionary,
    1131

The American book of days, **900**

The American census handbook, **354**

*The American College of Physicians complete home
    medical guide,* **832**

American college regalia, **573**

American conservatism, **476**

American Council of Learned Societies, **704,
    1684**

American Council on Education, **549, 555**

The American counties, **1670**

American decades primary sources, **1635**

American Dental Association, **828**

American dental directory, **828**

The American dictionary of criminal justice, **284**

American drama criticism, **1531**

The American economy, **451**

American educators' encyclopedia, **536**

American foreign relations since 1600, **468**

American generations, **421**

American Geological Institute, **744**

American Heart Association, **931**

American Heritage crossword puzzle dictionary,
    611

American Heritage dictionary of idioms, **620**

*The American Heritage dictionary of the English
    language,* **606**

American Heritage science dictionary, **693**

*The American Heritage Spanish dictionary: Spanish/
    English, Inglés/Español,* **683**

*The American Heritage Stedman's medical
    dictionary,* **814**

*The American Historical Association's guide to
    historical literature,* **1597**

American history and life, **1605**

*The American Horticulture Society A-Z
    encyclopedia of garden plants,* **784**

American Hospital Association, **827**

American incomes, **422**

*American inventors, entrepreneurs, and business
    visionaries,* **393**

American Jewish Committee, **145**

American Jewish yearbook, **145**

American Kennel Club, **1001**

*The American Library Association guide to
    information access,* **1**

American library directory, **46**

The American marketplace, **423**

American masculinities, **338,** 340

American Mathematical Society, **798**

*The American Medical Association complete medical
    encyclopedia,* **833**

American Medical Association manual of style, **647**

American men, **339,** 364

American men and women of science, **703**

American musical theater, **1191**

The American Muslim, **141**

American national biography, **1686**

American national biography online, **1684**

American nature writers, **1532**

American Patchwork and Quilting, **1267**

American plays and musicals on screen, **1192**

The American political dictionary, **477**

American Psychiatric Association, 208, **214, 223**

American Psychoanalytic Association, **218, 224**

American Psychological Association, 183, **186, 187, 188, 189, 213, 220, 225**

American Psychological Association 2004 membership directory on CD-ROM, **213**

American Radio Relay League, **755**

American Reference Books Annual (ARBA), 62

American religious leaders, **113**

American shelter, **1038**

The American sign language handshape dictionary, **630**

The American songbook, **1245**

American Theological Library Association, **86**

American universities and colleges, **555**

American University, **1673**

American women, 339, **364**

American women sculptors, **1078**

American women writers, **1452**

American writers, **1533, 1534**

Americans at play, **1379**

Americans at war, **809**

America's top-rated cities, **355**

America's top-rated smaller cities, **356**

Amico, Eleanor B., **366**

AMICO Library, 1017

Amit, Vered, **379**

Ammer, Christine, **620, 633, 882**

Anatomy of wonder, **1514**

Anchor Bible Commentaries series, 98

Anchor Bible dictionary, **98**

Ancient writers: Greece and Rome, **1561**

Anderson, Corrie, **1339, 1358**

Anderson, John W, **863**

Anderson, Nancy D., **797**

Anderson, Sean, **291**

Andrews, John F., **1560**

Annenberg political fact check, **497**

Anson, Jack L., **574**

Antique trader antiques and collectibles price guide, **1284**

Anzovin, Steven, **1623**

Appiah, Anthony, **308**

Apple, Hope, **1502**

Applebaum, Wilbur, **736**

Applied science and technology abstracts, **688**

apsa.org, **224, 225**

Arabic-English lexicon, **658**

Ariadne's book of dreams, **191**

Aronson, Amy, 338, **340**

Aros, Andrew A., **1155**

Arrington, April, **213**

The ARRL handbook for the radio amateur, **755**

Art across America, **1068**

Art full text, **1017**

Art history resources on the web, **1023**

Art in the modern era, **1071**

Art index retrospective, **1018**

Art Museum Image Consortium, 1017

Art Museum Image Gallery, **1019**

Artcyclopedia, **1024**

Artfact, **1025**

ArticleFirst, 35

Artist beware, **1253**

Artists, **1080**

Artist's and graphic designer's market, **1070**

Artists communities, **1069**

Artists from Latin American cultures, **1079**

Artist's illustrated encyclopedia, **1052**

ArtLex art dictionary, **1026**

Arts and humanities citation index, 691

ArtSource, **1027**

Asian American short story writers, **1439**

The Asian databook, **314**

AskART, **1028**

ASPCA complete cat care manual, **995**

ASPCA complete dog care manual, **1000**

The Associated Press stylebook and briefing on media law, **648**

Association for Computing Machinery, **722**

Association for Library Service to Children, **15, 1478**

Association for Psychological Science, **226**

The astronomical almanac online, **707**

Athletic scholarships, **569**

ATLA religion database, **86**

Atlas of American history, **1629**

The atlas of Canada, **1647**

Atlas of human anatomy, **852**

Atlas of the United States, **1648**

Atlas of the world, **1638**

Atlas of world art, **1072**

Audi, Robert, **76**

The Audubon Society field guide to North American rocks and minerals, **745**

August, Ernest R., **341**

Ausiello, Dennis, **815**

Auto repair reference center, **760**

AV market place, **545**

Avery index to architectural periodicals, **1020**

Axelrod, Alan, **700**

Axford, Elizabeth C., **1205**

Ayto, John, **951, 1405**

The A-Z of card games, **1348**

An A-Z of food and drink, **951**

B

Baby and child health, **860**

The baby boom: Americans born 1946 to 1964, **424**

Background notes, 396, **1671**

The backpacker's field manual, **1319**

Baechler, Lea, **1458**

Baggaley, Ann, **854**

Baha'i faith, **162**

Baigrie, Brian S., **738**

Bailey, John, **1354**

Bailey, Liberty Hyde, **785**

Bainbridge, William Sims, **723**

Baird's manual of American college fraternities, **574**

Bajac, Quentin, **1112**

Baker, Beth A., **947**

Baker's biographical dictionary of musicians, 1206, **1220**

Baker's biographical dictionary of popular musicians since 1990, **1250**

Baker's student encyclopedia of music, 1206, **1208**

Balaban, Naomi E., **696**

Balanchine, George, 1139, **1139**

Balletcompanies.com, **1137**

Balter, Lawrence, **987**

Banham, Joanna, **1043**

Banham, Martin, **1195**

Banker, Leslie, **971**

Banker, Pamela, **971**

Banks, Arthur S., **511**

Bankston, Carl L. III, **271, 305, 325**

The bargain buyer's guide, **903**

Bargain hunter's secrets to online shopping, **904**

Barker, Robert L., **352**

Barnard, Alan, **385**

Barnes, Ian, **1631**

Barnhart, Robert K., **614**

Barone, Michael, **496**

Barr, Catherine, **525**

Barret, Leonard E. Sr., **168**

Barron, Neil, **1514**

Barron's finance and investment handbook, **428**

Barron's guide to graduate business schools, **556**

Barron's guide to law schools, **557**

Barron's guide to medical and dental schools, **558**

Barron's profiles of American colleges, **559**

Barron's real estate handbook, **463**

The bartender's best friend, **887**

Bartle, Lisa R., **1517**

Bartlett, John, **1420**

Bartlett, John G., **810**

Bartlett's familiar quotations, **1420**

Barzun, Jacques, **1494**

Baseball, **1321**

Baseball America directory, **1322**

Baseball America's Almanac, **1323**

The baseball bibliography, **1324**

Baseball desk reference, **1325**

The baseball timeline, **1326**

Bashe, Patricia Romanowksi, **1249**

Bashe, Philip, **985**

Basic business library, **388**

Basic catalog of plays and musicals, **1182**

Basic facts about the United Nations, **498**

A basic guide to cycling, **1344**

A basic music library, **1203**

Bates, Karen Grigsby, **943**

Bayer, Patricia, **1104**

Bazler, Judith, **742, 762**

The bead directory, **1255**

Beadwork, **1256**

Bear, Mariah, **560**

Bear's guide to college degrees by mail and Internet, **560**

Beaumont, Stephen, **894**

Beaver, Frank E., **1143**

Beck, Charlotte, **387**

Beck, Joe, **982**

Becker, Charlotte B., **179**

Becker, E. Lovell, **820**

Becker, J. Alex, **235**

Becker, Lawrence C., **179**

Bednar, Nancy, **1275**

Beer, Jeremy, **476**

Beers, Mark H., **842**

Behave yourself! **938**

Beisner, Robert L., **468**

Bell, Catharine E., **795**

Bell, Daniel, **1304**

Bellenir, Karen, **280**

Bellingham, Jane, **1229**

Benbow-Pfalzgraf, Taryn, **1093, 1134, 1452**
Bender, James F., **625**
Benét's reader's encyclopedia, **1399**
Bennet, Alice, **653**
Benson, Eugene, **1572**
Benson, Sonia, **316, 321**
Benvie, Sam, **780**
Benyo, Richard, **1383**
Berenbaum, Michael, **150**
Berkshire encyclopedia of human-computer interaction, **723**
Berkshire encyclopedia of world sport, **1302**
Berlin, Adele, **159**
Berry, Mary, **920**
Bertucci, Mary Lou, **481**
Best books for children, **525**
Best customers, **425**
The best plays theater yearbook, **1201**
Bettelheim, Adriel, **276**
Bible atlas, **90**
Biblical literacy, **146**
Bibliography of bioethics, **177**
Bieber, Doris M., **649**
The big book of blues, **1224**
Big book of home how-to, **973**
The big book of home plans, **910, 911**
Big book of knitting stitch patterns, **1258**
Bigelow, Christopher Kimball, **126**
Biggs, Matthew, **937**
The Billboard book of top 40 hits, **1239**
The Billboard book of top 40 R and B and hip-hop hits, **1240**
The Billboard illustrated encyclopedia of jazz and blues, **1222**
The Billboard illustrated encyclopedia of music, **1209**
The Billboard illustrated encyclopedia of opera, **1229**
Billiard Congress of America, **1346**
Billiards, **1346**
Biographical dictionary of American educators, **589**
Biographical dictionary of congressional women, **518**
Biographical dictionary of psychology, **236**
Biographical dictionary of social and cultural anthropology, **379**
Biographical dictionary of twentieth-century philosophers, **84**
Biographical directory of professional basketball coaches, **1336**

Biographical directory of the U.S. Congress, **519**
A biographical handbook of education, **590**
Biographies of women mathematicians, **803**
Biography and genealogy master index, **1685**
Biography index, 1686
Biography reference bank, **1686**
Biography resource center, 313
Biological abstracts, **765**
Biological and agricultural index, **766**
Biology resources in the electronic age, **762**
BiologyBrowser, 691
Bird, Lonnie, **1278, 1282**
Birx, H. James, **381**
Bjarkman, Peter C., **1328**
Black, J., **452**
Black American colleges and universities, **561**
Black and Decker, **962, 963, 976**
Black firsts, **309**
Black heritage sites, **310**
Black heroes, **311**
Black members of the U.S. Congress, **520**
Black women in America, **312**
Black's law dictionary, **478**
Blackwell dictionary of sociology, **267**
The Blackwell encyclopaedia of social work, **347**
The Blackwell encyclopedia of management, **461**
Blackwell encyclopedia of modern Christian thought, **123**
The Blackwell encyclopedia of social psychology, **192**
Blandford, Steve, **1146**
Blank, Robert H., **275**
Blazek, Ron, **1600**
Bleiler, Richard, **1486, 1497**
Blocker, Jack S. Jr., **279**
Bloom, Abigail Burnham, **1460**
Bloom, Ken, **1245**
The bluebook, **649**
Bobick, James E., **696**
Boettcher, J. C., **390**
Bogdanov, Vladimir, **1238**
Bogus, Ronald J., **627**
Bolaffi, Guido, **298**
Bollard, John K., **626**
Bonadella, Julia R., **1585**
Bonadella, Peter C., **1585**
Book Awards, **1411**
Book lust, **2**
Book news, 62
The book of Jewish values, **147**

The book of spells, 247
The book of the states, **499**
Book of the world, **1639**
The book of world-famous music, **1210**
Booklist online, **16**
Books in print, **25**
Bopp, Richard E., **13**
Borchert, Donald, **78**
Bordman, Gerald, **1191, 1198**
Borgatta, Edgar F., **270**
Boston Women's Health Book Collective, **885, 886**
Boucquey, Thierry, **1431**
Boulware, R., **401**
Bowes and Church's food values of portions commonly used, **952**
Bowker, John, **89**
The Bowker annual of library and book trade information, **67**
Bowker's complete video directory, **1156**
Bowling, beatniks, and bell-bottoms, **1607**
Boyce, Charles, **1103, 1555**
Boyd, Pat Williams, **572**
Boyer, Paul S., **1621**
Bracken, James K., **1397**
Brackman, Barbara Ann, **1268,** 1269
Bradshaw, Paul F., **129**
Brahms, William Bernard, **1626**
Branch, Robert Maribe, **526**
The branch librarians' handbook, **68**
Brands and their companies, **437**
Breen, Walter, **1292**
Bremser, Martha, **1133**
Brenner, Morgan G., **1337**
Breslow, Karen, **569**
Brettler, Marci Zvi, **159**
Brewer's dictionary of modern phrase and fable, **1404**
Brewer's dictionary of phrase and fable, **1405**
Brewer's politics, **479**
Brewster, Janice, **913**
Brians, Paul, **1594**
Brickell, Christopher, **784**
Briggs, Asa, **1694**
Brigstocke, Hugh, **1062**
Bristow, M. J., **1214**
Britannica elementary encyclopedia, 42
Britannica student encyclopedia (Compton's), 38, 42
Britannica's original sources, 42
British writers, **1544**

Broadcast communications dictionary, **1168**
Broadcasting and cable yearbook, **1178**
Broadway musicals, 1943–2004, **1193**
Bromley, Geoffrey W., **100**
Brooklyn Public Library Business Library, **414**
Brooks, Tim, **1170**
Broughton, Simon, **1251**
Brown, Lesley, 602, **608**
Brown, Marianne Gluszak, **630**
Brown, Muriel, **1479**
Brown, Raymond E., **94**
Brown, Susan W., **1500**
Bruce, Colin R., **1290, 1291**
Bruce, Jenni, **793**
Brukner, Peter, **1351**
Bryant, Clifton D., **295**
Bryman, Alan, **253**
Buchanan, Ian, **1376**
Buchanan, Paul D., **302**
Buckland, Raymond, **246**
Buckman, Robert T., **1669**
Buddhism, **117**
Buffington, Robert, **1617**
Buhle, Mari Jo, **483**
Buhle, Paul, **483**
Building an affordable house, **912**
Building blocks of matter: A supplement to the Macmillan encyclopedia of physics, **808**
Building your own home for dummies, **913**
Bunson, Margaret R., **1612**
Bunson, Matthew, **132, 1612**
Burchfield, R. W., **623**
Burden, Ernest E., **1046**
Burg, Daniel B., **1350**
Burgess, Michael, **1517**
Burgess, Stanley M., **128**
Burgoyne, John, **932**
Burlingame, Dwight, **351**
Burnham, Stephanie, **1257**
Burns, Deborah, **1012**
Burns, J. M., **404**
Burns, Paul, **136**
Buros, Oscar K., **222**
Buros Center for Testing, **227**
Business cycles and depressions, **399**
Business organizations, agencies, and publications directory, **409**
Business plans handbook, **455**
Business rankings annual, **414**
Business source premier, **396**

Business statistics of the United States, **415**
Business: The ultimate resource, **398**
Butler, Alban, **136**
Butler's lives of the saints, **136**
Butterfield, Jeremy, **684**
Butterworth, Neil, **1233**
Buttlar, Lois, **524**
Byars, Mel, **1055**
Bynoe, Yvonne, **1247**
Bynum, W. F., **698**

C

Cabibbo, Andrea, **763**
Cahill, Sean, **335**
Calasibetta, Charlotte Mankey, **1276**
Calhoun, Craig, **250, 273**
Calloway, Stephen, **1042**
The Cambridge biographical encyclopedia, **1687**
The Cambridge companion to Australian literature, **1570**
The Cambridge companion to Native American literature, **1450**
Cambridge dictionary of philosophy, **76**
Cambridge encyclopedia of the English language, **600**
The Cambridge encyclopedia of the world's ancient languages, **594**
The Cambridge gazetteer of the United States and Canada, **1653**
The Cambridge guide to American theatre, **1194**
Cambridge guide to English usage, **621**
The Cambridge guide to literature in English, **1395**
The Cambridge guide to theatre, **1195**
The Cambridge Italian dictionary, **675**
The Cambridge world history of food, **953**
Campbell, George L., **595**
Campbell, Malcolm, **1367**
Campbell, Oscar James, **1554**
Canada, **1669**
Canada Post, **55**
Canadian almanac and directory, **27**
Canadian Atlas Online, **1649**
Canadian fiction, **1571**
Candelaria, Cordelia, **317**
Cannon, John, **1620**
The career guide, **465**
Carey, C. W., **393**
Caring for your baby and young child, **983**
Caring for your school-age child, **984**
Caring for your teenager, **985**

Carley, Rachel, **1050**
Carlson, Karen J., **884**
Carmichael, D. R., **417**
Carnegie Library of Pittsburgh, Science and Technology Department, **696, 702**
Carpenter, Humphrey, **1471**
Carpentry and trimwork step-by-step, **974**
Carr-Gomm, Sarah, **1059**
Carroll, Bob, **1359**
Carroll, Bret E., **338, 340, 1634**
Carroll, M. R., **1369**
Carson-Dewitt, Rosalyn, **870**
Carvajal, Carol Styles, **685**
Cashmore, Ernest, **1307**
Cassell, Dana K., **294**
Cassell's chronology of world history, **1601**
Cassell's Latin dictionary: Latin-English, English-Latin, **679**
Cassin-Scott, Jack, **1099**
The Cat Fanciers' Association complete cat book, **996**
Cat owner's manual, **997**
Catalog of federal domestic assistance, **348**
A catalogue of crime, **1494**
Catholic almanac, **132**
Catholic Bible Association of America, **97**
Caujolle, Christian, **1112**
Cavanaugh, Christopher, **190**
Caves, Roger W., **361**
Cecil textbook of medicine, **815**
Central Europe profiled, **1672**
Chadwick, Ruth, **178**
Chambers, John Whiteclay, **1619**
Chambers dictionary of etymology, **614**
Champagne, Duane, **323**
Champion, Dean J., **284**
Champion, Larry S., **1550**
Chapman, Antony J., **236**
Chapman, Robert L., **636, 646**
Character actors, **1164**
Charted knitting designs, **1260**
Charter schools, **572**
Chase's calendar of events, **901**
Cheffers, John, **1364**
Chemistry, **713**
Cheney, Frances Neel, **3**
Chesterman, Charles W., **745**
Chevalier, Tracy, **1529**
Chevallier, Andrew, **871**
The Chicago manual of style, **650**

Chicano literature, **1446**

Chiefs of state and cabinet members of foreign governments, **521**

Child, Julia, **929**

Child abuse sourcebook, **373**

The children's and young adult literature handbook, **1462**

Children's Book Council, **1477**

Children's book prizes, **1476**

Children's books and their creators, 1467

Children's books: Awards and prizes, **1477**

Children's literature, **1463**

Children's literature review, **1464**

The children's song index, 1978–1993, **1242**

Children's television, 1947–1990, **1169**

Childress, James E., **182**

Chilvers, Ian, **1053, 1063**

China, **1608**

China profiled, **1672**

Ching, Francis D. K., **1051**

Chingjung, Wu, **662**

Choice, 12, **17**, 24

Choice reviews online, 17

Chris, Jeffery, **1274**

Christensen, Jo Ippolito, **1265**

Christensen, Karen, 360, **1302, 1314**

Christianson, Stephen G., **900, 902**

Christie, Robert W., **848**

Ciment, James, **254**

CineMedia, **1157**

Claire Shaeffer's fabric sewing guide, **1273**

Clapham, Christopher, **799**

Clark, Amy Holsappe, **569**

Clark, Andy, **569**

Clark, Audrey N., **1662, 1665**

Clark, Duncan, **1227**

Clark, M., **669**

Clarke, Michael, **1054**

Clarke, Peter, **164**

The classic epic, **1562**

Classic home cooking, **920**

Classical and medieval literature criticism, **1563**

Classical Greek and Roman drama, **1564**

Classical music, **1225**

Classical music reference, 1220

Classical studies, **1565**

Classics in the history of psychology-Freud (1914/1917), **228**

Cleaning, **966**

Clements, William M., **386**

Cline, Elizabeth, **903**

Cline, Maryanne, **80**

Clute, John, **1485, 1515**

Cocks, L. R. M., **746**

A code of Jewish ethics, **148**

Coerver, Don M., **1617**

Cohen, E. Richard, **805**

Cohen, Morris L., **471**

Cohen, Richard E., **496**

Cohen, Saul B., **1654**

Cohen, Selma Jeanne, **1135**

Coile, D. Caroline, **1003**

The coin atlas handbook, **1287**

Coin world almanac, **1288**

Coins and currency, **1289**

Colgate, Craig, **412**, 413

College basketball's national championships, **1337**

College blue book, **562**

The College Board guide to high schools, **563**

College Entrance Examination Board, **563**, 576

College money handbook, **570**

College student's guide to merit and other no-need funding, **571**

Collins, Bud, **1393**

Collins, Jane, **860**

Collins, John William, **542**

The Collins big book of art, **1073**

Collins German-English, English-German dictionary, **667**

Collins Robert comprehensive French-English, English-French dictionary and thesaurus, **663**

Collins Spanish dictionary, **684**

Collinson, Diane, **84**

Colman, Andrew M., **195**

The Columbia companion to modern East Asian literature, **1576**

The Columbia companion to the twentieth-century American short story, **1519**

The Columbia dictionary of Shakespeare quotations, **1549**

The Columbia gazetteer of the world, **1654**

The Columbia Granger's index to poetry in anthologies, **1503**

The Columbia Granger's index to poetry in collected and selected works, **1504**

The Columbia Granger's world of poetry online, **1505**

The Columbia guide to Asian American literature since 1945, **1440**

The Columbia guide to contemporary African American fiction, **1435**
The Columbia guide to online style, **651**
Columbia guide to standard American English, **622**
The Columbia guide to the literatures of Eastern Europe since 1945, **1577**
Comay, Arié, **673**
Comfort, Nicholas, **479**
Comic book encyclopedia, **1086**
Commire, Anne, 1474, **1475**
Community colleges, **572**
Companies and their brands, **438**
Companion to American children's picture books, **1465**
Company profiles for students, **439**
Compendium of the world's languages, **595**
Complete atlas of world history, **1630**
Complete book of insurance, **459**
Complete book of sewing, **1274**
Complete catalogue of plays, **1183**
Complete directory to prime-time network and cable TV shows, 1946–present, **1170**
The complete dog book, **1001**
Complete do-it-yourself manual, **975**
The complete encyclopedia of needlework, **1262**
The complete encyclopedia of stitchery, **1263**
Complete encyclopedia of the freshwater aquarium, **1006**
Complete encyclopedia of the saltwater aquarium, **1007**
The complete fashion sourcebook, **1091**
The complete guide to bed and breakfasts, inns and guesthouses in the United States, Canada, and worldwide, **1675**
The complete guide to home plumbing, **976**
The complete guide to home wiring, **977**
The complete guide to prescription and nonprescription drugs, **867**
The complete guide to psychiatric drugs, **868**
Complete guide to quilting, **1267**
The complete Hebrew-English dictionary, **672**
The complete history of costume and fashion, **1092**
Complete home improvement and repair, **961**
The complete home veterinary guide, **990**
Complete horse care manual, **1009**
The complete household handbook, **967**
The complete illustrated guide to furniture and cabinet construction, **1278**
The complete illustrated guide to joinery, **1278**
The complete illustrated stitch encyclopedia, **1264**
Complete outdoors encyclopedia, **1377**
The complete pet bird owner's handbook, **993**
The complete photo guide to home improvement, **962**
The complete photo guide to outdoor home improvement, **963**
Complete photo guide to sewing, **1274**
The complete quilting course, **1267**
The complete rhyming dictionary, **627**
Complete stories of the great ballets, **1139**
The complete swimming pool reference, **1392**
Complete trimwork and carpentry, **978**
The complete vampire companion, 242
Compton's (Britannica student encyclopedia), **38,** 42
The computer glossary, **724**
Computer sciences, **725**
Conception, pregnancy, and birth, **879**
The concise Corsini encyclopedia of psychology and behavioral science, **193**
Concise dictionary of modern medicine, **816**
Concise dictionary of scientific biography, **704**
Concise dictionary of world place-names, **1655**
The concise encyclopedia of hockey, **1369**
A concise encyclopedia of Islam, **142**
Concise encyclopedia of special education, **537**
The concise geography encyclopedia, **1656**
The concise Oxford dictionary of archaeology, **380**
The concise Oxford dictionary of art and artists, **1053**
The concise Oxford dictionary of art terms, **1054**
Concise Oxford dictionary of ballet, **1132**
The concise Oxford dictionary of mathematics, **799**
The concise Oxford dictionary of music, **1211**
Concise Oxford dictionary of politics, **480**
The concise Oxford dictionary of world religions, **89**
Condition of education, **583**
Conelly, Robert B., **1151**
Confucianism, **118**
Congdon, Kristin G., **1079**
Congress A to Z, **500,** 504
Congressional Quarterly, 490, 491, 495, 501, 502, 503
Congressional Quarterly's desk reference on American government, **501**
Congressional Quarterly's desk reference on the presidency, **502**
Congressional Quarterly's politics in America, **503**
Conley, Brenda Edgerton, **572**
Connor, Billie M., **1188**

Conn's current therapy, **834**
Conoley, Jane Close, **222**
Conran, Terence, **972**
Conroy, Wendy A., **236**
Considine, Glenn D., **700, 717**
The consumer drug reference, **869**
Consumer health complete, **811**
Consumer Reports buying guide, **905**
Consumer sourcebook, **906**
Consumers Union of United States, **869, 905, 969**
Contemporary architects, **1039**
Contemporary artists, **1081**
Contemporary authors, **1427, 1428**
Contemporary authors autobiography series, **1428**
Contemporary black American playwrights and their plays, **1436**
Contemporary designers, **1082**
Contemporary dramatists, **1480**
Contemporary fashion, **1093**
Contemporary gay American novelists, **1441**
Contemporary gay American poets and playwrights, **1442**
Contemporary lesbian writers of the United States, **1443**
Contemporary literary criticism, **1413**
The contemporary novel, **1499**
Contemporary novelists, **1500**
Contemporary photographers, **1113**
Contemporary poets, **1506**
Contemporary quotations in black, **1421**
Contemporary theatre, film, and television, **1125**
Contemporary youth culture, **374**
The Continuum complete international encyclopedia of sexuality, **343**
Contraceptive technology, **880**
Coogan, Michael D., **104**
Cook, Chris, **505**
Cook, Dorothy E., **1525**
Cook, James Wyatt, **1401**
Cook, Richard, **1221**
Cooke, F., **793**
The cook's essential kitchen dictionary, **921**
Cool stuff and how it works, **694**
Cooper, C. L., **461**
Coppens, Linda Miles, **369**
Corbett, Doris, **1364**
Cordón, Luis A., **211**
Cordry, Harold V., **1419**
Corréard, MarieHélène, **666**

Corsini, Raymond J., **205**
The Corsini encyclopedia of psychology and behavioral science, **194**
Cosgrave, Bronwyn, **1092**
Costello, Elaine, **632**
Costume and fashion, **1094**
The costume page, **1029**
The costumer's manifesto, **1030**
Council of National Library and Information Associations (U.S.), **67**
Council of National Library Associations, **67**
Council of Science Editors, Style manual committee, **656**
Council of State Governments, **499**
The counter-creationism handbook, **767**
Countries of the world and their leaders yearbook, **1657**
Country monitor, 396
The Country Music Foundation, **1237**
Country profiles, 396
Country review, 396
Country study series, **1673**
CountryWatch, 396
Cowan, Robert, **359**
Cox, C. Brian, **1569**
Cox, Gerry, **1303**
Cox, Jeff, **934**
Cox, Mary, **1070**
CQ researcher online, **28**
Crabtree, Caroline, **1256**
Craddock, Jim, **1161**
Crafter's Choice, **1264**
Craig, Edward, **82**
Craig, Steve, **1363**
Craighead, W. Edward, **193, 194**
Craine, Debra, **1136**
Crampton, Luke, **1248**
CRC handbook of chemistry and physics, **718**
Creating keepsakes, **1270**
Creative Homeowner Press, **910**
Creative Publishing International, **1274**
Credo Reference, **58**, 62
Cribb, Joe, **1287**
Crime fiction II, **1495**
Crime in the United States, **285**
Cromley, Elizabeth, **1042**
Crosby, F. L., **130**
Cross, Gary S., **1380**
Crowther, Nicky, **1345**
Cruickshank, Dan, **1045**

Crystal, David, **600, 731, 1687**
C-SPAN, **469**
Cuhaj, George, **1291**
The cultural encyclopedia of baseball, **1327**
Curl, James Stevens, **1041**
Current biography, 1686
Current biography yearbook, **1688**
Current issues: Macmillan social science library, **258**
Current medical diagnosis and treatment, **835**
Current obstetric and gynecological diagnosis and treatment, **835**
Current pediatric diagnosis and treatment, **835**
Current surgical diagnosis and treatment, **835**
Currie, Phillip J., **791**
Curtis, Nancy C., **310**
Curtis, Rick, **1319**
Cutter, Charles, **160**
Cutter, Charles H., **1669**
CyberDance, **1130**
Cyclopedia of literary characters, **1409**
Cyclopedia of world authors, **1429,** 1448

D

D and B business rankings, **440**
Daintith, John, **715**
Dakin, Nick, **1007**
Dalby, Andrew, **596**
Dalby, Arnold, **657**
Dalley, Arthur F., **852**
Dalzell, Tom, **639**
Dance annual directory, **1121**
The dance handbook, **1138**
Daniel, LaNelle, **1531**
Daniels, Estelle, **165**
Danilov, Victor J, **1310**
Darnay, Arsen, **358**
Darvill, Timothy, **380**
Dassanowsky, Robert, **301**
Datamonitor, 396
Dating and sexuality in America, **344**
Daum, Kevin, **913**
Davidson, Alan, **958**
Davies, Martin, **347**
Davies, Penelope J. E., **1074**
Davis, Caroline, **998**
Davis, Elisabeth B., **764**
Davis, Elizabeth A., **1203**
Davis, Jeffrey, **1169**
Dawes, John, **1006**
Dawson, Kara, **538**

Day, A. Colin, **105**
Day, Daphne, **665**
Day, David, **981**
The DC Comics encyclopedia, **1087**
de Blij, H. J., **1648**
De Pree, Christopher Gordon, **700**
Dearborn real estate education, **464**
Death and dying sourcebook, **292**
DeCherney, Alan H., **835**
DeFrancis, John, **660**
Deisher, Beth, **1288**
Delahunt, Michael, **1026**
Delaney, John J., **137**
DeLoach, Charles, **1553**
Demeny, Paul George, **357**
DeMiller, Anna L., **593**
Demographics of the U.S., **426**
Dempsey, Amy, **1071**
Dennis, Matthew, **945**
Derks, Scott, **1627, 1628**
Design and applied arts index (DAAI), **1021**
The design encyclopedia, **1055**
Designer scrapbooks with Mrs. Grossman, **1271**
Deutsch, Babette, **1512**
DeVito, Carlo, **1308**
Dewey, Russell A., **234**
Diagnostic and statistical manual of mental disorders: DSM-IV-TR, text revision, 208, **214**
Diagram Group, **852**
Diamant, Lincoln, **1168**
Diamond, Dan, **1372**
Diamond, Marie Josephine, **1431**
Diamonds around the globe, **1328**
DiCanio, Margaret, **326**
Dickinson's American historical fiction, **1492**
Dickson-Carr, Darryl, **1435**
Dictionary of accounting terms, **419**
Dictionary of American children's fiction, **1466**
Dictionary of American classical composers, **1233**
Dictionary of American history, **1609**
Dictionary of American proverbs, **1417**
Dictionary of American slang, **636**
Dictionary of American young adult fiction, 1997–2001, **1466**
Dictionary of architecture and construction, **1040**
Dictionary of architecture and landscape architecture, **1041**
Dictionary of art, **1056**
A dictionary of biology, **768**
Dictionary of Christian art, **1057**

Dictionary of Christianity in America, 107
Dictionary of computer and Internet words, 726
A dictionary of costume and fashion, 1095
A dictionary of economics, 452
Dictionary of engineering materials, 758
Dictionary of fictional characters, 1410
Dictionary of film terms, 1143
Dictionary of finance and banking, 429
Dictionary of finance and investment terms, 430
Dictionary of furniture, 1103
A dictionary of genetics, 769
A dictionary of geography, 1658
Dictionary of gods and goddesses, 172
Dictionary of historic documents, 1610
Dictionary of insurance terms, 460
Dictionary of Irish literature, 1582
Dictionary of Italian literature, 1585
Dictionary of Jewish lore and legend, 149
Dictionary of languages, 596
Dictionary of literary biography, 1430
Dictionary of literary biography yearbook, 1430
Dictionary of medical syndromes, 836
A dictionary of modern design, 1058
The dictionary of multimedia, 727
Dictionary of Native American literature, 1451
A dictionary of physics, 806
A dictionary of psychology, 195
Dictionary of race, ethnicity and culture, 298
Dictionary of saints, 137
Dictionary of sociology (Lawson and Garrod), 268
A dictionary of sociology (Scott and Marshall), 269
The dictionary of sports, 1303
A dictionary of superstitions, 237
Dictionary of symbols in Western art, 1059
Dictionary of the esoteric, 238
A dictionary of the history of science, 735
Dictionary of the social sciences, 250
The dictionary of urbanism, 359
Dictionary of women artists, 1083
Dietz, Marjorie J., 787
Digest of education statistics, 584
Dillmont, Thérèse de, 1262
Dillon, Michael, 1608
Dimmitt, Richard B., 1155
The Dinosaur Society's dinosaur encyclopedia, 788
The dinosauria, 789
Dinosaurs, 790
Directories in print, 47
The directory for exceptional children, 546
Directory of American scholars, 591

Directory of business information resources, 410
Directory of financial aids for women, 571
Directory of physicians in the United States, 829
Directory of unpublished experimental mental measures, 221
Directory of venture capital and private equity firms, domestic and international, 456
Disability sport and recreation resources, 1309
Diskin, B. A., 463
Distinguished Asian Americans, 315
Dixon, T., 442
Dodds, Steve, 1016
Dodson, Peter, 789
Dogs, 1002
Doherty, Gerard M., 835
Dollinger, Malin, 857
Doniach, N. S., 674
Dorland, W. A. Newman, 817
Dorland's illustrated medical dictionary, 817
Dorn, Georgette M., 1613
Douglass, Judith Spungen, 952
Doundoulakis, James, 844
Douville, Judith A., 712
Dow, James R., 173
Downes, J., 428, 430
Dox, Ida G., 821
Drabble, Margaret, 1547
Drake, Miriam A., 69
Dramatists Play Service, 1183
The dream encyclopedia, 196
Drinks, 888
Drozdowski, Ted, 1222
Drug abuse sourcebook, 281
Drug use, 282
Drummond, Edward H., 868
Drury, Nevill, 238, 248
DSM-IV made easy, 214
DSM-IV-TR casebook: A learning companion to the Diagnostic and statistical manual of mental disorders, 215
Duckles, Vincent H., 1204
Duffy, Cathy, 529
Dun and Bradstreet, 440
Duncan, Joyce, 1306
Dunning, John, 1175
Dun's Marketing Services, 465
DVD and video guide, 1158
Dworkin, Rita, 1499
Dyson, Anne Jane, 1546
Dziemianowicz, Stefan, 1487

E

Eadie, Jo, **346**

Eagleson, Robert D., **1556**

Earth science resources in the electronic age, **742**

East and Southeast Asia, **1669**

Eastman, Mary H., **1468**

Eatwell, John, **453**

eBay: The world's online marketplace, **1031**

Ebert, Roger, **1154**

EBSCO Academic Search Premier, **35**

EBSCO Content Solutions, 43, 45

EBSCO Psychology Databases, **183**

EBSCOhost, **396**

Economic competitiveness, 396

Economy, Peter, **913**

Eddleman, Floyd E., **1531**

Edelson, Paula, **1311**

Edney, A. T. B., **995**

Education, **524**

Education and technology, **538**

Education index, **533**

Education research complete, **534**

Education state rankings, **585**

Educational media and technology yearbook, **526**

The educator's desk reference (EDR), **575**

Educators guide to free family and consumer education materials, **527**

Educators guide to free films, filmstrips and slides, **527**

Educators guide to free guidance materials, **527**

Educators guide to free health, physical education, and recreation materials, **527**

Educators guide to free Internet resources—elementary/middle school edition, **527**

Educators guide to free Internet resources—secondary edition, **527**

Educators guide to free multicultural materials, **527**

Educators guide to free science materials, **527**

Educators guide to free social studies materials, **527**

Educators guide to free videotapes—elementary/middle school edition, **527**

Educators guide to free videotapes—secondary edition, **527**

Edwards, Elwyn Hartley, **1011**

Edwards, Richard L., **349**

Egelson, Paula E., **221**

Egolf, K., **420**

Ehrlich, Eugene, **625**

Eigen, Lewis D., **486**

Eighth book of junior authors and illustrators, **1469**

Eisenberg, Ronald L., **158**

Ekerdt, David J., **277**

Elder, John E., **1532**

Elections A to Z, **504**

The Element encyclopedia of witchcraft, **239**

Elementary education, **572**

Elementary teachers guide to free curriculum materials, **527**

The elements of design, **1104**

The elements of legal style, **652**

The elements of style, **1042**

Elias, Edward E., **659**

Elias, Elias A., **659**

Elias Modern dictionary: English-Arabic, **659**

Ellingham, Mark, **1251**

Elliot, Stephen, **613**

Ellwood, Robert S., **114**

Emanuel, Muriel, **1039**

Ember, Carol R., **363**

Ember, Melvin, **363**

Emerton, Bruce, **573**

Emily Post's etiquette, **939**

Emily Post's wedding etiquette, **940**

Emmons, Mark, **1140**

Enciclopedia estudiantil hallazgos, 45

Enciclopedia universal en español, 42

Encyclopaedia Britannica, **42**

Encyclopaedia Britannica online, 42

Encyclopaedia Britannica online school edition, 38, 42

Encyclopaedia of the social sciences, **251,** 252

Encyclopedia Americana, **39**

Encyclopedia Americana online, 43

Encyclopedia Judaica, **150**

Encyclopedia of abortion in the United States, **274**

The encyclopedia of addictions and addictive behaviors, **197**

Encyclopedia of African American business history, **400**

Encyclopedia of African-American religions, **108**

Encyclopedia of African history, **1611**

Encyclopedia of aging, **277**

Encyclopedia of American business, **401**

Encyclopedia of American education, **539**

Encyclopedia of American folk art, **1060**

Encyclopedia of American gospel music, **1236**

Encyclopedia of American historical documents, **1636**

Encyclopedia of American holidays and national days, **944**

The encyclopedia of American religions, **109**
Encyclopedia of American religious history, **110**
The encyclopedia of American soccer history, **1389**
Encyclopedia of American women in business, **402**
Encyclopedia of ancient Asian civilizations, **1612**
Encyclopedia of ancient Egypt, **1612**
Encyclopedia of angels, **87**
The encyclopedia of animals, **793**
Encyclopedia of anthropology, **381**
Encyclopedia of applied ethics, **178**
Encyclopedia of applied psychology, **198**
Encyclopedia of aquarium and pond fish, **1008**
Encyclopedia of Arabic literature, **1543**
Encyclopedia of archaeology: History and discoveries, **382**
Encyclopedia of archaeology: The great archaeologists, **383**
Encyclopedia of artists, **1084**
Encyclopedia of associations, **48**
Encyclopedia of associations: International organizations, **48**
Encyclopedia of associations: Regional, state and local organizations, **48**
Encyclopedia of atmospheric sciences, **746**
The encyclopedia of beading techniques, **1257**
Encyclopedia of biodiversity, **770**
Encyclopedia of bioethics, **771**
Encyclopedia of biology, **772**
The encyclopedia of blindness and vision impairment, **875**
Encyclopedia of British writers, **1545**
Encyclopedia of business and finance, **431**
Encyclopedia of business information sources, **389**
Encyclopedia of capital punishment in the United States, **286**
Encyclopedia of capitalism, **403**
Encyclopedia of careers and vocational guidance, **466**
Encyclopedia of Caribbean literature, **1573**
Encyclopedia of children and childhood, **375**
Encyclopedia of classical philosophy, **77**
Encyclopedia of clothing and fashion, **1096**
Encyclopedia of community, **360**
Encyclopedia of computer science and technology, **728**
Encyclopedia of computers and computer history, **729**
Encyclopedia of corporate names worldwide, **441**
The encyclopedia of country music, **1237**
Encyclopedia of crime and punishment, **287**

Encyclopedia of criminology, **288**
Encyclopedia of cryptozoology, **794**
Encyclopedia of cults, sects, and new religions, **163**
The encyclopedia of deafness and hearing disorders, **876**
The encyclopedia of death and dying (Cassel et al.), **294**
Encyclopedia of death and dying (Howarth and Leaman), **293**
Encyclopedia of dinosaurs, **791**
Encyclopedia of disability, **877**
Encyclopedia of dog breeds, **1003**
Encyclopedia of drugs, alcohol, and addictive behavior, **870**
Encyclopedia of early Christianity, **124**
Encyclopedia of earth and physical sciences, **743**
Encyclopedia of education, **540**
Encyclopedia of educational research, **541**
Encyclopedia of ethics, **179**
Encyclopedia of evaluation, **199**
Encyclopedia of evolution, **773**
The encyclopedia of exercise, sport, and health, **1351**
Encyclopedia of family life, **325**
The encyclopedia of fantasy, **1485**
Encyclopedia of feminist literary theory, **1453**
Encyclopedia of feminist literature, **1454**
The encyclopedia of figure skating, **1352**
Encyclopedia of food and culture, **954**
Encyclopedia of genetics (Reeve), **774**
Encyclopedia of geology, **746**
The encyclopedia of ghosts and spirits, **240**
Encyclopedia of global change, **750**
Encyclopedia of gothic literature, **1490**
Encyclopedia of herbal medicine, **871**
Encyclopedia of Hinduism, **119**
Encyclopedia of historical archaeology, **384**
Encyclopedia of holidays and celebrations, **945**
The encyclopedia of horses and ponies, **1010**
Encyclopedia of human development, **200**
Encyclopedia of human emotions, **201**
Encyclopedia of human rights, **481**
Encyclopedia of interior design, **1043**
Encyclopedia of international games, **1304**
Encyclopedia of Islam and the Muslim world, **143**
Encyclopedia of Latin American history and culture, **1613**
Encyclopedia of Latin American literature, **1588**
Encyclopedia of Latino popular culture, **317**
Encyclopedia of leadership, **404**

Encyclopedia of lesbian and gay histories and cultures, **331**

Encyclopedia of lesbian, gay, bisexual, and transgender history in America, **332**

Encyclopedia of library and information science, **69**

Encyclopedia of Major League Baseball clubs, **1329**

Encyclopedia of management, **462**

The encyclopedia of marriage, divorce and the family, **326**

Encyclopedia of medical devices and instrumentation, **818**

Encyclopedia of medieval literature, **1400**

The encyclopedia of memory and memory disorders, **202**

The encyclopedia of men's health, **881**

The encyclopedia of mental health, **203**

The encyclopedia of Native American religions, **111**

Encyclopedia of natural medicine, **864**

Encyclopedia of new religious movements, **164**

The encyclopedia of North American sports history, **1305**

Encyclopedia of North American trees, **780**

The encyclopedia of nutrition and good health, **873**

Encyclopedia of ocean sciences, 746

Encyclopedia of outdoor and wilderness skills, **1378**

Encyclopedia of paleontology, **792**

Encyclopedia of pets and pet care, **991**

Encyclopedia of philosophy, **78**

Encyclopedia of pieced quilt patterns, **1268**, 1269

The encyclopedia of popular music, **1246**

Encyclopedia of population, **357**

Encyclopedia of presidential campaigns, slogans, issues, and platforms, **482**

Encyclopedia of Protestantism, **125**

The encyclopedia of psychiatry, psychology and psychoanalysis, **204**

Encyclopedia of psychology (Corsini), **205**

Encyclopedia of psychology (Kazdin), 187, **206**

Encyclopedia of public relations, **405**

Encyclopedia of racism in the United States, **299**

Encyclopedia of radio, **1171**

Encyclopedia of rap and hip hop culture, **1247**

Encyclopedia of recreation and leisure in America, **1380**

Encyclopedia of religion, **88**

Encyclopedia of Renaissance literature, **1401**

Encyclopedia of retirement and finance, **432**

Encyclopedia of rhetoric and composition, **1528**

Encyclopedia of Russian history, **1614**

Encyclopedia of saints, **138**

Encyclopedia of school psychology, **207**

Encyclopedia of science fiction, **1515**

Encyclopedia of science, technology, and ethics, **695**

The encyclopedia of scrapbooking tools and techniques, **1272**

Encyclopedia of sewing machine techniques, **1275**

Encyclopedia of sex, **345**

Encyclopedia of sexually transmitted diseases, **850**

Encyclopedia of small business, **457**

Encyclopedia of social and cultural anthropology, **385**

Encyclopedia of social work, **349**

Encyclopedia of sociology, **270**

Encyclopedia of soils in the environment, 746

Encyclopedia of special education, 537

Encyclopedia of swearing, **637**

Encyclopedia of television, **1172**

Encyclopedia of terrorism, **289**

Encyclopedia of the American Civil War, **1615**

Encyclopedia of the American Left, **483**

Encyclopedia of the ancient Greek world, **1612**

Encyclopedia of the city, **361**

Encyclopedia of the elements, **714**

Encyclopedia of the essay, **1529**

Encyclopedia of the modern Olympic movement, **1375**

The encyclopedia of the musical theatre, **1196**

The encyclopedia of the paranormal, **241**

Encyclopedia of the Roman Empire, **1612**

Encyclopedia of the scientific revolution, **736**

Encyclopedia of the solar system, **708**, 746

Encyclopedia of the United States cabinet, **484**

Encyclopedia of the world's minorities, **300**

Encyclopedia of the world's zoos, **795**

Encyclopedia of 20th-century architecture, **1044**

Encyclopedia of twentieth-century photography, **1114**

Encyclopedia of urban America, **362**

Encyclopedia of urban cultures, **363**

The encyclopedia of vampires, werewolves, and other monsters, **242**

Encyclopedia of weather and climate, **751**

The encyclopedia of witches and witchcraft, **243**

Encyclopedia of women and sport in America, **1313**

Encyclopedia of women social reformers, **365**

The encyclopedia of women's health, **882**

Encyclopedia of world biography, **1689**

Encyclopedia of world climatology, **751**

Encyclopedia of world geography, **1659**

The encyclopedia of world religions, **114**

Encyclopedia of world trade, **406**
Encyclopedia of world writers, **1431**
Encyclopedic dictionary of mathematics, **800**
Enghag, Per, **714**
English, Richard A., **349**
English novel explication, **1546**
English-Italian, Italian-English, **676**
English-Russian, Russian-English dictionary, **681**
Enos, Theresa, **1528**
Entertainment awards, **1128**
Entrepreneur press, **458**
Erb, Uwe, **758**
Ergas, Aimee G., **1080**
ERIC: Education Resources Information Center, **535**
Erickson, Hal, **1176**
Erlewine, Stephen Thomas, **1238**
The ESPN baseball encyclopedia, **1330**
ESPN college football encyclopedia, **1355**
ESPN sports almanac, **1300**
Espy, Willard R., **629**
Essential cat, **998**
The essential guide to children's books and their creators, **1467**
The essential Kabbalah, **151**
The essential kitchen, **922**
The essential Shakespeare, **1550**
The essential Talmud, **152**
Essential Wicca, **165**
Ethics, **180**
Ethnologue, **597**
Etz Hayim: Torah and commentary, **153**
Europa world yearbook, **1674**
European political facts of the twentieth century, **505**
Evans, Graham, **488**
Everett-Heath, John, **1655**
Everyone's guide to cancer supportive care, **856**
Everyone's guide to cancer therapy, **857**
The exotic pet handbook, **1013**
Expedia, **1676**
Extreme searcher's Internet handbook, **740**
Eyre, Harmon J., **859**

F

Facts on File, **1098, 1632**
The Facts on File companion to classical drama, **1566**
The Facts on File companion to the American novel, **1535**
The Facts on File companion to the American short story, **1520**
The Facts on File companion to the British short story, **1521**
Facts on File dictionary of astronomy, **709**
Facts on File dictionary of biology, **775**
The Facts on File dictionary of cell and molecular biology, **776**
The Facts on File dictionary of chemistry, **715**
The Facts on File dictionary of clichés, **633**
The Facts on File dictionary of foreign words and phrases, **617**
The Facts on File encyclopedia of word and phrase origins, **615**
Facts on File encyclopedia of world mythology and legend, **173**
The Facts on File physics handbook, **807**
Facts on File: Weekly world news digest with cumulative index, **29**
Fagan, Brian M., **387**
Fahey, David M., **279**
The Fairchild dictionary of fashion, **1276**
Families in America, **327**
Family Handyman, **975**
The family in America, **986**
Famous first facts, **1623**
Farmer, David Hugh, **140**
Farmer, William R., **92**
Farris, Jerri, **964**
Fashion in costume, 1200–2000, **1097**
Fashions of a decade, **1098**
Favorite hobbies and pastimes, **1254**
Fawcett, Jan, **203**
Federal Bureau of Investigation, **285**
Federal Citizen Information Center (U.S.), **909**
Federal regulatory directory, **490**
Fedstats, **260**
Feminist writers, **1455**
Ferguson, Everett, **124**
Ferro, Frank, **7**
Fiction catalog, **1488**
Fielden, Greg, **1318**
Fielding, Lori, **266**
Fifth book of junior authors and illustrators, **1469**
Figueredo, D. H., **1573**
Film and television, **1140**
Film cartoons, **1144**
The film encyclopedia, **1145**
Film studies dictionary, **1146**
Financial aid for African Americans, **571**

Financial aid for Asian Americans, **571**
Financial aid for Hispanic Americans, **571**
Financial aid for Native Americans, **571**
Financial aid for the disabled and their families, **571**
Financial aid for veterans, military personnel, and their dependents, **571**
Findling, John E., **1375**
Fine Cooking magazine, **927**
Fiore, Frank, **908**
Firefly encyclopedia of astronomy, **710**
Firefly geography dictionary, **1660**
Firefly guide to gems, **747**
Firkins, Ina Ten Eyck, **1186**
Fishbane, Michael, **159**
Fisher, David, **256**
Fisher, Helen S., **358**
Fisher, Ronald, **1633**
Fisk, Margaret, **48**
Fitzhenry and Whiteside book of Canadian facts and dates, **1602**
5,500 quilt block designs, **1269**
Fleming, John, **1047**
Fletcher, Banister, **1045**
Fletcher-Janzen, Elaine, **537**
Flora, Joseph M., **1542**
Flowerdew, Bob, **937**
Flynn, Roger R., **725**
Flynn, Tom, **81**
Foakes, Mary, **1549**
Foakes, Reginald, **1549**
Foerstel, Karen, **518**
Fogle, Bruce, **997, 999, 1000, 1004**
Folsom, W. D., **401**
Fons, Marianne, **1267**
Food and Nutrition Information Center, **955**
The food substitutions bible, **923**
The foodlover's atlas of the world, **956**
Foreign relations of the United States, **514**
Forest, James J. F., **543**
Forman, Robert J., **1564**
Forsythe, David J., **1678**
Fortin, François, **1385**
Foster, David W., **1589**
Foudray, Rita S., **1479**
Foulkes, Christopher, **890**
The foundation directory, **49**
Fournier, Robert, **1106**
Fourth book of junior authors and illustrators, **1469**
A fourth treasury of knitting patterns, **1260**

Fowler, H. W., **623**
Fowler's modern English usage, **623**
France, Peter, **1579**
France profiled, **1672**
The franchise annual, **442**
Francoeur, Robert T., **343**
Franks, Don, **1128**
Frawley, William, **598**
Frazier, Nancy, **1064**
Freed, Melvyn N., **575**
Freedman, Alan, **724**
Freedman, David Noel, **98**
Freeman, William, **1410**
Freidel, Frank, **1598**
Freud, Sigmund, **228**
Friedman, J. P., **463**
Frohnen, Bruce, **476**
Fuld, James J., **1210**
Fun and games in twentieth-century America, **1381**
Fundamental reference sources, **3**
Funding sources for K-12 education, **547**

G

Gaines, L. M., **390**
Gale Digital Archives, **48**
Gale directory of databases, **730**
Gale directory of publications and broadcast media, **50**
The Gale encyclopedia of alternative medicine, **865**
The Gale encyclopedia of cancer, **858**
The Gale encyclopedia of children's health, **861**
Gale encyclopedia of medicine, **812, 819**
The Gale encyclopedia of mental disorders, **208**
Gale encyclopedia of multicultural America, **301**
The Gale encyclopedia of psychology, **209**
Gale Virtual Reference Library, **58, 59, 62**
Gale's Ready Reference Shelf, **47, 50, 730**
Gall, Susan B., **209, 316**
Gallaudet dictionary of American sign language, **631**
Gallerstein, Gary A., **993**
Gambling in America, **1361**
Ganderton, Lucinda, **1266**
Ganzl, Kurt, **1196**
Garland, Henry, **1580**
Garland, Mary, **1580**
Garner, Bryan A., **478, 624, 652**
Garner's modern American usage, **624**
Garoogian, David, **314, 319, 355, 356**
Garrod, Joan, **268**

Garvin, Peggy, **493**

Gasnier, Vincent, **888**

Gates, Gary J., **333**

Gates, Henry Louis, **307**, **308**, 311

Gay and lesbian Americans and political participation, **506**

The gay and lesbian atlas, 333

Gay and lesbian literary heritage, **1444**

Gay and lesbian literature, **1445**

Gay travel A to Z, **1677**

Gaze, Delia, **1083**

Gelfant, Blanche H., **1519**

General information concerning patents, **701**

General science index, **689**

Generation X: Americans born 1965 to 1976, **424**

Genreflecting, **1489**

Georef, **744**

Georgakas, Dan, **483**

George-Warren, Holly, **1249**

Gerhardstein, Virginia B., **1492**

Germany profiled, **1672**

Gibaldi, Joseph, **654**

Gibbs, Nick, **1281**

Gibbs, William T., **1288**

Giemza, Bryan Albion, **1542**

Gifford, Clive, **1656**

Giglio, Anthony, **891**

Gillespie, John T., **525**, **1462**

Gillette, Gary, **1330**

Ginther, Catherine, **281**

Giordano, Ralph G., **1381**

Giuliani, George A., **530**

Glare, P. G. W., **680**

Glasner, D., **399**

Glazier, Stephen, **645**

Global Insight, 396

Globetrotting pets, **1678**

Glossary of film terms, **1147**

A glossary of literary terms, **1406**

A glossary of netspeak and textspeak, **731**

Glover, Linda K., **706**

Glut, Donald F., **790**

Goehlert, Robert U., **472**

Goethals, G. R., **404**

Goldman, Bert A., **221**

Goldman, Lee, **815**

Goldmann, David R., **832**

Goldstein, Norm, **648**

Golenbock, Peter, **1318**

Golf Digest's best places to play, **1365**

Gonzalez, Alexander G., **1456**, **1583**

González, Deena J., **320**

González-Wippler, Migene, **169**

Good Housekeeping Institute, **967**

Goode, J. Paul, **1640**

Goode's world atlas, **1640**

Goodfellow, William D., **1244**

Goodman, Fay, **1374**

Goodman, J. E., **428**, **430**

Goodman, Jordan, **283**

Google, **63**

Google Earth, **1641**

Google Moon, 1641

Google Scholar, 63

The Google story, 63

Gordon, Raymond G. Jr., **597**

Gottlieb, R., **410**

Goudie, Andrew, 750

Goulart, Ron, **1086**

The Gourmet cookbook, **924**

Gove, Philip Babcock, **605**

Grant, Barry K., **1146**

Grant, John, **1485**

Grant, Michael, **1567**

Grant, Richard P., **763**

Grant's atlas of anatomy, **852**

Gray, Jeffrey, **1537**

Gray's anatomy, **853**

Great American writers: Twentieth century, **1536**

Great beer guide, **889**

Great books for boys, **4**

Great books for girls, **5**

Great Hispanic Americans, **318**

Great world writers: Twentieth century, **1432**

Greek and Latin authors: 800 B.C. to A.D. 1000, **1567**

A Greek-English lexicon, **670**

Green, Ariadne, **191**

Green, Christopher D., **228**

Green, Jeff, **1241**

Green, Thomas A, **1373**

The Green book of songs by subject, **1241**

Greenberg, Blu, **155**

Greenberg, Doreen L., **1313**

Greenberg, Michael I., **810**

Greenberg, Milton, **477**

Greene, Gilbert J., **353**

Greenfield, Edward, 1225, **1226**

Greenfieldt, John, **1488**

The Greenwood dictionary of education, **542**

Greenwood Digital Collection, **60, 62**

The Greenwood encyclopedia of African American literature, **1437**

The Greenwood encyclopedia of American poets and poetry, **1537**

The Greenwood encyclopedia of multiethnic American literature, **1538**

Greenwood encyclopedia of science fiction and fantasy, **1516**

The Greenwood encyclopedia of world folklore and folklife, **386**

Greer, John Michael, **245**

Gregory, Richard L., **217**

Greydanus, Donald E., **985**

Griffith, H. Winter, **867**

Griffiths, Tom, **1392**

Grimal, Pierre, **175**

Grimes, Barbara F., **597**

Grimm, Robert T. Jr., **350**

Groden, Michael, **1408**

Grolier multimedia encyclopedia, 43

Grolier Online, 43

Gross, Ernie, **1301, 1603**

Gross, John M., **1219**

Grossman, Andrea, **1271**

Grossman, John, **653**

Grossman, Mark, **484**

Grove art online, 1022

Grove Music Online, 1215, 1223

Grove's dictionary of art, 1056

Grun, Bernard, **1604**

Grundy, Valerie, **666**

Grzimek, Bernhard, **777**

Grzimek's animal life encyclopedia, **777**

Guerrier, Katherine, **1267**

Guide to British poetry explication, **1507**

The guide to cooking schools, **925**

A guide to critical reviews, **1120**

A guide to critical reviews, part 1: American drama, 1908–1982, **1120**

A guide to critical reviews, part 2: The musical, 1909–1989, **1120**

A guide to critical reviews, part 3: Foreign drama, 1909–1977, **1120**

A guide to critical reviews, part 4: The screenplay from The Jazz Singer to Dr. Strangelove, **1120**

A guide to critical reviews, part 4, supplement 1: The screenplay, 1963–1980, **1120**

Guide to French literature, **1578**

Guide to getting financial aid, **576**

Guide to information sources in engineering, **752**

Guide to information sources in mathematics and statistics, **797**

A guide to Jewish prayer, **154**

Guide to poetry explication: American poetry, **1508**

Guide to reference, **6**

Guide to summer camps and summer schools, **548**

Guide to the evaluation of educational experiences in the armed services, **549**

Guide to world language dictionaries, **657**

Guiley, Rosemary Ellen, **87, 138, 240, 242,** 242, **243, 244**

Guinness world records, **30**

Guthrie, James W., **540**

Guttmann, Allen, **1314**

Guyton, Arthur C., **855**

Gwinnell, Esther, **197**

H

Habitat for Humanity: How to build a house, **914**

Hage, Christine Lind, **73**

Hager, Alan, **1545**

Haggerty, George, **331**

Haider-Markel, Donald P., **506**

Hainsworth, Peter, **1586**

Hall, John E., **855**

Hall, Kermit L., **510**

Hall, Linda D., **389, 409, 437, 438**

Hall, Timothy L., **113**

Halliday, Tim, **1014**

Halliwell's film, video and DVD guide, **1159**

Halliwell's who's who in the movies, **1165**

Hallmark, Kara Kelley, **1079**

Hammond, Scott J., **482**

Hand, N., **429**

Hand, Raymond Jr., **625**

Hand tools, **1279**

Handbook of American women's history, **1624**

Handbook of death and dying, **295**

Handbook of denominations in the United States, **112**

Handbook of Latin American literature, **1589**

Handbook of marriage and the family, **328**

Handbook of private schools, **550**

Handbook of Russian literature, **1593**

Handbook of U.S. labor statistics, **416**

A handbook to literature, **1407**

The handy science answer book, **696**

Hanlan, J. P., **407**

Hanlon, Thomas W., **1386**

Hansen, Brad, **727**

Hanstock, Terry, **256**

Harder, Kelsie B., **1417**

Hargraves, Orin, **629**

Harling, Michael, **1369**

Harmon, Deborah A., **572**

Harmon, William, **1407**

Harner, James L., **1396**

HarperCollins Bible dictionary, **99**

*The HarperCollins reader's encyclopedia of
    American literature,* **1539**

*Harper's encyclopedia of mystical and paranormal
    experience,* **244**

Harpham, Geoffrey G., **1406**

*Harrap's new standard French and English
    dictionary,* **664**

Harries, Dan, **1157**

Harris, Cyril M., **1037**, **1040**

Harris, J. C., **463**

Harris, Joseph, **202**

Harrison, Charles Hampton, **581**

Harrison's principles of internal medicine, **815**

Hart, James D., **1540**

Harte, John, **847**

Hartz, Paula R., **120**, **122**, **162**, **171**

The Harvard concordance to Shakespeare, **1551**

The Harvard dictionary of music, **1212**

Harvard guide to American history, **1598**

Harvard Medical School guide to men's health, **883**

Hatch, Jane M., **900**

Hatcher, Robert A., **880**

Haun, Larry, **914**

Havlice, Patricia Pate, **1243**

Hawes, Joseph M., **986**

Hawkins, Lawrence E., **749**

Hay, William W., **835**

Haywood, John, **1630**

Head, Dominic, **1395**

Headquarters USA, **411**

Health and wellness resource center, **812**

Health, United States, **837**

Heath, R. L., **405**

Heberle, Dave, **915**

Hedblad, Alan, **730**

Heidler, David S., **1615**

Heidler, Jeanne T., **1615**

Heilbron, J. L., **739**

Helbig, Alethea K., **1466**

Heller, James S., **70**

Heller, Jules, **1085**

Heller, Nancy G., **1085**

Hellman, Paul T., **1661**

Helmer-Citterich, Manuela, **763**

Helms, M. M., **462**

Henderson, Harry, **728**

Henderson, Helene, **948**

Henderson, Joe, **1383**

Henderson, Lesley, **1498**, **1513**

Hendrickson, Linnea, **1463**

Hendrickson, Robert, **615**

Henkenius, Merle, **980**

Henshaw, Edmund Lee, **522**

The HEP Higher education directory, **564**

Herald, Diana Tixier, **1489**

Herbs and spices, **926**

Hériteau, Jacqueline, **786**

Herron, Nancy L., **257**

Hess, Robert K., **575**

Hessenbruch, Arne, **734**

Heuff, Dick, **1137**

Hewstone, Miles, **192**

Hickok, Ralph, **1305**

Higginbotham, Evelyn Brooks, **307**, 311

Higham, Charles, **1612**

Higher education in the United States, **543**

Higher Education Publications, **564**

HighlyCited.com, 691

Hill, Levirn, **561**

Hill, Sam S. II, **219**

Hillier, Jim, **1146**

Hinchey, Patricia H., **572**

Hine, Darlene Clark, **312**

Hine, Robert, **768**, **775**, **776**

Hirschfelder, Arlene B., **111**

Hischak, Thomas S., **1192**, **1198**, **1199**

The Hispanic databook, **319**

Hispanic literature of the United States, **1447**

Historic asylums, **229**

Historical abstracts, **1606**

Historical atlas of the American Revolution, **1631**

Historical dictionary of terrorism, 291

*Historical dictionary of the Civil War and
    Reconstruction,* **1616**

Historical dictionary of the Olympic movement,
    1376

Historical encyclopedia of American labor, **407**

Historical fiction, **1493**

Historical gazetteer of the United States, **1661**

Historical guide to the U.S. government, **507**

Historical maps on file, **1632**

Historically black colleges and universities, **572**

A history of architecture, **1045**

History of art, **1074**

History of Indian literature in English, **1581**

History of modern science and mathematics, **738**

The history of the psychoanalytic movement, 228

A history of women photographers, **1115**

H-Net: Humanities and Social Sciences Online, **261**

Hobbs, James B., **642**

Hobson, Archie, **1653**

Hock, Randolph, 65, **740**

Hoffman, Penny J., **1680**

Hogan, Robert, **1582**

Holden, Amanda, **1231**

Holder, R. W., **638**

Holiday symbols and customs, **946**

Holidays and anniversaries of the world, **947**

Holidays, festivals, and celebrations of the world dictionary, **948**

The holy Qur'an, **144**

The home book of quotations, classical and modern, **1422**

The home health guide to poisons and antidotes, **838**

Home improvement 101, **964**

The home plumbing handbook, **979**

The homeowner's ultimate tool guide, **1015**

Homeschooler's guide to free teaching aids, **527**

Homeschooler's guide to free videotapes, **527**

Homophones and homographs, **642**

Honour, Hugh, **1047**

Hoobler, Dorothy, **118**

Hoobler, Thomas, **118**

Hooper, David, **1349**

Hoover's handbook of American business, 396, **443**

Hoover's handbook of emerging companies, 397, **444**

Hoover's handbook of private companies, 397, **445**

Hoover's handbook of world business, 397, **446**

Hoover's MasterList of U.S. companies, **447**

Hoover's Online, 397

Horkheimer, Foley A., **527**

Horn, Maurice, **1089**

Hornblower, Simon, **1618**

Hortus third, **785**

Household safety sourcebook, **968**

Household spending, **427**

How not to say what you mean, **638**

How to be a perfect stranger, **115**

How to break an egg, **927**

How to clean and care for practically anything, **969**

How to design and build your ideal woodshop, **1280**

How to organize just about everything, **970**

How to plan, contract, and build your own home, **915**

How to run a traditional Jewish household, **155**

How to use the library, **7**

Howard, Angela, **1624**

Howarth, Glennys, **293**

Howatson, Margaret, **1568**

Huang, Guiyou, **1439**, **1440**

Hubbard, Jan, **1338**

Hubin, Allen J., **1495**

Hudgeons, Marc, **1291**

Hudgeons, Thomas E., **1290**

Hudson, Karen E., **943**

Hughes, Geoffrey I., **637**

Human body, **854**

Human body on file, **852**

Hurt, C. D., **686**

Husband, Janet, **1501**

Husband, Jonathan F., **1501**

Husfloen, Kyle, **1284**

Hussain, S. B., **403**

Hussar, William J., **587**

Hutchinson, S., **749**

Hutera, Donald, **1138**

Hyman, Paula E., **157**

I

ICON Group, 396

IHS/Global, **754**

Illes, Judika, **239**

Illingworth, Valerie, **709**

Illustrated dictionary of architecture, **1046**

An illustrated dictionary of ceramics, **1105**

Illustrated dictionary of practical pottery, **1106**

The illustrated encyclopedia of costume and fashion, **1099**

The illustrated golf rules dictionary, **1366**

The illustrated history of antiques, **1107**

The illustrator in America, 1860–2000, **1110**

Impara, James C., **222**

In an influential fashion, **1100**

in-cites, 691

Index to children's plays in collections, **1184**

Index to fairy tales, **1468**

Index to fairy tales, myths, and legends, **1468**

An index to one-act plays, for stage, radio and television, **1185**

Index to Organism Names, 691

Index to plays, **1186**

Index to plays in periodicals, **1187**

The Indiana companion to traditional Chinese literature, **1575**

Industry research using the Economic Census, **390**

Information sources in science and technology, **686**

Information sources in the social sciences, **256**

Informed decisions, **859**

InfoTrac, 35

Ingold, Cindy, **372**

Injury facts, **839**

Inman, Roger, **1177**

Instituto geografico de Agostini, **1637**

Interagency Council on Statistical Policy, **260**

International Association of Universities, **565**

International Bible commentary, **92**

The international book of days, **902**

International business etiquette: Asia and the Pacific Rim, **941**

International business etiquette: Europe, **941**

International business etiquette: Latin America, **941**

International dictionary of ballet, **1133**

International dictionary of films and filmmakers, **1148**

International dictionary of films and filmmakers, vol. 1: Films, **1148**

International dictionary of films and filmmakers, vol. 2: Directors, **1148**

International dictionary of films and filmmakers, vol. 3: Actors and actresses, **1148**

International dictionary of films and filmmakers, vol. 4: Writers and production artists, **1148**

International dictionary of medicine and biology, **820**

International dictionary of modern dance, **1134**

International directory of little magazines and small presses, **51**

International encyclopedia of dance, **1135**

International encyclopedia of human rights, **485**

International encyclopedia of linguistics, **598**

International encyclopedia of marriage and family, **329**

International encyclopedia of the social and behavioral sciences, **252**

International encyclopedia of the social sciences, **252**

International encyclopedia of the social sciences: Biographical supplement, **252**

International encyclopedia of the social sciences: Social science quotations, **252**

International encyclopedia of the stock market, **433**

International encyclopedia of women and sports, **1314**

The international handbook of sociology, **272**

International handbook of universities, **565**

International motion picture almanac, **1162**

The international standard Bible encyclopedia, **100**

International television and video almanac, **1180**

The Internet, **741**

The Internet for cell and molecular biologists, **763**

Internet Mental Health, **230**

Internet Movie Database, **1142**

Internet Public Library Social Sciences Subject Collection, **262**

Internet Shakespeare Editions, **1552**

Inter-play, **1481**

Introduction to reference work, **8**

Introduction to the world's major religions, **116**

Ireland, Norma O., **1468**

Irish women writers, **1456**

Irons-Georges, Tracy, **1429**, 1448, **1449**

Isaacs, Alan, **806**

Isaak, Mark, **767**

Isralowitz, Richard, **282**

Issues and controversies on file, **31**

Italy profiled, **1672**

Iverson, Cheryl, **647**

J

Jackson, Albert, **981**

Jackson, Cynthia L., **572**

Jackson, Michael, **889**, **896**

Jacob, Merle L., **1502**

Jacobs, E. E., **416**

Jacobs, Pamela F., **764**

Jacques-Edouard Berger Foundation: World art treasures, **1032**

Jaine, Tom, **958**

James, Bill, **1332**

Janik, Del Ivan, **1459**

Janik, Vicki, **1459**

Janson, Anthony, **1074**

Jarman, Beatriz Galimberti, **685**

Jay, Antony, **487**

Jenkins, Fred W., **1565**

The Jewish holidays, **156**

Jewish Publication Society, **158**, 159

The Jewish study Bible, **159**

Jewish women in America, **157**

Jewitt, Jeff, **1278**, **1282**
Jews in American politics, **508**
Jimenez, Phil, **1087**
Joachim, David, **923**
Joel Whitburn's top country songs, 1944–2005, Billboard, **1235**
Johanson, Cynthia J., **1066**
The Johns Hopkins guide to literary theory and criticism, **1408**
Johns Hopkins symptoms and remedies, **840**
Johnson, Allan G., **267**
Johnson, Keith A., **235**
Johnson, Robert V., **879**
Johnson, Torrence, **708**
Johnston, Larry, **960**, **974**
Johnston, Sarah L., **1493**
Johnston, William M., **85**
Johnstone, Michael, 247, **247**
Jones, Constance, **119**
Jones, Henry Stuart, **670**
Jones, Jeffery A, **1309**
Jones, Lindsay, **88**
Jones, Timothy K., **134**
Jones, Toni Stokes, **572**
Jordan, Michael, **172**, **1338**
Jose, Colin, **1389**
Joshi, S. T., **1487**
Joy of cooking, **928**
The JPS guide to Jewish traditions, **158**
JPS Hebrew-English Tanakh, **159**
Judaica reference sources, **160**
Judd, Patricia A., **957**
Julia's kitchen wisdom, **929**
Junior book of authors, **1469**
Just, Tim, **1350**

K

Kahane, Ahuvia, **674**
Kahn, Ada P., **203**
Kahn, Cynthia M., **992**
Kale, Tessa, **1503**
Kaliski, B. S., **431**
Kane, Joseph Nathan, **1623**, **1664**, **1670**
Kanellos, Nicolás, **318**, **321**, **1447**
Kapel, David E., **536**
Kaplan, Justin, **1420**
Kaplan, Steven M., **212**, **757**
Karp, Rashelle S., **388**, **1190**
Karre, Andrew, **977**
Kartographisches Institut Bertelsmann, **1639**

Kasper, Dennis L., **815**
Kasser, Barbara, **908**
Kastan, David Scott, **1548**
Kastenbaum, Robert, **297**
Katz, Ephraim, **1145**
Katz, Solomon H., **954**
Katz, William A., **8**, **10**, 74
Katzner, Kenneth, **681**
Kavenik, Frances M., **1624**
Kayal, Alawi D., **144**
Kazdin, Alan E., **187**, **206**
Keck, Leander E., **93**
Keller, Dean H., **1187**
Keller, Harald, **758**
Keller, Michael A., **1204**
Kelley, A. M., 453
Kelley, J. N. D., **139**
Kellman, Steven G., **1402**
Kellogg, Ann T., **1100**
Kemp, Thomas Jay, **354**
Ken Schultz's fishing encyclopedia, **1353**
Kenkyusha's new English-Japanese dictionary, **678**
Kenkyusha's new Japanese-English dictionary, **678**
Kennedy, Joyce Bourne, **1211**
Kennedy, Michael, **1211**
Kent, Michael, **823**
Kerchelich, Karen, **609**
Kernfeld, Barry Dean, 1215, **1223**
Kester-Shelton, Pamela, **1455**
Khan, Karim, **1351**
Kieft, Robert, **6**
Kim, Hyung-chan, **315**
Kimmel, Michael S., 338, **340**
King, Anita, **1421**
King, C. Richard, **1315**
King, Robert C., **769**
Kingsbury, Paul, **1237**
Kingsbury, Stewart A., **1417**
Kinser, Kevin, **543**
Kipfer, Barbara Ann, **636**, **646**
Kiple, Kenneth F., **953**
Kirk, Connie Ann, **1465**
Kister, Kenneth F., **599**
Kister's best dictionaries for adults and young people, **599**
Kiyosi, Ito, **800**
Klatell, Jack, **843**
Klebba, Caryn E., **591**
Kline, Victoria, **1509**
Kloesel, Christian J., **1546**

Kloetzel, James E., **1296**
Knight, Denise D., **1443**
Knitter's handbook, **1259**
Knowles, Elizabeth, 61, **1424, 1425**
Koegler, Horst, **1132**
Kohn, George Childs, **1610**
Koocher, Gerald P., **219**
Kort, Carol, **1076**
Kosek, Jane Kelly, **705**
Kovalchick, Ann, **538**
Kovel, Terry, **1285**
Kovels' antiques and collectibles price list, **1285**
Kowaleski-Wallace, Elizabeth, **1453**
Kramarae, Cheris, **368**
Kramer, Jack J., **222**
Kranz, R., **392**
Krapp, Kristine M., **861**
Krasilovsky, M. William, **1219**
Krause, Chester, **1290, 1291**
Kreiswirth, Martin, **1408**
Krikos, Linda A, **372**
Krismann, C. H., **402**
Kron, John, **1351**
Kuhn, Laura Diane, 1206, **1208, 1213, 1220**
Kulik, Peter H., **700**
Kuper, Adam, **255**
Kuper, Jessica, **255**
Kurian, George T., **507**
Kushner, Harvey W., **289**
Kutler, Stanley I., **1609**

L

Lagowski, J. J., **713**
LaGuardia, Cheryl, **10,** 74
Landau, Sidney I., **820**
Lands and peoples, 43
Landsberg, Brian K., **509**
Lane, Carole A., **1692**
Lane, Edward William, **658**
Lane-Poole, Stanley, **658**
Lang, Jovian P., **12**
Lange, Norbert Adolph, **719**
Langenscheidt's new Muret-Sanders encyclopedic dictionary of the English and German languages, **668**
Lange's handbook of chemistry, **719**
The language of sailing, **1387**
Lanier, Pamela, **1675**
Larkin, Colin, **1246**
Larousse encyclopedia of wine, **890**

Larousse gastronomique, **930**
Last lines, **1509**
Latham, Alison, **1216,** 1217, **1217, 1232**
Latin America, **1669**
Latin America profiled, **1672**
Latin American mystery writers, **1590**
Latin American science fiction writers, **1591**
Latin American writers—Supplement I, **1592**
Latino and Latina writers, **1448**
Lauer, Josh, **737**
Laughlin, Kay, **1242**
Laurence, Vincent, **914**
Laver, James, **1094**
Law of schools, students, and teachers in a nutshell, 577
Law School Admission Council, **567**
Lawson, Edward H., **481**
Lawson, Tony, **268**
Lawther, Gail, **1267**
Layton, Robert, 1225, **1226**
Leaman, Oliver, **293**
Lederman, Ellen, **878**
Ledésert, Margaret, **664**
Ledésert, R. P. L., **664**
Lee, Steven W., **207**
Leeming, David, **174**
Legal information institute, **470**
Legal research in a nutshell, **471**
Lehman, Jeffrey, **301,** 306
Leibo, Steven A., **1669**
Leikin, Jerrold B., **833**
Leininger, Phillip, **1540**
Lemke, Robert F., **1291**
Lemmer, Thomas G., **964**
Lenderman, Lois, **632**
Lenman, Robin, **1116**
Leo, John R., **1508**
Leonard Maltin's movie guide, **1160**
Lerner, Brenda Wilmoth, **181**
Lerner, K. Lee, **181**
Lessem, Don, **788**
Lester, Katherine, **1090**
Levi, Anthony, **1578**
Levin, Simon A., **770**
Levinson, David, **201, 287, 360, 1302**
Levinson, David L., **572**
Lewis, Audrey, **9**
Lewis, James R., **163, 196**
Lewis, Richard J. Sr., **721**
Lewis, Samella S., **1077**

Lewis-Beck, Michael S., **253**
LexisNexis, 313, **448**
LexisNexis Academic, **36**
LexisNexis corporate affiliations, **448**
Liangbi, Wang, **661**
Liao, Tim Futing, **253**
The librarian's copyright companion, **70**
Librarians' Internet Index, **64**
Library journal, **18**, 24
Library of Congress portal application issues group, **74**
Liddell, Henry George, **670**
Lide, David R., **718, 805**
Lieber, David L., **153**
Lie-Nielsen, Thomas, **1278, 1282**
Life and death in the United States, **296**
Light, Jonathan Fraser, **1327**
Likoff, L., **466**
Lima, Carolyn W., **1461**
Lima, John A., **1461**
Lindberg, Christine A., **644**
Lindner, Eileen W., **135**
Lineker, Gary, **1390**
Linffors, Bernth, **1574**
Linguistics, **593**
Linn's world stamp almanac, **1293**
Lipsky, Martin S., **833**
Litchfield, Michael W., **965**
The literary filmography, **1149**
Literary research guide, **1396**
Literature criticism from 1400 to 1800, **1414**
The literature of chemistry, **712**
Litin, Scott C, **841**
Litterer, David, **1389**
Litz, A. Walton, **1458**
The lives and times of the great composers, **1234**
Livingston, Alan, **1111**
Livingston, Isabella, **1111**
Livingstone, E. A., **130**
Lluch, Alex, **1682**
Lluch, Elizabeth, **1682**
Lock, Stephen, **824**
Lockhart, Darrell B., **1590, 1591**
Loeb, Catherine, **372**
Logasa, Hannah, **1185**
Loizou, A., **433**
Lomeli, Francisco A., **1446**
Long, Mike, **229**
Long, Phillip W., **230**
Longe, Jacqueline L., **812, 819, 858, 865**

Longman dictionary of geography, **1662**
Lord, Charles R., **752**
Lord, John, **699**
Lorimer, Lawrence T., **1325**
Luce, T. James, **1561**
Lucie-Smith, Edward, **1067**
Lushington, Nolan, **7**
Lusk, Jon, **1251**

M
Macey, J. David, **1437**
MacKay, James, **1298**
Mackrell, Judith, **1136**
The Macmillan book of proverbs, maxims and famous phrases, **1418**
Macmillan dictionary of political quotations, **486**
Macmillan encyclopedia of death and dying, **297**
Macmillan encyclopedia of energy, **753**
Macmillan encyclopedia of physics, **808**
Macmillan Library Reference USA, **258**
Macquarrie, John, **182**
Madame Audrey's guide to mostly cheap but good reference books for small and rural libraries, **9**
Madden, W. C., **1320, 1335**
Maddex, Robert L., **485**
Maddox, Taddy, **531**
Magalini, Sabina C., **836**
Magalini, Sergio I., **836**
Magazines for libraries, **10**, 74
Magida, Arthur J., **115**
Magill, Frank N., **79, 1403, 1409, 1429, 1448, 1449, 1457**
Magill's cinema annual, **1150**
Magill's encyclopedia of science: Plant life, **781**
Magill's literary annual, **1402**
Maginnis, Tara, **1030**
Maguire, Mike, **290**
Maisel, Louis Sandy, **508**
Major acts of Congress, **509**
Major League Baseball official rules, **1331**
Making life more livable, **878**
Malinowski, Sharon, **324, 1445**
Malinowsky, H. Robert, **687**
Mallalieu, Huon, **1107**
Mallion, Bill, **1376**
Malone, John Williams, **1352**
Malone, Maggie, **1269**
Malone, Maura, **316**
Maloney, David J., **1108**

Maloney's antiques and collectibles resource directory, **1108**

Maltin, Leonard, **1160**

Malyon, John, **1024**

Managing for results, **71**

Mancini, Julie R., **993**

Mandel, Howard, **1222**

Mann, Elise, **1255**

Mann, Thomas, **11**

Manser, Martin H., **617, 661**

Mansion, J. E., **664**

A manual for writers of term papers, theses, and dissertations, **653**

Manuila, Alexandre, **820**

Mappy Road Guide, **1642**

MapQuest, **1643**

Maps on file, **1644**

March, Ivan, **1225, 1226**

Marchesani, Robert F., **574**

Marcus, Jeff, **1336**

Margen, Sheldon, **874**

Margolis, Simeon, **840**

Marill, Alvin H., **1173**

Marinelli, Janet, **783**

Markoe, Arnie, **1316**

Marlow-Ferguson, Rebecca, **544**

Marquis Who's Who on the Web, **1690**

Marriage customs of the world, **330**

Marsh, Earle, **1170**

Marshall, Gordon, **269**

Marthaler, Berard, **127**

Martial arts of the world, **1373**

Martin, Elizabeth, **768**

Martin, Fenton S., **472**

Martin, Judith, **942**

Martin, Mick, **1158**

Martin, Richard C., **143**

Martin Greenwald Associates, **1632**

Martinez, Joseph G., **1507**

Martinez, Julio A., **1446**

Martinez, Nancy C., **1507**

The Marvel encyclopedia, **1088**

Mason, Francis, **1139**

Massis, Bruce E., **72**

Masterpieces of women's literature, **1457**

Masterpieces of world philosophy, **79**

Masterplots, **1403**

Materials and techniques in the decorative arts, **1109**

Math forum, **802**

Mathison, Sandra, **199**

MathSciNet, **798**

Matisic, Kristina, **907**

Matlins, Stuart M., **115**

Matt, Daniel C., **151**

Matthews, Dawn D., **373, 849, 968**

Maunder, Andrew, **1521**

Mautone, Nick, **895**

May, Herbert G., **91**

Mayhew, Susan, **1658**

Mayne, Richard, **1387**

Mayo, Diane, **71**

Mayo Clinic book of pregnancy and baby's first year, **879**

Mayo Clinic family health book, **841**

Mazor, Dave, **1164**

McArthur, Tom, **601**

McCabe, Timothy Lee, **772**

McCall, Douglas L., **1144**

McCann, Michael, **1253**

McClendon, Jo, **526**

McColl, R. W., **1659**

McConnachie, James, **1251**

McConnell, Charles, **979**

McDarrah, Fred W., **1117**

McDarrah, Gloria S., **1117**

McDonough, J., **420**

McFadden, Christine, **922**

McFadden, Lucy-Ann, **708**

McFadden, Margaret, **371**

McGrath, Alister E., **123**

McGraw-Hill concise encyclopedia of chemistry, **716**

McGraw-Hill concise encyclopedia of science and technology, **692**

McGraw-Hill dictionary of scientific and technical terms, **697**

McGraw-Hill encyclopedia of science and technology, **692**

McHugh, Michael P., **124**

McKean, Erin, **607**

McLean, Iain, **480**

McMillan, Alistair, **480**

McMurray, Emily J., **705**

McNeil, W. K., **1236**

McNicoll, Geoffrey, **357**

McVicar, Jekka, **937**

Mead, Frank Spencer, **112**

Means illustrated construction dictionary, **916**

Medical school admission requirements (MSAR), **566**

Medicine, health, and bioethics, **181**

Mehrotra, Arvind Krishna, **1581**

Mehus-Roe, Kristin, **1005**

Meisami, Julie S., **1543**

Mellone, Michael A., **1297**

Melloni's illustrated medical dictionary, **821**

Melton, J. Gordon, **108, 109, 125**

Meltzer, Annabelle H., **1557**

Members of Congress, **472**

Men and masculinities, 338, **340**

The mental health diagnostic desk reference, **216**

Mental Help Net, **231**

Mental measurements yearbook, 183, **184, 222**

Mercatante, Anthony S., **173**

Mercer dictionary of the Bible, **101**

The Merck index, **720**

The Merck manual of diagnosis and therapy, **842**

The Merck manual of health and aging, **842**

Merck manual of medical information, **842**

The Merck veterinary manual, **992**

Mergent's handbook of common stocks, **434**

Merriam-Webster's biographical dictionary, **1691**

Merriam-Webster's dictionary of synonyms, **643**

Merriam-Webster's geographical dictionary, **1663**

Merrick, Janna C., **275**

Merton, Robert King, **252**

Meserole, Harrison T., **1398**

Metaphors dictionary, **634**

Metraux, Alfred, **170**

Metzger, Bruce M., **104**

Metzger, Phil, **1052**

Mexico, **1617**

Micarelli, Charles, **1294**

The Micarelli identification guide to U.S. stamps, **1294**

Michael, Thomas, **1290**

Michie, Jonathan, **259**

The Middle East and South Asia, **1669**

Middle grades education, **572**

Middle school teachers guide to free curriculum materials, **527**

Mieder, Wolfgang, **1417**

Miler, Eugene, **556**

Milgate, Murray, **453**

Millar, James R., **1614**

The millennials: Americans born 1977 to 1994, **424**

Miller, J. Mitchell, **288**

Miller, James, **1625**

Miller, Michael, **904**

Miller, Tice L., **1194**

The million word crossword dictionary, **612**

Mills, Watson E., **101**

Milne, George W. A., **782**

Min, Pyong Gap, **299**

Minderovic, Zoran, **804**

Miner, Earl, **1587**

Miner, Margaret, **1423**

Mishler, Clifford, **1290**

Miskelly, Matthew, **906**

Miss Manners' guide to excruciatingly correct behavior, **942**

Mr. Boston official bartender's and party guide, **891**

Mitcham, Carl, **695**

Mitchell, Charity, **1530**

Mitchell, David F., **221**

Mitchell, James V. Jr., **222**

Mitchell, S., **421**

Mjagkij, Nina, **52**

MLA handbook for writers of research papers, **654**

MLA international bibliography of books and articles on modern language and literature, **1398**

Mobil travel guides, **1679**

Mochedlover, Helene, **1188**

Modern American women writers, **1458**

Modern British women writers, **1459**

Modern Irish writers, **1583**

Modern South Asian literature in English, **1594**

Mokyr, J., **454**

Molin, Paulette Fairbanks, **111**

Monger, George, **330**

Monro, Isabel S., **1525**

Moore, Deborah Dash, **157**

Moore, John L., **504**

Moore, Stephen, **867**

More book lust, **2**

More junior authors, **1469**

Morgan, Kathleen O'Leary, **585**

Morgan, Rodney, **290**

Morgan, Scott, **585**

Morin, Alexander J., **1225**

Mormonism for dummies, **126**

Morrell, Robert E., **1587**

Morris, Desmond, **1002**

Morrison, James, 214

Morton, Brian, **1221**

Mosby's dictionary of medicine, nursing and health professions, **822**

Moss, R. W., **391**

Mossman, Jennifer, 342, **367**

Mostow, Joshua S., **1576**

Mother of all art and art history links page, **1033**
The motion picture guide, 1927–1984, **1151**
The motion picture guide annual, **1151**
The Mount Sinai Medical Center family health guide to dental health, **843**
Movies made for television, 1964–2004, **1173**
Müller, Thomas Christian, **511**
The multicultural dictionary of proverbs, **1419**
Munson, Carlton E., **216**
Munson, Robert S., **1254**
Murdin, Paul, **710**
Muret, Eduard, **668**
Murphy, Bruce, **1399**
Murphy, Larry G., **108**
Murphy, Timothy F., **334**
Murray, Linda, **1057**
Murray, Michael, **864**
Murray, Peter, **1057**
Murray, Tim, **382, 383**
Museum of American folk art encyclopedia of twentieth-century American folk art and artists, **1061**
The Museum of Broadcast Communications, **1174**
The music index, **1207**
Music reference and research materials, **1204**
Music since 1900, **1213**
Musical America, **1122**
Musson, James, **1602**
Mustazza, Leonard, **1149**
Muth, Annemarie, **292**
Myers, Jay, **1602**
Myers, Tamara, **822**
Mystery and suspense writers, **1496**

N

NADA official used car guide, **761**
Nagel, Carol DeKane, **321**
Nagel, Rob, **321**
Nagyszalanczy, Sandor, **1015, 1283**
Naked in cyberspace, **1692**
Nalen, James, **266**
Narins, Brigham, **733**
NASCAR encyclopedia, **1318**
Nash, Gary B., **1629**
Nash, Jay Robert, **1151**
Nathan, Lauren, **835**
National anthems of the world, **1214**
The National Arboretum book of outstanding garden plants, **786**

National atlas of the United States of America, **1650**
National Automobile Dealers Association, **761**
National Book Award, 1411
National Center for Education Statistics, **583, 584**
National Center for Health Statistics, **232**
National directory of children, youth and families services, **376**
National directory of chiropractic, **830**
National Education Association of the United States, **578**
National electrical code, **756**
National Fire Protection Association, **756**
National Geographic almanac of American history, **1625**
National Geographic atlas of the world, **1645**
National Geographic encyclopedia of space, **706**
National Geographic historical atlas of the United States, **1633**
National Hockey League, **1371**
National Hockey League rule book, **1370**
National Information Center for Educational Media, **528**
National Institute of Mental Health, **233**
National Organization for Rare Disorders, **845**
National profile of community colleges, **586**
National Reference Center for Bioethics Literature, **177**
National Register, **133**
National Safety Council, Statistics Department, **839**
National Technical Information Service, **690**
National trade and professional associations of the United States, **412, 413**
A Native American encyclopedia, **322**
Native Americans in sports, **1315**
Natividad, Irene, **316**
Nauman, Ann Keith, **590**
Naxos Music Library, **1228**
Naylor, Colin, **1113**
NBC handbook of pronunciation, **625**
NCAA playing rules, **1384**
NEA handbook, **578**
Nebula Awards, 1411
The needlepoint book, **1265**
Nehmer, Kathleen Suttles, **527**
Nelson, Emmanuel S., **1434, 1441, 1442, 1538**
Nelson, Jeffrey O., **476**
Nelson, Roxanne, **988**

Nelson, Sandra S., **71**

Nemeh, Katherine H., **313**

Nemeroff, Charles B., **193, 194**

Ness, Bryan D., **781**

Netter, Frank H., **852**

Neuborne, Ellen, **989**

New Age encyclopedia, **166**

The new American Heart Association cookbook,
  931

The new basic black, **943**

The new best recipe, **932**

The new Bill James historical baseball abstract,
  1332

The new biographical dictionary of film, **1166**

New book of knowledge online, 43

The new book of popular science, 43

New Catholic encyclopedia, **127**

The new complete book of herbs, spices, and
  condiments, **933**

New complete dog training manual, **1004**

New complete guide to sewing, **1274**

New complete sailing manual, **1388**

New dictionary of the history of ideas, **80**

The new Encyclopaedia Britannica, **40**

The new encyclopedia of fishing, **1354**

The new encyclopedia of golf, **1367**

The new encyclopedia of the cat, **999**

The new encyclopedia of the horse, **1011**

The new encyclopedia of the occult, **245**

The new encyclopedia of unbelief, **81**

The new Grove dictionary of jazz, 1215, **1223**

The new Grove dictionary of music and musicians,
  1215, 1223

The new Grove dictionary of opera, 1215, 1223,
  1230

The new Harvard guide to women's health, **884**

New historical dictionary of the American film
  industry, **1152**

New house/more house, **917**

The new illustrated encyclopedia of billiards, **1347**

New international dictionary of Pentecostal and
  charismatic movements, **128**

New interpreter's Bible, **93**

The new interpreter's dictionary of the Bible, **102**

The new Jerome biblical commentary, **94**

The new men's studies, **341**

New Oxford American dictionary, **607**

The new Oxford companion to literature in French,
  1579

The new Palgrave, **453**

The new Partridge dictionary of slang and
  unconventional English, **639**

The new Penguin opera guide, **1231**

New Princeton encyclopedia of poetry and poetics,
  1510

New religions, **167**

New Strategist, **278**, 339, **339**, 364, **364, 423,
  424, 425, 427**

New Strong's concise concordance of the Bible, 95

New Strong's exhaustive concordance of the Bible,
  95

New Testament abstracts, **96**

New Westminster dictionary of liturgy and worship,
  129

New York Public Library, **1034**

The New York Times film reviews, **1153**

The New York Times theater reviews, **1197**

The Newbery and Caldecott awards, **1478**

Newbery and Caldecott medalists and honor book
  winners, **1479**

Newby, Gordon, **142**

Newcomb, Horace, **1172**

Newman, Harold, **1105**

Newman, Peter K., **453**

Newman, Stanley, **612**

Newnham, Jeffrey, **488**

Newton, Keith, **1504**

Newton, Michael, **794**

NFL rules digest, **1356**

NICEM film and video finder online, **528**

Nicholls, Peter, **1515**

Nicknames and sobriquets of U.S. cities, states, and
  counties, **1664**

Niemi, Richard G., **516**

Nienhauser, William H. Jr., **1575**

Night sky atlas, **711**

Nineteenth-century British women writers, **1460**

Nineteenth-century literature criticism, **1415**

Ninth book of junior authors and illustrators, **1469**

Nobel Prize Internet Archive, 1411

Noonan, Raymond J., **343**

Nooy, Winifred Ver, **1185**

Norcross, John C., **219**

Nordic, Central and Southeastern Europe, **1669**

Norman, Jill, **926**

Norris, Frederick W., **124**

North American women artists of the twentieth
  century, **1085**

Northrup, Cynthia Clark, **406, 451**

Norton, Mary Beth, **1597**

The Norton anthology of children's literature, **1470**

Notable African American writers, **1438**

Notable American philanthropists, **350**

Notable last facts, **1626**

Notable Latino writers, **1449**

Notable mathematicians, **804**

Notable playwrights, **1482**

Notable twentieth-century scientists, **705**

Noyer, Paul Du, **1209**

NTC's dictionary of American slang and colloquial expressions, **640**

NTC's Hebrew and English dictionary, **673**

NTIS, **690**

La nueva enciclopedia cumbre, 43

Nunn, Eleanor F., **572**

Nunn, Joan, **1097**

Nussbaum, David, **929**

NYPL Digital, **1034**

O

Oakes, Elizabeth H., **1533**

Oboler, Suzanne, **320**

O'Brien, Nancy P., **524, 542**

O'Brien, Patrick Karl, **1646**

Occupational outlook handbook, **467**

Oceans, **749**

O'Connell, Erika Kruse, **1118**

O'Connor, Ann, **500**, 504

O'Connor, Maureen, **1571**

Odagiri, Hiroko, **1587**

Odean, Kathleen, **4, 5**

Odelberg, Wilhelm, **1695**

Oerke, Bess Viola, **1090**

The official ABMS directory of board certified medical specialists, **831**

The official blackbook price guide of U.S. postage stamps, **1295**

The official blackbook price guide to U.S. coins, **1290**

The official blackbook price guide to U.S. paper money, **1291**

Official Catholic directory, **133**

Official guide and record book, **1371**

Official guide to ABA-approved law schools, **567**

Official National Football League record and fact book, **1357**

The official NBA encyclopedia, **1338**

Official NBA guide, **1339**

Official rules of the National Basketball Association, **1340**

Official rules of the NCAA (basketball), **1341**

Official rules of the Women's National Basketball Association, **1342**

Official WNBA guide and register, **1343**

Ogden, Tom, **1200**

Oglesby, Carole A, **1313**

O'Gorman, Jack, **12**

Ohles, John F., **580, 589**

Ohles, Shirley M., **580**

O'Keefe, Donna, **1293**

Old Testament abstracts, **97**

Older Americans, **278**

Oldershaw, Cally, **747**

Olendorf, Donna, **777**

Oliver, John E., **751**

Olson, Kent C., **471**

On the air, **1175**

One hundred one stories of the great ballets, **1139**

100 top picks for homeschool curriculum, **529**

1001 computer words you need to know, **732**

O'Neil, Maryadele J., **720**

O'Neil, Patrick M., **1432**

Onians, John, **1072**

Onions, Charles T., **616, 1556**

Opie, Iona Archibald, **237, 1472**

Opie, Peter, **1472**

Orbitz, 1676

Orey, Michael, **526**

The organic cook's bible, **934**

Organizing black America, **52**

The original dog bible, **1005**

Ornelas, Kriemhild Coneè, **953**

Orr, Tamra, **318**

Orser, Charles E., **384**

O'Shea, Mark, **1014**

Osmólska, Halszka, **789**

Ost, Jason, **333**

Ostrom, Hans, **1437**

Otfinoski, Steven, **1124**

Ottemiller's index to plays in collections, **1188**

Our bodies, ourselves: A new edition for a new era, **885**

Our bodies, ourselves: Menopause, **886**

Overstreet, William, **511**

Oxford American writer's thesaurus, **644**

Oxford atlas of world history, **1646**

Oxford Bible atlas, **91**

The Oxford book of health foods, **957**

Oxford Chinese dictionary: English-Chinese, Chinese-English = [Ying Han, Han Ying], **661**

Oxford classical dictionary, **1618**
Oxford Companion series, 61
Oxford companion to American law, **510**
The Oxford companion to American literature, **1540**
Oxford companion to American military history, **1619**
The Oxford companion to American theatre, **1198**
The Oxford companion to archaeology, **387**
Oxford companion to Australian history, 1621
Oxford companion to British history, **1620**
The Oxford companion to Canadian literature, **1572**
The Oxford companion to chess, **1349**
The Oxford companion to children's literature, **1471**
The Oxford companion to classical literature, **1568**
The Oxford companion to English literature, **1547**
The Oxford companion to food, **958**
The Oxford companion to German literature, **1580**
Oxford companion to Irish history, 1621
The Oxford companion to Irish literature, **1584**
The Oxford companion to Italian literature, **1586**
The Oxford companion to music, **1216**, 1217
Oxford companion to Scottish history, 1621
Oxford companion to the Bible, **104**
Oxford companion to the English language, **601**
The Oxford companion to the history of modern science, **739**
The Oxford companion to the mind, **217**
The Oxford companion to the photograph, **1116**
Oxford companion to United States history, **1621**
The Oxford companion to Western art, **1062**
The Oxford companion to wine, **892**
Oxford companion to world mythology, **174**
The Oxford dictionary of American quotations, **1423**
The Oxford dictionary of art, **1063**
Oxford dictionary of chemistry, **715**
Oxford dictionary of dance, **1136**
Oxford dictionary of English etymology, **616**
The Oxford dictionary of foreign words and phrases, **618**
The Oxford dictionary of modern Greek: Greek-English, English-Greek, **671**
Oxford dictionary of modern quotations, **1424**
Oxford dictionary of music, 1211
The Oxford dictionary of musical terms, **1217**
The Oxford dictionary of musical works, **1232**
Oxford dictionary of national biography, **1693**
The Oxford dictionary of nursery rhymes, **1472**

The Oxford dictionary of plays, **1483**
Oxford dictionary of political quotations, **487**
Oxford dictionary of popes, **139**
Oxford dictionary of quotations, 61, **1425**
Oxford dictionary of saints, **140**
Oxford dictionary of scientific quotations, **698**
The Oxford dictionary of sports science and medicine, **823**
Oxford dictionary of the Christian Church, **130**
Oxford dictionary of the Jewish religion, **161**
Oxford dictionary of world religions, **89**
Oxford dictionary of zoology, **796**
Oxford Digital Reference Shelf, 61
The Oxford encyclopedia of British literature, **1548**
The Oxford encyclopedia of children's literature, **1473**
The Oxford encyclopedia of economic history, **454**
The Oxford encyclopedia of food and drink in America, **959**
The Oxford encyclopedia of Latinos and Latinas in the United States, **320**
Oxford English dictionary, **602**
Oxford English dictionary: Additions series, **602**
Oxford English dictionary online, **603**
The Oxford English-Hebrew dictionary, **674**
The Oxford guide to library research, **11**
Oxford handbook of criminology, **290**
The Oxford history of board games, **1362**
Oxford history of Christian worship, **131**
The Oxford illustrated companion to medicine, **824**
Oxford Latin dictionary, **680**
Oxford Paravia il dizionario inglese-italiano, italiano-inglese, **677**
Oxford Reference Online, **61**, 62, 1216
Oxford rhyming dictionary, **628**
The Oxford Russian dictionary, **682**
The Oxford Spanish dictionary: Spanish-English/English-Spanish, **685**
The Oxford style manual, **655**
Oxford-Duden German dictionary: German-English, English-German, **669**
The Oxford-Hachette French dictionary: French-English, English-French, **665**

P

Paciorek, Michael J, **1309**
Padlan, Kevin, **791**
Page, Martyn, **854**
Page, Tim, **893**
Pagel, Mark D., **773**

Palgrave's dictionary of political economy, 453
Palmer, Helen H., **1546**
Palmer, Louis J. Jr., **274, 286**
Palmer, Peter, **1330**
Pareles, John, **1249**
Parenthood in America, **987**
A parent's guide to first aid, **988**
Parks directory of the United States, **1680**
Parlett, David Sidney, **1348, 1362**
Parmar, Priya, **374**
Parrott, Cecil, **175**
Partnow, Elaine T., **1426**
Partridge, Christopher, **167**
Partridge, Eric, **639**
Party punches, **893**
Past worlds: HarperCollins atlas of archaeology,
  377
Pasztor, Suzanne B., **1617**
Patterson, Michael, **1483**
Paul, Lissa, **1470**
Paxton, John, **505**
PDR guide to terrorism response, **810**
Peacock, John, **1091, 1101, 1102**
Pearce, L. M., **455**
Pearl, Nancy, **2**
Pederson, Jay P., **1518**
Pelle, Kimberly D, **1375**
Pendergast, Sara, **1081, 1082, 1148, 1607**
Pendergast, Tom, **1081, 1148, 1607**
The Penguin concise dictionary of art history, **1064**
The Penguin concise guide to opera, **1231**
*The Penguin dictionary of architecture and
  landscape architecture,* **1047**
Penguin dictionary of classical mythology, **175**
The Penguin dictionary of geography, **1665**
Penguin dictionary of international relations, **488**
The Penguin dictionary of psychology, **210**
The Penguin guide to compact discs and DVDs,
  1225, **1226**
The Penguin guide to jazz recordings, **1221**
Pennington, Jean A. Thompson, **952**
Penston, Margaret, **710**
PEP archive, 183, **185**
The perfect smile, **844**
The performing arts, **1119**
Periodical Abstracts, 35
Perkins, Agnes R., **1466**
Perkins, Barbara, **1539**
Perkins, George, **1539**
Perrault, Anna M., **1600**

Pesticides, **782**
Peters, Pam, **621**
Peterson, Bernard L. Jr., **1436**
Peterson, Gary W., **328**
Peterson, Marion L., **376**
*Peterson's colleges for students with learning
  disabilities or ADD,* **568**
Peterson's 440 colleges for top students, **568**
Peterson's four-year colleges, **568**
Peterson's graduate and professional programs, **568**
Peterson's graduate schools in the U.S., **568**
Peterson's nursing programs, **568**
Peterson's private secondary schools, **551**
Peterson's short term study abroad, **551**
Peterson's smart choices, **568**
Peterson's study abroad, **551**
Peterson's two-year colleges, **568**
Peterson's vocational and technical schools—east,
  568
Peterson's vocational and technical schools—west,
  568
Pevsner, Nikolaus, **1047**
Pfister, Gertrud, **1314**
*The Phaidon atlas of contemporary world
  architecture,* **1048**
*The Phaidon atlas of contemporary world
  architecture: Travel edition,* **1049**
Philanthropy in America, **351**
Phillippe, Kent A., **586**
Philosopher's index, **75**
Photographer's market, **1118**
The photography encyclopedia, **1117**
Physicians' desk reference, **872**
*Physicians' desk reference for nonprescription drugs
  and dietary supplements,* **872**
Picken, Mary Brooks, **1095**
Pickeral, Tamsin, **1010**
Pickering, David, **617**
Pierangelo, Roger, **530**
Pinney, Chris C., **990**
The Pinyin Chinese-English dictionary, **662**
Piper Resources, **492**
Pizzorno, Joseph, **864**
A place for God, **134**
Plake, Barbara S., **222**
*Planning for results: A public library transformation
  process,* 71
Plano, Jack C., **477**
Plant, **783**
Plaut, W. Gunther, **153**

Play index, **1189**
Playdatabase.com, **1484**
Plays for children and young adults, **1190**
Plimer, I. R., **746**
Plumbing, **980**
The pocket decorator, **971**
Podell, Janet, **1623**
Podnieks, Andrew, **1369**
Poehner, Donna, **1118**
Poetry criticism, **1511**
Poetry handbook, **1512**
Policy documents and reports, **579**
Political handbook of the world, **511**
Political risk yearbook, 396
Political science resources on the Web, **473**
Pollack, Neuman F., **556**
Pollock, Sandra, **1443**
Ponzetti, James J. Jr., **329**
Poole, Hilary W., **741**
Popular contemporary writers, **1433**
Popular Mechanics complete home how-to, **981**
Popular psychology, **211**
Popular song index, **1243**
Porter, Joy, **1450**
Porter, Liz, **1267**
Porter, Marsha, **1158**
Porter, Roy, **698**
Post, Peggy, **939, 940**
Post, Stephen Garrard, **771**
Pound, Richard W., **1602**
Pournelle, Jerry, **732**
Powell, Michael, **938**
The practical encyclopedia of martial arts, **1374**
The practical library manager, **72**
Preminger, Alex, **1510**
Premium beer drinker's guide, **894**
Prestel dictionary of art and artists, **1065**
Preves, Richard, **917**
Price, Sandra P., **256**
Prichard, Mari, **1471**
Prince, Mary Miles, **649**
Prince's Bieber dictionary of legal citations, **649**
The Princeton companion to classical Japanese literature, **1587**
Pring, J. T., **671**
Pringle, David, **1491**
Pritzker, Barry M., **322**
Private colleges and universities, **580**
Pro football guide, **1358**
Proffitt, Michael, **602**

Project Vote Smart, **512**
Projections of educational statistics to 2014, **587**
Pronouncing dictionary of proper names, **626**
Proquest, 35, **395**
PRS Group, 396
Pruyne, Terry W., **1317**
PsycARTICLES, 183, **186**
PsycBOOKS, 183, **187**
PsycEXTRA, 183, **188**
Psychoanalytic Electronic Publishing, 183, **185**
Psychodynamic diagnostic manual (PDM), **218**
Psychologist's desk reference, **219**
psych.org, **223**
PsychWeb, **234**
PsycINFO, 183, **189**
Public colleges and universities, **580**
Public interest group profiles, **491**
Public Library Association, **71**
The public library start-up guide, **73**
Public schools USA, **581**
Publication manual of the American Psychological Association, **220**
PubMed, **813**
Pugh-Gannon, Joanne, **1275**
Pulitzer prizes, **1412**
Purdy, Dennis, **1333**

Q

Quah, Stella R., **272**
Queen, Edward L., **110**
The queer encyclopedia of the visual arts, **1075**
The quilter's companion, **1267**
Quilter's complete guide, **1267**
Quinn, Edward G., **1554**
Quirk, James P., **1360**
The quotable Shakespeare, **1553**
The quotable woman, **1426**

R

Race relations in the United States: A chronology, 1896–2005, **302**
Racial and ethnic diversity, **303**
Racial and ethnic diversity in America, **304**
Racial and ethnic relations in America, **305**
Radnedge, Keir, **1390**
Rae, Andy, **1278**
Raising the bar, **895**
Rajtar, Steve, **950**
Rakel, Robert E., **834**

Rand McNally commercial atlas and marketing guide, **1651**

Randel, Don Michael, **1212**

Randem, Mette, **895**

Random House American Sign Language dictionary, **632**

Random House historical dictionary of American slang, **641**

Random House Webster's crossword puzzle dictionary, **613**

Random House Webster's unabridged dictionary, **604**

Random House Webster's word menu, **645**

Rappaport, Helen, **365**

Rasmussen, R. Kent, **325**

Rass, Paula S., **375**

The Rastafarians, **168**

Rawson, Hugh, **1423**

Reader's Digest, **106, 1274**

The reader's encyclopedia of Shakespeare, **1554**

Readers' guide full text, mega edition, 37

Readers' guide retrospective, 1890–1982, 37

Reader's guide to lesbian and gay studies, **334**

Readers' guide to periodical literature, 37

Reader's guide to the history of science, **734**

Reader's guide to the social sciences, **259**

Reader's guide to women's studies, **366**

The real wood bible, **1281**

Reber, Arthur S., **210**

Reber, Emily S., **210**

Recent reference books in religion, 85

Recommended reference books in paperback, **12**

Recreation, **1382**

Reed, Amy Charlene, **893**

Reed, Ida, **1204**

Reed, Walt, **1110**

Rees, Dafydd, **1248**

Reeve, Eric C. R., **774**

Reference and information services, **13**

Reference and research guide to mystery and detective fiction, **1497**

Reference and user services quarterly, **19**

Reference guide to American literature, **1541**

Reference guide to science fiction, fantasy and horror, **1517**

Reference guide to short fiction, **1522**

Reference library of American men, **342**

Reference library of American women, **367**

Reference library of Native North America, **323**

Reference services review: RSR, **20**

Reference sources in science, engineering, medicine, and agriculture, **687**

Reference Universe, **62**

Reference works in British and American literature, **1397**

Regan, Mardee Haidin, **887**

Reheuser, Rob, **1339**

Reichl, Ruth, **924**

Reid, Daniel G., **107**

Reilly, Edward J., **1321**

Reiner, Robert, **290**

Renovation, **965**

Reproductive issues in America, **275**

Reptiles and amphibians, **1014**

Requirements for certification of teachers, counselors, librarians, administrators for elementary schools and secondary schools, **582**

Resch, John P., **809**

Resources for college libraries, **14**

Resources in education, 535

Reynolds, Barbara, **675**

Reynolds, Cecil R., **537**

Richard, Birgit, **374**

Richter, William L., **1616**

Riess, Jana, **126**

Riess, Steven A, **1329**

Rigden, John S., **808**

Riggs, Thomas, **1480, 1506, 1522, 1541**

Riley, Noel, **1104**

Rinzler, Carol Ann, **933**

Ritter, R. M., **655**

Rittner, Don, **772**

Rivers, Vickie, **68**

The road atlas: United States, Canada and Mexico, **1652**

Robbers, James E., **866**

Le Robert and Collins senior, **666**

Roberts, Albert R., **353**

Roberts, Robert North, **482**

Robertson, Allen, **1138**

Robertson, Robin, **935**

Robinson, Jancis, **892**

Robinson, Judith Schiek, **474**

Robuchon, Joël, **930**

Rock and roll year by year, **1248**

Rockman, Connie G., **1469**

Rockwell, Kenneth S., **1557**

Rodriguez, Robert, **318**

Roemer, Kenneth M., **1450**

RogerEbert.com, **1154**

Roget's international thesaurus, **646**

Roget's thesaurus of the Bible, **105**

Rogowski, Gary, **1278**

Rojas, Raúl, **729**

Rojek, Chris, **273**

Rolland, Jacques, **921**

The Rolling Stone encyclopedia of rock and roll, **1249**

Rollyson, Carl E., **1482**

Romaine, Deborah S., **881**

Rombauer, Irma von Starkloff, **928**

Ronzio, Robert, **873**

Room, Adrian, **441, 1404**

Rose, Cynthia, **1635**

Rose, Sharon, **321**

Rosenak, Chuck, **1061**

Rosenak, Jan, **1061**

Rosenbaum, Ernest H., **856**

Rosenbaum, Isadora, **856**

Rosenblum, Naomi, **1115**

Rosenfeld, Susan C., **1636**

Rosenfield, P., **417**

Rosi, Mauro, **748**

Ross, Stanley Ralph, **1151**

Roth, Bruce, **213**

Roth, John K., **83, 180**

Rothamel, Susan Pickering, **1272**

Rothfeld, Glenn S., **881**

The rough guide to classical music, **1227**

The rough guide to world music, vol. 1: Africa, Europe and the Middle East, **1251**

The rough guide to world music, vol. 2: Latin and North America, the Caribbean, Asia and the Pacific, **1251**

Roundtree, Bob, **862**

Routledge encyclopedia of philosophy, **82**

Routledge historical atlas of religion in America, **1634**

Routledge international encyclopedia of women, **368**

Roy, Christian, **949**

Rubin, H. W., **460**

Rubinstein, Charlotte S., **1078**

Ruffner, Frederick G., **48**

Ruiz, Fernando Pages, **912**

Running encyclopedia, **1383**

The Running Press pocket guide to beer, **896**

Ruppert, James, **1508**

Russell, Cheryl, **303, 422, 424, 426**

Russell, John J., **412, 413, 1068**

Russell, Malcolm B., **1669**

Russell, Roy, **685**

Russell Sage Foundation, **49**

Russia and the Commonwealth of Independent States, **1669**

Rutter, Hadyn, **1366**

Ruud, Jay, **1400**

Ryan, Bryan, **321**

Ryan, James D., **119**

Ryan, Joseph M., **575**

Ryan, Mildred Graves, **1263**

S

Sabath, Ann Marie, **941**

Sacks, Arlene, **572**

Sacks, David, **1612**

Sadie, Stanley, 1215, **1215**, 1223, **1229, 1230**

Safire, William, **489**

Safire's new political dictionary, **489**

Sage encyclopedia of social science research methods, **253**

The Sage handbook of sociology, **273**

St. James encyclopedia of labor history worldwide, **408**

St. James guide to horror, ghost and gothic writers, **1491**

St. James guide to science fiction writers, **1518**

Sakenfeld, Katharine Doob, **102**

Salem, James M., **1120**

Salem Press, **1438**

Sales, Arnaud, **272**

Salinas, Robert C., **294**

Salkind, Neil J., **200**

Salud en español, 811

Same-sex marriage in the United States, **335**

Sander, Reinhard W., **1574**

Sanders, D., **668**

Sanga, Jaina C., **1595, 1596**

Santelli, Robert, **1224**

Santería, **169**

Sardegna, Jill, **875**

Sardo, Julie Zetterberg, **1029**

Saterstrom, Mary H., **527**

Savage, George, **1105**

Sax, N. Irving, **721**

Sax's dangerous properties of industrial materials, **721**

Sayre, John R., **472**

Scagell, Robin, **711**

Scandinavia profiled, **1672**

Schemel, Sidney, **1219**

Schlachter, Gail Ann, **571**

Schlager, Neil, **408, 737, 777**

Schlemowitz, Joel, **1147**

Schlessinger, Bernard S., **388, 1190**

Schlessinger, June H., **1190**

Schmidt, Diane, **764**

Schmied, Wieland, **1065**

Schmittroth, Linda, **324**

Schneider, Elizabeth, **936**

Scholarships, grants and prizes, **570**

Scholze-Stubenrecht, Werner, **669**

School library journal, **21,** 24

Schools abroad of interest to Americans, **552**

Schor, Edward L., **984**

Schroy, Ellen T., **1286**

Schultz, Ken, **1353**

Schwartz, Howard, **176**

Schwartzman, Steven, **801**

Science and its times, **737**

Science and technology desk reference, **702**

Science citation index, 691

Science Fiction Writers of America, 1411

ScienceWatch.com, 691

Scientific style and format, **656**

Scofield, John, **1222**

Scott, John, **269**

Scott, Robert, **670**

Scott specialized catalogue of United States stamps and covers, **1296**

Scott's standard postage stamp catalogue, **1296**

Screen world, **1163**

The Scribner encyclopedia of American lives: Sports figures, **1316**

Scutella, Richard M., **915**

The search, 63

Search Engine Watch, 63

Sears, James T., **337**

Seasons of our joy, **156**

Sebastian, Anton, **735**

A second treasury of knitting patterns, **1260**

Secondary schools, **572**

Secondary teachers guide to free curriculum materials, **527**

Segel, Harold B., **1577**

Segen, J. C., **816**

Self-taught, outsider and folk art, **1066**

Seligman, Edwin R. A., **251,** 252

Sellen, Betty-Carol, **1066**

Selley, Richard C., **746**

Sennott, R. Stephen, **1044**

Sequels, **1501**

Settich, Robert J., **1278**

Seventh book of junior authors and illustrators, **1469**

Sexuality, **346**

Sexually transmitted diseases sourcebook, **851**

Shaeffer, Claire B., **1273**

Shakar, M. H., **144**

Shakespeare A to Z, **1555**

A Shakespeare glossary, **1556**

Shakespeare on screen, **1557**

Shakespearean criticism, **1558**

Shalinsky, Audrey, **378**

Shamos, Michael Ian, **1347**

Shamus Awards, 1411

Sharp, Michael D., **1433**

Shearer, Barbara S., **1599**

Shearer, Benjamin F., **1599**

Sheehy, Noel, **236**

Sheets, Anna J., **324**

Sheimo, M., **433**

Shelov, Steven P., **983**

Sherby, Louise S., **1695**

Shiffman, Jody R., **1585**

Shillington, Kevin, **1611**

Shim, J. K., **418, 419**

Shinto, **120**

Shoemaker, Merle Wesley, **1669**

Shoes, **1101**

The shopping bags, **907**

Shoquist, Jennifer, **850**

Shores, Elizabeth F., **986**

Short story criticism, **1523**

Short story index, **1524, 1525**

Short story index: Collections indexed 1900–1978, **1526**

Shorter Oxford English dictionary on historical principles, **602, 608**

The shorter Routledge encyclopedia of philosophy, **82**

Showalter, Elaine, **1458**

Showman, Richard K., **1598**

Shu, Jennifer, **860**

Shulman, Martha Rose, **956**

Shuman, R. Baird, **1536**

Shumsky, Neil L., **362**

SIBMAS: International directory of performing arts collections and institutions, **1123**

Siegal, Mordecai, **996**

Siegel, J. G., **418**, **419**
Siegel, Jonathan P., **486**
Siegfield, David, 63
Sienkewicz, Thomas J., **1562**
Sikhism, **121**
Sills, David L., **252**
Silvey, Anita, 1467, **1467**
Similes dictionary, **635**
Simon, Harvey B., **883**
Simon, Joanna, **898**
Simons, Linda K., **1119**
Simpich, Joe, **213**
Simpson, Donald Penistan, **679**
Simpson, Eva, **1604**
Simpson, J. A., **602**
Singer, Ronald, **792**
Singh, Nikky-Guninder Kaur, **121**
Sixth book of junior authors and illustrators, **1469**
60 years of notable children's books, **15**
Sizes, **699**
Skolnik, Fred, **150**
Skrzypczak, Edmund R., **678**
Skutsch, Carl, **300**
Sleight, Steve, **1388**
Slide, Anthony, **1152**
Sloan, Dave, **1358**
Sloan, Stephen, **291**
Slonimsky, Nicolas, 1206, **1213**, **1220**
Smallin, Donna, **966**
Smart medicine for a healthier child, **862**
Smith, Andrew F., **959**
Smith, Carter, **1629**
Smith, Darren L, **1680**
Smith, Greg, **1177**
Smith, Jessie Carney, **309**, **311**
Smith, John B. Sr., **313**
Smith, Linda C., **13**
Smith, Marianne Page, **893**
Smith, Myron J., **1324**
Smith, Raymond A., **506**
Smith, Sharron, **1571**
Smith, Tony, **1627**
Smith, Verity, **1588**
Smithsonian global sound for libraries, **1252**
Smullen, J., **429**
Snodgrass, Mary Ellen, **1289**, **1490**
Snyder, Tim, **914**
Sobczak, A. J., **1409**
Social issues in America, **254**
The social science encyclopedia, **255**

The social sciences, **257**
Social sciences citation index, 691
Social sciences index, **249**
Social trends and indicators USA, **358**
The social work dictionary, **352**
Social workers' desk reference, **353**
Sociology, **266**
Sociology basics, **271**
SocioSite, **263**
Sola, Ralph De, **609**
Sole, Carlos A. Jr., **1592**
Solomon, Burt, **1326**
Something about the author, 1474, **1475**
Something about the author: Autobiography series,
    1474
Sommer, Elyse, **634**, **635**
Sommer, Mike, **635**
Song sheets to software, **1205**
SongCite, **1244**
Songwriter's market, **1218**
Sonneborn, Liz, **1076**
Sorenson, G. J., **404**
The Sotheby's wine encyclopedia, **897**
South Asian literature in English, **1595**
South Asian novelists in English, **1596**
Southern Africa profiled, **1672**
Southern writers, **1542**
Sparano, Vin T., **1377**
Sparks, Linda, **573**
Spawforth, Antony, **1618**
Speake, Jennifer, **618**
Spears, Richard A., **640**
Special education, **572**
Special educator's complete guide to 109 diagnostic
    tests, **530**
Speech index, **1530**
Speight, J. G., **719**
Spencer, Dale, **368**
Spencer, Jonathan, **385**
Spencer, Thomas S., **1068**
Spevack, Marvin, **1551**
Spielberger, Charles Donald, **198**
Spieler, Marlena, **920**
Spies, Robert A., **222**
The spirit book, **246**
Spitzer, Robert L., **215**
Sport in American culture, **1306**
Sports, **1385**
Sports and games of the ancients, **1363**
Sports culture, **1307**

Sports, exercise and fitness, **1299**

Sports museums and halls of fame worldwide, **1310**

Sports nicknames, **1317**

The sports rules book, **1386**

Springer, Otto, **668**

Sprug, Joseph W., **1468**

Stafford, Diane, **850**

Stage it with music, **1199**

Stahl, Dean, **609**

Staines, Joe, **1227**

Stallebrass, Pam, **1256**

Standard and Poor's 500 guide, **435**

Standard and Poor's register of corporations, directors and executives, **449**

Standard and Poor's stock reports, **436**

Standard catalog of U.S. paper money, **1291**

Standard catalog of world coins, 1901–2000, **1290**

Standard catalog of world coins: Eighteenth century, 1701–1800, **1290**

Standard catalog of world coins: Seventeenth century, 1601–1700, **1290**

Standard catalog of world paper money, vol. I: Specialized issues, **1291**

Standard catalog of world paper money, vol. II: General issues, **1291**

Standard catalog of world paper money, vol. III: Modern issues, **1291**

Standard directory of world coins: Nineteenth century, 1801–1900, **1290**

Standring, Susan, **853**

Stankus, Bill, **1280**

Stanley, Harold W., **516**

Stanley, Montse, **1259**

Stanley Works, **978**

Stansfield, William D., **769**

Stark, Daniel, **612**

Starkey, Paul, **1543**

State and local government on the Net, **492**

State and regional associations of the United States, **413**

State names, seals, flags, and symbols, **1599**

State-by-state profiles of community colleges, **588**

Statistical abstract of the United States, **32**

Stawser, C. J., **415**

Stedman, Thomas Lathrop, **826**

Stedman's abbreviations, acronyms, and symbols, **825**

Stedman's medical dictionary, **826**

Steele, Valerie, **1096**

Steen, Michael, **1234**

Stein, David E., **153**

Stein, Gordon, **241**

Stein, Marc, **332**

Steinberg, Shirley R., **374**

Steinmetz, Sol, **614**

Steinmetz, Suzanne K., **328**

Steinsaltz, Adin, **152, 154**

Sterling, Christopher H., **1171**

Sterling Publishing Company, **1258**

Stern, David J., **1338**

Stets, Marah, **895**

Stevenson, Angus, 602, **608**

Stevenson, Burton Egbert, **1418, 1422**

Stevenson, Tom, **897**

Stewart, Bruce, **1584**

Stewart, John, **1193**

Stitch sampler, **1266**

Stoppard, Miriam, **879**

Storey's horse-lover's encyclopedia, **1012**

Stowe, Doug, **1278**

Strassfeld, Michael, **156**

Straub, Deborah Gillan, **316, 321**

Strauss's handbook of business information, **391**

Strong, James, 95, **95**

Strugatch, Warren, **844**

Student atlas of anthropology, **378**

Student rights, **572**

Sullivan, Eileen Crowley, **1364**

Sullivan, Leila Gonzales, **586**

Summer opportunities for kids and teenagers, **551**

Summers, Claude J., **1075, 1444**

Supernatural fiction writers, **1486**

Supernatural literature of the world, **1487**

Surf the ages, 45

The surgery book, **846**

Survey of social science: Sociology series, 271

Sussman, Allen E., **876**

Sussman, Marvin B., **328**

Sutton, Amy L., **851**

Sutton, Roberta Briggs, **1530**

Sweetland, James H., **3**

Szeman, Imre, **1408**

Szymanski, Marianne M., **989**

T

Taitz, Emily, **116**

Takebayashi, Shigeru, **678**

Taoism, **122**

Tapping the government grapevine, **474**

Tarr, David R., **500**, 504

Taunton's Complete Illustrated Guide series, 1278, 1282

Taunton's complete illustrated guide to box making, 1278

Taunton's complete illustrated guide to choosing and installing hardware, 1278

Taunton's complete illustrated guide to finishing, 1278

Taunton's complete illustrated guide to sharpening, 1278

Taunton's complete illustrated guide to using woodworking tools, 1278

Taunton's complete illustrated guide to woodworking, 1282

Taunton's complete illustrated guide to working with wood, 1278

Taylor, Wendell H., **1494**

The team by team encyclopedia of Major League Baseball, **1333**

Technical manual and dictionary of classical ballet, 1131

Television and cable factbook, **1179**

Television cartoon shows, **1176**

Television production handbook, **1177**

Telushkin, Joseph, **146, 147, 148**

10,000 garden questions answered by 20 experts, **787**

Tenenbaum, Barbara A., **1613**

Tennant, Richard A., **630**

Tenney, Merrill Chapin, **103**

Terras, Victor, **1593**

Terrell, Peter, **667**

Terrorism, **291**

Tests, **531**

Textbook of medical physiology, **855**

Thackery, Ellen, **208**

Thames and Hudson dictionary of art terms, **1067**

The Thames and Hudson dictionary of graphic design and designers, **1111**

Theatre world, **1202**

Theis, Paul A., **522**

Third book of junior authors, **1469**

This business of music, **1219**

This day in American history, **1603**

This day in sports, **1301**

THOMAS: Legislative Information on the Internet, **513**

ThomasNet, **759**

Thompson, John, **1625**

Thompson, Sally Anne, **15**

Thompson, Sue Ellen, **946**

Thompson, Wayne C., **1669**

Thompson, William Norman, **1361**

Thomson, David, **1166**

Thorburn, John E. Jr., **1566**

Thorn, John, **1334**

350 small home plans, **918**

Thyen, O., **669**

Tierney, Lawrence M., **835**

The time almanac, **33**

Timeline of art history, **1035**

The timetables of history, **1604**

A title guide to the talkies, **1155**

To be continued, **1502**

Tobacco in history and culture, **283**

Toll-free phone book USA, **53**

Tony awards, **1129**

Tools, **1016**

The Torah: A modern commentary, **153**

Tortora, Phyllis G., **1276**

Toshiro, Watanabe, **678**

Total baseball, **1334**

Total football, **1359**

Total hockey, **1372**

Total tennis, **1393**

Townsend, Chris, **1378**

Toxics A to Z, **847**

Toy tips, **989**

Toye, William, **1572**

Traditional festivals, **949**

Traveling with your pet, **1681**

Travelocity, 1676

Travers, Len, **944**

Treasures in full: Shakespeare in Quarto, **1559**

A treasury of knitting patterns, **1260**

Tree of souls, **176**

Tremblay, Carl, **932**

Trench, Lucy, **1109**

Trigg, George L., **805**

Trivieri, Larry, **863**

Truitt, Evelyn Mack, **1167**

Trumble, William R., **602, 608**

Tsur, Naomi, **673**

Tucker, Martha A., **797**

Tuitean, Paul, **165**

Turabian, Kate L., **653**

Turkington, Carol, **202, 838, 876**

Turner, Barry, **1672**

Turner, Bryan S., **273**

Turner, Jane, 1056, **1056**

Turner, Jeffrey S., **327, 344**

Twentieth-century Caribbean and black African writers, **1574**

Twentieth-century crime and mystery writers, **1498**

Twentieth-century fashion, **1102**

Twentieth-century literary criticism, **1416**

Twentieth-century romance and historical writers, **1513**

Twentieth-century short story explication, **1527**

Twentieth-century short story explication: An index to the third edition and its five supplements, 1961–1991, **1527**

Two hundred years of the American circus, **1200**

2005 online shopping directory for dummies, **908**

2006 consumer action handbook, **909**

Tyler, Todd W., **651**

Tyler, Varro E., **866**

Tyler's herbs of choice, **866**

Tyrell, Ian R., **279**

Tyrrell, John, **1215**, 1223

U

Uhle, Frank, **1382**

UK today, **1672**

Ulrich's periodicals directory, **54**

The ultimate dictionary of sports quotations, **1308**

The ultimate encyclopedia of caged and aviary birds, **994**

The ultimate encyclopedia of fortune telling, 247

The ultimate encyclopedia of soccer, **1390**

The ultimate encyclopedia of spells, **247**

The ultimate guide to college football, **1360**

Ultimate guide to the world's best wedding and honeymoon destinations, **1682**

The ultimate home and property maintenance manual, **982**

The ultimate house book, **972**

The ultimate mountain bike book, **1345**

Understanding your medical laboratory tests and surgical biopsy reports, **848**

Unger, Harlow G., **539**

Unique games and sports around the world, **1364**

United Nations Department of Public Information, **498**

United States Golf Association rules, **1368**

United States government Internet manual, **493**

United States history, **1600**

United States holidays and observances, **950**

United States Olympic Committee, **1344**

United States Postal Service, **56**

United States Soccer Federation laws of the game, **1391**

United States Tennis Association, **1394**

University of Michigan Documents Center, **473**

Unterman, Alan, **149**

Upton, Clive, **628**

Upton, Eben, **628**

U.S. Census Bureau, **32, 264**

U.S. Census Bureau home page, **264**

U.S. Centers for Disease Control and Prevention, **232**

U.S. Central Intelligence Agency, **521**

U.S. Chess Federation's official rules of chess, **1350**

U.S. Congress, House, Office of the Clerk, **519**

U.S. Courts, **494**

U.S. Department of Agriculture, **779**

U.S. Department of Agriculture, National Agricultural Library, **955**

U.S. Department of Health and Human Resources/National Center for Health Statistics, **837**

U.S. Department of Labor, **467**

U.S. Department of State, 396, 514, **514**

U.S. first day cover catalogue and checklist, **1297**

U.S. Geological Survey, **1650**

U.S. government manual, **515**

U.S. Library of Congress, **513**

U.S. National Agricultural Library, **778**

U.S. National Archives and Records Administration, Office of the Federal Register, **493, 515**

U.S. National Library of Medicine, **813**

U.S. Nautical Almanac Office, **707**

U.S. Office of Management and Budget, **348**

U.S. Patent and Trademark Office, **701**

U.S. Senate, **520**

The USA and the world, **1669**

USA.gov, **475**

Using the biological literature, **764**

USTA rules, **1394**

UXL Asian American almanac, **316**

UXL Asian American biography, **316**

UXL Asian American chronology, **316**

UXL Asian American reference library, **316**

UXL Asian American voices, **316**

UXL encyclopedia of Native American tribes, **324**

UXL encyclopedia of world biography, **1689**

UXL Hispanic American almanac, **321**

UXL Hispanic American biography, **321**

UXL Hispanic American chronology, **321**

UXL Hispanic American reference library, **321**
UXL Hispanic American reference library cumulative index, **321**
UXL Hispanic American voices, **321**

V

Valade, Roger M., **705**
The value of a dollar: 1860–2004, **1628**
The value of a dollar: The colonial era to the Civil War, 1600–1865, **1627**
Van der Maas, Eduard M., **128**
Van Nostrand's concise encyclopedia of science, **700**
Van Nostrand's encyclopedia of chemistry, **717**
Van Nostrand's scientific encyclopedia, **700**
Vandervort, Donald W., **961**
Vaughan, J. G., **957**
Vaughn, William, **1084**
Vegan planet, **935**
Vegetables from amaranth to zucchini, **936**
Vegetables, herbs and fruit, **937**
Veregin, Howard, **1640**
Vertical file index, **532**
Victor, Terry, **639**
VideoHound's golden movie retriever, **1161**
Villaverde, Leila E., **572**
The visual dictionary of American domestic architecture, **1050**
A visual dictionary of architecture, **1051**
Visual Education Corporation, **258**
Vital statistics on American politics, **516**
Vitt, L. A., **432**
Vogel, Amber, **1542**
Vogel, Colin, **1009**
Vogue knitting, **1261**
The Vogue/Butterick step-by-step guide to sewing techniques, **1277**
Voice of youth advocates, **22**
Volcanoes, **748**
Von Alt, Kenneth A., **554**
Voodoo in Haiti, **170**

W

Wainwright, Geoffrey, **131**
Walker, Barbara G., **1260**
Walker, Barbara K., **1527**
Walker, J. E. K., **400**
Walker, Janice R., **651**
Walker, John, **1159, 1165**
Walker, Lester, **1038**

Walker, Warren S., **1527**
Wallner, Anna, **907**
Walsh, Michael, **139**
Walsh, Peter, **970**
Walter Breen's complete encyclopedia of U.S. and colonial coins, **1292**
Walton, Rachel, **862**
Wangu, Madhu Bazaz, **117**
Ward, Gary L., **108**
Ward's business directory of U.S. private and public companies, **450**
Warman's antiques and collectibles price guide, **1286**
Warren, Lynne, **1114**
Washington information directory, **495**
Waskow, Arthur J., **156**
The Watkins dictionary of magic, **248**
Watson, Aldren A., **1279**
Way, Lawrence W., **835**
Weaver, William Woys, **954**
Web of Science, **691**
Webby, Elizabeth, **1570**
Weber, R. David, **571**
Webster, John G., **818**
Webster's third new international dictionary of the English language, **42, 605**
Weil, Danny K., **572**
Weiner, E. S. C., **602**
Weingand, Darlene E., **66**
Weir, R. E., **407**
Weishampel, David B, **789**
Weiss, Dorrie, **634**
Weissman, Paul, **708**
Welch, Robert, **1584**
Wellner, Alison Stein, **1379**
Wellness foods A to Z, **874**
Wentworth, Harold, **636**
Werblowsky, R. J. Zwi, **161**
Werlock, Abby H. P., **1520, 1535**
Wertkin, Gerard C., **1060**
West-Duran, Alan, **1448**
Westerfield Tucker, Karen B., **131**
Western Europe, **1669**
Westfahl, Gary, **1516**
Westheimer, Ruth K., **345**
Westminster dictionary of Christian ethics, **182**
Weston Jesuit School of Theology, **96**
Wetterau, Bruce, **501, 502**
Whaley, Mary, **63**
What American women did, 1789–1920, **369**

Wheeler, Marcus, **682**
Whitburn, Joel, **1235, 1239, 1240**
Whiteley, Sandra, **1**
Whitford, Frank, **1065**
Whitson, Kathy J., **1454**
Whitworth, Belinda, **166**
Who was who on the screen, **1167**
The whole brain atlas, **235**
Who's who among African Americans, **313**
Who's who in American education, **592**
Who's who in American politics, **522**
Who's who in contemporary gay and lesbian history, **336**
Who's who in finance and business, **394**
Who's who in gay and lesbian history, **336**
Who's who in international affairs, **523**
Who's who in the Bible, **106**
Who's who in the twentieth century, **1694**
Who's who of American women, **370**
The who's who of Nobel Prize winners, 1901–2000, **1695**
Whyld, Ken, **1349**
Wiegand, Wayne A., **1489**
Wiget, Andrew, **1451**
Wiggins, David Kenneth, **1312**
Wigoder, Geoffrey, **161**
Wikipedia, **44**
Wiley electrical and electronics engineering dictionary, **757**
Wiley's English-Spanish, Spanish-English dictionary of psychology and psychiatry, **212**
Wilhide, Elizabeth, **972**
Wilkins, David G., **1073**
Willenbrink, Rose Ann, **1130**
William Shakespeare, **1560**
Williams, Hywel, **1601**
Williams, Martha E., **730**
Willis, John, **1163, 1202**
Wilmeth, Don B., **1194**
Wilson, Dreck Spurlock, **1036**
Wilson, Jeffrey, **861**
Wilson, John D., **1402**
Wilson, Kenneth G., **622**
Wine, **898**
Wines of the world, **899**
Winks, Robin W., **1496**
Winn, Peter S., **294**
Wired for the future, 71
Wischnitzer, Edith, **558**
Wischnitzer, Saul, **558**

Witcombe, Christopher L. C. E., **1023**
Withers, Sara, **1257**
Wolman, Benjamin B., **204**
The women of the All-American Girls Professional Baseball League, **1335**
Women's issues, **371**
Women's studies, **372**
Wood, Clement, **627**
Wood, Hanley, **911**
Woodall's North America campground directory, **1683**
Woodard, Roger D., **594**
Woodford, Chris, **694**
Woodham, Jonathan M., **1058**
Woodshop dust control, **1283**
Woodstra, Chris, **1238**
The words of mathematics, **801**
Words to rhyme with, **629**
The world almanac and book of facts, **34**
The World Book encyclopedia, **41**
The World Book encyclopedia of people and places, **1666**
World Book Online Reference Center, **45**
World Book research libraries, **45**
World education encyclopedia, **544**
World encyclopedia of comics, **1089**
World encyclopedia of flags, **1622**
World encyclopedia of stamps and stamp collecting, **1298**
World of computer science, **733**
World of learning, **553**
World philosophers and their works, **83**
World radio TV handbook, **1181**
The world today, 2000, **1672**
WorldCat, **26**
Worldmark encyclopedia of the nations, **1667**
Worldmark encyclopedia of the states, **1668**
Wotherspoon, Garry, **336**
Wright, Richard A., **288**
Wright, Russell O., **296**
The writer's market, **619**
The WWW Virtual Library: Social and Behavioural Sciences, **265**

Y

Yaakov, Juliette, **1526**
Yahoo! **65**
Yahoo! to the max, **65**
Yearbook of American and Canadian churches, **135**
Young, Robyn V., **804**

Youngson, Robert M., **846**
Youth, education, and sexualities, **337**
Yuan, Zhu, **661**

Z

Zaczek, Ian, **1073**
Zand, Janet, **862**
Zevnik, R., **459**

Zeyl, Donald J., **77**
Zia, Helen, **316**
Zimmerman, Bonnie, **331**
Zipes, Jack, **1473**
Znamierowski, Alfred, **1622**
Zondervan pictorial encyclopedia of the Bible, **103**
Zoroastrianism, **171**
Zuk, Judith D., **784**
Zumerchik, John, **753**